G000243123

ADVANCED PERFORMANCE MANAGEMENT

An International Perspective

By

Eoin McGettigan

Published by
Chartered Accountants Ireland
Chartered Accountants House
47–49 Pearse Street
Dublin 2
www.charteredaccountants.ie

© The Institute of Chartered Accountants in Ireland 2015

Copyright in this publication is owned by the Institute of Chartered Accountants in Ireland. All rights reserved. No part of this text may be reproduced or transmitted or communicated to the public in any form or by any means, including photocopying, Internet or e-mail dissemination, without the written permission of the Institute of Chartered Accountants in Ireland. Such written permission must also be obtained before any part of this document is stored in a retrieval system of any nature.

This publication is designed to provide accurate and authoritative information in regard to the subject matter covered. It is provided on the understanding that the Institute of Chartered Accountants in Ireland is not engaged in rendering professional services. The Institute of Chartered Accountants in Ireland disclaims all liability for any reliance placed on the information contained within this publication and recommends that if professional advice or other expert assistance is required, the services of a competent professional should be sought.

ISBN: 978-1-908199-99-7

Typeset by Datapage
Printed by Replika Press Pvt. Ltd.

MIX
Paper from
responsible sources
FSC® C016779

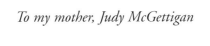

To my mother, Judy McGettigan

Contents

Preface

This book is about the performance management of multinational enterprises (MNEs). It has a particular focus on the island of Ireland. It also has a bias toward the financial aspects of performance management in the MNE.

The book comprises 18 chapters divided into five parts followed by three appendices:
- Part I, The Rise of the Multinational Enterprise, charts the growth of international trade and the rise of the MNE, focussing particularly on the island of Ireland. It also examines the role of corporate governance, ethics and the professional accountant within MNEs.
- Part II, Economic Factors influencing MNEs, explores macroeconomic factors and how they affect the MNE. It examines exchange rates, inflation and interest rates together with the international capital markets and details how international trade logistics are carried out, including the management of working capital across borders.
- The three chapters in Part III, Decision-making in Multinational Enterprises, examine how MNEs make decisions, particularly investment decisions, and how MNEs implement those decisions and change in general.
- Part IV, Treasury Management in an International Environment, examines how the treasury function deals with the challenges presented by trading in an international context. There is special focus on the management of foreign-exchange risk and the sourcing of finance for the MNE.
- Part V, Management Systems in Multinational Enterprises, looks at the types of systems and processes that the MNE uses to manage critical parts of its activities. In particular, it focusses on pricing, enterprise management systems and performance management.
- Appendix A presents 15 detailed case studies from past papers of the Chartered Accountants Ireland FAE Elective in Advanced Performance Management, on which most of the review questions included at the end of each chapter are based.
- Appendix B then provides extensive suggested solutions to these review questions.
- Appendix C comprises essays by or interviews with senior management of three Irish multinationals, relating these to relevant elements of the main text:
  - Appendix C.1 is an essay on the international dimensions of trading for Dairygold, one of Ireland's oldest and largest co-operative societies, by its Chief Executive, Jim Woulfe.
  - Appendix C.2 is an essay on the expansion of National Toll Roads (NTR) into the US by Michael Walsh, former Group Finance Director.
  - Appendix C.3 is an interview with Patrick Coveney, CEO of Greencore Plc, a publicly quoted MNE headquartered in Dublin that has transformed itself from the Irish Sugar Company, a state-owned sugar beet processor, into a major international food company. Many of the issues it faces and manages form part of the content of this book.

Acknowledgements

It would not have been possible to complete this book without the help and support of a number of people. First, I would like to acknowledge the invaluable encouragement of Becky McIndoe and the publishing team at Chartered Accountants Ireland. In particular I want to recognise the incredible help and patience of Director of Publishing, and my editor, Michael Diviney. Before writing this book, I would never have believed the level of support and collaboration I would need from Michael. He was just amazing.

My lecturing colleague Joe Healy was a huge help, especially during the editing process. Karen Russell and Diarmuid Breathnach kept me encouraged. Thank you also to Gerry and Fiona Gallagher who kick-started me into the writing process.

To the students of Chartered Accountants Ireland whose inquisitive minds helped shape the structure of this book. To Michael Walsh, Jim Woulfe and Patrick Coveney, thank you for your amazing generosity and contributions.

To my father Tony who constantly said he could not wait to read the final publication.

To my daughters, Aisling, Siobhán and Cáitríona, your support was invaluable in keeping me motivated.

Finally, to my wife Breeda, who said "if you ever contemplate writing a book again I'm going to hit you with this one".

Cork
December 2015

PART I

THE RISE OF THE MULTINATIONAL ENTERPRISE

CHAPTER

International trade has grown dramatically since the end of the Second World War. This growth is continuing with the use of new technologies and reductions in barriers to trade fostering an ever increasing volume of commercial activity between nations. The multinational enterprise (MNE) has become the dominant organisation structure used by participants in international trade. In Part I of this book we will examine the rise of the MNE. **Chapter 1** explores the history of international trade on the island of Ireland. In **Chapter 2** we examine why businesses become MNEs. We go on to examine the nature and formats of the differing types of international trade in **Chapter 3**, particularly how MNEs carry out that trade. In **Chapter 4** we look at how international trade manifests itself in Ireland. We also examine why the island of Ireland is a good place to do business. In **Chapter 5** we examine how business ethics and corporate governance have developed with regard to MNEs and try to imagine where these issues are going. The final chapter in Part I, **Chapter 6**, explores the role of the professional accountant in the MNE and how he or she can support its growth and development.

1

THE HISTORY OF INTERNATIONAL TRADE IN IRELAND

CONTENTS

LEARNING OBJECTIVES

Having read this chapter, you will understand:
* the evolution of international trade in Ireland;
* how to assess Ireland's international trade roots; and
* how to identify the factors that drive international trade.

1.1 INTRODUCTION

It is often assumed that international business only really started in the 20th Century. While it is true that international business escalated hugely in the 20th Century, it has been carried on for millennia. Though the majority of commercial and financial instruments that are used to carry out international trade are only 100 years old at most, trade activity can be traced back to prehistorical times, before humankind's activities were recorded in writing.

Some would argue that, by definition, international trade could only have started around the time of the French and American Revolutions when the concept of nations, rather than city states or monarchies, came to the forefront of how societies might organise themselves, that it was only with the development of nation states, together with currencies attaching to those nations, that international trade could develop. Technically, this is correct, in the sense that a strict interpretation of *international* trade requires there to be *nations* between which the trade is conducted. However, the student of international business can learn much from the broader history of trade between the different peoples on this planet and from the evolution of international trade over thousands of years. Driven by the desire for improved standards of living and increasing consumption, new technologies have developed to move goods and services around the globe with ever greater efficiency, allowing increased economies of scale and greater degrees of specialisation of labour.

While a large part of the world's population still live in poverty, it can be said as a general statement that international business has been a driver of improved standards of living for humankind. It is this overall improvement in standards of living that propels governments, enterprises and individuals to persist with removing obstacles to international trade. These initiatives, together with the pursuit of returns for investors, provide the background to much of this book.

As trade has increased, so has the complexity of the systems that support it. These systems need to be understood by today's business organisations. An absence of such understanding can lead a firm to take unnecessary risks by entering markets it does not understand, leading to losses. The uninformed manager can lead the business they serve into the seemingly calm waters of international trade without realising the dangerous currents and rocks that lie just below the waterline. How these risks and obstacles can be managed and controlled, enabling the enterprise to achieve its goals, is the subject of this textbook. As a starting point to this journey we will travel back through history to pre-history, to the roots of international trade in Ireland.

1.2 THE ORIGINS OF TRADE BETWEEN IRELAND AND ITS NEIGHBOURS

Long before the idea of the nation state emerged, Ireland had a history in international trade. A stone axe, its edges sharpened by patient chipping and smoothing, is among the exhibits in the National Museum of Ireland, on Kildare Street in Dublin. Estimated to be 9,000 years old, the axe was found in Culmore, County Derry, in 2003. It is made from a particular type of mudstone not found in Ireland. This baffled archaeologists at first. Furthermore, the shape of the axe is not consistent with Irish axes from that era. Subsequent analysis of the mudstone's composition and the axe's shape led to the startling conclusion that the axe is English, probably originating in what is now Lancashire. It is one of the earliest examples of trade between the peoples of the islands of Ireland and Britain. What makes researchers believe that the axe was traded in exchange for something else, rather than carried here by migrants? The answer lies in understanding how people lived in ancient Ireland.

The people of Mesolithic Ireland (the middle Stone Age) lived in extended family structures from which, generally, they did not travel very far. Practical skills, such as hunting and farming, and techniques were shared among neighbouring communities through word of mouth. In studying artefacts, such as the Culmore axe, archaeologists have been able to identify patterns of techniques. Items from a given area, from proximate communities, are remarkably similar to each other, made from the same materials, to the same shape and size, using the same techniques.

It also evident, on the basis of their different characteristics, that some ancient artefacts found in Ireland were made elsewhere. Such movement of goods cannot solely be explained by migration. If the Culmore axe was brought to the island by migrating peoples from Britain, then other implements of similar progeny would have been found in the same area. The fact that nothing similar, either in composition or by manufacturing technique, has been found locally leads to the deduction that the axe was brought by a trader and exchanged for something else, such as animal hides. The Mesolithic people on the island of Ireland must have traded goods with their prehistoric counterparts overseas.

Copper trading on the Nile Delta can be traced back 6,000 years to 4,000 BCE (before the common era). Copper was in demand, first as a metal in its own right, for making implements, then technologies developed to combine copper with other metals to make superior, more durable alloys for farming implements as well as weapons. The Nile Delta was a natural area for irrigation cultivation with a rich soil and access to river transport. Thus, the new technologies combined with the natural environment led to increased demands for copper, demands that could not be met from scant local sources, hence the need for trade with other peoples.

Humankind's earliest writings and large-scale settlements can also be traced to this era (the early Bronze Age). Thus, the earliest international trade followed a natural instinct in man, a social animal, to enquire of and learn from his fellow humans. Food surpluses created by improvements in farming techniques and technologies created a circle where trading boundaries expanded. Shortages in one area were exchanged for surpluses in another; for example, in Mesopotamia, a shortage of natural resources, such as copper and tin, but a surplus of barley led to the development of some of the earliest currencies. Goods were bought and sold through their equivalent value in barley. Since barley was bulky and thus expensive to transport, equivalent weights in lead were designed to act in place of the barley. Barley would be deposited with a 'Barley Banker' who would give an equivalent lead weight, which could then be re-exchanged for the barley at a later stage.

The drivers of international trade have broadly remained the same over the millennia. Exchanges must be facilitated by transportation technologies and an exchange mechanism. Even in the highly globalised and connected world of today, these drivers and enablers remain the same.

The Growth of Trade in Early Bronze Age Ireland

> The early archaeology of copper mining (c. 2,500 BCE) shows us that international trade is long established on the island of Ireland. Early Bronze Age farmers first imported copper implements, then mined it themselves using imported technologies and, finally, exported the bulk of their production.

Three thousand years before the common era (3,000 BCE), or 5,000 years ago, the early inhabitants of Ireland worked primarily with implements made of wood and stone. Even though they were beginning to cultivate land and livestock, they continued to use the technologies of the preceding 2,000 years. Stone axes designed for hunting were less effective for regular toil on the land than the copper axes and knives which have also been found among the belongings of these early farmers. These metal objects were probably their most treasured possessions.

Metallurgical testing of the oldest of these copper implements shows that the copper was mined in continental Europe. Archaeologists believe the axes would also have been made on the continent and brought to Ireland by early traders. The existence of these items shows that in early Ireland, trade with the European continent had developed from beyond the occasional stone axe to more substantial copper implements.

Some 500 years later the local population began to mine its own copper. Thus, having imported copper items for centuries, the people inhabiting the island of Ireland now began to see the benefit of mining the copper for themselves. The earliest mine was at Ross Island near what is now Killarney, County Kerry. Ross Island is in the middle of a large lake called Lough Leane and it was a rich source of copper. The mining process, which probably originated in continental

Europe, was complex. A fire was lit at a rock face that contained the copper. Through a process of heating the rock then rapidly cooling it through a combination of water and brute force exerted through stone implements, slabs of rock containing the copper were separated from the cliff face. These slabs were then heated to high temperatures in large pits in which fires had been set, which caused them to become brittle, releasing their hidden treasure.

The copper was then formed into small ingots. Later, these ingots were shaped into implements by craftsmen, who often worked close to where the mining took place. However, there is evidence that such craftsmen also worked many hundreds of miles from where the copper had been mined and where the ingots had been formed. This means that the community that mined the copper traded with a distant community of craftsmen. The absence of writing and record-keeping in this prehistorical era means it is not possible to identify with any certainty what the reciprocally traded items were. Given that there is no physical evidence remaining, one can suppose that the traded items were perishables, such as live animals, food or textiles.

The mining process described above was resource- and labour-intensive. It took many tonnes of wood to set the fires that were necessary. As many as 100 miners would be needed to work the mine, which in turn required large amounts of food to feed them. It is not clear how this food was obtained, but it is believed that nearby farmers produced it. Thus, collaboration was needed between at least two specialised groups (farming and mining), as well as a method of value exchange, which, at its simplest, is likely to have involved some sort of equivalence established between the food the farmers produced and the copper the miners extracted. This was most likely done by direct barter or by using the cow as a unit of currency (by the middle Bronze Age the unit of currency most widely used in Ireland was the cow).

When dealing with international trade, such issues still face us today and systems of common understanding have been developed to allow for the easy exchange of goods and services produced in one country to be exchanged with a buyer in another country. To enable the trading process, there must be an exchange system, a method of distribution and some legal certainty as to property rights and entitlement. The overall system leads to specialisation of labour, which in turn creates greater surpluses, which are then further exchanged for more scarcities. The student of international trade would be well served to always bear in mind these dynamics born from our past.

Trade, particularly in copper, with neighbouring islands and with continental Europe continued to develop as the late Stone Age moved to the early Bronze Age. In this era, the sea levels were lower than they are at present by some 40 metres. Though treacherous, the journey from the island of Ireland to Britain was much shorter than it is now. Furthermore, Britain was still connected by a land bridge to continental Europe, allowing even greater migration of peoples. It is not possible to ascertain what items the early Irish received in return for their copper exports. Thus, while we can say with some certainty that Ireland was exporting from the island over 4,000 years ago, we cannot say what was being imported in exchange in this prehistorical, pre-money era. There is evidence of the level of trade that may have been carried out by the examination of the remnants of the early copper mines. As much as 370 tonnes of copper is estimated to have been mined in Ireland during the Bronze Age; however, less than 1% of this is accounted for in finds on the island, leading to the conclusion that most of the copper mined in Ireland was exported.

Farming during the early centuries of the Bronze Age (c. 2,000 BCE) was in its earliest forms. The development of farming meant that settled communities were beginning to evolve, providing people with stability and certainty. However, as no one location could provide all of the resources needed for human existence, trade between communities began to grow. Communities would have specialised in the production of what their immediate environment could allow. For example, while copper was available in Ireland, it was not so easily found in Britain. In contrast, tin could be sourced in Britain, especially in what is now Cornwall, but was not easily found in Ireland. Thus, bronze, an alloy of these two metals, required tin from Britain to be mixed with copper from Ireland.

In order for the inhabitants of Ireland at this time to adopt the new bronze implements they needed to either import tin and make the implements themselves, or export copper and import finished articles. Not to do so was to eschew the improvements to standards of living afforded by the newly discovered technologies allowed by bronze.

1.3 TRADE WITH THE ROMAN EMPIRE

Rome's victory over Carthage in the Second Punic War in the 2nd Century BCE heralded a period of rapid expansion for the Romans. By 50 BCE Julius Caesar had conquered Gaul (France), and in 43 CE the Romans invaded Ireland's nearest neighbour, Britain. The inhabitants of Ireland had already established trade with Britain and, to a lesser degree, continental Europe. This trade was now set to move up a gear.

Referring to its wintry climate, the Romans called the island of Ireland 'Hibernia'. It is accepted history that the Romans never conquered Ireland, though not because they could not. According to the Roman historian Tacitus, the Roman governor of Britain, Agricola, claimed that: "Ireland could be reduced and held by a single legion with a fair force of auxiliaries".[1]

One theory suggests that the Romans were interested in the tin deposits of Britain, but as Ireland had no tin they were not really interested in going any further west. Furthermore, while there is some evidence of a Roman fortification at Loughshinny in North County Dublin, the Romans built on the existing or nascent trade between Ireland and Britain rather than invading. In the decades that followed the Roman invasion of Britain, trade between the islands increased, and there is further evidence of well-developed trade activity between Ireland and the rest of the Roman Empire. In maps drawn up by Ptolemy in the 2nd Century CE, the coastline of Ireland is shown in good detail. The names of the dominant Celtic tribes and their respective regions are also detailed. Ptolemy was a Graeco-Roman living in Alexandria, Egypt. For him to have this level of information means that the Romans of the time must have had a high level of interaction with Ireland since the invasion of Britain 100 years earlier. Indeed, Tacitus, writing in the 1st Century CE, mentions that Ireland differs little from Britain, and that the Romans have knowledge of most of its harbours through the merchants who trade there.

By the 1st Century CE Ireland was most likely exporting food, clothing, animal hides and slaves via traders who operated within the wider Roman Empire. Mention of the slave trade may surprise many modern readers. However, in Roman times the notion of human rights and individual freedoms were many centuries away. As societies across the globe developed elite classes, there also emerged inferior classes of people. These people would have worked for their keep and could be bought and sold the same as any other chattel of the time. Prisoners of war were also treated as a slave class. Roman Britain needed slaves to support its 'villa farm' system

---

[1] Waddell, J. (1998). *The Prehistoric Archaeology of Ireland*. Dublin: Wordwell.

and to work in the mines. Some of the slaves were provided from Ireland. Irish clans also conducted raids on the Scottish and Welsh coast where captives would be taken away to later become slaves. It is widely believed that this is how St Patrick arrived in Ireland.

These 'goods' would have been exchanged for pottery, metal utensils and, for the first time in Ireland, money. Roman copper coins have been found in Kilkenny, silver coins at Ballinrees, County Derry and gold coins at Newgrange, County Meath. The Newgrange finds could well be votive offerings by merchants or pilgrims, but the copper and silver finds are possible results of trade exchange between Ireland and the Roman Empire.

Small pieces of Roman pottery have been found at a number of sites in Ireland. There have also been finds of a Roman bronze ladle in County Meath and a small Roman handbell in County Kildare, offering us conclusive proof that there was interaction between the Romans and the inhabitants of the island. The settlements where the artefacts were found indicate that the indigenous population had assimilated these items rather than that Romans had settled in Ireland, bringing the items with them; again, this confirms the existence of trade between the communities.

Some Roman individuals did settle in Ireland, however, and it clear that by 100 CE there were Romans living for a while in small communities and trading with the locals. A burial site discovered in County Kilkenny in 1852 revealed a person buried in accordance with the Roman ritual of the time. The burial site, a mound protected by stones, held a sealed green jar containing cremated human remains.[2] This burial method was common in the 1st Century CE throughout the Roman Empire. The intricacy of the burial points to other people versed in Roman burial methods having been present after the person died. It would also suggest some type of permanent or semi-permanent presence in the area of a trading outpost or even a Roman settlement.

By 400 CE Irish wolfhounds were appearing in Rome, much to the awe of Roman citizens.[3] By now the Roman Empire was coming under increased attack from the barbarian tribes of Northern Europe, especially at its periphery. Under the Emperor Theodosius, Christianity became the official religion of the Roman Empire in 381 CE. By now the Empire itself had split in two, with the capital of the western Empire located in Rome and the eastern Empire in Constantinople (now Istanbul).

The idea of the nation state was beginning to develop and with it, increased trade. Nations suggest a legal structure that can be enforced by the rulers. A legal structure, particularly property law, underpins trade and enables the development of international trading. Property ownership, protected by law, allows for more certainty in trade in that the owner of one good can confidently exchange this right with the owner of some other goods.

The movement of people became much more widespread and with it trade increased. Trade and the development of standardised currencies brought about increased economic activity and the emergence of a new class of professional traders. Not producing anything themselves, this new merchant class instead saw opportunities to match supply and demand, taking a margin in the process. Traders and merchants would play a significant role in the development of business in the centuries to come. Their contribution to international business was especially

---

[2] Bourke, E. (1989). "Stoneyford: A first century Roman burial from Ireland". *Archaeology Ireland*, 57(3:2).

[3] Slaymen, S. (1996). "Romans in Ireland". *Archaeology Magazine*, 49(3).

important as they operated across kingdoms. They could speak different languages and kept accurate records. These skills, albeit rudimentary at the time, are still a critical part of the toolkit of an international business.

Increased trade between Ireland and its neighbours led to a gradual infiltration of Celtic culture. While it is not clear how this culture came to intermingle with the indigenous culture, linguists can tell that the language spoken by inhabitants of Ireland by 100 CE was of the Goidelic languages, as spoken by Celtic groups from the Iberian Peninsula. There were four waves of Celtic migration into Ireland stretching from 600 BCE to 100 CE.

While the Celts of this era traded with both Britain and continental Europe, this trade was not the substantive part of economic activity of Ireland. Ireland had now a mainly agricultural economy and most of the population would have little better than a subsistence standard of living. Studies of pollen residues from the period 100 CE to 200 CE show that oats, wheat and barley were the main farm outputs. However, cattle were the prized possessions of farmers. Indeed, as mentioned above, the unit of wealth at the time was a cow, or more precisely a cow and a calf. One's wealth, and therefore status, was defined by the number of milking cows one possessed. Incessant cattle raids required that farmers bring their animals into enclosures at night to keep them safe.[4] These enclosures were predominantly circular earthen mounds with wooden stakes on top and the remains of as many as 40,000 have been discovered in Ireland.

1.4 PRE- AND EARLY-CHRISTIAN IRELAND

During the Bronze and Iron Ages, trade with their neighbours had allowed the inhabitants of Ireland to embrace the latest technologies. However, as the Roman Empire declined, Ireland also entered its own 'Dark Age'. The island's growth in international trade stagnated between 300 and c. 550 CE and it remained a relatively underdeveloped backwater of Europe.

However, there was still trade with the Continent. One example of this is demonstrated by the physical layout of the 'Fair at Carman', which was held once every three years in north Kildare, and was in existence from 400 CE until c. 1000 CE. This was a major event in the lives of the people of Leinster at this time. The fair would begin on 1 August and last for six days. We know from the Book of Leinster that much of the activities of the fair were given over to entertainment: musicians and poets jostled with gymnasts and horsemen to entertain the masses.

In addition to the festivities, however, was the more serious business of commerce. The commercial aspects of the fair were conducted in a specially designated area divided into three sections: for the buying and selling of food and clothes; for trade in livestock and horses; and, finally, for foreign merchants to sell their goods. These merchants would have come from Britain and continental Europe. Their wares would have been predominantly gold and silver items and fine cloths, such as silk. They would have traded for local wool, woollen garments and animal skins. The use of money would not have been as developed as it had been in the Roman Empire.

These traders faced many of the same issues that face international business today. The logistics of transporting goods across vast distances must have been quite a task in a violent time when bandits were not unusual. How the trader would calculate the appropriate exchange value for

---

[4] Lucas, A. (1989). *Cattle in Ancient Ireland*. Boethius.

his wares presented another challenge: he would need to consider the possible value on continental Europe of the Irish products he was receiving in exchange. Likewise, the indigenous Irish buyers needed to be able to place a value on the product of their labour. For example, how would they calculate the exchange value of squirrel skins versus silk cloth from the Orient?

The Celtic culture still predominated on the island of Ireland at this time, during the first 500 years CE. Society was regulated through the Brehon Laws, which originated from the aggregated cumulative decisions of judges. As there are no written records of these judgments, the application of the law relied upon oral recollection. The training for a judge, or Brehon, was lengthy and arduous, involving the committing to memory of a vast array of previous judgments. The code was primarily a civil one rather than criminal, and dealt mainly with the protection of property, inheritance, marriage, and the righting of wrongs by the application of punishments and restitution. The Brehon Laws facilitated trade by providing a means of identifying property ownership together with remedies in case an exchange of property between two parties went wrong. This rule of law in Ireland greatly facilitated the growth of trade domestically, which in turn laid the foundations for international trade.

1.5 TRADE IN THE MIDDLE AGES

Economic activity in Ireland in the Middle Ages (from 400 CE to 1500 CE) can be broken down into two distinct phases: the period up to the arrival of the Vikings (around 800 CE) and the period afterward (from 800 CE up to 1500 CE). In the pre-Viking period Ireland was made up of agricultural communities, primarily self-sufficient and self-contained. Extended families lived in fortified circular settlements called 'raths' and produced all their own needs with little or no commercial interaction with others or communities outside of the island. Seen from outside, not much was going on in terms of foreign trade. The decline of the Roman Empire and subsequent erosion in the rule of law in Western Europe led to a reduction in the amount of long-distance travel and trade from Ireland. However, on the other side of Europe trade was increasing as merchants from the Middle East began to increase their influence on the silk routes to and from the Orient. The newly founded religion of Islam in the 6th Century 600 CE, with its positive view of trading, encouraged expansion of trading relationships and conquest. By the end of the 1st millennium CE, Muslim control of Mediterranean trading was almost complete and their armies had pushed well to the east of India.[5]

Foreign trade in the north-western islands of Europe was not growing at the same scale, however. These peripheral regions were of little interest to the newly dominant Middle Eastern traders. The further west of Baghdad you were, it seemed, the less likely that the rising tide of world trade was to affect you. Ireland did not benefit from the growth in trade because of its isolation and became less developed than the peoples to the east of it, which eventually led to Ireland becoming weaker than its neighbours:

> "Only the Irish remained almost impenetrable to foreign custom. For unaccounted reasons, probably rooted in social custom, they continued to cherish isolated farmsteads and to raid one another's cattle. Thus, they missed almost entirely the economic growth sweeping the rest of Europe".[6]

---

[5] Bernstein, W. (2008). *A Splendid Exchange*. New York: Atlantic Monthly Press.

[6] Lopez, R. (1971). *The Commercial Revolution of the Middle Ages, 950–1350*. Englewood Cliffs, N.J.: Prentice-Hall.

It is still a facet of modern international development that a modern economy with technological development strengthens a nation and leads to raised standards of living for its people.

While there is some evidence that the isolation of Ireland as described above by Roberto Lopez may have been the case during the early medieval period, it does not stand up to scrutiny as time goes on. Increasingly, both archaeological and written evidence of foreign trade from this period has been found, pointing to the importation of wine, olive oil, glass and grain. If these items were being imported, then there had to be an exchange method, either by way of money or in kind, to 'swap' domestic produce for the imported goods. Written accounts exist of the main exports from Ireland during this time, which appear to have been animal hides, hunting dogs, butter and slaves.[7] There is also evidence of the export of shoes and finished clothing, such as cloaks.

For centuries on the island of Ireland people lived in agricultural communities, a granular societal structure that hindered the growth of an export trade; local agricultural communities were unlikely to combine and specialise to produce more than their immediate needs demanded. In order to produce a surplus that could be exported, there would need to be a structured coordination of agricultural or industrial activity. Either each farmstead produced a modest surplus, or some nobleman or member of the elite caused there to be a concentration of production targeted for the purposes of trade. The latter is more likely and it was through the emergence of an elite ruling class that surpluses began to be created, presumably in the expectation of demand for the products from abroad. To imagine a future demand for a product and then cause it to be made requires a degree of planning and control. Thus, this medieval Irish business class was forecasting demand, causing production of surpluses on the island and then interacting with traders from abroad.

The export of butter is an interesting facet of this pre-refrigeration age. We know that butter was exported from Ireland in the early 19th Century without refrigeration, so it is quite possible that butter was exported from Ireland in the 9th Century. There is mention of Irish butter in the *Life of Columbanus*, where monks are consuming Irish butter in Northern Italy.[8]

Viking and Norman Ireland

When the Vikings arrived in Ireland around 800 CE, they established the first urban settlements, many of which were the foundations of today's towns and cities. These settlements with their concentrated populations could not be self-sufficient in food, so trade in general had to grow dramatically. As the Viking settlements were connected to communities outside of Ireland there was a dramatic increase in the level of foreign trade, dominated primarily by the Vikings with their maritime skills.

We have seen how the trade in slaves was a feature of commerce to and from Ireland since at least the 1st Century CE.[9] The Vikings took the import and export of slaves to a new level, setting up Ireland's first slave market in Dublin. Though it is uncertain if Ireland was a net importer or exporter of slaves, it is clear that slave trading was as integral a part of commerce at this time as it was throughout the world.

---

[7] Doehaerd, R. (1978). *The Early Middle Ages in the West*. Amsterdam: North-Holland Pub. Co.

[8] Krush, B. (1902). *Scriptores Rerum Merovingicarum IV. Hannoverae*: [Societas Aperiendis Fontibus Rerum Germanicarum Medii Aevi].

[9] Charles-Edwards, T. (2000). *Early Christian Ireland*. UK: Cambridge University Press.

FIGURE 1.1: IRELAND IN 1014 CE[10]

After a few generations, the inhabitants of the Viking settlements at Dublin, Limerick, Cork and Waterford became more integrated into the existing culture and social structure of the remainder of Ireland. What had been fortified encampments of invading Norsemen became the first cities of Ireland, acting as trading hubs through their maritime and riverine attributes. Since the Vikings came from Scandinavia, much of the trade they conducted was with their home population and its extended reach (Greenland, Iceland, Normandy and parts of maritime Britain). The exports from Ireland at this time were cereals and other foodstuffs, animals and slaves. Gold, silver and silks were also being imported and craftsmen in the urban settlements fashioned the gold and silver into brooches and other valuable artistic pieces. These could be exchanged for agricultural output from the farms which lay in the hinterland, and were still predominantly controlled by the indigenous Irish clans.

---

[10] Showing the Viking settlements of Cork, Dublin, Limerick, Waterford and Wexford. Adapted from McGettigan, D. (2013). *The Battle of Clontarf, Good Friday, 1014.* Dublin, Ireland: Four Courts Press.

The next significant increase in foreign trade came with the arrival of the Normans in 1169 CE. Originally arriving in Ireland to take sides in the endless squabbles between the tribal kings, the Normans found rich pickings on the island. The Normans were originally Norsemen who had based themselves in what became Normandy in Northern France. They invaded England in 1066 and took control of much of the country. By 1169, when the Normans invaded Ireland, Henry II was the first Norman King to proclaim himself King of all England. Previous Norman kings controlled much of England but not all of it.

The Normans brought with them to Ireland new methods of agriculture and of land ownership. Under the Brehon Laws, land was held by the extended clan with complex rules for how its benefits were to be divided up between the clan members. However, under the Normans, land was owned by an individual who farmed it through a tenant system for profit. Thus, the agricultural activity of Ireland changed from being one primarily of subsistence to one of producing surpluses for profit. This new 'for profit' agricultural system brought about an economic boom in Ireland. Foreign trade increased dramatically and the new landowners integrated the island even more with the trade routes of Europe and further afield. The Normans were not interested in land that could not be farmed profitably and concentrated their domination on lowlands with good connections to the port cities that had originally been set up by the Vikings.

Outside of the wider Dublin area, the Hiberno-Normans quickly began to integrate with the original Irish inhabitants and from the earliest days of Norman settlement in Ireland there was suspicion and jealousy among the Normans in Britain (Anglo-Normans) towards the Normans who had colonised Ireland (Hiberno-Normans). This tension between the two groups of Normans meant that foreign trade activity did not flourish in Ireland. Usually, an increase in commercial activity ought to lead to an increase in the export and import trade of a region. However, until the 1500s, such foreign trade did not increase substantially in Ireland; the Hiberno-Normans found that their Anglo-Norman cousins in Britain were not overly enthusiastic about trading with them. Since Britain was, and still is, a natural market for Irish produce, this hesitancy hindered the growth of the export trade.

Continuous wars with France drew English attention away from commerce with Ireland; the use of ships to cross the Irish Sea was seen as both perilous and a poor use of scarce resources. As a result, foreign trade from Ireland slowly stagnated. From the mid-14th Century, the devastating effects of the Black Death throughout Europe also served to dampen foreign trade from Ireland. The movement of people was severely curtailed by populations terrified of bringing the bubonic plague into their area. Trade throughout Europe slackened as people shuttered up their towns and villages, hoping to evade death.

As the 14th Century drew to a close, Hiberno-Norman estates shrank in size as they were subdivided amongst Norman heirs, which led to in-fighting and a reduction in their power. The Gaelic chieftains began to exercise increased control on the island as the Norman influence waned. These internal power shifts meant that while there was great turmoil and change in Ireland, its trade with the rest of the world remained static.

Until the time of King Henry VIII in the 16th Century, the trading relationship between Ireland and the rest of Europe had remained relatively stable after its initial blossoming following the arrival of the Normans. In 1536, Henry broke from Rome and began to assert himself in Ireland, displacing the Hiberno-Norman FitzGeralds, who had become the dominant dynasty. This time saw the beginning of the development of Ireland as a major producer of agricultural products for export. The intensity of the farming increased and, with it, the production of surpluses. Surpluses were also maximised by rationing levels of production made available to the indigenous peasantry. In a seismic change from the past, land was now mainly owned and controlled by absentee landlords with the focus on profit. Exports included timber for shipbuilding, salt beef, pork and butter. For the following 200 years Ireland increasingly became a supplier of foodstuffs and raw materials to England. The mix of exports remained broadly the same until the 1780s, when there began to be a switch away from salt beef to grain production due to increased competition from American and Scandinavian producers.

FIGURE 1.2: EXTENT OF NORMAN DOMINATION IN IRELAND BY 1300 CE

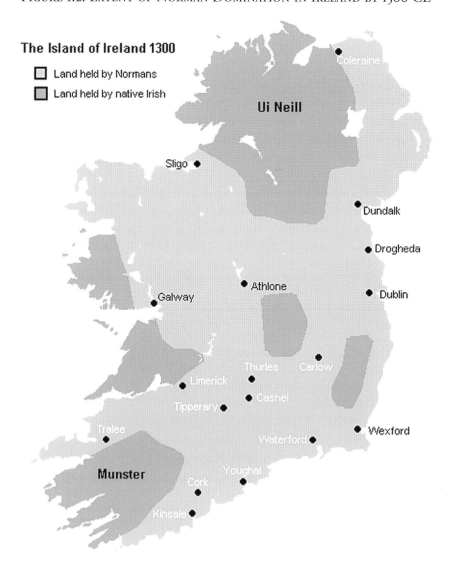

During the 1700s there was significant infrastructure development in Ireland with the construction of two major canals and improvements to the road networks, which facilitated increased agricultural output from the areas serviced by the new routes.

1.6 THE INDUSTRIAL REVOLUTION

Aside from major industrialisation in the north of Ireland, centred on Belfast, both in shipbuilding and textile manufacturing, the Industrial Revolution of the 18th and 19th Centuries did not generally impact upon Ireland to the extent it did in most of Northern Europe. In the 19th Century, Ireland was still primarily a producer of raw material for onward processing in the factories of Britain and continental Europe. It also remained an important food producer. While the Guinness brewery and the Jacobs biscuit factory were significant operations and employers in Dublin, the rest of Ireland was mainly made up of small holdings producing food and raw materials for the export market.

Indicative of the growth of Belfast as an economic centre in the 19th Century, its population in 1800 is estimated to have been 20,000; by 1900 this had grown to 400,000, eclipsing Dublin as the most populous city on the island. Improvements to its docklands in the early 1800s facilitated the export of linen and led to the development of a shipbuilding industry from the 1840s. While mass emigration due to the Great Famine in the mid-19th Century further impoverished the rest of the island, Belfast was booming. The spin-off industries from shipbuilding led to the world's largest rope manufacturing factory being based in Belfast.

Following the devastating reduction in population on the island as a result of the Famine, economic activity stagnated for a while and then began to grow again. The development of a railway infrastructure opened up the island to greater movement of goods. In 1845 there were 100 miles of rail track in Ireland; by 1855 this had grown to 1,000 miles. One tonne of coal used to take five days to get to Galway by canal. This could now be achieved in 10 hours by train. The movement and mobility of finished goods, raw materials and workers improved. As a result, exports from Ireland began to increase, particularly from factories in cities with rail links to ports.

A lesson for today's multinational enterprise (MNE, see **Chapter 2**) in understanding where to locate foreign manufacturing plants can be drawn from this history. Availability of the right type of workforce must be coupled with infrastructure links in order to achieve the economies needed for the successful development of trade. Indeed, infrastructure improvements often herald consolidation of industries as economies of scale can be more readily achieved if distribution and logistics are improved. For example, there were over 200 breweries on the island of Ireland in the early 1800s. This had reduced to around 40 by the time the railway network had reached its full scale. Larger breweries could now get their products to their customers more effectively using the railway system. Smaller, better-run breweries took advantage of the new reach the system provided and they expanded, taking market share from their less able competitors.

As the 19th Century drew to a close, Ireland had seen the industrialisation of the north-east and the depopulation of the rural countryside. Both of these changes dramatically altered the nature of foreign trade on the island.

1.7 THE TWENTIETH CENTURY

When compared to the preceding 19 centuries, the 20th Century saw more change and, in particular, greater scale, in the nature of international trade into and from the island of Ireland. The north-east of the island, particularly Belfast, continued its industrial production in textiles and shipbuilding, and Belfast remained Ireland's dominant industrial city. The remainder of the island continued to be a predominantly agriculture-based economy. Imports tended to be luxury goods and the factors of production that could not be made locally, i.e. mainly machinery and raw materials.

The partition of the island in 1922 and the consequent creation of Northern Ireland and the Irish Free State (subsequently the Republic of Ireland) meant that two stories of foreign trade developed. Northern Ireland continued to have a strong trading relationship with Britain and most of its exports and imports were connected to that relationship. Meanwhile, the nascent Republic of Ireland struggled to gain traction in its foreign trade as it endeavoured to set up the infrastructure needed to run a freestanding economy. The Free State Government engaged in an economic war with the UK that led to severe trade restrictions between the two countries from 1932 to 1938. Even though this dispute with the UK officially ended in 1938, the Free State and subsequently the Republic of Ireland continued with a policy of protectionism until the late 1950s. Investment in infrastructure improvements, such as electrification, took time to fund and implement. Education, housing and healthcare all needed investment in order to improve standards of living and economic capability. As the infrastructure lagged behind that of most of Northern Europe, standards of living did not keep pace. Emigration from the new republic continued at a pace, particularly in the 1950s.

Northern Ireland's infrastructure was more developed, in part due to the economic benefit derived from its strong manufacturing heritage and associated wealth. While Northern Ireland continued to serve its traditional markets, inward investment was hard to come by. As the textile industry came under pressure from cheaper production elsewhere, job losses began to take their toll. The UK had been involved in two world wars in the 20th Century; the loss of life and of economic assets was huge. After the Second World War, the dismantling of the British Empire commenced. Large parts of the Empire that had traditionally been part of an extensive trading network fell away to become fully independent countries in their own right. The knock-on effect was to reduce demand for exports from Britain, including Northern Ireland.

The stagnation of international trade continued more or less on both parts of the island until both the UK and the Republic of Ireland joined the European Economic Community (EEC) in 1973. Up until this time, the main foreign trading partner of the Republic, for imports and exports, had been Britain. There was also a strong commercial relationship between Northern Ireland and Britain. After joining the EEC, unprecedented new foreign markets were opened up to companies in Ireland. The removal of trade barriers heralded a major change. First, import increased as goods that had been subject to tariffs and import controls became available for the first time or at considerably cheaper prices. These imports added to overall economic activity but mainly displaced existing domestic production on the island – domestic production that had become inefficient for one reason or another. Secondly, and more importantly, producers on the island began to seize the opportunities the new markets presented by focusing on sectors where they could compete more effectively. The governments put in place agencies that would endeavour to attract industries to Ireland to manufacture products to then sell on to the newly opened-up markets. US companies in particular were attracted to the island, encouraged by the bond of a common language and an educated workforce. Standards of living on the island, however, were still behind Britain, the rest of Northern Europe and the US. Consequently, the first wave of inward investment saw MNEs taking advantage of this relatively cheap but educated workforce.

As the EEC expanded, becoming the European Community (EC) in 1993 and then European Union (EU) in 2009, the labour cost differential was slowly eroded. The success of world governments in reducing, but not yet eliminating, trade barriers meant that even cheaper labour forces could be found. Inward investment into Ireland based on labour cost differentials declined and the nature of the export industry in Northern Ireland, and particularly the Republic, moved towards skills-based knowledge economies. As we shall see in **Chapter 4**, Ireland has become increasingly an exporter of services rather than tangible goods. These services, mainly from the software industry, reflect the higher added value that can be achieved through a well-educated workforce. These types of exports add more value to the economy as a whole, improving domestic demand for consumer products through the redistribution of wages.

Figure 1.3 below shows the relative benefit to the Republic of Ireland in the growth of exports since joining the EEC in 1973 compared to the UK. Taking 2005 prices as constant in order to factor out inflation, the average annual growth in exports for each decade is calculated for both the Republic of Ireland and the UK. The average annual growth in the 1970s, factoring out inflation, was 7.3%. This was a dramatic increase and was improved upon in the two decades that followed. The growth did not just come from joining the EEC. The dividend for investment in schools and hospitals, together with electricity and housing also helped. Global improvements in logistics technology and computerised monitoring systems meant that a previously isolated island on the edge of Europe could become more connected. These changes encouraged growth.

FIGURE 1.3: GROWTH IN EXPORTS: CONSTANT 2005 PRICES[11]

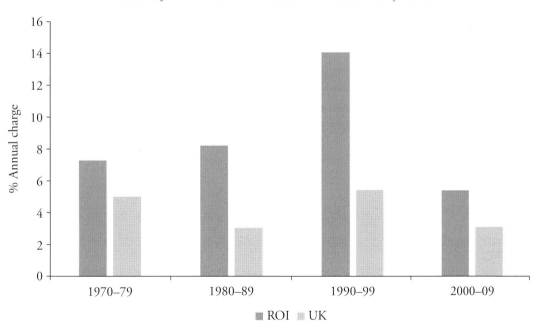

The relative change in imports in the same period is not as dramatic, as can be seen in **Figure 1.4** below.

Imports into the Republic of Ireland differ from imports into the UK decade by decade. However, taking the last 40 years together, the average growth in imports into the Republic has lagged the UK: 3.7% average compared to the UK figure of 4.5%. Taking the exports over the

---

[11] United Nations' statistics and the author's calculations.

40 years, the Republic is well ahead with an average of 8.7% compared to a growth of 4.1% in the UK. Both countries have shown growth in international trade over the last four decades, but two interesting features emerge:

- the growth in the Republic of Ireland has been twice UK levels; and
- the Republic's numbers are more volatile, which suggests a more open economy that is more dependent on the ebbs and flows of world trade demand curve and its own capability to meet those demands.

FIGURE 1.4: PERCENTAGE ANNUAL CHANGE IN IMPORTS (2005 CONSTANT PRICES)

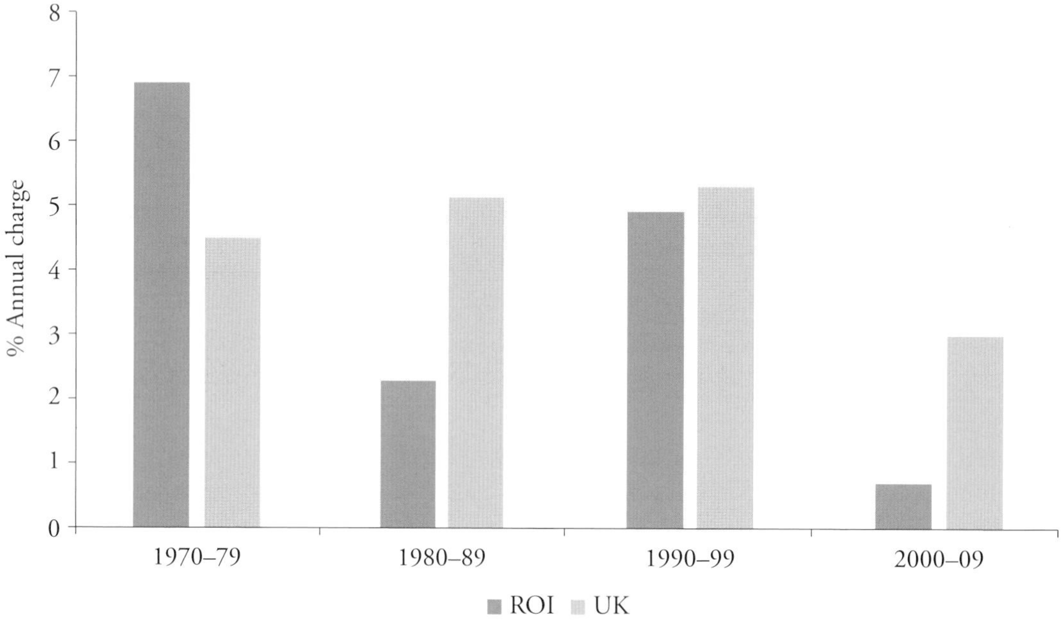

1.8 CONCLUSION

Trade across great distances has been a feature of humankind's existence for many thousands of years. In this chapter, we have seen that humans have been trading surpluses with each other since the Stone Age. Over time, such surpluses were created intentionally for the purpose of trade and, in turn, the distances over which these goods were traded increased. The creation of surpluses led to geographically based expertise and specialisation of outputs based on the local availability of natural resources. As surpluses increased so did production scarcity, which arose from the increased focus of resources on the production of the surpluses to the detriment of other possible production outputs. By specialising in producing one good, the extra surplus can offset the production that has been foregone; thus, trade creates an interdependency between otherwise unconnected peoples. This interdependency, together with improved standards of living, is the basis upon which most governments are eager to encourage international trade.

The island of Ireland has been involved in exporting and importing goods and services for millennia. As the Bronze Age developed so did Ireland's trade with its neighbouring islands and continental Europe. The Roman invasion of Britain, along with the subsequent invasions of

Ireland by the Vikings and the Normans, led to even more trade routes opening up, availing of the invading peoples' pre-existing trade routes. They also brought new technologies and legal structures that supported the production of surpluses, commercial certainty and the seeking of profit.

During the Industrial Revolution in the 19th Century, Belfast became the main industrial centre on the island while the remainder of the country increased its food production capability through mechanisation and expanding farms. In the 20th Century, the newly formed Republic of Ireland was subject to protectionism and trade barriers, which resulted in its economic growth and standard of living stalling while Northern Ireland remained a strong industrial producer. In 1973, both the UK and the Republic of Ireland joined the European Economic Community, which heralded a period of unprecedented growth in exports and imports for both countries. Standards of living improved, especially in the Republic of Ireland.

The factors that underpin trade over long distances have not changed much over the six millennia that the peoples of Ireland have engaged in it. Those factors are:
- the ability to produce surpluses;
- the anticipation of scarcities elsewhere;
- mechanisms to transport goods and services over long distances;
- a clear, certain and enforceable legal system; and
- an agreed exchange system.

International trade has become increasingly sophisticated and complex, but these five factors remain the bedrock of such trade and it is worth reverting to this list from time to time as you progress through this textbook.

One of the main features of the growth of international trade has been the creation of profit-seeking enterprises that aim to produce surpluses which they exchange for money or in kind across the globe. The growth of these organisations, multinational enterprises (MNEs), is the topic of the next chapter.

QUESTIONS

Self-test Questions

1.1 Why do communities engage in importing and exporting activity?
1.2 Explain how membership of the EEC (now the EU) has benefited foreign trade on the island of Ireland.
1.3 Why was Belfast so much more vibrant economically than the rest of the island during the Industrial Revolution?
1.4 Explain the benefits from infrastructure investment for international trade.

2

WHY BUSINESSES BECOME MULTINATIONALS

CONTENTS

LEARNING OBJECTIVES

Having read this chapter, you will understand:
- the nature and definition of the multinational enterprise;
- theories of why countries and companies trade internationally;
- the growth of international trade, especially over the last 50 years;
- why enterprises seek to expand internationally;
- what structures MNEs adopt in their international expansion;
- how agency costs increase as an MNE expands; and
- the role of the professional accountant in an MNE.

2.1 INTRODUCTION

In **Chapter 1** we saw that even before nation states existed, people traded across large distances. For this to happen, communities needed to be organised to such a degree that:
- local surpluses could be created to meet expected scarcities elsewhere;
- local scarcities could be met by exchanging local surpluses for surpluses created elsewhere;
- a means of transporting surpluses efficiently across large distances was available;
- an exchange system was developed; and
- a legal system capable of enforcing property rights was in place.

These five factors are still critical to successful international trade. Producers need to be able to make surplus goods and services and transport these efficiently to the markets in which they are demanded.

The producers need an exchange system through which they receive a return for their endeavours. The exchange system allows the producer to exchange the surplus for money, which can in turn be used to acquire a scarcity that they desire, or return a profit for their investors.

In this chapter we will see how humankind has increasingly organised itself to facilitate international trade. Since Adam Smith developed the concept of free trade in the late 1700s and demonstrated how it benefits all nations, governments have worked to remove barriers to the movement of goods, persons and capital. Though this process has not been rapid, often being tempered by parochial interests, fears of job losses or sovereignty, etc., the movement of goods has been increasingly facilitated by the development of transport infrastructures and the reduction or abolition of tariffs and quotas.

The development of the 'corporation' as a separate legal entity has also played a part in the growth of international trade. The corporation has become a vehicle through which surpluses are created and traded. The structure and framework these corporations, or multinational enterprises (MNEs), take when executing international trade is described in this chapter. In the final section we will explore the role of the accountant in the multinational enterprise and highlight how the finance function adds value in such organisations.

2.2 THE MULTINATIONAL ENTERPRISE ('MNE')

There are many books about international business and each adopts its own definitions of the various types of enterprise involved. In this book, I refer to an organisation involved in international trade as a **multinational enterprise** ('MNE'). The United Nations Conference on Trade and Development (UNCTAD) describes an MNE as:

> "an enterprise comprising entities in more than one country which operate under a system of decision-making that permits coherent policies and a common strategy."[1]

I use a somewhat wider definition of an MNE in this book in order to include enterprises that interact commercially with entities in more than one country. By widening the definition in this way we can include enterprises that import or export to other countries without actually owning entities there. Since most MNEs begin their international activities by exporting or importing, it helps understand MNEs more completely by including all enterprises that engage in trade with entities in other countries. Thus, in this text I define an MNE as:

> 'an enterprise that trades with entities in more than one country or comprises entities in more than one country that can make collective decisions through an integrated decision-making framework'.

In this book, the term 'MNE' is used to denote any business enterprise involved in international trade. Participation in international trade may take many forms:
- parent company with subsidiaries in other countries;
- subsidiary company with parent in another country;
- importing from or exporting to other countries;
- operating a foreign franchise either as franchisor or franchisee;
- operating as a licensee or licensor for a non-domestic principal.

---

[1] See http://unctad.org (UNCTAD is the principal organ of the United Nations General Assembly dealing with trade, investment and development issues).

The definition I use is deliberately wide enough to cover all enterprises that trade with entities outside their domestic jurisdiction. Where necessary I will examine the specifics as they apply to particular subsets of this wider population of MNEs, e.g. subsidiaries of foreign companies operating in Ireland. Thus, in general, the 'MNE' referred to in this text is an entity that carries on trade outside of its domestic home economy.

In **Chapter 1** we introduced the ancient nature of trade between different peoples from different geographic areas across significant distances. Since before written records began, as far back as 4000 BCE, the people of these islands have been trading with their neighbours and further afield.

The first cause behind international trade is the production of surpluses to trade for scarcities. Trade originates in meeting needs and wants that can only be addressed by trading with a distant party, people, or nation as the good or service desired does not exist in the home country. For example, the early Irish imported tin from Cornwall to mix with copper to make bronze implements as there was little or not in Ireland.

The same basic position is what drives the oil industry. Both the developed and developing world needs oil and its by-products to further grow and develop their economies. However, most countries cannot meet their oil needs from their own domestic supplies. Instead, they must trade with those countries that have an excess of oil, mainly Middle Eastern states which deliberately produce surpluses that can then be sold to those for whom oil is scarce. With the money they receive for the oil they can buy goods and services that are scarce in their home country. Indeed, the most profitable company in the world in 2014 was an American oil company, Exxon Mobil, and Europe's most profitable oil and gas company in 2014 was Royal Dutch Shell.[2]

The second cause of trade across seas and borders is that it enables people and organisations to meet their needs more efficiently. Some locations are more suited to the production of a product than others. For example, Ireland can produce milk all year round with minimal supplemental feeding and housing of dairy cows. Our mild maritime climate allows for an efficient production process compared to other parts of the world, which allows Ireland to compete on global markets even though the average farm size in terms of herd numbers pales into insignificance when compared internationally. This relatively simplistic description of Ireland's dairy industry is an example in action of the law of comparative advantage, which seeks to explain why some countries can produce surpluses more efficiently than others. This is explained in more detail later in this chapter.

As shown in **Figure 2.1** below, international trade in goods has grown from US$185 billion in 1964 to US$18,798 billion by 2013, over a 100-fold increase in 50 years. The growth of international trade in services has been even more pronounced. Why has this happened? Do the two causes of international trade outlined above explain the tremendous growth of MNEs?

In the next section I will seek to explain why there has been such a dramatic increase in international trade over the last five decades, first exploring some theories and concepts of international trade and then discussing how successive governments throughout the world have increasingly fostered and nurtured it. There have been obstacles along the way, and there is still much that could be done, but the route to improved living standards at a global level through international trade has been established.

---

[2] http://fortune.com/2015/06/11/fortune-500-most-profitable-companies/(accessed September 2015).

FIGURE 2.1: GLOBAL IMPORTS: US$ BILLIONS AT CURRENT PRICES AND EXCHANGE RATES[3]

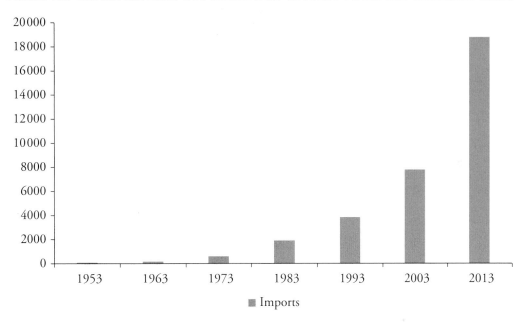

2.3 THEORIES OF INTERNATIONAL TRADE

Scholars have analysed trends in trade since the 1960s in order to determine why international trade occurs and, in particular, why it has grown so dramatically. They want to understand what benefits this increase in international trade has brought to humankind and, if there have been benefits, to develop agreed ways to encourage more international trade.

To fully understand the nature of international trade and its related theories we must go back a bit further than the 1960s to examine the first theories of international trade as they emerged in the 1600s. We will then trace how these theories have developed, particularly how the advent of democratic capitalism as an economic model influenced international trade theory and practice.

Mercantilism

One of the earliest theories on why nations should encourage international trade was **mercantilism**. Extant from the late 1500s through to the 1800s, the essence of this theory was that nations accumulate wealth by maximising exports and minimising imports, thereby running a balance of trade surplus. The idea was to build up significant reserves as a result of selling and exporting more than the nation imported. The reserves would normally be represented by significant gold reserves. Mercantilism was given real-life expression through government policies which sought to place tariffs on imports in order to protect the home production market.

A belief central to mercantilism was that trade between nations was a 'zero sum game', i.e. if a nation imported products, then it denied itself the economic benefit of producing those

---

[3] World Trade Organisation, International Trade Statistics 2013, www.wto.org/statistics.

products itself. The economic 'pie' is finite; therefore nations should focus on maximising the size of their slice by limiting the amount available to others. Put another way, global trade is limited in size and the way a nation gains wealth is by taking from other nations.

An effect of the European Renaissance was a greater focus on scientific measurement of most aspects of man's worldly existence, including international trade. Imports and exports were measured more accurately and the scientific approach served to increase the fervour with which successive European monarchs and leaders believed in the mercantile system. By doing everything possible to further exports and minimise imports, countries competed in ways that would feed into a drive for colonial conquests and incessant warring over territory and supply routes. For example, the British restricted trade by and with its colonies in North America with the imposition of trade embargos. It also sought to ensure that the colonies only produced raw materials and that value would be added in the home economy through the reworking of those materials. This resulted in wide-scale smuggling as the inhabitants of the colonies sought to buy better priced products from nations competing with Britain, and also frustration, which eventually boiled over into the American Revolution from 1765 to 1783.

An iconic event in the struggle for American independence, the Boston Tea Party in 1773, involved the dumping of tea from an arriving cargo ship into Boston harbour thereby rendering it unsaleable. This act of protest came as a direct result of the British government's imposition of mercantile policies. The East India Company had been given the monopoly for the import of tea into Britain. The company was not allowed, however, to export tea to the colonies but had to sell tea at wholesale prices to British exporters, who would then export it to the colonies. These exporters sought to make a high profit on this trade since the 'colonials' could only legally buy tea from British exporters, which led to widespread tea smuggling, particularly by Dutch traders.

The British government sought to reduce the overall effect of the smuggling in 1767 by giving the East India Company a 25% rebate on any of its tea that was re-exported to the colonies. In essence, the East India Company could undercut its competitors since it was in receipt of a rebate from the British Government whilst both the existing legitimate traders and smugglers received no such rebate. In order to part-finance the cost of this rebate, the British Government sought the imposition of a tax on tea exports to the colonies; however, this only exacerbated the smuggling situation in the colonies. As a result, the additional taxes were repealed in 1770 and the British Americans were once again enjoying teas from the East India Company. However, in 1772 the rebate was reviewed and reduced; this, along with the re-introduction of taxes for tea imported and consumed in Britain, led to a dramatic reduction in consumption. The East India Company continued to import tea despite the fact that it was not being sold. The effect was the creation of a 'tea mountain', and to dispose of the ever-increasing stock, the solution was simple: sell it off to the colonies. Rebates were introduced again for re-exported tea and the East India Company was allowed to export directly to the colonies. Ironically, this was designed to 'drop' the price of tea in the colonies; however, the resultant price drop was a major upset to the British American tea traders who had built up legitimate and illegitimate business in the importing and reselling of tea in the British Americas. In December 1773 demonstrators boarded ships containing 'cheap' tea belonging to the East India Company and dumped it into the harbour, rendering it unsaleable.

The immediate effect of the protest was to upscale the level of instability and insurrection in the British Americas. The event became a symbolic moment in the striving for independence by the British Americans. The policies implemented by the British government of the time were firmly rooted in mercantile concepts where the idea was to add value in the home country while preventing added value activities in the colonies by the imposition of taxes, tariffs and rebates.

The legacy of mercantile systems has prevailed right up to the present. One can see the competition between free-trade thinking and legacy mercantile policies in, for example, how the European Union has subsidised the production of certain food products for export to markets outside the EU. The producers in the target markets are often unhappy about this practice. It means that some EU exports into a non-EU market can be bought for less than the cost of producing the product. The practice then leads to reciprocal policies being implemented by non-EU companies, thereby reducing the attractiveness of international trade. In this way, government policies in both the home country and the export market can have a profound impact on MNEs. (We will return to this topic in greater detail in **Chapter 12**.)

The Development of Free Market Ideas

As the American Revolution began to gather pace, new ideas regarding trade were emerging in Europe. These ideas grew from philosophical considerations that started to emerge in the late 17th Century concerning the nature of freedom and, in particular, the freedom to conduct one's life in the pursuit of happiness.

The greater focus on scientific measurement brought about the European Renaissance and resulted in new theories about how the world worked. Born from the discoveries about gravity, the solar system and the nature of the universe, ideas began to emerge about how societies should be governed. Philosophers such as Jean-Jacques Rousseau and John Locke developed concepts concerning the freedom of man. In particular, they considered whether monarchs had divine provenance and whether church and state should be inextricably linked. They argued that man existed in and for himself and was entitled to self-determination through representative governance systems. They deduced that existing governance systems, essentially hereditary monarchies with varying degrees of democratic influence by the propertied classes, were legacy systems deriving from feudal structures. These ideas began to be translated into governmental systems that might actually be capable of pragmatic implementation through democratic structures and the overthrow of feudal monarchies. The '*ancien régime*' was appalled at the vista of the mob electing its own leaders and common ownership of property. These ideas also led to a logical conclusion that slavery was immoral and should be abolished, despite the fact that in the 18th Century slavery was still an important component of commercial efficiency, especially in the colonies run by the British, Spanish, French and Dutch empires.

While the ideas of mercantilism were still being effected throughout the world in the late 18th Century, new ideas about trade and commerce were developing. These ideas were driven by a belief that long-term, sustainable wealth creation for all arises from free markets, and not from restricting markets and trade.

Absolute Advantage and Comparative Advantage

These beliefs and concepts, from an international trade perspective, were first developed by Adam Smith. Writing in 1776, Smith, a Scottish philosopher and political economist, encouraged free international trade.[4] If products could be made more efficiently in another country, then a nation should take advantage of this **absolute advantage**. The idea is at the root of international trade and has led to the development of many more sophisticated ideas about international trade;

---

[4] Smith, A. (1776). *An Inquiry into the Nature and Causes of the Wealth of Nations*. London: Strahan and Cadell.

however, all of them have at their centre the idea that free trade should be encouraged, and that goods and services should be sourced from those providers who can most efficiently create them.

Remember, the existing system was to take as much of the pie for oneself, preventing, not encouraging, trade with others. Smith and others eschewed this notion, understanding that some nations were more efficient at producing certain goods than others. This superior capability at producing certain products can be explained by a nation having better resources than another, physical, cultural, intellectual and so forth. The realisation that international trade is not a zero sum game encouraged a more liberal *'laissez faire'* view to take hold. The principle of absolute advantage supported the notion that every nation could benefit from international trade through specialisation. Indeed, further derivatives of the theory showed that even a country that is inefficient in production of all its outputs can still benefit from specialisation.

Specialisation is the favouring of the production of an excess of a country's needs to the exclusion of other products in order to create a surplus that can be traded in exchange for scarcities. Even if the factor of production in which an inefficient country specialises does not achieve the degree of efficiency that could be achieved by its trading parties, it will still be to the benefit of both parties for the specialisation process to occur. This development of the theory is called **the law of comparative advantage**, which was developed by David Ricardo, an English economist, and which proposes that specialisation by a country can improve the overall wealth of that country. The theory of specialisation and the comparative advantage it provides a nation rests on the fact that some countries have natural endowments that allow them to produce goods and services at a lower **opportunity cost** than others. In **Example 2.1** below we can see how a below-average accountant, who earns less per hour than his gardener, is still better off employing the gardener and focusing on his accounting work. This is because the law of comparative advantage means the gardener can complete the task faster than the accountant. The opportunity cost of the accountant mowing his own grass inefficiently is that he loses his income from doing his clients' books.

EXAMPLE 2.1: OPPORTUNITY COST

Assume I need to do two tasks: first, complete accounts for clients and, secondly, mow my garden lawn. I am not the best accountant in the world but I can earn €20 an hour doing accounts compared to an average of €30 an hour for seasoned professionals. I can work a maximum of 50 hours a week to cover both tasks. My lawn is big and I only have a push lawnmower. Accordingly, it takes 10 hours to mow my lawn. Thus, I can only work 40 hours in the week on accounting since I need 10 hours to do my lawn. As a result, my weekly income is 40 hours at €20, or €800.

A local gardener will mow my lawn with his modern machine for €30 an hour, but it only takes him 2 hours. Accordingly, I stop spending 10 hours doing my lawn and use that time instead to do an extra 10 hours paid accounting work. I earn an extra €200 doing this work. From this extra money I pay the gardener for 2 hours at €30 an hour, that is €60. I am €140 better off by adopting my new strategy, i.e. my additional earnings of €200 less the €60 I need to pay the gardener.

So, even though the gardener earns more per hour than I do, and I earn less than the average accountant, I am better off to stick with my accounting and pay the gardener to do my lawn. This is because the opportunity cost of me doing the garden myself (€200 earnings foregone) is greater than the cost of having someone else do it (€60). Since the opportunity cost is higher than the cost of getting the lawn done by someone else, I am better to 'specialise' in accounting and eschew gardening. These concepts can be applied to the affairs of nations and MNEs.

Opportunity cost can be explained as the profit or benefit foregone by using resources to produce a chosen output as against another. It is a critical concept for countries in developing international trade strategies. It is also extremely valuable as a concept for MNEs in formulating their internationalisation strategies. The law of comparative advantage is linked inextricably to opportunity cost. A country, or an MNE, has a comparative advantage if it can produce a good or service at a lower opportunity cost than its competitor. Therefore, to understand comparative advantage the MNE manager must also understand opportunity cost and how it pertains to the MNE's chosen activities.

Example 2.2 below explains the law of comparative advantage further by showing how, even without absolute advantage in production efficiency, two nations can benefit from specialisation. The implication is that this same concept applies when scaled up to include all nations.

EXAMPLE 2.2: THE LAW OF COMPARATIVE ADVANTAGE

Imagine the entire world consists of only two countries of the same size: Beeland and Zedmania. Beeland uses 80% of its resources to produce food and 20% of its resources to produce farm machines. Beeland's use of its resources produces 1,200 food units and 100 machine units.

Zedmania, on the other hand, uses 80% of its resources to make farm machines and 20% to produce food. In doing so, it produces 800 machine units and 200 food units. Each country consumes all of what it produces. This consumption pattern is what leads each country's production pattern.

As can be seen, Beeland is more efficient at producing food than Zedmania. It makes 15 units of food for every 1% of resource used (i.e. 1,200 food units divided by 80), while Zedmania can only produce 10 units of food for each 1% of resources used (i.e. 200 food units divided by 20). However, Zedmania can make 10 machine unit for each 1% (i.e. 800 divided by 80) of resources used while Beeland can only make five units for each 1% of resources.

Then, Beeland decides to increase its resource allocation to the production of food from 80% to 90%. Beeland will now make an additional 150 food units for which it has no consumption demand in its own country. However, it now has a shortage of 50 machine units since the 10% additional resources used to produce food had to be taken from machine production.

At the same time, and in collaboration with Beeland, Zedmania decides to increase its production of machines to 900 units and to cut back on food production. Using 90% of its resources to produce machines, Zedmania now makes 100 units more than it needs but has left itself short of food by 100 units. This arises as it has reallocated resources from food production to machine production.

What will each country do with its surplus? Beeland has 150 surplus food units while Zedmania has a shortage of 100. On the other hand, Zedmania has 100 surplus machine units and Beeland is short 50 units. So, they trade: Beeland exchanges 100 of its 150 surplus food units for 50 of Zedmania's machine units. Both countries have now met each of their respective internal consumption demands. Critically, each country has also got a surplus of production left over. In the case of Beeland, they have 50 units of food production in stock while Zedmania has 50 machine units.

The essence of this example is that by each country specialising in the production of the goods in which they have the greater efficiencies, both countries can meet their internal consumption demand and still have extra surplus remaining. (In our example the world only consists of two countries, so the surpluses can either be stored for future use or traded with the other country. The main purpose of the example is to illustrate that countries can benefit from specialising in producing those outputs for which they have a comparative advantage.)

We can see that even in a world comprising just two countries, Beeland and Zedmania, and two production categories, food and machines, there is some complexity. Imagine, then, the complex interactions that take place when all the real world's countries are considered and all categories of production and service industry. It is almost impossible to conceive that a model could be developed that would optimise global production patterns. Thus, it is left to the markets, by which I mean that the idea that all the world's governments could get together and centrally plan production output in order to maximise output in accordance with the law of comparative advantage does not stand up to scrutiny: the variables are too numerous and the political judgements needed are too complicated.

Centrally planned economies have been shown historically to have inbuilt flaws where vested interests eventually cause over-production in some products and inbuilt inefficiencies. For example, the communist system introduced in Russia in 1917 was a centrally planned economic system. At a high level, the idea was that by central control of the factors of production, demand could be met and the surpluses, like those excesses created in **Example 2.2**, could be shared among the population, i.e. the workers whose efforts created the surpluses. The system eventually collapsed in a mire of inefficiency and corruption. The complexities of centrally controlling production and matching the production to demand proved too onerous to manage.

Free trade has come to be recognised by most of the world's democratically elected governments as the route to best use of the planet's collective resources in meeting the aggregate needs of people. Global capitalism is recognised by the majority of governments as the most effective way to ensure that production patterns optimise the world's resources.

Most countries of the world are members of the World Trade Organization, the WTO, which seeks to mediate agreements between its members to organise production and trade agreements in ways that optimise scarce resources while improving the standards of living of citizens in a 'sustainable' way (sustainable because the planet's resources are not infinite). Markets must be tempered by regulation, as global resources are limited in supply. Quality and safety standards must also be enforced in order to prevent the exploitation of people and natural resources; especially, but not exclusively, in poorer countries.

These necessary regulations add to the complexity even further. It is in this multi-layered and complex environment that MNEs must develop and execute strategies that will add value for the enterprise and, ultimately, their shareholders.

EXAMPLE 2.3: OPPORTUNITY COST AND COMPARATIVE ADVANTAGE

At its most basic, the concept of opportunity cost recognises that any choice of action will require the utilisation of resources and that these resources could have been used for another purpose. Where the benefit foregone by one country is low compared to that of another country, the first country has a comparative advantage. For example, imagine Beeland produces rice less efficiently than Zedmania. However, the land in Beeland is not capable of being used for growing any other crop other than rice. Therefore, the opportunity foregone in producing rice is zero, since no other crop can be grown. In Zedmania, however, they could use the land to produce another crop, say tomatoes, efficiently. The law of comparative advantage would propose that Beeland should increase production of rice even though it does so less efficiently than Zedmania. Zedmania would then decrease its rice production and focus on tomatoes. The overall effect is a benefit to both countries and an increase in food available when both countries are taken together.

As we have seen above, Ireland has a comparative advantage in producing dairy products. This advantage flows from the fact that our mild climate means that it is possible for dairy cows to be out of doors longer than most other countries. Accordingly, we are better off specialising in dairy production even though we leave ourselves short of other agricultural products, such as grain. We could use land in Ireland for increased grain production at the expense of dairy production, but this would run counter to the law of comparative advantage. We are better to focus on having more land given over to dairy production and to use the economic benefits of this production to finance the importation of the extra grain we need.

Imperfect Markets

While the concepts of absolute advantage, comparative advantage and opportunity cost are useful for understanding the dynamics of international trade, it is important to note that these concepts assume perfect markets. A **perfect market** is one in which:
• products are identical (e.g. a Spanish orange is identical to an Israeli orange);
• all market players are 'price takers', which means no producer can dictate the price for their output;
• all market players have relatively small market shares;
• buyers have complete knowledge about prices available in the market place;
• market players can enter or leave the market with ease.

The five attributes of a perfect market provide a simple framework upon which to build economic theories. In the real world, however, very few markets have all five attributes. Therefore, most markets are imperfect and can be considered the norm, though the existence of imperfect markets does not render theories developed on the basis of perfect markets useless.

MNEs must tailor their strategies to factor in the effects of imperfect markets. For example, the existence of a patent for a particular drug creates imperfect market conditions. The patent prevents new entrants from easily entering the market. It also allows the owner of the patent to have a large market share, and, in some cases, to set whatever price they wish. The patent will also allow the MNE that owns that patent to consider expansion into other countries that will honour the patent even if the MNE has no comparative advantage for such expansion. In this way, imperfect market conditions can present opportunities for MNEs to consider expansion into other countries – opportunities that may not be possible were perfect market conditions to prevail.

A further example of an imperfect market is the electricity market on the island of Ireland. In the Republic of Ireland there are many consumer-facing brands, such as Electric Ireland, Energia, etc. However, all of them must buy their electricity supply from ESB Networks, which runs the infrastructure that manages the electricity supply network under licence from the Commission for Energy Regulation (CER). The CER also regulates the economic factors affecting the market, setting the prices ESB Networks pay electricity generators and the prices it charges the consumer-facing companies, such as Energia. Increasingly, the generation of electricity and the consumer-facing supply of electricity have become liberalised. However, the network, i.e. the pylons, wires and sub-stations, remains a monopoly. In other words, the network is an imperfect market. As mentioned, prices are set by the CER and not by market forces. This imperfect market means that MNEs from outside Ireland who wish to enter the network business will find themselves locked out by dint of the licence and monopoly situation. On the other hand, MNEs wishing to enter the Irish market to generate electricity using wind turbines, for example, will find that the imperfect market creates an opportunity for them. This is because the CER is focused on encouraging new entrants into the electricity generation market, especially those using renewable resources. The CER prices are set at a level that is high enough to encourage new entrants. This imperfect market condition provides an opportunity for new entrants.

We can see that MNE managers need to be constantly aware of how pure market forces, such as supply and demand, comparative advantage and opportunity cost, are impacted by imperfect market conditions, as many, if not most, opportunities can come the way of MNEs due to imperfect market conditions rather than through the operation of perfect markets.

Comparative Advantage and the Growth in International Trade

Of course, the law of comparative advantage and the concept of opportunity cost apply to commercial organisations as much as they do to countries. But do they explain the growth in international trade of the last five decades?

A number of factors have come together to accelerate the growth of international trade. The development of technologies that allow for easier transfer of funds across the globe has helped to create opportunities for investment in projects that would hitherto have been too difficult to finance. These global flows of capital encourage greater exploitation of comparative advantage, both by countries and commercial enterprises. Over the last five decades the growth in international trade has flowed from trade between countries to a certain extent, but the greatest portion of the growth has come from the increase in the number of MNEs and the international trade in which they engage. We will now consider the models used by MNEs to take advantage of the climate for international trade fostered by many of the world's government's through the auspices of international trade organisations such as the World Trade Organization (WTO) and UNCTAD, as well as through the World Bank and the International Monetary Fund (IMF).

2.4 BUSINESS MODELS FOR INTERNATIONAL TRADE

The success of free trade over mercantilism has led to the slow but steady support of international trade by successive governments throughout the world. During the 19th Century and the Industrial Revolution in particular, the idea of the company as a separate entity also developed.

Prior to this development, organisations tended to be owned and run by extended families and were grouped around class structures: the propertied classes owned and controlled food production and other activities related to the ownership of land, while the other groupings were built around skills and artisanship. A family might own and run a shop and would probably employ a small number of people. However, the advent of the Industrial Revolution brought about increased division of labour and specialisation, which led to larger organisation structures that could not be run by a small number of employees. Nor could they rely upon the traditional feudal serfdom that was historically evident in the agricultural sector.

As a result of these challenges, a new and professional manager class developed. Investor groupings came to be increasingly drawn from commercially-minded, profit-seeking individuals rather than extended family groupings. There emerged, therefore, a new type of organisation, run by professional managers on behalf of investors who could liquidate their investments by the sale of their shares to other parties. (In **Chapter 5** we will see how the use of managers to run MNEs on behalf of the owners introduces new challenges concerning corporate governance.)

These new forms of organisations, the corporation, were the main vehicle for international trade by the early 20th Century as well as being the main drivers of domestic commerce. The multinational enterprise has truly emerged in the last 50 years. Governments and states still involve themselves in international trade transactions, particularly where there are state monopolies on a specific natural resource such as oil, or where the risk involved is too great for commercial enterprises to undertake, for example infrastructure development in the undeveloped world.

The MNE as a form of organisation has become the predominant vehicle for conducting trade on an international basis. However, the MNE may engage in international trade through a number of different business models. These models have developed over the years from simple importing and exporting to owning companies in foreign jurisdictions and endeavouring to operate them from the home country. One can think of the models as a continuum from simple import/export to full-scale ownership. There are a number of models that sit on this continuum, each representing different forms of risk/reward, and sharing together different frameworks for command and control of the relevant trade. These models are not generally mutually exclusive, however, and most large-scale MNEs may have a number of the different models in operation throughout their organisation.

1. Acquisition

An MNE can expand into a new country by acquiring an enterprise already operating there. For example, in 1987 Tesco expanded into the Irish market by the acquisition of Power Supermarkets, which operated as Quinnsworth in the Republic of Ireland and as Crazy Prices in Northern Ireland. Thus, Tesco expanded its operations in the UK and internationally by this one acquisition. The company disposing of Power Supermarkets to Tesco was ultimately controlled by a Canadian family, the Westons. So, in this example, one MNE disposed of a subsidiary while another, the acquisitive Tesco, expanded its international enterprises. Another more recent example is the acquisition of the Irish airline Aer Lingus by the owner of British Airways, IAG. This €1.4 billion takeover allowed IAG to expand its operations into Ireland. Previously, this airline MNE had a modest presence in the Northern Ireland market and almost no presence in the Republic of Ireland.

2. New Entity

An MNE can enter a new market by setting up a new entity in the target country. For example, American fashion retailer Abercrombie & Fitch established its operations in Ireland by setting up a new entity rather than acquiring an existing operator and converting it to its own operating model. Similarly, Google also entered the Irish market by setting up an entity in Dublin; indeed, it has used this base to expand their European operations. These new entities will most often be fully-owned subsidiary companies, owned and controlled by the parent company based back in the domestic country.

3. Franchising

The methods of international expansion discussed above can be capital intensive and have many attendant risks, examples of which could include choosing the wrong location or buying underlying problems that are not obvious from the original examination of the books. A further method, which can help reduce risks and capital requirements, is franchising. In this model, the expanding entity (the 'franchisor') will find an operator in the target country to run an enterprise according to its defined principles. The expanding MNE will define many factors of the marketing mix to which the operator, called the 'franchisee', must adhere. In return for giving access to their brand and know-how, the franchisor will receive a franchise fee. McDonald's uses this model for expansion, both internationally and domestically in the US, its home country.

4. Licensing

As a method of international expansion, licensing is similar to franchising in that it involves a lesser commitment of resources, especially capital, by the expanding MNE. The **licensor** sells a right to use its intellectual property, such as a trademark or a patent, to a **licensee**, normally for a fixed period of time. For example, PepsiCo, the global MNE behind the soft drink Pepsi, licensed Britvic Ireland to produce Pepsi in the Irish market. The product must be made to the precise defined formula in order to comply with the terms of the licence. Marketing programs need to be approved by the licensor in order to protect their brand – see **Appendix C.3**. This means that PepsiCo can expand into the Irish market without having the cost of building expensive bottling plants and distribution capability.

5. Joint Ventures

Recognising that foreign markets can often operate differently from the home market, expanding MNEs often use a joint venture to help reduce risk and capital requirements. The operating entity in the target country is jointly owned by the expanding MNE and its joint venture partner, often an existing operator in the target country. Indeed, in China, the government insists that MNEs expanding into their country must form a joint venture with a government-owned entity.

Fyffes, the Irish-based fruit supplier, managed much of its multinational expansion by forming joint ventures in target countries with existing fruit and vegetable operators in those countries. They sometimes buy out the joint venture partner if the venture was successful.

6. International Trading

This method of engaging in international business is the oldest, and possibly the most common, judging by the number of enterprises engaged in it. Essentially, international trading is where an entity expands its operations across borders by either buying goods from trading partners or selling goods to international customers. For example, in Ireland, Topaz, the fuel retailer, imports oil which it refines into motor fuels for sale in its forecourt operations. Often, over time, organisations involved in international trading tend to develop by using other forms and structures of international trade, such as operating subsidiaries, if the opportunity presents itself.

The six models described briefly here are explained in more depth in **Chapter 3**. We will also see that while other models of international trade do exist, most are subsets of the six models outlined above. For example, the setting up of a sales office in a new country is a subset of the 'new entity' MNE model for conducting international trade.

2.5 INCREASED ENTERPRISE VALUE AND INTERNATIONAL TRADE

In exploring why international trade, and MNEs, have grown so rapidly in the last five decades, we have considered six models for international trading. In order to determine how these models have contributed to the growth in international trade, we must first examine why enterprises exist in the first place, and why international trade is attractive to an enterprise in terms of it delivering on its goals and aspirations, particularly for its investors.

The *raison d'être* of a business will inevitably influence if and why it seeks to expand internationally. It follows, therefore, that any explanation of the benefits of international expansion by an enterprise will need to examine what stakeholder needs and expectations might be met by such an expansion.

While many companies or business entities have mission statements, visions, and long-term goals, in the final analysis they exist to provide a return on the investment made by their owners, normally shareholders. This return derives from an income received by way of distributions to the investor shareholders combined with an increase in the value of their initial investment. The distributions can be seen as the regular return required by the investor in return for providing funds to the entity. The shareholder investor will also expect that the entity will increase in value. But how is this value to be assessed?

Weighted Average Cost of Capital

An entity's current value is derived from the aggregate of its future cash flows, discounted to today's value by an appropriate discount rate. This rate is normally the **weighted average cost of capital** (WACC).

> Weighted average cost of capital (WACC) is a percentage that represents the weighted average cost of all of the entity's individual sources of finance.

Thus, in order to value a business entity, one takes all the future expected cash flows and discounts these cash flows back to today's value. All business strategies should be expected to increase the entity's value over time. Once an entity becomes an MNE, the estimation of the future cash flows becomes a bit more complex. This is because these cash flows are often in another currency. In order to assess the value of the MNE, these foreign currency cash flows need to be converted to the home currency at an expected future exchange rate. Predicting exchange rates is a difficult exercise as we will see later in **Chapter 8**. The MNE will need to develop strategies to have some confidence in the future exchange rates, and therefore, in the valuation of the enterprise. These strategies form a key part of how the finance function adds value in the MNE.

In addition to the complexity of foreign exchange, there are other challenges to using discounted future cash flows to arrive at an MNE's value. An MNE manager analysing enterprise value may not have access to future cash flows, particularly if they are trying to value a

third-party MNE as against one they manage themselves. In these cases other valuation models can be applied. These models include:
- multiplying annual profits by a figure comparable to other, similar enterprises;
- looking at the value of the assets of the entity less its liabilities;
- multiplying annual dividends by a figure comparable to other similar entities whose value is known.

Having said that, the context in which I am describing MNE valuations is one where the managers are making decisions about international expansion. In these cases, one would expect the managers to be able to prepare forecasted cash flows that will arise from the activities in which they propose to engage.

EXAMPLE 2.4: MNE VALUATION AND THE IMPACT OF EXCHANGE RATES

A Swiss company has a wholly owned subsidiary in France. At the end of 2014 the finance function predicted cash flow from its French subsidiary is €1 million per annum for three years: 2015, 2016 and 2017. The WACC is 10%. The exchange rate for the last three years has been that 1€ = 1.2CHF. The finance function believes, not unreasonably, that this rate will prevail for the three relevant years. Thus, the €1 million per annum income is translated to CHF1.2 million per annum. Discounting each year by the WACC of 10% produces the following present value of CHF3.25 million.

Calculations of present value of the French € cash flows:

2015 = 1.20m
2016 = 1.08m (being 1.2 × 0.909)
2017 = 0.97m (being 1.2 × 0.909 × 0.909)

Total CHF3.25 million

Therefore, the valuation of the French subsidiary at 2014 based on the finance function's estimate that the rate would remain at 1€ = CHF1.2 is €3.25 million.

However, in early 2015 the Swiss Government removed its 'pegging' to the euro leading to a massive increase in the value of the Swiss Franc. From mid-January 2015 the exchange rate between the two currencies has been averaging at around 1€ = CHF1.05. If the finance function of the Swiss MNE now uses this number to calculate the value of the future cash flows from the French subsidiary, it arrives at a new, lower number of CHF2.85 million. This drop in value of 12% is entirely due to the fluctuation in the exchange rate.

Now, to calculate the value assuming the 'new' rate will prevail of 1€ = CHF1.05:

2015 = 1.05m
2016 = 0.95m
2017 = 0.85m

Total CHF2.85 million

The French subsidiary has maintained its performance, but the value to the Swiss parent has fallen from CHF3.25 million to CHF2.85 million, a 12% decline in value brought about by unforeseen exchange rate movements.

It is important at this point to distinguish between the use of the WACC for the purposes of valuing an entity and the selection of a discount rate for the purposes of assessing a specific project's viability (see **Chapter 11**). In particular, the use of the WACC as a discount rate for the expected cash flows from new international investments may lead to incorrect assessments. This is because the risk profile for international expansion may well be different from that of the domestic market. The MNE must find some way to reflect these differences in the selection of an appropriate rate. Once again, this is an area where the finance function in an organisation can add significant value for the MNE. The use of the capital asset pricing model is a tool that is useful in this context and this is also explored further in **Chapter 11**.

In summary, the need for an enterprise to grow its value while distributing a return to its providers of capital leads it to search for new opportunities in which to invest. Once it cannot see any more opportunities in its domestic market, it will often seek out international opportunities. Many of the world's governments facilitate the international expansion of enterprise both directly and individually through incentives and other encouragements, and indirectly collectively through trade agreements and the initiation of international trade associations. In encouraging international trade in these ways governments reveal their belief in the law of comparative advantage; that all nations can be better off if international trade grows. Governments and states largely rely on MNEs to deliver this growth and, therefore, these improvements in national and global wealth and well-being.

In summary, enterprises use international expansion to meet their investors' demand for increased returns. In addition, governments, collectively and individually, also want to encourage international trade as it fosters improved standards of living for their citizens. Thus, two aspirations, profit and improved living standards, combine to drive the growth of MNEs.

2.6 INTERNATIONAL CO-OPERATION TO ENCOURAGE MULTINATIONAL ENTERPRISES

As global capitalism continued to grow, the world's countries and their governments sought to encourage international trade, albeit in a regulated fashion. As technological advances allowed for greater movement of goods and capital, governments began to increasingly create the economic environments that would encourage international trade. While the process has been going on for at least the last 150 years, it is since the end of the Second World War in 1945 that the changes have been most dramatic. These changes, designed to encourage free trade, have been critical to fostering the growth of MNEs. It is certain that MNEs would not have prospered to the same degree had these changes not happened.

Europe

The idea of a common market in Europe began to really take hold after the Second World War when the leaders of the Allies recognised that differing standards of living between countries could have been an influencing factor in determining the preconditions for war. The leaders of the Allies imagined that if there were a convergence in the standards of living of European nations, with the poorer nations improving faster, then the likelihood of further European wars could be reduced.

On the basis of the theory of comparative advantage, the idea was to create the conditions that would foster international trade within Europe. In 1951, the European Coal and Steel Community

(ECSC) came into being after the Treaty of Paris (1951). This developed into the European Economic Community (EEC) or 'Common Market' by the time of the Treaty of Rome in 1957, further developing with the Common Agricultural Policy in 1962. Though the six European Member States that founded the EEC did have enlargement as a goal, they were slow to accept new members. For example, Ireland and the UK (together with Denmark) did not join until 1973.

Joining the EEC had (and still has) a profound and positive effect on the international trading of the UK and Ireland. European MNEs began to export into Ireland and the UK. Indeed, some MNEs found trade so attractive they eventually set up operations in Ireland and the UK. For example, Marth, a German sausage casing company, set up an Irish subsidiary, the Irish Casing Company, in 1972. The company exports various types of sausage casings throughout the world.

At the same time, Irish and UK companies began to find it easier to access continental European markets. Finding new markets for their products encouraged UK and Irish MNEs to expand some of their operations, such as manufacturing and customer service, into those countries.

US companies also began to see the opportunity, especially from the 1970s onward, to gain access to the new wider European market by setting up operations within the EU. The shared language meant that many US MNEs gravitated toward Ireland and the UK as the location of first choice.

Today the EEC, now the European Union (EU), comprises 28 Member States and is a significant global trading block, one in which free trade has been actively encouraged and legislated for. The EU also acts on behalf of its Member States as a negotiating party to international trade agreements. Belief in comparative advantage to improve the living standards of all states is behind the drive towards the total freedom of movement of goods, capital and people. There is still some way to go, however, before free trade principles are applied on a world-wide basis, despite the evidence of its undoubted success in an EU context. Indeed, it can be argued that the EU protects itself from global trade by the imposition of tariffs and quotas on goods and services from outside the EU. Nevertheless, as the global movement of capital becomes increasingly easy, restrictions on international trade will tend to decrease. For example, at the time of writing, the EU and US are finalising the Transatlantic Trade and Investment Partnership (TTIP) to improve free trade between the US and the EU. This drive for the expansion of free trade principles will continue as long as nations continue to believe in the shared benefits for all participants.

The Euro

In 1969 the EEC set itself the goal of a common currency. The benefits of this were seen to be the elimination of foreign exchange risk, the easing of the movement of peoples, more ready price comparisons, particularly for consumer products, and the ability to set common interest rates across the Community. Not all Member States were keen to give up this critical element of their sovereignty. However, the majority of countries in the EU have either joined the euro or are committed to doing so once certain defined criteria have been met.

From a business perspective, the existence of the single currency certainly facilitates the international business of today's MNEs. The requirements on countries who wished to join the euro were set out in the Maastricht Treaty of 1992:
- a long-term interest rate no more than 2% greater than the average of the three countries with the lowest inflation;
- inflation no more than 1.5% greater than the average of the three countries with the lowest inflation;

- participation in an exchange rate mechanism limiting the maximum variation in exchange rate with the euro to 15% in the two years prior to joining;
- net government spending deficit of no more than 3% of GDP;
- government debt no greater than 60% of GDP.

As can be seen, the main goals are driven by inflation and interest-rate stabilisation, and fiscal rectitude by governments regarding spending. One of the intentions is to create an environment that will encourage MNE activity. By creating a single currency foreign exchange rate, risks are eliminated. Therefore, MNEs can invest in other Eurozone countries without needing to be concerned about adverse movements in exchange rates that are beyond their control damaging their investment. In addition to this benefit, euro-denominated countries can now only adjust economic underperformance by improving internal performance ratios, such as cost competitiveness. Prior to the euro, Member States could adjust their economy by altering interest rates and, in extreme circumstances, devaluing their currency.

The free trade strategies adopted by the EU, together with the benefits of the single currency within the Eurozone, have combined to produce real growth in international trade between EU Member States. In fact, the share of total exports represented by intra-EU exports is the highest of all free trade areas in the world at 68%,[5] which is testament to how well these strategies have worked.

FIGURE 2.2: EVOLUTION OF INTRA-EU28 EXPORT TRADE 2002–2013 (€BNS)[6]

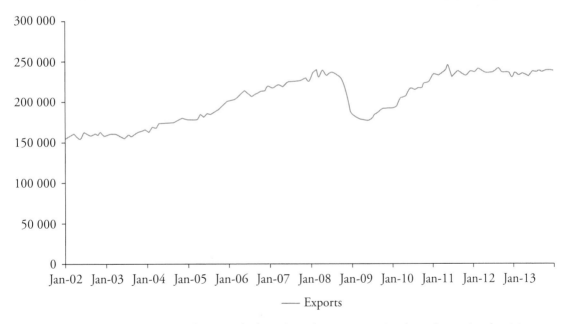

In **Figure 2.2** above the growth in trade between the 28 EU Members States in the 11 years from 2002 to 2013 is clearly evident. The intra-EU28 trade in 2002 was just over €150,000 billion per annum. This trade had grown to almost €225,000 billion per annum by 2013. At the same time, a tight control has been maintained on inflation within the EU.

---

[5] www.ecb.europa.eu
[6] http://ec.europa.eu/eurostat

The US and the Americas

In the US there has also been a desire by successive governments to ease restrictions on trade and therefore encourage MNE activity. In 1993, the North American Free Trade Agreement (NAFTA) lifted barriers between Mexico, Canada and the US. The resultant increase of trade went both ways. For example, US companies began to establish manufacturing entities in Mexico to benefit from the lower labour costs there; Mexican food producers now had access to the US market for their produce, which had previously been denied to them since the tariffs, taxes and embargos rendered the US market inaccessible to the aspirant Mexican MNE.

The overall effect of the NAFTA was to increase trade between the three countries and to increase the aggregate wealth of the nations involved, again in accordance with the law of comparative advantage.

Taken collectively, the trade between the US, Canada and Mexico increased by over 100% in the first 10 years of the operation of the treaty, from US$306 billion in 1993 to US$621 billion in 2003.[7]

In Latin America there has been a trend toward encouraging MNEs to take ownership or part-ownership in local firms as a way of improving international trade. This strategy has paid off, with an increase in investment in Latin America by foreign-owned MNEs over the last few decades.

A free trade area called Mercosur has been set up in South America that further encourages trade between its member countries. Brazil, Argentina, Uruguay and Paraguay are full members; Bolivia, Chile, Colombia, Ecuador and Peru are associate members.

Asia

The attraction of Asia to MNEs is obvious when one considers its huge populations (China, India, Indonesia, etc.) However, Western MNEs have found it difficult to penetrate Asian markets to the extent that they would like; despite the easing of some restrictions, many Asian markets remain difficult to access. One area where Asian governments have encouraged inward investment is in the building of manufacturing capacity for consumer goods to be exported into global markets. In order to achieve this manufacturing capacity, the governments ease restrictions on the building of factories that will manufacture goods that will subsequently be exported. The rationale for these policies is that there ought to be no displacement of existing domestic operators or jobs since the manufacturing jobs referred to are manufacturing goods to meet demand in other countries and therefore will not displace domestic demand.

The policies have been generally successful in providing employment. Many international MNEs have manufacturing entities or contracts with Asian firms. The vast availability of workers and comparatively low wages allow for economic manufacturing in Asia for onward sale in Western markets. This is particularly true for clothing and footwear. For example, over 75% of the goods sold by Primark (the low-price retailer founded by Arthur Ryan on behalf of the Canadian Weston retail dynasty in Ireland as 'Penneys') are made in Asia. In the meantime, Asian MNEs in the electronics and car industries, for example Samsung and Kia from South Korea, have gained significant market share for their products among western consumers. The growth of these companies first came from an ability to service foreign demand: only

---

[7] Office of the United States Trade Representative, 2003. See https://ustr.gov/trade-agreements/free-trade-agreements/north-american-free-trade-agreement-nafta

latterly have they been meeting domestic and intra-region demand. In 1985, Asian countries, including Japan, had US$88 billion of the global consumer electronics production, dwarfed by the production in the US alone which was $147 billion. By 2005, Asian production had reached $965 billion while the US production had grown to just $221 billion.[8]

Worldwide

We have seen that trade agreements to foster MNE activity can take a number of forms. Some agreements are between two or three individual countries, such as the NAFTA. Other agreements create tariff-free zones inside which participating countries are encouraged to trade, while those outside the zone are restricted, such as the EU.

Countries even negotiate agreements at product category level where restrictions might be eased for one category of import in return for the allowing of exports of another category. This method of setting tariffs can become quite complex. Normally, a country will seek to have tariffs reduced on goods and services in which it has a comparative advantage and wishes to export. These tariff agreements will be reciprocal, with complicated formulae being used to calculate how benefits in tariff reductions for one product sector can be equivocated to reductions in tariffs in a different product sector by the counterparty. For example, in May 2011 the EU negotiated a reciprocal trade agreement with South Korea: imports into the EU of 'eligible products' were given a tapered rate of duty, eventually leading to a 'nil preferential rate of duty'. In return, the South Koreans agreed to impose a 'nil preferential rate of duty' on exports from the EU into their country on 'eligible products'. The two lists of eligible products are dissimilar. For example, wines can be exported to Korea from the EU with the 'nil rate' applying; however, tariffs will apply to wine imported into the EU from Korea.

In 1993 over 110 countries, including Ireland and the UK, formed an agreement on world trade, the General Agreement on Tariffs and Trade (GATT), which had the goal of removing trade restrictions between the participating countries over a 10-year period. While it is fair to say that the goal has not been fully achieved, many restrictions have been lifted. As the world's economies converge on a capitalist model of economic development, so restrictions have continued to ease. It is the easing of these restrictions, coupled with advances in financial systems, information technology and supply chain management capabilities, which have created the environment that has allowed MNEs to prosper.

2.7 MOTIVES TO BECOME A MULTINATIONAL

As we have seen, international economic activity has grown tremendously over the last five decades and the world's governments have collaborated to encourage this in a belief that the rising tide of increased economic development will lift all boats. While there is a long way to go before we can say that all trade restrictions have been lifted, there is no doubt that the easing of trade restrictions has fostered and encouraged the growth of MNEs.

We now turn to the question as to why an enterprise would seek to internationalise. What would motivate an organisation to take on the risks and uncertainties associated with expanding its activities to outside its own borders? We will look at the motives under two broad

---

[8] Adapted from Reed Electronics Research, *Yearbook of World Electronics Data, 2010.*

classifications: proactive and reactive (see **Appendix C.2** for an Irish MNE's CEO account of international expansion).

Proactive Motives for Developing a Multinational Enterprise

Economies of Scale

Business entities will tend to expand across borders where they can achieve economies of scale in production of goods or services. If a home market is too small to allow a business to produce at an optimum level, it will look to foreign markets to give it access to the volumes needed to produce more efficiently. This is particularly true in industries that require significant investment in production capability for a standardised product, such as the motor car industry.

Opportunism

Sometimes an enterprise may see an opportunity to make a sale internationally without necessarily having a long-term strategy to internationalise. These opportunities can arise from attendance at trade fairs or can be from unsolicited approaches from potential customers who have heard about the firm's products or services. The opportunity is seized by the enterprise and the export sale is made. In this way the organisation becomes an MNE within the wide definition of the term used in this text.

Management Drive

The drive of a firm's management to expand the size of the enterprise they manage is often underestimated as a key motive for international expansion. Limited by the scale of a domestic market, management can see opportunities for growth across international borders. Management's desire to expand internationally, however, will not sustain a firm's international trade on its own (see **Appendix C.3**). The products and services must meet customer needs in the target market. For example, Tesco decided to expand into the US grocery market in 2006. Its management had a strong desire to expand internationally. A number of senior executives relocated to California. There was no apparent demand from consumers in the US for Tesco to enter the market; there did not appear to be any economies of scale to be realised; nor did the US grocery market represent a clear opportunity given that it was already a mature and developed market with intense competition between existing operators. The main motivation for the expansion was the optimism and ambition of Tesco's senior management and board. The new retail offer, Fresh & Easy, the brand Tesco used in the US, failed to attract enough customers and Tesco retreated from the US in 2013, at a final exit cost of £1.2 million. Another example, outlined in **Example 2.5** below, demonstrates how Ford's management desired international expansion but lacked the capability to use the acquisition of Land Rover and Jaguar to enhance shareholder value.

EXAMPLE 2.5: 'HUBRIS' AT FORD

In the 12 years to 2000, the US automobile company Ford endeavoured to expand its market share in Europe through the acquisition of well-known European brands, such as Jaguar, Volvo, Land Rover, and even 'uber' luxury car brand Aston Martin. Obviously, management at the time believed that they had a clear international strategy even though many observers struggled to identify it. Jacques Nasser took over as CEO in 1999 after more than 30 years in the company. Ford was then the most profitable car company in the world, with profits of US\$7.2 billion on sales of over \$160 billion. Nasser announced that he would re-invent Ford from being "a boring old car maker whose shares achieve a price-earnings ratio of only ten, into a consumer-products and services company commanding a multiple of more like thirty".[9] Ford bought Land Rover for $2.9 billion in 2000 and Jaguar for $2.4 billion in 1989. It sold both marques to the Indian automobile company Tata in 2008 for $2.3 billion, thereby eroding $3 billion in value. The fact that both brands have been growing strongly since their disposal would indicate that the Tata management have a better strategy.

Management's desire to pursue plans that are not fully aligned to shareholder goals is not new. It may well be the case that Tesco and Ford were just casualties of the natural phenomenon of business risk. Nonetheless, both companies were at the peaks of their domestic performances when the management led them to what ultimately were failed international expansions.

Product Life Cycle

Products have life cycles. They are 'born', develop into maturity, and ultimately die off. Marketers develop strategies to prolong product life cycles in order to sustain profits and recover product development costs over a longer time frame. Simplistically, products that have just been developed tend to have a smaller market share and sell for relatively higher price. As the volumes increase, the price drops but the return on the investment continues to increase as the increased sales volumes compensate for the falling prices. The life cycle concept envisages an eventual decline in volumes and prices as the product reaches 'old age'. (For further detail about the product life cycle, see **Chapter 16**, especially **Figure 16.5**.)

Firms can extend the life cycle of products by introducing them to new, international markets. This strategy is particularly appealing for products that have short life cycles, as is illustrated in **Example 2.6** below.

EXAMPLE 2.6: INTERNATIONALISING TO EXTEND PRODUCT LIFE CYCLES – HEELYS

Heelys®, a children's footwear product, was launched into international markets at differing points in the product's life cycle. Based out of Carrollton, Texas, Heelys are a children's footwear product that incorporates a wheel into the heel of the shoe allowing the wearer to accelerate to great speeds by raising the front of their foot and exposing the wheel and gliding along on one's heels. Once the front of the foot is returned to the normal position, the wheels recede into the heel and it can be used like a shoe. They are a recognised fashion 'fad' similar to hula hoops or Rubix Cubes. As the product was declining in Denmark, it was at maturity phase in Germany and was just being launched in Ireland. In this way, the MNE stabilised manufacturing volumes and extended the life of the product. It was also able to spread its management and marketing resources more evenly over a longer period of time as each marketplace was dealt with in succession. Sales eventually declined, but not until after a very successful international sales effort.

Diversification

Organisations sometimes realise that they are over-reliant on their home market for future cash flows. When examining future potential risks from a cash flow generation point of view, a firm may realise that 'all its eggs are in the one basket'. A concentration of earnings being generated from one domestic market may expose the company and its shareholders to unnecessary risk of volatility in

---

[9] www.economist.com/node/230457 (accessed September 2015).

earnings or erosion in value. This exposure arises because any adverse macro environmental effects in the home market cannot be counteracted by earnings from another market.

Enterprises therefore may endeavour to minimise this risk by diversifying the sources of their future cash flows. The diversification can be in the form of entering contra-indicated industries in their home market. Contra-indicated in this context means choosing an industry sector that is most likely to be in the ascendance while the existing sector is in decline. (The example of the sunscreen manufacturer diversifying into umbrellas comes to mind: if sunscreen sales are down, it is possible that umbrellas will be up!)

More often, to reduce reliance on its home country cash flows, a firm will seek to expand into a foreign market within its sphere of expertise and competence. Careful attention needs to be given, however, to the correlation of both countries' markets' performance if this strategy is to be effective in reducing risk. International expansion alone may not eliminate demand risk profiles: if the MNE chooses to enter a foreign market whose demand curve is similar to that in its home market, then the risk will not have been diversified. If demand for a firm's products in its home market is positively correlated with demand in the target foreign market, then the strategy of international expansion may grow the scale of the company but will not reduce risk. This is because if there is a decline in the home market, there will also be a decline in the foreign market. It follows, therefore, that while a firm may have expanded its operations and grown overall, it will not have diversified the risk.

For example, a hotel operator with ski hotels in Italy will not diversify risk by the acquisition of ski hotels in France. The demand for rooms in ski hotels in both countries is likely to be positively correlated.

The MNE seeking to expand internationally to diversify risk should seek neutrally or negatively correlated countries in which to locate their new markets. Managers can sometimes seek to legitimise foreign expansion as a risk reduction strategy without truly understanding that the strategy can actually be **increasing** the firm's risk exposure.

Incentives

For the reasons discussed, to encourage internationalisation of business activity, a country's government can seek to incentivise firms to expand internationally or to invest in their country through inward investment. These incentives can take the form of taxation benefits, capital grants, mentoring or consultative supports.

Most countries have connections with the wider world through their diplomatic structures, including embassies and consulates. Governments can use this extended international reach to introduce home country businesses to prospective international customers. They can also use this international network to showcase the home country as a place to do business. Governments may also fund specific agencies to further their goal of attracting foreign direct investment (FDI) or encouraging export activity. In the Republic of Ireland the main body supporting FDI is the Irish Development Authority (IDA). In Northern Ireland it is Invest NI, which also supports firms based in Northern Ireland who may wish to export their products or services. The main support agency for encouraging export activity in the Republic of Ireland is Enterprise Ireland. (See **Chapters 19** and **20** for further details on the workings of these agencies.)

Resource Acquisition

A firm's strategy may depend on achieving competitive advantage by securing continuity of supply of a scarce resource. This resource may be physical, such as the output from a mine, or it may be intangible, such as a patent. In order to minimise risk or enhance profit margins, a business entity may seek to acquire its source or supplier. Many companies have expanded internationally in order to secure such resources, which also makes it more difficult for competitors to acquire them. Consequently, there can be three main benefits to expanding internationally to acquire resources:

- ensuring continuity of supply of the resource adds greater security to future cash flows and hence the value of the MNE;
- acquiring exclusive supply of a scarce resource can give a competitive advantage over others in the marketplace;
- Owning the supplier of a scarce resource can help improve profit margins, as all of the margin is available for the MNE. Supply-chain efficiencies can also arise in the case of physical goods as the supply and demand curves ought to be more readily apparent to the operators since they are both part of the same entity. (The price at which goods are 'sold' within an MNE's entities is called the transfer price. Transfer pricing is covered in more detail in **Chapter 16**.)

Reactive Motives for Developing a Multinational Enterprise

Reactive motives are where and when a business internationalises in reaction to something in its marketplace rather than as a proactive strategy.

Competition

A firm may see that its competitors in a home market have expanded operations internationally and, fearing that they may become disadvantaged in some way, the firm then also seeks to expand and become an MNE.

Domestic Market Saturation

In response to the home market becoming saturated, a firm may seek expansion opportunities internationally. As market share increases in a home market, it becomes more difficult to increase market share. This is especially true in a mature market where there are a number of strong players and the total market is not growing. In order to deliver on its own growth aspirations, a business may have no choice but to expand internationally as an MNE.

Excess Capacity

Forecasting customer demand is an inexact science. Incorrect forecasts can lead to excess production. Firms will often seek to offload over-production in foreign markets. The advantage is that they can sell the excess production for once-off prices. A firm will hope that the sale into a foreign market will not affect the home market, although this is not always the case. For example, it can happen that a manufacturer with excess stock sells it off into a foreign market only to find it turning up again in its home market at prices that can often be below what the manufacturer is able to achieve domestically. Earlier in this chapter we saw the example of the 'tea mountain' in Britain after tax increases had rendered the price of tea sourced by the East India Company too expensive for British tea drinkers. The East India Company considered selling off the tea at a reduced price into the continental European market. However, it decided against this as it expected that the tea would be smuggled back into the British market, undercutting the existing supplies from the company. It chose to export it much further distances, to British America instead, even though the costs of transportation were considerably higher.

The improvements in supply-chain efficiencies in recent years together with the easing of restrictions on the international movement of goods has meant that manufacturers need to be cautious of exporting excess product at marginal cost prices into foreign markets. Also, while a manufacturer may seek to limit the markets into which a foreign buyer can sell the product, such attempted restrictions may often fall foul of competition law. For example, a UK manufacturer may supply a German wholesaler with excess stock on condition that the stock is not re-sold into the UK market; such a restriction could easily infringe EU competition law.

Seasonality

Some products' demand curves follow a seasonal pattern. This is especially true of consumer goods such as textiles and, to a lesser degree, food products. Light summer clothing, for example, sells in the northern hemisphere in May to July, but sells in the southern hemisphere from November to January. Consequently, a manufacturer may find it necessary to trade globally in order to reach its relevant markets at the relevant times of year. Even within Europe, products that appeal to customers in winter in Mediterranean countries can have summer markets further north. An example of this is outerwear, such as light coats, which are suitable in January in Southern Spain and in July in Dublin or Belfast.

Customer Demand

A potential customer may make an unsolicited order for a firm's product or service, often facilitated by a search using a search engine like Google. If the customer is based in a country other than the home country, this can lead to the firm expanding internationally purely as a reaction to the customer's demand. This type of unsolicited order often occurs where markets are physically or culturally connected, as in the following example.

EXAMPLE 2.7: WESTLAND SALADES

Salad manufacturer Westland Salades[10] in the Netherlands finds that a retailer from Belgium has ordered some of its products. The Belgian retailer has become aware of the product from seeing it in Dutch shops near the border.

On the face of it, the fulfilment of such orders would seem to be profit enhancing. However, there are many complexities connected with fulfilling an international customer order. Much of this book deals with these complexities, and firms should be careful to fully understand the total cost of expanding internationally by meeting customer demand on a reactive basis. In particular, the nascent MNE should be wary of the hidden costs of dealing with a foreign country's regulatory and fiscal codes as well as of competitors to which it may expose itself when expanding so spontaneously.

Investor Demand

Investors may often believe that the business in which they have invested will be worth more if it has a presence in international markets rather than just operating domestically. The logic is that a firm expanding internationally will not just have greater scale, and hopefully profits, but will also have greater exposure to the investment market, thus creating greater demand for the shares in the entity. A business that only has operations in Ireland might

---

[10] http://westlandsalades.nl/

never appear on the radar of foreign investors. Having said this, it is the seeking of econo-mies of scale that drives most investors to encourage the management of companies to expand internationally. As we will see in later chapters, these economies of scale are not easily achieved and, in almost all cases, international expansion adds complexity to an organisation's affairs.

Governments are also keen to see home companies expand internationally. A government or its agencies may encourage a firm to expand even though the firm may not have formed that strategy itself. As a minimum, a firm may actually start exporting as a result of such encouragement. Whether this reactive approach to becoming an MNE is profitable in the long run will depend on how the new MNE formulates its strategies in response to the new situation.

Agency Theory and International Expansion

There has been much research into how management may lead a company into international expansion when other strategies may have been more effective in delivering upon the investors' goals.[11] A good example of this phenomenon is the international expansion of Australian beer producer, Fosters. Following home market dominance, Fosters started an international expan-sion drive in 1992. In the period 1992–2000 Fosters lost AUS$400 million on its international expansion into the UK, Canada and Asia. Some analysts of the poor results have speculated that the Foster's management team were acting in the mistaken belief that it is expected of firms dominant in their home country that they expand internationally. Gaining an understanding of how such invisible pressure comes to bear on a firm's management is problematic, not least because it is difficult to get into the minds of executives at the point that these decisions are made. Agency theory has been put forward as a framework for understanding how these behav-iours can arise and the complex motivations that underlie them. Agency theory is used to explain the 'costs' to an enterprise that arise from the difference in goals and motivations between an enterprise's owners and its managers. If an enterprise is owned and managed by one person, then the owner's goals and the management goals can be said to be 'ad idem', in other words, of the same mind. In these circumstances it is simple to understand motivations. However, as a business grows, the distance between the owners and the managers often grows as well; the potential for conflicting goals becomes greater. Management's goals will not neces-sarily coincide with the goals of the enterprise's shareholders. At its extreme, in large, global Plcs, the owners may not even know the management and will never meet them.

Consider an MNE's management's desire to diversify activities in order to reduce risk or overexposure in a given market. A shareholder may take the view that they do not need the MNE to diversify in order to manage this risk as they can do so themselves by investing in a diverse portfolio of companies. The shareholder could argue that the MNE's management is diversifying to reduce risk exposure purely as a management goal and not a goal driven by shareholder value enhancement. (See **Chapter 11, Section 11.5** for a discussion of the Modigliani–Miller Theorem, which is relevant to this topic.)

Agency Costs The costs associated with the conflicting goals of owners and management are known as 'agency' costs because they arise from the necessary separation of the manage-ment of the enterprise from its owners, such separation creating a principal–agent relation-ship. In an international firm these costs can go up when compared to a domestic firm of

---

[11] See, for example, Dick, H. and Merrett, D. (2007). *The Internationalisation Strategies of Small-country Firms*. Cheltenham: Edward Elgar.

the same size. This escalation arises because of a temptation for managers of subsidiaries to endeavour to maximise the value of the subsidiary without regard to the overall MNE's goals or those of the shareholders. These forces of self-determination of management at local, subsidiary level are powerful and should be a major consideration for the management of all MNEs. Organisation design and reward system structures should seek to support congruence between the goals of the subsidiaries, the parent and, most importantly, the owners. These topics are discussed further in **Chapter 6**.

2.8 INTERNATIONAL BUSINESS AND THE PROFESSIONAL ACCOUNTANT

At its most simple, a firm's value is the discounted value of its future cash flows. To calculate this value one must estimate those future cash flows and choose a suitable discount rate. In an international business the estimation of the future cash flows is more complex. The choosing of suitable discount rates also becomes more complex. It is the MNE's business activities that generate the cash flows that ultimately provide a return to the investors and providers of finance. It is the accountant who must provide the professional expertise to ensure the least amount of volatility possible in the production of these estimates. (In **Chapter 11** we examine in greater detail how the MNE estimates future cash flows and uses these estimates together with discount rates to assess the feasibility of future plans and strategies.)

When one gets into the detail of any facet of today's MNE it is possible to forget the above statements and their relative simplicity. Despite this difficulty, the professional accountant in the MNE must not lose sight of the bigger picture and remember that to truly add value, he or she must be mindful of maximising the certainty of cash flows while endeavouring to minimise risk and select appropriate discount rates.

The selection of appropriate discount rates is critical for prudent investment appraisal. Since all future cash flows will arise from investments of one form or another, the discount rate's importance cannot be overstated. The greater the certainty of future cash flows, the lower the discount rate that needs to be factored into the calculations and, thus, the lower the discount rate applied to a firm's cash flows, the higher the value of the enterprise. If there is absolute certainty about cash flow, then it can be as good as risk-free.

All actions and advices of the accountant and the finance function in the MNE can be distilled down to advising, executing and supporting actions that:
• improve the certainty and quantum of future cash flows; and
• reduce the discount factor by improving the risk profile of the enterprise.

Achieving these two headline outcomes involves many supporting activities by the finance function, including ensuring good stewardship of assets, solid timely reporting and a strong compliance culture. These tasks are aided by the professional accountant's training and derived numeracy. He or she is normally at the centre of many of the data-collection activities in an MNE and can consequently be in a better position to gauge and measure many of the causes of cash flow volatility. The finance function is also best positioned to assess risk profiles across the organisation.

It is important to remember that there is no absolutely risk-free business activity. Therefore, there will always be risk in a business. The accountant must devise methods to measure risk and assess and advise whether it is appropriate to the investors' appetite for risk and relevant investment strategy. For example, investors in an oil exploration business have a different risk appetite from those who invest in an insurance company. The accountant must reflect these differing environments when making their own deliberations and advising their colleagues on what steps to take or strategies to implement.

A good manager can be identified by their ability to predict the consequences of their actions. The accountant plays a critical role in formulating these predictions and guiding the appropriate actions. (See **Chapter 6** for a more complete examination of the role of the accountant in the MNE.)

2.9 CONCLUSION

We saw in **Chapter 1** that humankind has always had a propensity to produce surpluses and to trade these surpluses for scarcities. As society developed, this trade became more commonplace. The idea of free trade advocated by Adam Smith in the late 1700s took hold as a concept during the 1800s and international trade began to gain support as a route to improved standards of living for all societies. Since the Industrial Revolution in the 1800s the ability to produce surpluses efficiently through specialisation of labour and mechanisation of processes has led to increased global trade. As the 20th Century developed, together with increased prevalence of democratic governance structures, the free movement of goods, persons and capital greatly increased the level of international trade. The emergence of the idea of the corporation as a separate and individual entity in its own right also facilitated the growth of international trade.

The models with which corporations can expand their business internationally have been discussed in this chapter. These take different forms as the enterprise seeks to minimise risk in order to maximise returns for its investors. We also looked at the reasons why corporations expand internationally, examining motives that are proactive. We also saw that in some instances the MNE will expand in reaction to macro or micro environmental forces that act on it. The relationship and different motives of owners of MNEs, their shareholder investors and management can become misaligned. The costs of this misalignment, known as 'agency costs', increase as an organisation expands internationally.

We also saw that the professional accountant and the finance function have particularly important roles to play in helping an MNE to manage its international business.

QUESTIONS

Self-test Questions

2.1 What is the law of comparative advantage?
2.2 In what way does increased certainty about future cash flows improve the value of an MNE?
2.3 Describe a number of proactive motives for international expansion.
2.4 List four forms an MNE might adopt to structure its international trade.

Thought-provoking Questions

Question 2.1
You are the CFO of an Irish company that owns and operates 'vintage' sweet shops. The CEO wonders whether the company could expand internationally. He asks you to write a short

report outlining the different structures the company could implement if it were to expand internationally.

Question 2.2

You work for a firm of management consultants. A client has asked for an analysis as to why companies expand internationally. List six reasons for international expansion.

Review Questions

(See Suggested Solutions to Review Questions in **Appendix B**.)

Question 2.1: TinyTots Baby Food Limited

Having read the TinyTots Baby Food Limited case study in **Appendix A**, propose and explain a new structure that would help the company overcome the present problems being experienced with the international expansion.

Question 2.2: Boyne Aviation Limited

Having read **Chapter 2** and the Boyne Aviation Limited case study in **Appendix A**, detail the actions Boyne Aviation Limited should take in terms of managing costs and revenues in order to change the business model to that of a low-cost operator and prepare a forecast statement of income and expenditure for Boyne using industry KPIs.

3

TYPES OF INTERNATIONAL BUSINESS AND TRADE

CONTENTS

LEARNING OBJECTIVES

Having read this chapter, you will understand:
- the value chain concept;
- how a firm carries on international business;
- how an MNE can select which model works best for its business;
- how MNEs can structure themselves to manage the international dimension of their affairs;
- the continuum from an atomised structure, where an MNE either buys or sells to third parties in different countries, to fully integrated international organisation structures;
- the advantages and disadvantages of the different structures; and
- whether and how far to centralise or decentralise decision-making.

3.1 INTRODUCTION

Chapter 1 gave a brief history of long-distance trade between peoples. This propensity to trade was driven by a desire to improve standards of living, which was achieved by producing surpluses locally and trading these surpluses in return for scarcities. In **Chapter 2** we saw how this propensity to trade surpluses has led to continued growth in international trade, particularly in the last 50 years, and we were introduced to theories of why countries and enterprises wish to expand their trade internationally. **Chapter 2** looked briefly at the types of business model used by multinational enterprises (MNEs) to expand their business internationally. In this chapter we will examine these models in more detail and seek to understand what drives an MNE to select one model over another for its international trade, first exploring the concept of the **value chain**, which provides a framework for analysing how an enterprise adds value. Understanding how value is added can help the nascent MNE to determine whether internationalisation is an appropriate strategy to follow. Having analysed how value is added, the MNE can also determine which internationalisation model to adopt.

The various methods or models for carrying on international business can be viewed as points along a continuum, from 'no ownership of foreign assets' at one end, moving through contractual arrangements, franchises and joint ventures, to where an MNE operates its international business through the ownership of firms operating in its chosen countries.

Figure 3.1 below is a graphical representation of the internationalisation continuum or spectrum. At one end, the MNE has invested very little capital outside its domestic market and engages in international trade through importing or exporting. The continuum is helpful as it portrays the 'life cycle' of an MNE. While an MNE may enter the international market at any stage on the continuum, the further to the right on the spectrum it enters, the more capital it puts at risk. A new company or a start-up will almost always gravitate toward the left-hand side of the continuum, only making heavier capital investments as it gains confidence and capability from past successes.

FIGURE 3.1: MNE OPERATIONAL MODELS: THE INVESTMENT CONTINUUM

3.2 THE VALUE CHAIN

A useful way to consider any enterprise is to think of it in terms of a process that ultimately delivers value for shareholders by creating added value that customers are willing to pay for. The phrase 'added value' is used often in strategic planning and simply involves a proposition that the value of the output of an enterprise is greater than the value of the inputs.

The most common schematic for understanding the value chain was developed in 1985 by Michael Porter (see **Figure 3.2** below). Porter's schematic proposes that an enterprise's activities are broken down into two types: primary and support. Products pass through primary activities, with some value being added to them as they progress. Support activities, as the name suggests, support the primary activities across the organisation.

FIGURE 3.2: THE VALUE CHAIN[1]

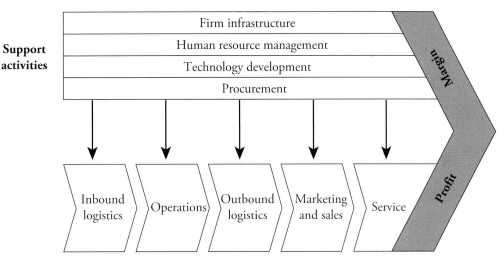

Primary activities

Porter (1985) identified five primary activities and four support activities. The primary activities through which products travel, gaining value as they go, are supported by four supplemental activities. The five primary activities are:

- **Inbound logistics** – the activities that source, store, and organise raw material goods and services are needed for the MNE to provide the goods and services it supplies its customers.
- **Operations** – All the activities that take the inputs and turn them into outputs.
- **Outbound logistics** – The activities involved in storing and distributing the outputs.
- **Marketing and sales** – Informing potential customers of the MNEs outputs and the actions required to deliver the outputs to the customers.
- **Service** – The actions required to ensure the outputs remain effective for the customer after the output has been sold.

The four support activities that enable and facilitate the execution of the five primary activities are:

- **Firm infrastructure** – The activities that tie the MNE together through functions such as accounting and finance, strategic planning, legal affairs, public and investor relations.
- **Human resource management** – The activities of hiring, retaining and firing the personnel needed by the MNE to carry out the other activities.
- **Technology development** – The software, hardware and other technologies needed to transform the inputs into the outputs and enable the support activities.
- **Procurement** – The activities that acquire all the inputs and resources for the MNE.

These support activities provide enabling infrastructure to the five primary activities through which the products pass. The model proposes that all of a firm's activities can be organised into one of the nine activity clusters. The MNE ought then to identify how much of its profit margin derives from each of the activity clusters. In this way the MNE can determine exactly why it is able to make a profit. In other words, why customers are willing to pay the

---

[1] Adapted from Porter, Michael E. (1985) *Competitive Advantage: Creating and Sustaining Superior Performance*. New York: The Free Press.

MNE for the outputs it produces, and, more importantly, which part of the activities it carries out that the customers value the most and are therefore prepared to pay most for.

The value chain concept is useful in breaking down an enterprise's activities into logical, interconnected processes, particularly when analysing where, within an MNE's complex structure, the value is being added. This analysis can then be further employed to develop strategies to maximise added value by carrying out the activities in those countries that add the most value. For example, Apple may design its products in California but it manufactures them in China. It has determined that value is added best through this combination. Apple will have deployed an analysis of how it adds value in order to inform this decision-making process: the value chain concept is a tool that aids this analysis. Apple will have used their understanding of their customers to determine which parts of the value chain customers most value – the design, the manufacturing, the operating system, and so forth. By assessing what value the customer places upon each of these elements of the value chain, Apple can gain an understanding of what its customers are actually paying for when they part with their hard-earned cash for the latest iPhone. The assessment of the value chain components calls for judgement since it cannot be determined with scientific certainty what parts of the value chain the customer values most. It follows, therefore, that MNEs that best understand their customers' needs and wants will be able to make best use of the value-chain concept for the purposes of decomposing their business into identifiable added-value processes.

The value chain can be identified across divisions and subsidiaries that form part of a larger organisation, creating a larger value system. Armed with an enterprise-wide set of interconnected value chains, one can systematically grasp the complete picture, understanding the interactions that occur between the differing parts of the organisation.

If one considers that the value chain can be used to model all enterprises on the planet, not just one's own enterprise, then it is possible to envisage a large network of interconnected value chains representing the total evolution of any product from its raw material all the way to its consumption by the consumer. Indeed, to truly grasp the full potential of value chain analysis, this system-wide approach is to be encouraged.

Analysis of the value chains of an enterprise's suppliers or customers can enable a firm to understand its role in the entire chain more thoroughly, which will inform strategic decision-making and help create a more sustainable enterprise. In **Example 3.1** below we can see how Musgrave used the value-chain concept to decompose the elements of its business model. Through this decomposition it gained an understanding of what the customer valued most, with which it was able to build a sustainable value chain in partnership with its retailers, i.e. the people who actually own the SuperValu and Centra stores.

EXAMPLE 3.1: MUSGRAVE AND THE VALUE CHAIN

In the 1990s, Musgrave Group Plc, a grocery wholesaler that controls the SuperValu and Centra retail brands in Ireland, analysed the value chain of its customers, the individual retailers who owned and operated the stores. They saw that their customers, the retailers, had complex inbound logistics: each store might receive 20 to 30 deliveries per day. Musgrave saw that if it could simplify the inbound logistics activities for the retailers, it would improve added value. Musgrave's outbound logistics activities were connected to the inbound logistics activities of their customers since the goods Musgrave sold and delivered were, in turn, the goods that the individual retailers bought and acquired. Musgrave decided that it would pre-assemble the retailers' orders at its central depots and consolidate all the day's requirements into one large delivery. This consolidated delivery replaced the myriad of smaller deliveries and improved efficiencies within the retailers' operations, which meant that the retailers could devote more time to the other added-value activities in their stores, such as sales and marketing. The resultant efficiencies and improvements in quality of chilled and fresh produce saw SuperValu and Centra become the largest retail operation in the Republic of Ireland. The brands have also gained significant market share in Northern Ireland using the same approach to the value chain.

We will refer to the value chain again as we look at the different types of international business that can be undertaken by an MNE in the following sections.

3.3 IMPORTING

For many enterprises, the first time they get involved in international commercial transactions is when they start to import a product from a foreign country. Enterprises start importing when they determine there is demand in the domestic economy for some product that is not available or produced locally. For example, almost all wine consumed in Ireland is imported since there is very little wine production on the island. The opportunity to import also arises when the firm's procurement function notices that a product that is currently being sourced in the home market can be purchased in another country at a better price, or with better quality for the same price.

In most cases, these first forays into international business arise out of opportunism rather than strategy. For example, a buyer may see a potential supplier's wares at a trade show, get a price and start from there. What seems, at first glance, to be the relatively straightforward purchase of a product from abroad quickly becomes more complex. This is because there are more issues to consider when importing than buying from a supplier 'down the road': the cost of transporting the goods from abroad can be higher, there are possible foreign exchange considerations, as well as obvious issues of quality control and returning damaged or faulty goods. Lead times will often be longer, upfront payments may be required, import duties may apply and there may be other taxes, such as VAT. So, what looks like a simple matter of buying goods for a better price can end up having many attendant, and sometimes hidden, costs. Nonetheless, using the value chain model to analyse the situation, the MNE can arrive at the correct decision. In **Example 3.2** below retailers have determined through their analysis of the value chain that customers will pay more for some domestically produced product categories, such as beef, but not others, such as strawberries.

EXAMPLE 3.2: VALUE CHAIN AND BEEF IMPORTS

Consumers on the island of Ireland are particularly keen to know that their beef is sourced in either the Republic of Ireland or Northern Ireland. A retailer such as Dunnes Stores or SuperValu will know from its value chain analysis that consumers are willing to pay for Irish beef and that sourcing cheaper beef from other countries will not add value since the point of origin is important, and hence part of the value added delivered by the retailers. However, the retailers also know that there is not the same loyalty to Irish strawberries and, accordingly, the retailers will often source strawberries from other countries in order to provide all year availability and better prices.

Importing is the core activity for some enterprises. In other words, the value added by the inbound logistics part of the value chain represents a major part of the profit margin that these MNEs generate. For example, there are importing businesses that do nothing other than source raw materials or finished goods in foreign countries for other firms who recognise the opportunity of foreign sourcing but do not want the complications involved in dealing with foreign entities. Such importing businesses will develop specialist knowledge of the global markets from which they are sourcing and can add significant value for their stakeholders from their small piece of the value chain. For example, Pan Euro Foods is a specialist food importer operating from a facility in West Dublin. It specialises in sourcing and importing new and innovative products that offer commercial and competitive benefits to its customers. Therefore, a restaurant chain, for example, may use the services of Pan Euro Foods to import products for them rather than getting involved in trying to master the complexity of foreign-country sourcing and importing themselves. Importing specialists learn the idiosyncrasies of trading across different jurisdictions, how the 'red tape' works and, more importantly, how to stop it from stifling business.

IMPORTING: ADVANTAGES AND DISADVANTAGES

Advantages	Disadvantages
• Lower cost than locally sourced products • Ease of access to new products • Low entry and exit costs • Possible to get domestic country exclusivity	• Foreign exchange risks • Additional distribution costs • Possible tariffs and import duties • Competitors may source same products

In summary, the value chain concept allows a firm to ascertain if there is a foreign sourcing opportunity. By further analysing how value is added or could be added by the sourcing of goods internationally the MNE can decide whether it should pursue that opportunity itself or outsource it.

3.4 EXPORTING

Importing is often the most common first 'toe in the water' for firms on the internationalisation journey. Similarly, exporting is very frequently the first or second step in the internationalisation process for an MNE. Many firms first get involved in international trade because a potential customer from another country makes an inquiry about the firm's product. They may have seen the product at a trade fair or simply by conducting a search on the Internet. In any case, it often happens that a firm with no internationalisation plans receives an unsolicited order from a potential customer and this can bring the first realisation that it has a real opportunity to do business beyond its own borders. This activity is often called 'casual exporting'.

As with importing, exporting to a foreign country is not as straightforward as fulfilling an order domestically. First, one has to consider the transport costs of getting the product to the new customer. Then there are the complications of ensuring that the new customer pays for the goods. The newly emerging MNE must also consider what currency to invoice in and what taxes apply. It will also have to consider whether there are import or export regulations with which it needs to comply. In some circumstances, firms will be concerned about what the new customer intends to do with the product. For example, is the new customer intending to sell the product on into another market at a significant mark-up, reducing the firm's opportunities for further expansion?

Finally, there is the issue of how to set prices for products the MNE may wish to export. Sometimes firms will look at new export orders as 'one-offs' and price them either exceptionally high to make a 'super profit' or at slightly above marginal cost on the basis that if they make some contribution to fixed costs from the transaction, it was a good day's work. Either approach is opportunistic.

The first, high-price approach takes the view that a once-off opportunity to make a 'killing' has presented itself. Minded that the firm has no long-term interest in supplying the international market, the MNE sets a price that rewards it for the extra effort to process a once-off export order.

The other approach, marginal pricing, looks at the opportunity as a chance to make a once-off contribution to fixed costs that will not impact upon the pricing model the enterprise uses in its normal markets. Accordingly, it should view the opportunity as a special and make the sale for any price that returns a positive contribution to fixed costs. Since it is a once-off, no fixed costs are absorbed or allocated into the order. It is important that the enterprise's existing domestic customers do not react negatively if/when they find out about any one-off marginal pricing activity undertaken in the export market. They may demand the same prices for themselves. This would lead to major problems since marginal pricing makes no contribution to fixed overhead, a contribution that is necessary for any sustainable ongoing business. However, if a business is serious about seizing the opportunities presented by entering foreign markets, it needs to be more than just opportunistic. It needs to take a long-term strategic view. This will lead to greater consideration being given to the appropriate pricing model to adopt and a greater focus on the costs associated with serving a foreign market.

Exporting and the Value Chain

We have touched on how a firm might start exporting by responding positively to orders from abroad. However, once an enterprise has established that there is a market for its products in a foreign jurisdiction it can then structure its organisation to support such activities. If we think about the value chain, we can see how some primary activities will be altered and adjusted and some of the support activities will need refocusing in order to maximise added value. For example, the outbound logistics activities will need to be rearranged and recalibrated if the enterprise is now going to serve a foreign market. Distribution options will need to be appraised: does the firm use its own transport to send the goods or should it use an export haulier? The decision will be made based on which approach adds most value for customers, who may want, and be prepared to pay, for next day delivery. This may not be possible using the firm's own transport but might be possible using more expensive air freight. The decision will be made based upon the excess between what the customer will be prepared to pay and the associated costs, in other words, the added value.

Sales and marketing activities are another part of the enterprise's value chain that will need to be reassessed in order to fulfil export orders. It is unlikely that the existing domestic sales efforts will be able to generate orders from customers in another country. There may be new languages to learn, different competitors, different VAT and tax regimes to take into account. All these variations between the domestic market and the foreign market will most likely lead to a different approach and structure from the nascent MNE's sales and marketing activities. The product itself may need some reformulating or repackaging to conform with the foreign market's requirements.

Consideration of how to execute the value-added activities within the value chain once the enterprise operates outside its home country presents complexities requiring solutions that are not just simple extensions of how the business operates domestically. In other words, the activities that add value in foreign markets will differ in nature and substance from the activities in the domestic market. The problem is to identify which activities are impacted and to introduce new processes to sustain the international export orders. Solving these problems can often lead to distractions from serving existing domestic customers. Hidden costs can start to arise as resources are diverted away from the home business to solve issues relating to meeting export customers' needs. The MNE manager also needs to be aware of how there can be some attraction to the excitement of dealing with the export business. This excitement can exacerbate the diversion of resources. Many firms will attempt to solve this challenge by setting up a separate export and shipping department just to handle the international sales and logistics function. However, this function will still need to be aligned with the other parts of the value chain, particularly production and marketing.

EXPORTING: ADVANTAGES AND DISADVANTAGES

Advantages	Disadvantages
• Additional sales • Increased economies of scale • Diversification of market risk • Increase product life cycle • Sell off excess production or over-stocks	• Extra costs, especially logistics • Product modification • Financial risks, especially bad debts • 'Red tape' • Market knowledge must be obtained

3.5 AGENCIES AND LICENSING

Faced with the challenges of dealing with suppliers in foreign countries, in the case of importers, or overseas customers in the case of exporters, an MNE must look for the solutions that most closely align with its strategy.

For example, imagine an MNE whose strategy is to expand its sales to South America. Recently it has been fulfilling orders from India on an ad hoc basis. It currently has no strategic intent to develop its activities in Asia. This MNE must reappraise the strategy in light of the export business to Asia. It can either reformulate its strategy and begin to focus increased resources on Asia or continue to develop its South American strategy. What it should avoid is investing in the Asian export activity without a clear strategic plan as to what it hopes to achieve and how.

Having decided that the international activity, either importing or exporting, is not a once-off, the MNE must then decide how to integrate the fulfilment of this part of the value chain into the wider activities of the business.

One of the ways an MNE may engage in trade in a foreign market is to appoint an agent to act on its behalf. The appointment of an agent can be greatly helpful to the MNE since it means it has a person in its target country who knows how the market operates. Usually the agent receives delegated authority to act on behalf of the MNE up to certain pre-defined levels. The MNE accelerates its understanding of the market since the agent will usually have built up experience and knowledge of the trade and will normally have pre-existing relationships in the foreign marketplace.

Agents can be used to sell the MNE's products into a foreign market. They can also be used to help procure and source raw materials that the MNE needs for production inputs, although this use of agents is less common. The relationship between the agent and the MNE is usually governed by an agency agreement or a licence agreement. This agreement will set out the obligations and duties on both parties, including how income is to be earned and the territory concerned, and will usually be for a definite time period.

Export Sales Agents

In its simplest form, a firm will export the product made in its home market (e.g. Ireland) to a foreign market in response to spontaneous orders by foreign customers. ('Product' in this chapter, and generally throughout the text, refers to goods and services: any tangible good like a machine, or intangible good like software, or any service such as IT consulting or server hosting.) However, once the export markets have been identified as being strategically important rather than just opportunistic, the MNE must decide how to best meet customers' needs and generate sales. One solution is to appoint a sales agent in the export market. The agent will enter into a contract or 'agency agreement' with the Irish exporter, which will cover matters such as:
- products to be sold and pricing;
- the region to which the agreement applies;
- marketing strategies and funding;
- commercial terms connected with, *inter alia*, ownership of the goods, credit terms and limitations to the agent's overall range of activities;
- duration of the agreement;
- agency commission terms;
- dispute resolution and termination; and
- the jurisdiction in which any dispute will be decided.

The agent then operates sales and marketing functions on the ground in the target market on behalf of the Irish exporter. The advantage for the exporter is that it does not have to set up an operation in a market where it is unfamiliar with the laws, language, etc. However, there are also disadvantages. The agent will own the relationship with the customer, and this relationship is critical in all businesses. As sales grow, the exporter's reliance on the agent will also grow. The agent will come to know many of the parts of the exporter's value chain that appeal to the ultimate customer. The bargaining position of the agent can become increasingly strong unless the exporter keeps it in check by also maintaining its own relationship with the customer. In **Example 3.3** below we can see that Umbro exports from its UK business into the ROI using specialist export sales agents. It keeps control of the relationship with the customers in ROI by forming relationships with them through, and in conjunction with, the sales agent.

EXAMPLE 3.3: UMBRO AND EXPORT SALES AGENTS

Umbro, the sportswear brand, manages its sales and marketing in Ireland through an exclusive agent. In order to ensure it maintains a good relationship with its retail customers in Ireland, it hosts events and conferences to which those retail customers are invited. Its executives will also arrange reciprocal visits between the retailers and the main Umbro business.

In this way there is a three-way relationship, with Umbro conducting its business through its Irish agent but at the same time maintaining a relationship directly with its retail customers.

EXPORT SALES AGENTS: ADVANTAGES AND DISADVANTAGES

Advantages	Disadvantages
• Speed to market • Reduced learning curve as agent is an expert in export market • Agent has established contact in the marketplace • Sales growth can be faster • Multiple new markets can be entered using a variety of agents • Less costly than direct engagement	• Commission costs reduce overall profitability • Agent will seek to negotiate prices in the export market • Exporter often restricted to using only one agent in a given market • Relationship with the end customer can be diluted

Licensing

As export sales grow, some MNEs begin to examine the value chain even further, looking beyond just the sales and marketing activities. For example, an Irish exporter may begin to see that there are opportunities to manufacture some or all of its products in a foreign market. There can be manufacturing cost reduction opportunities to be gained or it may just be that it is better to manufacture the products closer to the customers. Whatever the strategic rationale, the Irish exporter now seeks to seize an identified opportunity by manufacturing its products outside of Ireland.[2]

One method of executing a manufacturing facility outside of Ireland is to have a licensing agreement with a manufacturer in the target location. The advantage of this approach is that many of the start-up complexities can be avoided and set-up costs kept to a minimum, especially the fixed costs of setting up a new manufacturing location. Such fixed start-up costs can be particularly onerous when a firm has uncertain or volatile demand forecasts, which is often the case when expanding into a new market.

Where a firm wishes to have a manufacturing capability in another country operated and owned by a separate organisation, it will normally enter into a licence agreement with that manufacturing firm. The licence will normally cover:
• specifications and listings of the products to be made;
• cost and pricing arrangements;
• service-level agreements, including quality standards, lead times and customer order fulfilment targets;
• commercial terms, including credit terms, risk allocation and working capital finance;
• intellectual property rights and restrictions;
• restrictions of trade; and
• duration of agreement and termination.

It is also critical that any agreement specifies the jurisdiction of the laws governing the agreement, e.g. the laws of Ireland. The civil law system prevailing in most of continental Europe means that it differs from the common law principles of the UK and Ireland in many respects. The legal systems

---

[2] In some circumstances, the manufacturing facility is not being set up in the foreign country to serve a new sales market but rather to service existing customer markets from a more efficient production facility. Also, it can sometimes be the case that a sales agent will become a manufacturer under licence.

in many parts of Asia are also significantly different. As world governments have tried to encourage international trade the differences between legal systems have narrowed, especially for commercial contracts. However, when things go wrong and the remedies sought are through the courts, the MNE manager can find the concepts and processes of other legal systems surprisingly different. (See **Chapter 12** for further examination of legal risks for MNEs.)

While a manufacturing licence can give an Irish firm access to the benefits and efficiencies that may come from using another organisation's competencies to further its own strategic goals, there are also potential pitfalls to this approach. Some of the disadvantages are:

- The Irish firm comes to rely on the licensee and loses core manufacturing capability within its own organisation.
- The licensed manufacturer comes to know a lot about how the Irish firm's products are made.
- It can be complex to agree an appropriate price for the manufacturer that rewards the seeking of efficiencies. If a fixed price is agreed any improved efficiencies are profit for the manufacturer. If the price is variable, based on costs, there is no incentive for the manufacturer to seek efficiencies.
- Relationships with raw material suppliers can become more distant, increasing the firm's reliance on the manufacturer.
- If the manufacturer also has responsibility for sales, the Irish firm can become increasingly remote from its customers.

These disadvantages can be minimised by putting in place the appropriate organisational resources to manage risk, especially those risks around supplier relationships and intellectual property.

LICENSING: ADVANTAGES AND DISADVANTAGES

Advantages	Disadvantages
• Cost-effective route to market entry • Lower capital requirements • Tariff controls in export country may be minimised or avoided altogether • Possibility for higher return on capital invested	• Loss of control • Licensee could take control of key relationships and intellectual property (IP) • Misalignment of corporate values • Licensor does not develop core competencies

Royalties

Licenses can often include royalty payment provisions where the user of the intellectual property, the 'knowhow', pays a simple flat fee or a percentage of sales to the owner for its use. The nature of the fee structure depends on the product or intellectual property being deployed. The royalty fee structure will normally be related to and proportionate to the benefit derived by the user. For example, Company A pays a royalty fee to Company B for use of its technology in the manufacture of widgets. The royalty fee is €1 per widget manufactured. The more widgets Company A makes, the more royalty fees it pays Company B. The recognition of royalty income for accounting and taxation purposes is normally on a remittance basis. Royalty income paid to an ROI company is income in ROI and taxed accordingly. The reader should be aware that there are complex tax rules around royalty income. These rules are constantly changing and will no doubt change further with the development of base erosion and profit shifting (BEPS) initiatives by the OECD countries.

Import Sales Agents

We have looked at a situation where an Irish manufacturer seeks to supply its foreign customers on a more structured basis using an agent. Likewise, a manufacturer in a foreign market may wish to service the Irish market in a more structured way. In order to do this, the foreign manufacturer may seek to appoint an Irish sales agent to manage and run its sales effort in Ireland. This situation presents an opportunity for Irish sales and marketing companies. Traditionally, these companies also managed stockholding and the distribution for foreign manufacturers.

EXAMPLE 3.4: TATE & LYLE AND IMPORT SALES AGENTS

In the 1980s Tate & Lyle used an Irish import sales agent, J.V. McDaniels (JVM), to manage all its sales and marketing activities in the Republic of Ireland. JVM also held stock of Tate & Lyle's products in its warehouses in order to more speedily serve the Irish customers. JVM, a subsidiary of Irish conglomerate James Crean Plc, performed the same function for other non-Irish brands from the same premises, using the same sales staff and marketing personnel. In this way JVM was able to share the fixed costs of running sales, marketing and distribution across a large number of brands. The brand owners benefited from these economies of scale and the benefits were split between JVM and the brand owner in a variety of ways, depending on the license agreement negotiated.

In the past there were many such agencies in Ireland, but their number has slowly decreased as the EU has removed a range of trade restrictions. A manufacturer could give solus rights to an agent, preventing any other operator from selling its products in the Irish market. As time has progressed, and trade restrictions have been lessened or removed altogether, an agent or distributor in another country could buy extra stock from the same manufacturer and export it to Ireland themselves, thereby competing with the manufacturer's appointed Irish agent. Nevertheless, the use of agents as a method of establishing a presence in the Irish market is still prevalent.

Ireland-based Licensed Manufacturer

In the same way that an Irish firm may decide to license its product to be made and sold in a foreign market, a foreign manufacturer may see advantages in having its product made in Ireland by an Irish licensee. It may see the complexities of setting up its own factory as overly capital or resource intensive. To get around those complexities, the foreign enterprise may appoint an Irish manufacturer to make the products for it under a licence. When the licensing route is chosen, the Irish manufacturer produces the product to the specifications laid out by the parties in the licence agreement, the main contents of which would be the same as those outlined above for the case of an Irish firm licensing a foreign manufacturer.

The Irish division of Britvic manufactures Pepsi Cola beverages under a licence agreement with PepsiCo. Beverage companies often adopt this model as the cost of distributing liquids, where there is a low value/high weight ratio over long distances, can be prohibitive.

Exit Benefits

As well as ease of set-up, another advantage for a foreign manufacturer in using a licensee in Ireland or the UK to manufacture its products is the ease of exit. As a general rule, complexity equates to cost and it is much more complex to close down a foreign subsidiary than it is to cancel a manufacturing licence.

This issue has been a concern among employee representative groups in Ireland and the UK for some time. An otherwise profitable foreign company can cancel a manufacturing licence with its Irish or UK licensee, who may not have the reserves to make anything other than the bare minimum in compensatory payments. There is seen to be an inequity in these situations. A profitable foreign enterprise is seen to avoid making redundancy payments by dint of the fact that its manufacturing in Ireland or the UK is carried out by a licensee rather than directly by itself. The licence agreement will often cover the issues that arise on termination, including decommissioning costs and employee compensation schemes. Nonetheless, the issue remains as what is sometimes seen as the unacceptable face of international trade and globalisation.

3.6 JOINT VENTURES

As we have seen, two of the main disadvantages of operating in foreign markets using agents or licensees are:
- loss of direct control of the licensed elements of the value chain; and
- reduction in the quality of the relationships with suppliers or customers.

In addition to these two problems, a third also arises. It is very difficult to construct an agreement that motivates the agent to improve the efficiency of what they are doing for the manufacturer. In particular, there is little incentive for the agent to innovate or be creative. This problem arises because of the nature of licence agreements. Normally an agent will receive a fixed percentage or piece rate for providing the services on behalf of the manufacturer. If the agent finds ways to improve products or services, the fixed rate ensures that any benefit flows to the manufacturer. If the rate is more variable, the licensee may cut costs to such a degree as to cause a deterioration in the quality of the service provided to the ultimate customer, thus damaging brand values. A way must be sought that shares the benefits of any improvements or innovations; one way to share the benefits, and the risks, is to create a **joint venture**.

As the term name suggests, a 'joint venture' is where two or more business entities combine their resources to achieve an agreed common goal. While joint ventures are found in all forms of business and commercial activities, not just in international business, the 'JV' structure can lend itself very well to allowing enterprises to overcome the real risks and obstacles to growing internationally.

Joint venture shareholding need not be 50/50 owned by the parties involved. Indeed, joint ventures do not need to be corporate legal entities, though they normally are. The main purpose of a joint venture is that the parties collaborate in both the initial risk investment and then, if successful, the future benefits. All parties will bring some capital to the venture, either real or intellectual. For example, in 2012 Irish seafood companies Atlanfish and Rockabill Shellfish formed a joint venture to exploit the opportunity to service the consumer demand for whitefish in China. They formed a brand together, 'Atlantic Gold'. By combining their resources and expertise, both seafood companies helped reduce their respective risks and shared important product knowledge and processing capability. In this way, they were able to expand into a foreign market without overly risking the existing businesses.

In an international business context one can see how a joint venture can be useful. An MNE wishing to enter a new market can see that there are risks, particularly if it is unfamiliar with the market. An existing operator in the marketplace may have reached a point where it feels it cannot grow existing brands or operations any further. A joint venture provides both parties with an opportunity to address a strategic goal. The potential exporter delivers on its strategic goal of international expansion while its JV partner delivers on its growth strategy without having the expense of developing a new brand.

> In China, it is a requirement that firms entering the Chinese market must do so using a joint venture structure. The other party in the joint venture must be a firm owned by the Chinese government.

JOINT VENTURES: ADVANTAGES AND DISADVANTAGES

Advantages	Disadvantages
• Faster access to new markets • Sharing of different skill-sets • Sharing of risk • Can enter several markets at the same time • Knowledge of local cultures	• Shared benefits means lower profits • Complex agreements • Slower decision-making, more parties involved • Misalignment of corporate values and culture

3.7 FRANCHISING

A franchise is a long-term collaborative business relationship between a franchisor and one or more franchisees. The franchisor grants the franchisee privileged rights to carry on a business, and the business model along with its intellectual property will be owned and developed by the franchisor. The franchisee will be allowed to use the brand names, intellectual property and business know-how of the franchisor, usually in a designated geographic area. They will be obliged to maintain certain standards and to buy designated products from the franchisor. They will also benefit from the marketing and promotional expertise of the franchisor and, in return, the franchisee pays the franchisor a fee. The franchisee usually commits the capital expenditure needed to run the business, and will recruit and pay the staff required to carry on the business.

Franchising can be particularly attractive to brands wishing to internationalise their business. It can facilitate rapid expansion, especially in predominantly consumer-facing or service-oriented brands. This is because the capital requirements, local knowledge and recruitment, are all delivered on the ground by the franchisee, allowing the franchisor to develop and execute the larger national marketing strategies. Under a franchise agreement, the brand owner (the franchisor) provides sales and marketing support to the franchisee, which operates the brand in the specified territory. The franchisee normally pays the franchisor a fee based on performance, normally sales. Some of the world's best-known brands have expanded domestically and internationally using the franchise format. For example, McDonald's and Burger King have reached global consumer markets using this approach. The franchisor relies on picking good operators to deliver the brand in accordance with its required standards of store fit-out, product quality, customer service and hygiene. The franchisee commits to adhere to the rules of the franchisor's system. There is a constant tension between the two as the franchisee operator tries to deliver pragmatic solutions to local issues while the franchisor tries to enforce national or even global standards.

In some cases, a major franchisor will grant a regional 'master' franchise. The master franchisee can then roll out the brand through the issuance of sub-franchisee agreements within locally defined territories. For example, the Subway sandwich chain operates a system where a master franchise is granted and the recipient of the master franchise then seeks other franchisees. This is the way Subway operates in Ireland.

Franchisees often complain about the franchisor granting too many franchises, thereby diluting the profitability of individual outlets by cannibalising turnover. 'Cannibalising turnover' describes a situation where the sales of a firm's products or outlets involve simply a switch in consumption from an existing product or outlet to another rather than true additional sales. Where a newly opened outlet is close to an existing one, the additional sales in the new outlet can lead to a reduction in sales in a nearby existing outlet.

The main advantages and disadvantages of franchising to the *franchisor* can be summarised as follows:

FRANCHISING: ADVANTAGES AND DISADVANTAGES – FRANCHISOR

Advantages	Disadvantages
• Lower capital requirements than the fully-owned model • Speedy roll-out • Less need for local operations management and recruitment • The power of pooled commitment from franchisees for buying and sourcing • Focus of locally owned franchisee	• Lower returns than fully integrated business model • Loss of some control over the brand • Varied delivery of standards by franchisees

The main advantages and disadvantages of franchising to the *franchisee* are as follows:

FRANCHISING: ADVANTAGES AND DISADVANTAGES – FRANCHISEE

Advantages	Disadvantages
• Established brand, already proven • Support systems already in place • Pooling of purchasing power with other franchisees • Depth of back-up available compared to being a standalone business • Access to national or global marketing message	• The need to comply to standards that may not fit local business needs • Lower margins as franchise fees eat into profit • Some loss of independence

Franchising has been especially successful where the business model is labour-intensive and consumer-facing. The retail, catering and hospitality sectors seem to be best suited to franchising and many of the world's best-known brands in these business sectors operate through some sort of franchising system. Examples include Holiday Inn hotels, Burger King, Benetton, McDonald's, Subway, Seven-Eleven and Ritz Carlton. You can see that the brands operate at the 'cheap and cheerful' end of the market as well as at the premium end.

3.8 FOREIGN DIRECT INVESTMENT

As discussed in the Introduction to this chapter, and shown in **Figure 3.1** (p. 50), the various modes of internationalising a business can be viewed as points along a continuum, from 'no ownership of foreign assets' at one end, moving through contractual arrangements, franchises and joint ventures, to where an MNE operates its international business through the ownership of firms operating in its chosen countries. Foreign direct investment (FDI) is at one end of a continuum of potential international expansion models, where one end involves no ownership of assets in foreign jurisdictions and the other end of the continuum involves outright ownership of assets. The largest MNEs tend to operate a model whereby they own and control the organisations throughout the world, which they use to achieve their business goals and to meet and deliver on their corporate strategies. This model, called **foreign direct investment**, requires the MNE to invest directly in owning and operating assets in foreign jurisdictions.

In this section we examine why MNEs would choose FDI as a route to internationalisation over the other methods discussed in this chapter, looking at the two main methods for expanding internationally using FDI: acquisition of an existing entity; and setting up of a new entity. (In **Chapter 4**, we will look at why governments and states, in this case the Republic of Ireland and Northern Ireland, are keen to encourage FDI and at what incentives they offer to facilitate it.)

Acquiring an Existing Entity

One of the most common ways for an organisation to expand internationally is to acquire an existing operation in the foreign market it wishes to enter. Having identified the market, the MNE will then search for existing firms that meet certain predetermined criteria.

However, the advantages of entering a market by acquiring an existing business can be offset by risks, such as acquiring a failing entity or management, or customer departures in the immediate post-acquisition phase (see **Appendix C.3**). The MNE therefore needs to be careful not to overpay for the business it is acquiring.

Valuing a business is an inexact science at the best of times; valuing a business in an unfamiliar country is even more uncertain.

There are five main ways to value a business that a MNE is considering acquiring:
- assets: especially pertinent if the business being considered is a property company or another type of company with significant tangible assets;
- price/earnings ratios: useful when sustainable future profits can be determined and a benchmark multiplier is readily found;
- discounted cash flows: using future cash flows discounted back to today's value with an appropriate discount rate;
- sector 'rules of thumb': some industries have established 'rules of thumb' for valuing businesses in the sector, such as a multiple of weekly turnover or a multiple of client billings;
- entry costs: a valuation method that uses the estimated cost of building an equivalent business from scratch.

Each of the above methods provides a useful framework for estimating the value of a business. However, these estimates do not mean that if the MNE pays this valuation it will create value for its own shareholders, because the acquisition of an existing subsidiary must be relevant to the strategy of the acquiring MNE. For example, if an Irish dairy processor acquires a mobile phone operator in Taiwan at a reasonable price/earnings ratio, unless there is a clear strategic rationale for this extraordinary international foray, the acquisition would quickly begin to struggle as the new Irish owner grapples with the intricacies of an unfamiliar market, culture, language and business sector. In order to avoid these pitfalls it is always recommended that any acquisition of an existing business is assessed using a robust capital investment appraisal process (see **Chapter 11**). Just because a business is worth €5 million, does not mean it is worth €5 million to the acquiring MNE. Using discounted cash-flow projections has become one of the more established ways of estimating the value of a particular acquisition target to the acquiring MNE.

While taking future predicted cash flows and discounting those cash flows back at an appropriate rate may sound simple, how does the MNE predict the cash flows? What discount rate should the MNE choose? What level of possible future synergies should be taken into account? What value should be attached to the strategic dimension of expanding internationally? These are some of the key questions that need to be asked when making decisions on what is the right price to pay for an acquisition target in a foreign country. There is also the need to resist the natural tendency to justify a higher price once the 'momentum' of the deal begins to take hold. Buying new businesses can be exciting. Once the firm gets into the process, it can create its own momentum. Warning signs may not be sufficiently noticed or may even be simply ignored.

> In 2011 Teva, the Israeli pharmaceutical company, paid $6.8 billion for Cephalon, a US specialty drug manufacturer. Former executives say the deal was rushed through and due diligence was not thorough. Most analysts believe Teva overpaid for the acquisition. The siren call of accelerated growth that may be achieved by entry into a foreign market can affect the decision-making of otherwise clever and experienced business people. When making the acquisition, Teva forecast revenues for 2015 of $31 billion. At the end of 2014 it was estimating 2015 revenues to be between $19 billion and $20 billion.[3]

In order to ensure that a possible acquisition of an existing business 'does what it says on the tin' an MNE will undertake an investigation into the business, a process that is normally termed 'due diligence'. Sometimes an MNE will use its own internal resources and personnel to perform the due diligence. This approach has the advantage of using internal, competent people who should be aware of industry nuances and what the acquiring MNE is looking for in its new acquisition. However, internal resources can be biased toward completing the acquisition or busy in also running day-to-day operations of the firm. It is more normal for a firm to appoint external advisors, typically the management consultancy arm of an accounting firm, to carry the due diligence exercise in conjunction with management. Where matters of extreme sensitivity or commercial secrecy are involved, the use of an external firm can be a stipulation of the seller of the business. This would be especially true if the acquiring firm and the target firm were seen to be competitors, or possible competitors, as is often the case.

In summary, there are real advantages to an expanding MNE acquiring an existing operation as a route to developing international market entry. The potential disadvantages can be foreseen and planned for through appropriate due diligence and a clear business strategy.

Setting up a New Entity

When no suitable acquisition target can be found, the aspiring MNE may look to create its own firm from scratch in the new foreign market. This can often be the preferred route when the firm is locating in the new country because of its attractiveness from a cost perspective.

When one looks at the value chain, one can see that there is a 'flow' through the chain. Raw materials are procured, go through various processes, and are then sold, ideally at a profit.

---

[3] Kimes, M. (2014). Teva Returns to Roots after 'Nuthouse' Board Ousts CEO. [online] Bloomberg. Available at: http://bloom.bg/Ns09KE (accessed July 2014).

Where an international expansion is driven by strategic considerations that are towards the start of the value chain, i.e. relating to the cost of inputs or raw materials, setting up a new business in the new country may make more sense. In this case, the added value rationale would not be based on the sales and marketing part of the value chain (sales and marketing added value almost always requires local knowledge of customers and the setting up of a regionally focused sales effort). If the expansion is based on reducing manufacturing costs, or improving process efficiencies, then the need to acquire existing competence in the target country is reduced. Indeed, such new subsidiaries often do not sell onward to external customers but rather supply other subsidiaries of the same parent entity, which then carry out the sales and marketing function in the appropriate market. The price at which the subsidiary sells its output to its fellow subsidiaries is called the 'transfer price' (see **Chapter 16**).

Starting up a subsidiary has many advantages for the MNE, not least in that the firm can design exactly what it wants. However, it has attendant costs, especially in that the subsidiary will not generate any income until it has been fully set up and commissioned. There is also the challenge of conveying to a new workforce in a different country exactly what the parent is looking for in terms of strategy and culture. These challenges can be overcome with good project planning and people management skills.

FOREIGN DIRECT INVESTMENT: ADVANTAGES AND DISADVANTAGES

Advantages	Disadvantages
• Access to a foreign market • Trade barriers may be reduced • Production costs can be reduced • Access to natural resources	• Capital intensive • Cultural difference • Corporate value systems misaligned • Risk of over-paying

Organisational Structure in a Foreign Subsidiary

Having decided to set up a new subsidiary or acquire an existing business, the MNE must decide how to run its business in the foreign market. At a high level, this decision can be distilled into two options:
• centralise control at the head office; or
• decentralise authority to the subsidiary.

When discount retailer Poundland entered the ROI market it branded its stores 'Dealz' rather than 'Poundland'. It did not acquire an existing operator. It started from scratch in one store in Portlaoise. The business is primarily run from the UK head office, with limited local decision-making. There were 40 Dealz stores in ROI by mid-2015. Poundland had decided to run the business in ROI with centralised control from Poundland head office in the UK.

A different approach was adopted by Spar South Africa. It entered the ROI and UK markets in 2014 through the acquisition of an 80% stakeholding in existing operator BWG Foods. It left the existing management in charge and exercised limited control over the Irish and UK business. Decision-making authority seems to have been left with local management at the original BWG head office in Dublin. Both methods can be successful depending on the strategic rationale for the acquisition, managerial competence and the market sector involved. (See **Chapter 18** for a further discussion on organisation design in the MNE.)

A third way, a hybrid approach, is often the compromise solution but requires clarity about who is responsible for what. A hybrid involves a matrix structure where function heads in a country report both to the central functional leader and to the CEO in charge of the country. If such clarity around accountability is absent, then performance can be suboptimal as the firm bickers with itself about who was supposed to do what and when. **Example 3.5** below, about Laya Healthcare, illustrates the effect of a number of different management control philosophies in one business.

EXAMPLE 3.5: LAYA HEALTHCARE

Laya Healthcare was originally formed in 1997 by British health insurer BUPA, which had started a company from scratch in Ireland at a time when the only other health insurer was VHI, which was state-owned. BUPA retreated from the Irish market in the mid-2000s and sold the business to the Quinn Group, which was expanding from cement products into insurance. They rebranded it Quinn Healthcare and repositioned the offer to be more closely aligned with the 'value for money' Quinn brand. As the Quinn Group struggled after the financial crisis in the late 2000s, management saw the opportunity to acquire the business in 2012. They rebranded it 'Laya' and, with the support of their Swiss underwriters, set about growing market share. In January 2015 the global insurance giant, AIG, announced it was to acquire Laya from the management as part of its global expansion plan. AIG has stated that the existing management will continue to run the business as before, suggesting that AIG will adopt a decentralised approach to organisation structure and leave a high degree of autonomy with the Irish management.

The structure decision is further complicated when one considers the functions that exist within an MNE. For example, should the finance director of a subsidiary be responsible to the local subsidiary CEO, or to the group finance director based at head office? There is no right answer to the thorny issue of organisation design. However, here are pointers as to which structures suit which situations.

A useful way of thinking about this organisational dilemma is to consider the matter from the customer's perspective. Does the customer need or demand local responsiveness or is the customer prepared to engage at a global or continental level? One then needs to consider the product or service. Is the product standardised at the global or continental level or does it require local tailoring? Answering these questions can help the MNE understand how to structure its organisation. In **Figure 3.3** below we can see that where the customer is organised globally, the sales efforts of the MNE also need to be organised globally. An example of a 'globally organised customer' is one where the purchase decision is made centrally for an entire global entity. For example, Intel purchases its raw materials centrally for all production. A potential seller to Intel will need to organise itself to have a relationship with the central purchasing office that makes the decisions.

When the customer is local, that is, the purchasing decision is made locally, then the organisation needs to have its sale efforts focused on that local market. However, if the product is global but the customer is local, then the manufacturing will be organised on a global basis but sold with local subsidiaries. An example of a global product with local purchasing customers is the corrugated packaging market serviced by Irish Plc, Smurfit Kappa Group. The product is mass manufactured in enormous plants but is sold locally to end-users who buy in their own market. This requires Smurfit to have global manufacturing capability and local sales efforts. Another example is the thread business of Coats Plc. The thread is mass manufactured in plants that harness economies of scale. However, the textile manufacturers who buy the thread are a mixture of large global manufacturers and smaller, locally based ones. Therefore, Coats needs to organise the sales and marketing activities on a local basis even though the manufacturing is on a global basis.

Where the customer is local and requires a localised product, then it is best to decentralise as much authority as possible to the local subsidiaries. If the product is global and its customers are global, then authority can be centralised and the company can act on a global basis. Suppliers of raw materials to global manufacturers can be organised this way. Commodity manufacturers are also often structured in this way.

Figure 3.3 shows how four organisation structures can emerge from considering two variables. The vertical axis represents the continuum of the benefits of economy of scale manufacturing, where upward is toward greater economies of scale from mass production. The horizontal axis represents global customer market consolidation on the left toward fragmented and localised customer demand on the right.

FIGURE 3.3: GLOBAL/LOCAL ORGANISATION STRUCTURE DESIGN

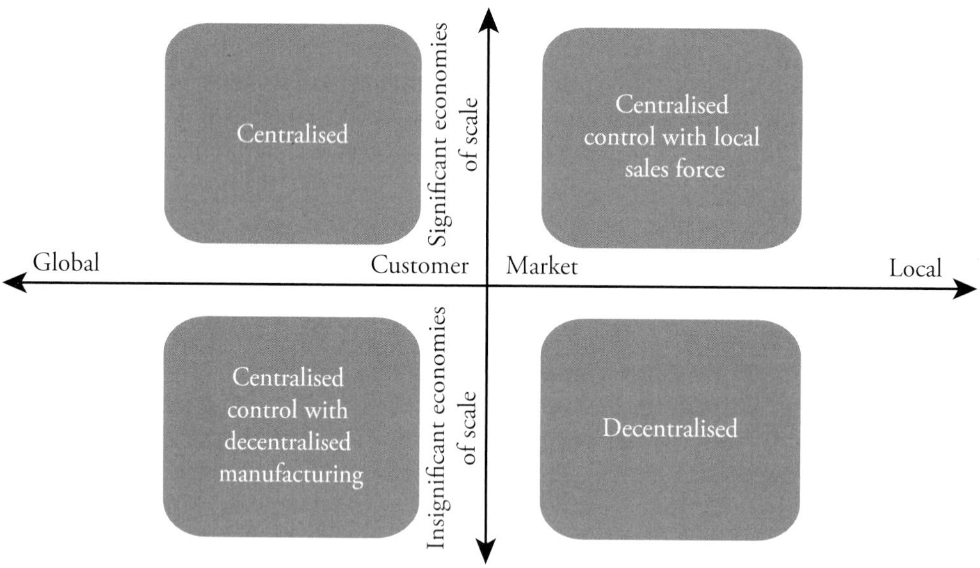

Whatever organisation design is arrived at, bearing in mind that there is never a right or a wrong structure, each design will bring its own advantages and disadvantages.[4]

Decentralised Structures

While the choice between decentralised structures or centralised seems simple, the reality is much more complex. Most enterprises organise themselves along functional lines with departments set up to specialise in, for example, finance, HR, manufacturing, etc., even if they are not an MNE. When the MNE starts its internationalisation process it needs to decide whether to keep this structure. The simplest structure for decentralisation is to keep existing functional reporting to the local CEO or general manager. This is what AIG has said it will do with

---

[4] Argyris, C. (1957). *The individual and organization: some problems of mutual adjustment*. Indianapolis: Bobbs-Merrill.

Laya Healthcare in **Example 3.5** above. One of the drawbacks of this approach is that synergies can be harder to achieve because the local management of the subsidiary remain empowered to run their division according to their local priorities. Taking actions or executing changes that deliver benefits for the wider group of companies within the MNE will rarely be a priority for these local managers since their main focus will be on delivering results for their local division.

When Musgrave Plc acquired Budgens Plc in 2002, it decided to operate a decentralised management structure. However, it also sought to extract benefits from the acquisition by way of synergies through the centralisation of some procurement functions. One of the cost centres chosen for centralisation was insurance. The Group Head Office now sought to negotiate insurance costs for the entire group, including the previously autonomous Budgens division. In order to do this the Budgens management team, who had previously negotiated their own insurance policies, now had to cede control of this negotiation to executives from Group Head Office, which was located in another country. The executives from the Group offices could never know as much about the 220 stores, warehouses and offices that comprised Budgens as the local management did. The local management believed that the process could leave the business exposed to uninsured risks. Their fears were further compounded by the fact that the group recharged out the insurance costs based upon an allocation formula that meant that while the overall group insurance costs were reduced, the costs for the division went up.

The disadvantages of a decentralised structure can be hard to quantify since they often manifest themselves through dysfunctional behaviour patterns rather than readily identifiable cost increases. Those behaviours lead to increased costs or, more frequently, missed opportunities for efficiencies.

The advantages and disadvantages of a fully decentralised structure include the following:

DECENTRALISED STRUCTURES: ADVANTAGES AND DISADVANTAGES

Advantages	Disadvantages
• Faster decision-making • Authority is devolved closer to the 'coalface' • Greater responsiveness to local market changes • Better empowerment and motivation in the division	• Synergy benefits are difficult to achieve • Lack of standardisation of approach • More costly structure as functions are duplicated • Less awareness of global market changes, i.e. 'the big picture'

Centralised Structures

At the other extreme, the MNE can organise itself on a fully centralised basis. In this situation there is little authority in the divisional subsidiaries, which are primarily cost centres, and all decision-making is at the centre. The advantages and disadvantages of this structure are as follows:

CENTRALISED STRUCTURES: ADVANTAGES AND DISADVANTAGES

Advantages	Disadvantages
• Clarity of control and decision-making • Economies of scale are easier to achieve • Standardised products and service provision • Lower costs as functions are not duplicated	• Lack of responsiveness to local customer and market demands • Can be slower moving and bureaucratic • Divisions can be demotivated as they have little control over what they are asked to do

Hybrid Structures

Most enterprises will adopt a structure that is predominantly centralised or decentralised. They will then **adapt** this structure to incorporate market and organisational goals. Consequently, they end up with a hybrid of both types. Once a foreign subsidiary has been acquired or set up, the MNE will seek to impose some degree of control on its operations. As time passes, the central office will begin to realise that some functions are better run with mostly local control, whilst others benefit from a degree of central control and standardisation. Consequently, some functions may report directly to local management while other functions may report to the group head of that specific function. The finance function is one which is often organised so that the country finance directors take their lead from the group finance director rather than the country CEO. This can lead to complicated relationships since at the local country board meetings, some executives report to the country CEO and others might report to the head of function back at the head office. These complications are part of the organisation challenges posed by the internationalisation process. The key to success with hybrid structures is to ensure that the organisation gets the best of both worlds instead of the worst of all worlds.

FIGURE 3.4: HYBRID ORGANISATION STRUCTURE

	Finance	Sales	HR	Manufacturing	Logistics	IT
Country A		X		X	X	
Country B		X		X	X	
Country C		X		X	X	
Head Office	X		X			X

Figure 3.4 above describes a simple hybrid organisational structure for an MNE. In this example, the enterprise has centralised finance but has decentralised its sales function into each country. While such structures have advantages, they can also present very real managerial challenges. Indeed, much underperformance arises from not properly overcoming the human problems associated with organisational complexity. One such problem is figuring out who prioritises a department's activities.

For example, the country CEO may wish the sales director and her team to focus on driving extra business from existing customers. However, the group may have an overarching goal of finding new customers and the group sales director may wish the country-specific sales force to focus its efforts primarily on finding new customers. The local country sales director may not know which activity to prioritise resources to and will seek guidance to clarify which goal should take precedence. This means the country CEO and the group sales director will need to agree between them which activities to prioritise; however, if they cannot agree, they will push the decision further up the organisation and the final arbiter, the group CEO, will then have to make the decision. Pushing decisions up the organisation can be a feature of a hybrid organisation structure. Most well-functioning organisations will develop processes to manage such complexities and to minimise the distraction that such organisational 'turf wars' can create. These issues may seem childish, but anyone who has worked in an MNE will testify as to the powerful nature of the conflicts that can arise from such apparent trivialities. (See **Chapter 18** for more on this topic.)

The advantages and disadvantages of hybrid structures are as follows:

HYBRID STRUCTURES: ADVANTAGES AND DISADVANTAGES

Advantages	Disadvantages
• Efficient use of central resources • Decentralised decision-making • Shared mission and values • Think global/act local	• Complex organisation structure • High potential for conflict • High administration costs • Corporate politics

3.9 CHOOSING AN INTERNATIONALISATION MODEL

In this chapter we have examined six types of structure that facilitate international trade for the MNE:
• Importing/Exporting
• Agencies
• Licensing
• Franchising
• Joint Ventures
• FDI/wholly-owned subsidiaries.

These six business models can be thought of as a continuum where at one end there are no assets in the foreign markets, and at the other end there is the wholly-owned subsidiary model where the MNE owns and operates its own entities in the foreign market. Each of the six models has different variant 'sub-models'. For example, the licensing model may involve licensed production, as in the case of many soft drinks companies. Irish bottlers will make and bottle the soft drinks under licence from the main brand-holder. In a different form of licensing, a manufacturer might have the licence to make a certain product for the Irish market. The TV programme *The Apprentice* is an example of this. Originally developed by US presidential hopeful Donald Trump, the programme was produced by Shinawil Productions for TV3 in Ireland. It is one thing to know and understand these different models, but how does an MNE choose which model to use? An ancillary question is whether these models are suitable for all business sizes.

To answer the second question first: size does matter; the smaller an entity, the more likely it is that the investment required for setting up a wholly owned subsidiary in another country will be prohibitive. The managerial complexity and the capital involved may expose the MNE to too much risk. Therefore, it is likely that smaller companies or start-ups will use less capital-intensive models to further their expansion goals. This means that the start-up will be more likely to use models such as importing/exporting or agencies. (For a good example of how an MNE will use different models of international trade at the same time, see **Appendix C.3.**)

Returning to the first question: how does the MNE decide which model to use?

The first step is to analyse what activity the MNE wishes to carry out using the value chain approach. Identify which activities the MNE wishes to carry out in a foreign jurisdiction and why. Ask the question: can this activity only be carried out by the MNE itself or could it be done by others? If it can only be done by the MNE, then the choice is simple: the MNE will need operations on the ground in the foreign country.

If the activities can be carried out by others, the question then should be posed: what level of control does the MNE need to exercise? The greater the degree of control needed to fulfil the MNE's goals, the stronger the relationship will need to be with the parties it may engage to carry out the work. Franchise agreements and licences have greater control measures than simple exporting or importing. Value chain analysis can help here since it is the added value that the control brings that the MNE must assess. There is no point in having excessive control on what is happening in the foreign market if the customer is not willing to pay for the additional costs that such control brings.

If control is not something that adds significant value, then a simple import or export model may be all that the MNE needs.

The final assessment is to use the value chain to determine the risk versus the reward of the particular model selection. This step involves estimating which parts of the value chain are critical to the customer and how and where these are best carried out. In doing this assessment the MNE should endeavour to allocate capital resources to the different frameworks chosen and assess the likely impact on return ratios.

For example, management of a shoe manufacturer in Newcastle, County Down, expect to be able to sell their shoes in France and are contemplating setting up a warehouse in Dijon with an associated sales force. After attending a trade fair in Cologne, Germany, their potential customers tell them they would be just as happy to order the goods from their existing warehouse in Newcastle. Therefore, no additional revenue or margin can be achieved by setting up in Dijon. In this instance, return on capital would fall if the MNE invested in the facilities in France. The extra investment is not rewarded by additional added value in the mind of the retail customer.

A Decision Matrix for the Most Appropriate Model

The MNE can use a decision matrix such as the one at **Figure 3.5** below to help with the decision-making process. Each of the seven elements of the value chain can be assessed using the matrix, allowing the MNE to decide how best to proceed.

For example, an MNE assessing the production operations element of the value chain of an intended expansion into Spain uses a decision matrix like that shown in **Figure 3.5**. First, it determines that this activity can be done by someone else without impacting upon the price the customer is willing to pay, i.e. one of first four models will suit its needs. It further determines that it only needs partial control of this process. This means that a simple ad hoc import/export model for this service will not work – it needs to have some sort of contractual control over the process – which leads it to focus on agency, licensing or franchising as the model of choice.

The MNE then goes on to assess the level of investment needed if the activity were to be performed by the MNE versus the price that would need to be paid to an outside service provider. It compares this level of investment versus the additional margin it would gain by not having to pay an outside provider. The MNE, determines that there are many firms providing manufacturing capabilities in Spain and that prices for these services are keen – much better value than trying to perform the activity itself. The MNE also believes it would like to tie in a manufacturing service provider through an agreement so that it does not run the risk of the provider sharing commercially sensitive information with competitors. This leads it to focus on some type of agency or licence arrangement. Even though tying in with a third party presents operational risk, especially if the relationship goes wrong, it is the MNE's assessment that it is worth doing for the security of continuation of service provision. The alternative would be to risk sporadic service as providers would prioritise customers with whom they had the strongest agreements. It determines that the investment required for franchising is too high and focuses on the agency or licence business model.

The MNE's analysis shows that there is little difference between the share of added value each model would produce. However, the risk assessment indicates that for its particular business sector, a licence agreement would present less business risk than an agency agreement.

The MNE finally concludes that for the expansion into Spain the manufacturing operations element of the value chain should be carried out using a licensed manufacturer.

The MNE can use the same approach for all elements of the value chain. The final analysis will propose to the MNE's managers a structure that can be used for planning the future expansion in a structured methodological fashion.

FIGURE 3.5: DECISION MATRIX TO HELP SELECT AN APPROPRIATE MODEL
FOR INTERNATIONAL EXPANSION INTO SPAIN

	Import/ Export	Agency	Licensing	Franchising	Joint Venture	FDI/Wholly owned sub.
Activity to be done by someone else	Yes	Yes	Yes	Yes	No	No
High level of control	No	Partial	Partial	Partial		
Investment/return		Good	Good	Poor		
Share of added value		Medium	Medium			
Risk profile		Medium	Low			

Figure 3.5 represents just one approach to deciding how to select the most appropriate model. Most MNEs will use a structured analysis coupled with qualitative problem-solving sessions to come to a conclusion. They will then zone in on one or two practical options. Each of these options will be assessed in more detail, often using discounted cash flows, or some derivative thereof, to assess the option that produces the best return for the business.

Models for Market Entry

We have looked at the different models that an MNE can deploy to carry out international trade. I mentioned that many MNEs will be using one or more of these models at any one time depending on the stage of maturity of the business in the relevant country. The choice of model will also be dependent on what part of the value chain is being carried out in the particular country. It is useful at this stage to consider what models an MNE might use at the early stages of entry into a new foreign market. The table below classifies the different market-entry models broken down between direct market entry and indirect market entry. The table also classifies the different models between whether the MNE is going to engage in the production and marketing elements of the value chain, or just the marketing.

TABLE 3.1: CLASSIFICATION OF MARKET-ENTRY MODELS

Value Chain Elements	Direct Market Entry	Indirect Market Entry
Marketing and operations	FDI (own subsidiaries) Joint ventures	Franchising Licensing Agency contracts
Sales/marketing	Import agents Wholesalers Sales office/branch	Ad hoc, casual exporting Catalogues/telesales Export agents Internet sales

Once an optimum model has been chosen, the MNE will need to assess its legality in the target country of operation. Some countries force foreign entities to adopt specific business models in order to carry out operations in their jurisdiction. China and Saudi Arabia, for example, insist on the use of joint venture structures with MNEs as the only way that foreign-owned entities can commence trade in their countries. It is important to assess what model is most appropriate for the MNE **before** cross-checking it to the legal system of the country involved. To do otherwise may lead the MNE to trying to 'shoe-horn' what is appropriate for its business sector into a model that is not going to work. MNE managers need to know how their processes add value and then, having gained that understanding using tools like Porter's value chain, decide which international business model best suits their added value framework. Indeed, it is often the case that MNEs will use different models for different parts of the globe depending on the value added dynamic in each market.

3.10 CONCLUSION

In the first two chapters we saw how international trade has developed over time, particularly at the dramatic growth in international trade over the last 50 years, and how the law of comparative advantage explains how the growth of trade can improve the standards of living for all nations involved. The rise of the corporate entity since the Industrial Revolution has been an enabler in the growth of trade between nations. In this chapter we looked at how the corporate entity in its multinational form structures itself to facilitate the complexity involved in trading across borders.

With our wide definition of an MNE established, we examined different business models they can employ for international trade. These can be graphed on a continuum, at one end of which the MNE has no assets in any foreign jurisdiction and simply imports from or exports. As the continuum progresses, the MNE is increasingly invested in foreign jurisdictions through licence agreements, the use of agents or franchisees, then onward to joint venture to eventually owning outright its own operations.

Traditionally, MNEs have grown from domestic enterprises by following a path similar to the asset ownership continuum. Of course, an MNE can start its internationalisation process at any point on the continuum depending on the circumstances that prevail. Once an MNE owns a subsidiary in another country, it must decide how to manage that entity. We explored three broad organisational structures – centralised, decentralised, and hybrid – and examined the advantages and disadvantages of each type and suggested ways for an MNE to decide which structure best suits its specific marketplace and corporate culture. Finally, we looked at how MNE's might choose which model for international business best suits their business. The use of frameworks such as Porter's value chain can greatly aid this decision-making process.

In **Chapter 4** we will look at how Irish MNEs have developed and look at some specific companies that have been successful in the execution of their international expansion. We will also examine how FDI is carried out on the island of Ireland, in particular focusing on what makes Ireland an attractive place in which to do business.

QUESTIONS

Self-test Questions

3.1 Outline the advantages and disadvantages of a centralised organisation structure.
3.2 Explain what benefits an MNE may get from a joint venture.
3.3 How does a franchise system work?

Thought-provoking Questions

Question 3.1

You are the CFO of a highly successful chain of fast-food restaurants, HotFoot, based in Belfast. The CEO wishes to explore expanding into the Spanish market. He has asked you to prepare a high level outline of the various methods that the business could use to expand into Spain. He has further asked you to recommend which approach HotFoot should use to achieve its expansion goal. HotFoot has a standard operating model where menus and restaurant design are set down at the head office. Each outlet is managed according to the formula set down by the head office.

Question 3.2

Ego Global Plc, EGP, is an MNE operating in five European countries and headquartered in Limerick, Ireland. It manufactures wood-burning stoves at its plant in Poland and sells these through its sales and marketing subsidiaries in each of the other four countries. Its administrative headquarters is in Bruff, County Limerick, where the CEO and founder lives. All activities are controlled from Bruff. The organisation is centrally organised, with the Finance, Sales and Manufacturing directors based in the offices in Bruff and reporting directly to the CEO.

You have recently joined Ego Global Plc as CFO. The finance director has been increasingly worried about the slowness of the organisation in responding to its customers' needs. By way of example she explains that emissions regulations in France have meant that EGP's stoves are no longer compliant with the law. The regulations were 24 months in formulation, but EGP only found out about them when sales of new stoves began to fall below budget. She has also told you that manufacturing quality problems in Poland have led to increased costs since many stoves are proving faulty. The manufacturing director, who doesn't speak Polish, has said he cannot get a straight answer about these problems from his line managers at the plant in Poznan, Poland. She asks you, as the new kid on the block, to give a quick assessment as to whether the organisation structure is behind some of these problems and to propose how EGP might structure itself differently.

Review Questions

(See Suggested Solutions to Review Questions in **Appendix B**.)

Question 3.1: Kebabs Ltd

Having read the Kebabs Ltd case study in **Appendix A**, identify the potential market-entry routes for Kebabs into the German market and discusses the key issues relating to each option. Recommend the most suitable market-entry option.

Question 3.2: TinyTots Baby Food Limited

Having read the TinyTots Baby Food Limited case study in **Appendix A**, develop an exit strategy for the manufacturing plant that will maintain TinyTots' operational capability and enhance company value.

Question 3.3: Redbarn Brewery

Having read the Redbarn Brewery case study in **Appendix A**, detail the considerations surrounding the various market-entry strategies open to Redbarn Brewery in entering the US market.

Question 3.4: EuroHub

Having read the EuroHub case study in **Appendix A**, discuss the various market entry strategies available to EuroHub in entering the Chinese market and recommend the most appropriate strategy.

4

IRISH BUSINESS IN AN INTERNATIONAL CONTEXT

CONTENTS

LEARNING OBJECTIVES

Having read this chapter, you will understand:
* why countries develop international trade patterns;
* some theories about why countries have different foreign business profiles, including the Heckscher–Ohlin model of factors of production and Porter's Diamond;
* the nature of imports into Ireland;
* the nature of exports from Ireland;
* who the major Irish MNEs are;
* who the foreign MNEs operating in Ireland are;
* what governments do to encourage exports and FDI;
* what supports and agencies exist in Ireland for exporting and to encourage foreign direct investment (FDI);
* why the island of Ireland is a good location for MNEs to invest and do business;
* some of the main tax structures and benefits available for MNEs in the Republic of Ireland and in Northern Ireland; and
* the case for FDI into Republic of Ireland and Northern Ireland.

4.1 INTRODUCTION

In the first three chapters of this book we have explored why international trade has grown so strongly over the last five decades and how the corporation has evolved as the main vehicle through which international trade is carried out. We have defined what we mean by the multinational enterprise (MNE) and have looked at the different models MNEs can use for international expansion.

In this chapter we will look at why certain **countries** specialise in one form of international trade rather than another, examining relevant theories that seek to explain this specialisation: the Heckscher–Ohlin model and Porter's Diamond. We will also assess the larger Irish MNEs and see which foreign MNEs are operating in Ireland. We will consider these companies to get a sense of the diversity and nature of some of the largest MNEs operating on the island. From your familiarity with some of these MNEs and their associated brands, you will probably already have a sense of how these MNEs have grown and expanded. Of course, there are also some MNEs that, while not having a high consumer profile, are still significant contributors to the overall economy on the island, and examples of these are also included in our discussion.

The chapter concludes by examining what makes Ireland a good place in which to do business. We look at what structures are in place to encourage FDI. We also take a high level picture of the taxation and corporate structures that MNEs can use when operating on the island of Ireland. In the next chapter we will then explore how these MNEs are governed on behalf of the various stakeholders in their activities.

4.2 'THE HECKSCHER–OHLIN MODEL' – FACTORS OF PRODUCTION

As we have seen in **Chapter 1**, for millennia the inhabitants of the island of Ireland have been involved in overseas trade, exporting raw materials and manufactured products to trading partners elsewhere, both in Britain, Europe and further afield, even before the concept of 'countries' came into being. While Ireland is not alone in being involved in foreign trade from the dawn of history, the island does 'punch above its weight' given its isolated position at the western edge of Europe, which poses a question: why do some countries excel in specific aspects of business and trade when compared to other countries?

There have been many theories over the centuries that have attempted to explain what drives trade between countries and, in particular, what drives successful trade. By the early part of the 20th Century the term '**factors of production**' was being used to describe the inputs in the production of a good or a service. The main theory concerning factors of production from this time is the **Heckscher–Ohlin (H–O) model**, developed in the early 1930s and finessed in the decades since.[1] As with many theories that stand the test of time, it has an elegant simplicity. At its core, it proposes that countries will specialise in producing goods that use those factors of production that they have in abundance. Likewise, a country will import goods that require factors of production in which it is scarce. The main factors of production are land, labour and capital.

As we will see later in this chapter, the services sector in Ireland has grown much faster than the tangible goods sector. The provision of services requires a high degree of the labour factor of

---

[1] See Ohlin, B. (1967). *Interregional and International Trade*. 2nd ed. Cambridge, MA: Harvard University Press.

production, usually skilled labour, as compared with either land or capital. Indeed, the 'know-how' of labour, especially in the provision of services, has become known as 'intellectual capital'. Intellectual capital, although intangible, is a very real factor of production. It is discussed further in **Chapter 18**.

The H–O model built on Ricardo's theory of comparative advantage (see **Chapter 2**) by developing mathematically driven theorems to explain how trade equilibriums occur between countries. Using these theorems it was possible to explain much of the international trade patterns of the 19th Century. The mathematics of the model are beyond the scope of this text, but the theory is useful for understanding international trade. For example, Saudi Arabia has an abundance of oil, which it exports. It has a scarcity of suitable pasture land so it imports beef. The H–O model makes predictions as to how prices for traded products will develop over time. The key prediction derived from the model is that prices for both the factors of production and end-for-end products will converge if a free and competitive market is allowed to develop. This prediction is not without its critics who point to, for example, wide disparities in labour rates. However, the H–O model proposes that labour rates, along with the price of other factors of production, should begin to converge as international trade barriers are removed. Critics would argue this has not happened; proponents argue it is happening, just not as fast as people may wish. The wage rate inflation in China suggests that the H–O model may well be correct: average annual wages in China increased from CNY 24,932 in 2008 to CNY 52,388 by 2014.[2]

The H–O model can be mapped onto historical data. The mapping exercise validates the H–O model as its predictive trends correlate closely with the actual trade patterns of international trade in the 18th and 19th Centuries. However, there have also been some critics who have pointed out that trade patterns predicted by the H–O model for the 20th Century have not been entirely accurate. For example, the H–O model proposes that labour intensive industries would be the main exporters from countries where labour was abundant and access to capital was scarce. However, in the 1940s and 1950s the US exported labour-intensive goods and imported capital-intensive goods, the opposite of the H–O model predictions. This anomaly was known as the 'Leontief Paradox' after the economist who first discovered it in 1954, Wassily Leontief.

The H–O model is predictive in nature. Of course, with the benefit of hindsight, we can see whether its predictions have come to pass. What economists and mathematicians have seen is that the predictions using the H–O model are broadly right. Some economists have further fine-tuned the formulae in order to 'retro-fit' the model's predictions onto the actual outcome achieved. The implication is that these adjusted formulae might be even better predictors of the future.[3] As the 20th Century progressed, two of the factors of production became increasingly mobile: labour and capital. Developments in transport technologies, together with greater political encouragement of international trade, meant that the migration of people (labour) became easier. Capital flows became much simpler, especially with the development of computers and the lifting of restrictions on the movement of capital. These changes have fundamentally altered the nature of international trade, facilitating the major increases we have seen in the last 50 years (see **Chapter 2**).

New theories have since been developed to help explain and predict the future direction of international trade. Understanding these theories, even at a high level, can help the managers

---

[2] www.tradingeconomics.com/china/wages (accessed October 2015).
[3] Vanek, J. (1962). *International Trade*. R.D. Irwin.

of MNEs identify the appropriate strategies to adopt in order to seize opportunities and manage risk. The management of these issues is especially important for Irish MNEs; the economy of the Republic of Ireland is 'open' in that over 50% of economic activity is derived from international trade. Northern Ireland also derives over 50% of its economic activity from international trade when one includes trade with Great Britain as international. (The Department of Enterprise, Trade and Investment in Northern Ireland refers to trade with GB as 'external trade'. I have added this external trade to true international trading in determining that NI is an open economy with over 50% of its economic activity derived from 'international' trade.)

4.3 PORTER'S DIAMOND

An analysis of international trade patterns since the end of the Second World War reveals trade flows that cannot be explained by theories based solely on the nature of the factors of production in the respective countries. Certain nations develop proficiency for producing certain goods that cannot be explained by a factor production theory, such as the Heckscher–Ohlin model, alone. In 1990, Michael Porter devised a model to explain these patterns of international trade,[4] proposing that international trade between nations was derived from four primary elements:
- firm structure, strategy and rivalry;
- demand conditions;
- related and supporting industries;
- factor conditions (originally the main element considered by earlier 'factors of production' theories).

These four interrelated elements can be represented as points on a diamond as follows.

FIGURE 4.1: PORTER'S DIAMOND[5]

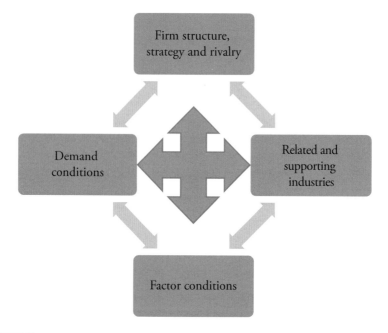

[4] Porter, M. (1990). *The Competitive Advantage of Nations*. New York: Free Press.
[5] Adapted from Porter, M. (1990). *The Competitive Advantage of Nations*. New York: Free Press.

The **factor conditions** element of Porter's Diamond draw from earlier theories, such as the Heckscher–Ohlin model, but augment them by considering the nature of the factors, especially the skill-set of the labour force. (Remember: the Heckscher–Ohlin theory proposes that a country will manufacture those goods that require factors of production that the country has in abundance, and import goods where the factors needed to produce them are in scarce supply.) For example, Ireland exports dairy products and imports oil.

The **firm structure** element concerns itself with the nature of the firms operating in the country being assessed, including the degree to which they need to compete with each other in the domestic market and what their overall strategies are. The idea is that competition between businesses in a domestic market will lead to superior performance and efficiency, which can then allow those firms to penetrate foreign markets. Likewise, poor internal competition and structure will see domestic firms' activities replaced by foreign imports. For example, the telecoms company eir (formerly Eircom) in the Republic of Ireland has struggled to compete with foreign telecoms companies coming into the market upon deregulation.

Domestic **demand conditions** give rise to domestic production. Porter noticed that exporting firms that began by meeting strong domestic demand had advantages over firms that had no domestic demand for their output. Ireland, for example, has a high domestic demand for butter. It is also a major exporter of butter. The diamond model would contend that there is a relationship between high domestic demand and the excellence in production capability that allows Ireland to be a major player in the global butter market.

The fourth point of the diamond involves the concept of **related and supporting industries**. Porter's Diamond model proposes that successful performance in industries that are related to the MNE's core industry in the home country give rise to a country advantage. The success of the related industries creates a virtuous circle of improvement, enabling the main industry to stay ahead of competition from operators in other countries. For example, success in microchip manufacturing in the 1970s and early 1980s in California led to the creation of support structures facilitating the growth of computer manufacturing by Apple, and eventually the explosion of software development companies such as Google and Oracle.

People who work in a successful industry can gain insights into how to solve problems in related industries. This cross-fertilisation is an important dimension that gives certain countries advantages over others when it comes to specific related industries.

Porter's Diamond can be used to understand why certain countries, and their MNEs, become successful and world-leaders in their field. The model allows for the analysis of a firm and its environment, which can inform the decision-making of an MNE. This is particularly useful when considering possible takeover targets or international location strategies. For example, an analysis carried out by students at the University of Sao Paulo in Brazil (Teixeira) found that Porter's Diamond was a useful tool in explaining and analysing the successful internationalisation strategies of one of Brazil's largest MNEs, the food company JBS-Friboi. To illustrate this expansion further, in June 2015 JBS-Friboi acquired one of Northern Ireland's largest employers, Moy Park, from another Brazilian company, Marfrig.

Porter's Diamond is also useful for understanding the relative dominance one country may have in a particular sector, especially when considering whether and how to compete in that sector. An MNE can also use it to ascertain the relative strengths of a particular nation's competitive advantage and, in particular, whether there are risks to the country's position that can be deduced from using the diamond to analyse the position.

Brian McCarthy worked in the foreign exchange department of AIB. While there, he saw the opportunity to develop a more customer-focused solution for VAT refunds for tourists visiting Ireland. In 1981 he founded Fexco, which has become a company employing 2,000 people and has services in 28 countries driven by an entrepreneurial spirit fostered at its head office in Killorglin, County Kerry. The original market opportunity for Fexco came from the fact that Ireland is a particularly strong player in the global tourism market. In order to encourage even greater numbers of tourists, the Irish Government has allowed for the reclaiming of VAT paid by tourists from outside the EU. Thus, Fexco came into operation by meeting a domestic demand market. From there it developed technologies that allowed it to move into other related industries, supported by an increasing focus on the technology sector within the Republic of Ireland. The initial competence that Fexco developed while engaging in activities to meet the strong domestic demand for technologies to aid the processing of the VAT refunds for tourists has allowed the firm to develop a competitive advantage over other firms operating outside Ireland. This advantage has meant that Fexco can now compete on the global market in the financial transaction services sector.

4.4 THE NATURE OF IMPORTS INTO IRELAND

Earlier in this chapter we examined the H–O model and Porter's Diamond. These two models seek to explain and understand the nature of trade between nations. The H–O model focuses on factors of production and was augmented by Porter's Diamond in 1990 after the sustained growth in international trade after the Second World War. Porter's Diamond still includes factors of production as one of the four drivers of international trade but also adds another three: demand conditions; related and supporting industries; and firm structure, strategy, and rivalry. Together these theories propose that a nation will import certain products in which it does not have a comparative advantage.

We will now examine the nature of imports into Ireland to gain an understanding of how this island operates economically in global markets. The purpose of including this information is to help the reader gain an understanding of the nature of the trade that Ireland undertakes with its international trading partners. The vast majority of importing and exporting activity on the island is conducted by MNEs, the performance management of which is the subject of this textbook. In **Chapter 1** we saw that the early Irish imported tin, which cannot be found in Ireland. The tin was mixed with copper to form bronze, a much superior alloy to pure copper, for the purpose of making agricultural tools in particular. Copper, and subsequently bronze, was exported from Ireland to areas where copper was in short supply or non-existent.

In the intervening millennia, Ireland has continued to import both raw materials and finished products. By 2014, imports to the Republic of Ireland were €54 billion per annum. The volume of goods imported has grown 138% since 1990 while indices show that prices for imports have increased by only 32%. The growth in the volume of goods imported is much greater than the growth in the value of those goods; the Republic of Ireland has been importing goods from the rest of the world in increasing amounts as prices for those goods have fallen.

FIGURE 4.2: SOURCES OF GOODS IMPORTS 2014: REPUBLIC OF IRELAND[6]

€53.6 billion

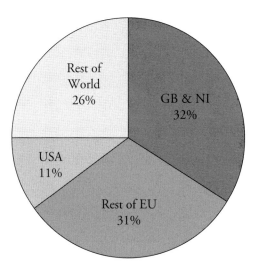

The data from the CSO for 2014 show that 63% of Ireland's imports are from fellow EU Member States, with over half of that number coming from either Great Britain or Northern Ireland. The Republic of Ireland imports a wide variety of products and commodities, as can be seen from **Figure 4.3** below.

FIGURE 4.3: GOODS IMPORTS % BY CATEGORY 2014: REPUBLIC OF IRELAND[7]

€53.6 billion

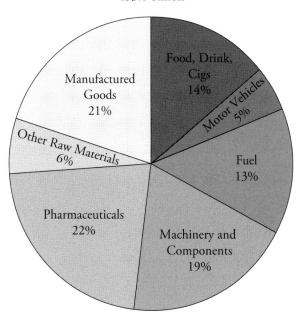

---

[6] Central Statistics Office, www.cso.ie/en/releasesandpublications/er/gei/goodsexportsandimportsde-cember2014/ (accessed May 2015).

[7] www.cso.ie/releasesandpublications/er/gei/goodsexportsandimportsdecember2014/ (accessed May 2015).

As one might expect in a country with no motor vehicle manufacturing, motor vehicle imports are significant at 5%. Also, as Ireland has no major fuel resources of its own, fuel is 13% of all imports. Ireland is a major food producer, so it is surprising to see food imports at 14% of all imports, or around €7 billion per annum. However, the level of food imports is comparable with other EU Member States. Imports of pharmaceuticals represent 22% of all imports and is the largest single category. Machinery and components at 19% indicates that the ROI has a need for the machinery necessary to carry out the processing activities it engages in, especially farming and food-processing. Much of the machinery importation is for use in the country's agricultural production industry and in other manufacturing activities.

Imports into Northern Ireland for 2013 stand at £5.9 billion, not including imports from Great Britain. Non-GB exports from Northern Ireland run at €5.2 billion, which shows that in 2013 NI had a balance of payments deficit with its non-Great Britain trading partners.[8]

4.5 THE NATURE OF GOODS EXPORTS FROM IRELAND

Following the above discussion of what goods are imported into Ireland, we now look at the goods that are exported from Ireland. Exports of goods from the Republic of Ireland ran ahead of imports in 2014 at €89.1 billion versus imports of €53.6 billion.

The Republic of Ireland runs a trade surplus with its main external trade partners, with the exception of the UK (in 2014 imports from the UK exceeded exports by almost €4 billion).

FIGURE 4.4: DESTINATIONS OF GOODS EXPORTS 2014: REPUBLIC OF IRELAND[9]

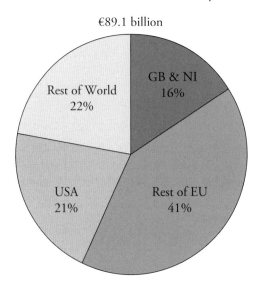

There has been a massive increase in exports from the Republic of Ireland over the last two decades. The volume of goods exported from ROI has grown 361% since 1990 while

---

8   Author's calculations based on data from detini.gov.uk.

9   www.cso.ie/releasesandpublications/er/gei/goodsexportsandimportsdecember2014/ (accessed May 2015).

indices for prices show a modest increase of only 3.9%. The huge disparity between the volume index and the price index shows that the Republic of Ireland's manufacturers have remained extremely competitive, even taking into account the low inflation rates prevailing since 2009.

FIGURE 4.5: GOODS EXPORTS % BY CATEGORY 2014: REPUBLIC OF IRELAND[10]

€89.1 billion

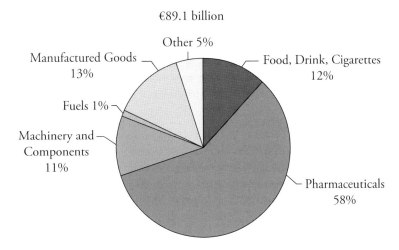

The export data for 2014 shows that the Republic of Ireland is now an industrial exporting economy rather than an agri-food economy. This is an indication of how the economy has developed since the middle of the 20th Century. Originally a food-producing, agrarian nation, Ireland has become increasingly industrial in nature. A number of factors have contributed to this development:

- removal of trade barriers, especially within the EU;
- a young, well-educated workforce;
- easing of controls on the flow of capital;
- an attractive tax environment.

Export data for Northern Ireland is more difficult to assess as the data is often aggregated into UK statistics. In recognition of this challenge, the Department of Enterprise, Trade and Investment in Northern Ireland prepared an analysis in March 2014 to try to address the information deficit.[11] The Department classifies goods manufactured in Northern Ireland but sold either to Great Britain or exported from the UK as 'external trade'. In 2013 external trade from Northern Ireland showed a solid performance given world market conditions. Total exports from Northern Ireland were £6.1 billion excluding exports to Great Britain, rising to £14.3 billion when one includes external trade to GB.[12]

---

[10] *Ibid.*

[11] Department of Enterprise, Trade and Investment, *Measuring Northern Ireland's Exports*, www.detini.gov.uk

[12] Northern Ireland Manufacturing Sales & Export Survey, latest results published 3 December 2014. www.detni.gov.uk

FIGURE 4.6: DESTINATIONS OF GOODS EXPORTS 2013: NORTHERN IRELAND

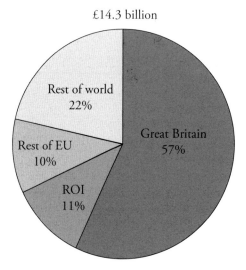

£14.3 billion

The breakdown of this external trade also makes interesting reading.

FIGURE 4.7: PERCENTAGE SHARE OF EXTERNAL TRADE FROM NI (2013)[13]

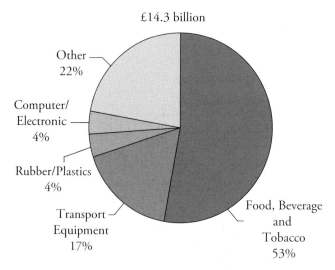

£14.3 billion

Approximately 50% of exports from Northern Ireland are food and beverage products. The next largest category is transport equipment at approximately 17%. In the 19th Century the part of the island that now comprises Northern Ireland would have been more industrialised while the remainder of the island would have been very much focused on agricultural production. The globalisation of ship-building and textiles manufacturing in the last 50 years has led to a reduction in these activities in Northern Ireland, resulting in the situation we see today where most of Northern Ireland's external trade is from the food and beverage sector. Interestingly, when one drills into the numbers a bit further, one sees that the 78% of the external trade in this sector is with Great Britain. This implies that Britain is a very critical market for Northern Ireland food producers.

---

[13] Results from the Northern Ireland Manufacturing Sales & Export Survey 2013/14, Northern Ireland Statistics and Research Agency, 3 December 2014.

Services

One of the great transformations of economic activity on the island of Ireland has been the growth in economic activity related to services, i.e. activities that generate revenue but that do not have a physical manifestation or characteristic. By way of an example, a computer keyboard made for export is classified as goods or merchandise in the statistical gathering process, while the software written to run the keyboard is classified as a service.

The services sector in the Republic of Ireland in 2013 accounted for €92 billion in exports and €92 billion in imports. A more detailed breakdown of the export and import of services is available for 2013, as shown in **Table 4.1** below. An examination of the table shows that there are large amounts of imports allocated to 'Royalties/Licences' – €34 billion, or 37% of the total. The strong performance of this category indicates how successful Ireland has been in attracting MNEs into using it as a base for locating their intellectual property. These MNEs are then licensing out their intellectual property to third parties and other members and subsidiaries of their groups around the world.

TABLE 4.1: EXPORTS AND IMPORTS OF SERVICES BY CATEGORY, 2012 AND 2013[14]

	€ million					
	2012[1]			**2013**		
Item	**Exports**	**Imports**	**Net**	**Exports**	**Imports**	**Net**
Services	**85,527**	**92,504**	**−6,978**	**92,292**	**92,113**	**178**
Repairs & Processing	1,322	1,167	155	1,406	726	680
Transport	4,609	1,675	2,934	4,396	1,640	2,758
Tourism and travel	3,022	4,609	−1,588	3,370	4,669	−1,301
Insurance	8,986	6,516	2,470	9,021	5,922	3,099
Financial services	7,732	5,077	2,655	8,157	5,172	2,985
Royalties/Licences	3,879	33,847	−29,967	4,140	35,796	−31,658
Communications	569	1,087	−518	591	1,076	−485
Computer services	36,150	350	35,800	38,957	347	38,608
Total other business services	17,750	37,967	−20,218	20,575	36,550	−15,975
Research and development	766	7,094	−6,328	1,060	5,181	−4,121
Operational leasing	7,537	1,434	6,104	7,497	1,393	6,103
Legal, accounting and other professional services	*	839	*	*	1,158	*
Advertising and market research	*	3,895	*	*	3,990	*
Trade related services	1,924	12,444	−10,519	2,296	12,589	−10,294
Architectural engineering and other technical services	288	89	197	310	*	*
Other	4,961	12,169	−7,208	5,831	*	*
Other services n.e.s.	1,511	214	1,297	1,681	217	1,464

[1] Revised.
* Suppressed for confidentiality reasons but included in 'Total other business services' total.

---

[14] CSO, International Trade in Services 2013, Statistical Release, 22 January 2015, 11am, Table 1.

The standout number on the exports side relates to computer-related services – almost €39 billion – or 40% of total services exports. The success of the Republic of Ireland in this category reinforces successive Irish governments' focus on the 'knowledge economy'. Exports of computer-related services in 2013 dwarfed exports of food and agricultural produce by more than 300%. Insurances and financial services added another almost €17 billion in export sales in the year.

Data concerning the exports of services from Northern Ireland is more difficult to find than for the Republic of Ireland. The Northern Ireland Statistics and Research Agency (NISRA) estimates the export sales of services for Northern Ireland were just under £500 million in 2011. When compared to the Republic of Ireland, this suggests that there is an opportunity for Northern Ireland to grow its knowledge economy. That said, Northern Ireland competes with other regions of the UK for inward investment and, as such, is operating in a different environment to the Republic. (Further discussion on how the respective authorities in NI and ROI try to attract inward investment and encourage exports is provided later in this chapter.)

4.6 IRISH MULTINATIONALS – REPUBLIC OF IRELAND

We are concerned here with the performance management of MNEs, and from an island of Ireland perspective. To illustrate the impact of MNEs on the Irish economies it is useful to consider the largest employers on the island and to identify which of these are MNEs. In this and the following section we will look at these large MNEs in ROI and then NI, and briefly explain the nature of those that started here and expanded abroad, as well as foreign-owned multinationals operating from the island of Ireland.

TABLE 4.2: TOP 10 COMPANIES IN IRELAND BY EMPLOYEE NUMBERS

Rank	Company	Employees	Turnover €bn
1	CRH	75,706	18.9
2	Smurfit Kappa	41,523	8.1
3	Kerry Group	24,492	5.8
4	Tesco	14,925	2.6
5	Dunnes Stores	14,000	3.4
6	Boston Scientific	11,800	5.0
7	AIB	11,384	111 assets
8	Bank of Ireland	11,255	130 assets
9	ICON plc	10,300	1.0
10	Perrigo	10,220	3.8

When measured in terms of employee numbers, seven of the top 10 companies in the Republic of Ireland are Irish-owned multinationals.[15] The top three of these, CRH, Smurfit Kappa and Kerry Group, all started their operations in Ireland and subsequently grew from their Irish base. The other Irish MNEs that appear in the top 10 are Dunnes Stores, AIB, Bank of Ireland and ICON plc.

---

[15] The Irish Times 1000 Companies 2014, www.top1000.ie/companies (accessed October 2015).

In the case of four of the seven, being from Ireland does not, in and of itself, appear to bring any immediate advantage regarding international expansion. Kerry Group could be seen to leverage its growth off an Irish heritage in food production, particularly dairy. The other two companies are banks, AIB and Bank of Ireland, each of which became involved in international business as they grew to meet their clients' growing needs by both acquiring and set up new operations in the UK and further afield. (See **Appendix C.3**.)

Note: I have used employee numbers as the measure here in order to better reflect the economic impact of the MNE. If turnover were used, the results would have been different, but not substantially, though some international companies would have entered the top 10 as they have large turnovers but do not have commensurate employee numbers in Ireland.)

CRH (Ranking: 1)

Ireland's largest company measured by employee numbers, CRH plc, is headquartered in Dublin. It is involved in supplying the construction industry throughout the world. CRH is interesting in that its business is one that may not appear at first glance to lend itself to globalisation. This is because the core products, cement, aggregates and asphalt are extremely expensive to transport over long distances; therefore, the key to success in this sector is to have a source of supply that is proximate to the customer. However, CRH has been able to use a standardised approach to the management of its business that gives customers reassurance and confidence in the quality and reliability of both the product and the service. It has mainly expanded internationally by acquiring existing operators and converting them to the CRH way of doing business.

> "CRH plc was formed through a merger in 1970 of two leading Irish public companies, Cement Limited (established in 1936) and Roadstone, Limited (1949). The newly-formed group was the sole producer of cement and the principal producer of aggregates, concrete products and asphalt in Ireland. In 1970, the Group had sales of *c.* €27m, *c.* 95% in Ireland.
>
> Since that time, CRH's strategic vision has been to be a responsible international leader in building materials, delivering superior and sustained shareholder returns, while reducing its dependence on individual markets and achieving a balance in its geographic presence and portfolio of products.
>
> CRH today is one of the world's leading building materials companies, with a business that spans 35 countries and which serves all segments of construction industry demand. CRH subsidiary companies employ approximately 76,000 people at over 3,400 locations around the world, and in 2013, generated sales of €18 billion.
>
> The Group's major businesses are in the developed markets of Europe and North America, and it has growing positions in certain developing economies in Asia. Operations focus on three closely related core businesses: primary materials, value-added building products and building materials distribution."[16]

There is no uniquely Irish reason for the success of CRH in the sense that Ireland has a particular historical or geographic advantage in cement production over and above any other country. The success must be down to some other factor, which could be the management philosophies adopted by the company as it went about acquiring and integrating business around the world.

---

[16] http://www.crh.com/our-group/group-profile/history (accessed February 2015).

CRH developed an acquisition and integration methodology that allowed it to acquire businesses in foreign jurisdictions and hold on to the customers and the key staff. The framework CRH developed must have been superior to other competitors' approaches or it would not have such a long and steady track record of success.

Smurfit Kappa (Ranking: 2)

Smurfit Kappa is an Irish success story. Originally an Irish-based packaging manufacturer, Smurfit realised the need to expand as economies of scale in the production of cardboard, in particular, began to threaten its Irish business. What the team at Smurfit saw in the 1970s was that larger, more economical production plants were being built. These plants were of such a scale that they would be too big for the domestic demand requirements. Therefore, if Smurfit wanted to compete, and survive, it would need to build or acquire these large production facilities. If it was to make that size of investment, it would need to find new markets for the output outside of Ireland. This led Smurfit to expand both by acquisition, exporting and building and investing in new facilities in foreign countries.

> "Smurfit Kappa is one of the leading providers of paper-based packaging solutions in the world, with around 43,000 employees in approximately 350 production sites across 33 countries and with revenue of €8.1 billion in 2014.
>
> We are located in 21 countries in Europe, and 12 in the Americas. We are the only large-scale pan-regional player in Latin America.
>
> With our pro-active team we relentlessly use our extensive experience and expertise, supported by our scale, to open up opportunities for our customers.
>
> We collaborate with forward thinking customers by sharing superior product knowledge, market understanding and insights in packaging trends to ensure business success in their markets.
>
> We have an unrivalled portfolio of paper-packaging solutions, which is constantly updated with our market-leading innovations.
>
> This is enhanced through the benefits of our integration, with optimal paper design, logistics, timeliness of service, and our packaging plants sourcing most of their raw materials from our own paper mills. Our products, which are 100% renewable and produced sustainably, improve the environmental footprint of our customers.
>
> Our headquarters are in Dublin with regional headquarters in Paris (Europe) and Miami (the Americas).[17]

As with CRH, there is no reason in particular why an Irish company should be successful in the development of an international packaging business. Perhaps, as with CRH, there is a special value system that the Irish management can bring to international expansion that is superior to the competitors from other, larger nations. Obviously there is also the personal drive and vision that the founding owners can bring to a business. In the case of Smurfit Kappa, this would have been through the founder, Jefferson Smurfit, and followed on by his sons, Michael and Jefferson, and currently by the founder's grandson, Tony Smurfit.

---

[17] http://www.smurfitkappa.com/vhome/com/AboutUs/WhoWeAre/Pages/Default.aspx (accessed August 2015).

Kerry Group (Ranking: 3)

Kerry Group had modest beginnings in the south-west of Ireland over 40 years ago. Originally a farmer-owned co-operative, it has been transformed into a successful, publicly traded, multinational corporation and a leading player in the global food industry. Its sales for the year 2014 were €5.8 billion with profits of €636 million.

> "With operations established in 24 countries across five continents, EMEA markets account for 38% of sales, Americas markets 44% and sales to Asia Pacific markets represent 18% of total Group sales.
>
> Kerry Group is quoted on the Dublin and London stock exchanges, with a market capitalisation in excess of €9 billion and some 30,000 shareholders. Since its inception, Kerry's Board, management and suppliers have progressively worked to grow the Kerry organisation and lead its evolution through three separate corporate entities:
> (A) Private Dairy Processor
> (B) Dairy Co-operative
> (C) Public Company
>
> Kerry's origins date back to 1972 when as a private company, three shareholders; the State owned Dairy Disposal Company, a Federation of eight small farmer Co-operatives in Kerry and the Erie Casein Company Inc. from the US, committed to invest approximately €200,000 to finance a €1 million dairy processing facility in Listowel, Co. Kerry, for the manufacture of milk protein (casein) for export to the US.
>
> Ownership of the company, then known as North Kerry Milk Products Ltd (NKMP) was shared with the Dairy Disposal Company holding 42.5%, the Federation 42.5% and Erie Casein 15%. The linkage to Illinois based Erie Casein provided a guaranteed market for the edible casein output, which was a relatively new dairy product for Ireland. In its first year NKMP processed 16 million gallons of skim milk to produce 2,000 tonnes of casein with a workforce of about 40 people and reported profits of €127,000 on a turnover of €1.3 million."[18]

Unlike CRH and Smurfit Kappa, one can see an Irish aspect to the success of Kerry. Ireland has long been at the forefront of dairy production: butter has been exported from Ireland as far back as Roman times, and the cow has been at the centre of Irish commerce for the last two millennia. Having said that, history does not guarantee a successful future. Kerry Group grew out of a joint venture arrangement between three parties: the Dairy Disposal Company (the state-owned dairy processing company), a group of eight small dairy co-ops, and US-based Erie Casein Company. The strategy was to make casein, a milk processing by-product, and export it to the US. We can see that Kerry's early origins involved one of the business types suggested in **Chapter 3** as a route for MNE's to grow: the joint venture. Eventually, Kerry bought out some of its joint venture partners and became a fully quoted Plc in 1986. Why did the Kerry Group grow so successfully when others, who were bigger than it in the 1970s, did not?

What sets Kerry Group apart is the vision and energy of a trio of young managers who all happened to arrive into the North Kerry Co-Op around the same time. Denis Brosnan was CEO from the foundation of NKMP in 1972. With Denis Cregan as his operations director and Hugh Friel as his finance director, the trio drove the performance of the company through a

---

[18] *Kerry Group Corporate History.* See http://www.kerrygroup.com/docs/history/Kerry_Group_Corporate_History_24-2-14.pdf

steady and well executed international expansion. The expansion involved a combination of acquisition of existing companies and the building of brand new facilities. From the mid-1990s Brosnan was talking about a vision to turn Kerry into a food ingredients business rather than purely a dairy and consumer foods company. The setting out of this vision and putting in place of the steps to deliver it sets Kerry apart from other Irish food-processing businesses of the time.

Dunnes Stores (Ranking: 5)

The fourth of the five companies that appear in the top 10 Irish companies by employee numbers and are also MNEs is Dunnes Stores, which is different from CRH, Smurfit Kappa and Kerry Group in that it is a retailer rather than a manufacturer. Unlike the other three, its main activities are in Ireland, with its international arm making up approximately 20% of its revenues in 2014.

Originally from Rostrevor, County Down, Ben Dunne (Snr) opened his first store on Patrick Street in Cork on 31 March 1944. He was a retailing visionary: he saw the success of Marks and Spencer in Britain and adapted their formula to an Irish context. He would buy factory seconds and end-of-line goods from Marks and Spencer, re-label them as 'St. Bernard' and sell them at great value prices. He also encouraged Irish textile manufacturers to supply him with mass-produced, low-priced clothing and footwear. At a time when clothing was predominantly made at home or by tailors, Dunne introduced the Irish shopper to 'off-the-rail' products.

Since his vision was essentially to emulate the best of what he saw elsewhere in the world of retailing, it is difficult to see what competitive advantage Dunnes Stores could have that would afford it international success. However, in the 1960s he met Sam Walton, the founder of the largest retailer in the world, Walmart, on a trip to the US. Dunne saw the Walmart way of selling food and thought about bringing the concept to Ireland. The idea was novel at the time: the grocery items would be placed on fixtures arranged in aisles around the store, allowing customers to choose their own products as they wandered around the store. Despite being told it would never work in Ireland, he decided to give it a try. Dunnes Stores opened Ireland's first self-service grocery store in Cornelscourt, County Dublin, in 1966. The model worked and Dunnes embarked upon an expansion drive that eventually saw the company have operations in Ireland, the UK and Spain.

"Dunne opened his first Dublin branch in 1957 on Henry Street, followed by a super-store on South Great Georges Street in 1960. This was a 'personal choice' store – the first of its kind in Ireland. Shoppers were allowed to browse through the items on racks before making a purchase – a completely new idea in Irish retailing. So began the aim of Dunnes Stores to innovate in order to put customers first."

"From the 1970s onwards, Dunnes Stores expanded all across Ireland and further afield. In 1971, the first Northern Irish store opened, and many others soon followed. Expansion continued in the 1980s in Spain, and later into Scotland and England. Dunnes Stores branch numbers in January 2015 were
- 116 branches in the Republic of Ireland
- 23 in Northern Ireland
- 6 in England
- 5 in Scotland
- 5 in Spain."[19]

---

[19] http://www.dunnesstores.com/our-story/content/fcp-content (accessed February 2015).

Turnover numbers are not publicly available for Dunnes Stores as the company is a privately owned, unlimited entity. However, it is estimated the business has sales of over €3 billion and is highly profitable with low gearing, meaning that the business has borrowed very little capital from the banks and uses shareholders' cash to trade together with working capital. The philosophy of Dunnes Stores is to have the business reliant on as few third parties as possible. Consequently, it avoids leasing properties where it can, not wanting to allow any bargaining power to landlords. It does not negotiate with its staff through trade unions and it does not borrow from banks if it can be avoided. The vision is that 'if our customers leave us, we have only ourselves to blame'. It is a philosophy that has made Dunnes the target of much criticism as it is seen to be divisive and not inclusive. Nonetheless, it seems to have served the shareholder well as the business has maintained market share over the 10 years from 2005 to 2015.

AIB (Ranking: 7)

AIB was formed in 1966 when three existing banks, Provincial Bank of Ireland, Royal Bank of Ireland, and the Munster and Leinster Bank, were acquired by the newly created Allied Irish Banks, an entity set up to facilitate the merger. It expanded into the UK in the 1970s in response to customer needs for retail banking facilities beyond its core Irish operations. Following on from the initial successes in the UK, the bank expanded internationally through the 1980s and 1990s: in 1983 it invested in First Maryland Bancorp in the US and in the 1990s it began investing in Poland, eventually acquiring the majority shareholding in two banks there. In 2010 AIB sold its interests in the US and Poland in order to raise capital in response to the financial crisis that hit most banks around the world following the collapse of Lehman Brothers in 2008. AIB also acquired interests in banking in Bulgaria and in the Baltic region. In late 2010 the Irish Government acquired 92.8% of AIB, effectively nationalising the bank. The bank is now substantially focused on the Irish market.

Bank of Ireland (Ranking: 8)

Bank of Ireland is one of Ireland's oldest companies, formed by the Bank of Ireland Act in 1781. It grew over the next century as the Irish economy grew and banking in general became increasingly necessary to facilitate commercial interests. The bank first paid interest on deposits in 1864, reflecting the start of the bank as a commercial enterprise in and of itself rather than merely a guardian for deposits and a provider of loans. It expanded into the US in 1988 with the acquisition of First New Hampshire Bank. It sold its interests in the US bank in the late 1990s.

While already having operations in the UK through its branch network in Northern Ireland, the bank subsequently acquired the Bristol and West Building society in 1996. This expansion led it into the then lucrative UK mortgage market. It sold this business in 2005. Its activities in the UK are now primarily focused on the financial services it provides through its relationship with the Post Office, the UK's postal service branch network. The bank is now primarily focused on the Irish market and international advisory services through its corporate banking arm.

ICON Plc (Ranking: 9)

ICON plc was founded in Dublin in 1990 by two doctors, John Climax and Ronan Lambe. The initial small team of five has grown to a global workforce in 2014 of over 10,000 in 37 countries. It has mainly grown organically although it has made some strategic acquisitions, such as Veeda Laboratories in 2009. It expanded into China through the acquisition of BeijingWits in 2012.

The company offers a broad range of specialised services to help pharmaceutical, biotechnology and medical device companies to bring new drugs and devices to market faster. ICON's services support their clients through the full product life cycle. This means that ICON needs to have competence in early product development and pre-clinical trials right through to helping clients commercialise their new products by advising on manufacturing processes and production capability.

It is apparent from looking at the seven Irish MNEs that are in the top 10 that having a strong vision and culture is as important for international expansion from Ireland as any unique 'Irishness'. When an MNE is considering international expansion, it is vital that the enterprise has a clearly defined recognition of what will make its operations successful in another country.

4.7 IRISH MULTINATIONALS – NORTHERN IRELAND

Two of Northern Ireland's top-10 companies, again measured by employee numbers, are MNEs originating from the province.[20] Interestingly, both are involved in the agri-food industry.

TABLE 4.3: NORTHERN IRELAND TOP 10 COMPANIES BY EMPLOYEE NUMBERS

Rank	Company	Employees
1	Moy Park	11,534
2	Tesco	9,762
3	Bombardier	5,014
4	Four Seasons	4,885
5	Asda	4,575
6	Translink	3,957
7	Firstsource Solutions	3,602
8	Dunbia	3,259
9	Royal Mail Group	3,520
10	Almac Group	3,201

Moy Park (Ranking: 1)

Moy Park is a hugely successful operator in the global poultry sector. With modest beginnings in Moygashel, County Tyrone, in its early days it was a farming enterprise with interests in dairy, potatoes and egg production. One of the by-products of egg production is selling-off the male birds needed to foster egg-laying but not needed subsequently for the egg production process. Moy Park started the selling of poultry as a side-line revenue channel from its main business during egg production.

However, the owners saw that the sale of poultry to grocery stores was becoming a larger market as traditional shopping habits changed: consumers were no longer keeping hens and chickens and

---

[20] Belfasttelegraph.co.uk, Top 100 NI companies 2015, http://www.belfasttelegraph.co.uk/business/top-100-companies/

were increasingly buying from grocery stores and, later, supermarkets. In 1960 Moy Park acquired the Ulster Farmers' Cooperative and in 1963 began selling into the British market. This first foray into the external trade market was a major step for the company. They developed the expertise and competence to process larger, long-term contracts together with the skills needed to supply customers who were based a long distance away from their processing operations.

The company continued its expansion by acquiring or building new facilities to increase its production capability. In 1996 it was acquired by a global food company, OSI Group. OSI gave it access to capital resources that allowed the business to start to acquire businesses in Britain. In 2008 OSI sold Moy Park to the Brazilian Food company Marfrig. Moy Park became part of a global food company. In 2013 Marfrig consolidated its diverse European operations into Moy Park. Moy Park now found itself running the entire European operations of Marfrig from its headquarters in Dungannon. While still mainly focused on poultry, the business is now operating in the meat sector. The reorganisation of Marfrig's European business resulted in Moy Park having 12,000 employees by the end of 2013.

During the 2014 World Cup in Brazil, many people in Ireland may have been surprised to see the Moy Park brand prominently displayed on advertising alongside football pitches. From its humble beginnings, there is clearly a major drive to increase awareness of the Moy Park name and to turn it into a global consumer brand. Moy Park has become a globally recognised brand. In June 2015 Moy Park was taken over by Brazilian food company JBS for $1.5 billion.

Dunbia (Ranking: 8)

Dunbia is a large multinational enterprise involved in the production and sale of meat products on a global basis. Again, the roots of the company are modest, starting as it did with the opening of a small butcher shop by the Dobson family in Moygashel, County Tyrone (coincidently the same town in which Moy Park was founded!)

In 1998 the company expanded outside of Northern Ireland with the purchase of Rose County Foods in Clitheroe, Lancashire. The international expansion continued, mainly by acquisition, and the company rebranded from Dungannon Meats to Dunbia in 2006. It now employs 3,300 and exports meat products all over the world. It is still run by the Dobson family.[21]

4.8 FOREIGN MULTINATIONALS IN IRELAND

Republic of Ireland

Three of the top 10 Irish companies, measured by employee numbers, are foreign multinationals with significant numbers employed in Ireland: Tesco, Boston Scientific, and Perrigo.[22]

Tesco (Ranking: 4)

As we saw in **Chapter 3**, Tesco entered the Irish market by acquiring the supermarket chain Quinnsworth. Tesco is a UK-based multinational grocer with interests throughout the world. Its international expansion has led to criticism from analysts as expensive investments have

---

[21] Source: www.dunbia.com
[22] Source: www.top1000.ie, 2014.

failed to deliver the promised returns, starving the core UK business of cash. However, the Irish business has always been profitable for Tesco and remained a success in its expansion pro- gramme until 2014. In the face of an accounting scandal and falling sales Tesco recorded sub- stantial losses for 2014 of over £6 billion. The Irish operation was particularly hit by this turn of events and Tesco had to adjust the profits of its Irish operation downwards by £63 million due to an accounting mistreatment of rebate payments from suppliers. Nonetheless, it remains a strong player in the Irish grocery sector with a market share of close on 25%.

Boston Scientific (Ranking: 6)

Boston Scientific was formed in 1978 by Pete Nicholas and John Abele. Abele was looking for an investor for the company he headed, Medi-Tech, and Nicholas was an investor looking to expand his investment portfolio. The two saw growth potential in Medi-Tech's vision for less invasive intervention approaches to patient care.

The company went public in 1992 and its main product line was the Taxus stent, which is a type of catheter designed to stave off heart attacks and help repair damaged arteries. The prod- uct requires 'cleanroom' manufacturing processes and demands high attention to quality and hygiene in the manufacturing process and throughout the supply chain. These requirements are best met by highly qualified personnel and advanced manufacturing techniques, which fits well into the profile of Ireland and its workforce as promoted by the Irish Development Authority (IDA). The role of the IDA is to attract foreign multinationals into the Republic of Ireland (see **Section 4.9** below).[23]

Boston Scientific is now a global player in the development and manufacture of a suite of medical devices, not just stents. It makes catheters, platinum coils, pacemakers and a range of other devices. It has annual revenues of over US$7.3 billion in 2014 and employs 25,000 around the world.

Boston Scientific first invested in facilities in Ireland in 1994. It now has three manufacturing sites in the Republic of Ireland: Clonmel, Cork and Galway. The investment by the firm in Ireland was supported by the IDA and it is now the largest medical device employer in the country.

The investment in Ireland can be understood in terms of the comparative advantage Ireland provides in its well-educated, English-speaking workforce, proximity to European markets and relatively competitive labour costs for university graduate-level personnel.

Northern Ireland

Five of Northern Ireland's top 10 companies, again measured in terms of employee numbers, are British or foreign MNEs. Interestingly, three of these achieved their prominence in Northern Ireland by acquiring existing large-scale Northern Irish-owned businesses.

Tesco (Ranking: 2)

Tesco entered the market in Northern Ireland by acquiring the supermarket chain Crazy Prices. It quickly rebranded the stores to Tesco and has continued to hold a dominant position in grocery retailing in Northern Ireland.

---

[23] See http://www.idaireland.com/how-we-help/case-studies/boston-scientific/

Bombardier (Ranking: 3)

Bombardier came to Northern Ireland through the acquisition of one of the world's first aircraft production companies, Short Brothers. Shorts itself was formed in 1908 and relocated to Northern Ireland after the Second World War and was eventually acquired by the giant Canadian aircraft manufacturer Bombardier in 1989. The UK government agreed to write off £390 million in debts to facilitate the acquisition for the relatively modest price of £30 million. The Belfast operation has remained strong and has specialised in the manufacture of aircraft wings that form the key component of Bombardier's aircraft production business. The company employs 5,000 people in its Northern Irish operations.

Asda (Ranking: 5)

Asda, part of the US giant Walmart, entered the Northern Ireland market in 2005 by acquiring the Northern Ireland stores from UK retailer Morrisons, which had acquired the stores as a side benefit of acquiring the UK chain Safeway. Safeway had bought the stores from the Tony O'Reilly- owned Fitzwilton Group. The Fitzwilton Group originally acquired them from the Moore family, who ran them for many decades under the name Wellworths.

Asda has grown its business in Northern Ireland with the construction of new stores, especially at the edge of major towns and cities.

Almac Group (Ranking: 10)

Almac Group is involved in the research and development of pharmaceutical products on behalf of over 600 pharmaceutical company clients. It is also involved in the commercialisation of those drugs that become viable for the marketplace. It is leading the way in specialist areas of cancer treatments and global clinical trials.

Other notable foreign multinationals in Northern Ireland are Sainsbury's and Caterpillar.

Sainsbury's

Sainsbury's started its operations in Northern Ireland by building its own brand-new store in Sprucefield, just outside Belfast. Unlike its competitors, it grew its business in Northern Ireland by building new stores rather than acquiring existing operations and rebranding them. Sainsbury's now employs 3,000 people in Northern Ireland and has an estimated turnover of £400 million.

Caterpillar

Caterpillar is a $56 billion turnover company manufacturing and supplying industrial machinery and equipment primarily to the construction industry. As an MNE, it employs 131,000 globally. In 1999 it acquired FG Wilson, a major Northern Ireland player in this sector, keeping the company's trading name and brands for many years. In 2013 Caterpillar rebranded the Northern Ireland operation from FG Wilson to Caterpillar; it has retained the FG Wilson product brand, however, recognising customer loyalty that has been built up over the decades. FG Wilson was founded by Fred Wilson in 1966 and built a reputation for making solid, reliable, high-quality generators. It has received many awards for the excellence of its products. The Caterpillar subsidiary employs 3,000 people in its own right.

4.9 GOVERNMENT SUPPORT FOR MULTINATIONAL ENTERPRISES

At the beginning of the chapter I explained how the international trade patterns of countries emerge using the H–O model and Porter's Diamond framework. In order to encourage the growth of international trade from the island, both the Republic of Ireland and Northern Ireland's governments have sought to facilitate and enable enterprises to foster their international trade. The governments have set up agencies to work with companies by offering them advice and, in some cases, financial incentives to embark upon the internationalisation path. The nature of these agencies fall into two distinct categories:
- aid to indigenous companies that are seeking to expand internationally; and
- aid to international companies that wish to expand their facilities into Ireland.

Agencies Supporting Indigenous MNEs

Enterprise Ireland is the main agency tasked with encouraging exports from the Republic of Ireland.[24] Its role is to help indigenous Irish businesses export into international markets. The track record of Irish exports has been impressive, as can be seen in **Figure 4.8** below:

FIGURE 4.8: EXPORT SALES – REPUBLIC OF IRELAND (€BNS)[25]

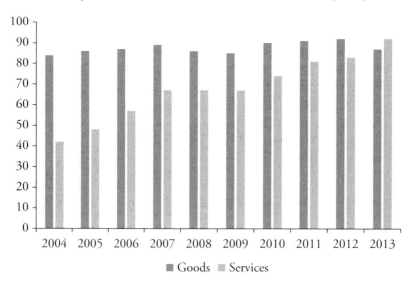

Even during the collapse in the global economy during the banking crisis of 2008 and 2009, exports from the Republic held up well. It is also interesting to note the growth in the export of services, which is now almost at the same level as goods exports.

Enterprise Ireland works with MNEs by providing them advice and mentoring. They also have offices throughout the world in countries where Irish exporters are most likely to find markets for their output. These offices provide Irish MNEs with on-the-ground information that would be difficult or expensive to obtain if the MNE was operating on its own. These services are

---

[24] See www.enterprise-ireland.com
[25] Adapted from data from www.CSO.ie

particularly advantageous to smaller enterprises that do not have the resources to conduct in-depth market research themselves.

In Northern Ireland, nascent MNEs can use the services of UK Trade and Investment (UKTI) to provide advice and support to enable and encourage exports into foreign markets.[26] There are also local support services in Northern Ireland, such as Enterprise Northern Ireland.[27]

Agencies Supporting Inward Investment

Governments recognise the benefits of inward investment from foreign multinationals. Both the Republic of Ireland and Northern Ireland have development agencies whose role it is to find and encourage foreign MNEs to invest in their respective jurisdictions. In April 2015 Enterprise Ireland announced that exports from indigenous Irish MNEs (companies such CRH, Smurfit Kappa, Kerry Group, etc., discussed in **Section 4.6** above) to the rest of the world amounted to €19 billion for 2014. This represents just 11% of total exports from the Republic of Ireland. By implication, 89% of all exports of goods and services from the Republic of Ireland are made by foreign MNEs who have located their operations in the state. This figure shows just how important to the Irish economy these foreign MNEs are.

In the Republic of Ireland the main agencies are:
• IDA Ireland (formerly the Industrial Development Agency);[28] and
• the Department of Jobs, Enterprise and Innovation.

IDA Ireland's role includes encouraging FDI in Ireland by foreign MNEs. It helps MNEs new to the ROI to set up; it also helps existing MNEs with their expansion and growth strategies. IDA Ireland offers a range of services, including:
• property search and location advice;
• helping build relationships between ROI institutions and MNEs;
• providing market research, statistics and other information beneficial to MNEs.

IDA Ireland also works with other state agencies. In addition, it runs a large number of research and development programmes, some of which include direct and indirect funding options for MNEs. In Northern Ireland the main agencies are:
• Invest Northern Ireland;[29] and
• the Strategic Investment Board.[30]

Invest Northern Ireland (Invest NI) is Northern Ireland's business development agency. It has a number of supports in place to encourage inward investment. It is also involved in encouraging NI companies to look to expand their operations into new markets. Part of the UK's Department of Enterprise, Trade and Investment, Invest NI offers "the Northern Ireland business community a single organization providing high quality services, programmes, support and expert advice" (www.investni.com).

Invest NI is particularly interested in supporting MNEs or potential MNEs that can offer what it terms "high returns" for the Northern Ireland economy. This focus on high returns allows

---

[26] See www.gov.uk/government/organisations/uk-trade-investment
[27] See www.enterpriseni.com
[28] www.idaireland.com
[29] www.investni.com
[30] www.sibni.org

Invest NI some prioritisation of its efforts and leads it to focus on certain sectors. The priority sectors for Invest NI are:
- aerospace and defence;
- business and professional services;
- construction;
- creative industries;
- financial services;
- food and drink;
- ICT and electronics;
- life and health sciences;
- materials handling;
- renewables and energy;
- security;
- tourism.

An MNE thinking about expanding into Northern Ireland in any of these sectors will receive significant support from Invest NI, which works with MNEs to secure new investment, find suitable locations and sites, as well as providing HR advice, specialist advice on R&D and marketing and, in some cases, capital investment grants or equity investment.

There is also an all-Ireland agency called InterTradeIreland, which was set up in 1998 under the Belfast Agreement, and whose role is primarily to increase the attractiveness of the island of Ireland as an investment home by focusing on mutually beneficial opportunities to improve competitiveness.

These agencies operate throughout the world, looking for businesses that might usefully expand their operations into Ireland. The agencies will promote Ireland as a good place to do business. However, their role is more than just promotional activity: they have a suite of incentives that they make available to foreign MNEs. These incentives range from making facilities available to the MNE, capital grants, market research, and advisory services on location and personnel selection.

4.10 IRELAND AS A BUSINESS LOCATION

Introduction

A focus of this book is the performance management of MNEs. The enterprises considered are both those that have expanded from these shores and also those that have come to this island. In **Chapter 3** we introduced foreign direct investment (FDI) as an operating model chosen by large-scale, global multinationals. In all instances such MNEs will have made decisions about their investment in a foreign country based on its suitability as a place to do business. In **Chapter 7** we will look at how the economic and political climate of a country affects an MNE's decision-making. MNEs will examine different attributes of a country in order to ascertain its suitability, either as a market for its products or a location to carry out some of its processes. These attributes can be quantifiable and measureable, or be qualitative in nature. An MNE will make these assessments both before making an inward investment in a country, and on an ongoing basis as it assesses and monitors performance. Inward FDI has been identified by many of the world's governments, including those of Ireland and the UK/Northern Ireland, as being of critical importance to the development and strength of their economies.

In this section we will explore
- why the island of Ireland is a good place to do business for MNEs;
- the main corporate structures available to MNEs in the Republic of Ireland (ROI) and Northern Ireland (NI);
- some of the main tax structures and benefits available for MNEs in both jurisdictions; and
- how one would make a case for FDI into ROI or NI.

The Republic of Ireland

Since the financial crisis in 2008 many of the world's developed economies have struggled to recover and start to grow. The Republic of Ireland has recovered faster than many of the world's other developed economies. FDI has been a major contributor to ROI's return to economic recovery. The ROI Government has been proactive in setting up support structures to encourage MNEs to invest in the country.

Resources in this area have been stepped up since the financial crisis. In particular, the Government has tried to create a business culture attractive to foreign MNEs by investing in education, reducing 'red tape' and trying to ensure that there is a conducive fiscal, legal and technological infrastructure. Almost 1,000 MNEs have located their major European hub in ROI. Among the main reasons that MNEs locate in ROI include:
- membership of the European Union ensuring access to other EU markets;
- a corporation tax rate of 12.5% (with a relatively simple corporation tax calculation and compliance process);
- good availability of a skilled, English-speaking workforce;
- the youngest population in Europe;
- strong productivity levels; and
- good technological and transport infrastructures.

As introduced in the previous section, the major agency responsible for encouraging and fostering FDI in Ireland is IDA Ireland. (The main agency responsible for encouraging FDI and exports from ROI into other countries is Enterprise Ireland.) Providing the education systems and technology infrastructure to support it, the Government's strategy has been to increasingly focus on skilled jobs in what is termed 'the knowledge economy', referring to the use of knowledge to create value in an economy, which differs from more traditional forms of value creation, i.e. taking raw materials and processing them into products. The main growth sectors in terms of FDI are:
- medical devices;
- bio-pharmaceuticals;
- cloud computing and Internet;
- 'clean tech' (processes that eliminate waste and reduce the environmental footprint);
- financial services;
- software development and ICT;
- engineering; and
- business services.

ROI has also responded to the economic crisis by addressing some of the uncompetitive cost drivers in the market. "Ireland's competitiveness has improved dramatically since 2008."[31] For example, office rents have fallen and commercial rates have stabilised. Dublin is the 49th most expensive city in the world in 2015; it was 16th in 2008.[32]

---

[31] See www.idaireland.com
[32] See http://www.iMercer.com/uploads/GM/col2015/e654123/index (accessed August 2015).

The International Financial Services Centre (IFSC)

Ireland has been particularly successful in attracting financial institutions to the International Financial Services Centre (IFSC) in Dublin. Currently, more than 250 financial MNEs have operations established in the IFSC; this has supported the creation of a large local network of support lawyers, accountants and other associated specialists.

A recent innovation in Ireland has been the establishment of a framework to accommodate Shari'ah compliant investment funds. An Islamic financing regime was established to allow Islamic financing houses to use Ireland as the base location for their EU product offerings.

One particularly successful sector of financial services in the IFSC has been leasing, particularly small-ticket item leasing and aircraft leasing. ROI tax law allows for the taxation of lessor companies on their accounting profits in respect of short-life assets. These provisions can be an attractive alternative to often more burdensome taxation regimes that use imposed depreciation policies as the system for calculating taxable profits.

Education

The Irish education system also contributes to the relative attractiveness of the country to MNEs seeking to invest. The high level of participation in meaningful third-level education ensures that ROI has one of the most appropriately educated workforces in terms of having the skills that can attract FDI. In 2014, Ireland ranked ninth overall in the world in terms of achievement in higher education.[33]

MNEs are interested in the competencies of the people they might employ. They are also interested in the state of the education system generally. This is because the infrastructure supports, such as healthcare, the legal system, education and general governmental administration, will be carried out predominantly by people employed in the public sector rather than by MNEs. If a country focused only on creating skills suitable for commercial entities' it may leave itself short of the necessary skills that provide the basic foundaions for the conduct of commerce.

Ireland is regarded as having a world-class education system. According to the United Nations Human Development Report Ireland, in 2013 it was ranked 11th in the world on its education index.

FIGURE 4.9: THE UN EDUCATION INDEX 2013

Country	Ranking
Norway	1
USA	5
Germany	6
Ireland	**11**
UK	**14**
France	20
Spain	27

---

[33] See thelearningcurve.pearson.com/index/index-ranking (accessed July 2015). The index is a composite of a number of education data banks examining links between education and skills development.

As mentioned earlier in this chapter (and also discussed in **Chapter 7**), MNEs will examine a number of a country's attributes in order to support its FDI decisions. Measures associated with the relevant country's economy are some of the most important attributes examined. We will now look at some of the measures, from an ROI point of view, that MNEs will examine in order to determine it is a suitable FDI target.

The Economy

The first measure is real GDP growth, see **Figure 4.10** below. (For a more complete explanation of why GDP is important, see **Chapter 7**.) Ireland is one of the fastest growing economies in Europe which means that it is attractive for inward investment, particularly for MNEs seeking new markets for their products. Growing economies also encourage MNEs because infrastructure in the country is likely to be at least maintained if not developed as the economy grows.

FIGURE 4.10: ROI – REAL GDP GROWTH[34]

	2009	2010	2011	2012	2013	2014	2015(f)	2016(f)
Ireland (ROI)	−7	−0.4	0.7	0.9	0.2	4.8	3.9	3.3
United Kingdom	−4.4	2.1	0.7	0.2	1.7	2.6	2.7	2.3
France	−2.7	1.5	1.7 (f)	0.0	0.3	0.4	1.2	1.5
Germany	−5.1	3.7	3.0	0.9	0.5	1.6	1.6	1.7
Spain	−3.7	−0.1	0.7	−1.4	−1.2	1.4	2.5	2.0
Euro area	−4.3	1.9	1.5	−0.6	−0.4	0.9	1.5	1.6
United States	−3.5	3.0	1.7	2.2	2.2	2.4	3.1	3.1

A second measure that MNEs will look at is unemployment levels. Falling unemployment suggests that the education system is producing increased amounts of newly skilled or reskilled labour, which can make meaningful added value contributions to the economy. A country that has a productive workforce also has less pressure on resources from unemployment support costs. However, it should be also noted that if unemployment is too low, MNEs may be somewhat deterred; unemployment levels below 4% normally entails recruitment problems. The ROI levels of 8.8% remain low enough not be too unwieldy a burden on the exchequer and high enough to ensure an availability of employees for inbound FDI-minded MNEs.

FIGURE 4.11: ROI – UNEMPLOYMENT (% OF LABOUR FORCE)[35]

	2009	2010	2011	2012	2013	2014	2015(f)	2016(f)
Ireland (ROI)	11.9	13.7	14.4	14.7	13.0	11.3	9.8	8.8
United Kingdom	7.6	7.8	8.0	8.0	7.6	6.2	5.4	5.4
France	9.5	9.8	9.7	10.2	10.3	10.2	10.1	9.9
Germany	7.8	7.1	5.9	5.5	5.3	5.0	4.9	4.8
Spain	18.0	20.1	21.7	25.0	26.1	24.5	22.6	22.1
Euro area	9.6	10.1	10.2	11.4	11.9	11.6	11.1	10.6
United States	9.3	9.6	8.9	8.1	7.9	6.2	5.5	5.1

---

[34] IMF, *World Economic Outlook*, April 2015 (f = forecast).

[35] IMF, *World Economic Outlook*, April 2015.

As we will see in **Chapter 8**, a country's inflation rate is an important measure for an MNE considering FDI. If inflation is too high, the 'real value' of investments will fall rapidly while at the same time costs can be expected to rise. On the other hand, inflation levels of zero and below are normally signs of a stalled economy. As **Figure 4.12** shows, ROI has had inflation of below 2% for six years, a trend that is expected to continue. Therefore, MNEs investing in ROI can have some certainty over potential cost increases for the foreseeable future.

FIGURE 4.12: ROI – INFLATION (HARMONISED INDEX OF CONSUMER PRICES)[36]

	2009	2010	2011	2012	2013	2014	2015(f)	2016(f)
Ireland (ROI)	−1.7	−1.6	1.2	1.9	0.5	0.3	0.2	1.5
United Kingdom	2.2	3.3	4.5	2.8	2.6	1.5	0.1	1.7
France	0.1	1.7	2.3	2.0	1.0	0.6	0.1	0.8
Germany	0.2	1.2	2.5	2.1	1.6	0.8	0.2	1.3
Spain	−0.2	2.0	3.1	2.4	1.5	−0.2	−0.7	0.7
Euro area	0.3	1.6	2.7	2.5	1.3	0.4	0.1	1.0
United States (CPI)	−0.3	1.6	3.1	2.1	1.5	1.6	0.1	1.4

Population, Demographics and Workforce

The 2011 Census for the Republic of Ireland showed the population to be 4,588,252, an increase of 8% on the previous census figure from 2006. Increasing population is of interest to an MNE for two reasons:
• more people provide larger markets for the MNE's products;
• increasing populations generally lead to a larger pool of available workers.

In its publication *Facts about Ireland*, IDA Ireland states that the ROI has the youngest population in Europe with 40% of the population under 29 years old. "Our young workforce is capable, highly adaptable, mobile and very committed to achievement."[37] This young population is attractive to MNEs, especially those looking for a skilled workforce as against new markets. There is a twin benefit of a young population demographic:
• a larger pool of people at working age;
• a lower percentage of older people reliant upon the State for pensions and healthcare, leading to less pressures upon the exchequer and allowing for greater investment in infrastructure and lower taxation.

Figure 4.13 shows that 40.2% of the ROI population is under 29 in 2015. This percentage is not expected to change over the coming five years. MNEs can therefore invest in ROI knowing that there will be no major medium-term changes to the demographic profile of the country in terms of a young, skilled and available workforce.

---

[36] IMF, *World Economic Outlook*, April, 2015.
[37] *Facts about Ireland* (Autumn 2015). Available at www.idaireland.com/docs/publications/Facts_Ireland_2015

IDA Ireland also provides the following table, sourcing it to Eurostat 2015, as shown in **Figure 4.13**:

FIGURE 4.13: % POPULATION UNDER 29 YEARS[38]

Country	Total
Ireland	40.2
France	36.5
UK	37.2
Netherlands	35.3
Poland	35.2
EU	32.2
Spain	30.8
Germany	30.1
Italy	29.2
Hungary	32.5
Switzerland	33.1

The ROI's workforce appeals to many MNEs as it has a high number of well-educated, young people. The figures below show how the ROI workforce ranks in terms of talent compared to some other, competing countries.

The International Institute for Management Development (IMD) compiles a general analysis of competitiveness between countries in order to determine which are best to do business in and publishes the results annually (see **Figure 4.14** below). One of IMD's measures looks at the workforce of a country and compares its skill-set to the requirements of MNEs. Based on this assessment for 2014, ROI had the sixth best workforce in terms of meeting the needs of a modern MNE. The assessment looked at age profile, level of education, skill-sets and other measures of workforce competence and availability. It is of major importance to MNEs that the countries into which they invest have available skilled workers.

FIGURE 4.14: WORLD TALENT RANKING OF WORKFORCE 2014[39]

Country	Ranking
Ireland	6
USA	12
UK	20
Czech Republic	37
Spain	45
Japan	28
Poland	36

---

[38] Source: Eurostat 2015 as published in IDA Ireland, *Facts about Ireland* (Autumn 2015).
[39] IMD, *World Competitiveness Yearbook* 2014.

It is one thing to have a workforce that has the right age profile and set of competencies. An MNE will also want to know what proportion of that workforce is available. ROI scores very well in this regard, as shown in **Figure 4.15**. This is an effect of Ireland's good education system, coupled with its young population and relatively high levels of unemployment.

FIGURE 4.15: SKILLED LABOUR AVAILABILITY 2014[40]

Country	Ranking
Ireland	1
Japan	29
USA	15
Czech Republic	28
Germany	37
Spain	16
UK	21
Poland	38

Business Structures Available in the Republic of Ireland

As we have seen in **Chapter 3**, any MNE wishing to engage in FDI will need to decide what form the investment will take. This decision normally involves considering whether to set up a subsidiary company or whether to choose a different type of structure. The structures normally used for FDI in ROI are as follows:

Limited Company In a liability company, the liability of the owners (members or shareholders) of the company for debts incurred by the company is limited to the amount that they have agreed to contribute to the company. A limited company can either be a public limited company (PLC) or a private limited company. A plc may seek subscriptions from the public and apply to have its shares quoted on a stock exchange whereas a private company is prohibited from inviting the public to subscribe for shares in the company. A private company can be limited by shares or guarantee. The majority of Irish companies are private companies limited by shares. There is also an option to form or be a designated activity company limited (DAC) by shares (or by guarantee with share capital), which is a type of private limited company but with very specific objectives.

Unlimited Company These companies are similar in nature to limited companies but do not have the protection of limited liability for shareholders; there is no limit on the liability of the owners for the company's debts. Consequently, the accounting and filing disclosure requirements are not as onerous as is the case where the shareholders have limited liability.

Partnership This business structure consists of a group of people who wish to carry on a business together. Their collaboration is normally documented in a partnership agreement, which covers such things as how much each partner should invest, how profits will be shared, etc. The members of a partnership are personally liable for the debts of the partnership. This liability is not limited to the proportion in which a partner has invested in the partnership. In other

---

[40] IMD, *World Competitiveness Yearbook* 2014.

words, for example, a 10% partner is liable for all the debts if the creditors cannot recover from the other partners. A partnership might be used by professional practices setting up in Ireland but, in the main, will not suit the purposes of most MNEs.

Foreign Company An MNE does not need to set up a ROI subsidiary. It can trade in Ireland using a branch structure. While this approach seems simple, in reality it can be quite cumbersome to administer because the 'branch' must comply with ROI taxation and reporting legislation, which in turn means that some way must be found of separating out the ROI branch results from the rest of the MNE's operations. The 'branch' may need to register for VAT and PAYE and comply with other tax codes. Using a separate legal structure makes this 'extraction' of the necessary accounting and fiscal information more straightforward.

(***Note:*** the types of vehicle that an MNE can use are broadly the same for the ROI and Northern Ireland (see below).)

Filing Requirements in the Republic of Ireland

All Irish companies, including subsidiaries of MNEs, must file an annual return with the Companies Registration Office (CRO). The company may also be required to file a set of accounts with the annual return.

Irish Companies Whether it is trading or dormant, all Irish companies must file an annual return at least once in every calendar year. An annual return comprises details of the company's:
• directors;
• shareholders and share capital;
• secretary;
• registered office.

In most cases, an audited set of accounts must be filed with the annual return. Smaller companies may be allowed to file abridged accounts and, in some cases, very small enterprises are exempt from needing to have an audited set of accounts.

Foreign Companies If a foreign-owned MNE operates in the ROI using a branch or a place of business, it will still have filing requirements, even though it will not have an incorporated entity in the jurisdiction. A branch is required to submit basic information, such as the registered office of the MNE and its consolidated accounts to the CRO. The MNE is not required to file separate branch accounts, however.

Audit of an MNE's Subsidiaries in the Republic of Ireland

Irish Companies An MNE's Irish subsidiaries will require audited accounts unless they can claim an exemption as a **small company**. Under the Companies Act 2014, audit exemption is available to small companies, parents and subsidiaries in small groups, companies limited by guarantee, certain unlimited companies and dormant subsidiaries. The qualifying criteria for a 'small company' are satisfied by a company in relation to a financial year in which it fulfils two or more of the following requirements. A company loses 'small' status if it does not satisfy these criteria for two consecutive years:
• average number of employees: 50;
• turnover not exceeding €8.8 million;
• balance sheet total not exceeding €4.4 million.

The small company audit exemption does not exempt a company from having to prepare full accounts and to have those accounts available at the company's annual general meeting.

As mentioned above, there is an important exemption to filing annual accounts available to subsidiary companies. The exemption allows the consolidated financial statements of the holding undertaking (the MNE) to be submitted with the annual return instead of the subsidiary's accounts. For example, Tesco's subsidiary in ROI does not need to file accounts. The Tesco Group accounts will suffice, as long as the conditions mentioned below are met. This particularly useful exemption is particularly relevant to MNEs with subsidiaries incorporated in ROI. The exemption can be availed of if the group holding company:

- irrevocably guarantees the liabilities of the subsidiary;
- a copy of the irrevocable guarantee is filed with the annual return;
- the shareholders of the subsidiary have all consented to the guarantee;
- the shareholders of the holding company have been made aware of the guarantee.

Of course, in some circumstances an MNE may not want to guarantee the liabilities of its subsidiary in ROI. In these cases, the subsidiary company will need to prepare annual accounts and file them with the annual return. MNE managers must decide which route they wish to pursue. Filing annual accounts in a relatively small market, such as the ROI, may mean that competitors can glean important commercial information. However, if the MNE wishes to avoid this level of disclosure, and possible scrutiny, it will need to guarantee the ROI subsidiary's liabilities.

Foreign Companies A company branch in Ireland that is not required by its own state law to have an audit has no obligation to have an audit for Irish filing requirements.

Financial Reporting

The financial statements of most Irish companies may be prepared in accordance with either international financial reporting standards (IFRS), as adopted by the EU, or in accordance with generally accepted accounting principles (GAAP) in Ireland. Financial reporting standards generally accepted in Ireland are those issued by the UK Financial Reporting Council (FRC), which are amended for Irish company law when relevant (for example, as published by Chartered Accountants Ireland).

The Companies (Miscellaneous Provisions) Act 2009, as amended by the Companies (Amendment) Act 2012, provides an exemption, subject to fulfilling certain conditions, until 2020, to the requirement for foreign companies reporting under US GAAP that operate in Ireland to prepare separate accounts using either Irish GAAP or IFRS. This is a significant benefit to US MNEs and other MNEs that prepare their accounts in accordance with US GAAP. Essentially, it avoids those companies having to prepare a second set of accounts for filing in ROI. This exemption expires in December 2020.

Tax Benefits of Investing in the Republic of Ireland

The ROI tax regime has some major attractions for MNEs. Some of the benefits include:

- the availability of a 12.5% corporation tax rate for trading activities;
- tax relief on research and development expenditure;
- exemptions on withholding taxes on interest and dividend payments to EU and some double-taxation-treaty countries;
- universally accepted transfer pricing regulations;
- beneficial income tax treatment for workers transferred from abroad;
- tax relief on foreign dividends;
- double taxation treaties with 72 countries (August 2015);
- no capital gains tax on disposals of subsidiaries by Irish holding companies.

In 2013, the ROI total tax rate for corporations was 25.9% compared to an average of 41% in the EU and the European Free Trade Area (EFTA). This rate is an amalgam of profits taxes, labour taxes and other types of taxes. Ireland ranked with the 4th lowest rate in the EFTA region. This amalgamated rate is of interest to MNEs as it combines all possible taxes in order to determine which country has the lowest overall rate. Some countries may compensate for low corporation tax rates by, for example, having higher labour taxes applicable to employers.

Trading Losses The ROI tax regime offers MNEs some favourable options when it comes to the treatment of losses. It is worth going into a bit more detail on the treatment of losses in ROI since many MNEs using a group structure will avail of this system at one point or another. The reason for this is that, within an MNE group structure, subsidiary companies may be set up from time to time to carry out a particular task or project, such as acquiring property or applying for planning permission. Often these subsidiaries may incur a loss. The favourable treatment of such losses is a very real advantage to an MNE operating in ROI.

Losses incurred can be offset against trading income of the same and the immediately preceding accounting period. Any unused losses can then be offset against non-trading income, including chargeable gains. Trading losses can also be carried forward for use against future profits. Also, and very importantly for MNEs with a large group structure, losses in one company can be offset against profits from another company within the same tax group in the same accounting period. There are specific rules regarding shareholdings that help define whether a company is a member of a group for tax purposes or not.

The reliefs available to groups can also be available to Irish parent companies in certain circumstances for losses incurred by non-Irish subsidiaries. This relief is an important attraction to MNEs looking to headquarter their operations in the ROI.

Taxation of Dividends As mentioned in **Chapter 16**, MNEs may often manage the balance sheets (also known as the statements of financial position) of subsidiary companies by paying dividends from subsidiaries up to the parent. Such payments are exempt from withholding taxes, which allows the group to structure its affairs in such a way as to optimise the structure of the group from both a tax and a commercial point of view. Ensuring that cash surpluses generated in one part of the MNE can be used to fund investment in other parts of the group without increasing the taxation burden is an important advantage for MNEs with operations in ROI.

In addition, dividends received by an Irish company from another Irish company are exempt from Irish corporation tax. Where dividends are received from EU companies (or companies where ROI has a double taxation agreement), they are taxed at the corporation tax rate of 12.5%. The exemptions allow MNEs to pay dividends intra-group without triggering taxation liabilities where the subsidiaries are Irish, and at 12.5% where they are from other EU companies. MNEs use these allowances to move cash around their group structure efficiently.

On the other hand, however, dividends and other distributions (including certain types of interest) are not tax deductible in the calculation of tax profits. Therefore, an MNE cannot reduce its taxation liability by payment of dividends.

Tax Administration An attractive facet of the ROI taxation system is the ease with which an MNE can meet its taxation filing and returns obligations. The system is administered by way of self-assessment. The MNE will normally complete one corporation tax return for each company within the MNE. This single return is relatively easy to complete and submit. The ROI has an excellent electronic pay-and-file system. Only 43% of the 189 economies surveyed in the *Paying Taxes 2015* survey had electronic payment systems.[41]

The *Paying Taxes* report also highlights that the average time taken to comply with the tax system in ROI is 80 hours. This compares very favourably with an EU/EFTA average of 176 hours. ROI is fourth highest in this league table. There are very real benefits for the MNE in reduced administration and compliance costs.

Tax Treatment of Foreign Workers   The ROI Government is keen not to put obstacles in the way of MNEs setting up in the country. In recognition of the fact the MNEs will need to transfer certain executives to ROI, especially during a start-up or investment phase, special taxation treatment has been put in place.

An MNE's foreign executives will normally become liable to ROI income tax once they meet the residency rules of 183 days in one year or 280 days in two consecutive years. Such an executive will be taxed on their ROI income in total. Foreign income will be taxed only on the basis upon which it is remitted to Ireland.

A special assignment relief programme (SARP) is also in place. This programme effectively reduces the income subject to tax of foreign executives by 30% subject to certain guidelines, rules and limits. It is an important part of the suite of attractive benefits available to MNEs considering locating in ROI or transferring key executives to ROI from other parts of the MNE.

Summary of the Case for FDI in the Republic of Ireland

ROI has a very real attraction for MNEs. Its attraction falls into a number of categories, including the following.
- Location: while part of an island, the country has excellent transport links to Britain and the wider European continent.
- Language: English is the country's first language and still the default language for many MNEs.
- Legal structures: the legal system in ROI is well established, with common law origins (similar to England, the US, Canada, Australia, etc.). Protection of private property rights and enforcement of contracts is dependable and secure.
- Workforce: the workforce is highly skilled and, as of 2015, there is a ready availability.
- Economy: having improved its competitiveness through the recession of 2008 to 2011, ROI now has a strong economy showing the fastest growth in the EU. A strong economy reduces the pressures on the exchequer and allows for greater investment in infrastructure into the future.

Northern Ireland

In **Chapter 1** we discussed the economic profile of Northern Ireland (NI). In particular, we emphasised its history as a manufacturer and exporter of goods and services, from the legacy of ship-building and linen industries to the agri-food success stories of today.

---

[41] *Paying Taxes 2015: The global picture* (Pwc and the World Bank Group, 2015). See www.pwc.com/ payingtaxes (accessed July 2015).

As with the Republic of Ireland, FDI is critical to the continuing economic development of Northern Ireland, whose Government has been focused on ensuring an economic environment conducive to FDI. Microsoft, Seagate and Caterpillar are just some of the global MNEs that have based their operations in NI.

Some of the reasons that they have chosen NI include:
• a highly educated, English-speaking workforce;
• competitive cost structures;
• access to the wider UK and EU markets;
• incentive packages.

NI has an attractive cost-efficient business environment, which helps attract MNEs to making investments in the province. MNEs have become major players in the following sectors of NI's economy:
• international financial services;
• information and communications technology (ICT);
• renewable energy;
• call centres and business support services.

One of the goals of the NI Government is to achieve annual FDI of £375 million. NI has a strong track record in attracting inward investment; £2.9 billion of inward investment was sourced through Invest NI from 2002–2003 to 2010–2011.[42]

The UK economy is now recovering from a long recession. However, the NI economy is lagging the overall UK recovery, although it is outperforming Scotland and Wales on some key measures. For example, proportionately, NI has lost more jobs than England or Wales but has fared relatively better than Scotland. Overall, the recession has led to a real reduction in wages in NI, particularly private-sector wage levels. NI private sector wages are 17% below the UK average. While this makes for lower standards of living in NI, on the other hand, it contributes to NI's cost competitiveness and attractiveness as a base for FDI by MNEs.

Another attractive feature of NI is the widescale availability of skilled graduate labour. In 2010, 10% of graduates remain unemployed six months after graduating, a significant rise from the figure of 4.4% in 2006.

While the productivity of the workforce in general in NI remains below UK averages, this represents a real improvement opportunity for the NI economy.[43] If low productivity can be improved, average wages will increase together with standards of living. This is one of the key reasons for the NI Government's drive to attract FDI. MNEs bring new ways of working, modern management practices and processes, which should in turn lead to improved productivity.

Large companies contribute to over 50% of economic activity in the UK as a whole. In NI this figure is below 25%. There is a much greater reliance on small and medium-sized enterprises. NI also relies more heavily on public sector economic activity than the rest of the UK.[44]

---

[42] *Economic Strategy: Rebuilding and Rebalancing the Economy* (Northern Ireland Executive, March 2012).

[43] Economic Research Institute of Northern Ireland, *Measurement and Benchmarking of Competitiveness – The Cost of Doing Business in Northern Ireland* (December 2005). See Eservices.afbini.gov.uk/erini/pdf/eriniresrpt01.pdf (accessed October 2015).

[44] See "A new kind of trouble", *The Economist*, 24 Janurary 2015: www.economist.com/news/britain/21640334-guns-mostly-silent-ulster-can-begin-deal-its-lamentable-economy-new-kind (accessed October 2015).

Employment and Labour Costs

The unemployment rate in June 2015 for Northern Ireland, at 6.5%, is above the UK average of 5.6%. However, it is significantly better than the EU average of 9.6% and the rate in ROI of 9.8%.[45] This means that MNEs will have greater availability of workers generally than other parts of the UK, but not as much as in ROI, or the EU in total.

At the time of writing, the numbers claiming unemployment assistance have fallen in recent months in NI, a sign of economic recovery. As mentioned above, NI has the most competitive labour costs in the UK, which makes it an attractive location from a cost point of view, especially if productivity issues can be addressed. This is borne out by statistics showing that NI has created 22 jobs per 10,000 of population in the first half of 2015, second in the UK only to London (26 jobs per 10,000).[46] Both regions lag behind ROI, which is around 50 jobs per 10,000 of population.

Population, Demographics and Workforce

The Northern Ireland Statistics and Research Agency (NISRA) estimated that the population of NI was 1.84 million people as at 30 June 2014,[47] incorporating slight growth on the previous year but also, significantly, the first growth in net migration since 2010. In other words, more people are coming to live in NI than are leaving. Birth rates continue to be greater than the death rate. The result is that NISRA expects the population to continue to grow, reaching 1.9 million in 2020. Growth after 2020 is expected to be slower, taking a further 15 years to hit 2 million in 2035.

NI has a young population relative to much of Western Europe. However, it is aging. The median age, where half the population is under this age, has risen from 28 years in 1985 to 38 years in 2015. This aging is expected to continue and NISRA expect that by 2027 there will be more over-65s in NI than children.

Education

Northern Ireland's education system is widely recognised as being of a very high calibre. This is especially true of its third-level education system. Its higher education institutions (HEIs) perform very well when compared to the rest of the UK.[48] The NI Government has allocated a high proportion of public expenditure to HEIs compared to other parts of the UK.[49] In addition, a higher percentage of persons who start degree programmes in NI stay the course and complete their studies (84.3% compared to the UK average of 81.8%).

MNEs are interested in the availability of a skilled workforce. NI's strong HEI sector means that MNEs coming to NI can be confident of being able to source a well-educated, dedicated and skilled workforce.

Business Structures Available in Northern Ireland

As we have seen, an MNE wishing to engage in FDI will need to decide what form the investment will take. This decision normally involves considering whether to set up a subsidiary

---

[45] See www.detini.gov.uk/stats-labour-market-unemployment (accessed August 2015).
[46] See www.detini.gov.uk/publications/deti-monthly-economic-update_august_2015 (accessed August 2015).
[47] See www.nisra.gov.uk/publications/default.asp10.htm (accessed August 2015).
[48] See www.delni.gov.uk (accessed August 2015).
[49] See www.hesa.ac.uk/stats-finance (accessed October 2015).

company or whether to choose a different type of structure. The business structures normally used for FDI in NI are discussed below.

Most MNEs will set up a company in order to conduct their business in NI. A **company** is a separate legal entity from its shareholders. Accordingly, the shareholders' liabilities are limited to their investment in the original share capital of the enterprise. Most MNEs will form a company in which they, i.e. the MNE's, will be the sole shareholder. In some instances, an MNE may form a joint venture with other shareholders.

Public statutory information on NI companies is kept and available at Companies House. Company formation and dissolution is governed by the Companies Act 2006, which commenced on 1 October 2009 and covers all of the UK. Previous to this, NI companies were registered with the Companies Registry Northern Ireland (CRNI). This register has now combined with Companies House. Consequently, companies in NI are UK companies rather than NI companies.

One or more persons are permitted to form a company for any lawful purpose by subscribing to a Memorandum of Association (setting out the company's objectives). A company will not be incorporated unless it appears that the company, when registered, will carry on an activity in Northern Ireland. Prior to the formation of a company, the Memorandum and the Articles of Association (regulating the manner in which the affairs of the company are conducted) are required.

There are a number of different types of company:

Limited Company The shares of a limited company are owned by its shareholders. The liability of the shareholders is limited to the greater of the amount of the nominal value of the shares or the amount agreed to be paid in respect of the issue of the shares. A limited company can either be a public limited company (plc) or a private company. A plc may seek subscriptions from the public and apply to have its shares quoted on a stock exchange. (This benefit, seeking public subscriptions for capital, places greater onus on the company with regard to its reporting requirements and its governance structures.) A private company is prohibited from inviting the public to subscribe for shares in the company. A private company can be limited by shares or guarantee (which can be with or without share capital). Private limited companies are by far the most common type of company in NI.

Unlimited Company An unlimited company has no limit on the liability of the members. Therefore, the shareholders are personally liable for the debts of the company, should the company fail to discharge them.

Partnership MNEs may choose not to form a company. They may operate a partnership. A partnership is a formal collaboration of two or more persons in order to carry on a business together. However, it is rare that MNEs adopt this structure, though it does happen in professional services practices such as global accounting firms or legal practices. (See above under **Republic of Ireland** for more on partnerships.)

Foreign Company Finally, an MNE may decide not to form a company in NI/UK and instead operate a **branch** or a **place of business**. Both forms of business must be registered with Companies House.

A 'branch' is a division of an MNE that has a degree of permanence, which is normally evidenced by a separate management structure and a degree of financial independence. A 'place of business' is less independent and normally just carries out an ancillary service for the MNE. By way of example, a retailer may have a branch in NI that could be a stand-alone shop with its own management team, bank account, etc. Another MNE may only have an ancillary activity being carried out in NI, such as invoice processing. This activity might be deemed to be a 'place of business' rather than a branch. The distinction is important as both are treated differently from a taxation and reporting point of view.

Another form of business entity available to an MNE in NI is a **Societas Europaea (SE)** or **European Company**. This is a form of public limited company that can operate on a pan-European basis. SEs can operate in each country and the country, a Member State of the EU, must acknowledge and respect that the SE can operate in adherence to the company law in the state in which it has its registered office and legal personality. In other words, an SE can operate to the law in its home country as against the host country. This simplifies many things for the MNE. In particular, it means it can have a unified management team and board rather than creating separate subsidiary boards in each operating Member State to comply with their individual regulations. It also means that the MNE's reporting is much simpler since it can operate to the one set of reporting regulations.

Filing Requirements in Northern Ireland

All UK companies must file an annual return. As the name suggests, this return must be filed at least once every 12 months. In addition, some companies are required to file accounts with their annual return.

All companies must prepare accounts but not all companies have to file those accounts with their annual return. The requirement to file accounts is governed by regulations covering the nature, size and scale of the company.

Private and public limited companies must file their accounts with the annual return. They must also file an audit report with these accounts. There are certain exemptions to these regulations. Unlimited companies do not need to file accounts save in certain circumstances; nor do partnerships have to file accounts. The reason unlimited companies and partnerships do not need to file accounts is because the owners of those entities are personally liable for the debts undertaken by the company or partnership.

Smaller companies can often file shortened versions of their accounts, providing less detailed information than would be the case for larger entities.

For MNEs operating in NI, or in the UK generally, the requirement to file accounts and returns will be dictated by the business structure they have chosen to use. Normally, this will be a limited company structure and the associated filing requirements will be regulated by the Companies Act 2006.

Financial Reporting in Northern Ireland

NI companies may prepare their financial statements in accordance with either International Financial Reporting Standards (IFRS), as adopted by the EU, or in accordance with generally accepted accounting principles in the UK (UK GAAP). Financial reporting standards generally accepted are those issued by the UK Financial Reporting Council (FRC).

In addition, the EU requires listed EU companies to prepare consolidated financial statements in accordance with the interpretations set out by the International Accounting Standards Board (IASB) such as those standards have been adopted in the EU. (**Note:** the requirement does not cover all IASB standards since not all standards have been adopted. As will be seen in **Chapter 6**, the lack of a fully standardised global set of accounting conventions is a problem both for MNEs and for the wider investment community.)

Tax Benefits for MNEs Investing in Northern Ireland

Northern Ireland has been very progressive in ensuring an attractive tax environment for MNEs considering setting up there. Some of the main advantages when compared to other European countries, including EU Member States, are:

- low personal taxation;
- low social-welfare contributions;
- no local taxes on profits or surpluses;
- generous tax allowances for MNEs[50];
- substantial shareholdings exemption on disposals of subsidiaries by NI holding companies;
- tax relief for foreign dividends;
- no withholding tax on dividends;
- generous tax reliefs for expenditure on research and development;
- extensive double taxation treaty network (the UK has over 100 double taxation treaties);
- generous income and capital gains tax incentives and reliefs for entrepreneurial investment;
- maximum 20% withholding tax rate on interest/royalty payments with the potential for a 0% rate;
- industry-standard transfer pricing rules.

NI is also in the process of establishing its own corporation tax rate, separate from the rest of the UK. Much of the debate up to now has been on how to distinguish whether a UK company is an NI company for tax purposes. It seems that the final determination will be made dependent on how much of the company's labour costs are incurred in NI and that the cut-off figure will be 75%, which means that, assuming the legislation is passed, NI will be able to set its own corporation tax rate from 2017.

Corporation Tax UK corporation tax applies to all profits (income and gains), wherever arising, from a UK/NI tax resident company. A NI branch or agency of a foreign resident company is also liable to UK corporation tax on profits (including gains on assets situated in the UK used for the purposes of that trade) derived from its UK/NI-based activity. These taxation rules would change when the new legislation is enacted.

At the time of writing (October 2015), the UK 20% rate applies to all profits and gains. If a new rate is introduced when the powers to do so is granted to the NI Government, companies will be required to split their profits and losses between NI and 'mainstream' profits/losses. This profit-splitting will be governed by complex tax rules governing the calculation of the profis to be split, the use of capital allowances and the carry-forward of tax losses.

NI Tax Residency MNEs that are resident in the UK are liable to UK corporation tax on their worldwide income. A non-UK resident MNE is liable to UK corporation tax on its UK-sourced trading income. An MNE is UK tax resident if it is incorporated in the UK. An MNE not incorporated in the UK can still be tax resident in the UK if it is 'controlled' from the UK. Whether an MNE is controlled in the UK is determined by a number of criteria, including:

- where shareholder meetings take place;
- where major negotiations and agreements take place;
- where directors' meetings occur;
- where the majority of directors live.

---

[50] See www.investni.com/invest-in-northern-ireland/competitive-operating-costs.html (accessed September 2015).

It is important for MNEs to ensure they have the correct taxation advice in order to ensure that their taxation position is optimised.

Taxable Profits   Having determined that a NI MNE, or its subsidiary, is liable to UK corporation tax (or NI/UK corporation tax from 2017 onward), the next step for the MNE is to assess the amount of tax to be paid. Normally, the MNE will start with the profits before tax in its applicable companies' accounts. These profits will then be adjusted to produce the taxable profits. The types of adjustments include:
- adding back depreciation charges and replacing those charges with the taxation equivalent capital allowances;
- adding back to profits costs that were not incurred 'wholly and exclusively' for business purposes;
- adding back general provisions for contingencies;
- reducing profits for special allowances, normally in the area of R&D.

The adjusted profit figure is that to which the current corporation tax rate (2015: 20%) is applied.

Trading Losses   If the adjustments described above result in a taxation loss, then the loss can be used in a number of ways to reduce other taxation liabilities:
- the loss can be offset against other profits in the same period;
- the loss can be used against future taxable profits, providing these profits are generated from the same trade;
- the loss can be used against profits from a previous period;
- losses can be used within a group of companies to reduce the overall taxable profits for the group within the same accounting period.

Clearly, it is taxation losses that are pertinent to tax calculations. A 'loss' in the normal accounts will not be relevant to tax until the tax computation has been complete. Sometimes a trading loss can become a taxable profit depending on the tax treatment of the items in the trading and P&L accounts.

There is no time limit on when trading losses can be used to reduce taxable profits. There may be restrictions on the utilisation of tax losses if there are changes to the nature of the trade being carried out, or the ownership of the MNE. Therefore, if an MNE incurs losses in, for example, closing down a division operating in NI, it will be unable to use these losses against its profits, unless those other profits are generated from the carrying out of the same trade.

As mentioned above, an MNE subsidiary may surrender its losses to other members of the group in order to reduce the group's overall taxation charge. Two issues are important for an MNE to consider in this regard:
- what types of 'tax losses' can be surrendered; and
- what constitutes a group for these purposes.

Many MNEs will have specific subsidiaries set up to carry out designated activities within the overall value chain. For example, an MNE may set up a subsidiary in Northen Ireland to manufacture components for other parts of the group. If this subsidiary makes a loss, it is important that it can be used, where appropriate, to offset profits in other parts of the MNE. Members of a MNE group may surrender:
- current year losses;
- excess management expenses (normally the management costs of running investment companies);

- excess charges on income (mainly now charitable donations);
- excess losses on non-trade intangible fixed assets (normally only trade losses can be used against tax liabilities);
- excess non-trading deficits on loan relationships.

It is beyond the scope of this text to examine how these 'losses' are calculated from a technical perspective. The key thing for the reader to appreciate is that there are 'tax losses' that can be surrendered to other group companies to reduce the overall tax burden in a group.

The second issue to understand is what constitutes a group for the purposes of receiving surrendered losses. Company S is a member of a group if it is a 75% subsidiary of another company, Company P. In that case the two companies, S and P, are said to be a 'group' for tax purposes. Any other companies that are also 75% subsidiaries of Company P are also members of the group. All group companies can surrender losses to other members of the same group.

Dividends Received On the basis that all dividends, and other income distributions, received by UK companies are taxable, regardless of the residency of the paying entity, dividends received by UK companies are taxable. In the case of MNEs receiving dividends from subsidiaries, however, there are a number of exemptions that may apply, which means that an MNE holding company will not normally pay corporation tax on the dividends it receives from subsidiaries that it controls, whether those subsidiaries are UK resident or not.

Dividends Paid Dividends paid from UK companies are not subject to a withholding tax. Furthermore, dividends paid are not allowable as a cost in the calculation of taxable profits.

Royalties Royalty payments by an MNE are allowable as a cost in calculating its taxable profits. Royalty payments to individuals and to non-UK resident companies must be subjected to a withholding tax at the basic rate. This is of particular interest to MNEs considering FDI since they may decide to base a headquarters in NI and charge any royalties to which it is entitled to the NI subsidiary. The NI subsidiary will be able to deduct these royalty charges from taxable profits.

Interest Loan interest paid by the MNE is an allowable deduction as a cost in calculating the taxable profits. A withholding tax at the basic rate must be deducted from payments made to individuals or to non-UK resident companies.

In order to be able to claim a deduction for intragroup interest payments, an MNE will need to be able to show that the company claiming the deduction is adequately capitalised. There are very complex tax regulations governing how these capitalisation tests are configured. In essence, the regulations try to prevent a situation where a MNE charges intragroup interest unnecessarily in high taxation jurisdictions to eliminate taxable profits in those countries, while other parts of the MNE located in low taxation jurisdictions receive the intragroup interest.

EU Directive 2003/49 This EU Directive abolished withholding taxes on interest and royalty payments made in one Member State to an associated company in another Member State. A company is said to be 'associated' if it has:
- a 25% holding in the capital of the other company;
- is owned 25% by the other company;
- both companies are 25% owned by a third company.

The Directive was introduced to reduce the administrative burden of implementing double taxation agreements between Member States where associates were paying dividends or royalties to each other, creating reversible incomes or costs in the respective tax calculations. The Directive simplifies the tax treatment of these payments immensely. It is an important advantage for an MNE based in NI (or indeed ROI), since it simplifies the tax compliance burden enormously.

Tax Compliance Since NI is part of the UK, MNEs operating there must comply with UK tax legislation. The UK system is one of self-assessment. The tax-paying MNE must determine its own corporation tax liabilities, generally once a year, and make the necessary payments. Both tax returns and payments must be made electronically using iXBRL, a language for tagging and presenting financial information language in a computer readable format.

Capital Gains Tax Exemptions on Share Disposals As a general rule, a UK company is liable to capital gains tax (CGT) on profits from the disposal of shares. However, if the MNE owns a substantial percentage of the company whose shares are being sold, an exemption can apply. Currently, if an MNE disposes of shares in a trading company and it owns more than 10% of the shares in that company, then, subject to certain rules, the profits on the sale may be exempt from CGT. This is a particularly attractive exemption for an MNE considering buying or setting up a business in NI as it means that, should it choose to exit the business in the future, it may not have to pay CGT on any profit made on the disposal.

R&D Tax Relief and Patent Box Some types of R&D expenditure can be written off against taxable profits at an enhanced rate of up to 200%. This means that the qualifying expenditure can be doubled when making the adjustment to profits to arrive at the taxable profits. For example, an MNE could spend £250,000 on R&D in a particular year. The relief will allow it to claim that it spent £500,000 when calculating the taxable profits. Clearly, this relief is particularly attractive to MNEs engaged in R&D activities.

In addition to being able to claim enhanced deductions for R&D expenditure, MNEs may also be able to avail of reduced corporation tax on profits emanating from any commercialisation of inventions that flow from R&D expenditure. Profits earned from patented inventions can be taxed at the lower rate of 10% since 2013. Though there needs to be a link between the patented income and the R&D expenditure, and there are complex rules as one might expect, essentially, if the MNE developed the invention in the UK, then it ought to be able to get the benefit of the 'patent box' reduced corporation tax rate.

Double Tax Treaty Agreements One concern of MNE managers is to avoid a situation in which the MNE is taxed twice on the same income. This can arise as the laws that govern how and where taxation liabilities arise differ from country to country. In order to mitigate against this, countries have entered into bilateral tax treaties with each other, which seek to ensure that entities, and individuals, are only taxed in one jurisdiction. Such treaties allow for:
- MNEs to claim tax relief in one country for taxes paid in another;
- for the elimination of uneccesary taxation of certain intragroup transactions, such as the imposition of withholding taxes on intragroup interest; and
- the handling of disputes between the different tax authorities (most of which can arise from the interpretation of transfer pricing rules (see **Chapter 16**).

If there is no double taxation treaty in place, an MNE may still find that it can get relief in the UK for certain taxes paid in other jurisdictions.

Tax Treatment of Foreign Workers If the employee of an MNE transfers to a part of the enterprise in NI/UK, then the employee becomes tax resident in the UK/NI if they spend more than 183 days there. They can also become tax resident in the UK/NI if they spend an average of 91 days a year over four consecutive years. The implications of tax residency can be quite substantial for the employee. A UK tax resident employee is taxed on their worldwide income. If the employee was non-resident, they would only be taxed in the UK on their income generated in the UK. It is therefore vital that MNEs understand the taxation implications for their employees as they move them into or out of UK/NI.

Summary of the Case for FDI in Northern Ireland

Investment in NI is attractive to the MNE for a number of reasons, many of which have been detailed in the preceding few sections.
- Location: within the EU and UK, with excellent transport links to both.
- Heritage: a strong history in commercial activity and international trade.
- Taxation: extensive double taxation agrements and attractive reliefs.
- Education: strong investment in higher level education.
- Productivity: room-to-improve productivity presents significant opportunity for innovative MNEs.
- Costs: costs, in particular labour, are lower than the UK average.

Preparing a Case for Foreign Direct Investment

Many MNEs will have a capital allocation process in order to determine where to invest capital to grow new products or services. Usually this process is incorporated into the MNE's annual budgeting process or its longer term strategic planning process. In either case, it may often fall to the MNE managers in each country to prepare a proposition for submission into the capital planning process. This proposition will have the objective of encouraging the MNE to invest capital in the MNE's local business unit.

Step 1 in preparing a case for FDI to present to a potential investor MNE is to invest time in understanding the MNE's strategy, critical to presenting a cogent rationale for inward investment. To prepare this analysis the local MNE Irish managers should:
- study the MNE's strategy and identify its key goals, especially target customers;
- use value chain analysis (see **Chapter 3**) to identify the critical elements relevant to the possible investment;
- consult internally and externally with stakeholders to truly understand what those stakeholders want from the MNE;
- assess which attributes of the Irish economy would contribute to an attractive investment, e.g. if the MNE considering FDI needs qualified engineers, the Irish team should quantify the numbers of qualified engineers available;
- benchmark the Irish attributes with other countries that may be attractive to the MNE.

Step 2 is to consolidate all the research and analysis into an organised report, which should start with an executive summary highlighting the main points. The body of the report should contain the relevant findings, describing how and why Ireland is a good place for FDI. Any data analysis can be attached by way of appendices.

Step 3 involves preparing a presentation. Many MNEs will request that the local management or agency who wish to attract the FDI make a presentation as to their rationale. This presentation is unlikely to be more than 20 minutes, with a further 40 minutes for questions and clarifications. Of course, these timeframes are only indicative and each MNE will have its own processes for assessing FDI proposals.

Step 4 is actually making the case to the prospective investor. In the case of an MNE, the case might be made to the capital committee or some other committee delegated by the MNE's board to carry out the appraisal. The Irish team should avoid the temptation to involve too many people in making the case. It is normally best if two, or at the most three, people make the case in person. This 'making of the case' will involve making the presentation described in **Step 3**. The report should have been circulated in advance to allow some level of preparation to be carried out. MNEs may also prescribe a format of cash-flow projections and investment appraisal, which is likely to be standardised for all submissions. (See **Chapters 11** and **12** for investment appraisal processes.)

In summary, the key to attracting FDI is to understand the MNE's strategic goals and then to map those onto the country's attributes. In this way, the case made will be relevant to the audience.

(The reader is referred also to *Investing in Ireland: A Guide to Foreign Direct Investment in Ireland and Investing in Northern Ireland: A Guide to Foreign Direct Investment in Northern Ireland* both published by Chartered Accountants Ireland and key sources for this section on Ireland as a business location.)

4.11 CONCLUSION

In this chapter we have looked at theories to explain why certain patterns of trade emerge and how MNEs fit into these patterns. We have also seen the importance of international trade to the island of Ireland. The top 10 employers in the Republic of Ireland are all MNEs: seven of them have grown from indigenous Irish companies, while the other three are foreign MNEs investing in Ireland. A similar picture emerges in Northern Ireland. For a flavour of the nature of these companies we looked at high-level summaries of the MNEs in the top 10 in Ireland and Northern Ireland.

The importance of the MNE sector to the economies on the island of Ireland are recognised by the fact that both governments have set up multiple agencies to aid the growth of MNEs. The work of these agencies is broadly broken down into those agencies that help indigenous companies export goods and services and agencies that help and support foreign MNEs locate on the island.

Ireland has been particularly successful in attracting FDI onto the island. Both Northern Ireland and the Republic of Ireland are attractive places for foreign MNEs to locate. In this chapter we have explored why this is the case. We have looked at the demographic attractions the island offers, particularly a young, well-educated workforce. This demographic coupled with excellent infrastructure and governmental supports means that Ireland should remain an attractive place to do business into the future.

International expansion increases the complexity of managing an enterprise. MNEs face more complexity than purely domestic enterprises as they need to deal with different legal and cultural environments together with relationships that need to be managed over long distances and multiple time zones. In the next chapter we will explore how these MNEs are run on behalf of their shareholders and other stakeholders, with a particular focus on corporate governance in MNEs and the role the finance function plays within the corporate governance frameworks.

QUESTIONS

Self-test Questions

4.1 Name two theoretical models of international trade.
4.2 Why do governments support MNEs?
4.3 Name five foreign-owned MNEs whose services you have used in the last 12 months.

Thought-provoking Questions

Question 4.1

You are the CFO of a small manufacturing company, Puck Ltd., based in Killorglin. Your CEO believes that there might be a market for Puck's product internationally. He has heard that there is some kind of government support for such activity, but does not know a lot about it. He has asked you to produce a 400-word report on what government agencies are involved and how they might be used.

Question 4.2

Explain the common attributes of indigenous Irish MNEs that have been successful in internationalising their business.

Review Questions

(See Suggested Solutions to Review Questions in **Appendix B**.)

Question 4.1: R&D Investment

Having read the R&D Investment case study in **Appendix A**, use Porter's Diamond model to aid R&D Investment to present the competitive advantages of locating an R&D facility in Ireland.

Question 4.2: Black Swan Inc

Having read the Black Swan Inc case study in **Appendix A**, advise on the key factors to be considered in selecting an appropriate location for a shared services centre investment and how to attract FDI for businesses operating in Ireland.

5

BUSINESS ETHICS AND CORPORATE GOVERNANCE IN AN INTERNATIONAL CONTEXT

CONTENTS

LEARNING OBJECTIVES

Having read this chapter, you will understand:
- the different theories of ethics (virtue, consequentialism and deontology);
- how ethics affects the business of a multinational enterprise (MNE) – the types of issues that arise and how the MNE should respond to them;
- what stakeholder theory is and how it relates to MNEs;
- how to identify stakeholders depending on the three attributes they might possess: power, legitimacy and urgency;
- how corporate social responsibility (CSR) has developed and is implemented (including some international guidelines for implementing CSR in an MNE);
- what corporate governance is and what approaches can be taken to it;
- the difference between rules-based and principles-based approaches to and codes of corporate governance; and
- the international dimension to corporate governance.

5.1 INTRODUCTION

International trade has developed over the centuries, particularly over the last 50 years. The advent of the company as a vehicle through which to conduct trade together with enabling global government policies and technological advances, has given rise to the globalisation of commercial activity. Most of the largest companies on the island of Ireland are either Irish companies that have expanded their operations into foreign markets, or are foreign companies that have expanded into Ireland. Almost all small and medium-sized companies are also involved in trading with international entities either through the importation of requirements or the export of finished or part-finished goods or services.

We have defined MNEs as enterprises trading with entities outside of their domestic markets, meaning that even the smallest office supply company, importing reams of photocopy paper from France, would be classified as an MNE. The challenges facing companies when engaging in international trade are broadly the same, irrespective of size. The solutions to these challenges might differ but normally only in scale and not in principle.

A company is a separate and distinct legal entity from the persons who own it, the shareholders. As companies become larger they need to employ people other than the shareholders to manage the functions and processes needed in order to produce output and satisfy customer needs. One of the challenges that face companies, therefore, is how to ensure that the persons who have been employed to manage the enterprise on behalf of the shareholders act in the best interest of those shareholders. An associated challenge is how to ensure that the company is managed in accordance with the value system of the shareholders and other stakeholders and that such management practices do not infringe on shared ethical principles. In this chapter we will examine these issues and propose some solutions that can be adopted by MNEs to ensure appropriate corporate governance and adherence to commonly understood ethical principles. **Chapter 6** will then go on to examine the role of the professional accountant in helping the MNE rise to these challenges, amongst others.

5.2 BUSINESS ETHICS IN A GLOBALISED WORLD

In recent times there has been much debate about ethics in business life. The collapse of Enron in 2001, the 2008 financial crisis, the Bernie Madoff affair and the Tesco accounting scandal are just a few of the financial headlines that have brought ethics in business into the spotlight. The collapse in 2013 of a textile factory in Bangladesh, with the loss of 1,137 lives, and the illegal logging in the Brazilian rainforests that led to protest during the 2014 World Cup are just a couple of examples of where commercial activity has fallen foul of understood ethical standards.

The investigation by regulatory authorities into corruption at FIFA, the world's governing body for soccer, is another recent example of serious questions being raised about ethical standards at the highest levels. Indeed, by October 2015, FIFA's own ethics committee was recommending the suspension of its President Sepp Blatter and Vice-President Michel Platini.

Yet another major scandal of global proportions is the use of technology by Volkswagen to reduce emissions from its vehicles when they were being tested by regulators throughout the globe but especially in the US. Volkswagen engineers built into cars' systems a computer program that could detect when the car was being tested for emissions. Once the vehicle's software detected it was being tested, it triggered a system that reduced the emissions until the test was over. In this way, millions of VW cars were accredited with emissions standards that were much lower than the reality of the cars' performance. This was a breach of trust on a number of fronts: **financial**, in that lower taxes are paid on cars with lower emissions; **environmental**, since the cars are emitting many more toxins than was believed to be the case; and **customer loyalty**, in that customers had absolute trust in the figures VW published about their emissions. Customers, in particular, and the wider public in general, have been astounded to think that such a large MNE would plan and execute such a major breach of trust.

In Ireland there have been high-profile incidents that have raised public concerns about 'low standards in high places'. The collapse of Anglo Irish Bank together with the associated bank guarantee has raised such serious questions that they were the subject of two separate enquiries in 2015. The collapse of the Quinn Group of companies and the subsequent court cases only serve to further the public sentiment that standards of probity are not where they should be.

In 2013 and 2014 there were a number of questions raised about the level of tax being paid by large-scale MNEs with operations based in Ireland. When one adds in the public reaction to frequent food contamination scares, the withdrawal of cars due to faulty steering, questions about planning permissions, etc., it is clear that there is a broad perception that businesses operate in an unscrupulous and self-interested fashion with no regard for societal norms of appropriate behaviour and fair dealings. Is there 'a whiff of sulphur from big business'?

The following questions arise:
- Is this negative reaction justified?
- Who decides what is right and wrong?
- Is complying with the letter of the law enough?
- What should MNEs, their management and professional advisors/employees do to ensure they adhere to appropriate ethical standards?

These questions are not new. For millennia traders have wrestled with the issue of balancing ethical standards with the goal of maximising profit. The earliest Chinese dynasties recognised the need to standardise weights and measures so that buyers could compare prices and not be taken advantage of by traders. It is quite amazing to think that in c. 200 BCE Chinese society had evolved to such a degree that this standardisation could be enforced by a central administration.

The Qin dynasty (221–206 BCE) reunited China after the centuries of war during the Zhou dynasty. Qin standardised administration and economic activity, setting up a framework for the conduct of trade. This included a system of standardised weights and measures. Though there is evidence of earlier systems existing, especially in Mesopotamia, the Qin dynasty's system most closely resembles today's systems. The standards were well documented and the infrastructure for enforcement was codified and understood by all citizens.

As the centuries passed, issues of ethics in business came to the forefront at times and receded at others. This ebbing and flowing of the prominence of ethical issues came about as the world's societies connected and disconnected with each other through commerce and war. By the time of the European Renaissance, the philosophical conundrums posed by making profits and conducting commerce were back on the agenda. Various schools of thought developed. On the one hand, some believed that the pursuit of profit, with concern for two simple principles, equity in transactions and the protection of private property, was all that was needed to have an efficient, equitable and just commercial environment. Others argued, however, that it was not enough to just consider the equity of transactions and the protection of private property; consideration should be given to what was good and right for the population as a whole, the common good. They also argued that there needed to be moral boundaries placed upon commercial transactions. (In *The Merchant of Venice*, Shylock's insistence on a pound of flesh by way of debt repayment is an example of how the 'letter' of a commercial transaction can conflict with what is commonly understood to be right.)

EXAMPLE 5.1: THE GREAT FAMINE

In Ireland during the Great Famine in the middle of the 19th Century, the trade in agricultural products other than potatoes continued while hundreds of thousands starved. Landlords, who legally owned the land and the outputs it produced, saw no issue with their continued extraction of rents by way of harvests from the land they owned while at the same time their tenant farmers starved as a result of the successive failure of potato crops. In the landlords' view they were extracting what was rightfully and legally theirs. Who were they to intervene in the unfortunate tragedies that befell their tenants? Indeed, in keeping with the '*laissez faire*' business philosophy of the time, the market will always sort out inefficiencies, and to artificially subsidise these poor tenants through charitable actions was to interfere with the operation of the efficient market. Thus the tenants starved and died whilst the landlords continued their rent extractions. Looking at these events through the lens of today's value system, we may recoil in horror. However, the rights and wrongs of the tragedy of the Great Famine suggest a number of larger questions:
- How is it decided what actions are permissible and appropriate?
- Is complying with the law enough to justify commercial actions?
- Is there a universal code of behaviour that can be adopted?

(This chapter attempts to provide answers to these questions.)

In the 17th and 18th Centuries, the slave trade was just another business. Though there were a few abolitionists, the majority of people considered slavery and indentured servitude as normal. When and where the debate began concerning the morality of the slave trade is hard to pinpoint. In the American colonies there were abolitionists protesting against the injustice of slavery from the middle of the 18th Century. However, the years after the French Revolution seem to show a fall-off in the slave trade in the countries that came under Napoleon's sphere of influence. Indeed, there were slave uprisings in the West Indies fuelled by the ideas of liberty inculcated by the French Revolution. Eventually, slavery was abolished in most areas of the globe by the middle of the 20th Century, though the working conditions of many people in today's globalised world have been described as akin to slavery. The conditions of the workers in impoverished parts of the world pose real ethical questions for the MNE and its managers.

What do such questions and issues mean for today's executive working in a profit-oriented MNE? There is a school of thought that the company executive has responsibility only to his or her employers, to make a profit constrained only by the law of the land. Milton Friedman, the US economist, put this view succinctly:

> "What does it mean to say that the corporate executive has a 'social responsibility' in his capacity as businessman? If this statement is not pure rhetoric, it must mean that he is to act in some way that is not in the interest of his employers. For example, that he is to refrain from increasing the price of the product in order to contribute to the social objective of preventing inflation, even though a price increase would be in the best interests of the corporation. Or that he is to make expenditures on reducing pollution beyond the amount that is in the best interests of the corporation or that is required by law in order to contribute to the social objective of improving the environment. Or that, at the expense of corporate profits, he is to hire 'hardcore' unemployed instead of better qualified available workmen to contribute to the social objective of reducing poverty.
>
> In each of these cases, the corporate executive would be spending someone else's money for a general social interest. Insofar as his actions in accord with his 'social responsibility' reduce returns to stockholders, he is spending their money. Insofar as his actions raise the price to customers, he is spending the customers' money. Insofar as his actions lower the wages of some employees, he is spending their money."[1]

The essence of Friedman's view is that producing sustainable wealth for the owners should be the only goal of the company executive. Ethical issues are relevant only in the sense that ignoring such issues may give rise to risks such as a reduction in the wealth of the business through disgruntled staff, customers, suppliers, etc. In other words, ethical issues are of concern only to the degree that they can be monetised.

Thus, we have on the one hand the view that executives charged with managing MNEs ought to behave in a way that respects a common good and a set of commonly agreed moral and ethical principles and, on the other hand, the view that the actions of the executives should be guided only by the pursuit of sustainable wealth on behalf of the shareholders with adherence to legal frameworks solely.

For executives managing today's complex MNEs there needs to be a way to decide what management actions are appropriate. A tension arises between doing 'what is right' and doing 'what is legal'. Executives will find these tensions exacerbated when competitor companies behave differently from the way they have chosen to behave. An MNE may find that its competitors can find new markets for their goods or sources of lower costs that allow them to gain competitive advantage in ways that may offend its sense of justice and fair play. The management and employees of an MNE can be faced with a very real dilemma when these situations arise. Does it seek the same advantages as its competitors but offend their own ethical standards, or do they stick to their standards and watch their profits fall?

What follows is an examination of how MNEs can reconcile the seemingly irreconcilable. This is possible because, in the long run, **what is good and ethical ought to produce a better environment in which to create long-term sustainable wealth**. This is a key point and can provide both a financial and moral justification for correct behaviours. If an action offends a sense of fair play and justice, then, almost by definition, it will lead, over time, to negative results. Thus, offending common principles of 'rightness' may lead to short-term gains but in the longer run will lead to an unsustainable position. In order to provide an MNE with a set of guidelines, one must examine the areas where ethical considerations of a wider social nature

---

[1] Friedman, M. (1970). "The Social Responsibility of Business is to Increase Profits". *New York Times Magazine*.

overlap with the ethical issues that may damage a company's future profit stream. The techniques to carry out this type of examination are discussed below.

Before we examine what systems and approaches an MNE might adopt to tackle these thorny issues, it is useful to gain a high-level understanding of some of the theories that underpin ethical decision-making and govern how one might distinguish right from wrong in a business context.

5.3 THEORIES OF ETHICS

For thousands of years philosophers have questioned the meaning of life, the nature of the universe, whether we have a higher purpose, and other matters that go to the heart of humankind's existence. Though this text cannot, of course, cover all of these topics, moral philosophy or ethics is one area of philosophy that does need some level of understanding in order to aid ethical decision-making.

Ethics concerns what is good and bad, right and wrong. It also concerns duties and obligations that flow from the consideration of what is right and wrong. It involves beliefs and values that guide the decision-making and behaviours of the individual. Business ethics is a subset of these wider considerations as they arise in the business context.

There are many theories of ethics and almost as many ways to classify those theories. I have used here a simplistic categorisation based on three schools of ethical thought in order to give a high-level picture of the main strands:
- virtue,
- utilitarianism,
- deontology.

Virtue

Aristotle, the 'father' of virtue-based ethics, believed that the whole world is interconnected and that each living thing within it plays its part in the whole. The part that each creature has to play in the world is based upon that individual living being's 'goal'. Each creature has a goal or purpose and as each creature strives to achieve its goal, it is doing good.

Man is a part of this world; within this ethical system, each person must consider their goal in life and then adopt a set of actions and behaviours that lead toward achieving this goal. Each person must contemplate his or her goal and then set about taking actions to achieve that goal. The actions taken on this path are 'good' if they lead toward the achievement of the goal. The Aristotelian system asserts that humankind's true goals are natural and, as they are natural, will tend to further universal improvement as everything and everyone is interconnected.

At first glance, this system looks very individualistic; however, it also considers the societal impact of all these individuals in pursuit of their personal goals recognising that the interconnected nature of the entire world, the 'cosmos', means that goals are constantly evolving and changing since the cosmos is also constantly changing. Individuals come together in order to share information about their goals and the pursuit of those goals. In so doing, they develop shared views on common goals. Individuals then collaborate to develop rules; common rules that, when observed and enforced, encourage and foster the pursuit of individual goals. In this way, society, a collaboration of individuals, formulates shared rules that need to be observed.

In the pursuit of goals the individual must act either individually or as part of a collaboration with others. Actions, however, cannot solely be in pursuit of one's individual goals to the exclusion of all other considerations. One needs a set of guiding principles that will help one distinguish between actions that are 'good' and those that are 'bad'. Following these principles in pursuit of true goals, one will be led to live 'the good life'.

Aristotle proposed that living 'the good life' involved exhibiting virtues, and these virtues were capable of being described. He further observed that virtues were the 'middle ground' of a behaviour type or characteristic. For example, on one side of the virtue of bravery is cowardice; on the other side, recklessness. The person following the 'good life' will consider the appropriate actions for the given situation and will choose wisely.

The main tenets of this school of thought are that:
• good flows from the actual acts of pursuing true goals that lead to happiness; and
• virtue guides behaviour.

For example, a CEO may be considering a new project, the construction of a new head office. Her own office forms part of the new construction. The project manager asks her how big the CEO office should be. She could get a huge office, bigger than all the rest of the offices, or she could get the same as the others, or even smaller. How can Aristotelian ethics help this decision? In the area of major spending, the virtue identified by Aristotle is 'magnificence'. Too little of the virtue is seen as stinginess and miserly, too much as vulgarity and tastelessness. On this basis the CEO would build an office demonstrating magnificence without being vulgar, on the one hand, or stingy, on the other. Thus, the CEO's office would represent the status of the role within the company in such a manner as to be neither ostentatious nor meagre. A CEO making the decision based on virtue ethics alone would select an office that exhibited these virtuous characteristics, neither vulgar nor mean, but yet 'magnificent'.

Utilitarianism

By the mid-17th Century, with 'the Age of Enlightenment', scientific reasoning became more prominent. By observing the physical world, the leading thinkers of the era began to formulate new ways of explaining it. Ethics, what is right and wrong, came under the gaze of this new thinking. The thought developed that whether an action was morally right depended upon the consequences that it brought about. The broad name of this scheme of ethics is **consequentialism**. By the 18th Century, scientific thought concerning consequentialist ethics had developed into a structured approach: the utilitarian view. The first proponent of this structured approach was Jeremy Bentham and, later, John Stuart Mill.

Their key insight was that the 'good life' was the one that led to the most happiness and least pain for the majority, rather than for just the individual pursing his or her individual (albeit true) goals. The main departure in thinking from Aristotle's view is that 'good' is to be defined by the consequences it has on overall happiness. The minimisation of pain and augmentation of happiness are the denominators of good. All 'good' actions must have the **consequence** of increasing the quantity of happiness or reducing the quantity of pain in the world. Mill in his essay, "Utilitarianism", defined happiness as pleasure and the absence of pain. He also differentiated between various types of pleasure, arguing that pleasures founded on humankind's higher faculties and capacities were superior to pleasures based on humankind's more primitive attributes: "it is better to be a human being dissatisfied than a pig satisfied; better to be Socrates dissatisfied than a fool satisfied."[2]

One can see the scientist's love of measurement influencing this school of thought. Systems were developed where the quantity of 'happiness' could be calculated by reference to the number of people affected, the sustainability of the happiness, and the 'halo' effect it might have in encouraging other actions that would lead to happiness.

We can see that the main difference between Aristotle's approach and the utilitarian approach is that Aristotle believed that good was defined by the action of doing what was right in accordance with virtuous behaviour, while the utilitarians believed that good is based on the consequences of actions rather than the actions themselves. The quantitative approach of utilitarianism has some advantages for the commercial manager in that it proposes a system of calculation in order to attempt to quantify the amount of 'goodness' or 'happiness' that will flow from a particular action or course of actions. It also provides a science of sorts behind the decision-making process.

If we reconsider our earlier example of the CEO's office selection, she will now need to consider the overall increase in 'happiness' that will flow from her decision, considering if there are other choices that could deliver more 'happiness'. (Remember: under this approach an action is 'good' if it increases the amount of happiness.) Perhaps with the money saved on a large office some artistic pieces could be bought for the main reception area of the office building. This artwork might bring happiness to many and increase the overall quantum of happiness. If the CEO's office is too small or meagre, she won't be able to do her job properly, leading to unhappy customers and shareholders. A balance needs to be made where the design of the office affords the ability of the CEO to perform her tasks efficiently but without depriving other projects, or indeed the shareholders, of cash. (We will see later, in the section on corporate social responsibility (CSR), how an approach related to these concepts helps decision-making in MNEs.)

Deontology

Deontology is the strand of ethics that emphasises **duty** as the main driver of ethical behaviour. The German philosopher Immanuel Kant formulated his thoughts as a counterpoint to what he saw as a moral deficit in consequentialism, the main strand of which became utilitarianism. In this school of thought it is the *intent* that matters, rather than the consequence. The motivation behind behaviour is what is critical in deciding whether it is good or not.

To illustrate this, let us take an example. A man helps a blind person to cross a busy road. He does so because he believes it is right to help others for no personal gain. Consider, then, another man who, seeing he is being observed by his neighbour whom he wishes to impress, helps a blind person cross the busy road. If he were not being observed, he would not have helped the blind person. He is motivated by vanity and self-interest. In the Kantian worldview, even though the actions are the same, the first man would be acting morally but the second man would not.

But what constitutes a valid motivation? In answering this, Kant argued that we all have duties, the main one being to govern our behaviour by asking ourselves whether the action we are

---

[2] Robson, J.M. (ed.), *The Collected Works of John Stuart Mill*. Toronto: University of Toronto Press, 1963–91, Vol. 10, p. 224.

about to take should be the one everyone should take universally. In other words, would I wish that everyone would act just as I am now about to act? The saying 'do unto others as you would have them do unto you' is a succinct way of capturing the essence of deontology.

> If we return to the CEO and her office decision, she would consider whether her choice should be one that should be applied universally. It might become clear that the bigger the office she chooses, the less likely that the selection could have universal appeal or practicality. The CEO would be more likely to select a modest office, only different from others if the demands of the role required those differences.

We can see that the three approaches, virtue, utilitarianism and deontology, lead to different considerations when making decisions. While the final action may still be the same, the CEO, in this case, will have considered different matters when reflecting upon her choices. We can expand this idea of considering all three approaches into wider ethical decision-making in business. Today's MNE manager need not select one philosophy to the exclusion of the others. By considering a dilemma using all three approaches (or indeed any other recognised ethical theory), the MNE manager can embrace a large number of possible 'correct' actions. Such considerations should improve the quality of the ultimate actions.

5.4 ETHICS AND THE MULTINATIONAL ENTERPRISE

Having considered that there are a number of different frameworks guiding appropriate behaviour for the individual, one must then consider whether these have any relevance for a corporate entity, particularly MNEs. It is often said that companies do not make decisions, people do. While it is true to say that a company has a *legal* personality separate from the people who work for it, it is quite a leap to argue that a company has its own *moral* personality in the same sense.

A company does not have its own sentient existence, its own free will, ability to make decisions or choose what is right or wrong. It is the people who make up the company that have these attributes. Each individual who forms part of an MNE is their own person, guided by their own moral compass. The individual free will of these constituent members of the MNE defines who they are as human beings. When the individual becomes part of an organisation, they must then make decisions in a more complex set of circumstances. Usually, decisions are made in groups such as boards, project teams and departmental committees. The individual finds themselves with other individuals faced with making decisions that often have a moral dimension.

> Imagine a clothing retailer that competes on price. Its clothes are fashionable, but most especially it is successful because its products are priced so cheaply that they are almost disposable. The retailer sources its goods from a third-party supplier which operates a factory in India. The buying team becomes aware that the factory is using child labour. The use of the child labour does not infringe the laws of the region in which the factory is located. If the factory was in Dublin or Belfast, it would not pass even the most basic inspection by the authorities. Upon questioning the supplier about the practice, the buying team learns that to bring the conditions up to 'Western' standards would add 85% to the ex-factory cost of the goods. What should the buying team do?

The buyers in the Milton Friedman camp would leave well enough alone and change nothing. The utilitarians would seek to improve conditions for the Indian workers. MNEs struggle to reconcile these different approaches on a daily basis. The remainder of this chapter gives some insights into how this challenge is being met by modern MNEs.

The Milton Friedman school of thought would say that the MNE's managers have no moral duty other than to make a profit for the owners and within the law. At the other end of the spectrum, utilitarians would believe that the MNE managers should be mindful of all the people affected by their decisions and actions and seek to act morally, guided by something more substantial than the goal of making profit – the goal of doing what is good for society, or at least that element of society that is impacted by the decision.

These two perspectives are not mutually exclusive, however. Consideration of how an action or decision may impact a wider set of stakeholders can lead to decisions that are more profitable for the enterprise in the long run. For example, adverse publicity about a company's actions can influence its customers' willingness to buy its products, suppliers' desire to extend credit, and prospective employees' desire to join the organisation. This negative sentiment should influence the MNE managers' decisions about continuing to pursue actions that *prima facia* can be justified by the pursuit of profit but may have longer term, hidden negative effects on profitability. This dilemma is at the kernel of ethical decision-making in business. What some would see as the 'woolly' realm of ethics and morally guided corporate behaviour can actually impact profits. Behaving morally and being seen to do what is right can create goodwill towards an organisation. Likewise, behaving immorally or amorally can damage goodwill. Given that 'goodwill' is the value attributed to an organisation over and above its actual asset value, decisions and actions that affect goodwill can have a real impact on shareholder wealth.

When one is dealing with ethical issues, it is difficult in most cases to precisely correlate a decision with its associated cost or benefit. The negative effects of a decision viewed as morally wrong are probably easier to assess, and possibly quantify, than the positive effects attributed to a decision seen as morally right. By this I mean that the damage done to a brand or an MNE's status by unethical actions will be easier to ascertain than the possible 'halo effect' of behaving in a morally responsible way. For example, if a retailer is caught using suppliers that are involved in child labour, the effect on profits might be felt immediately. Certainly, the negative press will be noticed. However, a retailer active in supporting child education in developing countries and who has no truck with the exploitation of child labour may enjoy few obvious or direct business benefits as a result. If it publicises its good deeds, it can be seen as self-serving. This difficulty in accounting for the detriments or benefits of ethical choices makes ethical decision-making more problematic than the more straightforward investment appraisal techniques with which accountants and project teams are already familiar.

Business organisations prefer to predict future outcomes of decisions in a quantifiable way. This quantification of possible future outcomes allows for future comparison of actual performance with expected or predicted performance. In this way, an MNE can quantify an expected outcome and then, subsequently, compare the actual performance to this expectation and thereby assess the quality of the decision-making process or the predictive capability of the MNE's managers. Many budgeting processes involve exactly these steps. The comparison of actual to predicted results is then used to make adjustments to the original plans and strategies and the cycle repeats. Therefore, the focus is on quantifiable measurement rather than qualitative measurement of outcomes. However, the measurement of the quality of ethical decisions is less scientific, more subjective and less capable of precise measurement. Consider **Example 5.2** below, where an oil firm can accurately measure actual output and compare it to its predictions. It is much more difficult to measure the possible environmental impacts of the oil well.

EXAMPLE 5.2: THE OIL WELL DILEMMA

An oil well might be expected to produce a measureable 10,000 barrels a day. It might end up producing a measureable 12,000 barrels. These are hard, tangible numbers. How does the MNE predict the environmental impact? Should the possible damage to the environment be netted against the economic benefit to the region that the oil well brings? There will be more jobs and therefore better infrastructure and greater opportunity for self-improvement for the inhabitants of the area where the well is located. MNEs need to come up with organisational structures and processes that ensure consistency in approach when dealing with these matters in accordance with values of the organisation. We will see later on in this chapter how MNEs can structure their processes to ensure consistency of approach to these thorny issues.

5.5 PROFESSIONALS AND ETHICS

Most people face ethical considerations at some stage in their lives, and because of the nature of their work and their trusted positions professional people regularly experience the need to make ethical decisions (e.g. the ethical dilemmas no doubt faced on a daily basis in hospital operating theatres).

In order to facilitate decision-making in the face of such dilemma, professional bodies have developed codes of conduct to guide their members. These codes serve two main purposes:
- to inform and guide the professional practitioner as to what behaviours are expected or allowed;
- to provide transparency to clients, patients, etc., as to what standard of behaviour can be expected.

The sanctions for breaching such codes are usually quite severe, even if a criminal offence has not occurred. By imposing severe sanctions for infractions by its members, professional bodies endeavour to ensure a standard of behaviour that preserves the ethos of the profession and keeps it in good standing with its client population.

The professional accounting bodies that operate in Ireland each have their own code of conduct. These codes go beyond describing what is legal or illegal: they are based on what is 'right and correct behaviour for the conduct of a professional accountant' and are built upon ethical principles. For example, the *Code of Ethics* of Chartered Accountants Ireland is grounded in 'five fundamental ethical principles':
- **Integrity** – to be straightforward and honest in all professional and business relationships;
- **Objectivity** – not to allow bias, conflict of interest or undue influence of others to override professional or business judgements;
- **Professional competence and due care** – to maintain professional knowledge and skill at a level required to ensure that clients or employers receive competent professional service;

- **Confidentiality** – to respect the confidentiality of information acquired as a result of professional and business relationships and, therefore, not disclose any such information to third parties without proper and specific authority, unless there is a legal or professional right or duty to disclose, nor use the information for the personal advantage of the professional accountant or third parties; and
- **Professional behaviour** – to comply with relevant laws and regulations and avoid any action that discredits the profession."

Also enumerated by the *Code of Ethics* are the **threats to compliance with the fundamental principles**, which include:
- **self-interest** – e.g. inappropriate use of company assets;
- **self-review** – e.g. determining the appropriate accounting treatment for a business combination after performing the feasibility study that supported the acquisition decision;
- **advocacy** – e.g. promoting the organisation's position using statements that may be false or misleading;
- **familiarity** – e.g. accepting gifts or preferential treatment the values of which are not trivial or inconsequential; and
- **intimidation** – e.g. a dominant personality attempting to influence the application of an accounting principle to achieve a preferred accounting outcome.

The application of ethical decision-making in the day-to-day business world is just as serious as it is in the operating theatre. To ignore such considerations is to ignore the very real opportunity that business and commerce presents to improve the quality of life for all its stakeholders, not just the shareholders.

5.6 CORPORATE SOCIAL RESPONSIBILITY (CSR)

As MNEs have grown in scale and number over the last few decades, so too have the concerns about how they impact upon the environment and society generally. The MNE is first and foremost a servant of its shareholders – it is there to add value for the investor. As the MNE expands its reach, it touches more and more people and communities, and its impact grows. Countries around the world are at different stages of development, ranging from poor and underdeveloped nations to highly evolved democracies with mature consumer societies. What is legally permissible in one country may be illegal in another. How do MNEs and the global society at large ensure that due recognition is being given to all who are impacted by an MNE's actions?

Since the 1950s the concept of corporate social responsibility (CSR) has developed. The essence of this concept is that companies (MNEs for our purposes) should take responsibility for the impact of their actions and decisions on not just shareholders but also employees, suppliers, customers, wider communities and the environment. There is an obligation placed on the socially responsible MNE to act ethically within society and not just focus on profits for its shareholders. Of course, as mentioned above, behaving ethically can often have the additional benefit of enhancing profits over the long term by improving goodwill and reducing reputational risk.

Making the case for CSR has fallen to world leadership figures who believe that a widespread adoption and adherence to these commonly understood principles would be of societal benefit to all. Often these thought-leaders come from outside the business world and are to be found amongst leaders of charities, religions, or collaborative organisations whose goals are more than just about making profits. Kofi Annan's view quoted below contrasts quite sharply with the Milton Friedman view discussed above. Annan draws particular attention to the role of the

MNE and the positive effect that globalised MNEs can have on the quality of life for the people of the world:

"There has been progress and the importance of corporate responsibility has entered the mainstream.

But we need to go further. For example, it is no longer enough for business leaders to say they meet national standards in the countries in which they operate.

If we are to make globalization work for all and not just a minority, if we are concerned about the sustainability of our planet, then businesses at local and global level must take the lead in driving up standards on labour and human rights and on the environment.

Nor is good enough for businesses again to ignore the impact of their reckless pursuit of profit at the expense of everyone and everything else."[3]

The graph in **Figure 5.1** below is taken from an analysis by the European Commission of 200 companies in the EU that have over 1,000 employees and some MNE activity. It shows that 68% of these MNEs have some adherence to CSR policies and indicates the level of commitment to the main global CSR standards. However, it also shows that 32% of these randomly selected companies do not have any CSR policy evidenced in their public documentation or websites. If the sample is representative, it suggests that there are still many companies that would more closely align themselves with Milton Friedman than with Kofi Annan.

FIGURE 5.1: ADHERENCE TO CSP POLICIES IN LARGE EU MNEs[4]

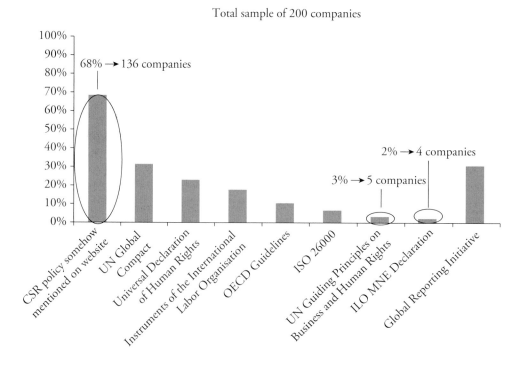

Total sample of 200 companies

---

[3] Kofi Annan, "Governance and Values", Speech, Oslo, February 2009.
[4] European Commission, 2013. *An Analysis of Policy References made by large EU Companies to Internationally Recognised CSR Guidelines and Principles*, March 2013.

The x axis lists the various CSR policies that the MNEs in the sample mention in their public documentation that they adhere to. (Global guidelines are dealt with in more detail further on in this chapter.)

Implementing CSR Policy in a Multinational Enterprise

To understand how managers may go about implementing CSR, we need to understand its basic components. According to Archie Carrol (1991), there are four components of social responsibility:
- legal,
- ethical,
- economic, and
- philanthropic.[5]

The components of CSR can be summarised into the four-letter acronym '**LEEP**', as set out in **Figure 5.2** below:

FIGURE 5.2: THE 'LEEP' COMPONENTS OF CSR

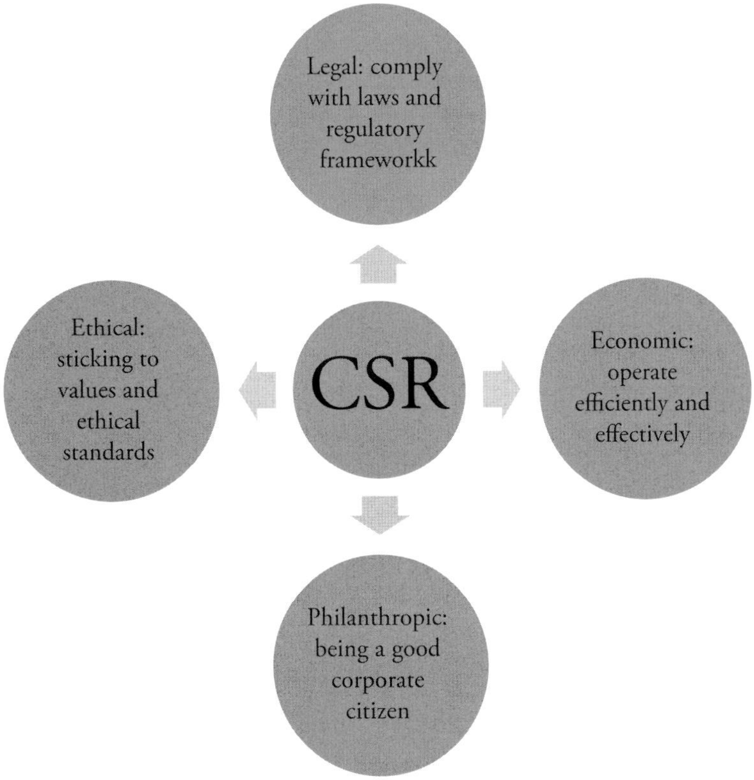

- **Legal** comprises the obligations on the MNE to comply with all laws and regulations pertaining to the countries and markets in which they operate.
- **Economic** component is concerned with the obligation on the MNE to produce a return on investment for the shareholders. It also includes an obligation to produce goods that are valuable to society, to create jobs, and to manage in an efficient way that is not wasteful.

---

[5] Carroll, A. (1991), "The pyramid of corporate social responsibility: toward the moral management of organizational stakeholders", *Business Horizons*, 34(4), 39–48.

- **Ethical** component means sticking to values and ethical standards. This component is about going over and above what is required by laws and regulations. Examples of this would include not over-stating the MNE's product capabilities in the marketing program, or not hiding important details in the small print of a service contract. Often a passing observer equates CSR with this ethical component solely; however, as we have seen, there are three other components to CSR in the context of an MNE.
- **Philanthropic** component captures the obligation on the MNE to be a good corporate citizen. For example, in 2014 coffee producer Kenco supported an initiative in Honduras to provide vulnerable young people with an opportunity to improve their lives by training them as coffee farmers. The idea was to show them that there was an alternative to the gang culture lifestyle that has become so problematic in the country.[6]

Carroll also proposed that these four components exist in a hierarchy where, without the support of the component on the level below, the higher up component would not function. Accordingly, he proposed a pyramid-type view of the four components, as shown in **Figure 5.3** below. The economic responsibility component supports the legal responsibility component, which supports the ethical responsibilities component, and so forth.

FIGURE 5.3: CARROLL'S CSR PYRAMID[7]

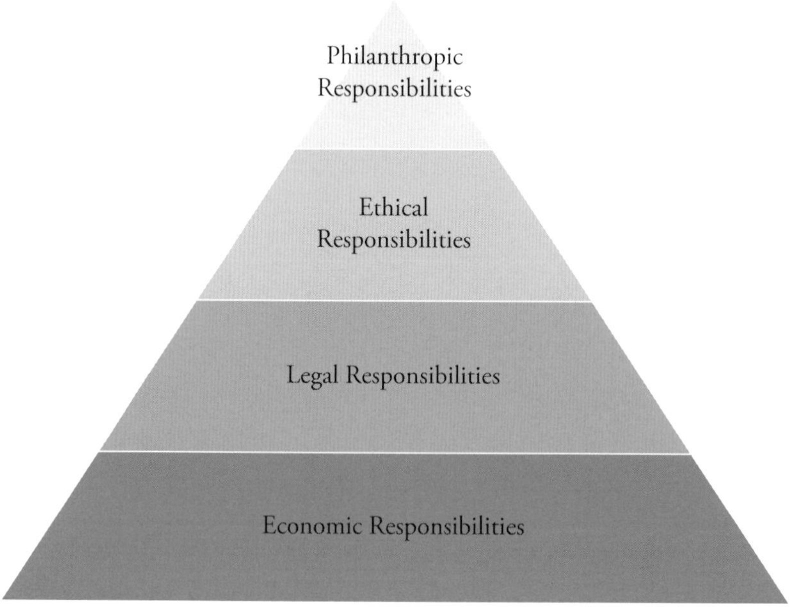

In 2004 Carroll introduced the notion of stakeholder groupings to the model.[8] This new linking of the LEEP components with the stakeholder concept meant that MNEs also needed to

---

[6] www.coffeevsgangs.com (accessed May 2015).

[7] Adapted from Carroll, A. (1991), "The Pyramid of CSR: Toward the Moral Management of Organisational Stakeholders", *Business Horizons*, July–August.

[8] Carroll, A. (2004), "Managing Ethically with Global Stakeholders: a Present and Future Challenge", *Academy of Management Executive*, Vol. 18, No. 2, 114–120.

consider how the four LEEP components apply to what Carroll identified as the five major stakeholder groups of the MNE:

- owners,
- customers,
- employees,
- local communities, and
- society at large.

To implement a CSR policy effectively, the MNE will need to consider each stakeholder and each component together. For example, looking at the legal component, how does the current legislation affect our customers? A specific example would be the law requiring retailers to seek 'proof of age' from customers wishing to buy alcohol. An MNE formulating CSR policy will need to come up with processes that allow it to comply with the legal requirement to seek the 'proof of age' while at the same time needing to ensure that *bona fide* customers are not overly discommoded.

A useful way to think about the LEEP components and stakeholders when formulating a CSR policy and an associated implementation plan is to recognise that there are four LEEP components and five stakeholder groupings. Therefore, there are 20 areas to be examined and considered by an MNE in formulating its CSR policy if they choose to use Carroll's method.

Not only does the LEEP component/stakeholder consideration need to take account of the current situation concerning each stakeholder group, but also how it might change in the future. By considering how such possible changes could impact the MNE and how the MNE might impact stakeholders, the MNE's managers can adopt and adapt strategies that reduce the risk of negative outcomes and maximise opportunities. So, taking our earlier example of the legal requirement for retailers in Ireland and the UK to obtain 'proof of age' when approached by customers looking to buy alcohol, imagine that the Government proposes to change the age requirement, raising it from 18 to 21. The CSR policy and its attendant strategies will need to be reformulated to take account of these changes. In this way, the CSR policy and strategy becomes a dynamic suite of practices and procedures rather than something that is cast in stone, never to change.

For CSR to work effectively in an MNE, it needs to be integrated into the strategic planning and leadership function of the organisation. CSR should be at the heart of an organisation, not merely a compliance activity carried out by a single department or team. MNEs that successfully implement meaningful CSR will usually have a board and a CEO who is committed to its principles.

Below is a statement on CSR from the website (www.greencore.ie) of the Irish food giant, Greencore Plc. As you can read in the interview with Greecore's CEO, Patrick Coveney, in **Appendix C.3** of this book, Greencore implements CSR through 'The Greencore Way', which is how Greencore links CSR with business strategy and execution.

"**Corporate Social Responsibility**

As a leading food manufacturer and major employer in the core markets in which we operate, we believe we have a duty to maintain strong integrity and sustainable corporate and social responsibility practices for the benefit of our people, our customers, our suppliers, the environment, our shareholders and our communities.

> We aim to operate in a sustainable and responsible manner. To embed and drive this approach within our organisation we have developed a framework, which we call 'The Greencore Way'. This framework is based on four core operating principles:
>
> 1. **People at the core**
> 2. **Great food**
> 3. **Business effectiveness**
> 4. **Cost efficiency**
>
> The Greencore Way sets out how we apply these principles to our behaviours and actions on a day-to-day basis. It also creates a vision and goals for our desired outcomes with our key stakeholders – our people, our customers, our suppliers, the environment, our communities and our shareholders. This report therefore discusses our vision and goals and how we are doing against each of these stakeholders."

Each of the LEEP components needs to be understood in the context of each of the stakeholder groupings. Since it is the people who make decisions in organisations, it is imperative that there is good communication throughout the MNE of the CSR approach chosen by the organisation. In other words, the CSR policy and LEEP components cannot be embedded in the organisation without embedding them into the thought processes and decision-making of its people. CSR policy and LEEP components are not like an air-conditioning system; you cannot just 'install' and plug them in to make them work. A communication system is needed. This communication system needs to be coupled with clear expectations of what behaviours are encouraged and an identification of those behaviours that are considered inappropriate.

Some organisations endeavour to implement their CSR systems through extensive rules and procedures. These compliance-based systems will typically have written rules, codes of conduct, behaviour measurement systems and sanctions for breaches and indiscretions. However, a drawback with this approach is that it is difficult to envisage all potential scenarios and, consequently, it is difficult to have scripted rules in place for all eventualities. It is also challenging to enforce moral behaviour on employees without a degree of cynicism developing, especially if the corporate ethical standards are at variance with individual employees' own values. For example, an MNE may seek to impose gender quotas on recruitment and promotion. Some managers may embrace rules that seek to enforce the quota system. However, some may bristle, especially if they do not have the same value system. Another source of dysfunction when trying to impose rules-based moral behaviours occurs when employees see that senior managers do not follow such rules themselves. For example, profanity may be frowned upon by the MNE and actively discouraged through the CSR policy. If the CEO is noted for colourful language and uses profanity in many scenarios, then employees who observe this behaviour will most likely take quite a cynical view of the policy and its associated rules and behaviour codes.

A different approach can be taken other than adopting a compliance-based approach. A more holistic implementation of CSR has been for an MNE to inculcate their values and core purpose through all decision-making in the organisation. While an organisation adopting this approach may still show some features of a compliance-based system, it has made the effort to instil CSR deeper into the DNA of the organisation. By developing shared values, an MNE can have more assurance that knowledge of these values will guide decision-making throughout the firm. In **Example 5.3** we can see how Twitter has embedded the principles of CSR through the proactive leadership of its founder, Biz Stone.

EXAMPLE 5.3: TWITTER AND CSR

Founded in the US, the micro-blogging company Twitter has been voted one of the best companies in the world for corporate culture and values.[9] The company's founder, Biz Stone, believes in the principles of CSR and talks about them often in his press briefings and media engagements. These high-visibility utterances set the tone. Twitter also actively encourages behaviours in accordance with the desired moral code and value system through team meetings, employee feedback systems, and internal communications systems. Twitter also makes its Code of Business Conduct and Ethics public and easily visible to customers.[10]

Global Guidelines for Corporate Responsibility

Though most large MNEs based in Europe have adopted CSR principles to some degree, as yet the adoption of CSR is not obligatory and all of the guidelines discussed below are just that – guidelines. Compliance with the guidelines is not audited by any external agency as they are aspirational and part of the global effort to improve corporate behaviour. This global effort is presently voluntary and is based on setting out best practices and making CSR an attractive option for MNEs.

An MNE wishing to adopt a CSR approach does not have to start from scratch. A number of guidelines have been set out at various global summits over the last 20 years, which can be used or referred to by the MNE in formulating its CSR policy. Some major initiatives developed by the various world organisations include:
- The OECD Guidelines for Multinational Enterprises (OECD Guidelines) includes guidelines for MNEs wishing to implement CSR.[11]
- The United Nations Global Compact.
- The Universal Declaration on Human Rights (Article 23 of which focuses on the rights of workers. Subsection 2 emphasises the "right to equal pay for equal work" and subsection 4 stresses that "everyone has the right to form and to join trade unions for the protection of his interests".)
- The United Nations Guiding Principles on Business and Human Rights. (Following on from the endorsement of the United Nations Guiding Principles on Business and Human rights in 2011, the Business and Human Rights Resource Centre created a set of tools that MNEs can use to help implement CSR in their organisations.)
- ISO 26000 Guidance Standard of Social Responsibility (ISO 26000).
- ILO Core Conventions and the Declaration on Fundamental Principles and Rights at Work (Instruments of the ILO).
- ILO Tripartite Declaration of Principles concerning Multinational Enterprises on Social Policy (ILO MNE Declaration).
- The Global Reporting Initiative (GRI).

---

[9] Fortune.com/2014/08/22/twitter-tops-list-company-culture/ (accessed May 2015).

[10] Files.shareholder.com/twitter_code_of_business_conduct_and _ethics (accessed May 2015).

[11] *OECD Guidelines for Multinational Enterprises*, www.oecd.org/corporate/1922428.pdf

While these guidelines may differ, they also share key similarities, albeit with differing levels of emphasis. In 2001, Kathryn Gordon identified eight themes that emerge from an analysis of six of the major global guidelines, or 'instruments', for corporate responsibility[12]:

* consumer protection;
* transparency in reporting and accountability;
* corporate governance standards;
* legal compliance, including corruption issues;
* involvement in local communities;
* protection of the environment;
* labour conditions and workers' rights; and
* basic human rights, child or slave labour, working hours.

The six global instruments for corporate responsibility that Gordon analysed are set out below.[13]

Caux Principles for Business (1994)

The Caux Round Table (CRT) is a network of business leaders that seek to promote improvements in the practice of business, especially international business, through enhanced observation and implementation of a set of moral principles. The group first met in Caux, Switzerland in 1986 and adopt what they term 'moral capitalism'. In 1994, CRT issued the CRT Principles for Responsible Business. The network encourages MNEs to become more 'moral' by implementing the CRT Principles for Business. There are seven core principles:

* respect stakeholders beyond shareholders;
* contribute to economic, social and environmental development;
* build trust by going beyond the letter of the law;
* respect rules and conventions;
* support responsible globalisation;
* respect the environment; and
* avoid illicit activities.

The CRT support MNEs in implementing CSR policies that follow these principles through support networks, consultative dialogues and guidelines. The guidelines are constantly updated with new strategies for implementation but, as you might expect, the core principles remain the same.

Global Reporting Initiative (GRI)

The Coalition of Environmentally Responsible Economies (CERES) is a non-profit organisation that promotes 'sustainability leadership'. As part of this initiative CERES encourages adoption of and adherence to its Global Reporting Initiative (GRI) Guidelines, which were first issued in 1999 but have since been finessed and updated on a regular basis. The GRI is a standardised approach to reporting that CERES hopes MNEs would adopt in their financial and other reporting processes. CERES seeks to encourage MNEs to publish reports in accordance with its guidelines by advocating best practice and, in some instances, meeting directly with shareholders or investors in order to demonstrate the benefits and advantages of adopting the GRI. Implementation of the guidelines is voluntary.

---

[12] Gordon, K. (2001), "The OECD Guidelines and Other Corporate Responsibility Instruments: A Comparison", OECD Working Papers on International Investment, 2001/05, OECD Publishing. http://www.oecd.org/corporate/mne/WP-2001_5.pdf

[13] Material adapted from *Business for Social Responsibility* (2000) and quoted in Gordon, K. (2001).

CERES measures the penetration of GRI by regular surveys, most recently in 2014.[14] The most recent report analyses the reporting of 613 of the largest public companies in the US and assesses their adherence to the GRI guidelines. Whilst CERES is happy that there has been some progress over the years in integrating sustainability into the operational and strategic decision-making of these corporations, they point to the slow progress as a cause for concern. An MNE wishing to adopt GRI does not have to be at the scale of the largest corporations. An additional advantage of GRI is that it is a non-financial reporting initiative and, as such, should not pose any disclosure or regulatory challenges from a financial reporting point of view.

Global Sullivan Principles (1999)

Reverend Leon Sullivan was an African-American minister who joined the board of US auto manufacturer General Motors in the 1970s. General Motors was a large employer in South Africa at the time, when the system of apartheid was still in effect. Sullivan developed a set of principles that sought to extinguish racially-motivated policies and behaviours in the workplace. In 1999 Sullivan reissued his principles, now reworked with the help of the then UN Secretary General, Kofi Annan, and several multinational companies. The idea was to encourage MNEs to publicly endorse the eight principles and to work them into their operational policies. The statement of the principles that an MNE would issue would be as follows:

"We will:

- Express our support for universal human rights and, particularly, those of our employees, the communities within which we operate, and parties with whom we do business.
- Promote equal opportunity for our employees at all levels of the company with respect to issues such as color, race, gender, age, ethnicity or religious beliefs, and operate without unacceptable worker treatment such as the exploitation of children, physical punishment, female abuse, involuntary servitude, or other forms of abuse.
- Respect our employees' voluntary freedom of association.
- Compensate our employees to enable them to meet at least their basic needs and provide the opportunity to improve their skill and capability to raise their social and economic opportunities.
- Provide a safe and healthy workplace; protect human health and the environment; and promote sustainable development.
- Promote fair competition including respect for intellectual and other property rights, and not offer, pay or accept bribes.
- Work with governments and communities in which we do business to improve the quality of life in those communities – their educational, cultural, economic and social well-being – and seek to provide training and opportunities for workers from disadvantaged backgrounds.
- Promote the application of these principles by those with whom we do business.

We will be transparent in our implementation of these principles and provide information which demonstrates publicly our commitment to them."

OECD Guidelines for Multinational Enterprises (revised 2011)

The Organisation for Economic Co-operation and Development (OECD) is concerned with the ethical dimension of managing enterprises with ever-increasing focus as MNEs have grown

---

[14] Gaining Ground: Corporate Progress on the CERES Roadmap for Sustainability, downloaded from www. Ceres.org/gainingground (11 May 2015).

in scale and standing since the 1970s. Countries who are members of the OECD and who have signed up to the Guidelines are expected to appoint National Contact Points (NCPs) to actively promote compliance within their respective countries. The guidelines were first introduced in 1976 and have been updated five times since then, most recently in 2011. The guidelines embrace nine core areas of business conduct and there are 60 standards in the guidelines associated with these areas. The guidelines are only recommendations and it is the responsibility of each country that has committed to the principles to promote adherence within its jurisdiction. Since MNEs operate internationally, most will find that they operate in a number of countries that have each committed to the guidelines, although it is possible that they may also operate in countries that have not made such a commitment. The general approach is for the MNE to engage with the NCP in the country where it has most of its commercial activities. There is also a section in the guidelines encouraging MNEs to operate cross-divisional information-sharing processes across the divisions of the MNE to inculcate best practice.

The OECD has published a useful brochure on the Guidelines, including a few examples of the guidelines in action in Africa.[15] The continent of Africa is rich in natural resources. Historically, the extraction of these resources by MNEs from outside the continent has been a source of human rights violations and environmental concerns. The OECD worked with stakeholders to put together guidelines for the ethical extraction of African mineral resources. The guidance led to a five-step framework that can serve as a template for MNEs wishing to engage in these extraction activities. Aside from the specific African examples, this brochure gives some helpful advice to MNEs considering how to implement CSR into their organisations. The NCP in Ireland is the Department for Jobs, Enterprise and Innovation and the NCP in the UK is the Department for Business, Innovation and Skills.

Social Accountability International (SA8000)

Social Accountability International (SAI) is an international voluntary advisory group made up primarily of trades unions, NGOs and civil society groupings. Like the other five systems for CSR implementation mentioned, implementation of SAI is voluntary. However, it includes an auditable standard, SA8000. Since the standard is auditable and therefore externally validated, the adherence to SA8000 can provide the MNE with external validation of its commitment to the standard and thereby to CSR principles. The SA8000 has been revised and updated a number of times since its inception in 1997, most recently in 2014. The application of the standard is modelled on the implantation of other quality standards in manufacturing and industry, such as ISO 9000 and ISO 14000. The approach of SA8000 is to set performance indicators which demonstrate the existence of standard behaviour and conduct. The external auditor then seeks evidence for the existence of the standard in operation through the explicit observation and measurement of the performance indicators. SAI also provides training to organisations wishing to implement SA8000.

United Nations Global Compact

The UN Global Compact is a policy initiative by the United Nations for MNEs that are committed to implementing CSR by having policies and procedures that are in accordance with 10 principles laid down which cover the areas of human rights, the environment, labour practices and anti-corruption. It has over 12,000 corporate participants and is in operation in over 145 countries. The 10 principles are:

---

[15] *Responsible Business Conduct Matters, OECD Guidelines for Multinational Enterprises*, https://mneguidelines.oecd.org/MNEguidelines_RBCmatters.pdf

"**Human Rights**
- Principle 1: Businesses should support and respect the protection of internationally proclaimed human rights; and
- Principle 2: make sure that they are not complicit in human rights abuses.

Labour
- Principle 3: Businesses should uphold the freedom of association and the effective recognition of the right to collective bargaining;
- Principle 4: the elimination of all forms of forced and compulsory labour;
- Principle 5: the effective abolition of child labour; and
- Principle 6: the elimination of discrimination in respect of employment and occupation.

Environment
- Principle 7: Businesses should support a precautionary approach to environmental challenges;
- Principle 8: undertake initiatives to promote greater environmental responsibility; and
- Principle 9: encourage the development and diffusion of environmentally friendly technologies.

Anti-Corruption
- Principle 10: Businesses should work against corruption in all its forms, including extortion and bribery."

The UN provides MNEs with supports and guidelines to help them implement the UN Global Compact. The UN published a report in 2011[16] that was the result of an in-depth survey of CSR practices, the largest of its kind ever undertaken. It found that although CSR is growing in importance and implementation is on the increase, the pace needs to be stepped up. It also found that just over a quarter of respondents believed that CSR was embedded into their corporate strategies and that these companies tended to be larger MNEs. MNEs commit to updating the UN Global compact with their progress annually and this update is made through the reporting of a Communication on Progress (CoP). Where an organisation fails to issue a CoP two years in a row, it is expelled from the scheme. In 2014 over 300 MNEs were expelled from the scheme for not complying with the CoP requirement, representing around 10% of all participating MNEs.

The UN Global Compact and the OECD Guidelines have the advantage of being supported by global collaborative organisations, which tend to be backed by member governments. This backing provides for fairly large budgets to support the initiatives and means that there are good supports available for MNEs wishing to implement CSR using the OECD Guidelines or the UN Global Compact framework.

Whatever the CSR approach or model chosen, it is important to tailor the framework to the individual MNE's own specific vision, mission and value system. If this tailoring exercise is not done, the risk is that the CSR initiative will become a box-ticking exercise rather than something meaningful for all stakeholders.

---

[16] Annual Review of Business Policies and Actions to Advance Sustainability, www.unglobalcompact.org/aboutthegc/annual_review

Stakeholder Theory

We have already mentioned 'stakeholders' in the context of CSR and explored the connection between the LEEP (legal, economic, ethical and philanthropic) components of CSR and stakeholders in order to best formulate strategies for incorporating CSR into the fabric of an MNE. We will now return to the concept of stakeholders. It is critical for any MNE implementing a CSR policy, whichever model is chosen, that it understands its relationships with its stakeholders. For this reason it is important to be able to identify those stakeholders and to pinpoint which relationships are appropriate for the MNE to have with each class of identified stakeholder.

In 1984, R. Edward Freeman proposed the concept of stakeholder management as a more appropriate business model than focusing solely on profit or shareholders. His observation was that all commercial enterprises, including MNEs, cannot focus solely on the pursuit of profit for their shareholders. He contended that an MNE will impact on other groups of people and institutions and that these impacts have counteracting forces on the MNE. If the MNE does not consider the position of these counterparties, it might underestimate the risks associated with negative responses, or miss opportunities that might be afforded by more collaborative relationships. To organise his thoughts and ideas about these relationships, he defined the other parties as **stakeholders**. He further sought to cluster these stakeholders into groups that had similar relationships to the MNE. He identified stakeholders as "any group or individual who can affect or is affected by the achievement of the organisation's objectives".[17]

Freeman's definition of a stakeholder is very wide. Indeed, for large, global MNEs, a manager might struggle to define who is *not* a stakeholder. In order to bring some sense of perspective to the definition and to focus management actions, Mitchell, Agle and Wood (1997) developed a stakeholder identification model,[18] which not only proposes a system to identify stakeholders but also suggests a method for deciding the level of priority to be given to each stakeholder depending upon certain attributes.

The core of the Mitchell, Agle and Wood stakeholder identification model is the notion that stakeholders will possess one or more of the following three attributes:
* the **power** to influence the MNE;
* the **legitimacy** of the stakeholder's relationship to the MNE;
* the **urgency** of the stakeholder's claim on the MNE.

The identification process involves assessing each stakeholder against these three attributes. The result of the allocation of attributes will produce a classification of all stakeholders into sub-groups where each sub-group will have one, two or all three of the attributes. The authors do not propose any specific treatment of each of the different classes of stakeholder depending on the number and type of attributes allocated to them. Rather, they have deduced that managers respond differently to each of these stakeholder classifications. They argue that by performing the analysis, an observer of MNE behaviour can gain greater understanding of the behaviour patterns that exist in the relationships between the MNE and its stakeholders. Building on that understanding, one can also predict how the stakeholders and

---

[17] Freeman, R. Edward (1984), *Strategic Management: A Stakeholder Approach*. Boston: Pitman.

[18] Mitchell, R., Agle, B. and Wood, D. (1997). "Toward a theory of stakeholder identification and salience", *Academy of Management Review*, 22: 853–886.

the managers' behaviours will change as stakeholders acquire or lose attributes as circumstances change.

Stakeholders Possessing One Attribute: Latent

If a stakeholder group possesses only one of these attributes, it is classified as 'latent'. Depending on which attribute they have, latent stakeholders are either dormant (power attribute), demanding (urgency attribute) or discretion (legitimacy attribute). While latent stakeholders need monitoring and some management, they are a low priority for management. Remember, the classification system designed by Mitchell, Agle and Wood does not propose that any class of stakeholder ought to be treated in a particular way. The research they carried out confirmed that stakeholders that fall into the different categories ARE treated in that way by managers in an MNE. The emphasis of the classification system is that if an analysis is carried out, it allows the MNE to know how different classes of stakeholder are being treated, assuming the MNE conforms to the observed behaviour patterns in the authors' research. More importantly, it helps the MNE to anticipate what actions it may need to plan for if stakeholders move from one classification to another. The anticipation of a classification change and the planned response can be very important.

For example, a residents' association representing the local community in the vicinity of an MNE's manufacturing plant may be classified by the stakeholder analysis as having some legitimacy since it represents stakeholders living in the immediate vicinity of the factory. Their lives are affected by the operation of the factory; deliveries and dispatches from the plant, noise of machinery and so forth. If the MNE applies for planning permission, it will need to engage in the planning process and advertise the plans locally. The planning authorities will seek observations and suggestions from interested parties. Now the residence association acquires some power since it can object to the MNE's plans and slow down the process. A good stakeholder analysis will anticipate this change in classification and provoke the management to engage with the residents' association in a meaningful way at the earliest stage possible, maybe even before any plans have been submitted to the local authority. In this way the stakeholders' views can be factored into the planning process, thus minimising the possibility of hostility and delays to the project.

Stakeholders Possessing Two Attributes: Expectant

If a stakeholder possesses two of the attributes, they acquire greater significance for the management of the enterprise. This level of stakeholder is labelled '**expectant**'. The sub types of expectant stakeholder are dependent on which of the two attributes they possess.

Power and legitimacy attributes combine to produce **dominant** stakeholders. These stakeholders have the power to influence the MNE and have a legitimate entitlement to do so. The residents' association in the example went from being classed as 'discretion' to 'power' as they progressed from having one attribute, 'legitimacy', to having a second, 'power', once the planning process was anticipated. However, there is no urgency about their relationship with the MNE. These two attributes combine to make them what's termed 'dominant'.

If the stakeholder has power and an urgent need but has no legitimate claim, then they are classified as **dangerous**. This is because, by implication, their claim is not legitimate but they have power to influence the MNE. For example, secondary picketing, where striking workers picket the premises of a connected party of the primary party they have the dispute with, such as a customer, is an example of this 'dangerous' stakeholder group. The picketers have power since they could stop entrance and egress from the MNE's business premises. They also have urgency associated with their need for a resolution of their issues. However, they do not have legitimacy since the MNE whose premises they are picketing has no control over the resolution of the disputed issue, nor are they legally involved. Secondary picketing is illegal in most countries, including the UK and, in almost all circumstances, in the Republic of Ireland.

The third type of stakeholder group classification that possesses two attributes is the one that has a legitimate relationship with the MNE and whose issue is one of an urgent or time-bound nature. By implication such a stakeholder has no direct power to influence the MNE and vice versa. Many lobby groups can fall into this classification. For example, a small group of an MNE's customers may object to the MNE's activities in some way, for example, animal welfare practices amongst the MNE's suppliers. The group is not sizeable enough to exert any meaningful influence on the MNE. The MNE's importance to the lives of the small customer group is not of a scale to mean it, the MNE, can exert any real power influence over the group. However, the group may engage in disruptive tactics, such as boycotting products supplied by the MNE or carrying out high-profile publicity events to try to influence the MNE's practices. An example of this class of stakeholder might be the 'Shell to Sea' campaign group in the West of Ireland.

EXAMPLE 5.4: SHELL AND STAKEHOLDER CLASSIFICATION

In 1996 a natural gas field was discovered off the north-west coast of Ireland. It was a large find and the first off the Irish coast since the Kinsale gas find in 1976. A joint venture between three parties was set up to commercialise the find. The three parties involved in the project were Shell E&P, which would operate the extraction process and build the site with 45% share of the venture, Statoil Exploration (Ireland) Ltd with 36.5% and Marathon International Petroleum Hibernia Ltd with 18.5%. Shell has proposed to develop the gas field by extracting the gas from below the seabed and bringing it ashore for refining and further processing. Shell believes this system to be in accordance with best practice in the industry. Local residents, amongst others, have objected to this approach. They believe there are risks to the local environment from the process and wish to encourage Shell to change their plans and to refine the gas off shore. The campaign by the objectors to the on-shore refinery is called 'Shell to Sea'. It has been very effective in gaining high profile for its argument and delaying Shell's development of the on-shore refinery. The group had very little actual power over Shell and vice versa. Nonetheless, the activities of the campaign have commanded huge efforts and resources on both sides.

Stakeholders Possessing Three Attributes: Definitive

Finally, if a stakeholder group possesses all three attributes, or power, legitimacy and urgency, then they will be treated as a top priority by management. The class of stakeholder possessing all three attributes is called **definitive** in this classification system. Research by Mitchell, Agle and Wood showed that stakeholders in this class will most certainly be gaining the attention of the MNE managers.

FIGURE 5.4: STAKEHOLDER IDENTIFICATION[19]

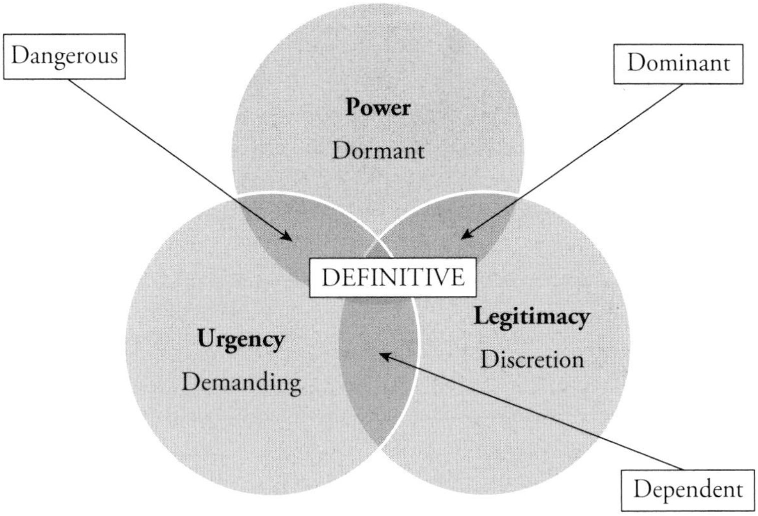

The stakeholder identification model provides the MNE manager with a useful classification system for identifying stakeholder groupings and prioritising management's planning in how to deal with each grouping. For example, stakeholders who are classified as having power and urgency but lacking legitimacy are labelled as 'dangerous'.

Groupings that possess no legitimacy are often discounted by managers in considering their plans and actions, e.g. "Why should we pay attention to people whose claims upon us are not legitimate?" This 'high moral ground' approach is eschewed by the model, which proposes that such stakeholders are 'expectant' in that they have two of the other attributes and should be prioritised as such by management. Environmental campaigners, illegally occupying a business's premises or otherwise seeking to prevent execution of legal actions by the MNE, might fit this classification.

EXAMPLE 5.5: ANIMAL RIGHTS AND STAKEHOLDER CLASSIFICATION

In May 2015 a group of animal welfare activists entered a restaurant in central Dublin. While two or three of them distracted staff by pretending to seek a certain type of table, others approached the water tank containing live lobsters and removed them from the tank. They took the live lobsters to the sea and released them. The whole activity was filmed by the action group and released onto YouTube. It was also released to the news desks of the major TV companies. The group were protesting at the imminent killing of the lobsters and described the matter as a 'life or death' affair and believed this issue transcended the obvious illegality of their actions. The restaurant concerned took quite a solid approach: they respected and acknowledged the campaigners' concerns about animal welfare and the plight of lobsters in particular, but expressed a wish that the protest might take a different form in the future. What they did not do was condemn the illegal actions taken by the protesters or suggest pressing for criminal charges, calling the police, or any other action that might

---

[19] Adapted from Mitchell, Agle and Wood (1997), see above n.18.

enflame the matter. So, although the actions of the campaign had no legitimate basis at law, the restaurant chose actions which accommodated the protests while subtly making their own feelings known without escalating the matter.

In 1984, Mary Manning, who was employed by Irish grocery chain Dunnes Stores, refused to handle oranges grown in South Africa as a protest against the apartheid system there. While there were trade sanctions against South Africa at the time, trade in agricultural produce was not banned as it was deemed by the UN to be disproportionately of benefit to the peoples oppressed by the regime in comparison to other forms of trade.

Nonetheless, many anti-apartheid supporters felt the trade sanctions did not go far enough and Mary Manning's trade union issued an instruction not to handle South African produce, which Mary followed. She was suspended by Dunnes for not fulfilling her contractual duties and for the following three years Mary and 10 of her colleagues picketed their employer's store in central Dublin.

The strike ended when the Irish Government banned the import of fruit and vegetables from South Africa in 1987. Such had been the worldwide support for the cause of the workers that when Nelson Mandela was released from prison in 1990, he visited them in Dublin. When Mandela died in 2013, the strikers were invited to his funeral and the matter was recounted to a whole new generation of shoppers. There is a street named after Mary Manning in Johannesburg.

The strike has left a long-lasting perception amongst some that Dunnes Stores is a profit-hungry, capitalist organisation that does not care about the welfare of its staff or its suppliers. However, it is impossible to know whether this sentiment has any meaningful commercial impact on Dunnes Stores as its market share has grown since the dispute ended, and has remained steady at 22% of the Irish grocery trade for the 10 years from 2005 to 2015.[20] Nonetheless, it is possible that Dunnes Stores might have had a much higher market share had there not been this underlying negative perception about the business stemming from this strike.

The strikers were stakeholders with the attributes of power and urgency. Their strike efforts exposed the cause to Dunnes' customers who had legitimacy in the sense that they were customers and therefore had some entitlement to raise any issues they had with the company. Almost 30 years later the strike is still remembered and talked about by the public, even though it only involved 10 members of staff.

Stakeholder analysis and management is a dynamic process that needs to be integrated into an MNE's management structure. It should not be viewed as a 'nice to have' or something to be delegated to the HR department. The process is dynamic since the world is constantly changing and the attributes possessed by each type of stakeholder change with it.

A management team should regularly go through the following process:
1. identify the organisation's stakeholders;
2. understand and describe the relationship the stakeholders have with the MNE;
3. classify attributes of each stakeholder group, using the model described above or some other stakeholder classification tool;

---

[20] www.kantarworldpanel.com/global/grocery-market-share/ireland/snapshot (accessed May 2015).

4. identify which of the 'LEEP' components of CSR apply to each stakeholder group;
5. formulate strategies for dealing with each class of stakeholder and a monitoring system. This monitoring system will ensure that the outcome of steps 1 to 4 above remain relevant for the MNE. One way of ensuring that the analysis stays relevant is to repeat it annually or twice a year, and to include the carrying-out of the process as a measure on the MNE's reporting system, say the strategic scorecard (see **Chapter 18** for a discussion of strategic scorecards).

CSR and the Law

We have looked at the challenge in deciding what is right or wrong from an ethical point of view. Managers must manage increasingly complex affairs in MNEs and need a systematic approach to guide the behaviours of the enterprise as it conducts its business around the world. The concept of CSR, the global guidelines for same, and the principles of stakeholder management give the MNE manager a toolkit to enable a structured approach to an area of management that can sometimes feel vague and full of rhetoric rather than substance.

In 2014, the EU introduced laws to ensure that large companies reported on non-financial matters in their annual reports,[21] which is evidence of the commitment of legislators to ensuring that companies, including MNEs, play a responsible role in society, are accountable and have regard to their stakeholders.

Under new rules to come into force in 2017, large companies (over 500 employees) in the EU will need to report on a 'comply-or-explain' basis on their environmental and social performance. If they fail to report this information, they will need to specify the reasons for this failure.

The companies in question will be required to disclose in their annual reports relevant and material information on policies, outcomes and risks, including the due diligence that they implement and relevant non-financial KPIs concerning environmental, social and employee-related matters, respect for human rights, anti-corruption and bribery issues and diversity on their boards. The due diligence dimension of this requirement might become quite onerous on an MNE. For example, an MNE may state that it seeks to only use products bought from suppliers who do not use child labour. The onus will be on the MNE to describe what due diligence it carries out to ensure that this pledge is translated into actual behaviour.

What the new EU Regulations demonstrate is that society at large will increasingly want MNEs to be concerned with more than just making profits for their owners. These changes in social expectations will lead to increased responsibilities on managers and executives in MNEs.

5.7 ETHICAL DECISION-MAKING MODELS

The MNE is a more complex entity to manage than a purely domestic enterprise. This complexity comes from the fact that business relationships and resources flow across borders into new jurisdictions where the same 'rules' do not apply. New rules, laws, customs and cultures must be considered, and with those considerations come new risks to be managed – risks that can and do affect future cash flows.

---

[21] Council of the European Union Press Release 26/2/2014, http://gr2014.eu/sites/default/files/hatzidakis%20COREPER.pdf (accessed March 2015).

In managing MNEs, managers historically concerned themselves with increasing profits for the owners of the business in compliance with the law. As we have seen, this relatively simple principle has been complicated by the development and general acceptance of stakeholder theory and CSR guidelines issued by some of the most important global authorities. It might not be enough anymore to make profit at the expense of other responsibilities. In the past, managers were measured, and rewarded, on their ability to produce profits for the firm. Now that MNEs have much more complex sets of obligations and goals, the tasking of managers becomes more complex: now the MNE must still deliver profits for its shareholders while also creating the environment that supports the other, non-financial goals and objectives of the organisation. But how does an MNE make sure its executives make decisions that are aligned to the organisation's value system? How does the MNE ensure an ethical and moral code is both observed and used to formulate decisions and actions?

Ethical decision-making models have evolved since the 1980s as business ethics have become more centre-stage. These models can be used by the MNE to ensure that a clearly understood and accepted process is applied throughout the decision-making process in the organisation. The 'right' decision may not always be made, but, as in other realms of the business world, a good process can improve the chances of the right decision being made. As we have seen, there are many ethical decision-making frameworks that an MNE can choose. In addition, professional bodies such as Chartered Accountants Ireland or the Law Society have ethical codes of conduct that can be used by members, and others, in formulating decisions. Members of those bodies may combine their professional body's guidelines with one or more of the more generic frameworks that exist.

There are many frameworks for ethical decision-making and which one an MNE adopts is a matter for each individual enterprise and its management. What is most important is for the MNE to *have* an ethical decision-making framework, whether developed in-house or adopted, and to ensure that it is well understood throughout the organisation and embedded into its processes and practices.

We will consider two such frameworks at a high level:
• Rion's five-stage model; and
• Hodgson's three-stage framework.

These two models are simple yet very practical in their application. The sequential steps involved in each of the two models afford a sense of structure and direction to the decision-making process and prevent circular discussions and considerations.

Rion's Five-stage Model

Dr. Michael Rion developed this practical and straightforward ethical decision-making framework in the 1990s.[22] It has particular appeal to MNE managers as it is specifically developed for the business environment, although it could be used in other non-commercial scenarios.

Rion formulated the model while he was director of Corporate Responsibility at Cummins Engine Company in the US. Cummins is a large manufacturer of engines, employing over 40,000 people throughout the globe. Rion saw the need for a practical decision-making

---

[22] Rion, Michael, Dr (1996). *The Responsible Manager: Practical Strategies for Ethical Decision Making*, Resources for Ethics and Management.

framework that was simple but also gave due consideration to the weighty issues involved in dealing with ethical issues. He developed a five-stage framework that led those involved through a process that culminated in a decision being made. Rion worked in the business world with Cummins and would have appreciated that procrastination is the enemy of prompt decision-making. He would also have understood that ethical considerations can lead to procrastination as decision-makers struggle to decide what to do while they search for guidelines in the grey areas of the ethics world. The five stages are:

1. **Why is this bothering me?** In posing this question first, the framework elicits whether the issue is really an ethical one or just a complex one. When considering the issue in this context, the MNE manager ought to try and classify the areas of concern, usually into one of the areas such as fairness, promise-keeping or avoiding doing harm. For example, an MNE manager may be grappling with the issue of locating an extension to a factory, but she knows that it will damage the local wildlife, and this bothers her. When answering the question of why this bothers her, she will recognise that it is because she would wish the MNE to avoid doing any harm.

2. **Who else matters?** The second step of the process involves considering all the stakeholders who might be impacted by the decision. Having identified who the stakeholders are, the idea is to consider the issue from each of their viewpoints. The decision-maker should also consider the impact the decision will have on each of these stakeholders.

3. **Is it my problem?** The third stage involves ascertaining whether the problem is the responsibility of the decision-maker, or of someone else. This consideration goes to the heart of duties and obligations. In an integrated and interdependent business world, most decisions involve a number of connected parties in the formulation of the decision. It is important that the decision-maker understands whether the decision to be made is actually their responsibility. Answering this question can be more difficult than first appears. Since we are dealing with ethical consideration, it is not a question about whether this is legally or technically the decision-maker's problem: it is a question of whether there is a moral obligation on the decision-maker to avoid doing harm or carrying out a good deed. For example, a manager may be aware that a manager in another department is harassing a junior member of staff. There may be no immediate connection between the two managers and, technically, it is not his concern. However, upon consideration of the issue, he decides it is his problem since he has a moral obligation to ensure appropriate and dignified treatment of all staff, even if they are not his direct reports. (Employer codes of conduct can help with this type of issue.)

4. **What do others think?** Having identified why the issue concerns him or her, who else is affected, and that the issue is his or her problem, the manager will now consult others about the issue. Seeking the views of others will usually introduce different or new perspectives on the same issue; other people may give different weighting to the information available to the decision-maker. However, it is important to recognise that seeking the views of others can also have the opposite effect. A matter that looked easily resolvable becomes muddy and unclear when the manager finds that there are many ways of approaching the same issue. However, as a general rule, eliciting views from others will help the decision-making process.

5. **Am I being true to myself?** The final step in the process involves deciding on a course of action and then appraising it with this question. This step validates the ethical justification of the decision. For example, the decision-maker can ask, 'would I be happy if this decision was in the newspapers?' as a self-check on its ethical validity. The decision can also be cross-referenced to any professional code of ethics to ensure that it complies with professional

guidelines and codes of conduct. If the decision passes the 'true to self' test, the manager should proceed to implement it. If not, the manager should go back through the process to arrive at an option that will pass this stage.

Hodgson's Three-stage Framework

In 1992, Kent Hodgson developed his thoughts about ethical decision-making in an appropriately titled book, *A Rock and a Hard Place: How to Make Ethical Business Decisions When the Choices are Tough*.[23] In it, he emphasises the need for organisational values and principles to be developed and adhered to within a business, and proposes a three-stage framework to aid ethical decision-making. The framework essentially involves developing a set of possible options and then choosing the one that has the most responsible general principles.

Hodgson's three-step framework offers the decision-makers in an MNE a pragmatic process for bringing together the business action options available and linking them with values and principles. The framework also combines accepted general principles, such as honesty, integrity and fair dealing into the process. Adopting the process allows the MNE manager to know that there is a structure that should produce effective, responsible and justifiable decision-making.

- **Stage One:** the situation is examined by getting the critical facts, identifying the key stakeholders, and identifying what each stakeholder wants to be done.
- **Stage Two:** establish the dilemma. In this stage, the decision-makers ascertain why each stakeholder wants their particular option to be done. For example, the sales people in an MNE may wish to launch a new product that has not yet been through all the quality checks that the manufacturing department would like to carry out. In stage two, the process would identify the options that deliver upon each stakeholder's wishes. Options that offend any legal or corporate code should be excluded at this stage.

  Having identified each possible option, the decision-maker must forecast the consequences of each option by envisaging the steps needed to implement the option, and the consequences of each of those action steps.

- **Stage Three:** in stage three, the decision-maker now examines all the possible options and identifies the general principles behind each of them. For example, the sales people in the above situation are working on the principle of maximising the return for the shareholder by wanting to launch the product as soon as possible. They may also want to satisfy a promise that the company made to its customers about when the product will be available. The manufacturing team want to complete their quality checks and are operating on the principle of ensuring product quality standards are being met. The premise of this third stage is that the option with the most responsible general principles supporting it is the one that is selected. This can be a subjective assessment in itself. However, option selections that involve ethical dilemmas will be aided and improved by the use of Hodgson's three-stage model.

Hodgson's model can been seen as being the selection of a decision from an array of options generated by consideration of what each stakeholder grouping would want. Rion's 5-stage model might be more internally focused, but it still involves stakeholder considerations. As mentioned earlier, whichever model the MNE chooses, the application of a framework will improve ethical decision-making quality and consistency.

---

[23] Hodgson, K. (1992), *A Rock and a Hard Place*. New York: AMACOM, American Management Association.

The use of established frameworks to aid practical, ethical decision-making produces superior choices. It encourages and supports structured analysis, which contributes to a more complete and evolved perspective on the decision facing the organisation. Such frameworks also provide an audit trail that allows retrospective examination of how a decision was arrived at and what aspects were considered. The examination of how decisions were made helps organisations improve future decision-making and learn from past successes and failures.

The current trend for MNEs in decision-making processes is that the profit considerations alone are not enough in today's interconnected world. MNEs must work out their organisational values and how these values can underpin their decision-making process. World bodies, academics and practitioners have developed sets of guidelines, processes and frameworks that allow the MNE manager to formulate appropriate courses of action.

5.8 CORPORATE GOVERNANCE

We have seen that MNEs need professional managers to manage them on behalf of the investor shareholders specifically, while acting responsibly toward the wider stakeholder community. We have seen, through a brief examination of ethics, that deciding what is right and wrong is not necessarily straightforward. We went on to examine how the field of CSR sought to marry ethics with corporate responsibility. In particular, we saw how stakeholder analysis can help identify who and what are going to be affected by corporate actions. In this section, we now move on to examining how the MNE can organise its own management, its governance, in order to ensure the best outcomes for all stakeholders.

As an organisation grows in size, a gap can arise between the owners of the company and those who are actually running the company. The shareholders elect a board of directors to represent their interests and hold executive management to account. Structures should then be put in place to allow the shareholders to hold the *board* to account. Sometimes, executive management are elected to the board of a company, such as the CEO and the CFO. The result can be confusion over the respective roles involved and who is holding whom to account. Boards of directors can sometimes align themselves too closely with management, seeing management as executors of their decisions and creating a feeling that a criticism of one is a criticism of the other. To clarify the situation and to define how various roles relate to each other, different codes of corporate governance have been drawn up around the world.

The *UK Corporate Governance Code*,[24] issued in 2010 and updated in 2012 and 2014, is the authoritative code for MNEs. In the Republic of Ireland, the UK code is seen as best practice and adherence to its principles is encouraged. The Irish Stock Exchange issued a supplementary 'Irish Corporate Governance Code Annex',[25] which is to be read in conjunction with the UK code and focuses mainly on Irish Plcs. The *UK Governance Code* establishes standards under five broad principles:

---

[24] *UK Corporate Governance Code* (FRC 2010, 2012, 2014).

[25] Irish Stock Exchange, *Main Security and Market Listing Rules and Admission to Trading Rules*, Appendix 4 (the "Irish Corporate Governance Annex") (ISE, 2011).

- **Board Leadership** where the code outlines how the board is composed and outlines its responsibilities.
- **Effectiveness** sets the standards underpinning how the board will be recruited with particular focus on its efficacy once it is operating.
- **Accountability** sets the standards covering how the board makes itself accountable to the shareholders and how it holds the management accountable.
- **Remuneration** is the standard of how directors' remuneration is set and, in particular, the transparency of board remuneration levels.
- **Relations with Shareholders** communicates the standard that the board is expected to reach in its communications with shareholders and the management of shareholder participation in the company.

All MNEs need management. Management involves the planning, coordination, motivation and control of the MNE. Broadly, corporate governance is the system by which management executes these activities. While in recent years the term 'corporate governance' has come to take on a narrower meaning linked with ethics in the boardroom, we can still describe general corporate governance structures and principles and apply these to MNEs in a way that also encompasses this narrower definition. Thus, corporate governance encompasses more than just the decision-making in the boardroom (the narrower definition), but the entire suite of management controls, processes, risk management and accountability.

The corporate governance laws, rules and codes of practice that have developed over the years have tended to focus primarily on shareholders' rights, the composition of boards, and executive remuneration. Governance laws and codes have also focused on processes to deal with ensuring independence and delivering equitable treatment of other governance matters, such as looking to the divisions of responsibilities and rights between shareholders, boards and executive management. Indeed, these checklists of rules and regulations might represent the codification of expected behaviours for boards and companies in general.

It is worth noting that it is possible to comply with these codes and still have a badly run company with little more than a token regard for corporate governance. The truism 'you can't legislate for morality' comes to mind. Having said that, it is useful to have a generally accepted, structured set of corporate governance guidelines, which allow external examination and assessment of what corporate governance principles are being applied in an organisation. Having a set of corporate governance guidelines at least sets a standard which is examinable and capable of being audited.

In this text we also consider the wider dimensions of corporate governance, equating good governance with good management. An appropriate system that delivers good management will, almost by default, deliver good corporate governance. (See **Appendix C.3**.)

This leads us to try to define what good corporate governance is. There are many texts on management strategy and organisation design and each will deal with various aspects of corporate governance. From an examination of those texts the reader can deduce some common themes.

The consultancy and advisory firm Applied Corporate Governance has developed 'Five Golden Rules'[26] for good corporate governance from its study of best practice in leading organisations:

---

[26] www.applied-corporate-governance.com (accessed May 2015).

1. Ethics: there is a clearly ethical basis to the organisation.
2. Aligned business goals: the organisation has appropriate goals, arrived at through the creation of a suitable stakeholder decision-making model.
3. Strategic management: the organisation has an effective strategy process that incorporates stakeholder value.
4. Organisation: the organisation is suitably structured to effect good corporate governance.
5. Reporting: the organisation has reporting systems that are structured to provide transparency and accountability.

The stakeholders in an MNE all have an interest in or are affected by the actions of that MNE. Some are actively involved in its decision-making processes; others are more removed from the core of the MNE but are still active in its operation. For example, non-executive directors are not involved in the day-to-day running of the MNE and do not have any executive power to control its activities. However, they do wield power and influence and can play an active, but less involved, role than an employee at the coalface.

In **Figure 5.6** you can see how the various stakeholders are linked to the MNE. The MNE is at the core, surrounded by the stakeholders who are most closely linked to it, such as employees, customers and so forth. Also linked to the MNE, but not as closely, is the wider community in which the MNE operates, including government agencies, shareholders and so on.

FIGURE 5.6: RELATIONSHIP OF STAKEHOLDERS TO THE MNE

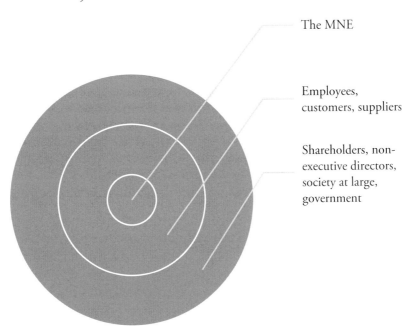

The MNE

Employees, customers, suppliers

Shareholders, non-executive directors, society at large, government

By understanding all of the MNE's stakeholders' needs, wants and perspectives, management and the board can formulate the appropriate structures of good corporate governance in keeping with best practice along the lines of the 'Five Golden Rules' outlined above by Applied Corporate Governance.

The Codification of Corporate Governance

The codification of corporate governance has stepped up in intensity due to some of the high-profile corporate collapses in recent decades, such as Enron (2001) and Lehman Brothers (2008). Enron, a US energy company, collapsed into bankruptcy in 2001 after institutionalised accounting fraud was discovered to have been behind its seemingly meteoric growth. In 2008, Lehman Brothers, a US financial services giant, collapsed into bankruptcy after its asset base was down-graded by the credit ratings agencies. It subsequently transpired that a contributory factor to the collapse was an overstatement of financial results, particularly the strength of the balance sheet (also known as the statement of financial position).[27] Examination after the events of what caused these collapses and the loss of shareholders' monies has led to the identification of issues that were poorly handled. Almost always the post-collapse investigations highlight a knowledge gap between what the shareholders were aware of and what the company was actually doing. Sometimes, there is a lack of knowledge at the board level, where management have either not informed the board what is happening, or have misled them. The result of the identification of these causes of company collapse, or 'malfeasance', has led to the introduction of more comprehensive codes of behaviour and structure for companies and their boards. Some of these codes carry legal obligations or are preconditions for listings on certain stock exchanges. An example of where adherence to a code is a precondition in order to obtain a listing on a stock market is the *UK Corporate Governance Code,* which an MNE must commit to adhering to before it can secure a listing on the London Stock Exchange.

Since the 1970s, the pace of codification of corporate governance has accelerated. As well as high-profile corporate scandals alluded to above, the main drivers of this have been:
- Globalisation and the rapid growth of MNEs has led to increasingly complex business models that are beyond the scope of what the shareholder can readily grasp or see. Hence the requirement that the shareholder and other stakeholders must be able to rely and trust that best practice is in operation.
- Concerns about transparency in financial reporting: increasingly complex financial instruments and derivatives together with large scale merger and acquisition activity have led to increased complexity in financial reporting. This complexity, together with the lack of global accounting standards, has meant that accounts have become more difficult to interpret over the decades. Investors and other readers of accounts placed increased reliance upon the standards that underpin the preparation of financial statements.
- Differentiation between foreign and domestic investors: investors have become more diverse, with many MNEs having shareholders from multiple countries across the world. Each investor may have a different expectation of what and how the business should be managed. The codification of standards ensures that an objective standard is applied by the MNE to its governance environment.
- Differences between countries and cultures: MNEs operate in different countries and what is legal in one country may be illegal in another. The application of an external code allows all stakeholders to know what standard the MNE operates to. It also means that competing MNEs must adhere to a common standard, thus ensuring that one may not take a 'short-cut' to gain an advantage on another.

---

[27] www.csmonitor.com/usa/2010/0312/Lehman-bros.-used-accounting-trick-amid-financial-crisis-and-earlier (accessed October 2015).

The OECD Principles of Corporate Governance

Following an extensive consultation process with its member countries, the OECD (the Organisation for Economic and Cultural Development) has drawn up five key principles of corporate governance. The principles were first published in 1999 and then updated in 2004. As of December 2014 they are again under review. They aim to inform governments of the principles they should seek to enshrine in the corporate governance cultures in their own countries. They are mainly concerned with issues related to the separation of ownership of an enterprise and its management. The principles are:

- **The rights of shareholders** Shareholders should have their rights to attend, participate in and vote at general meetings protected. They also should have the ability to appoint and remove directors from the board.
- **The equitable treatment of shareholders** All shareholders with the same class of share should be treated the same and rank *pari passu*.[28] Blockages to cross-border shareholdings should be removed to allow shareholders from around the world to have shares in the firm.
- **The role of stakeholders** All stakeholders should have their rights protected and should receive timely and relevant information. Stakeholders should be allowed to freely voice concerns over illegal or unethical behaviours.
- **Disclosure and transparency** All material items should be communicated to shareholders, including financial forecasts, material departures from expected results, financial reporting and governance matters.
- **The responsibility of the board** The board is responsible for guiding the company on behalf of the owners. Directors should be in receipt of the appropriate information to allow them to carry out their responsibilities.[29]

Governments and legislators around the world have endeavoured to use these principles to shape their own specific codes. While the principles may have been widely consulted in the formulation of various codes, differences have now arisen between codes of corporate governance in different parts of the world. These differences are primarily as a result of the different heritage of the legal systems and business cultures in operation around the world. In South Korea, for example, some of the largest enterprises, such as Samsung, are still controlled by family dynasties while not being majority-owned by them. Historically, the South Korean Government has been happy with this arrangement and even encouraged it. By 2014, however, the Government recognised that the current practices would not meet more developed corporate governance principles and are seeking to change the way these companies are being run. Whether they can make those changes remains to be seen.

Types of Corporate Governance Code

There has been ongoing debate internationally about the form that corporate governance codes should take. One school of thought, the OECD approach, is that the codes should be voluntary and principles-based. The other, more prescriptive approach, is that the codes should be legal and regulatory with rules governing what is allowed and permissible and what actions are prohibited. The Sarbanes–Oxley Act in the US, for example, follows this rules-based approach.

---

[28] *Pari passu* is a Latin phrase meaning 'with an equal step'. It is now commonly used to rank different parties as equal. In other words, two parties who are *pari passu* will rank equally in whatever matter is to hand and being considered.

[29] OECD Principles of Corporate Governance (OECD 2004).

Rules-based Codes   Rules-based approaches to corporate governance have at their heart measureable targets and outcomes. These systems tend not to focus on the underlying ethos but rather on a compliance environment. Put another way, either you have complied with the rule or you have not.

One of the challenges of rules-based systems is that the rules need to be well defined and leave no room or scope for ambiguity or misunderstanding. Achieving this level of definitive rule-making is easier said than done given the variety of ownership models and industry types that exist.

A further challenge for a rules-based system is that, of necessity, there needs to be a rigorous enforcement system. In other words, an entity could comply with the *letter* of the regulation while defying the *spirit* of it. This makes enforcement difficult because the basis of any challenge being made can be rebutted by the offending entity claiming that it has complied with the regulations.

The Sarbanes–Oxley Act in the US, introduced in 2002 after a number of high-profile corporate collapses, is the most widely applied rules-based corporate governance code in the English-speaking world.

For the MNE, rules-based systems can present problems and choices. Laws can only be enforced by the courts empowered to do so in a specific jurisdiction. Therefore, an MNE that operates across borders is presented with a choice: we must ensure that the organisation complies with the law, but which law? In a simple situation where there is one parent company that owns 100% of all the subsidiary companies, the position is relatively simple: comply with the laws of the country where the company is registered. But when the company is owned by international investors and where, through joint stock companies and other ownership structures, the subsidiary companies are companies registered in other countries with outside shareholdings, the issue becomes more complex. An Irish company may have a controlling interest in a US company through a 40% shareholding, with the remaining 60% owned by institutional international investors. The MNE must decide how to ensure it has the correct structures in place to comply with the relevant corporate governance codes in each jurisdiction. Because we are talking about rules-based systems, there is a legal onus upon the MNE to comply with the rules in the relevant country. Therefore, an MNE with operations in India and Mexico must comply with the rules based codes in both jurisdictions, or receive some type of waiver. Therefore, rules-based systems, especially where they are based on legislation, can present particular challenges for entities like MNEs that have operations in multiple jurisdictions.

Principles-based Systems   Principles-based systems set *qualitative* objectives in the sense that they tend to focus on relationships and an organisation's culture. The relationships between the MNE and its stakeholders are critical in a principles-based system. Standards of behaviour are set out that describe what principles should be applied to the conduct of each of the relationship types. The principles built around these themes do not lend themselves to prescriptive regulation since they are based upon behaviours and relationships which often present challenges for legislators. These challenges stem from the fact that all situations will be different and the relationships that exist in each MNE will differ from one MNE to another.

Where principles-based corporate governance guidelines are in place, the enforcement tends to be of a 'comply or explain' nature, meaning that an organisation must state whether it complies with a relevant code and where it does not, it must explain why.

One advantage of a principles-based system for MNEs is that it can be applied internationally, across borders. Once the principles are established by the parent company, they can be cascaded down throughout the organisation. The 'comply or explain' approach can be implemented throughout the group structure of the MNE, whether its organisational culture is centralised or decentralised. If an MNE had a listing on an exchange where a rules-based system applied, such as the US, it would have to comply with the regulations there.

While not enshrined in legislation, principles-based systems are often insisted upon by stock exchanges in order for a company to obtain a listing. For example, to be listed on the London Stock Exchange a company must comply with the *UK Corporate Governance Code*.

The Irish Stock Exchange (ISE) recognises that the *UK Corporate Governance Code* has set the standard for corporate governance internationally. The ISE has required, since 1995, that all companies listed on the exchange state in its annual report how the *UK Corporate Governance Code* (and its predecessors) has been applied to the company. Following a report in 2010 commissioned by the ISE and the Irish Association of Investment Managers (IAIM), the ISE strengthened the requirement through the publication of a new Irish Corporate Governance Annex (the 'Irish Annex'), which implements the nine recommendations that flowed from the 2010-commissioned report, setting out requirements for additional disclosures relating to board appointments and their operation, audit committees and remuneration, essentially giving an Irish flavour to the UK code, particularly with regard to the size of relevant organisations.

In other instances, a company will specifically say it has complied with the code, even though it is not strictly obliged to as it has not sought a listing. (Companies often do the same with regard to accounting disclosures, complying with the disclosure requirements of a Plc even though they may be privately owned.)

Rules-based systems can lead to a grudging, box-ticking compliance approach to corporate governance, which surely misses the point. Principles-based systems have the benefit of having access to internationally understood guidelines, such as the OECD's, with the MNE still having the choice not to implement certain parts if such implementation would be inappropriate. The MNE then has the opportunity to explain the deviation from the principles and the investor can decide what to do.

While there is an argument that there is greater transparency in the principles-based approach, because they set a broad visible code of behaviour, critics would say that as the principles are non-binding, unscrupulous managers can simply ignore them. A further criticism is that the principles may be worded so broadly that the intent becomes ambiguous.

In reality, most countries have developed a combination of the two approaches: legislating some aspects of corporate governance through rules-based systems and producing principles-based guidelines which are encouraged but remain voluntary. While this hybrid approach would appear to make the most sense, nevertheless the fact that different countries place different levels of emphasis on different parts of their corporate governance codes can lead to disparities across the globe.

International Codes of Governance

Over 100 corporate governance codes have been issued by various countries throughout the world.[30] Some of these are rules-based but most are principles-based, following the OECD's lead. The MNE manager must be aware of the governance codes in force in the countries in which the company operates. Even if the MNE has trading relationships, but does not have subsidiary operations in the relevant countries, it is still important to understand what frameworks are to be complied with by trading partners with whom an MNE develops relationships.

Where an MNE sources some of its goods from a supplier in a foreign country, the managers should ensure that the supplier complies with the relevant codes in its home country. If the supplier does not comply with the code pertaining to its own country, then it may signal other governance or compliance issues with the supplier. It also may signal infringements on the MNE's own ethics code. For example, an ethics code may state that an MNE will only source goods from suppliers that comply with local corporate governance codes.

Boards and Corporate Governance

It is the responsibility of the board of directors to ensure that good corporate governance is implemented in an MNE and that all relevant codes are complied with. Over time, two basic board structures have emerged. In many countries the **unitary** board system applies. This system is prevalent in the US, UK, Ireland, Australia and Canada, as well as in Russia and Japan. In this system there is one board comprising members of management who have executive roles in the company, and other directors who have no executive function (non-executive directors) within the business.

The other board structure is called the **dual** board system. In this system there are two boards, one a supervisory board, comprising entirely non-executive directors and the other, a management board, made up of executives. The dual board system is prevalent in Germany, Austria and Poland. There are advantages and disadvantages to both structures:

	Unitary Board	**Dual Board**
Advantages	Represent shareholders through non-executives	Represent shareholders through non-executives
	Direct relationships between management and non-executives	Strong objectivity since board is outside day-to-day influence
	The whole board sees the same information	Chairman and CEO power balance more effective
	Relatively inexpensive	All members are non-executive
Disadvantages	Powerful position of CEO	Lack of direct relationships between non-executives and management
	Possible lack of objectivity	Higher costs
	Group-think	Confusion as to whether both boards see the same information

---

[30] www.ecgi.org/codes/all_codes.php (accessed June 2015).

All directors' share dealings are governed by strict disclosure regulations in most developed stock exchanges, whether the unitary or dual mode applies. There will often be supplemental regulations governing how the remuneration of directors and senior management is set. While these regulations differ in their precise formulation around the world, essentially they adhere to the principle of the independence of the directors' remuneration-setting process together with shareholder approval requirements.

5.9 CONCLUSION

Worryingly, a number of recent surveys have raised the issue of risk-management at board level.[31] These surveys indicate that boards are spending no more time on risk management today compared to pre-2008, or are delegating the responsibility to board sub-committees. This is despite the identification by many of a deficit in this area being a contributory cause to the global recession of 2008 onward. One such survey is the "Improving board governance" global survey from McKinsey in 2013, which, under the heading "Room for Improvement", states that[32]:

> "While respondents say their boards are taking more responsibility for strategy, risk management is still a weak spot – perhaps because boards (and companies) are increasingly complacent about risks, as we move further out from the 2008 financial crisis. This is the one issue where the share of directors reporting sufficient knowledge has not increased: 29 percent now say their boards have limited or no understanding of the risks their companies face. What's more, they say their boards spend just 12 percent of their time on risk management, an even smaller share of time than two years ago.
>
> Despite the progress they report, directors identify the same factors that would most likely improve board performance as respondents did in the previous survey: a better mix of skills or backgrounds, more time spent on company matters, and better people dynamics to enable constructive discussions."

What we can conclude from the results of this survey is that while corporate governance issues have come to the fore in the minds of consumers and electorates, there is still some way to go before this awareness turns into actual improvement in performance. These issues are likely to remain at the forefront among senior managers and directors in MNEs for the next decade at least.

QUESTIONS

Self-test Questions

5.1 Describe three theories about ethics.
5.2 What are the main components of corporate social responsibility (CSR)?

---

[31] See, for example, *Global Risk Management Survey*, Deloitte.com (2013).
[32] "Improving board governance: McKinsey Global Survey", August 2013. See http://www.mckinsey.com/ insights/strategy/improving_board_governance_mckinsey_global_survey_results (accessed March 2015).

5.3 How might one go about identifying stakeholders?

5.4 Should all stakeholders be given the same amount of management time and effort?

5.5 What is the difference between a principles-based approach to corporate governance codes and a rules-based approach?

Thought-provoking Questions

Question 5.1

Bluberry Plc makes yoghurts in Mullingar and Munich. It sells these throughout Europe. You have recently been appointed as group financial controller for the company. The CEO is thinking of introducing a corporate social responsibility program into the business. He thinks it will look good on marketing material and at international trade fairs. He has asked you to produce a 500-word summary of how Bluberry should go about implementing such a CSR program.

Question 5.2

You are the country accountant for the Irish division of a major MNE operating in Banbridge. A directive from the head office informed all divisions that gender quotas will apply from 1 July 2014, which means 50% of all promotions and new recruits must be women. You notice that some department managers have been recording men as women in order to achieve their quota. What will you do and why?

Review Questions

(See Suggested Solutions to Review Questions in **Appendix B**.)

Question 5.1: Kebabs Ltd

Having read the Kebabs Ltd case study in **Appendix A**, discuss the environmental concerns arising from the information presented and devise key performance indicators (KPIs) as to how these can be monitored and managed.

Question 5.2: Trident Mobile Ltd

Having read the Trident Mobile Ltd case study in **Appendix A**, what are the key points that Trident Mobile Ltd will need to consider in terms of developing a corporate social responsibility policy in respect of its proposed operation in Kenya?

Question 5.3: BoneDri

Having read the BoneDri case study in **Appendix A**, outline the key issues of corporate and social responsibility that BoneDri will need to consider should it choose to establish a production facility in Bangladesh and what it can do to address these.

6

THE PROFESSIONAL ACCOUNTANT IN THE MULTINATIONAL ENTERPRISE

LEARNING OBJECTIVES

Having read this chapter, you will understand:
• the role of the professional accountant in the MNE;
• how the accounting profession is attempting to converge accounting presentation;
• the international auditing approach;
• the role of the accountant in performance management; and
• global ethical standards for accountants.

6.1 INTRODUCTION

In the first five chapters of this book we have explored the history of international trade and how the MNE has become its main vehicle, some of the major MNEs operating on the island of Ireland and how such MNEs are governed with a particular focus on stakeholder analysis and corporate social responsibility. Within this context, the finance function is one of the most critical functions in any MNE. Even where an MNE's organisation structure is extremely decentralised, the finance function will always have some overarching role in bringing all the information together for overall management and governance of the enterprise. The importance of accountants and the finance function is such that I have devoted this chapter to exploring the role of the accountant in the multinational enterprise.

It is a popular image of accountants (instance Monty Python's famous "Guidance Counsellor" sketch[1]) that they are 'boring' naysayers, who sit on the periphery with spreadsheets explaining why things cannot be done, investments cannot be made and costs must be cut. But this image could not be further from the truth.

There are 2.5 million accountants in the world according to the International Federation of Accountants (IFAC), working in commercial enterprises, public bodies, auditing and advisory firms and in the not-for-profit sector. They function at the heart of multinational enterprises. Many accountants rise to the top of the organisations they work in. Accountancy is the professional qualification most in evidence among CEOs of larger companies and Plcs.

To understand why accountants play such an important role in today's organisations, especially in MNEs, we need to step back a bit and look at the role of the accountant in general.

6.2 THE ROLE OF ACCOUNTANTS

The accountancy profession has traditionally been involved in either:
- **Accounting:** the keeping of accurate financial records for an enterprise and the extraction of meaningful financial statements from those records to aid decision-making; or
- **Auditing:** the audit of other enterprises' accounting records and financial statements.

The profession has built up a series of systems and procedures to standardise the methodologies for carrying out these two functions. These two traditional roles of the accountancy profession have been greatly augmented since the Second World War and the growth of the corporation. While auditing and accounting remain two of their most important functions, accountants now find themselves at the forefront of decision-making in MNEs, with roles in treasury, costing, investment appraisal and procurement, augmented functions that have become identified naturally with a profession that has numeracy, accuracy and ethical standards at its core. As we saw in **Chapter 5**, because accountancy is a profession, it has strong ethical guidelines, which overarch the behaviour standards and regulations set by the accounting profession's various membership bodies. Put another way, it is important to follow the spirit of the ethical guidelines rather than doing the minimum to comply with just the letter of the behaviour standards.

On a global level, the profession has sought to standardise approaches to both record-keeping, accounting and auditing so that the readers of financial statements can understand them irrespective of where they are prepared or by whom and, importantly, can rely on these statements. (**Note:** for any student of international performance management it is critical to be aware how accountants must make decisions (e.g. valuation, purchase of companies, supplier and customer credit ratings, etc.) based on the financial statements of companies based in other jurisdictions.)

---

[1] See https://youtu.be/4h-wVe9a6rQ (accessed November 2014).

When one looks at the organisation chart of a typical MNE, one will normally see a hierarchy centred on functions such as production, sales and marketing, etc., or on countries or regions, or a combination of both. The two organisation charts in **Figures 6.1** and **6.2** below show two of the most basic structures. **Figure 6.1** shows an organisation structured on a **functional** basis. Here the finance director has subordinate finance directors in each operating country. In **Figure 6.2** the structure is based around country structures. In these instances, the country finance directors will report directly to the CEO for that country. The group finance director will only have indirect authority over the individual country finance directors. Deciding which structures will work most effectively is a critical decision that MNE managers must make.

FIGURE 6.1: ORGANISATION STRUCTURED BY FUNCTION

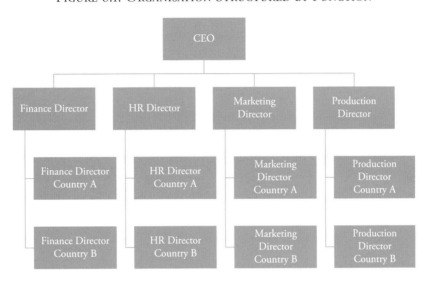

FIGURE 6.2: ORGANISATION STRUCTURED BY REGION/COUNTRY

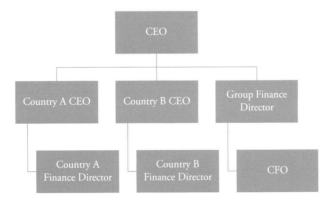

The finance function has visibility of what is happening in all the other functions and of the organisation. Even if the MNE is operating a decentralised organisational structure, the finance function will collate information centrally in order to prepare accounts and management information. This unique position means that accountants often have insights into the 'whole' organisation that are not obvious to other functions in the MNE. The modern accountant is expected to be able to use these unique insights and present them back to the

MNE's managers in a way that allows them to make improved business decisions that increase the overall value of the firm or reduce risk, or both. Accountants can also take these insights and use them to help managers predict the consequences of their actions more effectively, which is key to performance improvement and enhancing reliability of future cash flows.

In **Example 6.1** you can see how a relatively simple MNE with only two subsidiaries will need to ensure collaboration between its finance teams around the business if it is to make the right decisions regarding a potential acquisition.

EXAMPLE 6.1: COLLABORATION BETWEEN FINANCE TEAMS

Irish-based 'Quimby Plc' has a number of subsidiaries, two of which are in Spain. One is based in the Andalucía region and is focused on making par-baked bread products. The other subsidiary is in Murcia and processes tomatoes into a tomato puree. The management of the Andalucían subsidiary are aware of an opportunity to acquire a similar enterprise operating in Catalonia. The finance function in Andalucía want to prepare projected cash flows for the day-to-day operations of the proposed new acquisition in Catalonia. However, they will require input from the central finance function, which is more aware of the cost of capital for the proposed project. They will also have greater knowledge of the tax implications of any acquisition and legal implications. The finance team in the Murcia division may also have valuable information as the region is quite close to the proposed acquisition. A collaboration between the finance departments of the divisions and the central finance function will be required in order to produce the best quality information for the management of the MNE to make the best informed decision.

6.3 INTERNATIONAL STANDARDS FOR ACCOUNTANTS

Regulations for accountants differ throughout the world. These differences are understandable given the differing historical contexts of each jurisdiction, the nature of commerce and trade and indeed political representation. One must expect that the regulations governing an accountant in communist China will be different from those governing accountants in the United States or in France.

Irish Auditing and Accounting Supervisory Authority (IAASA)

The Companies Auditing and Accounting Act 2003 set up the Irish Auditing and Accounting Supervisory Authority (IAASA) in the Republic of Ireland. It is responsible for:
- examination and enforcement of certain listed entities' periodic financial reporting;
- supervision of the regulatory functions of the prescribed accountancy bodies (PABs), of which there are nine.

The latter of these two responsibilities is directly involved in ensuring the highest standards apply in the practice of the accounting profession in the Republic of Ireland. IAASA has set up a specialist unit, the Regulatory & Monitoring Supervision Unit (RMS), to deliver independent and effective supervision of the PABs. The PABs themselves then have their own regulations covering the behaviours and competences expected of their members. For completeness, the PABs regulated by IAASA are:

- Association of Chartered Certified Accountants (ACCA);
- Association of International Accountants (AIA);
- Chartered Institute of Management Accountants (CIMA);
- Chartered Institute of Public Finance and Accountancy (CIPFA);
- Institute of Chartered Accountants in England and Wales (ICAEW);
- Institute of Chartered Accountants in Ireland (ICAI);
- Institute of Chartered Accountants Scotland (ICAS);
- Institute of Certified Public Accountants in Ireland (ICPAI);
- Institute of Incorporated Public Accountants (IIPA).

Membership of a PAB is regulated by the individual professional bodies in accordance with their charter and their own professional standards and guidelines.

Financial Reporting Council (FRC)

The Financial Reporting Council (FRC) performs a similar function in the UK. The FRC is the UK's independent regulatory body and it is responsible for the promotion of high-quality corporate governance and reporting. The FRC uses a committee structure to carry out its functions. The Codes and Standards committee sets the standards that are expected from the bodies under the FRC's remit. The Conduct Committee oversees adherence to the codes set by the Codes and Standards Committee. The bodies covered by the FRC are the same as those covered by IAASA in the Republic of Ireland.

The management of an MNE needs to understand the qualification and competency levels of the accountants they are employing in the organisation. It is important for the MNE to know that the competency of individual accountants employed in a particular region or country is comparable to the standards elsewhere in the MNE, especially with the parent company. Accordingly, an MNE must not only make sure that its accountants have the necessary competence to comply with foreign country standards, they will also need to ensure they can adhere to overall reporting standard required by the parent company and its regulators.

The International Federation of Accountants (IFAC) endeavours to bring about a convergence in the accounting standards, if not the regulations, governing professional accountants across the globe. IFAC has no legal or regulatory powers and seeks to achieve its objectives by positioning itself as an authoritative body contributing to the consultation processes in global accounting standard setting. IFAC consists of over 160 membership bodies operating in 125 countries. In its own words, Its mission is to serve the public interest by "contributing to the development of high-quality standards and guidance; facilitating the adoption and implementation of high-quality standards and guidance; contributing to the development of strong professional accountancy organizations and accounting firms and to high-quality practices by professional accountants, and promoting the value of professional accountants worldwide; and speaking out on public interest issues."[2] IFAC does not produce any regulations or standards itself. Rather, through its global reach, it presents the voice of its members in accordance with its mission.

Most of the world's professional accountants are members of accrediting professional bodies that ensure their members have met specified competency levels and adhere to ethical standards.

---

[2] www.ifac.org/about-ifac (accessed December 2014).

These bodies are themselves normally accredited by the regulators in their relevant country. The professional bodies normally ensure the maintenance of competency standards through continuous professional development (CPD). The professional bodies are often specifically accredited by the legislation of their home country and empowered to permit their members to perform certain tasks not allowed to accountants who are not members of their bodies.

International Federation of Accountants (IFAC)

IFAC seeks to bring all these individual professional membership bodies into one global organisation in the drive for the improvements in the accountancy profession. A major focus of IFAC's work are ethical standards for the profession. While a complete and detailed regulatory framework governing accountants may not converge at a global level, the agreement of, and adherence to, ethical standards can go much of the way to creating a standardised profession globally. If all accountants adhered to global ethical frameworks, then readers of accounts prepared by them would be able to draw confidence from the fact that certain standards of ethics and behaviour had been adhered to in the preparation of the accounts.

6.4 INTERNATIONAL ACCOUNTING STANDARDS

The International Accounting Standards Board (IASB) sets standards for the preparation of financial statements through the publication of its International Financial Reporting Standards (IFRS). These standards are adopted by many countries around the world as the relevant accounting standard for their jurisdiction. The goal of the IASB is to create a set of accounting standards that are capable of implementation globally and, in so doing, to standardise financial reporting in a way that is meaningful for investors and other stakeholders.

One hundred and thirty countries either oblige or permit companies in their jurisdiction to produce their accounts in accordance with IFRS. (You can see a full list of the countries that permit or oblige the use of IFRS at www.iasplus.com/en/resources/ifrs-topics/use-of-ifrs.) However, local regulations can still overrule the adoption of all IFRS standards and companies may end up adopting only some of them.

Different stock exchange regulations and countries' legal requirements have meant that no one complete set of accounting standards applies throughout the world. This poses challenges for the MNE in that it needs to be compliant with the accounting regulations in the countries in which it operates, and each country may have different rules. Some countries will require the MNE to report in accordance with both local and global standards or, at a minimum, to reconcile the accounts produced under one standard to the accounts produced under another.

For example, an accountant in a US-owned MNE operating in Ireland may need to prepare accounts in accordance with IFRS to comply with Irish legislation and US GAAP to comply with parent company reporting regulations in the US.

The production of different sets of accounts under differing standards can become quite complex when one considers the possible number of permutations there can be in a large MNE operating in 30 or 40 countries, each with their own specific requirements. Computerised accounting systems have enabled this titanic task to be managed more effectively. In particular, the use of **enterprise reporting systems** (ERP) to capture data in a standardised way across the

MNE has enabled the finance function to present and organise data into many numbers of differing reporting formats.

Enterprise Reporting Systems

ERPs standardise reporting and data capture and their use means that an MNE can design a system to capture data and incorporate diverse reporting requirements across an entire, complex organisation (see **Chapter 15** for more detail on ERPs and SEMS). The starting principle is to identify the most granular data points and to capture all of these at source. These are the most basic level of transaction or activity the MNE engages in. For example, in a retailer one of the data points might be the sale of an individual item to an individual customer at a specific moment in time at a specific location. All these individual components of the basic transaction would be captured by the system. Then, by using powerful database analysis tools, this granular data can be organised to inform decision-making. As the data has been captured at its most basic level, it can be collated and presented in any fashion the MNE requires. Consequently, the data can also be organised to produce accounting information. In this way, the finance function can use the same data to produce, for example, management accountants, FRS compliant accounts and US GAAP compliant accounts. This ease of data organisation and manipulation has made the maintenance and production of a variety of financial statements formats much more manageable for the MNE.

When an MNE has differing business models across a variety of countries and currencies, the complexities can be enormous – some would say unmanageable. Large software companies such as SAP and Oracle specialise in helping companies overcome these challenges. Many management consultancy firms also specialise in implementing enterprise-wide systems. This topic is covered in more detail in **Chapter 17**.

The accountant's role in the design, implementation and maintenance of these systems is crucial. As one of the main roles of the accountant is the maintenance of the financial records and ERPs capture the source data for the production of those records, it is critical that accountants are integral to the design of the system and its ongoing management. If the ERP is being implemented across the entire MNE, then the central finance function must work in conjunction with all divisional finance teams to ensure the integrity of the implementation. The system also needs to capture the differing reporting regulations in each of the countries in which the MNE operates.

6.5 INTERNATIONAL AUDITING STANDARDS

We have seen that accountants work at the heart of the MNE. Accountants also play a large role in the auditing of MNEs. The International Auditing and Assurance Standards Board (IAASB) endeavours to standardise auditing approaches on a global basis in much the same way as the IASB does for accounts preparation and financial statements.

The IAASB sets out its objectives clearly as follows:

> "The International Auditing and Assurance Standards Board (IAASB) is an independent standard-setting body that serves the public interest by setting high-quality international standards for auditing, quality control, review, other assurance, and related services, and by facilitating the convergence of international and national standards. In doing so, the IAASB enhances the quality and uniformity of practice throughout the world and strengthens public confidence in the global auditing and assurance profession."

The IAASB's *Strategy and Work Program, 2012–2014* set the direction and priorities for its activities, with its efforts focused on development, adoption and implementation of international standards addressing audit, quality control, review, other assurance, and related services engagements.[3] The IAASB's medium-term strategy addresses the following "three main themes in the public interest:
• Supporting global financial stability;
• Enhancing the role, relevance and quality of assurance and related services in an evolving world; and
• Facilitating adoption and implementation of the standards."

As with the production of financial statements, the auditing process is different in various parts of the world. The standards published by the IAASB, called International Standards on Auditing ('ISAs'), are adapted by various countries to comply with their own legal and regulatory environments in consultation with the IAASB. As you can imagine, this process is neither speedy nor simple, leading to different versions of ISAs applying in different parts of the world, notwithstanding their common origins. For example, the designated regulatory body for auditing standards in the UK and Ireland is the FRC, which issues ISAs (UK and Ireland) and has, in the main, adapted these from the ISAs issued by the IAASB.

The two main systems of international auditing standards used in the English-speaking world are the ISAs, from the IAASB, and also those issued by the Public Company Accounting Oversight Board (PCAOB) in the US. The PCAOB believes it is necessary to have a separate audit standard setting body for the US as it contends that the investor market there is much more developed than elsewhere in the world and therefore needs auditing standards that reflect this investor climate.[4] The need for ensuring that the differences between the two standards issued by both groups are highlighted is apparent to both bodies, the IAASB and the PCAOB. For regulators, the existence of two standards poses challenges since, especially for MNEs, they may be operating in jurisdictions in which one or other standard may apply. In 2009, the EU published its findings from research conducted into the main, substantive differences between the two types of standard, which are as summarised below.[5] Highlighting these differences allows the readers of accounts, and the relevant audit reports, to know what work has been carried out by the auditors in coming to their conclusions on the accounts.

> "Based on the comparative analysis and the consultation of experts, we conclude that the number of areas for which substantive differences exist between the clarified ISAs and PCAOB standards is limited. There are only 5 areas for which experts perceive substantive differences that have a significant impact on the audit. These 5 areas are the following:
>
> (1) Assessing and reporting on internal control over financial reporting:
> Developing and implementing an effective system of internal control is a primary responsibility of management. Under PCAOB standards, an auditor is required to express an opinion about the quality of the client's internal control over financial reporting. ISAs do not have a comparable requirement, nor do they require an integrated audit (i.e. include an audit of the effectiveness of internal control as part of the audit of financial statements). It is important to

---

[3] IAASB, *Strategy and Work Program, 2012–2104* (IAASB, June 2012). See http://www.ifac.org/ sites/default/files/publications/files/IAASB%20Strategy%20and%20Work%20Program%20 2012-2014-final.pdf

[4] www.pcaobus.org/news/speech/pages/02282012_dcbar.aspx (accessed May 2015).

[5] EU Project No Markt/2007/15/F Lot 2–European Commission, available at ec.europa.ie

note that the PCAOB standards on internal control and integrated audit are a consequence of SOX 302 and 404.

(2) Use of another auditor for part of a group audit:
In contrast to PCAOB standards, ISAs do not permit the primary auditor to make any reference to the work of another auditor.

(3) Documentation:
Documentation requirements under PCAOB standards and ISAs follow a different approach. While PCAOB standards are perceived to be more prescriptive, ISAs are perceived to rely more on professional judgment (e.g., in contrast to ISA 230, AS 3 requires preparation and maintenance of an engagement completion memorandum). The issue was raised that there might be a link between documentation and enforcement. This question remains outside the scope of the study.

(4) Risk assessment and responses to assessed risks:
The approach to assessing and responding to risk within the ISAs differs from that of the PCAOB standards. International standards require the auditor to obtain a broad understanding of an entity and its environment, through specific risk assessment procedures in order to identify where there may be risks of material misstatements. This perspective includes that an auditor should understand the entity's business risks (for example, strategic and operating risks) and how the entity responds to them in the course of planning and conducting the audit, in order to assess the risk of material misstatements both at the financial statement and assertion levels. While the PCAOB is currently working on a major revision of their risk assessment standards, at the time of this report, there is no requirement comparable to the ISAs for assessing and responding to risk.

(5) Going concern:
PCAOB standards limit the foreseeable future to 12 months, while under ISAs it is at least, but not limited to, 12 months."

The professional accountant operating in an MNE must plan a way through these complexities in order to ensure that the MNE's audit process complies with the appropriate regulations in each jurisdiction where it has relevant operations. This task is made more complex by differing languages that may prevail in each of the jurisdictions. It is critical that the overall goal of producing reliable, meaningful, consistent and timely financial information is not lost in the sea of compliance work that may surround the accounts preparation and auditing processes in a large MNE.

6.6 TAXATION

Tax laws differ throughout the world. Understanding these differences and planning an MNE's affairs in order to minimise the tax burden on the organisation is part of the role of the professional accountant. The degree to which MNEs have optimised their tax affairs has been a topical issue for some years now in the international business arena. In particular, the Republic of Ireland's 12.5% corporation tax rate for limited companies has attracted much international public comment, not all of it favourable.

Nonetheless, it is the role of the management in an MNE to increase the value of the business on behalf of its investors while remaining aligned to the organisation's values and other stakeholder needs. This role therefore requires knowledge of international tax law and its applicability to the MNE's operations. This responsibility normally falls to the accountants within the business. As we saw above, the finance function typically has the best overall view of all the MNE's activities; it is thus best positioned to be the architect of structures that ensure compliance with the appropriate tax codes and seizing any opportunity presented to minimise the enterprise's taxation exposures. However, care must be given to the needs of other stakeholders in managing this situation. Various large MNEs, such as Apple and Amazon, have come under severe criticism from public representatives and media commentators for seemingly paying too little tax. Considering the value of brands and reputation, and their importance to sustaining long-term cash flows, these matters must be planned for in a coordinated and measured way. Management of the MNE must balance reputational issues with tax savings and seek to understand what path delivers the best long-term and sustainable benefit for the enterprise.

EXAMPLE 6.2: TAXING ISSUES FOR MULTINATIONAL ENTERPRISE[6]

"Amazon Under Scrutiny Over EU Tax Affairs

Online retail firm Amazon is facing a potential investigation by EU officials over its Luxembourg tax hub.

According to the *Financial Times*, the EU's competition commission has demanded that the country's Grand Duchy hand over documents of the tax status given to Amazon, including any potential state aid.

The retailer has come under increasing scrutiny over structures that allow customer revenue from member states to be assessed for taxation purposes at its Luxembourg hub.

The company has 800 staff at its headquarters, where £13.6bn in EU sales were logged last year, reportedly reducing its effective tax rate by 8%.

European Commission spokesman Antoine Colombani told Sky News: "As we have said publicly many times before, the commission continues to gather information about certain tax practices in several member states, in order to assess the situation from the point of view of EU state aid rules. However we will not make any comment on whether specific companies may or may not be covered by this information gathering exercise."

The US firm has come under criticism in the EU over warehouse working conditions, purchasing power over suppliers and claims it has a damaging effect on other retailers.

Amazon is the latest firm to see its tax status come under scrutiny amid a clampdown on favourable conditions given to certain multinational corporations.

EU investigations have already been launched into Apple in Ireland, Starbucks in the Netherlands and Fiat Finance in Luxembourg.

Starbucks has since announced a decision to move its EU headquarters to Britain.

---

[6] "Amazon Under Scrutiny Over EU Tax Affairs", Sky News 4 July 2014. See http://news.sky.com/story/1294863/amazon-under-scrutiny-over-eu-tax-affairs

Luxembourg has the highest per capita GDP in the world, according to the International Monetary Fund, while the World Bank and United Nations rank it third highest.

G20 member countries have agreed to greater cross-border tax information exchange, in a principle supported by the Organisation for Economic Co-operation and Development.

The EU intends to implement new rules about 'transfer pricing', where local divisions must buy goods and services from a parent firm located in another jurisdiction.

Westminster's Public Accounts Committee (PAC) chair Margaret Hodge previously called Amazon's finance arrangements an "extremely aggressive tax avoidance strategy".

She said: "We welcome this examination of Amazon's tax affairs and hope the investigation contributes to putting an end to profit-shifting. I only wish the British authorities would be so assertive."

In 2012, the PAC questioned top executives from Amazon, Starbucks and Google over their tax strategies and effective UK tax rates."

6.7 RISK MANAGEMENT

In the early part of this chapter I mentioned how the accountant plays a role in the corporate governance process of an organisation. This is especially true in an MNE because accountants and the finance function in general have a visibility and oversight of the entire organisation that other functions often do not have. As a result of this overarching view of the MNE, accountants are uniquely positioned to assess its risk profile and the activities in which it is engaged.

Most corporate governance codes recommend that company boards set up a subcommittee, or 'board committee', to manage risk. Often this risk committee is coupled with the audit committee and is called the 'audit and risk committee'. It is recommended best practice that the majority of the members of this committee be non-executive directors and that it be chaired by an independent non-executive director. The other members would normally be executive directors. Such segregation of duties and responsibilities between the executive management of the MNE and its shareholder-elected non-executive board members is a critical part of ensuring the objectivity of the audit committee.

In order to assess the levels of risk in the business, the audit and risk committee may ask executive management to prepare and maintain a **risk register**, which typically consists of a list of possible eventualities that pose risk to the future cash flows of the organisation, either directly or indirectly. The risks are then quantified systematically by reference to a combination of the likelihood of occurrence and the potential impact on the business. For example, while for a business based in Dublin an earthquake might have a huge impact in completely destroying a critical factory, since this is an extremely unlikely event, the risk would not feature high on its risk register. On the other hand, a strike by workers at the factory may have a less dramatic impact, but since it might be more likely to happen, it would feature higher on the risk register.

The risk committee reviews the risk register for completeness and briefs the full board of the company on its work. It also ensures that management have in place appropriate risk-management strategies for the main risks. These strategies should include mitigating action plans as well as plans to deal with the risk events should they occur. In this way, the likelihood of the risk event happening is reduced and, even if it does happen, the business has well-thought-out action plans to deal with it.

The finance function is often at the centre of the activities of the risk committee. One reason for this is that the assessment of risk needs to be based on an overview of the enterprise as a whole. Finance professionals in the MNE are often the best placed people to make this assessment. They also possess the numeracy skills and competence to quantify the possible effects of the risk event.

Even if the finance function is not directly involved in the workings of the risk committee, professional accountants ought to ensure best practice is being followed. As a professional working to recognised standards, it is incumbent upon the accountant to draw management's attention to areas where they feel the best practice is not being followed, particularly where this could have a possible impact on the future cash flows and stability of the MNE.

6.8 PERFORMANCE MEASUREMENT

Having mentioned risks to the future cash flows of a business, how does a business know what those future cash flows will be? It is here that the accountant comes to the fore. The finance function normally has responsibility not just for the maintenance of accounting records but also for the production of estimates of future performance, which are produced in collaboration with the functional managers of the business. The MNE has specific complications in this regard as, by definition, there is some degree of international or cross-border business activity. Most likely this will involve different currencies, laws and cultures. These facets of the MNE make predicting future performance more complicated.

Indeed, the accountant's role goes further than helping management predict future performance. Future performance arises from the business decisions made today. Each business situation will involve a number of possible decisions, each with a different possible outcome and associated risk profile. Thus, the accountant must inform the business as regards not just the possible future performance from one decision, but also outline the array of possible outcomes from a selection of possible decisions. A decision is then made, but the accountant's role is not over. The responsibility of the finance function is then to ensure that systems are in place to enable the managers to monitor their performance against the predicted performance to ensure that performance and prediction are aligned. If there is a misalignment, then corrective action needs to be taken or the decision revisited. Systems for aiding prediction of managerial performance and subsequent monitoring are most often part of so-called 'budgetary control systems' or 'capital appraisal systems'. Both systems are designed to support managerial decision-making and are normally managed by the accountants in the MNE. **Chapters 17** and **18** describe these systems and their implementation more completely.

6.9 CORPORATE GOVERNANCE AND ETHICS

While we discussed ethics and corporate governance in **Chapter 5**, it is worth emphasising the role of the accountant and the finance function with regard to best practice in corporate governance. Earlier in this chapter we saw how the standardisation of international reporting and auditing standards remains a 'holy grail' of the accounting profession. Differing legal and cultural frameworks around the world make standardised, global rules-based systems almost impossible to envisage, not to mention enforce. The alternative approach, however, of adopting instead a principles-based system is liable to misinterpretation at best and outright manipulation at worst (see **Chapter 5**).

A tension exists between rules-based and principles-based accounting standards and processes. To address this tension, the accountancy profession is seeking to introduce a third pillar on which to base the profession on a global basis. This third pillar is a global recognition of the ethical standards to which professional accountants must adhere. These standards, which sit well with global corporate governance standards, endeavour to ensure that the spirit of a global accounting and auditing standard is set, even if the policing of the letter of such a standard remains elusive. If all professional accountants are carrying out their work in accordance with these ethical principles, then the fact that there are different jurisdictional treatments of similar accounting issues matters less.

The ethics board of IFAC sets out ethical standards that should govern behaviour and performance of professional accountants across the globe. These standards include five principles, as follows:

"A professional accountant shall comply with the following fundamental principles:
- **Integrity** – to be straightforward and honest in all professional and business relationships.
- **Objectivity** – to not allow bias, conflict of interest or undue influence of others to override professional or business judgments.
- **Professional Competence and Due Care** – to maintain professional knowledge and skill at the level required to ensure that a client or employer receives competent professional services based on current developments in practice, legislation and techniques and act diligently and in accordance with applicable technical and professional standards.
- **Confidentiality** – to respect the confidentiality of information acquired as a result of professional and business relationships and, therefore, not disclose any such information to third parties without proper and specific authority, unless there is a legal or professional right or duty to disclose, nor use the information for the personal advantage of the professional accountant or third parties.
- **Professional Behaviour** – to comply with relevant laws and regulations and avoid any action that discredits the profession."[7]

You may recognise these five principles and much of the same wording from our discussion of the professional Code of Ethics of Chartered Accountants Ireland in **Chapter 5**. This is because the Institute is a member body of IFAC and its Code of Ethics is based on IFAC's articulation of ethical standards for professional accountants globally.

IFAC believes that adherence to these principles will introduce a degree of standardised behaviour across the profession. When these behavioural standards are taken in conjunction with IFRS, which govern accounts preparation, and the ISAs, which govern auditing, there emerges a picture of a global standard for the professional accountant. This standard is critical for the effective management of the finance function in the MNE. It aids the progression of free trade through encouraging and supporting transparency and clarity in accounting preparation and the auditing and presentation of information for consideration by investors and other stakeholders.

---

[7] International Ethics Standards Board for Accountants Fact Sheet, April 2014. See www.ethicsboard.org.

6.10 CONCLUSION

In Part I of this book we have examined why organisations internationalise their activities. We have seen how various economic theories support the global democratic desire to improve the standards of living for all peoples through free trade. In particular, we have examined the role of global institutions such as the WTO, whose *raison d'être* is the facilitation and support of free trade principles. However, with the freedom to trade comes the obligation to behave correctly. We have looked at the guidelines and regulations that have been put in place across the globe to ensure that organisations are managed in accordance with commonly understood and agreed standards of ethics and values. Adhering to these principles ensures that MNEs do not abuse the freedoms afforded them by the removal of barriers to trade and the freedom of movement of goods and people.

Professional accountants play a critical role in managing MNEs. In this chapter we saw that accountants are regulated by state institutions and professional bodies in their own jurisdictions. Most of these regulators design systems based upon international standards, which are produced by the IAASB and the IASB, both of which in turn being independent arms of the International Federation of Accountants (IFAC). Since the IFAC has no global legislative mandate, it must persuade each country to apply regulatory standards that mirror the standards for accounts preparation and auditing that it has produced. The individual professional bodies will also have codes of ethics and conduct that members must adhere to.

The finance function in an MNE is often one of the few functions that gains an overall view of the enterprise. This unique view arises as, at a minimum, financial information for the entire business and all its subsidiary operating divisions must be centralised for consolidation and preparation into an aggregate set of group accounts. The overall view allows the finance function special insights into the overall performance of the MNE. These insights can help the accountants to prepare meaningful management and accounting information that should improve decision-making in the MNE. I have mentioned before how risk is increased in the MNE due to increases in the scale and complexity of the organisation that internationalisation brings. Accountants play a key role in the management of this risk.

In Part II of this book we will examine the macro-economic factors that influence and affect MNEs. In Parts III, IV and V we will examine the different strategies and tactics that MNEs can adopt in order to manage these influences, seize the opportunities they present and minimise the risks that they present, in all of which the professional accountant's role is vital.

QUESTIONS

Self-test Questions

6.1 How does the accounting profession endeavour to standardise accounts presentation on a global basis?

6.2 What is the role of a risk committee?

6.3 What should you do, as a professional accountant, if the accounting standards in a country in which a subsidiary operates contradict the accounting standards in the country of the parent company?

Thought-provoking Questions

Question 6.1

You have just joined Blooming Plc, a fast-growing, US-based international grower of flowers, as a newly qualified accountant at the shared service centre in Belfast, which prepares the accounts for the entire Plc. To do this it requires submissions from each of the 15 operating subsidiaries, seven of which were bought in the last three months. Your boss, Ella Stem, has seen the need for new accountants to be recruited into each of seven recently acquired subsidiaries in Brazil, Spain, Poland, Canada, Mexico, Italy and, of course, the Netherlands. She has asked you to prepare a paper suggesting how Blooming Plc might go about this process. She is particularly interested in whether there is a need to have qualified accountants in each subsidiary or could costs be saved by using book-keepers.

Question 6.2

You are looking at the accounts of two public companies, one listed in the US and the other listed in the UK. Your client has pointed out that both companies have been audited, but he is worried that the audit process for both may not be consistent. He has asked you to describe in a briefing paper how the audit process of the two sets of accounts may have differed.

Review Question

(See Suggested Solutions to Review Questions in **Appendix B**.)

Question 6.1: Redbarn Brewery

Having read the Redbarn Brewery case study in **Appendix A**, detail the practical issues that Redbarn Brewery would need to address in negotiating any joint venture/licence agreement and, in addition, detail the practical implications for the finance function in Ireland if the joint venture were to be established.

PART II

ECONOMIC FACTORS INFLUENCING MULTINATIONAL ENTERPRISES

CHAPTER

In Part II of this book we will examine the economic factors that influence and affect MNEs. These economic factors fall into two categories: the issues that arise from the global economy, and those that arise in the individual countries in which the MNE operates. First, **Chapter 7** will look at the macroeconomic and political influences on the MNE. **Chapter 8** will then examine exchange rates, why they move and how such movements might impact upon future cash flows of the MNE and its balance sheet (also known as statement of financial position). In **Chapter 9** we will examine how the global capital markets operate and see that the freedom of movement of capital is an intrinsic part of international trade. Without ease of movement of capital, movement of goods and labour becomes problematic. Finally in this part, **Chapter 10** examines the nature of working capital in the MNE, particularly how an MNE's working capital requirements are impacted by the international dimension of its activities. This chapter also explains some of the terms that are commonly used in the carrying out of international trade on a day-to-day basis, particularly concerning the logistics and payment systems.

By the end of Part II the reader will have gained some insights into why international trade presents opportunities and challenges to the managers of MNEs. In Parts III, IV and V we will then examine the decision-making processes that MNEs can adopt to ensure that risks are minimised while the MNE seizes opportunities presented by international trade. In Part III we will look at investment appraisal decisions and implementing change in MNEs. In Part IV we discuss treasury management and its associated decisions, with special focus on foreign-exchange risks. In Part V we will then consider how MNEs make pricing decisions, implement decision-making support systems and measure performance.

ECONOMIC AND POLITICAL IMPACTS ON MULTINATIONAL ENTERPRISES

LEARNING OBJECTIVES

Having read this chapter, you will understand:
• the nature of macroeconomic impacts on the MNE;
• the difference between economic and political risk;
• how to identify economic risk issues;
• how to identify political risk issues;
• techniques to analyse and measure such risks; and
• how to use country-specific risk analysis techniques to aid an MNE's decision-making.

7.1 INTRODUCTION

In this chapter we take a high-level view of how global and domestic macroeconomic factors can impact on multinational enterprises (MNEs) and what, if anything, MNEs can do to minimise the detrimental effects and seize any opportunities presented.

Remember that, as we have seen in **Chapter 2** and will see in **Chapter 11**, the theoretical valuation of any investment is the present value of the future cash flows discounted by an appropriate rate to include a risk premium relevant to the MNE's risk profile.

I say 'theoretical valuation' because, in the final analysis, the value of any business is represented by what someone will pay for it. However, in this context, we are talking about decision-making processes that increase the value of an enterprise for the investors through adding value. In making each of these decisions, an MNE's managers do not contemplate selling the entire enterprise after each and every decision they make. Therefore, they need a framework to understand whether the decisions they make are likely to add value or not. The best way to do this is to measure the expected future cash flows from each decision, discounted at an appropriate rate to factor in the cost of capital. Through such measurement of expected outcomes they can determine which decisions to make on the basis that they add value and have a positive cash flow impact on the business. External observers often do not have access to a business's detailed cash flows. Thus, over time, a variety of valuation models have developed that attempt to externally value an enterprise based upon asset values, multiples of profits and so forth.

Anything that can affect the future expected cash flows can reasonably be expected to increase or decrease the value of the business. When we consider that the primary role of management is to maximise the value of the business for its owners, then it follows that managers need to be aware of matters that can affect the future cash flows and, by implication, the valuation of the enterprise.

The two variables in our high-level valuation model are future cash flows and the discount rate. The MNE manager therefore needs to be interested in the management of both of these variables. Maximising the future cash flows and, almost as importantly, reducing volatility in future cash flow projections should be priorities for the MNE executive. A second area of focus is to reduce the discount rate that the market feels is appropriate to the MNE's business profile. In **Example 7.1** we can see how the investors will ascribe a lower value to a business whose cash flows are less certain in their estimation. In this case 'certainty' is equivalent to 'risk'. The more certain that investors view the future cash flows of an MNE, the lower the return they require on their investment. A safe euro is always worth more than a risky one.

EXAMPLE 7.1: EFFECT ON VALUE OF RISKY CASH FLOWS

Imagine two businesses with the same predicted cash flow over the next 10 years. One business draws its cash flows from its operations in Germany and France; the other draws its cash flows from operations in Somalia and Liberia. Despite the fact the both MNEs have the same cash flow quantum projection, it is likely that investors will ascribe a higher value to the enterprise operating in the more stable commercial environment of Western Europe.

In this chapter we will examine how to quantify the reasons for these different valuations and how the MNE manager can manage the impacts of external influences on the firm. External influences that impact an MNE fall into two main areas:
• economic; and
• political.

When formulating business strategy MNEs often carry out an environmental analysis, which informs decision-making by examining the relevant environmental factors that can impact upon the future cash flows of the business. There are a number of frameworks that can be used to structure such analysis. One of these frameworks uses an acronym, PESTEL, to act as a type of checklist. The letters stand for **P**olitical, **E**conomic, **S**ocial, **T**echnological, **E**cological and **L**egal. Each factor interacts with the others to a greater or lesser degree. For example, climate change, a dimension of ecological factors, has impacted upon both the political and legal factors leading to the introduction of laws that seek to reduce emissions that cause climate change. In addition, awareness about this issue has led to social change with an increased awareness of the environmental impact of consumption patterns. Notwithstanding that the six factors interact with each other, breaking them down into these six main areas helps MNE managers to structure an analysis so that they can make informed decisions. In this chapter, we examine two of these factors: economic and political.

In **Chapter 12** we consider the social factor, in particular, how cultural differences can affect MNE decision-making. The technological, ecological and legal factors are discussed in various chapters as they arise. For example, technological changes have greatly enabled the development of the management systems needed to run an MNE. This topic is covered in **Chapter 17**.

We will first examine the **economic** factors and how they can be considered during the decision-making process in the MNE.

7.2 ECONOMIC FACTORS THAT IMPACT MULTINATIONAL ENTERPRISES

The economy of a country has an impact on the performance of commercial entities operating in that country, be they MNEs or domestic enterprises. An MNE may be dependent on an individual country because it:
- imports goods/services made in that country;
- exports goods/services to that country;
- manufactures products in that country;
- locates support functions in that country.

The cash flow that will arise in future years from each of these four scenarios is dependent on many variables. One of the drivers of the MNE's performance will be the financial stability and economic growth potential of a country on which it is in some way dependent. For example, if a country's economic performance is poor and the MNE is exporting to there, then demand might be dampened and performance undermined. On the other hand, if the economy is poor but the MNE is importing from that country, then there may be the possibility to obtain reduced costs as the country will be eager to maintain employment and economic activity. Therefore it is the economic position of the country in relation to what the MNE wishes to achieve that is pertinent for the MNE managers' decision-making process, not the country's absolute economic position. For example, a wealthy, high-income country may present real opportunities to an MNE seeking to sell luxury products, such as Rolex watches, but it would be a distraction for a company looking to make bargain-priced T-shirts.

In 2014 the owners of the Bausch + Lomb production facility in Waterford, which makes contact lenses, were able to secure cost reductions by way of reduced labour costs predominantly in return for longer term commitments to the plant. These cost reductions would have been more difficult to achieve if the Irish economy were in a stronger position at the time, with more demand in the labour market. IDA Ireland, the state agency tasked with obtaining inward investment into the Republic of Ireland, also played a role in securing the commitment.

EXAMPLE 7.2: BAUSCH + LOMB[1]

Bausch + Lomb to invest estimated €6m in Waterford plant

Eye-care multinational company Bausch + Lomb has announced plans to invest what is believed to be nearly €6 million in upgraded production systems in its Waterford facility.

The announcement follows last week's agreement with its employees on a cost reduction plan.

---

[1] RTÉ News, 25 June 2014. See http://www.rte.ie/news/2014/0625/626427-bausch-and-lomb-waterford/

The plan will see 200 of the 1,100 staff taking a redundancy package, and pay cuts of around 12% for the remaining staff.

Bausch + Lomb's Vice President of Manufacturing Angelo Conti met unions and management at the plant today to outline the investment and to discuss the future of the plant.

The investment, which will be supported by IDA capital grants, will be used to upgrade packing and inspection systems.

"The cost reduction agreement provides us with the opportunity to invest in the Waterford facility and better positions this facility to compete overall and develop into the future," Mr Conti said.

"With upgraded systems and an appropriately aligned cost structure in place, we will be able to turn our attention to regaining a leading market share position in contact lens and continuing the strong heritage of the Bausch + Lomb brand."

Economic Indicators of a Country

It is one thing to know that economic factors influence the performance of MNEs, but how does the MNE manager assess those economic factors and build them into the planning process? In this section we will examine how a country's economic performance might be assessed and, in so far as is ever possible, how those factors might change in the future thereby impacting upon the MNE. In particular, we are interested to know whether economies are growing, stalling or shrinking. The performance of the economy drives demand and this demand gives rise to the factors that influence the performance of the MNE.

There are three main indicators of a country's economic health:
- **Interest Rates** Higher rates tend to slow demand and capital investment in an economy. Lower interest rates stimulate demand and expenditure and discourage saving. Also, the theory of interest rate parity (see **Chapter 8**) proposes that a currency's exchange rate will weaken relative to the currencies of countries with lower interest rates.
- **Inflation Rates** Inflation gives rise to increasing prices, which may stimulate immediate expenditure and discourage savings. However, rising prices come from rising costs, which can erode consumer purchasing power if wages do not keep pace, leading to reduced demand in an economy. Generally, some inflation is good for an economy. A consensus view in the Eurozone and by the Bank of England is that an inflation rate of 2% is best for an economy. Inflation rates above or below 2% probably represent a negative indicator for a country. The greater the variance, the greater the issue.
- **Exchange Rates** Exchange rates affect both the cost of imports and the competitiveness of exports. If a currency is strong then imports will be cheaper, but exports will cost more for trading partners. Falling exports can affect overall production in the economy and reduce economic activity. A weak currency, on the other hand, can stimulate exports and make imports expensive. However, investors do not like to hold currencies that are falling in value and might be encouraged to sell off their holdings of the weakening currency, thus reducing the funds available for investment in that economy.

Of course, these three key economic indicators do not operate separately from each other. A more detailed explanation of how they connect and interact, and of the economic theories explaining this, is provided in **Chapter 8** (where we will also examine the theories of purchasing power parity, interest rate parity and the International Fisher effect, the main theories that help explain the interaction of interest rates, inflation and exchange rates. For this chapter it is only necessary to appreciate that these are important measures of an economy's health). The movement of exchange rates affects the future cash flows received by the MNE, thereby impacting, either positively or negatively, on the value of the MNE and the return for investors. The tools the MNE might use to manage these issues are covered in **Chapter 15**.

In addition to the three indicators listed above, an MNE will also look at other measures of the performance of a country's economy. An MNE is particularly interested in the level of commercial risk that it may be exposed to resulting from movements in the economies upon which it has some reliance for future cash flows. There are a wide number of measures that can indicate levels of risk associated with a particular country. Some of the major ones to consider are outlined below.

Gross Domestic Product (GDP)

Gross domestic product (GDP) is the total of goods and services produced in a geographically defined economy. For example, the GDP of the Republic of Ireland is the total value of goods and services produced within the borders of the Republic, even if these goods and services are ultimately exported. Year-on-year growth of GDP indicates a growth in economic production and is therefore a positive indicator for an economy. It is important for the MNE to know how the countries with which it is commercially involved are performing as this will eventually impact on cash flows. The GDP is a useful measure for determining that economic performance within a specific geographic area, such as a country.

There is also a measure called **gross national product (GNP)**, or **gross national income (GNI)** as it has recently been termed. GNP is an assessment of the total value of production of goods and services by the citizens of a country, whether in their home country or from assets based abroad. Thus, it is not a measure of the local country's domestic economy. It is a measure of the economic performance of the citizens of the country and the assets they own, wherever they are located. The output from assets owned abroad does not need to be remitted to the home country in order for it to be included in GNP. For example, the production of cars in a Japanese-owned factory in the US would be included in USA GDP but also in Japan's GNP.

The economic measures normally track each other, with GNP tending to be higher than GDP as a matter of course. Occasionally, however, the differences can be significant and lead to wrong conclusions if the wrong measure is taken by the MNE to make decisions. For example, in Ireland in the first decade of this century, what appeared to be GDP increases were in fact the result of accounting and bookkeeping tactics made by several major multinational corporations that wished to take advantage of Ireland's low corporate taxes. By using legitimate transfer pricing arrangements profits earned in other countries were brought into the Irish economy before being brought back to their non-Irish home (often the US). I look in further detail at transfer pricing in **Chapter 16**. Since the profits were being earned by the Irish-based subsidiaries the effect was to boost GDP numbers, even though there was no significant economic activity within the ROI to support the profit levels achieved.

Ireland is a small, open economy with a major dependence on international trade. This open nature of the Irish economy can give rise to large gaps between GDP and GNP, especially when one considers the large numbers of MNEs that locate their operations there. In most developed economies of a greater scale the gap between GDP and GNP is not as pronounced.

Normally an MNE will also look at the GDP per capita of the countries it is analysing. This measure will allow the MNE to compare counties of differing population sizes. Countries with higher per capita GDPs will more likely be stronger economically.

Unemployment

Unemployment numbers are a strong indicator of a country's economic performance. High unemployment indicates a slump in economic performance, low demand and, possibly, high levels of parallel economy operating outside the normal fiscal structures, i.e. the black market. It also indicates a strong demand for budget-consuming services from the central exchequer, such as social welfare payments. These are negative indicators for the MNE looking for positives on the demand side in the country concerned. If, however, the MNE is looking for a competitive source of labour, then high unemployment could suit its needs. Due to the laws of supply and demand, countries with higher levels of unemployment tend to have lower labour costs than countries with low unemployment. While governments do put in place 'floors' of the lowest wage allowable in labour markets by enforcing minimum wage legislation, it can generally be said that higher unemployment indicates lower wage levels.

Low unemployment is normally a sign of a strong economy, one that is functioning well and where most people in society who want to be, can be employed. There should always be *some* unemployment in an economy to take account of people switching jobs, disability, illness and so forth. A figure of 3.5% to 4% of the working population is often taken to be an ideal level as it means there should be enough people seeking work to take up new positions as the economy grows. A level of unemployment lower than 4% tends to create upward pressure on wages. An MNE that is looking for consumer demand in a country should take encouragement from a low unemployment level. An MNE seeking to base itself in a country in order to set up a new manufacturing base or service centre should be aware of low unemployment levels as this means that wage costs may be on the rise. This is especially true for skilled labour.

Budget Deficit

Governments collect taxes from individuals and corporations. They spend the money raised by taxes predominantly on infrastructure, social welfare, education and health in accordance with their democratically elected mandate, or some other such mandate as they may hold in non-democratic societies. Governments tend to spend slightly more or slightly less than they raise in taxes. It seems like good fiscal management to suggest they should never spend a lot more than they have raised in taxes. On the other hand, it can seem unfair if governments do not spend all the funds that were raised, as it means that money has been taken unnecessarily from taxpayers.

An MNE seeking to understand a country's economic position can learn much from the fiscal rectitude of that country. A country borrowing and spending too much on itself (i.e. more than it has raised in taxes) is a country with problems, either immediate or impending. While a budget deficit in one year might not herald disaster, recurring deficits with little or no will to tackle the issue indicates a government that will need to borrow increasingly large sums of money. This borrowing increases the country's demand for foreign currency and reduces demand for its own currency. It also reduces public spending in the economy as more tax receipts are diverted to paying back debt. These changes in the demand curve can impact the economy further and cause variations to predicted cash flows for the MNE.

A useful benchmark of fiscal rectitude is the euro convergence criteria that EU Member States are required to meet. In order to enter the third stage of the Economic and Monetary Union (EMU) and adopt the euro as their currency a country must commit to fiscal rectitude performance measures. These measures include the requirement that the government budget deficit, i.e. the ratio of the annual general government deficit relative to GDP, should not be more than 3%.

Balance of Trade

Another indicator of the health of a country's economy is its balance of trade, which is the net difference between a country's exports and its imports of goods and services. Conventionally, it is desirable for exports to be greater than imports, suggesting an economy that produces surpluses which it can then sell to other countries thereby increasing its own wealth. The relationship between the balance of trade, balance of payments and foreign exchange rates is discussed in **Chapter 8**. It suffices to say here that an MNE should include the measure in those being analysed in order to assess economic risk. A balance of trade surplus is a sign of a strong domestic economy. It may also signal a possible strengthening of that country's currency since demand for it will grow as purchasers of the country's exports need the currency to pay for the goods and services they have bought. Conversely, a deficit on the balance of trade, where a country is importing more than it is exporting may herald a decline in the value of that country's currency as it seeks foreign currencies to pay for its imports.

Within a fixed currency union, such as the Eurozone, these balance of trade pressures cannot resolve themselves through movements in exchange rates. Therefore, some other corrections will occur in the country's economy to counteract the balance of trade pressures. For example, a balance of trade surplus may give rise to inflation as the extra income in the economy arising from the proceeds of its exports will serve to stimulate domestic demand and therefore drive up prices. Currency unions also have tight rules about economic targets that member countries have signed up to through binding treaties; nonetheless, the absence of exchange rate fluctuations as a method of absorbing balance of trade pressures leads to other pressures for members of such currency unions.

7.3 POLITICAL FACTORS THAT IMPACT MULTINATIONAL ENTERPRISES

We are examining economic and political factors that can impact upon MNEs and, in particular, the volatility of predicted future cash flows. We have examined the economic factors. We now move on to the political factors. An organisation must balance minimising the volatility of its expected cash flows with maximising the returns on its capital employed (capital it has been given by investors). For an MNE, the situation is even more complex as the future cash flows derive from international activities where there are more variables to manage.

An increased number of variables means an increase in possible outcomes. One of the most important matters for the financial manager in an MNE to consider is the political situation of the countries connected to the future cash flows of the enterprise. These countries might not just be those where the MNE has actual operations. An exporting MNE will be interested in the economic factors affecting the political situation in the countries it hopes to sell to. An importing MNE will want to ensure that there are no disruptions to supplies and pricing from the countries it is importing from.

The MNE manager must have a systematic way of assessing the impact of these economic factors. Such a systematic analysis allows for easier comparative assessments between countries and adds some process to the very uncertain activity of assessing the viability and volatility of future cash flows. The main political factors that an MNE needs to consider are outlined below.

See also **Appendix C.1**.

Political Instability

The future cash flows of an MNE will be affected by the nature of the stability of the political infrastructure of a relevant country. The greater the stability, the greater the certainty around the future cash flow predictions. The rate of turnover of the government, i.e. the frequency with which it changes, can be a key indicator of political instability. Political stability may, however, be indicative of economic stasis, for example in a totalitarian regime like North Korea. Even if the government or ruling regime does not change often, stability risks remain. For example, the government may introduce new laws or impose new taxes that can affect the MNE. The degree to which a government endorses international trade agreements, supports commercial contracts and encourages free trade are good indicators of the degree to which it will support a stable trading environment for MNEs.

Another strong indicator of political stability is the degree to which new governments maintain existing legislation and bureaucratic structures. When the government changes in a country and the new government preserves the organs and legislative framework of the state, an MNE can take this as a clear sign of political stability. If, on the other hand, a new government seeks to introduce widespread changes to the civil service structures and the laws of a country, then the MNE can be certain of a degree of political instability that will have an impact upon its operations. Of course, that impact can be positive as well as negative; either way, it introduces volatility.

Consumer Sentiment and Public Opinion

With increasing globalisation, there can be a subtle, and sometimes not so subtle, backlash from consumers to the apparent omnipresence of global brands and MNEs. Some of this opposition is based on a political or philosophical belief that globalisation is the instrument of capitalism and works against the interests of ordinary people for the betterment of the super-rich. (see **Chapter 5, Example 5.4, 'Shell to Sea'**).

An MNE needs to do its research in order to anticipate any problems that may arise from a negative sentiment being expressed. Indeed, such possible negative sentiment may be enough to dissuade an MNE from entering a market altogether.

More of the opposition to globalisation is driven by pure self-interest, either collective or individual. For example, Irish pork producers are not pleased to see pork produced from outside Ireland available on local supermarket shelves. Another example is how, in 2014, the residents of a satellite town of Dublin protested vigorously against the opening of a Starbucks, preferring a locally owned coffee shop rather than a global MNE brand. An MNE needs to make an assessment of the likely impact of such public opinion on the future cash flows of the business.

Conversely, it can also be the case that consumers are positively disposed to the arrival of a global employer or service provider to their local market. In many cases, government agencies, such as the IDA in Ireland, will subsidise a market entrant and will encourage local support.

EXAMPLE 7.3: IDA IRELAND AND LOCAL SUPPORT

IDA Ireland helps MNEs source suitable sites for their activities in the Republic of Ireland. Indeed, in the IDA Ireland annual report for 2013, the chairman and CEO report highlights that property is a key part of its activities in attracting FDI.[2] IDA Ireland invested €467 million in supporting research, development and innovation projects in 2013 in furtherance of its goals to support inward direct investment. Often IDA Ireland will help the MNE to build the facility through the provision of the land for the site or by way of grant-aiding the construction costs.

IDA Ireland will often engage with local stakeholders to advocate for inward investment in the local community. It will also explain to stakeholders the benefits to the local economy of FDI and location of sites in a particular locality. The instances of widespread local opposition to IDA Ireland-supported inward investments are few and far between.

Bureaucracy

Bureaucracy (or 'red tape') may seem to be innocuous and 'just part of doing business'. However, it is often a less obvious, 'softer' barrier to entry and in some countries the never-ending web of complex and seemingly illogical rules and regulations can have a heavy commercial cost. MNEs needed to consider the implications of such 'red tape' on their business model when contemplating entering some countries, for example the former communist countries of Eastern Europe as governments struggled with the transition from centrally planned, government-controlled economies.

MNEs may need to collaborate with local businesspeople to try to ease the journey through the red tape. In some countries, foreign-owned MNEs are actually compelled to form alliances with local business in order to get licences to operate. In China, as we have seen in **Chapter 3**, MNEs that wish to do business there must form joint ventures with locally owned entities, often owned by the People's Republic of China. In this way the Chinese government ensures that the activities of the MNEs are in accordance with its own economic goals. Any MNE contemplating expansion into such markets needs to build in the costs of such arrangements into their forecasts in order to properly appraise the suitability of the investment.

Government Inconsistency

At the other end of the spectrum from bureaucracy can be a government's inaction to enforce commercial codes and contracts. In some circumstances the authorities might not actively enforce regulations covering beaches of contract, intellectual property rights, planning, and so forth. In such circumstances an MNE may find it has complied with expensive regulations in accordance with host country laws only to find itself competing with businesses that flout or ignore those same laws. An MNE will, rightly, seek to comply with the law in all the countries in which it operates. However, this may work to disadvantage its future cash flows in countries where such compliance only adds cost and does not add any competitive advantage.

---

[2] IDA Ireland, *Annual Report and Accounts 2013*, www.IDAireland.com

Corruption is a further area where government inaction can frustrate an MNE's ability to gain certainty concerning its future cash flows. One does not have to go back too far in history to find evidence of where kings and rulers would sell entitlements to collect taxes or issue licences to the highest bidder. The winning bidders would then be allowed to levy their entitlement onto the populace, often unfairly. This practice was prevalent in France in the 18th Century and was recently still a feature of some less developed countries, such as Burundi.[3] In the past, this system facilitated the collection of revenues from a population that was effectively ungovernable in any other fashion due to the lack of central systems of control. In a world before modern communications systems it was difficult to impose central rule across a wide area. Thus, the 'selling' of the right to collect taxes or levies was often the only way to exercise control.

Clearly, this approach is flawed in that it is easily open to corruption. As modern governmental systems developed along with accompanying communications technologies, such practices died out in modern democracies. However, it is still the case that where governments cannot exercise control on their citizens, civil service or armed forces, corruption can be so endemic as to cause damage to the commercial environment in which the MNEs can do business and ultimately damage the MNE's performance. For example, licences or government contracts can be awarded to whoever pays off the right official. The global business community has sought to hold MNEs to account through the introduction of ethical frameworks to guide behaviour (see **Chapter 5**). Thus, the solution to the issue is one involving changes to behaviour of states and their officers, as well as MNEs and their managers.

While this behaviour can happen in any country, it is true to say it happens in some countries more than others. To facilitate an analysis and awareness of corruption Transparency International ('the global coalition against corruption') produces an annual Corruptions Perceptions Index which "ranks countries/territories based on how corrupt a country's public sector is perceived to be". Scores range from zero (highly corrupt) to 100, where there is a perception of high degrees of integrity and low corruption.[4] The 2014 index analysed 175 countries. The five countries with the lowest levels of corruption were:

1. Denmark
2. New Zealand
3. Finland
4. Sweden
5. Norway.

On the low end of the scale, the bottom five countries were:

171. South Sudan
172. Afghanistan
173. Sudan
174. North Korea
175. Somalia.

MNEs should be aware of this index and any other sources of information that can aid their understanding of impacts to the predictability of cash flows. As you can see from the top five, all are countries with stable, democratically elected governments. The bottom five, on the other hand, are all either war-torn or have undemocratic governments, or no government at all.

---

[3] Collecting tax in Africa, www.economist.com/news/finance-and-economics/21601293-burundi-shows-how african-countries-can-reduce-their-dependence-on-aid, 26 April 2014 (accessed May 2015).

[4] See http://www.transparency.org/

(The UK is at position 14 in the league table, with a score of 78 out of 100. The Republic of Ireland was at joint position 17, with Hong Kong, The US and Barbados, with a score of 74.)

The other side of government inaction is state action and intervention. Governments may act unilaterally in imposing new taxes or regulations on MNEs. In many cases it is not easy to anticipate what dramatic moves a government may make as, in order to maximise its own position, a government may not wish to flag its intentions. This was certainly the case in Venezuela before Hugo Chavez was elected in 1999. The subsequent widescale nationalisation of industries was not flagged during the election as a keystone of post-election actions by the government. Miguel Octavio, a Venezuelan financial analyst, has a fairly negative view of the effects of nationalisation on the efficacy of that country's production capability, as can be seen from his brief commentary below. Aside from Octavio's subjective view, the main issue is that during the election Hugo Chavez did not highlight that he would embark on such widespread nationalisation and any MNEs were caught out by the unexpected turn of events.

> In Venezuela, Sidor, the country's steel producer, was privatised and sold to an Argentinean concern in 1997. The company became profitable and productive and paid yearly dividends, giving to the government the money to pay over to the workers who had become shareholders when the company was privatised. And then, one day, Hugo Chavez decided to nationalise Sidor and the oil pipe factory next door. Sidor, today, is producing less and losing money, and the oil pipe factory has shut down. And what happened to that dividend for the workers? They have yet to collect. In fact, Sidor's cash flow is so bad that the Venezuelan state oil company was forced to hand over US$800 million to prop it up temporarily. Except, of course, this subsidy will regularly be needed as, in its nationalised state, the company will always be inefficient and unproductive.[5]

Exchange Controls and Political Risk

Exchange controls can have a dramatic effect on cash flows for the MNE. An MNE converts the cash it generates in the various countries back into the home currency eventually. Over the long run, the surplus cash generated needs to find its way to the investors through improved share price value or real dividend payments. Unexpected exchange control variations (blocked funds) can cause the quantum of the cash that is converted back to the parent company currency to differ from expectations. MNEs need to be aware of existing regulations and policies regarding exchange control and possible future changes. This matter is covered in more detail in **Chapter 8**.

7.4 MEASURING COUNTRY RISK PROFILES

In order to assess the risks of doing business in a certain country an MNE needs a process by which it can assess those risks and compare the country's assessment to other countries. A way of doing this is to collect information pertinent to target countries in a structured and consistent way using country performance measures like the ones mentioned earlier in this chapter. This collected data should provide a profile of the country. We can call this profile a 'country risk' profile. We can compare a country's profile with other countries in which the MNE does

---

[5] www.moneyweb.co.za/archive/nationalisation-in-venezuela-an-inside-perspective/

business already. The MNE can also use the profiles to compare one or more countries in which it is considering investing resources. In this way the MNE affords itself a structured assessment process that allows it the best chance of making the right decision.

Having understood that the external influences or factors that impact an MNE fall into two areas, economic and political, the MNE manager then needs to have a systematic way of assessing those impacts. Such a system is important as it facilitates objective assessment and, perhaps more importantly, relative comparison. The assessment of future cash flows is difficult. Assessing the possible impacts of economic and political influences in an international context is even more problematic. By having a systematic approach, an MNE is afforded a method for comparison. As each country is assessed on the same basis it is possible to conclude that Country X is better than Country Y on this measure or that measure. This means that even if the absolute measure is difficult to ascertain scientifically, the analyst can at least say that one country differs from another on the basis that both countries were measured the same way. For example, measuring corruption might be an inexact science. However, if two countries' corruption levels, measured on the same basis, exhibit significantly different results, the MNE can at least make valid inferences from this variance, even though the actual measure itself may be unscientific in its calculation. Such processes call for judgement on the part of the MNE manager.

There are four main techniques that MNEs use to systemise their assessment of economic and political risk, which we will examine below in turn:
- qualitative analysis,
- quantitative analysis,
- the checklist method, and
- the Delphi technique.

Qualitative Analysis

Qualitative analysis uses subjective judgement based on unquantifiable information. In this regard the MNE managers will draw on their experience, the 'feel' for a place or market and other non-scientifically measureable information about the country.

MNEs may engage in either structured or unstructured qualitative analysis. Research has shown that half of MNEs do not conduct structured country analysis in any systematic way. These companies most likely carry out an unstructured analysis involving desk research, informal market analysis and most probably on-the-ground country visits. While sometimes eschewed by more quantitative leaning analysts, there is much to be said for experiencing a country in person. If managers are experts in their own fields of business they develop an intuitive 'gut feel' for what does and does not work. While it can be lazy not do further, more quantitative analysis, it would also be foolish to discard the intuition of experienced managers and to neglect their 'feel' for a country.

However, to aid inter-country comparison and to remove the subjectivity that can arise from just taking unstructured analysis, it is preferable to have a structured approach to the qualitative analysis.

A structured qualitative method uses some standardised format with a specifically stipulated scope and focus of analysis. Since it adheres to a uniform format across countries and is augmented by economic statistics, it is easier to make accurate and more reliable comparisons between countries. Still, considerable subjective judgement has to be made by analysts.

The political risk index provided by Business Environment Risk Intelligence (BERI) SA is an example of such a structured qualitative method rating country risk.[6] For example, if an MNE with operations in Ireland, Portugal and Spain is considering investing in the Czech Republic, it could buy some analysis from BERI for the Czech Republic and Portugal, where it is already operating. This allows it to make a comparison between a market it already knows, Portugal, and one it is considering investing in. BERI sells Quick Response Country Reports (QRCRs), which cover, among other things, a country's:

- business environment for MNEs
- political scenarios
- political and currency developments
- economic performance forecasts
- labour force evaluations.

The MNE can compare this analysis to countries with which it is familiar. It can also use the analysis to stress-test its forecast by imagining various scenarios outlines in the QRCR and assess the likely impact upon future cash flows.

Whatever qualitative analysis is used to assess the country risk, it is best if the MNE adopts a structured approach since such an approach allows for the reasonable comparison with other options available to the MNE. Such structured approaches also allow the MNE to compare actual performance in the future to the expectations that were imagined at the decision formation stage. Such post-event analysis helps MNEs learn about markets and international expansion.

Quantitative Analysis

Quantitative analysis as applied to country risk profiles or assessments involves the use of mathematical analysis techniques to understand the financial dynamics of a country. This technique often involves complex statistical models in order to simulate a country's performance and thereby inform the MNE managers in their decision-making.

There are several quantitative methods that can be used to analyse the various issues concerning country risk. These methods can be useful in establishing relationships between political, economic and financial factors on one hand and some indicator that reflects risk exposure or risky behaviour on the other. For example, the relationship between unemployment and consumer spending might be correlated to each other. By looking at past trends in the movements of these two variables, an MNE might be able to gain an understanding as to how spending in the country in focus might move in the future under various unemployment rate scenarios. The basic approach is to use historical data trends. The data is selected by reference to the areas of risk that the MNE believes may impact upon its performance. The trends in the data are examined in order to assess the likely future trends.

For example, if inflation has been growing in a country at 4% per annum for each of the last 10 years, the quantitative analysis might extrapolate how this trend will continue. It might also attempt to mathematically correlate this inflation trend with, for example, imported goods and services. Assuming the MNE was interested in assessing the likely level of imports into the country under assessment, the MNE could then produce some forecasts as to how the future may look. In this way, the MNE builds up a picture of a number of likely scenarios.

---

[6] See www.beri.com/

Each scenario will present a different set of possible outcomes for the performance of the MNE in its activities related to that country. Quantitative analysis applies statistical and mathematical techniques to create models or simulations in order to predict outcomes.

As the statistical models become more developed they will begin to use more than one variable for the formulation of likely scenarios. Such, more complex models of a country's economy are called **econometric models**. As such, econometric approaches are usually different from simple regression analysis in that they attempt to model more complex situations albeit mainly involving two variables.

For example, an analysis of two measures, say unemployment and sales of orange juice, might create a prediction that if unemployment falls by 2%, then demand for orange juice increases by 4%. The model may then attempt mathematical modelling to predict how unemployment might alter based on historical and predicted inflation rates. Thus, a more complete picture might begin to emerge through the modelling process that allows an MNE to make more scientifically based predictions about its future cash flows. Imagine that the MNE is interested in selling orange juice into this country. By modelling historical data it can begin to produce predictive data based on the economic and political risk profile of the country. These predictive models will allow the MNE to be able to build into its future cash flows the effects of macroeconomic variables on its own performance. If the MNE is comparing two country location options, it can compare and contrast the quantitative results from both markets and make its decision based on the one most likely to produce the desired results, in this case, increased sales of orange juice.

The Checklist Method

Another method for assessing economic and political risk is called the **checklist method**. This involves drawing up a checklist of important measures concerning the country or countries under consideration. The checklist can include quantitative data, qualitative assessments or both. The MNE will construct the variables to be included on the checklist based on its own internal experiences of what it looks for in a market. It may also seek advice from others who have been involved in the internationalisation process in the past. It may further involve development agencies like Enterprise Ireland, which help MNEs expand into international markets.

The checklist allows each item to have a scale of importance to be associated with it. For example, 'democratic government' might be an item that has a score of 10 out of 10 whilst the existence of 'consumer research panels' might be given a scale of 3 out of 10. In this way the checklist attaches different importance to each item on the list. By marking each item on the checklist the analysis will provide the MNE with an overall score for the country involved. This score can be compared with other countries that have been scored on a similar basis. Thus the MNE can make an informed decision. An MNE may, for example, decide never to invest in countries that produce scores under a certain threshold based on their internal country risk profile checklist.

It can be helpful for MNEs to use this checklist system as the comparisons that can be carried out between options can aid decision-making. It can also be used to compare how one country that was examined some years ago compared to a prospective new country with which the MNE is considering getting involved. For example, if five years ago a checklist analysis was done of Portugal in advance of a successful involvement by the MNE in that country, the MNE manager could then draw some comfort from the fact that an analysis of Czech Republic produced a similar scoring from the checklist system.

In **Figure 7.3** below you can see how such a checklist works in practice. I have used draft data from a project carried out by the Norman Paterson School of International Affairs for illustration purposes only.[7] Let us assume an MNE was contemplating an investment in either Senegal or Sierra Leone. The managers in the MNE would list the economic and political issues which they believe will impact upon the MNE's likelihood of producing the desired returns on investment. These are listed under the heading 'Issue'. The MNE would then weight the issues on a scale of 1 to 10 in order of their impact upon the MNE's planned investment. The MNE will then assign a score to each country through some type of internal process. This process may be a meeting of the teams involved where the participants work out a consensus score. More likely though, the MNE will ask each relevant person, both internal and possibly external to the enterprise, to assess the country on each issue and allocate a score. The scores will then be aggregated and an average score arrived at. This method has the benefit of eliminating group-think and smoothing out the possible effects of a dominant or biased view. The larger the pool of informed contributing scorers, the more objective the final result. The average scores are then multiplied by the weightings to arrive at a weighted average score. The weighted averages are totalled and divided by the number of issues (adjusted for their respective weightings) to arrive at a 'Risk Index Weighted Average' Score. In this example, Sierra Leone has a much higher score at 7.5 being 360.7/48, than Senegal at 5.4 (261.3/48). If the MNE was using Country Risk checklist as its only input into its decision-making, then it should proceed with the investment in Senegal and reject the Sierra Leone investment. The higher the Risk Index Weighted Average Score, the higher the risk. Higher risk investments are less attractive and should therefore require a higher return for investors.

FIGURE 7.3: RISK INDEX – SENEGAL VS SIERRA LEONE

Issue	Weighting	Senegal Average Score	Weighted	Sierra Leone Average Score	Weighted
History of Armed Conflict	8	5.4	43.2	9.3	74.1
Political Instability	5	5	24.8	8.3	41.3
Militarisation	5	4.3	21.7	3.8	18.8
Population Heterogeneity	4	4.3	17.3	6.7	26.7
Demographic Stress	5	6.1	30.7	6.1	30.3
Economic Performance	8	5.8	46.4	9.6	76.4
Human Development	3	6.0	18.0	7.9	23.6
Environmental Stress	5	5.0	25.0	8.5	42.5
International Linkages	5	5.0	25.0	5.4	27.0
	48		261.3		360.7
Risk Index Weighted Average			5.4		7.5

[7] Country Indicators for Foreign Policy Project, Norman Paterson School of International Affairs, August 2001.

The Delphi Technique

Originally developed for the US military in the early 1950s as a way of forecasting likely trends in military capability, the Delphi Technique was further developed by Helmer, Dalkey and Rescher in the 1990s.[8] The technique involves structured questions asked of acknowledged experts in a particular subject area. In the case of MNEs, these experts may be internal to the MNE itself but can also include external advisors. The process uses questionnaires which each member of the panel of experts completes. After the first round of questionnaires is completed, a facilitator will encourage the experts to revise their original answers in order to move the overall answers towards a consensus. A statistical analysis of the answers can also indicate the mathematically measured divergence of viewpoints. The greater the divergence of viewpoints, the greater the risk.

The Delphi technique draws from its roots in scientific analysis and problem-solving. It is based on the idea that group thinking can pollute objective analysis and that experts may alter their views, either to avoid or embrace a consensus view. The Delphi technique seeks to eliminate these natural human urges by collecting viewpoints independently and, often, anonymously.

A possible scenario for use of Delphi analysis could be that an MNE, aided by a facilitator, has drawn up a list of questions about a particular country. The questions would normally be capable of being numerically answered. For example, rating on a scale of 1 through 10 how stable the political system of Portugal is, with zero being very unstable and 10 being very stable. Then the MNE would draw up a list of experts whose views on the target country would be informed and valuable. Each of the experts is polled, separately and privately. It is important for the process that the experts are not identified to each other and that their views are kept confidential.

The results of the questionnaires are then aggregated and analysed statistically. Two important pictures emerge from the analysis. First, a shared view, unpolluted by consensus thinking, can be mathematically calculated. This could be done by calculating the simple average of the scored answers given by the participants. Secondly, the statistical variance of the answers can be determined. Simplistically, the use of the Delphi technique would propose that the greater the variance in viewpoints expressed by the experts, the greater the potential variability and volatility for future cash flows from the target country for the MNE.

In the real world, MNEs will use a combination of some or all of the techniques outlined above. In this way, the exposure of the MNE to economic and political influences can be assessed, usually in a numerically defined way, albeit without losing sight of the value of intuition and qualitative analysis.

7.5 CONCLUSION

Part II looks at the economic factors that influence and affect MNEs. In this chapter we looked at the economic and political factors. In particular, we examined how an MNE can assess the economic and political factors of the countries in which it is engaged. We examined

---

[8] Rescher, N. (1998) *Predicting the Future*, State University of New York Press, Albany NY.

how these factors are measured using indicators such as GDP, inflation, unemployment and others. These factors contribute to the two main types of external risk that an MNE is exposed to: economic risk and political risk.

We then went on to see how MNEs can use economic and political indicators to build up a risk profile of a country. The MNE can use this risk profile to compare and contrast different countries with each other. They can also use the risk profiles to inform decision-making within the MNE and to help forecast future cash flows. The greater the certainty of future cash flows, the lower the risk profile of the MNE for investors. Finally, we looked at some techniques and tools that can be used to structure the information garnered of differing countries of interest to the MNE. These techniques, such the checklist method and the Delphi Technique, can put some structure on the information collected. This structured approach aids decision-making and allows for post-event analysis. Learning from one's past is as important for MNEs as it is for humankind in general.

In the next chapter we will look at how exchange rates, inflation rates and interest rates affect the MNE. In particular, we will examine why these economic indicators are different between differing countries. These differences produce challenges for the MNE, challenges that can be managed, as we will see in **Chapter 15**.

QUESTIONS

Self-test Questions

7.1 What are the two main sources of external risk?
7.2 What types of analysis of the economic and political impacts of a country on an MNE can be carried out?
7.3 You are the financial controller of an Irish food manufacturer considering opening a factory in Zambia. What advice would you give the board regarding the steps it should take before committing to the project?

Thought-provoking Questions

Question 7.1
You are Caitriona Crosby, a newly appointed accountant in Flashdesi Plc, an international chain of fashion stores. Your boss, the group CFO, has told you that the company is thinking of expanding into the African market. The buyers and designers are looking at what products might sell in those markets. The finance function has been asked specifically to assess which country would be better to invest in from an economic and political point of view, Algeria or Egypt. You have been asked to describe how Flashdesi Plc should go about making its investment decision purely from a macroeconomic viewpoint.

Question 7.2
Your boss, Yvonne Cross, has told you that your firm, a management consultancy, is to prepare an assessment of the macroeconomic factors that may influence your client's performance in Brazil. She is thinking of using a technique she has heard of called the Delphi Technique in order to produce this assessment. She asked that you look into how the Delphi Technique

might be used in the preparation of this assessment. She knows nothing about how the technique works and has asked you to produce a 'one pager' outlining the process and how it might work for the client, Bramby Plc.

Review Question

(See Suggested Solutions to Review Questions in **Appendix B**.)

Question 7.1

Internationally, how do countries differ in their approach to property rights and corruption?

8

EXCHANGE RATES, INFLATION AND INTEREST RATES

CONTENTS

LEARNING OBJECTIVES

Having read this chapter, you will understand:
- the factors that influence exchange rates;
- the linkage between interest rates, inflation and exchange rates;
- how government policy can affect exchange rates;
- why currencies change in value, the intervention of governments and the effect of the demand and supply curves;
- the theory behind the balance of payments;
- the nature of arbitrage, in particular how it operates in foreign exchange and interest rate markets to prevent risk-free profits and ensure one exchange rate prevails for any two currencies;
- the International Fisher Effect, how inflation rate differentials interact with interest rates and exchange rates;
- purchasing power parity, and how prices adjust through the movement of exchange rates;
- how interest rate differentials affect exchange rates;
- the main contemporary theories concerning foreign exchange; and
- how looking at inflation rates can inform an MNE as to likely movements in exchange rates that will directly feed into its business decisions.

8.1 INTRODUCTION

In order to conduct international business there must be an exchange system to manage the flow of money across borders and between jurisdictions. For example, in order to pay a supplier from another jurisdiction a multinational enterprise (MNE) must have a method to transmit the necessary funds to the country that the supplier operates from. Likewise, an MNE that sells its products abroad must find ways to receive payment for the goods it has supplied.

The MNE operating in today's global economy will almost certainly be involved in, and exposed to, foreign exchange risks. Allied to these foreign exchange risks are the other monetary risks connected to interest rates and inflation. This chapter will set out the main theories that underpin these three risk areas. **Chapter 15** will then explain the various options open to the MNE to manage those risks.

In order to appreciate the nature of the risks associated with exchange rates we need to understand what exchange rates are and why they move. The first part of the chapter will explain how exchange rates have come about and what causes them to move. In particular, we will see how the exchange rate is related to the demand for a country's currency. Currencies are an asset and demand for that currency will be driven by attributes that make the asset attractive to investors. These attributes include the interest rate the currency earns, inflation rates in the currency's associated economy, the perceived risk of falling value and stability. Demand for a currency is also driven by the need to make payments to suppliers and service providers. The aggregate of such demand is measured as part of a country's balance of payments calculations. A component of the balance of payments of a country is its imports and exports; in other words, its external trade with other countries. Importantly, most of this trade comprises the activities of MNEs. The exchange rate is also subject to movement through government intervention. Having examined what drives exchange rate movements, we will then examine how these exchange rate movements are connected to interest rates and inflation. Through understanding these dynamics we will be in a better position to understand the tools that an MNE will need to use to manage the risks associated. We will examine a number of theories that seek to explain exchange rate movements:
- balance of payments;
- international parity approaches; and
- asset markets models.

8.2 THE BALANCE OF PAYMENTS

> The balance of payments (BoP) of a country is the aggregate of all transactions between residents of the country and residents of other countries. 'Residents' for this purpose includes individual citizens and all commercial entities, including companies and governments.

In order to gain an understanding of why exchange rates move we must first take a step back from examining MNEs and look at the macroenvironment in which MNEs operate. The main driver of exchange rate movement of a currency is the supply and demand for that currency. The most significant driver of demand, or supply, of a currency, other than government intervention, is the level of transactions the country and its citizens conduct with other countries. A country monitors this level of transaction through measuring its balance of payments (BoP). The BoP comprises all transactions with foreign countries. The BoP is made up of the two sub-classifications and therefore has two components:

- the current account; and
- the financial account.

Balance of Payments Current Account

The aggregate of all the payments for goods and services imported into a country is netted against the aggregate of all the payments for goods and services exported from the country. The resultant is called the **balance of payments current account**. If the value of the imports is greater than the exports then the balance of payments current account is said to be in deficit. On the other hand, if exports exceed imports then the account is in surplus. While the balance of payments is always measured in the home country's currency, to allow country-by-country comparison the values can be converted into a common currency. For example, to compare the BoP current account of the UK to that of South Africa, both current accounts might be converted from Stg£ and the Rand, respectively, into US$ to allow for comparison.

> An MNE's 'home country' is the country from which it is predominantly managed. Normally, it is the country in which the MNE has its headquarters. In most instances, it will be the country where the MNE was originally formed, although this is not necessarily the case.

Balance of Payments Financial Account

Citizens, firms and governments will also want to invest in stocks, shares and assets in foreign countries. The aggregate of a nation's foreign investments netted against the aggregate of the investment in that country by foreign-owned MNEs and individuals produces its **balance of payments financial account**. Investment overseas by home country MNEs represents a deficit on the financial account, while investment in the home country by foreign MNEs represents a surplus. The net of the two investment types produces either a financial account deficit or surplus.

Where foreign investment in a country exceeds that country's aggregate investments in other countries, then its financial account is in surplus. Note that an excess of exports produces a surplus on the current account while it is an excess of inward foreign investment that produces a surplus on the financial account. This is because surpluses arise from actions that cause a demand for the home currency. Thus, exports create a demand for the home currency as foreign entities seek to pay for the goods and services they have purchased. Likewise, foreign investment in the home country causes a demand for the home currency as foreign entities pay for whatever capital assets have been purchased.

The financial account and the current account must balance with each other. It is useful to think about BoP as being the accounting system of a country's external transactions with the rest of the world prepared under the **double-entry system**. Where the exchange rate of a currency is 'free floating' it means that the government allows the currency's exchange rate in terms of other currencies to be set by the market. Where a currency is 'free floating' the exchange rate will vary by an amount that will cause the current account to balance with the financial account.

> Double-entry is the accounting system where all transactions have two accounting entries, a debit and an equal credit. Since all entries have a debit and equal credit the total of all accounting entries will be zero.

As we have seen, there are two parts of the balance of payments account: the current account and the financial account. Either can be in surplus or deficit. Since the current account must balance to the financial account, it follows therefore that there can be three scenarios for a country's balance of payments:

• current account in surplus, financial account in deficit;
• current account in deficit, financial account in surplus; or
• current account and financial account are in equilibrium.

Like a company's statement of financial position, a country's balance of trade account will balance, with the current account surplus equal to the financial account deficit, or vice versa, or both being close to zero. This is because, at an atomised level, each transaction with a foreign country by an MNE creates both the debit and credit side of the balance of payments account. By 'atomised', I am referring to the consideration of each transaction at the individual level, each international export or import. This is considered further in the example of trade between Zedmania and Beeland in **Example 8.1** below.

EXAMPLE 8.1: BoP AND ITS LINK TO EXCHANGE RATES

Zedmania's currency is the Zolar. Imagine it has only one MNE, Zinc, which has just one transaction in a given year: the export of a machine for which it charges its trading customer, Blu, in Beeland, 1 million Zolars.

In Beeland, the customer Blu must buy 1 million Zolars in order to pay its supplier, Zinc. Beeland's home currency is the Buro. The exchange rate is 2 Buro = 1 Zolar. Consequently, Blu pays its bank 2 million Buros, which the bank then uses to buy 1 million Zolars from the bank in Zedmania. The Beeland bank then gives the Zolars to Blu who then pays Zinc, back in Zedmania.

However, the bank in Zedmania now has in its possession the 2 million Buros that it exchanged with the bank in Beeland. Thus, taken as a whole, Zedmania has a balance of trade surplus, or current account surplus, of 1 million Zolars and a finance account deficit of 1 million Zolars, being the 2 million Buros converted into Zolars at the exchange rate 2:1. Essentially, the exchange rate is automatically determined at the rate needed to balance the current account surplus of 1 million Zolars with the financial account deficit, which is represented by the 2 million Buros in the Zedmania bank.

Why Balance of Payments Matter to MNEs

The essence of the theory that underpins the balance of payments concept is that the exchange rate for a given currency is driven by the balance between the demand for that currency and its supply. The demand for a currency is driven by the requirement of foreign trading partners to acquire it in order to pay for goods exported from the home country. On the other side, the supply of that currency is driven by the amount of it that investors and the central bank of the home country make available for the purchase of foreign currencies with which to buy imports or make investments in other jurisdictions. The theory proposes that the rate of exchange adjusts in such a way as to keep the BoP balanced. When all the transactions are converted back to the home currency at the appropriate rates, then the BoP balances. Put another way, the exchange rate is the price of the home currency and the BoP represents its demand and supply curve. The rate is set at the intersection of the curves.

An individual country will have an exchange rate equilibrium for each of the currencies it has transactions with. In other words, every country will have its own set of foreign exchange rates between its currency and the currencies of the countries with which it transacts. Therefore, the entire global system of BoPs combine through foreign exchange rates to be in equilibrium at any moment in time. (Later in this chapter we will see how the global foreign exchange system works in order to ensure that this equilibrium is arrived at.)

Exchange rates are arrived at by the interactions of supply and demand for respective currencies. By way of example, examine **Figure 8.1** below. The horizontal axis represents the quantity of € demanded by holders of Stg£. The vertical axis represents the exchange rate between the € and the £. At the lower end of the vertical axis, owners of £ get more €s for their pound. At the upper end of the axis, each £ buys less €s. D_1 is the demand curve for €s by holders of £s. When the € is expensive, demand is lower. As the exchange rate drops, and each £ buys less €, the demand for € by holders of £ decreases. The line S_1 represents the supply of € made available by holders of € for exchange into £s. As the amount of £ each € can buy improves, so the supply of € available for purchase by holders of £ increases.

The exchange rate is determined by the intersection of the demand curve, D_1, and the supply curve, S_1. This intersection occurs at E_1, when £0.70 buys €1.

If the demand for € by holders of £ increases because of a deficit on the capital account between the two currencies, then a new demand curve arises, D_2. (Remember: a deficit on the capital account will most likely arise from a surplus on the balance of trade account, i.e. exports to € countries are greater than imports.) The new exchange rate is determined by the new intersection point E_2. In **Figure 8.1**, this is at the rate £0.80 buys €1. Therefore, £ has weakened *vis-à-vis* the €.

Imagine if the amount of € supplied was increased through the actions of the European Central bank. The effect of this would be to move the supply curve to the right, to a new position, S_2. Central banks sometimes effectively increase the supply of their currency by printing money. This practice is known as 'quantitative easing' or 'QE'. We will explore later in this chapter why central banks might do this. Assuming no change in the demand curve, the intersection point of demand curve D_1 and new supply curve S_2, is E_4. This happens at an exchange rate of £0.50 buys €1. Therefore, the increase of supply of € has led to a weakening of the € and a strengthening of £.

The final scenario depicted in **Figure 8.1** is where there is an increase in the demand curve to D_2 and an increase in supply to S_2. In our example, this happens at intersection point E_3. At this intersection, the exchange rate remains the same as in our first scenario, that is, £0.70 buys €1. One can deduce from this that central banks can maintain stable exchange rates by increasing or decreasing the supply of money in order to balance out the effects of increases or decreases in demand factors. We will see later how actions by governments and/or central banks can be a major determinant of exchange rates. Therefore, MNE managers need to be cognisant of government and central bank policies in this regard.

FIGURE 8.1: THE LAW OF SUPPLY AND DEMAND AND FOREIGN EXCHANGE RATES

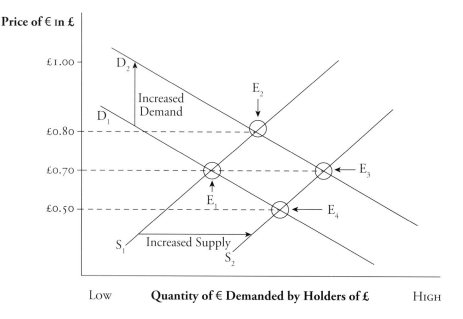

For MNEs it is important to understand that macroeconomic issues can and do affect exchange rates. In particular, issues that influence the balance of payments current account will feed into trends in foreign exchange rates, as illustrated in **Example 8.2**.

EXAMPLE 8.2: KOALA TRADES WITH NEW ZEALAND

An MNE, Koala Plc, manufactures in Australia and exports its products to New Zealand. Australia has been running a current account surplus with New Zealand and this is expected to grow over the next 12 months. All other things being equal, this will lead to strengthening of the Aus$ against the NZ$. This strengthening of the Aus$ will mean that Koala's products will become more expensive in New Zealand, which will have the effect of reducing demand volumes.

What is Best for a Country: Current Account Surplus, Deficit or Equilibrium?

In a developed country, such as Ireland or the UK, it is commonly understood that it is best to run a current account surplus, where exports are greater than imports. The corresponding deficit on the financial account means that there is a demand for the home currency. The downside is that the demand can lead to a strengthening of the home currency, causing prices of exports to rise and imports to fall, and so the balance of payments current account surplus reduces. Such is the nature of global international trade.

On the other hand, when a developing country runs a current account surplus, this normally arises out of a need to generate foreign currency reserves to pay back loan interest or capital. However, if a developing country can run a current account deficit, it means that the surplus on the financial account is being provided by the global financial community. This vote of confidence in the longer term development of the country is a positive sign. Therefore, as a general rule it is better for developed economies to run current account surpluses and for developing countries to run current account deficits.

However, there is a major global anomaly which belies this rule of thumb. Since 1980 the US has increasingly run current account deficits, which should have led to a weakening of the US dollar. The current account deficit should give rise to lower demand for dollars as US citizens and firms buy foreign currencies by selling their US$ to pay for the imports. This state of affairs would mean that foreign investors would be holding large quantities of US$, and of which there is a plentiful supply. However, the US$ has not weakened to the degree that the deficits have predicted. Essentially, this means that the foreign owners of US$ reserves are prepared to hold the dollars at an exchange rate higher than the macro-economic numbers would predict. Economists are unable to get consensus as to why this situation prevails. Some believe the current account deficit data is inaccurate. Others believe that foreign investors 'over-value' the US dollar as they see it as the world's only global currency. Indeed, the biggest purchasers of US Government bonds are international investors, particularly China, who seem to be holding the dollar as an investment in its own right rather than for any essential trade purpose. Whatever the reason, it has meant that the US has been able to run a current account deficit without seeing a corresponding erosion to the value of the dollar.

Limitations of the Balance of Payments Theory

While the theory of the balance of payments, and its resultant equilibrium of foreign exchange rates, has a certain elegance there are limitations to it.

Data Collection

The collection of a country's data is not without problems and not all relevant data can be sourced or collected. The balance of payments current account is often made to balance with the BoP financial account by the use of a 'correcting' or balancing figure.

Non-trade Demand

A further criticism of balance of payments theory is that it assumes that all international movement of currency arises from trade, i.e. the flow of goods and services or investments in stocks, shares and other assets. However, currency is an asset class in its own right. Investors may wish to invest in a currency because it is seen as stable or 'safer' than holding funds in another currency. Furthermore, investors may not necessarily sell a currency just because the exchange rate moves in a way that would make it appear logical to do so. For strategic reasons they may decide to hold the currency for the longer term.

> The Chinese government seeks to control the exchange rate of its currency, the Yuan. It does this by buying and selling currencies in order to achieve its desired exchange rate. China has vast foreign exchange reserves, over $2.5 trillion. The government-controlled banks use these reserves to control supply and demand for Yuan, thereby controlling the exchange rates of the Yuan. The rate is such that over the last number of decades goods made in China and exported globally are relatively inexpensive and, thus, enjoy high demand, which has meant that China has run balance of payments current account surpluses for many years.

The BoP theory would predict that the Yuan should appreciate as the demand for the currency rises as a result of these surpluses, eventually cancelling out China's competitive advantage. Standards of living in China should rise, imports should become cheaper. While these market and societal changes have happened to a certain degree, it has not been at the pace that the trade surpluses could support. In other words, the current account surpluses are such that the Yuan should have appreciated in value to a much greater degree, allowing the average Chinese citizen much greater purchasing power in terms of their ability to buy foreign goods. The switching of domestic consumption from domestically manufactured goods to imported goods would bring about improvements in standards of living as, by implication, consumers would not make the switch unless the imported goods were either cheaper, thus freeing up extra cash, or of a better quality, thus improving living standards. Consequently, the actions of the Chinese Government by not letting the Yuan find its own exchange rate on the open market distort the application of BoP theory in real life.

Though China's is not the only government that seeks to control exchange rates, nor even the most authoritative in doing so, nonetheless China is a huge global power and the effects of its Government's actions are widely felt. These effects are mainly that China-based exporters have a competitive advantage over other countries if the Yuan is undervalued through the management of the exchange rate by the Chinese government. The competitive advantage means that Chinese firms can undercut competitors from other countries. If the currency was allowed to rise, then the Chinese exports would increase in price, thus eliminating the competitive advantage over time.

Imperfect Markets

A further limitation is that the balance of payments theory assumes a '**perfect market**', one where there is complete information together with no transaction costs. There is also the presumption of transparency within the market. We already know that some governments do not allow their currency to trade freely on the world markets, i.e. they do not allow their currency to be completely subject to the laws of supply and demand in the market. Rather, they seek to control the exchange rates by imposing restrictions on their banking sector. Governments may also seek to employ other restrictions on a completely perfect market to either discourage or encourage certain types of commercial activity. Such distortions of the market must also distort any inferences and deductions that can be made by applying the balance of payments theory. (See also **Chapter 2**, for a broader discussion of imperfect markets.)

In September 2011 the Swiss National Bank, SNB, announced that it was going to 'peg' the exchange rate of the Swiss Franc, CHF, to the euro at a rate of €1 = CHF1.2 or less. The intervention was seen as a response to a strengthening CHF as investors sought out the currency as a 'safe haven' from the turmoils of the euro. The announcement in 2011 meant that the SNB would intervene in the market by increasing money supply, or restricting it, to ensure the rate remained below the agreed number, €1 = CHF1.2. In January 2015 the SNB surprised markets by removing the 'peg' and returning to a free-floating exchange rate. The CHF immediately strengthened by 20%. From 2011 to 2015 the exchange rate that prevailed was not a free market one and thus distorted the underlying assumptions of BoP theory.

However, the absence of a perfect market may also give rise to opportunities for MNEs in that the distortions create differences between markets which can be exploited. Indeed, many MNE strategies for expansion into foreign markets involve taking advantage of the differences that arise between markets. Often, these differences arise in the first place from government actions to limit the effects of totally free markets. For example, a government might provide grants to certain companies in order to attract them to set up activities in their country. Such grants are a distortion of totally free market mechanics since they introduce an artificial incentive to locate in an area that market forces alone would not support. An MNE may take advantage of these distortions to expand its own markets through availing of the grants. Much of the work of IDA Ireland was initially through the provision of financial incentives to foreign companies to locate in the Republic of Ireland (see **Chapter 4**). Competition authorities watch this type of activity very closely to ensure that it does not distort the market to the disadvantage of other operators in the market or, ultimately, the consumer.

8.3 A HISTORY OF EXCHANGE RATES

An MNE needs to be aware of its exposure to exchange rate movements and it must manage this exposure in accordance with the risk appetite of the enterprise and its stakeholders. Part of the awareness of foreign exchange matters involves understanding why and how exchange rates move. Earlier in this chapter we saw how the BoP theory influences movements in exchange rates. However, the BoP is not the only influence on exchange rates. As mentioned above, governments are hugely interested in exchange rates, particularly those of their home currency. As international trade has developed and grown, particularly since the Industrial Revolution, governments have become increasingly involved in the determination of exchange rates. To more fully understand how and why government actions are connected to exchange rate movements we need to look at the history of exchange rates, which to some degree is also the history of money.

The Gold Standard

When it first originated, the value of paper money was based on a fixed quantity of gold. The total amount of money printed by a government had to be 'backed' by an equivalent amount of gold in its vaults. Money supply remained relatively constant. The import of this connection between gold reserves and printed money meant that if a government printed more money without changing its gold reserves, the value of the currency would fall. This would happen since there would now be more printed money represented by the same amount of gold. There was no advantage to a government printing more money, all other things being equal, and so the money supply remained fairly constant. The supply of a given currency would normally only increase as the country's gold reserves increased, i.e. in an expanding economy. This system was standardised in 1876 into what was called 'the gold standard'.

Every country's currency within the gold standard system was given a fixed exchange rate at which that currency could be exchanged into a given amount of gold. As each currency had this rate attached to it, it was possible to calculate exchange rates between different currencies using the gold rate as the triangulation point.

> Historically, the government of Zedmania printed 100 billion Zolars. The currency in issue was backed by 10,000 gold bars in the vaults of its central bank. The government of Beeland had also printed 100 billion Buros. These were backed by 5,000 gold bars in its bank's vaults. There was half the amount of gold in the Beeland bank vaults compared to the Zedmania bank vaults. Consequently, the value of a Buro was half that of a Zolar, giving an exchange rate of Buros to Zolars of 2:1.

With the outbreak of First World War in 1914 the gold standard system was suspended. Not all countries abandoned the system but since some countries, such as the UK, suspended it, its usefulness as a system for exchange rate determination was impacted negatively. There were some attempts to re-introduce it when the war ended, but the Wall Street Crash of 1929 and the Great Depression that followed put an end to those aspirations. There were insufficient gold reserves to back most currencies. Despite attempts by some governments to link their currencies to the US dollar or the pound Sterling, this also failed as there was not enough confidence to exchange one currency for another at the committed rate. This lack of confidence led to constraints on foreign exchange activity, with a consequent reduction in the level of international trade. However, the US dollar remained backed by gold reserves and became the international 'world' currency of choice, followed by Sterling.

Bretton Woods

Near the end of the Second World War it became clear to the allied governments that international trade was a possible source of greater global financial and social integration. This integration could stabilise intra-country relationships in a way that might reduce the risk of wars between nations in the future. To facilitate greater trade between nations, however, there needed to be greater certainty of exchange rates and an easier system of movement of goods and money between trading nations. The Bretton Woods Agreement, which was entered into in 1944 and lasted until 1971, established fixed exchange rates between the participating countries. Governments committed to each other to intervene to prevent movement of their respective currencies outside a range of plus or minus 1%. Thus, the practice developed of government intervention to 'correct' free market forces. Governments would therefore intervene in the marketplace when they felt there was a risk that their currency exchange rate would move outside the 1% band agreed. The Bretton Woods Agreement also created the International Monetary Fund (IMF). Each participating country funded the IMF. The IMF, armed with those funds, was then able to help countries intervene in the markets when they hadn't the capability to do so themselves, for whatever reason. Thus a collaboration of the co-funded IMF and the individual countries' central banks ensured that the exchange rates for transactions did not fall outside the 1% variation band.

As mentioned earlier, from 1944 onward the US ran a cumulative trade deficit on its balance of payments account. This deficit was 'balanced' by foreign governments happy to hold dollars as a reserve, especially as the US dollar was capable of being exchanged into gold. Thus, the Bretton Woods Agreement also buffered the currencies from any volatile exchange rate fluctuations.

As mentioned earlier, Bretton Woods was also the occasion of the birth of the IMF, of which most countries are members and which still plays a major role in world trade. The goals of the IMF are to:
- promote stability in exchange rates;
- promote free trade;

- promote co-operation between countries on monetary issues;
- promote free movement of capital;
- provide temporary funds to correct international payments imbalances.

The IMF acts to encourage international trade. Its activities are of interest to MNEs as the goals of the IMF encourage and promote the conditions that foster greater MNE activity.

The Smithsonian Agreement

By 1971 some countries became nervous about continuing to hold US dollars and sought to convert their dollars to gold. The subsequent sell-off of dollars led to the Smithsonian Agreement. This landmark agreement revalued the dollar downward against all the major world currencies. The agreement also widened the bands of tolerance from Bretton Woods from 1% to 2.25%. The need to back the dollar with gold reserves was also dispensed with.

The Smithsonian Agreement represented a major shift toward allowing free market forces determine exchange rates while at the same time decoupling currencies from gold, thus fundamentally changing the nature of currency. Up until this time the US dollar was pegged to a fixed given quantity of gold. Other world currencies were pegged to the dollar, and thus, by implication, to the gold reserves held by the US Government. With the Smithsonian Agreement, for the first time, money could be printed without needing a matching increase in gold reserves.

The Plaza Accord

By the mid-1980s the world's currencies were exchanging with one another at rates dictated, more or less, by free market forces. However, while governments were not overtly managing exchange rates in the fashion of Bretton Woods or the Smithsonian Agreement, they were still involved in a more subtle way. Governments could still control interest rates for each currency and, through controlling interest rates, they could still influence demand. (An increase in interest rates ought to produce an increase in demand for the currency since the return is higher than it was previous to the rate increase. This increased demand should see a strengthening of the currency. However, as we will see later, these increases can be short-lived through the workings of interest rate parity theory.) They could also issue new money, thereby influencing supply. Therefore, although the commitment to act to maintain prescribed exchange rate bands had begun to disappear, governments, through the actions of their central banks, were, and are, still acting to influence exchange rates. Therefore, it remains important for the MNE to be aware that central banks take actions in the financial markets to support a desired exchange rate.

Such actions taken by central banks and their respective governments do not now take place against the backdrop of explicit agreements to exchange rate bands. However, there are agreements between governments that still influence exchange rates. One of the most important of these agreements in recent decades has been the Plaza Accord. In an attempt to quell rising inflation in the late 1970s, the US had raised its interest rates. While this did dampen inflation it also led to a rise in the value of the US dollar of over 50% from 1980 to 1985. This hampered exports and made imports cheaper, the knock-on effect of which was that the US began to run a current account deficit that reached 3.5% of GDP. US manufacturers were finding it impossible to compete on a global level. Japanese and German competitors, in particular, were taking market share from US manufacturers.

In 1985, the G5 nations (West Germany, France, Japan, the UK and the US) met in Washington and agreed multilaterally to reduce the value of the US dollar in the Plaza Accord. This accord signified a desire to co-operate constructively on managing exchange rates. So, on the one hand, you have an explicit support by the many of the world's governments to the principles of free trade and free market economics but, on the other hand, one can witness active intervention by governments in the operation of those self-same free markets. Defenders of these interventions point to the fact that the actions of governments and central banks are funded by and financed by citizens who themselves are operating in the free markets and elect the governments that are carrying out the interventions. Put another way, government, in these circumstances, are part of the free market system.

While one can argue that the market determines the price of one currency in terms of another, the Plaza Accord is an example of how governments can and do have a major bearing on what happens. In the two years after the Plaza Accord, the US dollar fell by 50% versus the Japanese Yen. Japanese exports to the US were becalmed and the US economy began to ramp up its exports, thereby reducing its current account deficit. Thus, the intervention tactics put in play by the Plaza Accord had the desired effect.

The Euro

In 1979, the governments of the EEC Member States agreed to fix exchange rates between their respective currencies. An artificial triangulation currency unit, the ECU ('European currency unit'), was created and all EEC governments committed to fix their exchange rates to it. The EEC governments agreed to ensure that the currencies within the system would not deviate from the fixed exchange rate by more than 2.25%, the same band of tolerance as required by the Smithsonian Agreement.

The ECU also became a currency in its own right and by 1990 international financial transactions began to take place in ECU. It was an electronic virtual currency that had no physical manifestation. However, as it was backed by EEC Member States, it was sometimes preferred by those engaging in foreign exchange transactions to the currency of one or other of the parties to the transaction. This held true for non-ECU currencies in addition to ECU participating currencies. For example, a US company might conduct transactions with an Irish company in ECU rather than the Irish Punt and the ECU was a much more substantial currency and could give the US entity some comfort as to its stability.

After the currency crisis of 1992–1993 the ECU's band of tolerance was widened to 15%, although most governments ensured that the actual operating rates were in a much narrower trading range. However, in the run-up to the crisis of 92/93 there was one casualty: Sterling had to leave the ECU mechanism due to unsustainable pressure on the currency. After its application for membership of the EEC had been vetoed twice by the French, the British Government had agreed in the early 1970s to the principle of monetary union within the EEC. It made this agreement, somewhat reluctantly, in order to ensure that its entry to the EEC would not be vetoed for a third time. Although not widely publicised at the time, their agreement meant that Sterling would become a participant in the ECU system.

By late 1992 the Bank of England was under pressure to maintain Sterling's rate within the system. It had raised interest rates to unprecedented levels to make the pound more attractive to investors. Interest rates could only be raised to a certain level before they began to impact business dramatically and thus, on 16 September 1992, Sterling left the ECU system (it has yet to return). The resultant 20% collapse in value of the pound led to a major recession in the UK, with thousands of firms going to the wall. While high interest rates were maintained to prevent further erosion in the value of Sterling, this strategy had the unwanted effect of dramatically reducing consumer spending.[1]

In January 1999 the exchange rates between the currencies participating in the ECU system were fixed permanently and irrevocably, thereby creating the euro, the world's second largest currency. The ECU was transformed into the euro at parity, that is, 1 ECU equalled 1 euro. The euro was therefore a new currency created by fixing the exchange rates of all its participant members irrevocably. By implication, the 'old' currencies theoretically exist in the background. The currency is not completely integrated in the way that the US dollar is – the participant Member States have not ceded their budgetary planning or fiscal systems to a centralised economic unit. Rather, each government has contracted with each other through the auspices of the EU, its structures and institutions, to maintaining certain financial disciplines.

The European Central Bank

One of the main institutions of the EU involved in the management of the euro system is the European Central Bank, the ECB. The ECB is governed by a system involving the central banks of each euro country and in consultation with non-euro countries, such as the UK. The ECB's main goal is medium-term price stability, defined as keeping inflation under 2% in the Eurozone. The removal of exchange rate risk between the countries participating in the euro was never the main goal of the ECB but rather an enabling benefit. Inflation, while targeted to be under 2% in the Eurozone area as a whole, can be under or over this rate in individual Member States. Before the creation of the euro, a country could manage its exchange rate pressures through intervening in its exchange rate with the rest of the currencies it traded with. As we saw earlier in the chapter, it could do this by adjusting interest rates or increasing or decreasing the money supply. These options are no longer available to an individual country operating within the euro scheme. Thus, the adjustments that might have occurred through exchange rate fluctuations must now, at the country level at least, happen through some other mechanism. These adjustments happen through price inflation or deflation within a specific jurisdiction. These price adjustments are not just to the price of consumer goods, but also to costs in the economy such as labour. In the ROI wage rates deflated in the years after the financial crisis. Had the Republic of Ireland not been in the euro the home currency would have devalued thus also bringing about a reduction in wage rates in the economy when translated into the currencies of its trading partners. Deflation or inflation above the 2% target, at an individual country level, is seen as a necessary systemic adjustment within the euro system, critical to keeping the whole system balanced and in equilibrium.

8.4 GOVERNMENT INFLUENCE ON EXCHANGE RATES

As we have seen, the history of exchange rates is one of actions taken by governments. Since the origination of currency, governments have been responsible for managing and controlling its supply. In recent history, governments have also sought to influence the demand for currency.

---

[1] Eglene, O. (2011). *Banking on Sterling: Britain's Independence from the Eurozone*, Lexington Books, London.

In the era of floating exchange rates governments cannot directly set the exchange rate they would wish for their currency. Instead, they try to influence exchange rates by exerting pressures on the levers that cause their movement (exchange rate movements are discussed further in the next section). Governments plan that by moving these levers the markets will respond accordingly and that the exchange rate will move in the desired direction. Of course, some countries still operate exchange rate controls and do not allow their currency float freely. In this section we will examine the different types of control systems governments use for the management of exchange rates. It is important for MNE managers to be aware of these different systems since they have a direct bearing on the possible exchange rate movement that may occur in the currencies in which the MNE operates.

Fixed Exchange Rates

Where a state operates a fixed exchange rate system for its currency, the exchange rate remains constant; the government intervenes to prevent movements in the exchange rate. In order to achieve this equilibrium, the state, through its central bank, must either reduce or increase reserves, depending on the balance of payments.

For example, if a country is running a current account surplus and the government wishes to manage a fixed rate system, then it must intervene to prevent the demand for the currency that results from the surplus from creating an increase in its value. The central bank must balance this current account surplus by adding to the country's foreign currency reserves by the amount needed to cancel out that surplus. The central bank would achieve this scenario by selling the domestic currency in exchange for the currency/ies in which the current account surplus. This leads to an increase in supply of the domestic currency. (The supply curve S_2 in **Figure 8.1** above is an example of such an intervention.) In this way the demand for more of the currency is met by an increase in **supply** of the domestic currency balanced by an increase in the foreign currency **reserves** of the country. If the central bank took no action, then the increased demand for the domestic currency would result in an increase in the price of the currency, that is, the exchange rate. As the double-entry principle applies, once government management of reserves causes the current account changes to be zero, then the changes on the capital account will also be zero. Therefore, there has been no change to either the supply or demand for the currency and, consequently, no change to the exchange rate. Put another way, the government intervenes to counteract demand curve pressures by either buying or selling the domestic currency at the desired fixed rate.

It would be very complicated for a government to engage in this matching process for all the currencies with which its country trades. In order to overcome this complexity a government will normally fix its rate relevant to a standard. This standard might be gold or the currency of one of its main trading partners. Sometimes the standard might be a weighted average of a basket of currencies.

> The Irish Government operated a fixed exchange rate with Sterling for most of the three decades running up to the European fixed exchange rate system (described above) in 1979. As the UK was Ireland's main trading partner and shared a land border, the Irish Government saw it as economically and politically important to maintain parity with Sterling.

While the main advantage of having a fixed exchange rate is the removal of exchange rate risk for international trade, another advantage is the fiscal discipline that maintaining the fixed rate imposes. Countries operating a fixed exchange rate cannot disregard running successive deficits or surpluses. As we have seen from the balance of payments theory earlier, running current account surpluses or deficits will cause the exchange rate to move since the normal rules of supply and demand will apply. If a government is following a goal of fixed exchange rates it must intervene in the market and use reserves to support the currency at the desired rate. Such supports cannot continue indefinitely as government reserves are finite.

Thus, one of the main disadvantages of a fixed exchange rate system is the cost of maintaining such government intervention. In particular, demand in the economy might need to be dampened down by the imposition of taxes in order to reduce imports and cut a deficit. Sometimes, when a government can no longer use its reserves to support continued deficits, it may need to devalue the currency.

EXAMPLE 8.3: THAILAND AND THE PROBLEM OF FIXED EXCHANGE RATES

In 1997 Thailand had to abandon its fixed rate exchange rate between the Baht and the US$. Thailand had been running current account deficits and was thereby stimulating demand for its own currency. This is because the current account deficits meant that the Baht was being held in increasing amounts by foreign banks. As the amounts held by foreign banks looked like they would continue to increase, the value of the Baht began to fall since there effectively was an oversupply. The Thai government had to 'buy back' the foreign held Baht in order to match the oversupply with demand. It had to use its foreign exchange reserves to do this. Reserves are finite and eventually will run out. Speculators can anticipate these problems and they engaged in transactions that increased the supply Baht by selling the currency into the market, thereby forcing the Thai government to buy even more Baht, using up even more reserves. In June 1997, with the support of the IMF, the fixed exchange system between the Baht and the US$ was discontinued. The Baht fell in value by 20% immediately and by January 1998 the Baht had lost 45% of its value against the dollar.

As the Thai example shows, expectations of such devaluations can lead to speculators betting against a currency, making it increasingly difficult for a government to continue to use its reserves to support the fixed exchange rate. In essence, over the long run, a government cannot maintain fixed exchange rates at rates inappropriate to the market fundamentals.

Pegged Exchange Rates

In 1971 the Argentine peso was pegged to the US dollar. This meant that the Argentine currency board needed to maintain dollar reserves equivalent to the total amount of pesos in issue. The system gave MNEs comfort that the Peso was backed by the US dollar. The system collapsed in 2002 when investors demanded to exchange their pesos for dollars during an economic crisis.

A pegged exchange rate is where a government 'attaches' its currency to another currency with which the pegged currency moves in tandem. A government normally achieves this 'pegging' by having its reserves in the currency to which it is pegged. Normally, a currency board appointed within the country will operate the system. The currency board must maintain reserves equivalent to the total money in issue. These reserves must be held in the currency to which the home currency is pegged. One can see the attraction for MNEs in operating in a country where such a system is in place. Instead of being exposed to the vagaries of a potentially unstable weaker currency, an MNE is effectively trading in a strong currency, the one to which the home currency is pegged.

> The Renmimbi is China's currency. It means 'people's money'. The term was introduced in 1949 when the communists won the civil war and the People's Republic of China was formed. The Yuan is the unit of the Renmimbi. An equivalent naming system exists in the UK where the currency is Sterling and the unit is the pound.

On 15 March 2014 the Chinese Government said that it would allow its currency, the Renmimbi, to float within a range of plus or minus 2% of a target rate to the US dollar. It would set the target rate each day. Up to that point the Chinese had operated a fixed rate system. This change to a pegged system was seen as a move toward allowing market forces to eventually prevail and to allow the Renmimbi to exchange with other currencies at the rate produced by market forces. China has run trade surpluses with the rest of the world, especially the US, for many years. A free-floating Chinese currency would have appreciated against the dollar, making Chinese exports more expensive and thus reducing the trade surplus. However, the currency has been pegged at a rate that some believe is artificially low, meaning that China continues to run surpluses that would otherwise be 'appreciated away' by a strengthening currency. In other words, some analysts believe the Chinese currency should be stronger than the Chinese Government and central bank currently allow. This strengthening of the currency, if it were allowed to happen, would make Chinese manufactured goods more expensive in the rest of the world, thereby reducing demand for those goods. At the same time, imports into China would become cheaper and this would stimulate Chinese consumption of foreign goods leading to an increased global demand for those goods. The Chinese Government might be wary of allowing too rapid an appreciation of its currency after seeing what happened to Japan when its currency appreciated strongly after the Plaza Accord (see above). While trade surpluses were indeed eliminated, a long period of low growth and deflation followed in Japan.

Free-floating Exchange Rates

Where a government does not intervene in the currency markets to influence its exchange rate, its currency is said to be 'free floating'. The market forces of supply and demand for the currency set its rate with other currencies. As demand for the currency increases, the exchange rate will strengthen. The corollary is also true. The supply and demand curves are influenced by economic matters in the home country. The supply and demand curves are also influenced by matters in other countries with which the home country trades. MNEs must identify their exposures to such movements in supply and demand curves and their associated exchange rate movements, and take appropriate risk management steps.

Set out below are some of the advantages and also disadvantages of a free-floating exchange rate system.

ADVANTAGES AND DISADVANTAGES OF FREE-FLOATING EXCHANGE RATES

> **Advantages** include:
> - No need for a government to hold foreign currency reserves.
> - Current account deficits and surpluses are automatically corrected.
> - Market forces weed out inefficient processes and sectors within the economy.
> - A government can avoid taking unpopular actions that are sometimes needed to support a fixed or pegged exchange rate.

Disadvantages include:
- Market forces can cause cyclical 'boom/bust' patterns to emerge in an economy. As exchange rates move up due to surpluses, exports become more expensive, dampening domestic production. As they subsequently move down, imports become more expensive, causing inflation.
- A policy of exchange rate '*laissez faire*' may prevent a government taking actions that would otherwise have been beneficial for its economy. For example, a government may stem inflation in a fixed rate system by buying its own currency and preventing its fall in value which would otherwise push up prices of imports. This action could be particularly important to a government where imports of raw materials are needed to produce the country's manufactured outputs. A government cannot do this directly in a 'laissez faire' system
- Foreign exchange risk is at its highest in a free-floating system. This may impact the actions of MNEs and discourage investment.

Levers of State Intervention

When one considers the history of exchange rates, it is obvious that state intervention has been prevalent, especially since the Industrial Revolution of the 1800s. Intervention by governments is easy to understand. Exchange rates are directly related to money, and money is printed by governments. Perhaps more fundamentally, exchange rates impact upon any economy that trades internationally. As the world's international trade has expanded dramatically in the past century, these impacts are all the greater.

In order to manage money supply and associated matters, such as interest rates and inflation, states have central banks. In all countries the government of the state will have a direct or, in some cases, an indirect influence on the actions of its central bank. The role of a central bank is to:
- print money;
- set interest rates;
- control credit in the economy;
- manage exchange rates;
- regulate the financial sector.

The main objectives of the central bank in a country are to maintain price stability, encourage economic growth and keep unemployment low. In some countries the central bank is an arm of government and controlled by it. In other countries, the central bank operates independently of government. In 1997 Gordon Brown's first major decision when he became Chancellor of the Exchequer in the UK was to decouple the Bank of England from government control. The Labour government of which he was part believed that the market forces should be let prevail. Nonetheless, the government still set the targets which the central bank must endeavour to deliver. These targets are especially focused on controlling inflation. While the Central Bank of Ireland is part of the administrative structure of the Irish State, one of its main roles is the maintenance of price stability through "the implementation of ECB decisions on monetary policy".[2]

Governments execute and implement their interventions in the foreign exchange markets through the actions of their central banks. Sometimes this intervention can be a direct instruction, but normally it involves setting targets for the economy and instructing the central bank

---

[2] www.Centralbank.ie/mpolbo/pages/introduction.aspx (accessed May 2015).

to manage the economy using what levers it can to meet those targets. The main target is connected to price stability and inflation. As we will see later, inflation is directly linked to foreign exchange rates and interest rates. Therefore, central banks will make interventions in order to keep the country and its currency as close to the targets as possible.

Central banks are normally motivated to intervene in the foreign exchange currency markets for one of four reasons, to:
- control inflation;
- maintain competitiveness;
- ensure financial stability;
- build foreign exchange reserves.[3]

In 2012 a survey of the governors of the central banks for the world major currencies provided further insights into why central banks intervene in the currency markets, ranking central banks' motives for intervening in the market in order of importance[4]:
1. curb excessive exchange market speculation;
2. maintain monetary stability;
3. build or reduce foreign exchange reserves;
4. discourage sharp capital inflows or outflows;
5. alleviate foreign exchange funding shortages in banks and MNEs;
6. smooth commodity price fluctuations;
7. maintain competitiveness.

In recent years central banks have also found it necessary to intervene in the foreign exchange markets in order to counteract the actions of speculators.[5] For example, speculators may buy a currency in anticipation of an increase in its value. Central Banks may counteract the speculators buy selling an equivalent amount of the currency in the market, hopefully rebalancing the money supply.

Intervention in the markets by central banks falls into two categories: direct and indirect, which we will examine in turn below.

Direct Intervention by Central Banks

Most direct intervention takes the form of buying or selling the currency on the **spot market**. The spot rate is the rate at which one currency can be exchanged for another immediately at the time of the quote. The spot market is the market where such spot rates are quoted. Central banks tend to favour reacting to movements that have already happened rather than using direct intervention as a pre-emptive tactic. Choosing reactive tactics makes sense, particularly when one considers that counteracting speculation is one of the main reasons for intervention. If central banks intervened on a pre-emptive basis they would be engaging in a form of speculation themselves, effectively speculating on what actions the real speculators might take.

Sterilised Intervention   When a central bank intervenes in the foreign exchange markets by buying or selling its home currency, it indirectly affects the money supply in its domestic economy because such actions consume or release money into that economy. The effect of these movements in money supply in the domestic economy may result in changes to other fundamentals, other than the foreign exchange rate. For example, increasing the money supply in the

---

[3] Moreno, R. (2005). "Motives for Intervention", *BIS Papers*, Vol. 23, pp. 1–8.

[4] Mohanty, M. S. and Bat-el Berger, www.bis.org/publ/bppdf/bispa73.pdf (accessed July 2015).

[5] Mohanty, M. S. Bat-el Berger (2013). "Central Bank Views on Foreign Intervention", *BIS Papers*, Vol. 73.

domestic economy can give rise to inflation. In simple terms, inflation can happen since there is an increase in the amount of money but the same amount of goods. Therefore, the price for those goods may rise, leading to inflation. In order to prevent these unintended consequences a central bank will engage in counteracting measures in and around the same time as it executes the direct intervention in the foreign exchange markets. When a central bank engages in these counteracting measures the intervention is said to be a 'sterilised intervention'.

> For example, if the Bank of England sold Sterling in order to weaken its currency, it would offset the money supply effect of the transaction by issuing Sterling bonds to commercial banks in the domestic economy for the same amount, leaving the money supply unchanged. On the other hand, if the Bank was using its foreign currency reserves to buy Sterling in order to strengthen the exchange rate, it would then 'sell' that Sterling domestically by using the funds to buy back previously issued bonds, thus giving the commercial banks a cash inflow that they would then use in the domestic economy.

At a high level one could pose the question: if a central bank takes off-setting actions and thereby leaves the money supply unchanged then what, if anything, would bring about a change in the exchange rate? In fact, academic research has indicated that in the medium term, sterilised foreign exchange interventions by central banks have no effect on exchange rates.[6] However, sterilised interventions can be effective in influencing short-term rates and are therefore useful to correct sharp fluctuations in exchange rates, in particular.[7] No doubt this is why governments and central banks persist with interventionist strategies.

Unsterilised Intervention   When a central bank does not exercise a counteracting transaction after direct intervention in the foreign exchange market, then the actual effect of the transaction is either an increase or decrease in the money supply of the home currency. For example, if the Bank of England wished to strengthen Sterling it would use foreign reserves to buy the pound on foreign exchange markets. If it engaged in no other transaction then the pounds it has bought would be taken out of general circulation in the wider economy because the Bank of England would just hold onto the Sterling it has bought and not release it into the wider economy through the banks. This is called a '**unsterilised intervention**'. Assuming the market to be in equilibrium prior to the intervention, the action of the Bank of England in our example would be to reduce supply of Sterling. Since demand remains unaltered from the intervention but supply has been reduced, then, using the law of supply and demand, the price for Sterling will rise.

Are Central Bank Interventions Effective?   The total value of transactions on world's foreign exchange markets (FOREX) is now over $5 trillion a day.[8] On a single day there could be more FOREX transacted than the combined value of all reserves of all the central banks. Global foreign exchange activity related to actual transactions of goods and services now accounts for less than 4% of all foreign exchange activity. The other 96% is currency trading in and of itself.

---

[6] Jurgensen, P. (1983), *Report of the Working Group on Exchange Market Intervention*, Washington, D.C. US Treasury.

[7] Fatim, R. and Hutchinson, M. (2003), "Is Sterilised Foreign Exchange Intervention Effective After All?" Royal Economic Society.

[8] Triennial Central Bank Survey of Foreign Exchange Turnover, *BIS*, April 2013.

Given the enormous scale of the market, direct intervention by central banks has become increasingly ineffective. As a result, there are fewer direct interventions by central banks in recent years. When the central banks do intervene, they like to do so 'under the radar', or covertly. This is because in order to make short-term gains FOREX speculators try to determine when a government might be about to intervene. The speculators then try to make their speculative moves based upon their assessments of when governments might act. By acting covertly the speculators are never quite sure whether an action in the market has been by a central bank, or another speculator. That said, the scale of the overall market increasingly mitigates against direct intervention as a route to any type of effective long-term management of a desired exchange rate. In the end, the market always wins.

Indirect Intervention

As the overall Foreign exchange (FOREX) market has grown in size and problems with the effectiveness of direct intervention have strengthened, governments and central banks have had to rely on other methods in order to influence the market in favour of their currency.

As we will discuss in more detail below, the spot rate between two currencies will move if there is a change in one or more variables between those currencies, including:
- rates of inflation;
- interest rates;
- government and central bank currency controls;
- income levels;
- sentiment of the market; and
- change in money supply.

While a country's government or its central bank may exercise influence over some or all of these variables, a government's ability to influence each of these factors is not equal. A government may exercise exchange rate controls with some rigour but it will find that controlling the income level of the economy is much more difficult. It must also be borne in mind that the variables are not unconnected. Interest rate increases, for example, may reduce consumer demand in an economy by discouraging borrowing and encouraging saving.

Foreign Exchange Controls As a method of controlling exchange rates and the inflows and outflows of its home currency a government, or its central bank, may restrict trade in its currency by constraining the amount of foreign currency its citizens can buy. It may also restrict the amount of its currency that can be bought by non-residents. In most circumstances, the government will also impose a fixed exchange rate to the permitted transactions. The wider the gap between the imposed exchange rate and one that buyers and sellers of the currency feel should be in place, the greater the opportunity for an 'unofficial' exchange rate market to open up. While governments will seek to control the development of such black markets in their currency, this can be difficult, especially if the rewards for operators in the market are high. In the final analysis, the real market forces influencing a currency will eventually come to bear on exchange rates. Accordingly, while governments can exercise exchange rate controls, they cannot isolate their currency from market forces over the longer term without incurring significant trade imbalances.

Interest Rates Governments and central banks can indirectly intervene in the foreign exchange markets by raising or lowering interest rates. Increases in interest rates increase a currency's attractiveness due to higher returns for investors holding the currency, all other things being equal. The increased return on holding the currency stimulates demand for it. Since the supply of the currency remains unchanged, the increased demand for the currency leads to an appreciation in its value according to the traditional laws of supply and demand.

The opposite is also true. Lowering a country's interest rates can lead to a reduction in demand for its currency and thus deflate its value. However, it should be noted that interest rate movements lead to other effects in the economy. For example, low interest rates can discourage savings, which can stimulate consumer spending. Indeed, some central banks when altering interest rates have made it abundantly clear that their motive is not to manage exchange rates:

> "Question: … Do you envisage taking any further action to try and weaken the (euro) exchange rate?
>
> …
>
> Draghi: I will restate here, the exchange rate is not a policy target … it's definitely very important for our outlook of price stability".[9]

We will examine the link between interest rate differentials and exchange rates in further detail later in this chapter, but first we will consider exchange rate movements on their own.

8.5 EXCHANGE RATE MOVEMENTS

Exchange rate movements are normally expressed as the percentage change in the spot rate between two relevant dates. This means that the movement in an exchange rate is relatively easy to calculate. **Example 8.4** below shows how to calculate a simple exchange rate movement of pounds Sterling versus euro. However, while this calculation may be straightforward, understanding why the movement occurred in the first place is more difficult. Forecasting how exchanges rate may move in the future is even more fraught with problems. Nonetheless, today's MNEs must endeavour to understand these issues. Future cash inflows and outflows in a foreign currency will translate back into the home currency at these future rates. Consequently, an MNE's revenue streams and profit margins can be directly impacted by movements in exchange rates, movements that are outside its control.

EXAMPLE 8.4: CALCULATING AN EXCHANGE RATE MOVEMENT

The spot rate for the pound Sterling to the euro on 2 May 20x4 was €1 buys £Stg 0.8217.

On 2 June 20x4 the spot rate was €1 buys £Stg 0.8120. (Source: Bank of England)

The movement in exchange rate is given by the formula:

$$\frac{Spot\ Rate\ Today - Spot\ Rate\ Historically}{Spot\ Rate\ Historically \times 100} = Percentage\ Movement\ in\ Exchange\ Rate$$

In our example this would be:

$$\frac{0.8120 - 0.8217}{0.8217 \times 100} = -1.18\%.$$

This means that the euro depreciated in value against Sterling by 1.18% in the period from 2 May 20x4 to 2 June 20x4.

---

[9] Mario Draghi at a press conference on 3 July 2014, in response to a question from a journalist. See https://www.ecb.europa.eu/press/pressconf/2014/html/is140703.en.html#qa

The exchange rate for a given currency at a particular moment in time is driven by market forces. In this sense, a currency is similar to any other traded commodity in that the price is driven by the laws of supply and demand. An increase in demand for a currency will cause it to appreciate. An increase in supply will cause it to depreciate. The global foreign exchange (FOREX) markets operate in such a way as to ensure that there is only one spot rate operating at any given moment in time. Thus, the exchange rate is in equilibrium as a result of the workings of the market and is a function of the supply and demand for the relevant currency. As there are many currencies in the world, so there are many exchange rates. A particular currency can rise when compared to another currency over a given period but fall in value when compared to a third currency. While the mathematics is relatively simple, the sheer preponderance of currencies can give rise to many calculations having to be made throughout the trading on one day, or even in one hour. However, the foreign currency markets are efficient in ensuring that the exchange rates between currencies are broadly reflective of the supply and demand for the respective currencies. How does the market create this efficiency that ensures the exchange rates quoted on the FOREX around the globe are timely and meaningful? To understand the answer to that question we must first understand the concept of arbitrage and how it applies in the FOREX markets.

Arbitrage

'**Arbitrage**' is the practice of exploiting price differences between marketplaces for the same product. For example, there are two bicycle shops on either end of a street, one of which is selling a particular Bianchi branded bicycle for €1,000, while the other is selling the exact same model for €5,000. Both have a steady demand for their wares despite the price difference. In our artificial world of examples, the customers of each shop are unaware of the price differentials. For the purposes of our example we should also ignore transaction costs and retail margins. An arbitrage opportunity exists. The arbitrageur is aware of the price differentials. An arbitrageur would buy Bianchi bicycles for €1,000 at one end of the street and sell them for €5,000 at the other end of the street. As the arbitrageur continues the practice, the price differential will narrow. Either the bike shop owner selling at €1,000 will increase prices or the other retailer will drop prices. This happens as the retailer selling at the lower price begins to see that volumes of sales are increasing dramatically whilst the more expensively priced retailer finds business is dropping away. Each will need to adjust to the market condition. The arbitrageur will continue to exploit the price difference until the prices for the bikes converge and there is no more risk-free profit to be made.

In the real world of foreign exchange trading, these opportunities exist momentarily. It is the activities of the arbitrageurs on the global markets that ensure that the price of the US dollar in terms of Sterling is the same in Hong Kong as it is in Frankfurt. If this were not the case, traders would buy on one market and sell in the other.

Imagine one US Dollar could buy 58p Sterling in Hong Kong and at the same time could buy 60p Sterling in Frankfurt. A trader has $100,000. Assuming no transaction costs, she could buy £60,000 Sterling in Frankfurt and then sell the Sterling in Hong Kong for 60,000 ÷ 0.58 = $103,448. The trader has made a profit of $3,448, being her current dollar holding of $103,448 less her original holding of $100,000. The operation of the global FOREX markets ensure that such discrepancies only exist for the briefest of times.

The global FOREX is operated between banks and foreign exchange currency traders. Their trading between each other ensures that price differentials between markets are eliminated quickly through the process of arbitrage. The result of the process is that there emerges a single exchange rate for each currency expressed in terms of another. It is important for an MNE to recognise that this system works and that exchange rates for free-floating currencies are universal, with one rate applying throughout the global market.

Arbitrage and Perfect Competition

As explained above, understanding the concept of **arbitrage** is important when considering exchange rate movements and the foreign exchange markets. Arbitrage is one of the factors that underpins the operation of what economists call 'perfect competition'. Much economic theory presumes the existence of perfect competition, or something approaching it. Foreign exchange markets exhibit most of its characteristics, which are:

- many buyers;
- many sellers;
- freedom of entry to and exit from the market;
- homogeneous products, meaning that all products in a particular market are interchangeable with each other;
- perfect knowledge on the part of buyers and sellers;
- perfectly mobile factors of production;
- no externalities from either production or consumption (in other words, no knock-on effects to other parties outside of the market);
- arbitrage.

As discussed above, one of the main reasons the FOREX might not be considered as having all the features of perfect competition is the influence of governments and central bank interventions. However, for the purposes of understanding the market we can say that it has near perfect competition. One of the features of perfect competition is the operation of arbitrage.

As we have seen, arbitrage is the practice of exploiting a price difference for the same product in two or more markets, and is illustrated below in **Example 8.5**:

EXAMPLE 8.5: ARBITRAGE IN ACTION – HONG KONG AND NEW YORK

If the euro could buy \$1.40 in Hong Kong and \$1.30 in New York at the same moment in time, 'arbitrageurs' would immediately buy dollars in Hong Kong for their euro and sell them in New York and get their euro back plus a profit. In this example, €1,000 could buy \$1,400 in Hong Kong. Selling the dollars in New York at €1 = \$1.30, which is the same as 1\$ = €0.7692, the arbitrageur would get €1,077 back (\$1,400 × 0.7692 = €1,076.88, round to €1,077). A handsome profit of €77 (or 7.7% return on the €1,000 invested) would have been made by exploiting the price difference between the Hong Kong market and the New York market.

In the real world, computer-generated trading results in a situation where, for all practical purposes, the same rate of exchange quoted for a given currency applies throughout the globe at the same time. Thus, any arbitrage opportunities that arise on the foreign exchange markets are mainly identified by computers and are for much smaller discrepancies than in our example, although the volumes are much larger.

To illustrate the level of trade in the global foreign exchange markets, including arbitrage, it is useful to consider some hard data. The World Trade Organization (WTO) estimates that annual global world trade in exported goods and services for 2013 was $22 trillion. Given that each export trade has an import on the other side of the transaction, the total foreign exchange market activity supported by goods and services would be around $44 trillion. The triennial report of the Bank for International Settlements, an organisation made up of 60 central banks, puts the April 2013 daily foreign exchange market at $5.3 trillion, or over $1,800 trillion per annum. The importance of these numbers is that the global market for foreign exchange dwarfs the element of it related to world trade by some 40 to one. The enormous trading on the foreign exchange markets for reasons other than goods and services is a significant factor in making the foreign exchange market efficient in providing risk-management strategies for the MNE. The market is broadly efficient, with the exception of transaction costs, and has almost perfect competition. We will see later on in the book how these factors help the MNE in its quest to minimise risk and ensure as much certainty as possible about future cash flows.[10]

Covered Interest Arbitrage

We have seen that the efficiency of the market would not allow differences in foreign exchange spot rates to exist for very long. Arbitrage trading eliminates these discrepancies very quickly. In our simple example of the euro and the US dollar being quoted at different rates in Hong Kong and New York, we could see how arbitrage trading could quickly make a profit. The profit opportunity quickly disappears as traders flock to the easy money.

Consider now the following example.

EXAMPLE 8.6: INTEREST RATE ARBITRAGE PROFIT

- €1 buys $1.30 in New York today.
- There is also a forward rate of exchange for 12 months' time of $1.10.
- Euro interest rates are 2% per annum in our example while $ interest rates are 4%.
- You have €1,000 to invest.
- You spend the €1,000 on buying $1,300, foregoing the 2% interest you could have earned.
- You enter a contract to sell your dollars in exchange for euro in 12 months' time at $1.10.
- You place your dollars on deposit and earn $52, being 4% of $1,300.
- You then sell your dollars in exchange for € in 12 months' time obtaining €1,229, being $1,352 converted at the contracted rate of €1 = $1.10.
- You now have €229 more € than you started with.
- When you subtract the interest rate foregone had you done none of this of €20, being 2% of your original cash pile of €1,000, you have made a profit of €209.

Extreme illustrative numbers have been used in the above example to highlight the concept. Foreign exchange arbitrage trading ensures that such profits as may arise from interest rate differentials between currencies do not last for long.

Example 8.7 below takes the example above into the real world, with the exception of transaction costs. All figures remain the same except that, as a result of arbitrage trading, the contracted future rate available in 12 months' time is €1 = $1.325.

---

[10] Bank for International Settlements, *Triennial Central Bank Survey*, September 2013.

EXAMPLE 8.7: EFFECT OF ARBITRAGE ON FORWARD FOREX RATES

- Convert €1,000 into dollars at $1.30, obtaining $1,300.
- Place the dollars on deposit for 12 months at 4%.
- Enter into a contract to sell the dollars at €1 = $1.325 in 12 months' time.
- Earn interest of $52 after 12 months.
- Sell the $1,352 in accordance with the contract at a rate of €1 = $1.325 obtaining €1,020.
- You now have €20 more than when you started.
- However, when you subtract the €20 interest you have foregone had you just placed the euro on deposit and done none of this, you find you end up with €1,000, the same as when you started.

Thus, arbitrage trading on the foreign exchange markets eliminates any possibility of making risk-free profits on exploiting the difference in interest rates between currencies. In fact, forward contract rates are a function of interest rate differentials, not predictions of what the rate might be at that time in the future. We address interest rates and exchange rates again further in this chapter.

Triangulated Arbitrage

The operation of the market is obviously more complicated than in our examples thus far. In particular, exchange rates exist between all currencies, and each other. This facet of currency markets leads to triangulated arbitrage. This is where arbitrageurs take advantage of small discrepancies between the prices of two currencies expressed in terms of a third currency.

Example 8.8 shows a real-world example with actual exchange rates operating on a particular day in July 2014. It demonstrates that the arbitrageurs' actions through large-scale buying and selling of currencies quickly (in micro-seconds) eliminate discrepancies between rates quoted by different banks around the globe, even between three currencies.

EXAMPLE 8.8: ARBITRAGE IN ACTION WITH REAL-WORLD RATES

On 5 July 2014 UK£1 could buy US$1.72. At the same time, US$1 could buy €0.73. By mathematical implication therefore, £1 should be able to buy €1.26 using £1 = US$1.72. And since US$1 = €0.73 then US$1.72 must equal €1.26. This implies that UK£1 must equal €1.26. When I checked the actual rate quoted on the morning of 5 July 2014, the actual quoted rate for Sterling to euro was £1 = €1.26. No surprise, the arbitrageurs had done their work and the derived rate for the Stg/€ using the US$ as the intermediary currency was the same as the actual rate quoted, £1 = €1.26.

Example 8.9 below introduces the concept of '**forward rate**', which is a rate that you can agree today with a bank that will apply to a given amount of a currency at a specified date in the future. (See **Chapter 15** for a more complete description of forward rates.) The example demonstrates how forward rates are today's **spot rate** adjusted for the interest rate differential between the two relevant currencies. This is an important point. Many casual observers think forward rates are some type of 'guesstimate' as to what the rate will be at some point in the future. They most certainly are not. It is worth repeating: forward rates are a function of today's rate and the difference in interest rates between the two currencies.

EXAMPLE 8.9: FURTHER ILLUSTRATION OF INTEREST RATE ARBITRAGE

Our arbitrageur has €100,000. She notices that US$1 buys €0.73 today. She also sees that she can exchange US$1 for €0.73 in six months' time. She notices that the $ interest rate is 4% per annum whilst the € rate is 2% per annum. So, she takes her €100,000 and converts it to $136,986 using the rate of US$1 = €0.73. She agrees a contract to exchange her $100,000 back into € in six months' time at 1$ = €0.73. Her $136,986 earns $2,740 over the six months. At the end of the six months our arbitrageur now has $136,986 plus $2,740 interest giving $139,726. She then converts the dollars back into euro at the contracted rate of $1 = €0.73, giving her a total of €102,000. On paper she has made a profit of €2,000 but she needs to take account of the fact that she could have made €1,000 in interest if she had left the funds in euro for the six months, given that € interest rates are 2% per annum. So her total profit of her foreign exchange transaction is €1,000.

However, we will remember that arbitrage prevents these 'easy' profits being made for long. In the real world, our investor would not have been able to agree a six month contract at $1 = €0.73. The rate would have been $1 = €0.723. How can we know this? This is because the actions of arbitrageurs will eliminate the opportunity to make risk-free profit and so the forward contract rate will be at a rate that the forward exchange rate will be at exactly the rate needed to eliminate any profits made from exploiting the interest rate differential between the two currencies. Thus, the exchange rate will be a function of the amount of euro that would have been earned if nothing had been done, €101,000 and the amount of $ earned by engaging in the transaction $139,986. By simple division:

$$\frac{101,000}{139,986} = 0.723$$

Another way of making this calculation is to consider the interest rate differential between the two currencies. $ interest rates are 4% and € rates are 2% per annum. Therefore, the calculation would be:

$$\text{Forward rate is } 0.73 \times \frac{1 + (0.02 \times \frac{6 \text{ months}}{12 \text{ months}})}{1 + (0.04 \times \frac{6 \text{ months}}{12 \text{ months}})} = 0.73 \times \frac{1.01}{1.02} = 0.723$$

8.6 EXCHANGE RATES AND HOW THEY RELATE TO INTEREST AND INFLATION RATES

Having established that arbitrage operates to ensure that a single exchange rate prevails on the global foreign exchange markets in respect of two currencies, we can now turn our attention to interest rates and how they relate to exchange rates.

Interest Rate Parity Theorem (IRP)

Each currency has its own interest rate, normally set by the central bank mandated to set the rate for the relevant currency. These rates differ from currency to currency depending on the decisions of the relevant central bank and its governing mandates and objectives. In the examples concerning arbitrage above, we looked at situations where the transactions occurred instantaneously. We are now going to consider transactions that occur across a time period. This is why interest rates must be considered as interest is earned over time. Therefore, when considering transactions with a time dimension to them, the arbitrageurs must also consider the interest rates that apply to the respective currencies in which they carry out the transactions.

> A **forward rate** is the exchange rate that one can agree today for the exchange of one currency for another at a future date.

From **Example 8.9** above we can see that the forward rates are a function of the interest rate differentials that apply to the respective currencies. Accordingly, no profit can be made by borrowing in one currency and depositing in another and eliminating risk by entering into forward contracts. The contract rates that will be available will be priced at exactly the rate needed to eliminate any risk-free profit that could have been earned. The reason for this is that the banks who quote the rates essentially execute the cash flows underpinning the transaction once a contract is entered into. When an MNE enters a contract for the exchange of a currency in, say, six months, the bank performs the cash flows immediately. For example, if a Sterling-based MNE enters a forward contract for a €1 million cash payment it must make in six months' time, the bank will borrow Stg£ today for six months, convert it into euro at today's spot rate and place it on deposit for six months. In six months' time it will give the euro to the MNE and receive Sterling at the appropriate rate in return. The rate will be calculated so as to eliminate any possible profit from exploiting the interest rate differential between the two currencies.

Expressing the above as a formula we can say that:

$$FR_{y,x} = \frac{1 + Ix}{1 + Iy} \times SR_{y,x}$$

Where

$FR_{y,x}$ = Forward Rate of one unit of currency y in terms of another currency, x
Iy = interest rate for currency y
Ix = interest rate for currency x
$SR_{y,x}$ = spot rate of one unit of currency y in terms of x

Bid/Offer Spreads

In the real world, interest rates for borrowing are slightly different, i.e. higher, than interest rates for deposits. There are also transaction costs to be taken into account, even though we exclude them for the purposes of our theory development. These costs give rise to a spread of quoted rates between what a bank will buy a currency for and sell it. This applies to both the spot market and the forward markets.

Purchasing Power Parity (PPP)

We have seen how interest rate differentials between currencies lead to changes in exchange rates. We have also seen how forward contract rates are a function of interest rate differentials and not expectations of movement in the actual rates. We now come to consider the notion of purchasing power parity (PPP).

The main premise behind PPP is that consumers will buy where prices are lowest. The development of the theory imagines a world without trade barriers and distribution costs in order to simplify the basic construction of the theoretic model.

Consumers will buy the same product from wherever in the global market they find the lowest prices for the same product. As a result, demand will shift from higher priced locations to lower priced locations. As a result of this demand shifting, prices will go up in the location with the lower prices, and prices will fall in the higher priced regions. Over time, prices will equalise across all markets. Thus, the PPP theory states that prices for the same product will equalise across the world when you ignore trade barriers and logistics costs.

In 1986 the *Economist* magazine started its Big Mac Index. The index based itself on the price of a BigMac burger. The price of the BigMac burger bought on the same day in different countries around the world is compared. The index is based on PPP and proposes that the derived exchange rate from comparing burger prices is the 'real' exchange rate and goes on to suggest over- or under- currency valuations by comparing this 'burger' rate to the real rate quoted on the FOREX. It is a light-hearted way of understanding PPP.

Imagine that there is only one currency in the world, the dollar. If a BMW car costs $80,000 in Ireland but costs $40,000 in the US, PPP proposes that consumers will shift their buying pattern to the US. This will give rise to an increase in demand in the US and a drop in demand in Ireland. The law of supply and demand means that such changes in the demand curve will give rise to price changes, upward in the US and downward in Ireland. The PPP theory suggests that the prices will converge to the same price.

Now consider that there are different currencies in each of the markets. In our example, let's assume €1 = $2, meaning that the BMW is €40,000 in Ireland and $40,000 in the US. The further proposition of PPP is that just because different markets have different currencies shouldn't affect the consumer behaviour, all other things being equal. Developing this thought further, the PPP proposes that where a price discrepancy between the same product quoted in different currencies arises, the currency exchange rate will adjust to eliminate the price discrepancy. These changes arise from the change in the demand curve for the respective currencies. Buyers from Ireland will buy $ so that they can then buy the car in the US. The increased demand for US$ and the sale of € brings about an adjustment to the exchange rate through the application of the laws of supply and demand. One can see the essence of PPP is that there is one 'world' price for every product. Local pricing and the associated exchange rate will vary in order to bring about this universal price.

It is not possible to consider the prices of all products available, one by one, in each market and examine their price behaviour relevant to PPP. An examination of all products would not only be unwieldly, it would also require major adjustments to be carried out to each item's price to factor in local considerations, such as taxation. Rather than do these enormous calculations, what actually happens is that the total price in each currency of a basket of products is examined. The assumption is that PPP applies and that the price of a basket of goods in one currency is equivalent to its price in another currency. In other words, the pricing is in equilibrium and PPP has operated. The next step is to consider price movements for the basket of goods. The movement in the total price for this standardised basket of products, both goods and services, over time is measured. This price movement is called **inflation**. PPP is then applied to inflation differentials between currencies. The principle remains the same; consumer behaviour will tend to equalise prices so that they converge to a one 'world' price. Therefore, changes in the price of the basket of goods in one country relative to another should be cancelled out by a movement in the exchange rate, leaving the relative prices for the basket of goods between the two countries the same.

Take a situation where on 1 January €1.00 = $1.30 and inflation in the US is running at 10% p.a., but is only 4% p.a. in the Eurozone. An item that was cost $1.30 in the US in January will cost $1.43 by December. Likewise the same item costs €1.00 in Germany in January and costs €1.04 by December. The theory of relative purchasing power parity says that the exchange rates will move in such a way as to eliminate the effect of this and the country with the higher rate of inflation will weaken against the country with the lower rate of inflation. In this instance the rate will go from $1.30 to approximately $1.375 (i.e. 1.10/1.04 × $1.30).

However, as mentioned earlier, the theoretic world of absolute PPP does not exist. Indeed, logistics costs and trade barriers do exist and have a large bearing on the pricing of products in different markets (for example, vehicle registration tax in Ireland). In order to build on PPP theory for use in real-world circumstances, PPP has evolved to include the idea of relative prices. Taking our example of the BMW once again, let us imagine that the price differences between the markets are explained by logistics costs and trade barriers. Thus, the consumer cannot exploit the price difference and supply and demand are in equilibrium. Relative PPP theory proposes that the price relativities between the two markets should remain the same, assuming no change to the logistics costs or the tariffs. Therefore, if the price in the US goes up by 10% to $44,000, then the exchange rate will alter to ensure the relativities remain the same. Assuming no other products existed, then the exchange rate between the euro and US$ would change from €1 = $2 to €1 = $2.2, a weakening of the dollar of 10%. This results from the fact that the relativities were in balance prior to the changes in prices. Now that prices in the US have gone up, consumers there will switch their demand to the now cheaper Ireland. This will push up demand for the euro needed to buy in Ireland and lead to a sale of dollars to acquire the necessary euro. These changes in demand lead to a weakening of the dollar and an increase in the value of the euro, relative to the dollar.

EXAMPLE 8.10: RELATIVE PURCHASING POWER PARITY (PPP)

A basket of goods cost 1,000 Zolars, $\hat{Z}$, in Zedmania on Day 1. In Beeland, the same basket of goods cost 2,000 Buro, B. The exchange rate is $\hat{Z}1 = B2$. If inflation in Zedmania is 5% per annum, then the basket of goods will cost $\hat{Z}1,050$ on Day 365. The inflation rate in Beeland is 10%, therefore the basket of goods there will cost B1,100 on Day 365. Purchasing power parity means that the exchange rate for $\hat{Z}$ to B will adjust from $\hat{Z}1 = B2$ to $\hat{Z}1 = \frac{2200}{1050} = B2.095$.

This can also be calculated as 1 Zolar will equal $2 \times \left(\frac{1.10}{1.05} \right) = 2.095$ Buros.

If the exchange rate did not adjust and stayed at $\hat{Z}1 = B2$, then a canny investor could buy the basket of goods in Zedmania on day 365 for $\hat{Z}1,050$ and sell them in Beeland for B2,200. He could then convert his B back into $\hat{Z}$ at the Day 1 unchanged rate and receive $\hat{Z}1,100$. He has netted a tidy profit if $\hat{Z}50$. Our earlier readings have shown that arbitrage quickly eliminated such risk-free profit opportunities.

Of course, the world markets consist of more than one model of BMW cars. In order to properly apply the PPP, economists use a basket of goods to measure relative prices across currencies and compare how the price of the basket of goods varies. Measuring the movement in price of a basket of goods is the same as measuring inflation. If the basket of goods chosen is relatively consistent across the world's currencies, a global measure of price relativities arises. Now, armed with a set of global price indices for the world's currencies, we can apply the theory of relative PPP to the world's currencies. The theory predicts that the exchange rates between two currencies will vary in accordance with the relative inflation rates between the two currencies.

An MNE can use the relative PPP to make a judgement about calculating possible exposure to foreign exchange risk. This is because inflation rate differences between currencies are measures that are relatively accessible and easy to calculate. Unfortunately, whilst a good guide, other factors also influence the exchange rate between two currencies, and these factors are more difficult to predict than inflation. Remember, there may be government intervention, balance of payment current accounts surpluses of deficits, speculators and so forth. These factors will also impact upon prevailing exchange rates.

FIGURE 8.2: DRIVERS OF FOREX RATES AND THEIR EFFECT

Driver of Change for Country X	Likely Effect on Currency of Country X
Balance of payments trade surpluses	Strengthen
High relative interest rates	Weaken
High relative inflation	Weaken
Country X's central bank buys currency X	Strengthen
Country X's central bank 'prints' new currency X	Weaken
Balance of payments trade deficits	Weaken
Currency X seen as a 'safe haven'	Strengthen

Inflation and the Fisher Effect

In the earlier paragraphs of this section we have seen how interest rate differentials and inflation rate differentials both explain movements in exchange rates between two currencies. Irving Fisher, a US economist of the early 20th Century, proposed that both inflation and interest rates could be combined in a general explanation regarding exchange rates. The main thrust of his idea is that investors will seek the same return for the same risk irrespective of the currency they are invested in. Taking this basic idea he then argued that any difference in interest rates between currencies was a function of inflation rate differentials between the currencies. This is a big statement. It means that investing in a currency with higher interest rate as a means of seeking a superior return is futile as the exchange rate will alter to erode the supposed superior return.

The proposition is almost counter-intuitive. It means that the currency with the higher interest rate will weaken by the time you come to convert your funds back into your original currency, eroding any gains one has made due to interest rate differentials. Intuitively one would expect a currency with a higher interest rate to appreciate in value due to the better return available. But the International Fisher Effect, as Fisher's idea has come to be known, proposes the opposite, all other things being equal. The argument is based on the combination of purchasing power parity theory and covered interest rate arbitrage concept. Relative inflation between two currencies will cause a fall in the value of the currency with the higher inflation in order to preserve purchase power parity, a one 'world' price for every product or, more correctly, a stability in the relative price of products between currencies.

In order to understand the Fisher effect more comprehensively it is useful to work through a mathematical derivation of it.

Domestically: nominal interest rate = real interest rate plus rate of inflation, formulaically expressed below as

$$NI_h = RI_h + I_h$$

where NI_h is the nominal interest rate at home, RI_h = real interest rate of the home currency and I_h is the home inflation rate, all expressed over the same time period.

In the foreign currency:

$$NI_f = RI_f + I_f$$

where NI_f is the nominal interest rate in the foreign currency, RI_f is the real interest rate in the foreign currency and I_f is the foreign inflation rate.

We have already said that the change in the exchange rate, ΔEX, between a home currency, h, and a foreign currency, f, is a function of the nominal interest rate differential between the two currencies. Expressed mathematically we can say that:

$$\Delta EX = \frac{1 + NI_f}{1 + NI_h} - 1$$

Expressed using the formulae developed above for stating the NI we can reformulate as follows:

$$\Delta EX = \frac{1 + RI_f + I_f}{1 + RI_h + I_h} - 1$$

As the International Fisher Effect, the IFE, proposes that real interest rates are the same irrespective of the currency, we can see that a unit of the home currency will buy more units of the foreign currency when $I_f > I_h$. In other words, where inflation is lower at home compared to the foreign currency, the home currency will strengthen against the foreign currency.

When the real interest rates and the inflation rates are relatively small, the formula can be simplified to say that the percentage appreciation/(depreciation) of the home currency in terms of the foreign currency can be expressed as:

$$\Delta EX = I_f - I_h$$

Using the simplified formula derived earlier we can work through an example. The UK£1 buys US$1.70 at today's spot rate. Inflation in the UK is 2% whilst US inflation is expected to be 3%. Using the simplified formula we would expect Sterling to strengthen by 1% so that £1 buys $1.717.

This can also be calculated as $1.70 \times \dfrac{1.03}{1.02} = 1.717$

8.7 CONCLUSION

In the chapters up to now we have explored the nature of international trade. We have seen how it has grown strongly, especially since the 1970s. MNEs have been to the forefront in driving this growth. We have explored how these MNEs manage their international expansion through the use of differing business models and frameworks, depending on their industry sector and their appetite for risk. We further examined how these MNEs should be run according to good corporate principles. We further identified the main locally owned MNEs and those foreign-owned MNEs operating on the island of Ireland.

As we were exploring these topics I will have always referred to the fact that MNEs operate in a more complex environment than purely domestic enterprises. This complexity comes from scale and reach issues but also from the challenges of dealing with different legal and cultural environments. MNEs also need to manage dealing with different currencies. In this chapter we have started to delve a little deeper into these complexities. We delve deeper in order to better understand the strategies and tactics the MNE might use to deal with the risks that such additional complexities introduce. Specifically in this chapter we explored how the foreign exchange markets operate. We have sought to understand why exchange rates move by examining the balance of payments theory and looking at government intervention. We have seen that different governments manage their country's exchange rate movements in different way. Some try to fix the exchange rate and others allow the rate to be influenced completely by market forces in what is called a 'free float'.

The chapter went on to examine three main theories that have been developed to explain exchange rate movements and to interlink interest rates and inflation rates to exchange rates. The theories are purchasing power parity theory (PPP), interest rate parity theory (IRP) and the International Fisher Effect (IFE). We have further explored how these movements are possible through the operation of arbitrageurs in the foreign exchange markets.

Later, in **Chapter 15**, we will examine the tools and techniques the MNE will use to manage exchange rate exposures. We will see how these tools are effective risk-management strategies and how they interrelate to the theories and principles introduced in this chapter. In the next chapter we look at how an MNE will raise the necessary long-term capital to carry out its desired operations.

QUESTIONS

Self-test Questions

8.1 What is the difference between a sterilised and a non-sterilised intervention by a central bank in the foreign exchange markets?

8.2 What are the advantages of a 'free-floating' exchange rate?

8.3 If annual inflation in the US and the UK were 10% and 5% respectively, what effect would this have on exchange rates according to the purchasing power parity theory?

8.4 What is the 'spot rate'?

8.5 On 1 June the exchange rate between Sterling and the euro was Stg£1 = €0.85. On 1 September of the same year the spot rate was Stg£1 = €0.73. Calculate the percentage change in the value of the euro and identify whether it appreciated or depreciated in value against Sterling.

Thought-provoking Questions

Question 8.1

You are the CFO of Quandry Ltd, a company with operations in the US, UK and the Eurozone (France). You have been given the following information regarding the three countries in which Quandry operates:

- The spot rate is Stg£1 = US$0.80 = €0.73.
- Annual interest rates are £4%, US$7% and €2%.
- Annual inflation is £2%, US$8% and €6%.

Your CEO, Peter Donow, has heard of the International Fisher Effect. He asks you to prepare a calculation to show what the spot rate would be one year from now assuming the only market effects are inflation and interest rates and that the IFE holds true. You sit down and start to figure out how you are going to calculate an answer.

Question 8.2

You are Emma Stockton, a newly appointed CFO of Green Dragon Ltd. Your CEO has asked you to help the board understand why exchange rates do not stay constant over time. She has heard it has to do with governments and central banks but is not quite sure. She has requested a 500-word summary for the board of the key drivers of movement of foreign exchange rates.

Review Questions

(See Suggested Solutions to Review Questions in **Appendix B**.)

Question 8.1: Smart Bathroom Fittings Ltd

Analyse the economic data presented in Appendix 1 of the Smart Bathroom Fittings Ltd case study in **Appendix A** and comment on the relative attractiveness of each of the countries for Smart Bathroom Fittings Ltd in expanding internationally. Comment on the limitations of the data provided.

Question 8.2: Trident Mobile Ltd

Analyse the economic data presented in Appendix 1 of the Trident Mobile Ltd case study in **Appendix A** and comment on the relative attractiveness of each of the countries for Trident Mobile Ltd in expanding internationally. Comment on the limitations of the data provided.

9

INTERNATIONAL CAPITAL FLOWS

CONTENTS

LEARNING OBJECTIVES

Having read this chapter, you will understand:
- the different types of international capital flows;
- the international agencies set up by collaborating states to facilitate international capital markets;
- how capital markets enable foreign trade; and
- how both the Republic of Ireland and Northern Ireland measure capital flows.

9.1 INTRODUCTION

Up to now we have considered the nature of international trade in the context of the trade in goods and services. We have seen how long-standing theories propound that these international flows produce better outcomes for the global society, tending, as they do, to produce improvements in standards of living for both exporting and importing nations. Empirical evidence supports these theories[1] and thus the economic goal of most liberal democracies, and some other governmental systems, is to encourage global trade and to support the infrastructures that facilitate its growth. A number of institutions have been set up through collaboration among states that share the same philosophies about the benefits of global trade. These include the G20, the International Monetary Fund (IMF), the World Bank and the World Trade Organization (WTO). Later in this chapter we will examine the operation of some of these institutions in greater detail.

---

[1] "10 benefits of the WTO trading system", www.wto.org/english/res_e/doload_e/10b_e.pdf

There are two aspects to international trade of relevance to the discussion to this chapter. First, there is the process of actually producing the good or service that is to be traded, what manufacturing processes are used, and so forth (though technical production processes are not the topic of this text). Secondly, there is the provision of capital to facilitate trade, whether this is international trade or trade to meet domestic demand. For example, a multinational enterprise (MNE) may provide capital to a foreign entity that it owns, or contracts with, so that the foreign entity can increase production to meet demand in its own domestic economy. This second aspect of international trade is just as important as the first since without capital, production does not happen. Thus, in this chapter we will look at this second aspect of international trade, the flows of capital that are needed to facilitate the execution of the primary aspect, which is the production of goods and services.

9.2 TYPES OF INTERNATIONAL CAPITAL FLOWS

International capital flows involve the movement of funds from one jurisdiction to another for the purpose of funding economic activity. For MNEs, such capital flows involve:
- the acquisition of shares in entities in foreign markets; or
- the provision of loans.

The first type of capital flow, share acquisition, can, in turn, be distinguished into two types:
- foreign direct investment; and
- foreign portfolio investment.

We will examine these two subdivisions first and we will then go on to examine capital flow in the context of the provision of loans to MNEs. (In this chapter we are looking at 'credit' in the sense of the credit provided being a source of the longer term financing needed for the MNE to carry out its activities.)

Share Acquisition

As outlined above, in the context of international capital flows, there are two kinds of shares acquisition. Where only a return is sought by the investor but not managerial control it is a called a **'foreign portfolio investment'**. Where managerial control or influence is sought the capital flow is called a **foreign direct investment** (FDI).

Foreign Direct Investment (FDI)

The OECD[2] defines ownership levels in excess of 10% of the voting rights in an acquired entity as foreign direct investment (FDI). FDI capital flows involve share acquisitions representing at least 10% of the share capital of the acquired entity. The OECD's definition differentiates between capital flows, or investments, that are made for the purposes of acquiring a return without exercising management control and those investments that are made in order to gain a longer lasting controlling influence on the acquired entity.

The OECD is interested in benchmarking these definitions in order that comparisons between countries' performances and level of FDI activity can be made.

So, FDI is about investment strategies that seek to exercise control; it is through exercising control that the investing entity seeks to optimise its overall return. Usually, the investing entity will wish to exercise managerial control because it seeks to integrate the activities of the acquired

---

[2] *OECD Benchmark Definition of Foreign Direct Investment* (4th Edition, 2008).

entity into the activities of the enlarged entity, the MNE. Sometimes this integration might be as simple as having integrated treasury and cash management systems. Normally, however, the integration is much more developed than just treasury or accounting systems. The MNE seeks to integrate the acquired entity's activities for the purpose of enhancing the overall value chain and thereby the profitability of the entire entity. In other words, it will seek to integrate activities such as production, operations, logistics and so forth.

Clearly, any entity that makes an investment in a foreign entity with an interest in influencing the management of that entity has a strategy that implicitly means the investor believes they can obtain returns superior to those which the existing management can obtain acting on their own, as illustrated below in **Example 9.1**. If an acquiring MNE did not seek to influence the managerial strategies of the acquired entity it would be preserving the status quo, meaning that returns to the investors would remain the same. Thus, how could the acquiring entity create value for its investors? Unless the acquiring entity's investors are prepared to accept a lower return on an acquired entity than enjoyed by the previous investor, one would always expect to see some influence exerted upon the acquired entity's management and strategy in the case of FDI acquisitions.

EXAMPLE 9.1: IAG TAKEOVER OF AER LINGUS

In early 2015, international airline group IAG launched a €1.4 billion takeover bid for Aer Lingus, representing around a 30% premium on the share price prevailing in the weeks before the bid was announced. The IAG management plan to grow the airline in ways that Aer Lingus could not achieve as a stand-alone company. Through this growth, IAG will hope to gain a superior return from the investment than the shareholders of Aer Lingus could achieve. This superior return expectation is what persuades IAG to offer a price higher than the market price prior to the bid.

In summary, the provision of capital through the FDI route is done for the purposes of exercising managerial control and extracting a superior return.

Foreign Portfolio Investment (FPI)

In contrast to FDI, foreign portfolio investment is where the investing entity makes the investment, through the acquisition of shares, for the purpose of acquiring a superior return to that which might be available in their domestic economy. Crucially, the portfolio investor has no interest in acquiring a management interest.

The portfolio investor is seeking a return on their investments. They seek out investments that fit their investment strategies, those that balance the risks the investor is taking with the returns that can be achieved. An investor will hold a number of investments in a 'portfolio'. When searching for returns the investor may notice that some asset classes in another jurisdiction provide superior returns than those that are available in their home market. A superior return in this regard is either a better rate of return on the investment than can be achieved in the home market for the same level of risk, or the same rate of return but for lower level of risk. The investor acquires assets in the foreign jurisdiction solely to have access to this superior return. They have no wish to exercise any managerial control over the entity, even though their investment might be quite large. For example, a German pension fund may make an investment in an Irish company purely to receive a return. It adopts a passive position with regard to its investment and does not seek to exercise any managerial control. It envisages no synergy nor does it seek to influence the management in the running of the Irish company except through voting on issues put to shareholders.

The Provision of Loans

At the outset of this chapter we saw that international capital flows fall into two categories:
• the acquisition of shares in entities in foreign markets; or
• the provision of loans.

We now move on to consider the second type of international capital flow: the provision of loans. International capital flows by way of loans are normally provided by commercial banks, financial institutions, central banks and international organisations, such as the World Bank and the IMF. These types of loan represent international capital flows since they are loans provided by parties in one jurisdiction to entities in another. International capital flows may also be generated by the issuance of bonds. In this instance, the MNE will issue bonds in a foreign country or countries rather than in its domestic market. The bonds will then be subscribed for by investors. In this way, capital flows to the MNE from a foreign jurisdiction, i.e. the market where the bonds are issued.

Capital Inflows to Less Developed Countries

Returns from invested capital can be higher in developing counties compared to developed countries. This is because less developed countries tend to have a scarcity of domestic capital due to less developed capital markets and the fact that a larger percentage of consumer income is spent rather than saved. It is hard to encourage saving in an economy where incomes are low. This shortage of capital leads to higher returns being available for investors into those economies. Indeed, in recent years capital outflows from developed countries have increasingly been into less developed economies.

There has been much research into whether these increased capital inflows have actually produced benefits for the emerging or developing countries, some of which indicates that the recipient countries' economies have not benefitted.[3] The argument against the encouragement and facilitation of inward capital flows as an improvement strategy for less developed countries can be summarised as follows. Providers of capital will seek to maximise returns and will extract a premium from the developing economies in return for making investment there. This premium starves those economies of some element of the profits generated by the investment, profits that would otherwise be invested back into the local economy and would fuel growth. The premium extracted from the developing country's economy can be at its highest when the capital provided is not used for productive purposes in the economy. As we saw in **Chapter 2**, mercantilism, the economic theory that prevailed before the emergence and application of free market theory in the 1800s, advocated the extraction of value from foreign jurisdictions. The extracted assets, normally raw materials, were shipped back to the home country and then processed into finished goods. The country whose assets were being extracted received little if any sustainable benefit from this activity. Some would argue that modern inward capital flows have the same effect as the outdated mercantilist extraction strategies. The superior returns demanded

---

[3] Hall, P.A. and Soskice, D. (2001), *Varieties of Capitalism: The Institutional Foundations of Comparative Advantage*, Oxford: Oxford University Press; Di Tella, R. and MacCulloch R. (2009), "Why Doesn't Capitalism Flow to Poor Countries?", *Brooking Papers on Economic Activity*, Spring.

from international investors for the risk of investing or lending into less developed countries forms a subtle form of value extraction that impoverishes the recipient nation.

However, while there is no settled view emerging from the research, there also seems to be much support for inward capital flows to developing economies as a means of improving standards of living. Of the two types of investment, FDI and PDI, FDI in particular seems to enable the development of an emerging economy's infrastructure. It also seems to aid the development of the recipient economy through the emergence of regulations, legal frameworks and commercial competencies, all of which serve to enable further growth. This is why so many governments are keen to encourage FDI and have set up agencies to do so.

9.3 AGENCIES THAT SUPPORT INTERNATIONAL CAPITAL FLOWS

As we have seen, most of the world's governments believe that global trade should be encouraged. Despite some opposition to this view in recent years, the preponderance of opinion at the governmental level remains supportive of the goal and the developed economies continue to put in place structures to facilitate global trade. Having said this, in the five years to 2013, the number of measures put in place by the world's governments restricting capital flows has also increased and the number of measures easing capital flows has been falling.[4] It seems counter-intuitive that there are increased restrictions on capital flows at the same time as the level of international trade is increasing so dramatically. It seems that as global trade and capital flows have gained in importance, countries that in the past were not hugely exposed to such factors, now find it necessary to enact regulations to prevent unfettered, and possibly uncontrollable, international development.

In this section, we will consider the main agencies that have been developed to encourage and enable international trade.

The International Monetary Fund (IMF)

In 1944, as the Second World War drew to a close, a United Nations Monetary and Financial Conference was held at Bretton Woods, New Hampshire, in the US, one of the outcomes of which was the formation of the International Monetary Fund, or IMF. Its goals are to:
- promote co-operation among countries on international monetary issues;
- promote stability in exchange rates;
- provide temporary funds to member countries with imbalances on international payments;
- promote free trade;
- promote free movement of capital.

The IMF's goals were set out in a charter signed and agreed to by the member countries, of which there are currently 184.

The executive board of the IMF is based in Washington, D.C., and comprises 24 directors drawn from the member countries. The executive is overseen by a board of governors, which has one representative from each of the 184 member countries. It is a complex governance structure but one that focuses on inclusion and consensus. Having said that, the voting rights in the IMF are linked to the contribution a member country makes to the funding of the institution.

---

[4] UNCTAD (2013), *Trade and Development Report*, Geneva: United Nations, pp. 22–23.

Thus, the wealthier countries have a greater say in how the funds are used. The result is that, in the eyes of some, the stringent terms attached to IMF funding might have the effect of increasing poverty in recipient countries rather than decreasing it.

Indeed, in the aftermath of the world financial crisis that was sparked off in September 2008 by the collapse of Lehman Brothers, dimensions of this debate were played out in Ireland as the country received funds in late 2009 and early 2010 from a 'troika' that included the IMF. A popularly held view was that the troika imposed unaffordable conditions on Ireland at a time when it was at its most vulnerable. In the final analysis, however, countries that require intervention funding rarely have a strong bargaining position. The IMF seeks to stabilise global markets and that involves placating creditor nations in conjunction with bailing out debtor nations.

As mentioned above, the IMF is financed by the contributions from its member countries. The contribution level is set by reference to the size of each individual member country's economy and its scale in international trade and commerce. The amount a country can borrow from the IMF in also linked to the amount it has paid in. Thus, the fund is really intended to be used to correct short-term instability, normally resulting from trade imbalances in an economy.

Since contributions to and lending from the fund are related to the size of a country's economy, all countries, regardless of their balance of payments position, have the same entitlements from and commitments to the fund on a pro-rata basis. Consequently, no capacity for long-term lending arises where excess contributions from 'healthy' economies could finance longer term funding to 'unhealthy' economies. This inability to fund long-term instabilities flows from the governance model, which does not create surpluses available for restructuring economies on a long-term basis. If longer term loans were available from the IMF, the organisation would become divided between the better-off economies as lenders, and the developing countries as borrowers. If this situation arose, then the IMF would find itself divided into two camps with competing objectives. In order to avoid this, the structures and governance of the IMF ensures that it is only involved in the provision of short-term restructuring loans. These loans almost always come with conditions attached. The conditions are such that they ensure the repayment of loans through a restructured fiscal environment in the recipient country coupled with longer term refinancing. In order to access the funds, countries must be able to demonstrate that their funding requirements are short-term (one month to five years). Where longer term funding is needed, the IMF will collaborate with other institutions to provide a solution.

MNEs should pay particular attention when any of the countries in which they operate, or depend on for trade, enter into supports from the IMF. Usually the conditions of receipt of IMF funding and support are recessionary in nature, usually meaning that public spending is cut, taxes are increased and consumer sentiment drops. All these factors have a detrimental effect on the recipient country's economy, especially in the short term, entailing higher unemployment, lower disposable incomes and a contraction in demand. That said, MNEs with sourcing operations in countries in receipt of IMF support may see improvements in the competitiveness in the economy, leading to possible lowering of sourcing costs. These lower costs can come from weakening exchange rates of the recipient country's currency and real improvements in competitiveness.

The World Trade Organization (WTO)

In 1993 the Uruguay round of international trade negotiations led to the General Agreement on Trade and Tariffs (GATT). One aspect of the GATT accord was the foundation of the World Trade Organization or WTO, the role of which is to provide a platform for the carrying out of trade negotiations between countries. This role is especially helpful where there are a number of countries taking part rather than bilateral negotiations.

The WTO also has a critical role in the resolution of trade disputes between nations. In simple terms, the member countries use their voting rights to carry out judgements in order to resolve disputes. While the trade negotiation process and the dispute resolution system is relatively easy to describe in theory, it can be very complex in its operation. The complexity flows from the interconnectivity of contemporary global international trade. Most member countries are connected to each other directly or indirectly through international trade. Therefore, no one country is entirely objective in its deliberations about negotiations or, in particular, dispute resolution. As a result, the solutions found can be complex and tend toward compromise on all sides.

Indeed, compromise is often what is needed. The WTO provides a hugely important platform for these sensitive negotiations and, despite criticism from some quarters, international trade is more generally enabled rather than hindered by its existence. Without the WTO there would be a tendency for some nations to discourage international trade in order to further their domestic political agendas.

The World Bank

The World Bank was also created towards the end of the Second World War at the Bretton Woods Conference (see above) to lend money to countries to further their post-war reconstruction and economic development. Today, it is now more closely aligned with poverty alleviation. Its original name was the International Bank for Reconstruction and Development, the IBRD. Indeed, the World Bank today comprises the original IBRD together with the International Development Association (IDA, not to be confused with Ireland's IDA). It is also headquartered in Washington, D.C., and has over 10,000 employees worldwide.

The World Bank offers low-interest loans, interest-free credits and grants to developing countries. It operates on a 'for-profit' basis, borrowing money on the world's financial markets and lending it to countries it expects will be able to pay the money back.

The World Bank is part of the World Bank Group, which has set itself two goals to achieve by 2030, to:
- end extreme poverty by decreasing the number of people living on less than $1.25 a day to less than 3%;
- promote shared prosperity by fostering the income growth of the bottom 40% for every country.[5]

The World Bank Group comprises five organisations. The World Bank is made up of two of these five institutions: the IBRD and the IDA. (For a description of the role of the other three, see below.) The World Bank is made up of 188 member countries who are its shareholders. They are represented by a board of governors who, in turn, delegate operational responsibility to 25 executive directors. There is an annual meeting where the board of governors meet together with the board of governors of the IMF.

The International Development Association

As mentioned above, the World Bank has two components, the original IBRD and, since 1960, the IDA (again, to be distinguished from IDA Ireland). The IBRD was formed on a

---

[5] See http://www.worldbank.org/en/about/what-we-do

self-sustaining basis and provides loans and advice to middle income and credit-worthy poorer countries. The IDA is the arm of the World Bank that provides finance to the world's poorest countries. It does this by way of providing loans, which it calls 'credits' and 'grants'. The credits and grants focus on the development of programs that will facilitate and encourage economic growth and improve peoples' standards of living.

The IDA is the single largest source of funds for the world's 77 poorest nations, 39 of which are in Africa. The money is lent on benign terms over terms of 25 to 38 years with little or no interest being charged. The IDA also provides grants to countries with distressed debt sourced elsewhere, normally to provide a means of avoiding default.

In addition to the credits and grants it provides, the IDA works with countries to secure debt forgiveness. (It is not just Bono that has this goal.) There are two main programmes for delivering debt relief: the Heavily Indebted Poor Countries Initiative (HIPC) and the Multilateral Debt Relief Initiative (MDR).

The International Finance Corporation

The International Finance Corporation (IFC) is the largest global development institution focusing on the private sector in developing countries. In fact, its support for the private sector is what distinguishes the IFC from other aid agencies operating in the financial sphere. As well as providing support through advice and project management, the IFC provides loans to the private sector and also takes shareholding positions in companies by investing directly in the equity.

Where it does lend money, it is typically 10% to 5% of a project's requirements, normally its capital needs. The rest of the funding must be achieved from normal lending markets. In this way, the IFC acts as an accelerant to get viable projects off the ground. The IFC also works with loan recipient companies to garner the extra funding they need. MNEs operating in developing countries need to be aware of the IFC and how it operates, as it could be a useful source of funds or advice.

The IFC also provides investment advice. An MNE looking to invest in certain countries can use the agency to help tailor its investment approach. The IFC tends to focus on facilitating investment in infrastructure, manufacturing, agribusiness and financial services markets. It has 4,000 staff, of whom 2,800 are in the field and the rest are based at its headquarters, again in Washington, D.C.

The Multilateral Investment Guarantee Agency

The Multilateral Investment Guarantee Agency (MIGA) is also part of the World Bank Group. Its function is to promote inward investment into developing countries. The MIGA works in countries where it believes it can have the most impact. These are normally countries to which either the IBRD or the IDA has provided funding or support, or countries that have been affected by conflict. The MIGA encourages inward investment by providing risk-management products that reduce the investing company's exposure to political risk in the investee country. In this way it garners much-needed private investment into volatile or underdeveloped countries. The manager in a MNE looking to invest in projects in these countries should be aware of the workings of the MIGA as there may well be risk-management approaches facilitated by the agency to enable investments that might otherwise fail the MNE's risk thresholds.

The International Centre for Settlement of Investment Disputes

Set up in 1966, the International Centre for Settlement of Investment Disputes (ICSID) is an autonomous institution formed by way of treaty by over 140 members of the IBRD, the original world bank. Its goal is to provide dispute resolution frameworks for the conciliation and arbitration of international investment disputes. It was established because potential investors were slow to invest if they did not have clear visibility on how disputes would be resolved. This reluctance on the part of investors was seen as a brake on the flow of private investment funds on a global level.

The ICSID does not conciliate disputes itself. It provides institutional and procedural frameworks for independent conciliation commissions that are constituted in each case. These independent conciliation commissions then plug into the procedural frameworks in order to come to a resolution. MNEs operating in developing countries should be aware of the benefits and risk reduction capabilities that the ICSID affords. For example, on 20 July 2015 arbitration proceedings were instituted using the auspices of the ICSID by Samsung Engineering Co Ltd against the Sultanate of Oman. The matter at issue is the handling of a state-tendering process by Orpic, the oil refinery business owned and operated by the Sultanate of Oman. The allegation is that Orpic closed down the bidding process after it had selected Samsung as the preferred bidder and had received a deposit from Samsung. It has not returned the deposit. The matter is still awaiting arbitration at the ICSID at the time of writing (October 2015). This example shows how the ICSID can help MNEs in dispute resolution, especially when operating in countries with significantly different legal infrastructures.

The Bank for International Settlements

The Bank for International Settlements (BIS) was established in 1930, making it the world's oldest international financial organisation. It has 60 members, which are central banks. These 60 central banks represent countries that in aggregate amount to 95% of the world's GDP.

The mission of the BIS is to serve the member central banks in their pursuit of monetary and financial stability. It also acts as a bank for the member central banks. BIS was founded on the belief that monetary and financial stability are preconditions for sustained economic growth. As we have seen, governments and their central banks are interested in sustained economic growth as they believe it is a root to improved living standards for all societies over the longer term.

The BIS has five main ways in which it seeks to achieve its goals:
- facilitating collaboration and discussion between central banks;
- promoting and encouraging dialogue with other non-central bank authorities that are responsible for promoting financial stability;
- carrying out research and policy analysis;
- acting as a counterparty to central banks in their financial transactions;
- being a trustee or agent in international financial operations.[6]

The BIS is a valuable resource for the MNE manager to gain access to well-funded research prepared on an impartial basis. An MNE carrying out desk research on potential markets or assessing country risk can avail of much information, statistics and analysis from the BIS.

---

[6] See www.bis.org/about/ (accessed November 2014).

9.4 IRELAND AND INTERNATIONAL CAPITAL FLOWS

Ireland is a major international financial centre. It has significant market share in the administration of mutual funds, insurance, leasing and some forms of international banking. Indeed, in 2013 the aggregate of foreign assets and liabilities managed in Ireland was some 3,600% of the country's GDP.[7] This level of what is called 'international financial integration' (IFI) is especially high for Ireland due, in part, to the success of the International Financial Services Centre (IFSC) in attracting and sustaining international financial institutions since its inception in 1987.

Ireland also has a high level of MNEs operating in the country. They make up almost 25% of gross added value in the economy and conduct a large amount of capital transactions and fund flows, some of which finance capital projects in Ireland, such as building new production plants, and so forth. However, a large amount of the capital flows are due to the management of group treasury functions that are carried out, in or through Ireland. As MNEs operating here seek to optimise their group cash management positions, these movements of funds lead to disproportionately high capital inflow and outflow figures for Ireland.

Interestingly, Irish pension funds are heavily invested in global securities and bonds while domestic equities and bonds are mainly subscribed to by foreign investors. One of the reasons for this is that the pensions regulator in the Republic of Ireland has specified the investment grade necessary for pension fund investments in Ireland, which has led to Irish pension funds, especially defined benefit schemes, investing in less risky assets. Once again, this contributes to Ireland's unique position as having much greater flows through its capital account than is warranted by its import and export trades.

Most media discussion regarding international trade in Ireland focuses on the import and export of goods and services and rightly so as these are key drivers of economic prosperity. We know from our discussion of balance of payments theory in **Chapter 8**, that the net of international trade in goods and services, together with the net of portfolio investments must be financed by the capital account. Therefore, the capital account is as valid a measure of the country's economic performance as the balance of payments current account. The capital account is a net figure arrived at by subtracting the capital outflows of a country from its inflows. A country's capital account is also the net balance of all its 'real economy' transactions. It is the other side of the double entry on the country's financial balance sheet (also known as a statement of financial position). The large amount of capital flows originating from Ireland's role as a global financial centre can mask the actual capital account funding implied by its real economy. This masking is further exacerbated by large foreign-owned MNEs 'parking' undistributed profits in Ireland. These profits, earned outside the country, are parked in their Irish entities but, if they remain undistributed, are not balanced by outflows to the ultimate owners. Thus, they create capital inflows into the country that are not connected to international trade in the real sense of that phrase. Any comparative assessment with other countries of the capital flows for the ROI must adjust for the effects of these anomalies to allow for meaningful comparison.

Trying to determine the capital flows for Northern Ireland is also problematic as the statistics are consolidated, partially at least, within the overall UK numbers. The balancing of the financial account with the balance of trade account happens at a UK level for Northern Ireland.

---

[7] Lane, P. (2014), *International Financial Flows and the Irish Crisis*. Dublin: Institute for International Integration Studies.

The OECD published a paper in 2011 contending, supported by empirical evidence, that large-scale inflows of capital into a country increase the likelihood of a banking crisis fourfold.[8] This is because the large inflows can create greater volatility in the domestic banking sector since the inflows are exposed to movements in global banking and economic sentiment. Therefore, while the report contends that ultimately global capital market integration is a good thing, it cautions that those countries with large inflows, such as the Republic of Ireland, are more greatly exposed to the volatility of the global financial markets and not just the inherent volatility of the Irish market. Consequently, it is important that there is accuracy in measuring the capital inflow numbers for Ireland. The MNE manager should also be interested in these numbers in order to manage risk in target countries or, indeed, in Ireland because volatility in a domestic banking sector can impact the operations of an MNE and its profitability. Excessive credit or a tightening of credit can impact the economy of a country greatly. Ireland was exposed to both factors during the boom and subsequent bust from 2003 to 2013.

9.5 CONCLUSION

In this chapter we looked at the movement of capital and the nature of capital flows. There are three types of international capital flows:
- foreign direct investment (FDI), where the MNE providing the capital seeks to exercise managerial control of the entity in which it has invested;
- foreign portfolio investment (FPI), where the investing MNE seeks a return on its investment but does not seek to exercise managerial control;
- credit, where the MNE providing the capital lends money to the recipient entity.

We also explored the global financial institutions that have been set up to encourage the movement of capital and to correct the imbalances that can occur in the international capital market system. The international community collaborates to create the environment to encourage international trade. In order to facilitate international trade it is essential to ease the flow of capital between countries and MNEs. A number of institutions have been set up that play a role in supporting the global capital markets, including the IMF, the World Bank, the International Development Agency, the Bank for International Settlements and the World Trade Organization.

As discussed in **Chapter 8**, the balance of payments (BoP) account of a state comprises two parts: the balance of payments current account (or balance of trade) and the balance of payments financial account. The two must equalise as they are the components of the double-entry system for international transactions of a country. Thus, if exports are greater than imports there must be a balancing amount on the BoP financial account, and vice versa.

The BoP financial account comprises three sources of funds: foreign direct investment (FDI), foreign portfolio investment (FPI) and the provision of credit. The net total of these three will balance to the surplus or deficit on the BoP current account. Therefore, to encourage international trade by facilitating ease of the movement of goods and services on its own will be like one hand trying to clap; it will not work. Freedom of movement of capital is as instrumental in the facilitation of international trade as the free movement of goods and labour.

---

[8] OECD (2011). "Getting the most out of international capital flows". OECD Economics Department Policy Notes, No. 6.

We also discussed how capital markets enable foreign trade. The BoP theory recognises that for each outflow of a good or service from an economy there needs to be an equal inflow of capital. This means that capital flows are as critical to world trade as freedom of movement of goods and labour. Thus, restrictions on capital movements have a distorting effect on the movement of goods and services. Therefore, any steps that can be taken to facilitate capital flows will encourage greater trade.

Both the Republic of Ireland and Northern Ireland measure capital flows; ROI has major capital inflows relating to the MNEs that use Ireland as a country to 'park' cash. These need to be adjusted for in calculating meaningful comparisons with other countries. NI's capital account is not calculated separately and is integrated into the overall UK capital account.

QUESTIONS

Self-test Questions

9.1 What complications exist in trying to determine the underlying capital account for Ireland or Northern Ireland?

9.2 Why does the BoP current account need to balance to the balance of payments financial account?

9.3 What is the difference between FDI and FPI?

Thought-provoking Questions

Question 9.1
You are the financial controller in an Irish MNE considering investing in a dam construction project in Zambia. Prepare a report for your board outlining the risk-management strategies that the company might adopt to minimise exposure to the currency volatility. What are the main headings your report would contain and why?

Question 9.2
You have recently joined Sheerbone Plc, a Boston-based MNE with operations in Banbridge, Northern Ireland. The board of Sheerbone is considering some long-term 'what-if' scenario planning. They have asked you to consider what might happen to capital inflows and outflows to the UK if the UK government introduced restriction on the flows of capital. What are the main points you would make to the board?

Review Questions

(See Suggested Solutions to Review Questions in **Appendix B**.)

Question 9.1
Explain the history and role of the International Monetary Fund (IMF).

Question 9.2
Explain the history and role of the World Bank.

Question 9.3
Explain the history and role of the Bank for International Settlements (BIS).

10

INTERNATIONAL TRADE AND WORKING CAPITAL

LEARNING OBJECTIVES

Having read this chapter, you will understand:
- the nature of working capital;
- the cash management options available to multinational enterprises;
- the benefits of a centralised treasury management system;
- sources of short-term finance for MNEs;
- the credit control function in an international setting;
- the payment methods that ensure the seller gets paid and the buyer gets the right goods;
- the terms of international trade;
- the different terms of sale that exist in the carrying out of international trade; and
- the area of letters of credit.

10.1 INTRODUCTION

In Part II of this book we have been examining how the external financial world impacts upon the operation of multinational enterprises (MNEs). In **Chapter 8** we looked at how the foreign exchange markets work and in **Chapter 9** how MNEs raise longer term funds in order to finance the pursuit of their objectives. In this chapter, we will explore the operation of the day-to-day financing needs of MNEs. In particular, we will examine how MNEs pay their suppliers in foreign jurisdictions together with how they, in turn, ensure that they get paid by their customers. These matters are much more complex when trading internationally than in a purely domestic enterprise.

When a domestic enterprise decides to internationalise, whether proactively or in response to market demands, it will be faced with making a number of choices. The nascent (MNE) must decide which countries to enter, how to finance its expansion strategies and how to minimise the attendant risks. The issues under consideration can be short or long term. By their nature, strategic considerations tend to be long term. However, the ongoing running of a business on a day-to-day basis involves short-term decisions, which ought to align with, and support, its longer term strategies. In particular, the MNE will need processes in place allowing it to finance its day-to-day operations, pay its supplies and receive payment for the goods and services it sells to its customers.

These matters may seem humdrum and not very exciting when compared to the weighty strategic issues that face the MNE and are the subject of other chapters in this book. However, the execution of the management of the day-to-day finances of an MNE is one of the most critical determinants of its success or failure. Left unattended and running out of cash will put an MNE out of business faster than running out of ideas. The management of these day-to-day finances is a key role of the accountant in an MNE.

Thus, in this chapter we will address the factors that need to be considered by an MNE in managing its day-to-day financing, particularly working capital. We will also explore how it manages the capital needed to finance those day-to-day activities.

10.2 WORKING CAPITAL MANAGEMENT

Elsewhere in this book we explore the sources of long-term finance available to MNEs (see **Chapters 9** and **11**). Essentially, these fall into two categories: debt and equity. The raising of finance from these two sources is normally carried out after projections have been done of the capital requirements of the business over a number of years, normally five to 10 years. These projections tend to have a smooth appearance in that outflows are normally one-off 'lump', capital payments and inflows are smooth cash-flow earnings that flow from the capital investments. The projections are 'smooth' since they are almost always an aggregate of individual transactions. This aggregation is necessary in order to be able to produce intelligible forecasts. If every single transaction was listed on a cash flow forecast it would run to many pages and pages and the reader would be unable to make any meaningful interpretation of them. Another reason for the smoothing is that the forecast is exactly that: a forecast. The MNE may expect that its sales for a particular month will be €1 million but it does not know the detailed composition of this €1 million until the transactions actually happen.

As mentioned earlier, these cash-flow projections are normally done on a month-by-month or year-by-year basis. However, the reality of the cash-flow position of an MNE is that the cash comes in and goes out on a daily basis – on any day there are cash-flow movements. The hope and intention is that when the daily movements are aggregated they will equate to the monthly, or yearly, expectations. In all cases, the annual cash flow of the MNE will be the sum of the monthly cash flows. The monthly cash flows are the aggregate of the weekly cash flows, the weekly cash flows are the aggregate of the daily cash flows, the daily are the aggregate of the hourly cash flows, and so forth.

An MNE must ensure that its management practices concerning cash flow are at and of a sufficiently granular level and nature. This means the system needs to be able to cope with the individual actual and expected transactions while at the same time summarise these transactions to present a 'snapshot' of what is happening in the MNE, thereby enabling the managers to manage.

For example, if cash receipts are banked once a day, then the MNE's processes must ensure that there is sufficient control on the daily lodgement process that the MNE can predict whether its overall cash position will be in line with expectations. A retailer might expect a cash inflow for the month of March to be €15 million. If, after 20 days trading, the daily lodgements have only totalled €5 million, alarm bells should be ringing. It would not be good management to wait until 1 April to discover that the bank account had a shortfall.

Fluctuations in daily cash flows stem from the day-to-day activities of the MNE as it seeks to pursue and execute its strategies. The better able the MNE is able to predict these short-term cash-flow movements, the better able it will be to plan how much of its cash resources or borrowings it needs to set aside to finance these daily movements. The amount it needs to set aside is '**working capital**', which is, as stated above, the capital needed to finance the day-to-day activities. It normally consists of the cash needed to buy stock, pay wages and other daily costs less any cash receipts from debtors. The MNE will normally have to pay these amounts out to its suppliers before it can get payments in from its own customers.

Most working capital management programmes seek to get paid for goods and services as quickly as possible while deferring payments to suppliers for as long as possible. Since all MNEs are trying to achieve the same thing, i.e. to get paid by customers quickly and have agreed prolonged payment periods with suppliers, there are competitive pressures at play. Generally, suppliers will be trying to get paid as quickly as possible and customers will be trying to defer payment as long as possible. Since all participants in the **value chain** (see **Chapter 3, Figure 3.2**) are both suppliers and customers of other participants in the value chain, these pressures exist at all points in the chain. Sometimes an MNE will differentiate its offer from its competitors by offering advantageous credit terms. In the consumer electronics or furniture sectors we often see this differentiation in offers such as 'interest-free credit' and 'nothing to pay for 12 months'.

10.3 CASH MANAGEMENT AND WORKING CAPITAL

The importance of working capital cannot be over-emphasised. As we have seen, in planning for the future, an MNE must ensure it has captured not just its long-term capital costs but also its short-term working capital needs. Special consideration should be given to the working capital cash-flow timings. Normally, budgets and five-year plans will be phased by month and year. Working capital requirements are daily and hourly. If the MNE's business is one where the inflows and outflows are not 'smooth', projections need to capture this level of detail. For example, if wages are paid weekly but inflows from customers only come in at the end of the month, the cash-flow management system needs to capture these irregular timings of the various cash flows. In **Example 10.1**, a manager thinks there is no problem with the January cash flow as it is an inflow of €200,000. However, because of the timings of the cash flow within the month of January itself, €400,000 will, in fact, be needed to bridge the gap between the outgoings at the start of the month and the receipts at the end of the month.

EXAMPLE 10.1: TIMING ASPECTS OF CASH FLOW FORECASTS

A budget for January might show cash inflows of €600,000 and outgoings of €400,000. A manager might think there is no issue, that there will be a total net inflow of €200,000. However, if the outflow happens on the first of the month and the inflow only comes in on

31 January, the situation 'on the ground' will be different. The manager will need to secure short-term additional funding of €400,000 from the 1st of the month until the 31st, when the inflow will arrive and the business would be back in surplus funds.

In an MNE that has subsidiary operations in other countries, the management of working capital will have two dimensions:
- working capital management in the MNE's subsidiaries (each individual subsidiary within the MNE will have its own day-to-day cash flow needs);
- enterprise-wide management (the working capital and associated cash flow requirements of the entire group of companies taken as a whole).

Importantly, there might be opportunities within a group for buffering working capital requirements in one part of the group with working capital surpluses in another part. In this way, the working capital requirements of the group as a whole can be minimised. MNEs often, but not exclusively, operate as a group of companies, whose shares are held by an over-arching 'parent' company.

The development of electronic banking together with integrated systems such as SEMS (see **Chapter 17**), has given MNEs much greater visibility in managing their cash positions. In the past, a flurry of phone calls would take place each morning to see what cheques were going to be put in the post, how much the daily lodgement would be, etc. Today, this inexact approach has largely been dispensed with and the use of cash flow forecast variance analysis together with real-time banking information allows for much tighter control on this critical aspect of an MNE's activities.

Centralised Treasury

In **Chapter 15** it is highlighted that an MNE must measure and thereby manage its exposure to foreign exchange fluctuations. We can see that the way to do this is by calculating the net exposure to the various currencies throughout the enterprise. I point out that the best way to structure this function organisationally is to have a centralised treasury function, which can capture all the relevant information from an MNE's subsidiaries and branches. Only at the centre can the net movements of foreign exchange throughout the group be fully grasped and, therefore, managed.

A centralised treasury function would also help greatly with the management of cash and working capital throughout the group. The rhythms of the group's working capital cash flows can be fully grasped only at the centre. In addition to having visibility of the working capital cash flows, a centralised treasury function can move funds around the group to ensure that the optimal position is taken in each jurisdiction. Obviously, this ease of movement of funds requires relative freedom of movement of cash between the relevant bank accounts operated by the MNE. For example, SABMiller, the FTSE20 brewing MNE, operates a centralised treasury function. An extract from its 2015 annual report gives some indication of the high level of responsibility delegated by the board to the treasury team. The group has "a treasury operating framework and group treasury team, accountable for all treasury activities, which establishes policies and manages liquidity and financial risks, including foreign exchange, interest rate and counterparty exposures, and incorporates group and regional treasury committees that monitor these activities and compliance with the policies" (SABMiller *Annual Report 2015*).

Figure 10.1 below shows the movement of cash flows around an MNE with a centralised treasury function. On the upper left of the diagram cash comes in to the various subsidiaries from customers. On the bottom left cash leaves those subsidiaries through the payments for goods and services. Any gaps that arise between receipts in and payments out represent a surplus or deficit in the cash flow of each subsidiary. These working capital surpluses and deficits are managed by the central treasury function. On the right side of the diagram are three providers of finance: shareholders, banks and bondholders. The central treasury receives funds from these three sources and also remits to them returns on their investments. When you consider the interaction between working capital cash flows and providers of finance, it is possible to grasp how a centralised treasury function is the most effective way to manage all these inflows and outflows. This is because a centralised treasury will have an overview of all the cash movements, an overview that is not easily attainable in any individual part of the group.

While it is generally accepted that a centralised treasury function allows for the best use of an MNE's cash resources, it can also be argued that this approach leads to a lack of local autonomy. However, the benefits are so compelling that it would be hard to see how the centralised approach would not be favoured in all but the most exceptional of circumstances. For example, restrictions of such freedoms, which exist in many of the banking systems of developing countries, can complicate this approach. Nevertheless, the value of a centralised overview of working capital cash flows is immense.

FIGURE 10.1: WORKING CAPITAL CASH FLOWS WITH A CENTRALISED TREASURY FUNCTION

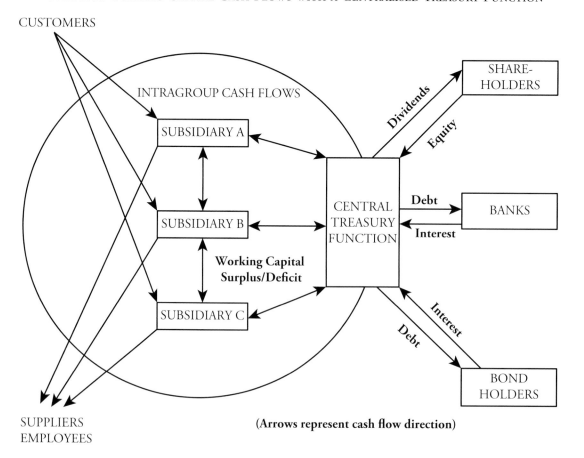

10.4 SHORT-TERM SOURCES OF CASH

Having identified the need for working capital, the treasury function of the MNE must then decide how to source the finance to meet this need.

Internal Sources of Finance

The first port of call for sourcing working capital or short-term financing is within the MNE itself. Cash-flow surpluses in one part of the group can be used to support cash-flow requirements in another part. Some MNEs structure their operations so that such counter-cyclical movements will work in their favour. In other words, they find investment opportunities that will generate working capital surpluses when other parts of the MNE have working capital requirements.

In any case, whatever the origin, an MNE should first assess its working capital surpluses and deficits on a group-wide basis to see if there can be a matching process that will obviate, or at least reduce, the need for external funds. This exercise will also highlight when there are working capital cash flow surpluses on a group-wide basis (see the discussion below on how to approach this positive situation).

Having identified those parts of the MNE group that need cash, the treasurer then moves funds from those subsidiaries or parts that are in surplus to those that need funding. Where movements of funds also involve conversion of funds from one currency to another, additional complications arise. (See **Chapter 15** for more on how this is managed.) In some cases, the central treasury function provides guarantees to the providers of loans to the subsidiary rather than actual provision of cash funds. There will usually be an intragroup interest charge made on a subsidiary that needs the funds, thereby providing income to those providing the funds. The taxation treatment of these intragroup interest charges is complex and dependent on the legislation prevailing in the relevant countries. While, in some cases, external interest payments can be tax deductible, there are restrictions on intragroup interest. The treasury function in the MNE will need to work with company's taxation specialists or advisors in ensuring that if there is an interest charging mechanism in operation, it optimises the MNE's position.

The governments of some countries will not allow the movement of funds from inside their borders. In other words they restrict movement of money, either into the country or, more usually, out of the country. Where these circumstances arise, an MNE may need to adopt other strategies to get the best value in the group for any surpluses that might arise. It may require its subsidiary or subsidiaries operating in the country with the 'blocked funds' to source its long-term capital requirements locally. In this way, short-term surpluses can be used to repay the longer term debt within the subsidiary's jurisdiction, meaning the funds do not need to leave the country.

Another strategy can be for a subsidiary in the country with the blocked funds to use its surplus to undertake a cash-consuming activity on behalf of the whole group but receive no internal income for it. For example, the MNE with the blocked funds may carry out R&D on behalf of the whole group. This would use up surplus cash in the 'blocked' country while at the same time benefiting the whole group, which would be charged for this service.

External Sources of Finance

Once any sources of internal financing have been explored, the MNE should then be able to identify the balance of funds still required. This exercise can and will be carried out on an ongoing basis. In other words, the MNE will use short-term forecasting to anticipate its short-term funding needs and to set up and quantify the necessary facilities. The MNE will also carry out real-time assessments of what is actually needed, which will be daily, and in some instances, hourly.

The MNE will identify what the short-term funding needs are and in what currencies. By moving funds around the group through the internal assessment mechanism, the treasury function will endeavour to source the external requirements in the location that is most advantageous from the overall group perspective. There are a number of considerations that will feed into this decision:

- location of availability of existing funding facilities;
- interest rates;
- foreign exchange exposures;
- transaction costs.

The short-term forecasting process will allow the treasurer of the MNE to pre-arrange short-term financing in anticipation of future requirements. These funding facilities will be pre-negotiated and will sit, undrawn, awaiting the day when the MNE will need them. When the day arrives that the working capital is needed, the funds will be drawn down in whichever jurisdiction most suits the circumstances.

In most circumstances, an MNE will have negotiated facilities in excess of what it needs based on its short-term forecasts. Most probably there will be an overall cap on what can be drawn from the aggregate of the facilities. For example, Scrod Plc may have negotiated short-term facilities, which it has not drawn down, of €5 million, £4 million and $8 million. Its overall banking agreements may state that it will not draw down more than €6 million from its short-term facilities at any one time. These overall facilities may be with one bank or a syndicate of banks. In any case, while it has these various facilities for working capital available to it in various countries, it can only tap into a portion of these facilities at any one time, depending on its needs. The skill of the treasurer is to have enough facilities to cover all eventualities without burdening the MNE with arrangement costs and facility charges. (Most of these facilities have costs attached to them even when they are not drawn down.)

Having identified how much the group will need in terms of external working capital financing, what options are available to the MNE in terms of raising the identified funds?

As mentioned above, the MNE may negotiate short-term facilities with banks to cover working capital requirements. (Longer term capital requirements and their sources are dealt with in **Chapter 14**.) The MNEs may also raise short-term working capital by issuing a number of different types of financial instruments. The most common that are issued for short-term working capital needs are Euronotes and Eurobank loans.

Euronotes

Euronotes have become more popular in recent years. (The term 'Euronotes' can be confusing. It does not mean that the currency involved needs to be the euro. It is just an unhappy co-incidence of labels.) Euronotes are unsecured loan notes that are issued by an MNE. They differ from normal bonds in that they have a shorter time horizon to maturity, reflecting their aptness for short-term financing requirements. The maturity dates are normally one month, three months or six months. An MNE will often redeem one issue of Euronotes with the issue of another round. Euronotes would be typically underwritten by a commercial bank. Indeed, commercial banks often use them as part of their own investment portfolio. They attract an interest rate, normally linked to the interbank overnight rates such as LIBOR or EURIBOR, plus a premium. Euronotes are essentially short-term promissory notes, a promise to pay, issued outside the country and currency of the issuer. For example, if an Irish company needed US dollars, it might issue a dollar note in the US.

Eurobank Loans

Euronotes may not be attractive to all MNEs due to their arrangement fees, set-up costs or complexity. A simpler source of short-term external finance is a loan from a bank, a Eurobank loan. (Once again, Eurobank in this context does not refer to the euro currency.) Sometimes an

MNE can have over 100 short-term Eurobank facilities arranged, which it will draw upon when and if they are needed.

Other Sources of Short-term Finance

Bank overdrafts, loans, Euronotes and Euroloans are provisions of short-term finance by institutions external to the trading activity of an MNE. The provision of credit by a supplier to a customer can lead to opportunities to gain access to cash for that supplier. The obligation by the customer to pay the supplier can be sold to a third party in return for cash. For example, a supplier may invoice a customer on Day 1 for goods supplied. The customer may have until Day 60 to pay. The supplier may be able to sell this Day-60 payment obligation to a third party in return for immediate or early payment. Thus, a finance institution like a bank will buy the Day-60 obligation to pay from the supplier at a discounted price, possibly on Day 1. When Day 60 arrives, the customer pays the supplier and the supplier immediately gives the money to the institution that provided the service, or the customer may directly pay the purchaser of the Day-60 obligation to pay. This activity is called 'invoice discounting' or 'factoring'. In an international context, a supplier MNE will find that it will need financial instruments that are capable of being enforced internationally in order to sell the payment obligations it has received from its customers. These instruments are discussed further in **Section 10.6**.

10.5 CREDIT CONTROL

One of the critical components of working capital is the management and control of cash inflows from customers, the idea being to get paid for the goods or services provided as quickly as possible. The longer the customer gets in credit, the more working capital the MNE will need to finance. MNEs, as with all businesses, ought to have a credit control policy that will stipulate the credit terms available to its customers. The operation of an MNE makes the credit control function more complicated. This complexity derives from:
• the multi-site, multi-country nature of MNEs;
• differing cultures in the various countries;
• language barriers;
• legislative and regulatory differences.

The decision that the MNE needs to make is whether to apply an enterprise- or group-wide policy on credit control or whether to allow local autonomy. This decision will be influenced heavily by the nature of the industry sector in which the MNE operates and the customary or accepted practices in that sector. In most cases, an MNE will adjust its practices to the appropriate dynamic in the country in which it is operating. Typically, it will also link credit control with the sales function, working to the maxim: "It's not a sale until it's paid for." In particular, where sales-incentive schemes are in place, it is important to link those incentives to the payment by the customer, not just the sale.

The growth of international trade over the centuries, coupled with the importance of credit, has led to the development of an established and standard set of arrangements and terms relating to the buying, selling and payment for goods that are traded internationally. This has led to a shared understanding of how trade is to be carried out and an international framework for the protection of traders' property rights and the right to be paid.

Since receiving payment for goods or services supplied is inextricably linked to the actual 'real' supply of those goods and services, it is important for the MNE manager to understand not only the mechanics of how payment is received but also how the supply of goods is evidenced to support such a payment. For this reason we should explore the terminology of international trade.

10.6 TERMINOLOGY OF INTERNATIONAL TRADE

A standardised terminology regarding international trade has developed over time. Originally driven by common terminology and documentation used by the banks to effect payment between traders, this terminology has now gained common acceptance in international business. The terms we will explore here fall into two categories, connected with:
• the sale of goods; and
• payment for goods.

Sale of Goods

In standard, 'domestic' trading, a buyer and seller agree a price for goods. This price will cover the purchase and sale of the goods at a given point. In international trade, however, there are a number of additional costs that do not occur, or that occur in a different way to purely domestic trade. These additional costs relate to the fact that the goods must be transported from one country to another. It needs to be clear at the point of purchase whether the price includes these additional costs. Put another way, the transaction between the buyer and the seller must clarify who is responsible for organising and paying for the different elements of the transportation of the goods.

Any MNE involved in the sale or purchase of goods internationally will need to be familiar with the standard set of concepts, practices and terms connected with the sale of goods. Organisationally, the specialist concerned with these phrases will be in the shipping or logistics department or within a specialist section of the finance department.

'Ex Works'

'Ex works' is a phrase denoting that the buyer takes possession of the goods at the seller's factory gate. The buyer must arrange for all onward transportation and shipping costs, together with appropriate insurance and other expenses, such as demurrage. **Demurrage** is the cost that must be paid to the operators of the ports and docks where the goods may be stored awaiting the arrival of the ship upon which they will be transported. Demurrage can also occur at the destination port as the goods lie in the dock awaiting collection by the buyer's transport for onward delivery. Ex works is very simple for the seller in that they do not need to manage any of the onward logistics. Ex works also often suits the buyer, especially where they are consolidating purchases in a geographic area. For example, a buyer may have commissioned a fleet of trucks to collect purchased goods from a number of factories and deposit them on a ship on which the buyer has booked the requisite amount of space. In these instances, the buyer may be able, through economies of scale and relationships, to get better terms for the provision of the logistics services than the seller can achieve.

For example, a large retailer such as Dunnes Stores might agree with the Chinese manufacturer of its own-label T-shirts to collect the goods it has ordered at the factory in Feidong, Northern China. This makes things simple for the Chinese manufacturer since it just needs to have the goods ready for collection at the designated time. For Dunnes Stores it is a bit more complicated. They need to arrange for a truck to go to Feidong and pick up the goods. They then need to somehow get the goods from there into their shops, which are predominantly located in Ireland. Therefore, they would expect the Chinese manufacturer to give them a better price for taking on all this extra work.

'Free Alongside Ship'

The seller delivers the goods to a preordained ship or loading point. The seller is responsible for getting the goods to that point. Upon arrival at the loading point, the buyer is responsible for all onward costs.

This arrangement may suit both parties where the seller is at the same time bringing goods to the port for other customers. Imagine the seller has five customers sailing from the port in Cork. It is more economical for the seller to bring the goods to the port and then deposit the goods ready for collection at the various ships rather than have the buyers send five trucks out to the seller's factory, each collecting their own specific order. The buyer is responsible for getting the goods onto the ship and all onward associated costs.

'Free on Board'

Under this term of sale, the seller pays for all the costs associated with getting the goods onto the ship. It is a term similar to 'free alongside ship' except in that the seller must also pay for the loading of the ship. Once the goods are on board the ship all further costs are borne by the buyer.

'Cost and Freight (C&F)'

With a C&F term of sale, the seller must organise and pay for getting the goods to the buyer's destination port. All the costs associated with the transportation are to be paid by the seller. Crucially, however, while the shipping costs are paid by the seller, title in the goods falls to the buyer once the goods cross the ship's rail. Accordingly, it is the buyer's responsibility to insure the goods against loss or damage once they are on board the ship, even though it is the seller who is paying the shipping costs.

'Cost, Insurance and Freight (CIF)'

As the name suggests, this arrangement is the same as C&F except that the seller also pays the insurance costs. Responsibility for the goods in terms of loss or damage remains with the seller until the goods arrive at their destination port. The buyer must take over all costs from the point of disembarkation.

'Delivered Duty Paid (DPP)'

The seller pays all costs of getting the goods to the point of destination nominated in the contract or sale of agreement. This arrangement involves the least amount of obligations on the buyer and places the onus on the seller to carry out the following:
• transfer of the goods from the factory to the embarkation port;
• organise and pay the shipping costs;
• pay all insurance and shipping costs;
• pay all import duties; and
• arrange for the delivery of the goods to the seller's nominated destination.

The 'delivered duty paid' method is particularly suitable for buyers that do not have a developed infrastructure to handle importation of goods, for example where the buyer is importing on a 'one-off' basis from a foreign country. DPP suits the seller when it has a large number of smaller export orders to one destination country in which there are multiple customers. There are economies of scale to be achieved by the seller in managing all the logistical complexity rather than it all being handled by each individual buyer/importer.

Payment for Goods

Having considered the various buyer/seller arrangements and their associated terminology, we now turn to how the seller gets paid.

Similar to contracts or agreements for the international sale of goods, there is a well-established and standard set of arrangements and terms relating to payment for goods. Originating in the banking sector, essentially they are ways in which the buyer endeavours to get paid and ways the seller commits to paying.

There are a number of methods that a seller of goods can use in order to get paid. These are listed below in order of commercial risk, beginning with the least risky method from the seller's perspective.

Prepayment

This is the most secure type of payment system from the seller's point of view. The buyer pays for the goods in advance at the agreed price. Only when the seller has received the payment for the goods do they release them into the possession of the buyer or their appointed agent. The drawbacks from the buyer's point of view are obvious:
- the goods may not match the required standard;
- the goods may arrive late;
- the buyer will be 'out of pocket' and must finance the cost of the stock for longer than would be the case with almost all other systems of payment. This is because the buyer will have paid for the goods in advance of receiving them. In most instances, the buyer will then need to sell the goods, or integrate them into their own finished product, before they receive any cash back from their own commercial activities; and
- the seller might just take the money and run, and not ship any goods at all.

The disadvantages to the buyer are of such a scale that all the payment arrangements described below are designed to eliminate some of these disadvantages while still retaining some degree of assured payment for the seller.

Letters of Credit

Letters of credit (also known as 'documentary credits') are one of the most common payment methods used for trading between MNEs in different countries.

The main point of a letter of credit is that a bank, usually the buyer's bank, will guarantee the seller that they will get paid as long as certain conditions are met. These conditions are normally linked to certifications that the goods are of the standard required or certifications concerning adherence to required delivery dates.

The chart in **Figure 10.2** shoes how a letter of credit (LC) works. There are five steps involved, from the original agreement between the buyer and the seller to the final payments of the seller by the buyer or his bank.

FIGURE 10.2: LETTER OF CREDIT PROCESS FLOWCHART

Stage 1
- Buyer and seller agree a contract for the supply of the goods
- Contract agrees a price and stipulates payment by letter of credit

Stage 2
- Buyer requests that his bank issue a letter of credit in favour of the seller. His bank is called the issuing bank
- Bank and buyer set up the terms of the letter of credit in accordance with the contract between the buyer and the seller

Stage 3
- Buyer's bank sends letter of credit to seller's bank, called the correspondent or advising bank
- Seller's bank checks letter of credit terms with the seller
- If the letter of credit requires the correspondent bank to guarantee payment, the LC is called a confirmed LC

Stage 4
- The goods are delivered by the seller to the buyer in accordance with the contract
- The documents required to give effect to the LC are collected by the seller and given to the advising bank
- The documents are sent by the advising bank to the issuing bank

Stage 5
- The issuing bank presents the documents to the buyer and demands payment
- The issuing bank pays the advising bank
- The advising bank pays the seller

There are a number of types of basic letter of credit:

- **Revocable letters of credit** allow the buyer to amend the letter of credit or even cancel it. Clearly, this type of letter of credit affords the seller very little security of payment.
- **Irrevocable letters of credit** cannot be changed by any party unless all parties agree to the change. 'All parties' include the issuing and advising banks. In some instances, a seller may not be comfortable with the guaranteed payment from the issuing bank since they may know very little about that bank. In those cases, the seller may ask its own bank, the advising or correspondent bank, to guarantee the payment. This type of letter of credit, as mentioned at Stage 3 above, is called a **confirmed letter of credit**, which gives the seller the added security of having the payment guaranteed by a bank with whom it has a relationship or in whom it has confidence.
- **Revolving letters of credit** can be used where a series of identical shipments is under consideration to cover all of them rather than issue one for each shipment.
- **Deferred payment letters of credit** arise when the parties do not wish to have payment by way of a bill of exchange (see below). This may be because of the stamp duty that bills of exchange attract in some countries. Instead, the issuing bank will give a letter of undertaking committing to make the payment.
- **Stand-by letters of credit** are normally used as safeguards. They are issued in the normal way but the issuing bank will only pay on presentation of specified evidence that the buyer has not paid their obligations under the sales contract.

Documentation involved in Letters of Credit The use of letters of credit has become widespread internationally as trade between MNEs has grown. There are a number of documents involved in the LC process that are worth explaining.

The summary process chart above in **Figure 10.2** does not detail the documents required to support the shipment of the goods. Nor does it explain the nature of the payments documentation between the banks involved in the letter of credit process. (The seller's bank is called the 'advising' bank; the buyer's bank is the 'issuing' bank.)

We will now examine these two aspects of the letter of credit approach to the payment for goods in more detail:
• the documents supporting the physical transfer of the goods;
• the documents supporting the payment for the goods.

Bear in mind, however, that these apparently more complex considerations do not alter in any significant way the core essence of the transactions. The purpose of involving 'issuing' and 'advising' banks is to figure out ways that the seller can ensure its gets paid and that the buyer can ensure it gets the goods in accordance with the original sales agreement. In other words, the buyers and sellers willingly involve these third parties, i.e. the banks, in order to devise a system that will ensure, in as much as is practicably possible, that the buyer will get her goods and the seller will get paid. (If the world was simple, buyers and sellers would just do deals between themselves and not involve the banks to this degree, though this does also happen once trust levels have built up, as we shall see later.)

Bills of Lading

A '**bill of lading**' is a document that underpins the actual receipt of goods in specified quantities and to required specifications. It is a critical part of the paper trail evidencing the movement of goods through the supply chain. The bill of lading will also identify who has responsibility for the goods at each stage of the supply chain process.

The bill of lading also acts as a receipt for the goods. This aspect of the bill of lading is issued when the goods are received, usually on board a ship. The bill of lading transfers the title, or ownership, of the goods to the designated entity.

While bills of lading today are usually automatically issued by computer and may differ in size and nature, they will normally contain the following:
• the parties involved (seller, shipper/carrier, buyer, banks);
• ports of loading and discharge;
• the total number of documents associated with the transaction and the number of copies (this numbering might seem somewhat archaic, but it allows the parties to know how many documents they should have and whether there are any missing);
• vessel name and voyage identifier;
• marks and numbers identifying the goods;
• description of the goods;
• gross weight and cubic size of the goods;
• received dates;
• shipping dates;
• who is paying for the freight.

The bill of lading will be signed by the ship's master (bills of lading are the document used when ships are the chosen method of transport. Air Freight and Land transport have similar documents – see below.) This signature is critical as it is evidence of the transfer of title of the goods from the seller to the buyer or the buyer's agent or bank, depending on the terms of the sales contract and the letter of credit (see above). While there will be copy documentation, including copies of the bill of lading, the original bills of lading are the ones that are most important. The original bill of lading, with the original signatures, must be presented back to the carrier, in this case the shipping company, at the destination port in order for the buyer to physically take possession of the goods. Accordingly, when the seller receives the original bill of lading after placing the goods on the ship, they, or their bank, will not release the bill of lading until the terms of the sales contract have been fulfilled. Once the conditions have been fulfilled, the bill of lading will be released to the buyer or his agent thereby allowing the buyer to gain possession of the goods at the destination port.

When the goods arrive at the destination port they remain either on the ship or on the quayside while they await matching with the bill or bills of lading. Once the original bills of lading have been presented to the shipping company it will release the goods into the possession of the nominated person, identified on the bill of lading. This process is called '**clearance**'. When the seller is being paid by a letter of credit, the banks involved will ensure that the terms of the sales contract have been adhered to and that all original bills of lading are accounted for before they finally present the bill of lading to the shipping company for release of the goods.

If there is a delay in the presentation of the bill of lading the goods will remain, un-cleared, at the port. In this instance they incur **demurrage** charges (see above), which can be very expensive.

It is clear that the control of the bill of lading can restrict the buyer's access to the goods until it has fulfilled the necessary conditions (normally payment) connected with the sales contract.

Waybills

Of course, not all goods travel by sea. Where road, rail or air transport is used, the parties use a document called a **waybill**, which has many of the features of a bill of lading except that it is **not** used to convey title in the goods. However, it can be used to restrict the buyer's access to the goods until certain conditions have been fulfilled.

Bills of Exchange

Bills of lading and waybills underpin the *physical movement* of the goods and who *owns* the goods and has responsibility for them at different points on their journey. They are an integral part of international trade and the associated payment systems. The second integral element in the document system for international trade is the **bill of exchange**, also known as 'trade drafts' or 'bank drafts' (see below). A 'bill of exchange' is the document that supports the *payment* for the goods. To differentiate between the earlier part of this chapter it is useful to think of the two main documents involved in international trade as follows:
• the bill of lading supports the transfer of the ownership of the goods; and
• the bill of exchange supports the payment for the goods.

While the bill of exchange is usually prepared by the issuing bank (buyer's bank), its terms will be specified by reference to the contract for sale between the parties together with the relevant letter of credit. For example, a bill of exchange may be payable after the elapsing of a certain time period, say 90 days. This payment term will have been part of the original sales contract between the parties. It will also have been referred to in the letter of credit. A bill of exchange differs from a promissory note in that a bill of exchange can normally be endorsed over to a third party who was not involved in the original transaction. Bills of exchange can be issued by an individual company or a bank. Where they are issued by a bank they are sometimes called 'bank drafts'.

Sometimes bills of exchange are traded, meaning the seller may be able to obtain payment earlier but at a slight discount to the full amount due. The trading in bills of exchange normally happens through 'discount houses'. Discount houses will buy the bills of exchange from the seller at a discount to the value that will eventually be paid on the settlement date relevant to the bill. The scale of the discount will depend on how the acquirer of the bill of exchange, or trade draft, perceives the risk that they will not be paid. Clearly, the stronger the bank that issues the draft and the closer it is to the maturity date, the less the discount the seller may need to take. The maturity date is the date upon which the payment will fall due. This date will be identified on the bill of exchange and specified in accordance with the letter of credit and the original sales contract.

The buying of bills of exchange is called **forfaiting**. This is where a third party, unconnected with the original trade, will buy a bill of exchange at a discount from the seller. They will then hold the bill until maturity and obtain payment for it from the issuing bank. They may also sell it on before maturity to another forfaiter. This system introduces increased liquidity into the international trade market as sellers can receive payment for their goods earlier than would normally be the case. Clearly, it is also a source of funds for working capital. Indeed, the discount rate is the cost of these funds and this cost should be compared to other sources of funds.

Drafts and International Transfers

The buyer can pay the seller for the goods by furnishing the seller with a bank draft or by making a transfer of funds to the seller's bank account. This type of payment for the goods often exposes the buyer to the risk that the goods are not of the quantity or quality that was agreed in the contract for sale. As mentioned previously, the buyer is exposed to risk if she pays the seller, using a bank draft, in advance of receipt of the goods. If the buyer does not need to pay for the goods using the draft or the bank transfer until after the goods are delivered, the seller runs the risk that the goods are not paid for at all. Consequently, one would only expect to see this method of payment for relatively small amounts or where a long-standing and trusting trading relationship has developed between the buyer and the seller.

Consignments

Consignment is a system whereby the seller sends stock to the buyer but does not transfer title in the goods until some subsequent event takes place, usually the sale of the goods onward by the buyer. Such an arrangement will normally be covered by a consignment-stock agreement that contractually binds each party to certain obligations, especially regarding care for stock and subsequent payment. Therefore, it is critical for the MNE supplying the consignment stock that it has confidence in the legal system of the country into which it is supplying the goods. The legal system will be its route of last recourse if the terms of the consignment-stock agreement are not adhered to. A simple example should explain more clearly.

EXAMPLE 10.2: CONSIGNMENT STOCK

Scrod Plc, an Irish exporter, sells €1 million of beef to A101, a Turkish grocery retailer, on consignment. Scrod delivers the beef to A101's warehouse. It retains title to the goods until A101 itself sells the beef through its stores. Only when A101 has sold the beef does the ownership of the goods change hands and the liability to pay Scrod becomes real. Under a consignment-stock agreement, A101 will communicate with Scrod on a daily or weekly basis as to the level of sales. Scrod will then top-up the stock holding with new deliveries that bring the overall stockholding back up to €1 million. This means that the seller can get the right amount of stock quantities into the foreign market without running a significant credit risk. On the other hand, the seller will need to rely of the bona fides of the buyer to care for the stock until it is sold.

Open Account Trading

Though more common in normal, 'domestic' trading, open account trading does occur between buyers and sellers in an international context, particularly when the parties involved have a long-standing relationship. Often they will also have a geographical proximity. Simply, it means that the seller supplies the buyer on credit and issues invoices when it sells the goods. The buyer then pays the seller's account when the invoices fall due.

Countertrade

Despite the increased sophistication in banking, accounting, shipping documentation and other systems to support international payment, the last few decades have seen a dramatic rise in countertrade. **Countertrade** is where the payment for the goods supplied is 'in kind' rather than in cash. Some studies have suggested that 30% of the world's trade involves some dimension of countertrade. Where countries have difficulty in establishing a solid value for their own currency, countertrade can be an attractive alternative.

The term 'countertrade' actually encompasses a variety of processes; the main ones are outlined below.

- *Barter* The direct exchange of one set of goods for another. (For example, New Zealand might supply China with mining equipment in return for China supplying New Zealand with rice.)
- *Counter Purchase* Where the seller commits to buying something from the buyer in order to secure the order. While such trading will follow the normal letter of credit structure, the point is that there will have been some reciprocal arrangement in order to secure the two transactions. The amounts do not necessarily need to match in terms of quantum. For example, Country A may agree to buy €10 million of potatoes from Country B if Country B agrees to buy €5 million of tomatoes from Country A.
- *Buy Back* A system where the seller agrees to take payment in the form of the output from the product supplied. This normally happens in a sector where large-scale manufacturing equipment is supplied. For example, a seller may sell equipment that makes steel bolts to a company in Poland. It would then receive payment for the machine by way of steel bolts that are produced by the machine it supplied. IKEA operates a variation on this theme where it buys the equipment needed for the manufacture of its flat-pack furniture from its suppliers. They sell on the equipment to manufacturers in Eastern Europe. The Eastern European manufacturers pay IKEA by supplying it with a given amount of the output from the machines that IKEA has supplied them with.
- *Offset* This is where the buyer insists that it supplies certain of the raw materials and components that the seller has incorporated into the finished product. The costs of these raw-material inputs is offset against the final selling price of the seller.

FIGURE 10.2: CERTAINTY OF PAYMENT FROM DIFFERENT PAYMENT METHODS

Payment Method	Certainty of Payment
Prepayment	Certain – paid upfront and in advance
Letter of credit/Bill of exchange/Bank draft	Certain – assuming bank does not fail
Draft/International transfer	Certain if before delivery Uncertain if after delivery
Consignment	Uncertain – enforced through consignment-stock agreement
Open account trading	Uncertain – enforced through legal structures
Countertrade	Certain – assuming goods are countertraded simultaneously

Export Credit Insurance

MNEs can insure themselves against the possible losses due to a customer defaulting upon their payment obligations. By taking out such insurance, an MNE protects itself from a number of risks that could lead to the non-payment for goods or services supplied. Export credit insurance (ECI) can protect against many of the payment risks to which an MNE is exposed, including the insolvency or bankruptcy of customers. ECI usually covers other risks that may lead to non-payment, such as war, terrorism or the inconvertibility of the customer's currency of payment. The specialist insurance products that provide ECI cover can be expensive, depending on the level of risk. Sometimes an MNE will seek to have the customer pay the insurance premiums as part of the overall transaction. The advantage of having certain payment may outweigh the cost of the ECI. This is a judgement that an MNE's managers will need to make.

10.7 CONCLUSION

In Part I of this book we have examined how international trade has grown and why. In Part II we went on to explore in more detail how the MNE carries out international trade. In particular, Part II seeks to explain the additional complexities that impact upon an enterprise that trades internationally as distinct from one that operates solely in a domestic economy.

In this chapter we examined specifically how an MNE manages its working capital when transacting business across borders. We also looked at how MNEs raise short-term finance to fund the working capital needed to carry on its trade. We then went on to look at how the MNE ensures it gets paid for the goods or services it supplies its foreign customers with. In particular, we looked at the types of financial instrument, such as letters of credit, that can be used to ensure both the interests of the buyer and the seller are protected. The roles of the banking systems in this regard are critical.

Next, in Part III, we begin to examine in more detail the organisational processes and strategies that an MNE can adopt in order to manage the challenges and complexities that international trade can bring. We will explore how MNEs organise their resources, appraise investment opportunities and manage risk.

QUESTIONS

Self-test Questions

10.1 Describe how international trade would be affected if banks did not provide any services in this area.

10.2 What is a bill of lading?

10.3 How would countertrade help an under-developed country such as Zambia?

10.4 Explain the difference in risk for a seller multinational enterprise between consignment stock and prepayment.

Thought-provoking Questions

Question 10.1

You are Ella Thinkwell, the CFO of Monkey Plc, a soft toy manufacturer. Your CEO is excited by the opportunity to export soft toys to the Indian market. He has asked you to prepare a short paper on what the working capital implications of such a move would be. What would such a paper contain?

Question 10.2

Your boss, Margaret Shoutout, is screaming. She is the Finance Director of Red Bicycle Ltd. You are Peter Pains, the company accountant with responsibility for international trade. You only joined last week. A major customer in South Africa has just gone into liquidation leaving Red Bicycle with a potential bad debt of €250,000. Margaret Shoutout demands that lessons be learnt. She calms down a bit and asks you to outline how the company can avoid taking such a credit risk in the future. You sit down, take a deep breath, and start to write down the various methods of managing a credit control risk in an international environment. What are the main headings of your paper?

Review Questions

(See Suggested Solutions to Review Questions in **Appendix B**.)

Question 10.1

Describe the operation of bills of exchange in international trade.

Question 10.2

Discuss export factoring as a way of reducing bad debt risk.

Question 10.3

Discuss export forfaiting as a way of reducing bad debt risk.

Question 10.4

Discuss the use of letters of credit as a way of reducing bad debt risk.

Question 10.5

Discuss export credit insurance as a way of reducing bad debt risk.

PART III

DECISION-MAKING IN MULTINATIONAL ENTERPRISES

CHAPTER

In this part, we will examine how international organisations make decisions. In particular, how decision-making in an international environment differs from that in sole country operations. These differences focus on cultural, economic and legal factors.

We will explore how MNEs evaluate and assess investment opportunities using financial and non-financial measures. The reader will also gain an understanding of how to manage change in an international environment, including assessment of legal, cultural, logistical and HR issues.

11

INVESTMENT APPRAISAL TECHNIQUES

CONTENTS

LEARNING OBJECTIVES

Having read this chapter, you will understand:
- the relationship between risk and return;
- how to calculate net present values (NPVs);
- how to select relevant discount rates for NPV calculations;
- the capital asset pricing model (CAPM), its derivative the international capital assets pricing model (ICAPM) and their uses in investment appraisal;
- how to evaluate the optimum capital structures for an MNE;
- how loan repayment schedules affect investment returns; and
- the factors that influence capital structures in different countries.

11.1 INTRODUCTION

Managers make choices. In an MNE, the manager's role is to assess the environment the MNE is operating in, choose from a number of possible strategic options and then invest in implementing the chosen options. The implementation phase of this process consumes the most resources. Therefore, it behoves the MNE manager to choose strategic options wisely before committing shareholders' resources to their implementation. In this chapter we will examine how MNE managers can choose which investments to progress and which to reject using financial investment appraisal techniques. In the next chapter we will examine the non-financial considerations that the manager should make in assessing which investments to progress. The final chapter in this Part, **Chapter 12**, "Implementing Change in an International Context", will examine how the MNE managers then implement change in their organisations.

Investors seek profit. Essentially, an investor wants to buy an asset, do something with it or transform it in some way so that it is worth more money than he has invested. The investor will either seek to gain the return by:
• selling the investment for more than he paid for it; or
• receiving cash flows from the investment that are greater than the interest cost (or opportunity cost) he is paying for the investment funds.

In other words:

Future Cash Flow less Investment Costs = Investment Return

This straightforward formula forms the basis for all investment appraisals. While such appraisals can become incredibly complex, particularly with the increase in computing power and the use of spreadsheets, the basic principle remains the same. The future cash flows from the investment must exceed the investment costs for the investor to be 'in the money'.

When one thinks further about this simple model, the subtleties become more apparent. In particular, one begins to think about risk. Imagine an investor sitting at a roulette table with €1,000 borrowed at 10% per annum, or €0.27 per day. He considers putting it on RED. If he wins, his return will be 100%, significantly greater than his cost of funds, which are just 0.03% for the day. He will receive his investment of €1,000 back from the croupier plus his winnings of €1,000. He can repay the €1,000 of debt the next morning, pay the interest cost of €0.27 and keep €999.67 in profit.

Based on our formula:

Future Cash Flow (€2,000) less Investment Cost (€1,000.27) = Investment return (€999.67)

Who could resist?

However, the reality is not so simple. Our roulette-playing investor could lose; the ball could land on BLACK. If that happened, the investment would be lost and worthless but 'the investor' would still need to repay the debt of €1,000 plus the interest costs of €0.27 per day. In this case our formula looks somewhat different:

Future Cash Flow (€0) less investment cost (€1,000.27) = Investment Loss (€1,000.27)

So, as the financial advisor to our investor, what would you suggest? How do you appraise the return when balanced against the risk? You need to come up with a systematic way of calibrating the risk/return relationship. It should be systematic because you need to be able to compare it to other investment opportunities, e.g. putting the cash on BLACK or on Number 22. It also needs to be capable of being assessed after the event when the assumptions can be tested against the actual results. The overlaying of these systematic approaches onto our simplistic investment formula is where investment appraisal starts to get complicated. But one should always remember that the above formula is the bedrock of all investment appraisals.

11.2 RISK AND RETURN

The complexities of investment appraisal primarily relate to modelling future cash flows while at the same time attempting to have a logical way of factoring in risk. This attempted modelling is made all the more difficult as the future cash flows have not happened yet. **Example 11.1** below shows how 'a euro today is worth more than a euro tomorrow'. Investors will value immediate cash more than the promise of cash. Therefore, to entice an investor to part with funds today he must be rewarded by the promise, and hopefully the delivery, of a larger sum than the initial investment. In other words, he will demand a return on his investment.

EXAMPLE 11.1: A EURO TODAY IS WORTH MORE THAN A EURO TOMORROW

Imagine an investor is faced with an opportunity to put €1,000 into a project, which project guarantees a gross return in five years' time of €1,000. So, the investor will put in €1,000 and get back her €1,000 in five years. This would be a difficult sell. Investors require a return on their investments over and above the cash put in. By investing in one project an investor is giving up the *opportunity* to invest in another project or to spend the money now. Put another way: 'a euro in the hand today is worth more than a euro in five years' time'. Consequently, the investor needs a return in five years' time to attract her into the investment. The euro today is also certain, she has it in her hand. A euro in five years' time has a degree of uncertainty to it: will she get it back, will the banks still be around, will the euro still exist as a currency? All these uncertainties mean that the euro today is worth more than a euro in the future.

But how much should the return be? Most economic and financial theories are based on the notion of a 'rational investor', i.e. investors will seek the highest returns for the least amount of risk. In answer to our question about how much should the return be, it should be at least as good as or better than the investor could achieve for a similar sized investment with the same attendant risks. 'Risk', however, is in the eye of the beholder; as future cash flows can never be certain, each investor might take a different view of the risk profile of the investment and hence judge the investment opportunity differently.

In order to introduce some objectivity and logical structure to the potentially subjective activity of investment appraisal, financial modelling techniques have been developed. A degree of consensus has emerged through usage as to which techniques are most useful in aiding investors in their decision-making.

It is important to add, however, that though it is tempting to allow these investment techniques to dictate actions, they are not infallible.

11.3 NET PRESENT VALUE AND INTERNAL RATE OF RETURN

We will begin our journey of understanding these logical constructs that aid investor decision-making with the concepts of net present value (NPV) and its close cousin, internal rate of return (IRR), which are at the heart of most financial investment appraisal techniques. They bring together the two facets of investments to which we have already been introduced:
1. that an investment must be made; and
2. that a return must be earned for the investor.

The NPV attempts to work out the level of return required and assess whether the future cash flows from the investment will exceed that level. The IRR attempts to calculate the return level of the future cash flow forecasts and compare this level of return to a desired level of return, accepting the project if the calculated forecasted rate of return exceeds the desired rate of return. Both calculations can be derived from the same cash-flow projections.

Net Present Value

We have already seen that, in general, a euro today is worth more than a euro tomorrow, or five years' time, or at any time in the future. (This may not be the case in the exceptional circumstances of negative interest rates and deflation). So, if an investor is promised a euro in five years' time, he needs to figure out what this future euro is worth in today's money. By implication, it is worth less than one euro today. To understand how much less, we must **discount** the value of the euro in five years' time in order to arrive at a value of the euro today. The quantum of the discount factor is sometimes also called the '**opportunity cost of capital**' because the discount rate used is the rate of return that could be achieved on similar types of alternative investment. In **Example 11.2** below we have to advise an investor as to which of two options to choose. We will use the net present value method to assess the options available and see how the formula for NPV is derived using the simple cash flows our example presents.

EXAMPLE 11.2: USING FORMULAE TO ASSESS INVESTMENT CHOICES

Imagine an investor with €1,000. She can invest in the Irish Government State Savings scheme at 3% per annum for five years. She is now presented with an opportunity to invest in Project X with a total return, including her original investment, of €1,000 in five years' time of €1,200 guaranteed. Advise her on what she should do.

If she invested in the State Savings scheme she would receive €1,159 in five years' time. This number is arrived at by adding compound interest of 3% to the €1,000 invested for five years. Clearly this is less than the €1,200 guaranteed by Project X. Therefore, she should invest in Project X.

Another way of assessing her options is to work back to today's value the value of €1,200 in five years' time. To work the value back to today's value we need to discount the €1,200 by 3% for each year:

$$PV = C_t \times \frac{1}{(1+r)^t}$$

Where PV = present value, i.e the value today
C = the cash flow in t years' time (in our example €1,200)
t = the number of timeframes, typically years and in our case five
r = the discount rate, in our example 3% or 0.03

When you slot the numbers into the equation you get:

$$PV = €1,200 \times \frac{1}{(1.03)^5} = €1,035$$

So, the present value in today's money of €1,200 in five years' time, taking an annual discount rate of 3%, is €1,035. Once again, we would advise our investor that she should put her money into Project X. Why is this?

The State Savings scheme delivers €1,159 in five years' time on an initial investment of €1,000. If you use the PV calculation on this return you get:

$$PV = €1,159 \times \frac{1}{(1.03)^5} = €1,000$$

So, the PV of the state investment is less than the PV of Project X, €1,000 versus €1,035. Therefore, given that the risk profile of both is the same, our investor should invest in Project X.

Our investor is investing €1,000 today in Project X for which she receives €1,200 in five years' time. The PV of €1,200 in five years' time at a discount rate of 3% is €1,035. Accordingly, her net gain in today's money is €35. Put another way, she could make €35 more by investing in Project X than she could by investing in the State Savings scheme which, for our purposes, has the same risk profile. The net gain, or more appropriately, net present value (NPV), is calculated by subtracting the initial investment from the PVs of the future cash flows.

Accordingly, the formula for NPV is

$$NPV = C_0 + \sum \frac{C_t}{(1+r_t)^t}$$

Where C_0 = initial cash flow, usually a negative or outflow representing an investment
C_t = cash flow for period t
t = number of time periods, usually in years
r = discount rate per time period.

In our example there is only one future cash flow, the return achieved in Year 5 of €1,200 from Project X. However, as one can see from the formula, to work out the NPV where there are cash flows over a number of years one just calculates the PV of each year's cash flow, one by one, and then adds all of these values together. One then adds the initial cash flow to this total, remembering that the initial cash flow is normally, but not always, a negative.

The rule, then, is that if the NPV is a positive figure, the investment is worth doing. If the NPV formula returns a negative figure, then the investment is not worth doing as the return to the investor is less than could be achieved with alternative investments.

You may have noticed that there are two major variables to grapple with when performing an NPV calculation:
• calculating as accurately as possible the future cash flows of the investment (see **Section 11.4**);
• choosing an appropriate discount rate (see **Section 11.5**).

When doing the NPV calculation for an MNE, the principles are exactly the same as outlined above. The complexity arises from calculating the future cash flows of a foreign investment, possibly in a foreign currency, and choosing an appropriate discount rate. (We shall come back to these challenges later in this chapter.)

The value of a project to an enterprise is the NPV of the future cash flows that arise from that project, discounted at the appropriate rate. One of the advantages of the NPV technique is that NPVs can be added together. Therefore, if all project NPVs in an enterprise were calculated and added together one could find the value of the whole enterprise. Foreign subsidiaries in an MNE can be viewed as projects. For the purposes of NPV calculations, projects are merely cash flow streams. NPV calculations can be performed on all cash flow streams. Therefore, it is possible to use NPV techniques as a method of valuing an MNE. Again, and it bears repeating, the critical variables are twofold:
- predicting the future cash flows; and
- selecting the most appropriate discount factor.

In most problems to do with capital investment appraisal, these two dimensions of the NPV calculations are always where the challenge lies. The actual arithmetic of the calculations is relatively straightforward, whereas predicting the cash flows is not. As the predicted cash flows are discounted at an appropriate rate, the term '**discounted cash flow**' (**DCF**) is sometimes used to describe the technique of valuing future cash flows. Put another way, the DCF is equivalent to finding the present value (PV) of the future cash flows. The NPV is simply the PV of the cash flows netted against the initial cash outflow. (**Note:** sometimes the initial cash flow can be an inflow, e.g. where a firm receives a deposit from a customer at the start of a project. In this case the initial cash flow would be a positive and would be added to the PV of the cash flows.)

Internal Rate of Return

As mentioned above, the internal rate of return (IRR) is the 'cousin' of the NPV. This is because the IRR uses a very similar formula to the NPV. In fact, the formula is the same except that the NPV is set to zero and the discount rate, r, is the value one is tasked to calculate. In other words, the IRR of a set of cash flows is the value of r that returns a nil NPV.

Before the advent of scientific calculators and spreadsheets one had to calculate the IRR by trial and error, choosing differing values and performing the calculation again and again until arriving at the number for r that produces a nil value for NPV.

Let's look at the formula again setting the NPV at zero:

$$NPV = C_0 + \sum \frac{C_t}{(1+r_t)^t} = 0$$

where:
C_0 is the initial cash flow, usually a negative
C_t is the cash flow in period t
t is the time period concerned, usually years
r is the discount factor (in this case the IRR)

Taking our stipulation that for the IRR we must make the NPV equal zero, then our task is to solve the equation and find the value of 'r'. Put another way, the IRR is the value of 'r', the discount rate in the NPV formula, that would make the NPV equal zero.

Unfortunately there is no easy way to calculate the value of 'r' that produces the answer NPV= zero. Unless one has a calculator that has an IRR function or a spreadsheet function, one will have to solve the equation by trial and error.

Using the same data as we used in Example 11.2, **Example 11.3** below takes this trial and error approach to try to find the IRR for Project X.

Once calculated, the use of the IRR is quite simple. If a project produces an IRR greater than the investing MNE's required return, then the project is acceptable. If the IRR is lower than the investing MNE's required return, then the project should be rejected.

EXAMPLE 11.3: CALCULATING THE IRR OF PROJECT X

Project X produces a cash flow of €1,200 in Year 5 from an initial investment of €1,000. Therefore:

$C_0 = (1,000)$
$C_t = 1,200$
$t = 5$
$r = $ IRR (the number we are trying to find)

The NPV must be set to zero. Therefore, putting the relevant numbers into the NPV formula we get the following:

$$NPV = C_0 + \sum \frac{C_t}{(1+r_t)^t} = 0$$

$$(1,000) + \sum \frac{1,200}{(1+r_5)^5} = 0$$

If we try using 5% for r and insert 0.05 into the formula we get:

$$(1,000) + \frac{1,200}{(1.05)^5} = (1,000) + \frac{1,200}{1.276} = (1,000) + 940 = (60) \neq zero$$

The resultant answer when we set r to 5% is not zero, therefore the IRR of Project X is not 5%. Let's try 3%:

$$(1,000) + \frac{1200}{(1.03)^5} = (1,000) + \frac{1200}{1.159} = (1,000) + 1,035 = 35 \neq zero$$

So, the NPV does not equal zero when we set r to 3%. Since 3% produced a positive NPV and 5% produced a negative NPV, we can assume the r that produces an NPV of zero lies somewhere between 3% and 5%. Let's try 3.8%:

$$(1,000) + \frac{1,200}{(1.038)^5} = (1,000) + \frac{1,200}{1.205} = (1,000) + 996 = (4) \neq zero$$

Setting r to 3.8% produces an NPV of 4, very close to zero. The number implies the IRR of Project X is very close to 3.8%. Since the NPV formula produces a slight negative of (4) we can deduce that the IRR is slightly less than 3.8%. Let's use 3.75% for our last calculation:

$$(1,000) + \frac{1,200}{(1.0375)^5} = (1,000) + \frac{1,200}{1,200} = (1,000) + 1,000 = ZERO$$

At last we have found, by trial and error, that the IRR of Project X is 3.75%.

As you can imagine, when there is a time period of many years involved with multiple cash flows this trial and error method becomes very cumbersome to manage. This is where spreadsheets have been a huge boon to the investment appraisal process. Most spreadsheet programs have an IRR calculation function. When using these functions one usually only needs to enter in the future forecasted cash flows and the relevant periods in which they occur and the spreadsheet makes the calculation. However, it is important to remember that it is the accuracy of the initial investment calculation and the associated future cash flows that are the key variables. I emphasise this because spreadsheets can lull the user into the illusion that there is some degree of scientific accuracy afforded the calculation since it was performed so swiftly and accurately by a computer. The key message is that it is not the calculation *per se* that informs the decision-making process, it is the accuracy of the information fed into the calculation in the first instance.

Calculation of the IRR can be a useful measure for the appraisal of an investment. It allows for quick comparison between mutually exclusive projects and between different industries. For example, if two projects are not dependent upon each other, then the IRR of one can be compared to the IRR of the other. The project with the higher IRR should be chosen.

The MNE can also compare IRRs that are earned in one industry versus IRRs in another industry sector. For example, the IRR in the mining industry can be compared to the IRRs achievable in pharmaceuticals. Such an analysis can help the MNE to understand the investment opportunities that are available to the investor population in general. These comparisons can give the investing MNE a 'feel' for the returns that can be expected, allowing it to gauge those returns against its own risk appetite.

Disadvantages of the IRR Approach
However, there are pitfalls and disadvantages with the IRR method of investment appraisal. The mathematicians among you will see that a problem arises when the cash flows for the project are positive in some years and negative in others. When this eventuality arises there may

be a number of solutions for *r* that produce an NPV of zero. There can also be situations where no IRR can be mathematically calculated, and where the NPV for a given Cash Flow A is higher than for comparative Cash Flow B but the IRR is lower. Thus, the investing MNE can be persuaded to choose Cash Flow B over Cash Flow A if it only referenced IRR.

These anomalies with the IRR method lead me to suggest that the NPV method of investment appraisal is preferable, will lead to more reliable decision-making and, ultimately, improved wealth for the investing MNE and its shareholders. The pitfalls of using IRR as an investment appraisal technique can be avoided by defaulting to the NPV method.

As we have seen earlier, there are two key variables involved when appraising an investment:
1. the prediction of future cash flows; and
2. the selection of an appropriate discount rate.

These will now be discussed in detail in the sections that follow.

11.4 PREDICTING FUTURE CASH FLOWS

Regarding the first variable, future cash flows, the preparation of cash flow forecasts is essential in the use of net present value (NPV) as a technique for investment appraisal. This can be a difficult task in MNEs given the number of factors that can affect the cash flows in investments in other jurisdictions. Nonetheless, this is what the management of an MNE must be able to do if they are to successfully maximise NPVs for the enterprise and, accordingly, shareholder wealth.

A basic method of appraising managers' performance and competence is to assess their ability to predict the consequences of their actions. And managers ought to plan actions that are aligned to the MNE's goals. These actions follow upon a process that usually involves the preparation of a set of possible options that could be decided upon. Managers then use their judgement, aided by decision-making support systems, including investment appraisal techniques, to select the most appropriate actions, the consequences of which are forecasted sometimes in narrative, but more often in numerical, projections of cash flow, profit and loss and balance sheet (also known as statement of financial position). These financial projections are then used to monitor performance and adjust actions as necessary. Sometimes this process will be part of the official cyclical budgeting and planning process of the MNE and not just carried out for the investment appraisal process. In either case, the principles remain the same.

In order to assess investment opportunities the manager must predict the cash flows that will arise from the investment to be made. Managers often rely upon the finance function of the MNE and its accountants to prepare such predictions. The dynamic between the accountant advisor and the manager in the preparation of these predictions is critically important. The manager brings market knowledge to the table, the accountant, technical competence, professional prudence and objectivity. Neither can delegate their responsibility in the relationship to the other. It will not benefit the MNE or its shareholders if the accountant subordinates their objectivity or professional prudence to unwarranted ambitions of the other managers involved in the investment appraisal. Neither should those managers subordinate their views to those of the accountant. A healthy debate should take place in a genuine attempt to arrive at a consensus view of the likely future cash flows and the other variables associated with the investment under consideration.

Cash Flows from Foreign Investments

Forecasting cash flows from foreign investments is more complicated than for domestic cash flows because of the additional complexity foreign enterprises bring. However, the principle remains the same: the manager and the accountant must attempt to forecast all the cash inflows and outflows associated with the project or entity under consideration.

The best way to gain a competency in cash flow projections is to do them followed, most importantly, by subsequent comparison to the actual results achieved. All too often companies and managers neglect to carry out thorough post-investment appraisals, which is understandable since, if an investment is performing well, the tendency is to press on and find more attractive propositions. On the other hand, if the investment performs poorly, managers are often so consumed in trying to get things back on track that they do not take the time to properly assess whether and how the original cash flow forecasts were flawed.

A further temptation in the prediction of future cash flows is to include expenditure already incurred. However, past spending should be disregarded in terms of future decision-making.

> For example, imagine €100,000 has been spent on Phase 1 of Project X and an MNE now must decide whether to progress to Phase 2. When forecasting the cash flows for this decision, no account should be taken of the cash already spent. This cash is gone and is therefore irrelevant to the decision. The previously spent funds are called a 'sunk cost'.

It can also be tempting to include cash flows that are irrelevant to the decision. For example, imagine that a supermarket has a bakery section that produces a cash flow of £30,000 per annum for the foreseeable future. The manager proposes to invest £60,000 and predicts the cash flow will rise to £35,000 per annum. The relevant cash flow is the increment of £5,000, (£35,000 – £30,000), not the entire £35,000 that is predicted for the future. The existing cash flow of £30,000 is irrelevant to the decision. In this example it is easy to extract out the existing cash flow. In real life it can be much more difficult. MNE managers, and their accountants, can often mis-allocate irrelevant cash flows to projects and proceed with investments that would not have made sense if the forecasts had included only relevant cash flows.

Elements of the Cash-flow Forecast

As we have seen, the calculation of the cash-flow projection, or future cash flows, is the first step in investment appraisal. Outlined below are the elements involved in the preparation of cash-flow projections for MNEs, many of which are the same or similar to those taken by purely domestic firms, though there are further considerations to be made for MNEs. Unfortunately, these extra considerations do not simplify the analysis. The rewards for expansion internationally can be great, but such expansion does increase the complexity of the business and affects all parts of the enterprise, including the investment appraisal process.

Initial Investment

Most projects require an initial investment to get started. In the case of an MNE this investment will usually come from the parent company and will include the funding needed to get things off the ground; for example, the acquisition of a premises for the new business, as well as the funding needed for start-up losses and working capital, such as stock. While it can be tempting to assume that ongoing revenues from the project will cover costs once sales start to materialise, it is important to assess the timings on the cash inflows from these sales. Normally, sales will be made on credit and the proceeds will take some time to appear as cash. In the meantime, wages and overheads will need to be paid. The calculation of the initial investment should include an amount to cover this initial cash requirement.

Sales Volume

The MNE will need to forecast as accurately as possible sales volumes and associated production costs expected from its investment. Sales demand will be the source of the MNE's expected return on its investment. Sales volume predictions are notoriously difficult, however, especially in new markets. For example, an Irish cheese manufacturer may decide to build a plant in Poland to service the Polish and Czech markets. Supported by market research and analysis, the MNE will look at the overall size of the market and make initial predictions of how much market share it will gain. Forecasting sales demand can be challenging and is a notoriously uncertain part of the investment appraisal process.

Pricing

The price at which the products or services of the MNE's investment will be sold must also be predicted. It is possible to compare the prices for competing products in the market, or similar markets, in order to estimate the selling price. Since the cash-flow forecast will last for the duration of the investment it is important to try to set prices not just for the first year but also into the future. As time periods extend the accuracy of prediction suffers. Prices may rise or fall over time and it is important for the accuracy of the cash-flow projection to make assessments of these inflationary movements.

Prices will also change over time in response to market conditions and product lifestyle phases (see **Chapter 16** where these issues are discussed in more detail). Suffice to say that they must be estimated in order to accurately predict the revenue streams that will feed into the cash-flow projections. This is because the product's selling price multiplied by expected volumes produce the revenue figure for the cash-flow projections.

Variable Costs

The calculation of an investment's associated variable costs can present challenges for the MNE. The projected variable costs to be incurred by carrying out the investment can be difficult to ascertain in advance, particularly in an MNE. Clearly, the more the MNE knows about the relevant marketplace the more capable its managers will be in assessing the likely costs. Comparisons can be made to existing production costs in the market or in similar markets. For example, labour costs in a Polish salad manufacturing operation might be a good indicator as to possible future costs in a cheese manufacturing plant. Cost inflation also needs to be considered; if cost inflation rates are different from price inflation rates, the profit contribution level flowing from the new investment will either erode or improve over time, depending on which is rising faster: sales prices or cost prices.

Fixed Costs

Fixed costs may be easier to forecast as they tend to be stable over a longer period of time and do not change according to increases or decreases in output. For example, it will be easier to forecast the rent cost for a factory location, subject to a proposed contract, in which to produce cheese than it will be to forecast the variable labour costs. Other fixed costs, such as insurance, should also be easier to calculate.

The question arises as to whether a fixed charge to cover parent company costs should be included. MNE parent companies often charge their subsidiaries an amount for the 'management' of the overall enterprise. Such charges often give rise to much 'in-fighting' in an MNE, with the subsidiary claiming to receive no benefit for the costs being charged and the parent arguing that the subsidiary should bear its portion of the wider MNE costs. Whatever the rights and wrongs of such charges, the MNE should only include them in its cash-flow projections for an investment to the degree to which they are incremental as a result of the project. If the costs are part of the existing head office structure and would exist whether the investment went ahead or not, they should not be included for the purposes of the assessment.

Timescale

The timescale of the investment, whether it is in an entity or a specific project, also needs to be determined. As the years move out, forecasting becomes less accurate. On the other hand, cash flows should settle down as the investment becomes more established. Thus, while forecasting far into the future presents problems, there should be some compensatory factors due to reduced volatility. It is also the case that as time lapses the discount factor on future cash flows increases, making errors in forecasting a distant cash flow less impactful than getting a near-term cash flow forecast wrong. In all cases, the MNE manager will need to know the duration of the cash flows that are needed to be calculated.

Terminal Value

Two factors need to be considered as an investment draws to a close:
- scrap values and decommissioning costs; and
- valuation of income streams in perpetuity where no known end date exists

Let us examine each in turn. The MNE manager needs to make an assessment of the final disposal value of the assets of the investment project at its end. Sometimes this will be a cost as there will need to be a decommissioning charge that can be related to labour or to assets.

> For example, imagine an investment has a lifetime of five years, at the end of which there remains the legacy issues of the assets and personnel involved. The assets can be sold and redundancy payments may need to be paid to staff. Revenues in the final year may be lower than expected as customers switch their business in anticipation of the MNE's exit from the investment. The MNE manager must build all these matters into the investment appraisal analysis.

Most investments, however, are initiated by MNEs with the intention of continuing them indefinitely. But how does one value future cash flows into infinity? Well, it can be done. There are two steps to the valuation of future cash flows into infinity.

First, determine the cash flows for each year appropriate for the situation at hand. If each year's cash flows for the first 10 years can be realistically calculated, the n, the starting point for the valuation of the perpetuity income is Year 11. The following formula gives the value in Year n of a future cash flow into perpetuity from Year $n+1$ onward:

$$V_n = \frac{C_n(1+g)}{(r-g)}$$

where:
V_n = the terminal value in Year n of a cash flow in perpetuity
C_n = the quantum of the perpetual cash flow value per period
g = the periodic growth rate of the cash flow
r = the discount rate

This formula produces the value in Year n of the relevant perpetual cash flow. This leads on to the second step. The value in Year n of the perpetual cash flow should be added to the cash flow generated in Year n by the investment and the aggregate discounted back to present values.

In **Example 11.4** we make an initial investment of €2.5 million in a project that has varying cash flows for the first four years and then grows at a constant rate of 2% in perpetuity. First, we calculate the value of the perpetual income stream, €2,465,000. We then add the value of the perpetual income to the given Year 4 cash flow of €145,000, giving a Year 4 total of €2,465,000. This derived Year 4 cash flow is added into the sequence of cash flows and the NPV calculation done using the formula. In this example the NPV is negative, −€224,000, and the investment should therefore be rejected.

EXAMPLE 11.4: TERMINAL VALUES OF CASH FLOWS

Consider an investment with the following cash flows. (All numbers in €000s.)

Initial investment: 2,500
Cash Flow Year 1: 120
Cash Flow Year 2: 140
Cash Flow Year 3: 160

From Year 4 onward the investment produces 145 annually, growing at 2% per annum in perpetuity.

You are required to calculate the NPV of the investment. You have been told the discount rate is 8%.

First, to calculate the value of the perpetual income stream that arises from Year 4 onward:

$$V_n = \frac{C_n\left(1+g\right)}{\left(r-g\right)}$$

Thus, in our example:
C_n = 145
g = 2%
r = 8%

Therefore, $V_4 = \dfrac{145(1.02)}{(0.8-0.2)} = 2,465$

The future cash flows now look like this:

Year 1: 120
Year 2: 140

Year 3: 160

Year 4: 145 plus 2,465 being the value in Year 4 of the in-perpetuity cash flow = 2,610.

We now apply the NPV formula:

$$NPV = C_0 + \sum \frac{C_t}{(1+r_t)^t}$$

$$NPV = (2,500) + \frac{120}{1.08} + \frac{140}{1.08^2} + \frac{160}{1.08^3} + \frac{2610}{1.08^4}$$

NPV = (2,500) + 111 + 120 + 127 + 1,918 = (224)

In this case, the investment produces a negative NPV at the 8% discount rate and should therefore be rejected.

Exchange Rates

Exchange rates present a problem for multinational enterprises in assessing investment opportunities because the question will arise as to which currency to use. Of course, it is possible to choose the currency of the subsidiary entity or project that is the object of the proposed investment and use discount factors pertinent to that currency to calculate net present value. However, given that the shareholders of the parent company are the final arbiters on the MNE's activities, it is advisable that the cash flows should be converted back to the parent company's currency and discounted at the rate of return pertinent to that currency. This is because it is the parent company's shareholders' cash, either directly or indirectly, that is being used to finance all investments. Therefore the returns should be assessed from the shareholders' perspective.

If it is decided to convert back to the parent company's currency, a significant issue arises: it will be necessary to forecast exchange rates into the future. Though an inexact science, this is, however, possible. Forward exchange rate markets exist and it is possible, if not to predict, at least to lock-in future exchange rates for the near term. This system normally can only help for the near to medium term. Using forward markets beyond two to three years becomes unrealistic. But project lifetimes are often longer than this. So, how does the MNE manager cope with this challenge?

One way is to use historical data to help set statistical ranges into which the future rates might fall. For example, by examining the last five years' exchange rates one can calculate the standard deviation of the rates of the host country currency versus the currency of the MNE's home country. One can determine with some statistical probability where the upper and lower ends of the range of possible exchange rates exist and then calculate a number of NPV scenarios at the different exchange rates. Such statistical analysis will also produce probability assessments at the given exchange rate ranges. The MNE can adjust, i.e. reduce, the expected cash flows by the probability factor to take account of the statistical analysis. In **Example 11.5** below, Tricky is trying to assess an investment in Zedmania, factoring in movements in the exchange rates of Tricky's home currency, the Buro and Zedmania's currency, the Zolar. Tricky uses three scenarios upon which to base its NV calculations, selected because it believes these have the highest probability of occurring based upon an analysis of historical exchange rates between the respective currencies.

EXAMPLE 11.5: FACTORING EXCHANGE RATE VOLATILITY INTO NPV ANALYSES

Suppose that Tricky Plc is a company based in Beeland, a 'Buro' denominated country. Tricky is considering valuing future cash flows from a potential Zedmania investment. The currency in Zedmania is the 'Zolar'.

Tricky's analysis of the historical volatility of the exchange rate between the Buro and the Zolar shows that there is a statistical probability of 95% that the exchange rate will vary by plus or minus 15% from the statistical mean of the last five years. Tricky would then produce cash flow models at a variety of exchange rates, the upper end of the range, the mean and the lower end of the range. Tricky might also reduce the expected cash flow projections by the probability factor of 0.95 in order to more accurately capture the expected cash flows. If all three scenarios produced a positive NPV, Tricky could proceed with the investment.

From the example above, we can see that there is quite a degree of judgement called for in the analysis of converting future foreign currency cash flows back to the home currency for the purposes of investment appraisal. It is another example of the increased complexity that arises when an enterprise starts to become an MNE.

Tax

The taxation of MNEs is a very complex area. The tax computations can be labyrinthine, requiring highly trained specialists to compute the actual liabilities. In forecasting cash flows for the purpose of appraising an investment, the task of calculating taxation liabilities can be even more complicated. This is partially driven by the fact that the MNE is trying to predict the future, the nature of which is uncertain. In calculating future cash flows from an investment, the MNE manager must attempt to calculate the tax charges and the timing of the cash flows associated with them. The tax charge will often be dependent on the capital structure chosen to finance the investment. Indeed, sometimes it may be the case that a project that fails the NPV test with one tax structure would pass it with another.

For example, one country allows 100% capital allowances on certain types of investment expenditure and another country does not. The corporation tax rate in both countries is 35%. The cash flows from the investment are precisely the same in both countries other than taxation. The NPV in the country with the 100% allowances will be greatly enhanced as the cash benefits of the initial investment will reduce the cash paid out in taxes and, by implication, improve the net returns on the investment.

The level of taxation of a particular project's cash flow will also depend upon the double-taxation agreement that exists between the home country and the overseas country. Three situations arise – the home country's taxation levels are:
• higher than the overseas country's taxation levels;
• the same as the overseas country's taxation levels; or
• lower than the overseas country's taxation levels.

Assuming there is a double taxation agreement in place, then the highest rate will always apply. The following example may aid understanding.

Irish Tax (ROI) %	Overseas Tax %	Implication
12.5	40	40% tax is paid in overseas country; no further tax is paid in ROI
12.5	12.5	12.5% tax is paid in overseas country; no further ROI tax
12.5	5	5% tax is paid overseas and an additional 7.5% is paid in ROI. Total tax paid is 12.5%

Where there is no double-taxation agreement, the project profits could possibly be taxed in both jurisdictions, leading to higher tax liabilities than would be the case where double-taxation treaties exist. (Remember: while it is profits that are taxed, it is the relevant cash flows that we are interested in for the purposes of NPV. Thus, **when the tax is actually paid** is the relevant cash flow item for our NPV purposes.)

Capital Controls

In assessing a prospective investment overseas, MNEs must take account of controls exercised by host country governments on the movement of capital and the remittance of profits back to the parent company. Controls on these movements can affect the cash flows back to the parent and reduce the attractiveness of the investment. These controls effectively lock capital into the overseas country. Such capital is referred to as '**blocked funds**'. Appropriate capital and debt structures should be chosen to optimise the shareholders' position. It is often important to plan for these at the outset. Indeed, such structuring decisions can help projects achieve higher NPVs and, by implication, shareholder wealth.

Options

Situations can arise where an investment in a project or subsidiary entity carries with it an option to make a further investment at some point in the future. For example, an MNE may have identified a site and investment opportunity to build a shopping centre in Bratislava. Once completed, the project might carry with it an option to build a further 200 apartments after Year 5 on the top of the shopping centre. In this situation, the investing MNE may or may not develop the apartments, depending on the price of apartments five years hence. The option might add some value to the proposition, and then again, it may not.

How should such an investment proposition be evaluated? One approach would be to perform the cash-flow projections on the shopping centre proposition and work out the NPV of this element of the investment. Then, separately, one could carry out a cash-flow projection for the apartments option and discount this cash flow back at the appropriate rate. This discount rate may be different from that of the shopping centre as the commercial property market is a different market from that for residential property. Since net present values can be added together to obtain an aggregate, the investing MNE can then add the value of the apartments option NPV to the shopping centre NPV. It is possible that though the shopping centre NPV would be negative, the overall project is made positive by a positive NPV for the residential property dimension.

11.5 SELECTING AN APPROPRIATE DISCOUNT RATE

The second key variable in calculating the net present value of an investment is the selection of the discount rate. While this normally involves the selection of just one number, the discount rate, it is just as critical as the forecasting of the cash flows. (Indeed, it would be a sorry state of affairs if an MNE were to reject an attractive investment over the incorrect selection of an appropriate discount rate.) Discount rates can sometimes be the MNE's cost of capital (see below). However, an MNE may choose a discount rate different from the MNE's overall cost of capital for investments with different risk profiles. I will expand on this later in this chapter.

Cost of Capital

The starting point for our exploration of the selection of an appropriate discount rate is an examination of the cost of capital for the MNE. The **cost of capital** is the rate of return the MNE needs to pay to its providers of finance in return for the use of the funds lent to it to carry out its activities.

In a simple world, MNEs would invest in projects calculated to pay a return greater than the cost of capital and reject those paying a return lower than the cost of capital. However, the world is not that simple. Investments in new projects or subsidiaries may involve more or less risk than the current risk profile of the business. Accordingly, it would be wrong to give a very risky investment the same cost of capital for NPV calculations as a low-risk project. This means that the discount rate applicable to investments should represent some assessment of the 'riskiness' of the investment. A rule of thumb would be that investments with a risk profile greater than the enterprise's current risk profile should have a discount rate higher than its current cost of capital. If the new investment has a much lower risk profile than the current MNE's overall risk profile, then the MNE may select a discount rate lower than the current cost of capital. A point worth noting regarding the current cost of capital for an MNE is that since investors and providers of debt are 'happy' with the existing returns they receive, the current cost of capital is an appropriate proxy of the current risk profile of the MNE. If the investors and debt providers become 'unhappy' with the return, this will normally be reflected in either a fall in the value of the equity or bonds issued by the MNE, which has the same effect as increasing the actual cost of capital as measured against the value of the funds invested. In summary, the true cost of capital is dependent on the use to which the capital is put.

So, we can say that cash flows should be discounted at a business's cost of capital **plus or minus an adjustment for risk**.

To return to calculating the cost of capital: an MNE finances its activities from two main sources of capital:
- shareholders, together with
- providers of long-term debt.

Each of these two groups requires a return. The providers of long-term debt get their return through the payment of interest. The shareholders get their return through dividends and capital growth. The cost of capital where an entity is financed by equal amounts of long-term debt and equity is:

$$r_c = (0.5)\ r_d + (0.5)\ r_e$$

where:
r_c = cost of capital
r_d = cost of financing long-term debt (usually bonds, preference shares or debentures)
r_e = cost of financing equity.

Weighted Average Cost of Capital

Unfortunately, while elegantly simple, this formula is not suitable for most cases because it does not take account of the fact that a business's ratio of debt to equity is seldom 1:1.

In calculating an MNE's cost of capital, we need to take account of its debt/equity ratio and adjust our calculation to allow for the fact that the company may hold more debt than equity, or vice versa. We also need to take account of the fact that interest costs on debt are tax deductible in calculating a firm's profits.

Therefore, the formula now becomes:

$$r_c = \left(\frac{D}{D+E} \right) r_d (1-t) + \left(\frac{E}{D+E} \right) r_e$$

where:
r_c = cost of capital
r_d = cost of financing long-term debt (usually bonds, preference shares or debentures)
r_e = cost of financing equity (normally calculated using the capital asset pricing model)
D = market value of total long-term debt
E = market value of equity
t = corporation tax rate

This formula is also known as the **weighted average cost of capital (WACC)** since it takes account of the different weightings of the two sources of capital, i.e. equity and debt.

The calculation of r_d, the costs of financing long-term debt, is normally straightforward since an MNE's debts will have associated interest rate costs. Therefore, the total required interest payments in any one period should be capable of being calculated relatively quickly.

The calculation of r_e, the cost of financing equity, is less straightforward because, as mentioned earlier, the providers of equity capital gain their return through a combination of dividends and capital growth. These twin sources of return introduce the complexity since their future value cannot be easily determined. To calculate r_e we need to use a theoretical model called the **'capital asset pricing model' (CAPM)**.

The CAPM states by way of formula that the return of equity required by an investor is given by the following:

$$r_e = r_f + \beta \left(r_m - r_f \right)$$

where:
r_e = the return on equity, or cost of equity from an MNE's point of view
r_f = the risk-free return in the market
r_m = the market return
β = beta, the MNE's variability coefficient to the market.

(I will return to the CAPM later in this chapter to more fully explain how it can be used to calculate the return required for investors, with particular focus on the MNE.)

One would imagine that the managers of an MNE would tend to prefer debt to equity as a source of capital as interest rates on loans are normally cheaper than equity in terms of the return required by investors. This is because share capital is the riskiest of the investments in an MNE's capital structure (see **Appendix C.3**). Shareholders are the last to get paid in any distributions. On the basis of the principle that a 'risky euro is worth less than a safe euro', the investor in shares will require a superior return to other long-term capital providers in return for this additional risk.

However, the more debt that an MNE holds the less profits that are available for its shareholders. Interest on debt must be paid, regardless of the performance of the enterprise. Therefore, in good times, there can be a large pay-out to the shareholders as the interest costs will not have increased. However, in lean times, the interest must still be paid, leaving little or nothing for the shareholders. Importantly, managers of an MNE must balance its debt levels with its equity levels in order to ensure that investment in it remains attractive for both stakeholder groups, that is, shareholders and debt providers.

The Modigliani–Miller Theorem

Investors in an enterprise can use their own funds or borrowed funds to make investments. Accordingly, an individual investor can, through individual borrowing, create the level of debt/equity that meets their own individual requirements. Therefore, they do not need to pay attention to an enterprise's debt/equity ratio. Rather, they will decide what level of debt/investment they are personally happy with and adjust their borrowings accordingly. A logical deduction to be drawn from this is that an enterprise's cost of capital will be a constant, irrespective of how much (cheaper) debt it takes on.

Franco Modigliani and Merton Miller, professors at the Graduate School of Industrial Administration of Carnegie Mellon University in the 1950s, were asked to teach corporate finance, even though they had no prior experience in this subject. In researching to prepare for the delivery of their course they found inconsistencies in the material that had been delivered previously at the university and worked together to reconcile these inconsistencies. In particular, they were interested in trying to understand whether the amount of debt to equity that an enterprise took on affected the returns the market required from that enterprise. Their analysis produced some surprising results. They deduced that an enterprise's debt/equity ratio had no bearing on its cost of capital.

Modigliani and Miller ('M&M') proposed, in 1958, after extensive analysis of past performances, that a firm's cost of capital, r_c, was a constant, assuming a free market and irrespective of the ratio of debt to equity. This means that no matter how high the levels of debt in an MNE, the shareholders' return on equity will adjust to ensure that the cost of capital remains the same. They were able to show that investors could, through personal gearing, effectively achieve their own desired level of aggregate gearing on any investment. Therefore, the level of gearing in a company has no bearing on its cost of capital. For example, an investor with a preference for high gearing could invest in a low-geared firm by borrowing a certain level of the investment himself. In this way, he would simulate a highly geared company by combining personal gearing with the low-geared company investment.

As with many financial theories, the Modigliani–Miller Theorem does not hold true at the extreme levels of debt. High debt levels introduce increased risk for the lenders, thus adding to the cost of capital. Another 'wrinkle' in the theory is the tax deductibility of interest charges. Interest is deductible for the purposes of calculating a firm's tax charge. However, in most cases, interest is not an allowable deduction for personal tax purposes. Thus, the investor cannot readily simulate a corporate gearing position through personal gearing as the net interest cost to the personal investor will be higher than for the equivalent corporate debt.

In summary, an MNE must seek to balance the tax advantage of higher debt with the disadvantage of higher levels of risk. As a general rule, the less volatile a firm's cash flow, the higher the level of debt it can sustain without negatively affecting the cost of capital.

Cost of Capital for Multinationals versus Domestic Enterprises

I have mentioned throughout this text that an enterprise trading internationally, an MNE, introduces increased complexity as a result of this international trading, which changes its risk profile when compared to a purely domestic enterprise. The risk profile of MNEs will have attributes that are not present in domestic firms. As a result, an MNE may have a different cost of capital compared to a purely domestic firm involved in the same industry.

There are two main differences in the nature of an MNE that can cause its cost of capital to differ from a purely domestic firm:
1. An MNE will have cash flows generated in different markets in different countries. Often, these markets are not as interdependent as domestic markets. Hence, the cash flows have a greater stability as they are more independent from each other than in a purely domestic enterprise. For example, a firm may find its cash flows in Brazil remain strong even though its Irish cash flows are under-performing. A domestic enterprise with only Irish cash flows would not have such a counterbalance.
2. On the other hand, an MNE may have exposure to foreign exchange risk that a domestic firm might avoid. Remember: the risk is not in exchange-rate fluctuations brought about by inflation differentials – these inflation-related movements are compensated for by higher or lower prices (see the discussion of purchasing power parity (PPP) in **Chapter 8**). The risk an MNE is exposed to in terms of cost of capital and exchange rates is the overall market risk connected to the countries in which it is doing business. For example, trade sanctions against Russia have introduced market effects on the Rouble, not connected to inflation. An MNE with exposure to the Russian market will have a different cost of capital from an equivalent domestic firm.

Investment Discount Rate

All enterprises have a cost of capital, r_c. When appraising an investment using the NPV method, the MNE manager must determine whether the MNE's existing cost of capital, r_c, is the appropriate discount rate to apply to the future cash flows of the proposed investment. It may not always be the case that r_c is the appropriate discount rate to use. An investment by an MNE in a project or a subsidiary entity should be appraised by following a simple, two-step approach:
1. forecast the future cash flows from the investment; and
2. discount the value of the investment's future cash flows back to 'today's' money using an appropriate discount rate.

When one **nets** the initial investment from the future discounted cash flows one gets the net present value of the investment. If the NPV is positive the investment should proceed; if it is negative it should be rejected.

We have been focusing on how to select an appropriate discount rate. Remember that an 'investment' in this context can be a project or an entire overseas entity. For the purposes of our considerations an 'investment' is simply a set of future cash flows.

An MNE's cost of capital is the discount rate that produces the value today of the entire future cash flows of that MNE. As a formula:

$$\textbf{\textit{Value of firm}} = \textbf{\textit{PV}}(\textbf{\textit{c}}_t) = \textbf{\textit{c}}_0 + \sum \frac{\textbf{\textit{c}}_t}{(1+r)^t}$$

where:
PV = present value
c_0 = initial cash flow
c_t = cash flow period t
r = cost of capital.

If an investment in a project or an entity has the same risk profile as the entire MNE, then the appropriate discount rate will be the firm's cost of capital. However, in an MNE it is often the case that the investment under consideration has a different risk profile from that of the overall firm. In **Example 11.6** below an Irish dairy company cannot just choose its existing cost of capital as a discount rate for an overseas project because it has a different risk profile.

EXAMPLE 11.6: INVESTING OVERSEAS – SELECTING A DISCOUNT RATE

A dairy-processing MNE based in Ireland is considering an investment in a plant in Tunisia, which is likely to have a higher risk profile than that of the overall existing MNE. Therefore, the MNE cannot simply use its existing cost of capital as the discount rate to be used to appraise the Tunisian project. Some adjustment to the firm's cost of capital must be made to account for the additional risk. In this example, the Irish dairy-processing company would need to add an amount, a premium, to its normal cost of capital to arrive at an appropriate discount rate for the assessment of the Tunisian project cash flows.

The question is: what is the appropriate premium and how can it be calculated?

One way of answering the question of what is the appropriate premium is to use the valuation model called the capital asset pricing model (CAPM). We saw earlier in this chapter how the CAPM is used to calculate the return the providers of equity capital require. When showing the formula earlier, we demonstrated how it is used to calculate r_e for the purposes of calculating the weighted average cost of capital (WACC). We were interested in the WACC since we had determined that this rate was a starting point in determining the appropriate discount rate to be used for the purposes of performing an NPV calculation. We will now use the CAPM again, this time to help us determine an appropriate rate to use for assessment of international projects.

The Capital Asset Pricing Model
The capital asset pricing model (CAPM)[1] emerged in order to answer the question of how to adjust the investing firm's cost of capital to factor in the specific risk associated with an investment. The model can be used to value an MNE or, as in our case, to help when

---

[1] Sharpe, W.F. (1964), "Capital Asset Prices: A theory of market equilibrium under conditions of risk", *Journal of Finance*, 19: 425–436.

selecting an appropriate discount rate for the purposes of discounting future cash flows. At the heart of this model is the idea that the return on an investment is made up of two components: a risk-free return *plus* the return specifically generated from the investment. Thus:

Investment return = risk-free return + investment-specific return

The model further proposes that the investment-specific return is a function of the overall market return net of the risk-free return. In other words:

Investment return = risk-free return + β(market return − risk-free return)

where β, beta, is the variance of the investment-specific return to the market return less the risk-free return.

This means that the investment-specific return has a variability, either up or down, which can be correlated to the overall market. The 'market' for the purposes of the CAPM is generally taken to be an index of all available 'risky' investments. Usually, a stock market index, such as the FTSE 250 or S&P 500, is chosen as a proxy for the market, depending on what investments are available to the investor. For example, a particular investment's return might increase by 10% when the market moves by 5%. This return is positively correlated to the market return by a factor of 2. When the market rises by 5%, this investment's return increases by 10%. When the market falls by 5%, the return would fall by 10%.

The formula for the capital asset pricing model is as follows:

$$r_e = R_f + \beta\left(R_m - R_f\right)$$

where:
r_p = rate of return required for investment, p, or the discount rate
R_f = risk-free rate of return
R_m = market return
β_p = the beta of the investment.

The overall return required for an investment is determined by the risk-free return adjusted by the investment's variability to the market return.

R_f, the risk-free return is the return an investor can gain by investing in a risk-free asset, e.g. government bonds, where such bonds are rated AAA.

R_m, is the market return, normally the FTSE 250 Index for UK companies or the ISEQ in Ireland. Stock market indices are used as a proxy for market return since they represent the return available to an efficient investor if they held a portfolio that consisted of all available 'risky' investments. The idea is that a stock market represents the aggregate of the investing decisions of all investors in the market at any one moment in time. Since the market is in equilibrium, all investment-specific risk has been eliminated because investors will hold portfolios that minimise investment-specific risk. The CAPM is based upon considerations of a single economy, which implies that the risk-free return is the risk-free return applicable to the currency of that economy. For example, the risk-free rate for Sterling is what would be used in doing a CAPM calculation for a UK investment. Likewise, the relevant market return is the market return available in that economy, in our example, the UK.

When one considers the options open to an MNE, one can see that the investment options extend beyond its home economy. In these circumstances, the MNE must endeavour to extend the measure of the risk-free and market returns to beyond a single economy. This extension, called the **international capital asset pricing model** (**ICAPM**), means selecting market indices that approximate as closely as possible to the total investment choices available to the MNE. (ICAPM is discussed in more detail below.)

It is possible to calculate the beta for listed companies or commodities by examining their past performance and tracking it against the overall market returns and the risk-free return. The level of variation, over the chosen timeframe, of the investment under analysis versus the overall market return less the risk-free return can be worked out. This variation, called the co-variance in statistics language, is the beta (β) of the investment. The MNE manager can then use this calculation of the β when the investment being appraised bears similarities to the stocks or commodities analysed. The discount rate used for the appraisal can be the expected return produced by the CAPM with the calculated β inserted.

Where the MNE is not a listed entity, the MNE manager can seek out similar investment types in order to calculate the β. Though this calls for some judgement and a degree of subjectivity, nonetheless, the process of using the CAPM for the determination of discount rates remains very useful, even if the entity is unlisted.

EXAMPLE 11.7: USING ICAPM TO CALCULATE A DISCOUNT RATE

An Irish-based MNE is considering investing in a cement factory in Argentina. It has determined that the risk-free return on Irish markets, in its home currency, is 1%. The MNE then compares the historical returns for companies involved in cement production in Argentina to global stock market returns less the risk-free return. It chooses to look at the last 10 years' data and determines that Argentinian cement businesses have a β of 1.3, which means that, historically, Argentinian cement businesses have variances in their returns by a factor of 1.3 versus global market returns.

The MNE is now in a position to choose a discount factor to apply to the future cash flows for their possible investment in Argentina. They believe the risk-free rate will remain at 1% and expect, based on market analysis, that the returns from global stock markets will be 7.8%. Using the CAPM formula they can calculate the expected return on their investment. They will use this expected return as the discount factor for the cash flows.

$$r_p = R_f + \beta_p(R_m - R_f)$$
$$r_p = 1.0 + 1.3\,(7.8 - 1.0) = 9.84$$

Therefore, based on the above calculations, the Irish MNE will discount the future cash flows of the possible Argentinian cement business investment at 9.84%. If the calculation produces a positive NPV, the investment will proceed. If it is negative, the investment will be rejected.

In this example we are assuming there is no debt involved; therefore the ICAPM cost of capital calculation produces the discount rate the Irish MNE will use. If there was a debt element, it would need to calculate the WACC using the CAPM as the rate required for the equity element at the appropriate weighting plus the cost of the debt at its appropriate weighting.

Finding the beta for an investment can present practical problems for MNE managers if quoted stocks or commodities with similar betas to the investment opportunity cannot be identified. Having said that, there is a large body of data available from publications such as the *Financial Times* or from Bloomberg, which provide the betas for traded commodities and shares and these can be used to **approximate** a project's beta. For example, if an MNE is considering investing in a pharmaceutical company in the US, it may be possible to calculate an appropriate beta by reference to the Beta for quoted food companies on the New York Stock Exchange (NYSE).

However, in some cases it will not be appropriate to look up a set of quoted data to select an appropriate beta for a proposed investment. This can arise where there is no comparable investment choice where the beta is readily available, such as where the investment under consideration is in a specialist market. In these cases, judgement will be required and in making such judgements the manager should:
- understand the determinants of the beta of the class of assets, i.e. the nature of risk/return profiles for the investments being considered;
- avoid manipulating the beta to account for the uncertainty in his calculation.

With regard to the second of these issues, the manager should avoid the temptation to increase the beta, and hence the discount factor, just because the Beta is difficult to determine. The β is one of the variables that feed into the CAPM formula, which produces the expected return on an investment. We are using this calculation to feed into the WACC calculation, which combines the cost of capital and the cost of debt to produce an appropriate discount rate for the purposes of investment appraisal. Where the β is difficult to determine, the cash-flow forecasts should be investigated and prepared more extensively. In particular, by using probability analysis of various possible outcomes, it may be possible to calculate an investment β appropriate for the NPV analysis. (It is beyond the scope of this text to examine such calculations in any further depth.)

The International Capital Asset Pricing Model

As discussed above, the capital asset pricing model (CAPM) is useful for calculating the appropriate discount rates to apply in assessing investments in a domestic market. What happens, however, when a MNE must consider capital projects or acquisitions in international markets? Does the CAPM still have a use?

The answer to the question is 'Yes', though there are some changes and clarifications required for the CAPM when we move into the international arena. The international capital asset pricing model (ICAPM) is an extension of the CAPM and integrates multi-currency, multi-market scenarios. It has the following features:
- The market return chosen for ICAPM analysis is the world market, not the domestic market.
- The risk-free return, R_f, is the risk-free return in the home currency, i.e. the currency in which the MNE bases its financial reporting.
- In appraising investments, managers need to account for foreign exchange risk to the extent that the risk has not been hedged.

Selecting an appropriate β is even more challenging for MNEs than for purely domestic firms. In the domestic firm, new projects are more likely than not to be closely aligned to the existing business. Therefore, the manager can choose the firm's existing cost of capital as the appropriate discount rate, particularly if the domestic firm is not diversifying but investing in projects that are broadly similar to its existing risk profile.

For an MNE, β selection has more practical problems, the most obvious of which is that the MNE's movement into the international arena means that the investment under consideration is unlikely to have a risk profile similar to the MNE's existing risk profile. Therefore, it is unlikely that the MNE's existing cost of capital can be used as the discount rate.

As we have seen, the CAPM suggests that the costs of capital for an MNE should be lower than for a purely domestic firm in a similar market because there ought to be less overall risk in an MNE since it has diversified income streams relative to a purely domestic enterprise. However, investment in an international project often carries more risk.

Let us examine in more detail why an MNE may have a lower cost of capital. One of the assumptions of the CAPM, and its derivative the ICAPM, is that markets are in equilibrium at any moment in time. The logical deduction from this assumption is that at any moment in time all investors are happy with the investments they hold. Any change in the investors' satisfaction will motivate them to either buy or sell investments. The CAPM proposes, therefore, that, at any moment in time, the entire market represents a perfect balance of investor sentiment.

A further assumption of the CAPM is that all investors will seek an efficient portfolio of investments, meaning they will optimise the level of returns versus the risk profile of the investments made. Therefore, investors will hold diversified portfolios that will seek to eliminate investment-specific risks. This leaves investors, taken as a collective, only exposed to the overall risk in the marketplace. For the CAPM, the marketplace is the domestic economy; for the ICAPM, it is the global economy.

Since the ICAPM proposes that investment-specific risk will be diversified by the marketplace investor, only overall market risk should be taken into account in calculating an enterprise's cost of capital. (Remember: we are using ICAPM to calculate the equity element of the cost of capital that we will combine with the cost of debt to produce a discount rate to be used in investment appraisal.) Overall market risk, as I have termed it, is often called '**systematic risk**'. Investment-specific risk is also referred to as '**unsystematic risk**'. Systematic risk should be lower for an MNE resulting from an MNE's ability to be diversified across a greater number of markets than a domestic firm. Since the MNE's exposure to systematic risk will be a function of the systematic risk in a number of economies, the ICAPM proposes that the MNE will be able to have a relatively lower cost of capital since markets will not all rise or fall at the same time. Some market falls will be off-set by market rises elsewhere; this off-setting helps the MNE achieve a lower cost of capital.

Unsystematic risk, or investment-specific risk, is deemed capable of being diversified away by investors opting to hold a diversified portfolio. It is therefore not relevant to ICAPM calculations. Having said that, some MNEs will attempt to diversify away their unsystematic risk rather than presume that the investor will do so. There is a debate as to whether this diversification is appropriate since the investor can achieve the same result by diversifying his or her own individual investments. In any case, some MNEs do diversify their risk, which leads to greater stability in income and cash flows.

Example 11.8 below illustrates the difference between diversifiable, i.e. unsystematic, risk and systematic risk. The gold prospector has highly volatile cash flows below, which are investment-specific risks. He has an almost guaranteed return if he does find gold. Historically, the β for gold is almost zero, meaning it is a good proxy for a risk-free return and is not correlated to market returns at all.

EXAMPLE 11.8: SYSTEMATIC AND UNSYSTEMATIC RISKS

A gold prospector is panning for gold in the Yukon. His cash-flow forecast is hugely volatile. He may find gold or he may not. His returns from any find he makes will be determined by the market rate for gold. The price of gold, or return on gold as an investment, has a low β, which is calculated by reference to the historical returns for gold compared to market returns. It is found that gold does not track market returns and is much closer to the risk-free return. Whether he finds gold or not is deemed to be a diversifiable risk. This is because an investor could invest in any number of projects, of which this gold mine would be just one. By investing in more projects, the investor is less likely to find that all projects will fail to provide the expected return at the same time. (Think of it as backing all the horses in a race. By spreading the risk the investor reduces the returns available but also reduces the risk.)

In this case, it is the forecasted future cash flows of the gold-panning activity that will be adjusted to take account of the possibility of either finding gold or not. Let us presume that the area where the prospecting is taking place presents a 1 in 10 chance of finding a kilo of gold every year. Gold is worth €30,000 a kilo. The future cash flows are calculated at €3,000 per annum, being €30,000 per kilo at 10% probability. This is the cash flow that would be discounted at the appropriate rate, which would be close to the risk-free rate of return. This low discount rate is because gold has a very low β, close to zero according to many analysts.

Remember:

$$r_p = R_f + \beta_p(R_m - R_f)$$

The β for gold is almost zero, therefore the required discount rate r_p is equal to R_f, the risk-free return. The volatility in gold mining is connected to the certainty of the cash flows, which is a diversifiable risk. An investor can minimise their risk of not finding gold by making investments in other projects. Based upon historical calculations of returns from gold, if the miner finds gold, he will be certain to make a profit from it. The conclusion from this illustration is that the risks associated with gold mining are unsystematic, that is, completely linked to whether you find gold or not. Investor returns from gold, systemic risk, is almost zero since, once found, gold is almost guaranteed to provide the risk-free return in the market.

We can see from this discussion that an MNE can use the ICAPM to produce a figure for the expected cost of equity to feed into the cost of capital calculation. The derived WACC, which uses the ICAPM calculation combined with the cost of debt, for investments under appraisal can be used as the discount factor to be applied to the future cash flows associated with the investment under consideration. The discount factor may be lower or higher than the MNE's current cost of capital, depending on the risk profile of the investment being considered relative to the existing risk profile of the MNE's current operations.

11.6 COUNTRY DIFFERENCES IN COST OF CAPITAL

It is important for the MNE manager to understand that the cost of capital differs across different countries. Understanding this is critical for the MNE manager because:
• cost of capital differences can be a source of competitive advantage;
• the portfolio of international operations and capital structures can be optimised;
• cost of capital differences can lead to different approaches to debt/equity ratios.

As we have seen, an MNE's capital structure is made up of equity, provided by shareholders, and debt, which is provided by lenders. The cost of capital is the *weighted* cost of sourcing these two forms of long-term financing. The 'weighting' calculation is carried out by using the market value of each component of the sources of capital. Each cost is 'weighted' in the ratio of the market value of the two components of the capital. **Example 11.9** below is a simple weighted costs of capital calculation.

EXAMPLE 11.9: WEIGHTED COST OF CAPITAL CALCULATION

Crosby Ltd has equity valued at €200 million. It provides shareholders with a 15% return per annum. It also has long-term debts valued at €400 million at an interest rate of 7% per annum. Calculate the weighted cost of capital.

Total capital: €200m + €400m = €600m

Weighted Cost of Equity: $\dfrac{200}{600} \times 15\% = 5\%$

Weighted Cost of Debt: $\dfrac{400}{600} \times 7\% = 4.67\%$

Add the two weightings together and,

Weighted Cost of Capital   **= 9.67%**

It follows then that if similar companies in different countries have different costs of capital, these differences must flow from differences in the cost of debt together with differences in the cost of equity.

Cost of Debt Differences

The cost of debt can be thought of as the risk-free rate of return demanded in an economy, plus an added premium for risk. The risk-free rate in a particular country will be dependent on a number of factors that combine to affect either supply or demand in the economy. The supply side is driven mainly by corporate and individual savings, while the demand for funds is influenced by private, corporate and government borrowing needs. This interaction of supply and demand requirements affects the risk-free rate of return. For example, if savings are high, the risk-free return in the economy will be lower since the availability of funds, i.e. supply, will be greater.

There are a number of factors in a country's profile that will interact with each other to influence the supply and demand for funds and, consequently, the risk-free return. These factors are of interest to the MNE manager since the risk-free return in an economy influences the cost of capital required in that economy.

- **Demographics** Age profiles, in particular, will have an influence on savings and consumption. Countries with an older age profile will have a greater propensity to save and this will tend to lower interest rates.
- **Monetary policy** Countries with different currencies will follow differing monetary policies, including the setting of criteria by central banks for the lending of money through the control of its supply. These criteria shape the availability of funds and hence interest rates. The Eurozone is an anomaly in that the monetary policies for a number of countries are set by the ECB. Indeed, the risk-free rate across the Eurozone is the same in all Member States.

- **Taxation** Countries have different tax legislation as to what items can be deducted in calculating taxable profits, particularly where taxes with a capital expenditure dimension are involved, such as R&D credits or accelerated depreciation. Taxation may also be used to encourage saving, which will tend to increase available funds in a country's capital markets. For example, pension contributions by both employers and employees are generally tax deductible in ROI.
- **Economic Conditions** The economic conditions in a country play a large part in setting its risk-free rate. Where a country has an unstable economic environment, a higher risk-free return will tend to be demanded. This does seem counter-intuitive since risk-free is risk-free, wherever one is in the world. Indeed, higher interest rates for risk-free debt in certain currencies should be explained by future inflation predictions. However, historical analyses of interest rates would show that rates tend to have a premium slightly above that which can be explained by inflation adjustment alone.

When the levels of supply and demand within two countries differ we can expect that the risk-free return demanded in those countries will also differ. However, as global capital markets become increasingly deregulated, the risk-free returns will most likely converge toward a global risk-free return.

The premium for risk demanded (the difference between the return from the market less the risk-free return) in different countries will also vary, and by more than the variants in risk-free returns. This is because the conditions that give rise to the risk premium required will differ between countries.

We will now examine in more detail what the determinants of the risk premium are in order to understand why they vary between different countries.

The biggest determinants of the risk premium required by investors or creditors in a country are connected to its prevailing economic conditions. These are not just linked to economic performance but also to the stability of the political and legal environments. Creditors and investors, the providers of finance, need to know they are going to be paid. The greater their doubt about getting paid, the higher the premium they will demand. Accordingly, if a country has a poor track record of enforcing property rights or commercial legislation, then the higher the premium a lender will require. Also, if there is instability in government or policy, lenders will worry about the collectability of their loans and its attendant interest. The threat of nationalisation of assets hangs over some developing countries while in other countries, there is a strong interdependency between the government and corporations leading to greater certainty of repayment and thus lower risk premiums. Credit ratings agencies, such as Standard & Poor's or Moody's, provide rating scores of countries, which give MNE managers an external assessment as to the risk profile associated with certain types of transactions involving the rated country. For more on ratings agencies and their impact upon risk, see **Chapter 14**.

Cost of Equity Differences

Cost of equity is the return demanded by shareholders. It is based on the 'opportunity cost' the shareholders place on their shareholding, i.e. investors leave their investment in a company providing the return is as good as they could achieve elsewhere for a similar risk profile. It stands to reason, then, that the cost of equity will change between companies as their risk profile changes. In **Example 11.10** below we can see how the cost of equity for dairy farming investments will be lower in Ireland than in Zambia due to the climate and infrastructure differences between the two countries.

The cost of equity for different firms in the same global market sector but operating in different countries will be different. Dairy farming in Ireland has a risk profile below that for dairy farming in Zambia. This is because Zambia does not have a climate suitable to dairy farming and has high associated costs. Accordingly, the cost of equity in both countries for a dairy farming company would be different.

The same could be said for copper mining, but in reverse because copper mining in Ireland is almost non-existent, despite the island's earlier successes in this activity (see **Chapter 1**). Copper mining is a hugely significant commercial activity in Zambia, however, with all the associated infrastructure and skills in place for many decades. Consequently, investors will demand a higher return on their equity for a copper mining investment in Ireland as compared to Zambia.

The cost of capital is made up of the risk-free cost of debt, the risk premium cost of debt and the cost of equity. We have seen from the earlier discussions in this chapter that each of these three components of the cost of capital can vary country by country. Differences in the cost of debt, added to differences in the cost of equity, give rise to differences in the cost of capital between countries. These differences will impact upon the MNE's decision-making concerning investment appraisal and optimum capital structure. They may also present the MNE with opportunities for gaining competitive advantage. In the next section, "Assessing Foreign Investments", we will see how the cost of capital helps determine investment strategies for MNEs. We will also explore how MNEs can exploit differences between countries in which they operate to help maximise returns for investors.

11.7 ASSESSING FOREIGN INVESTMENTS: FUNDING STRUCTURES

As we have seen, the cost of equity and the cost of debt are combined to arrive at an enterprise's cost of capital. An MNE contemplating a new investment needs to consider the capital structure most appropriate to that investment. This is especially so if the MNE has access to capital from different countries. As discussed above, some countries will have lower costs of capital than others. Why, then, would not all investing MNEs seeking capital just flock to the countries with the lowest cost of capital? There are a number of reasons why this does not happen:

- Sourcing capital where costs are low, in Japan for example, may not be appropriate for a UK company considering an investment in Spain. The costs of managing the exchange risks can outweigh any benefits.
- Furthermore, shareholders in the UK may not like new shares being issued in Japan, where shareholders will expect to be treated the same as UK shareholders, which will either mean increasing yields above Japanese norms or reducing yields to below UK norms. If equity costs rise to provide Japanese investors with the same return as UK investors, then the benefit is eroded. If costs fall, the implication is that the cheaper funds could have been sourced in the UK all along.
- Borrowing costs will be higher when the investment is in another jurisdiction. All creditors want to be paid and if there are possible increased costs associated with debt recovery, these will be factored by creditors into the debt.

In planning and assessing an investment opportunity the MNE must estimate the costs of the different financing options and choose the best option based on this analysis. In the example of Scrod Plc below you can see the various options that need to be considered in making what, in this case, is a relatively simple decision of what financing structure should be adopted to invest in a Turkish opportunity. As the number of investment opportunities increases, so does the complexity of the calculations. The number of financing options also serves to increase the number of possible options. It is critical for the MNE that it is well informed in making these decisions as it may reject profitable investment opportunities, or sub-optimise their funding, if they are not conversant with the techniques applicable for international investment appraisal.

EXAMPLE 11.11A: ASSESSING FUNDING STRUCTURES

Scrod Plc, an Irish-based MNE, is presented with a €40 million investment opportunity in Turkey for which its management team are trying to assess the optimum funding option. The following information is pertinent:

- Euro risk-free rate = 3%
- Turkish Lira (TRY) risk-free rate = 8%
- Risk premium required on euro debt = 3%
- Risk premium required on TRY debt = 5%
- Beta of the project = 1.5
- Expected € market return = 12%
- Irish corporation tax rate = 12.5%
- Turkish corporation tax rate = 20%
- The providers of credit will not advance more than 70% of the project costs. This requires the MNE to finance at least 30% of the project from equity.

	%	%
Cost of € debt	$(3 + 3) \times (1 - 0.125) =$	5.25
Cost of TRY debt	$(8 + 5) \times (1 - 0.2) =$	10.4
Cost of € equity	$3 + 1.5(12 - 3) =$	16.5

Scrod must now consider how these differing components of the cost of capital can combine into producing a weighted average cost of capital (WACC) for the project. They look at four possible options for capital structure and have assumed no exchange rate risks.

Option	Capital Structure	€ debt 5.25%	TRY debt 10.4%	Equity 16.5%	WACC %
1.	1. 70% € debt; 30% € equity	5.25 × 70% = 3.675%		16.5 × 30% = 4.95%	8.625
2.	2. 70% TRY debt; 30% € equity		10.4 × 70% = 7.28%	16.5 × 30% = 4.95%	12.23
3.	50% € debt; 50% € equity	5.25 × 50% = 2.625%		16.5 × 50% = 8.25%	10.875
4.	35% € debt; 35% TRY debt; 30% € equity	5.25 × 35% = 1.837%	10.4 × 35% = 3.64%	16.5 × 30% = 4.95%	10.427

From the four options examined the capital structure that gives the best WACC is Option 1, 70% € debt with 30% € equity. Indeed, since debt financing is so much cheaper than equity for Scrod, it would be best if it could finance even more of the investment with debt. However, the creditors will only advance 70%.

Adjusting WACC for Exchange Rate Exposure

In **Example 11.11A** above, the lowest WACC is gained by borrowing 70% of the financing needs in euro and using euro equity for the other 30%. However, the analysis did not take account of exchange rate exposure, to ignore which in project investment appraisal is unrealistic. Therefore, we must look at ways to include the exchange rate dimension into the appraisal process. Let us return to the Scrod Plc example to expand on our analysis.

EXAMPLE 11.11B.: ASSESSING FUNDING STRUCTURES

The Turkish Lira (TRY) is worth €0.35. That means that Scrod will invest €40 million sourced from euro-denominated lenders and shareholders and convert this to TRY114.4 million. Assume that the investment produces TRY cash flows. It is clear that the providers of capital are exposed to a risk of exchange rate movement that impacts their returns. The optimum WACC calculated above for Scrod Plc is 8.625%. (See workings in earlier example panel.) Management of Scrod Plc may decide to add an extra 5% premium to account for additional risk, i.e. a 'risk' premium to the calculated WACC of 5% to account for the exchange rate risk. This would give a new required return of 8.625% + 5%=13.625%. This new, risk-adjusted WACC of 13.625% is above the 12.23% Option 2 of the 4 options calculated in **Example 11.11A** above. This Option 2 WACC was calculated where the 70% debt portion is taken out in Turkish Lira rather than in euro. Therefore, when Scrod adjusts the WACC to take account for the exchange rate risk it ends up selecting Option 2 as the preferred option as against the initial Option 1. (The 5% risk premium chosen for this example was arbitrary. MNEs may have complex treasury and financial models to help them choose an appropriate premium. The main point is that the adjustment for the foreign exchange rate risk may lead to a different funding structure.)

There is a flaw with this method that is immediately obvious: because selection of the risk premium, in this case 5%, is entirely arbitrary, this may lead to projects being rejected that would have added value for shareholders. This could happen if the arbitrary premium is too high, leading to an unachievable level of return required from the investment. In any case, as mentioned in the example panel, the MNE may adopt some more scientific approaches to arriving at the required premium for the foreign exchange risk. It could also assess the cost of eliminating the exchange rate risk through using financial instruments designed for such applications. It would then factor the cost of using such instruments into the financing/investment decision-making assessment. We will explore the options available in more detail in the section that follows.

The attraction of the approach of putting a simple foreign exchange risk premium into the calculation is its simplicity. It can also be argued in its favour that if all projects are assessed on a consistent basis, the investments with the best returns will still be selected. Of course, even with a consistent approach, arbitrary allocation of risk premiums can lead to flawed decision-making.

So, we need to look more deeply into how to factor in the exchange rate risk into our assessment of international investments. We have seen that the application of an arbitrary risk premium has simplicity on its side, but may produce flawed results.

Deriving NPVs from Exchange-rate-adjusted Cash Flows

One of the best ways of dealing with foreign exchange risk in assessing foreign investments is to try to adjust the expected future cash flows for those risks. In **Example 11.11C** below we examine the options open to Scrod Plc.

EXAMPLE 11.11C: ASSESSING FUNDING STRUCTURES

As we have seen, the optimum WACC for Scrod Plc's investment is 8.625%, Option 1, before any exchange rate premium adjustment. The cash flows from the project are in TRY. One of the ways Scrod Plc could incorporate exchange rate exposures is to build the exchange rate into the future cash flow projections. This would involve the highly precarious art of predicting future exchange rates. (If Scrod could predict future exchange rates with certainty, they would make a fortune.) However, the fact that they cannot means that they will need to develop scenarios at differing exchange rate possibilities and then allocate probabilities to each of those scenarios. In this way, the exposure to the exchange rate is factored into the predicted cash flows, which are then discounted back at the WACC to produce the NPV for the investment. (*Note:* while this approach is more accurate than simply adding a premium for the additional risk, it still involves a degree of estimation.)

One of the drawbacks of the approaches to assessing foreign investment opportunities discussed thus far is that they only look at the cash flows from the investment and do not take into account the repayment of the debt. The cost of debt factored into the cost of capital, and hence into the discount rate being used, includes the interest cost of the debt, but not the repayment of the original sum borrowed. The approaches involved looking at cash flows from investments and discounting them at an appropriate rate. We have focused up to now on:
- improving accuracy in forecasting cash flows;
- selecting appropriate discount rates;
- selecting optimum funding structures (as illustrated in **Examples 11.11A–C**).

When an investment is being appraised in the domestic economy, NPV calculations provide a useful analytical tool for assessing and comparing investment opportunities. It also allows for ready comparisons with existing investments. Future cash flows are discounted back to today's money at a rate appropriate for the capital structure of the project. Since the cash flows from the project that are used to repay the debt are in the same currency, there is no need to factor into the calculations any possible exchange rate fluctuations due to timing differences. However, when the investment is international and cash flows are in another currency, then exchange rate considerations become more pertinent. In other words, the demand for cash to be used to repay foreign and domestic debt (domestic debt might be repaid from foreign cash flow) has exchange rate implications.

To illustrate these challenges and propose a solution, let us continue with our Scrod Plc example, considering now some further information.

Example 11.11d: Foreign Investment Appraisal

The project involves an initial investment of TRY114.4 million, which converts to €40 million at the initial exchange rate of 1TRY= €0.35. Following the initial investment there is a cash flow of TRY30 million in Year 1 and TRY180 million in Year 2 at which time the project terminates. The loan must be repaid at the end of Year 2. The exchange rate at the end of Year 1 is expected to be TRY1 = €0.31 and at the end of Year 2 TRY1 = €0.27. Cash flows from the investment project are converted at the year-end rate.

The options to be considered are whether to finance with 70% debt in TRY or in €. Remember, the providers of finance have insisted that they will only provide 70% funding. The table compares the two options. We start with the cash flows:

	€28m debt, €12m equity	TRY80m debt, €12m equity
Year 1 cash flow TRY	30,000,000	30,000,000
TRY interest costs before tax @ 13%		(10,400,000)
Net TRY income	30,000,000	19,600,000
Turkish tax @ 20%	(6,000,000)	(3,920,000)
Net Turkish profit	24,000,000	15,680,00
Convert to € at TRY1= €0.31	7,440,000	4,860,800
€ interest costs before tax @ 6%	(1,680,000)	
Tax benefit on interest cost	210,000	
Year 1 € cash flow	5,970,000	4,860,800
Discount at 16.5%	**5,124,463**	**4,171,673**
Year 2 cash flow TRY	180,000,000	180,000,000
TRY interest costs		(10,400,000)
Net TRY income	180,000,000	169,600,000
Turkish tax @ 20%	(36,000,000)	(33,920,000)
Net Turkish profit	144,000,000	135,680,000
Less: TRY loan repayment		(80,000,000)
Net Turkish cash flow	144,000,000	55,680,000
Convert @ 1TRY = €0.27	38,880,000	15,033,600
€ interest costs	(1,680,000)	
Tax benefit of interest cost	210,000	
€ debt repayment	(28,000,000)	
Net Year 2 € cash flow	9,410,000	15,033,600
Discount @ 1.165^2	**6,933,264**	**11,076,719**
Total Year 1+2 discounted cash	**12,057,727**	**15,248,392**
Less: initial equity investment	12,000,000	12,000,000
NPV	**57,727**	**3,248,392**

As can been seen from the above calculations for Scrod Plc's Turkish investment, using debt in Turkish Lira (TRY) returns a higher NPV (€3,248,392) than that from using the euro debt (€57,727), even though euro interest rates are lower. This is because the depreciating Turkish Lira is offset by the cost of servicing the Turkish loan repayments. Therefore, based on these calculations, Scrod should finance its project in Turkish Lira.

In this example we have used the discount rate of 16.5%, which is the required return on equity (see **Example 11.11A** above). *Note:* We use return on equity rather than WACC since the cash flow calculations take into account the servicing cost of the debt and its ultimate repayment. Since we are including the cost of servicing the debt and the debt repayments in the investment cash flows, we only use the equity investment amount of €12,000 as the initial outlay rather than the full cost of the investment. Accordingly, we are measuring the NPV of the equity investment, discounted at the equity cost of capital. This contrasts with the usual use of NPV which would include the full investment cost as the initial outlay and use the adjusted WACC as the discount rate to be applied to the cash flows.[2]

The above example shows the importance of working the cash flows through when looking at investment appraisal in MNEs. The cash flow should be worked out using the MNE's cost of equity as the discount rate and factoring the loan repayment into the cash flow projections. By including the loan repayment schedule, a clearer picture emerges of what decisions to make.

When one looks more closely at the calculations, one can see that the depreciation of the Turkish Lira is what made the Turkish debt option more attractive for Scrod. The company could explore a funding structure that would allow it to borrow euro at a lower interest rate and protect itself against the declining TRY by using hedging instruments such as those outlined in **Chapter 15**. However, the cost of such a structure should exactly match the benefits. Why is this?

We have already seen that the **International Fisher Effect** (IFE) (see **Chapter 8**) would negate any differences in exchange rates that flowed from interest rate and inflation rate differentials. The IFE proposes that interest rate and inflation rate differentials between currencies will be counterbalanced over time by movements in the exchange rates. Therefore, borrowing in euro at the lower interest rates and hedging the exposure would provide no additional benefit as the cost of the hedging instruments would equal the benefit from the interest rate differential between € and TRY. As the table in **Example 11.11D** shows, the strategy of borrowing in the currency of the investment, in this case Turkish Lira, seems to be the most effective way of internally protecting the investment against exchange rate movements. This approach reduces the impact of unpredictable movements in the exchange rate.

Capital Structure Implications of Foreign Investment Cash Flows

The capital structure of a company is made up of a combination of debt and equity. When it starts to invest in foreign projects or subsidiaries, the company's capital structure may become more complicated. The return required from investments in different currencies can be different than the return required for the original parent company, or the company taken together as a group.

---

[2] For more on this see Madura, J. and Fox, R. (2007), *International Financial Management*, Chapter 17, London: Thomson Learning.

The value of an MNE is the aggregate of its discounted cash flows, discounted back at the rate appropriate to each individual cash flow stream. The return required on an individual investment can vary due to the nature of the project or entity. It can also vary due to the nature of the capital structure put together to finance the investment. In our example, we have seen that Scrod Plc secured a higher NPV from a project that had 70% Turkish Lira debt and 30% euro equity than it could from the exact same project cash flows but with 70% euro debt and 30% euro equity. It follows then that MNEs must make decisions about the appropriate capital structure for their enterprise. The capital structure of an MNE will be made up of the aggregate of the capital structures of all its subsidiaries. Each MNE will have a unique set of dynamics and attributes that will shape its capital structure, some which will be dependent on the unique nature of the MNE itself, its industry, etc., and some which will be connected with the countries in which it does business.

Figure 11.1 below illustrates that there are a wide variety of possible funding sources that combine to produce the ultimate capital structure of an MNE. While the most common structure is where subsidiaries are financed by retained earnings and parent company or intercompany loans, each MNE will have its own unique capital structure depending on a number of factors which we will explore in the next section.

FIGURE 11.1: HIERARCHY OF CAPITAL STRUCTURE IN AN MNE

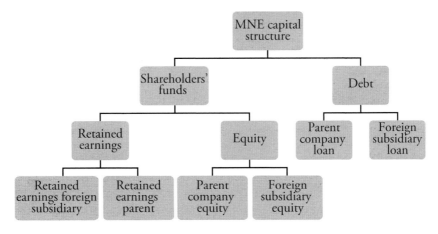

11.8 FACTORS SHAPING THE CAPITAL STRUCTURE OF A MULTINATIONAL ENTERPRISE

Level of Retained Earnings

MNEs that have retained high levels of profits over time rather than pay them out in dividends may be able to finance international subsidiaries from retained earnings. On the other hand, if high dividends or low profitability have depleted retained earnings then an MNE will need to add debt to its capital structure. This is especially true when the MNE is in strong growth mode and has not accumulated sufficient retained earnings to finance the investments needed for the growth. In such cases one would expect to see high levels of debt relative to equity.

Parent Company Guarantees

Parent company guarantees to creditors are sometimes required when subsidiaries are borrowing funds. The subsidiary may be able to borrow more than might be the case if it were stand-alone. In those circumstances one might see higher levels of debt in the subsidiary. On the other hand, though such guarantees will almost certainly reduce the parent company's borrowing capacity, they may be useful, particularly for borrowing in foreign currencies to match foreign currency cash flows.

Volatility of Cash Flows

The volatility of an MNE's cash flows can influence the level of debt that its management may wish to take on. Since debt has fixed servicing costs, specific amounts of cash flow must be set aside to meet these servicing costs. If debt levels are too high, there may be periods when the cash flow required to meet servicing costs are not available. Unless cash is put aside for the 'rainy days', the MNE might find itself breaching its banking agreements. Such pressures will tend to reduce debt levels in MNEs with volatile cash flows.

On the other hand, when cash flows are steady and do not vary much over time, debt levels tend to be higher. Remember our maxim: a safe euro is worth more than a risky one. Since, at most levels of debt, debt capital is more secure for the provider than equity capital, debt should always cost less than equity. Therefore, equity returns to shareholders will be maximised by having higher levels of debt. Having said that, personal gearing can always create the level of gearing an individual shareholder wants to achieve. This idea is at the heart of M&M Theorem discussed earlier in this chapter.

Credit Risk

The credit risk attached to an MNE will have a bearing on its ability to borrow and the costs of such borrowing. Credit risk is determined, officially at any rate, by ratings agencies who allocate risk grades to individual companies (MNEs). These ratings affect the cost of borrowing for an MNE. The riskier the MNE's debt, the more expensive it will be. The cost of debt has a direct influence on an MNE's decision as to how much debt to hold versus equity. The credit risk can be related to the calibre of the MNE's management, the nature of its investments, and the security or collateral it can provide. For example, a firm whose assets comprise very specialised machines for making a unique product will find their credit risk will be worse than a firm with the same cash flow profile but whose assets comprise real estate in a developed economy. The extent to which assets are readily realisable into cash is a determining factor.

Reliance on Local Management

We discussed agency theory in an earlier chapter (see **Chapter 2**). The MNE must rely on local management (its agent) to carry out its goals in the host country of its investment. This management challenge is made more difficult in an MNE compared to a purely domestic firm due to the particular nature and complexity of managing across borders. The goals of the foreign entity's management can become misaligned to the parent company goals. In particular, local management can focus on doing what is right for the local entity rather than what is right for the shareholders of the ultimate parent.

For example, cash may be needed in one part of the group for a very lucrative investment in Zedmania. However, the management in Buroland might not push their customers as hard as they could to get paid in the interest of keeping them happy. Taken to an extreme, the cash retained to fund working capital in Buroland could produce an inferior return to the investment in Zedmania. The parent company management in Ireland cannot readily assess the degree to which the Buroland management are maximising their cash flow or just easing their working life.

The management of an MNE must devise capital structures that reduce such possibilities for misalignment. Sometimes it is necessary to have some local equity to ensure that there is alignment. Allowing local country participation in the profits of the enterprise, and exposing them to possible loss, helps motivate local management and equity holders to behave in a way more aligned with the majority shareholders' goals. Many companies do this by allowing some shareholding to be held by local management, or local shareholders, who can ensure an appropriate focus in the host country.

Country Attributes that Shape Capital Structure

Interest Rates

Interest rates are a function of the supply and demand for money. They vary between countries for reasons explained elsewhere in this book (see **Chapter 8**). Since rates vary, it may not always be the case that an MNE would borrow in the country where it wishes to invest if interest rates there are too high. Conversely, an MNE might finance a project entirely with debt if the interest rates prevailing in the target country warrant it.

Tax

There is an entire specialist profession concerned with the provision of advice on optimal capital structures factoring in taxation. Remittances of profits by subsidiaries back to parent companies are treated differently in different jurisdictions. The tax treatment of interest charges, especially interest on intercompany loans, is fraught with complex legislation, much of it designed to prevent MNEs from using their global structures to avoid local taxes.

In Autumn 2015 the OECD/G20 published its final reports from Base Erosion and Profit Shifting (BEPS) project – its guidelines regarding the treatment of many of the taxation issues for MNEs resulting from a collaborative exercise involving member countries. The objective of this extensive work was to seek ways to prevent MNEs using legal loopholes in the extensive double-taxation agreements between member countries to reduce their taxation liabilities. One area of particular focus by the BEPS project was the use of inter-company loan structures and associated interest charges to 'shift' profits from higher taxation countries to countries with lower taxation charges. On this issue, BEPS focused on what is called 'thin capitalisation', where a company, usually an MNE subsidiary, is financed by high levels of debt rather than a more normal combination of debt and equity. This high level of debt gives rise to high interest charges that are deductible costs in arriving at taxable profits. BEPS has focused on seeking ways to reduce inordinately high debt levels in these types of subsidiaries by supplanting the high debt level with a notional 'normalised' capital structure for the purpose of calculating how much interest to allow as a deductible. (**Chapter 16** deals with this and other issues regarding intragroup charging systems.)

The MNE will need to consider how to arrange the capital structure of its subsidiaries in order to optimise the wealth of its shareholders, ensuring that maximum competitive advantage is taken. For example, interest on local currency debt is allowed as a deduction against profits in calculating the tax charge in most countries. Many countries do not allow the deduction of group interest charged by a parent to a subsidiary for the use of its funds. Therefore, an MNE might put local currency debt into the capital structure of the subsidiary when, all other things being equal, it would have financed the entity by a loan from the group.

Capital Movement Restrictions

Some countries impose ownership regulations on its citizens and corporations that limit investment from outside the jurisdiction. For example, they may do this by banning the sale of certain asset classes to anyone other than to fellow citizens. Consequently, the cost of equity in these countries can be low as there is a higher demand for opportunities to invest in local companies than would otherwise be case. The management of an MNE may wish to take advantage of this by raising equity in the foreign country, given that it may be able to obtain funds at a good rate.

In other situations, it can be a stipulation of a country's inward investment regulations that a local shareholder, sometimes the state itself, be involved in the financing of the subsidiary. In this way, many global MNEs end up with minority shareholders participating in their growth efforts in countries into they wish to expand.

> In China, for example, the government insists that many foreign-owned MNEs form joint ventures with Chinese enterprises or the state itself, if they wish to set up a business in China. In 2012, Jaguar Landrover (JLR), the automobile manufacturer, formed a joint venture with Chery Automobile Company, a Chinese state-owned enterprise. JLR's £1.1 billion investment in the JV will see them manufacture cars for the Chinese market.[3]

Foreign Exchange

In the example of Scrod Plc used earlier, we saw that the depreciation of the Turkish Lira led to a favoured option of financing the investment with Turkish Lira debt rather than euro. This demonstrated the general principle that exchange rate risk can be minimised by borrowing in the currency of the cash flows of the investment. (In **Chapter 15** we explore further how these risks are minimised in practical terms.) Thus, MNEs will design their capital structures to minimise risk for the same reward, or seek higher rewards for higher risk. An MNE may believe that a currency will depreciate. In these cases it will almost certainly seek to put local currency debt, or equity, into the capital structure.

The situation may be different if the MNE's home currency is weaker than the target host country currency. In these instances, an MNE may use funds from the weaker home currency to make the investment in the stronger currency. For example, a South African company might be happy to lend Rand from the parent to a stable euro-denominated subsidiary. However, in the final analysis, the cash flow must be remitted to the parent and, ultimately, the shareholders, for it to provide real value either through dividends or the increased net worth of the business.

---

[3] www.telegraph.co.uk/finance/newsbysector/transport/9684276/jaguar-landrover-seals-chinese-joint-venture (accessed May 2015).

Country Risk

Country risk presents a number of challenges to MNEs, most of which impact upon decision-making in areas other than its capital structure. These risks might be the risk of civil war, famine, and such like (see **Chapter 12** for further analysis of country risk). However, they do impact the capital structure decision also. For example, there may be a risk that restrictions are imposed on remittances outside the country in question. This can happen to prevent capital outflows at times of insecurity. If a subsidiary has local debt it can mitigate the effect of these restrictions. In some instances a country's government may seize assets belonging to an MNE's subsidiary. Again, the effects of these actions are minimised if the assets are financed by local creditors. Indeed, the financing by local creditors may be a type of 'poison pill' for any government thinking of confiscating an MNE's assets since the local creditors will surely vigorously resist such actions. Resistance from local creditors makes it more difficult for the government than would otherwise have been the case had the creditors been the subsidiaries' parent company or other multinational corporations.

> A **poison pill** is a defensive tactic used to prevent a hostile takeover of a company's shares or its assets. It involves the inclusion, usually through the capital structure, of some attribute that will make the target more expensive to assimilate if it is taken over. It usually lies dormant until it is activated by the predefined takeover activity.

11.9 CONCLUSION

Most MNEs start their existence as domestic companies. Then, over time, they grow and expand. Eventually, for some, this expansion takes them into the consideration of international markets. The firm becomes an MNE as it expands into foreign markets, selling to foreign customers, importing from foreign suppliers and, ultimately, investing in assets that are located in foreign jurisdictions.

In this chapter we have sought to understand how an MNE can assess whether a project or entity is worth investing in. To make this assessment I have advocated the use of an appraisal technique that involves calculating the future cash flows that derive from the investment. These cash flows are for periods out into the future. Remembering the principle that 'a euro today is worth more than a euro tomorrow', the MNE manager must come up with a way of reducing the value of the future cash flows to their value in today's money. The future cash flows are reduced by a discount factor that is appropriate to the investment. This discount factor will vary from project to project depending on the capital structure financing the investment and the non-diversifiable risk attached to it. To minimise risks associated with foreign exchange exposures it can sometimes be valuable for MNEs to include the debt repayment cash flows in the future cash flow projection. If the debt repayment is included then the discount factor to be used is the parent company's cost of equity and not the WACC.

QUESTIONS

Self-test Questions

11.1 Two accountants in Tullamore Vodka, an Irish spirits manufacturer, are asked to assess a potential investment in a vodka manufacturer in Poland. Each uses exactly the same future Zloty cash flows to perform a NPV calculation. One accountant produces a positive NPV and the other produces a negative NPV. Explain how this might happen.

11.2 Should a company assess a new investment opportunity from its subsidiary's point of view or from the parent company point of view? Explain the rationale for your answer.

11.3 How does the financing structure of a project affect the NPV?

11.4 Shamrock Plc is considering investing in Venezuela. It finished its appraisal process in June. In August the Venezuelan political situation worsened. Shamrock reduced its cash flow projections by 15% to account for these effects. Should it also alter the discount rate used?

Thought-provoking Question

Question 11.1

Catsee Plc has a possible project investment in Boston. You are the CFO, based in the head office in Dublin. The following details are relevant:

- Investment required; $30,000,000
- Annual cash flow; $2,000,000 in Year 1 growing at 15% a year for the following two years.
- Catsee Plc discount rate on US projects of this type: 14%
- Terminal value of investment at the end of year 3: $28,000,000
- Exchange rate Year 1; €1= $1.1, Year 2; €1 = $1.15, Year 3 €1=$1.25
- Catsee can borrow 100% of its investment requirement in dollars at 7% or euro at 3%
- US corporation tax is 30%
- Irish corporation tax is 12.5%
- Interest costs are allowable against returns.

Advise your board as to:
1. whether Catsee should proceed with the investment
2. if it does proceed, recommend a borrowing strategy.

Review Questions

(See Suggested Solutions to Review Questions in **Appendix B**.)

Question 11.1: Redbarn Brewery

Having read the Redbarn Brewery case study in **Appendix A**, assess the financial outcome of the various investment options open to Redbarn Brewery and consider the various risks relating to the analysis.

Question 11.2: Black Swan Inc

Having read the Black Swan Inc case study in **Appendix A**, evaluate and assess the opportunity facing Black Swan in establishing a finance shared services centre in the EMEA from a financial and non-financial perspective. In addition, estimate the annual cost savings and the investment required for set-up.

Question 11.3: Natural Food Company

Having read the Natural Food Company case study in **Appendix A**, evaluate and assess the international investment opportunity for Natural Food Company in relation to the Artisan Food Company and recommend whether or not the company should proceed with the acquisition.

Question 11.4: Hughes Engineering Limited

Having read the Hughes Engineering Limited case study in **Appendix A**, calculate the most competitive price range for the bid to supply and install specialised machinery for ADP's new plant.

This should range from: (a) the lowest price Hughes could bid in order to breakeven; to (b) the price Hughes could bid to maintain its normal profit margins on manufacturing and installation.

Question 11.5: Pillar Bank Plc

Having read the Pillar Bank Plc case study in **Appendix A**, review the memo from Ken in relation to outsourcing and critically evaluate its findings, considering the information with which Beta have provided Pillar Bank Plc.

Question 11.6: BoneDri

Having read the BoneDri case study in **Appendix A**, consider the financial implications of establishing a factory in Bangladesh and discuss any other key factors that should be considered (e.g. does this make sense or would it be better to increase capacity in Ireland?).

Question 11.7: Stent Manufacturing Limited

Having read the Stent Manufacturing Limited case study in **Appendix A**, compare the option of setting up an operation in Germany to one in south-east England from both a financial and non-financial perspective and advise Stent Manufacturing Limited as to how it should proceed.

Question 11.8: Trident Mobile Ltd

Having read the Trident Mobile Ltd case study in **Appendix A**, evaluate the possible investment by Trident Mobile Ltd in Kenya from both qualitative and quantitative perspectives and suggest a bid price for the contract.

Question 11.9: Smart Bathroom Fittings Ltd

Having read the Smart Bathroom Fittings Ltd case study in **Appendix A**, evaluate the possible investment by Smart Bathroom Fittings Ltd in South Africa from both a qualitative and a quantitative perspective.

12

NON-FINANCIAL FACTORS AFFECTING CAPITAL INVESTMENT APPRAISAL

CONTENTS

12.1   Introduction
12.2   Political Risk
12.3   Cultural Differences
12.4   Misalignment of Goals between Parent and Subsidiary
12.5   Conclusion

LEARNING OBJECTIVES

Having read this chapter, you will understand:
- the nature of non-financial factors that affect capital investment appraisal;
- how corruption is measured between comparative countries and how it can affect investment appraisal;
- how to suggest strategies to minimise the various types of non-financial risk;
- techniques for factoring political risk into investment appraisal;
- how to assess risks associated with cultural differences between countries;
- how to adjust cash flow forecasts to take account of probability analysis and perform simple NPV calculations; and
- how to factor in principal–agent relationship conflicts into investment appraisal.

12.1 INTRODUCTION

In the previous chapter we discussed the various techniques the management of a multinational enterprise (MNE) can deploy to appraise investment opportunities in non-domestic markets. We categorised an investment opportunity as being a set of future cash flows from an investment. An investment opportunity can be a specific capital project, the setting up of a subsidiary or the acquisition of an existing business. The investment's forecasted cash flows are then discounted by an appropriate rate to calculate its value in today's money. If the net discounted cash flows are positive, the investment is judged to be viable and it should proceed.

Though this appraisal technique is numerical in nature and produces answers that have the benefit of being 'concrete' in appearance, the MNE manager would be foolish to take its outputs as 'gospel'.

Any numerical techniques, such as NPV, are only as good as the quality of the information fed into them. Since the predictions of future cash flows are, at best, estimates, they are subject to some degree of uncertainty. In some cases, there can be greater certainty over cash-flow forecast numbers, e.g. where the lease on a building has been signed. In other cases, however, prediction might be more difficult and therefore more uncertain, e.g. forecasting income streams from a hotel in Afghanistan.

In **Example 12.1** below, concerning Venezuela's nationalisation policy, one can see that the actions of the government will have had a significant effect on the cash flows of the MNEs concerned. The expected cash flows from the various investments will have been replaced by the compensation cash flow. There have been disputes in many countries, not just Venezuela, about the level of compensation paid to MNEs in recompense for the loss of their investments.

EXAMPLE 12.1: EXPROPRIATION IN VENEZUELA[1]

"Venezuela's government has accelerated its rate of nationalisations and expropriations but tends to pay fair compensation to business owners. Takeovers include:
- A majority stake in four oil projects operating in the Orinoco river basin worth an estimated $30bn.
- A gas injection project belonging to Williams Companies and a range of assets from local energy-related service companies.
- A eucalyptus tree farm owned by Ireland's Smurfit Kappa.
- An Argentine-owned steel mill and Mexican cement company.
- Assets of the US-based AES Corp which was Venezuela's largest private power producer.
- Hundreds of large farms, including the UK-owned Vestey cattle ranch."

Predicting future cash flows is uncertain; just as uncertain is the prediction of the wider, non-financial environment in which the MNE will be operating. The non-financial environment may lack the perceived solidity of 'hard and fast' numbers, but its impact can be just as forceful as any financial dimension. In formulating its views about what options to select, an MNE must have a view as to the potential impact of non-financial issues on the future cash flows and/or the discount rate used to assess a project. In this chapter we will examine techniques that the MNE manager can use to assess the non-financial environment and show how to factor this assessment into the appraisal of investment opportunities.

EXAMPLE 12.1 – CONT.: EXPROPRIATION IN VENEZUELA[2]

"A portrait of the president greets you at reception, the managers espouse socialism, the guests wear red T-shirts and the décor promotes Latin American solidarity: welcome to Hotel Chávez.

What used to be the Caracas Hilton today soars over Venezuela's capital as a bold symbol of Hugo Chávez's leftist revolution, a 36-storey, state-run declaration of intent.

---

[1] Carroll, Rory, "Workers of the World, relax! Chávez takes over Hilton", *The Guardian* 22 October 2009. See http://www.theguardian.com/world/2009/oct/22/chavez-seizes-hilton-caracas (accessed November 2014).
[2] *Ibid.*

The government took it over from the US hotel chain two years ago as part of a sweep towards greater state economic control. Renamed Alba – 'dawn' in Spanish and also the acronym of Chávez's regional grouping, the Bolivarian Alliance for the Americas – the hotel hosts summits which condemn US imperialism and chart a brighter, leftist future.

'We are the first socialist hotel but hopefully not the last,' said Katiuska Camaripano, its general manager.

Last week it acquired a sister: the government seized the Hilton on Margarita island, Venezuela's tourist playground. It had angered Chávez during a meeting of African leaders he hosted at the hotel. 'The owners tried to impose conditions on the revolutionary government. No way. So I said, "Let's expropriate it." And now it's been expropriated.'

A presidential decree transferred its assets, including 280 rooms, 210 suites, shops, restaurants and a casino to the tourism ministry. A Hilton spokeswoman said the chain was 'evaluating' the government's action.

The state's Margarita acquisition may also be renamed Alba, consolidating the brand name. Venezuela has also partly funded a small Alba hotel in Managua, capital of its leftist ally Nicaragua, said Camaripano. 'It would be wonderful if we became part of a socialist chain.'

Two years after it became a political as well as geographic landmark, the Caracas Alba draws mixed reviews. Managers say it blends socialist values with business savvy and top-notch service. Critics say it is a dump in which nothing works.

There are some striking changes. Gone are the American and European managers and well-heeled foreign guests who used to snap up jewellery and cosmetics in the shops. Red-clad government officials and Cuban delegations have largely taken their place. 'Business is dead. All we'll sell is chewing gum and antibiotics,' lamented one store owner.

The Italian restaurant now serves more Caribbean fare such as chicken in coconut sauce and cachapa, a corn-based pancake. The gift shop offers a range of ceramic Chávez mugs and sculptures ranging from $20 to $240.

The bookshop which sold glossy magazines and Dan Brown novels has been replaced by a culture ministry outlet offering political tracts such as Transition Towards Socialism and Venezuela: a Revolution *Sui Generis*.

The titles are all subsidised, with some costing the equivalent of just 50p. 'The problem is people buy the books and sell them on for profit,' said Nicola Castilla, the bookshop clerk. 'It's not easy instilling a socialist conscience.'

Top floors offer superb views of downtown Caracas, the Ávila mountain and hillside slums, but the hotel's surrounding district, a hub of theatres and museums, has become dilapidated and crime-ridden. Many middle-class Venezuelans who used to visit now go only when participating in opposition marches. As they pass the Alba they chant 'out', apparently directed at the Cubans.

Managers say the 400 staff – who were retained from the Hilton era – reflect socialist values by doing voluntary work such as rubbish collection on their days off. The hotel says it does its bit by giving staff generous benefits not stipulated in their contracts, such as paying for babysitters, and by hosting poor children and hospital patients.

A basic room costs $286 a night but discounts are offered to the needy, said Rayneth Oleaga, a spokesman for the government agency that administers the hotel. 'It is for the people. It is accessible to all.'

The hotel has 900 rooms, but under Hilton management only 545 were in service, a number the Alba has increased to 782. Last year's 90% occupancy rate owed much to government delegations, said Camaripano. Occupancy this year has fallen to 65% but the hotel still makes a profit. 'We are getting a lot of ordinary tourists as well as official delegations.'

Travel agents dispute that. Venezuela's capital has a shortage of hotel rooms but foreign tourists often refuse to stay in the Alba, citing bad service, credit card rip-offs, musty smells, tatty furniture and overpriced food.

Online reviews have dwindled but the few that are posted tend to be scathing. 'I would never under any circumstances go back there, even if it were free,' said one former guest on tripadviser.com.

'It reminded me of hotels behind the iron curtain in the 60s, very depressing. I was glad to leave.'

This article was amended on 27 October 2009. The original referred to a grouping by its previous name, the Bolivarian Alternative for the Americas. This has been corrected."

In **Chapter 7** we examined the different types of country risks and how they impact upon decisions a MNE might make about where it invests. We also saw how these country risks shape how an MNE expands its operational horizons. These same risks also have an effect on exchange rates and are the same risks that impact on the capital expenditure appraisal process. In this chapter we will:
- expand upon the non-financial dimensions of country risk;
- examine how to carry out an assessment of the risks relevant to a specific country;
- explore how to factor risk assessment into the investment appraisal process.

The **non-financial** factors affecting investment appraisal discussed in this chapter are:
- political risk;
- cultural differences; and
- misalignment of goals between parent and subsidiary.

12.2 POLITICAL RISK

In this section we will examine the most important factors that an MNE should be aware of when considering political risk in the context of capital expenditure or investment appraisal. These include:
- nationalisation;
- contract nullification;

- tax legislation;
- foreign exchange controls;
- corruption;
- terrorism; and
- home country restrictions, e.g. where the home country restricts the activities of its citizens regarding countries they can do business with.

Nationalisation

Nationalisation risk is where a host country's government seizes an MNE's assets. Sometimes this can be done without any compensation being paid, which is one extreme. Sometimes compensation is paid but it is set unilaterally by the government carrying out the nationalisation. Even when there is negotiation about the nationalisation process and appropriate compensation, many of the cards will be with the host country (see **Example 12.1** above and how Hugo Chavez's Venezuelan government seized the assets of many MNEs).

In **Example 12.2** below, a joint venture between Canadian and Chilean MNEs to mine for gold and copper in the Reko Diq area of Pakistan was found to have been issued with its mining licenses "in conflict with the laws of the country". The Pakistan Supreme Court made its ruling some 20 years after the initial licenses were granted and the court findings will increase the uncertainties over future cash flows arising from the investment by the MNE joint venture company, TCC.

EXAMPLE 12.2: CANADIAN/CHILEAN JV LOSES CONTROL OVER MINES[3]

Supreme Court declares Reko Diq agreement void

ISLAMABAD: The Supreme Court on Monday declared the Reko Diq agreement void and in conflict with the country's laws, DawnNews reported.

In its ruling, a three-judge bench of the apex court, headed by Chief Justice Iftikhar Muhammad Chaudhry, stated that the agreement reached on July 23, 1993 was in conflict with the laws of the country.

The Supreme Court had been hearing the case constituting of identical petitions filed against the federal government's decision to lease out gold and copper mines in Reko Diq in Balochistan's Chagai district to the Tethyan Copper Company (TCC) — a Canadian and Chilean consortium of Barrick Gold and Antofagasta Minerals. Reko Diq sits over the popular Tethyan copper belt and is known to have the fifth largest deposits of gold and copper in the world.

The bench added that all amendments made to the agreement after its signing were unlawful and in contradiction with the agreement.

---

[3] Dawn.com, 7 January 2013. See http://www.dawn.com/news/776967/supreme-court-declares-reko-diq-agreement-unlawful

The court, in the 16-page short order, moreover admitted for hearing the petitions that had been filed pertaining to the agreement.

The bench, in its order, stated that the TCC no longer had any rights in relation to the Reko Diq agreement.

Admitting the petitions filed against the TCC for hearing, the bench ruled that the agreement was in violation of the country's rules and regulations.

Earlier in Dec 2012, the International Centre for Settlement of Investment Disputes (ICSID) had given a go-ahead to the Balochistan government and prominent nuclear scientist Dr Samar Mubarakmand to carry out the mining and smelting project in Reko Diq area. The ICSID had rejected the TCC's demand for 'provisional measures' for 'protecting' two of its deposit areas.

Cases pertaining to Reko Diq mining lease dispute were being heard in courts for the past five years.

Contract Nullification

Governments may revoke or nullify contracts with MNEs. A government may also choose not to pay an MNE according to the terms of a contract. Both cases have significant impact upon the MNE, which may have made its investments in accordance with a contract with the relevant government or other parties and then finds itself without the sales proceeds from products it has supplied once the contract is nullified.

Governments may also cancel licences issued to MNEs to carry out certain works or provide certain services. As seen in **Example 12.2** above, this is what happened in Pakistan, albeit through the Supreme Court. The revocation of a licence often deprives an MNE of its expected cash flows. The possibility of such revocations needs to be considered when appraising an investment. The greater the likelihood of such an action by a government, the greater the uncertainty of future cash flows that may have been forecast.

Tax Legislation

Governments can quickly change the basis on which an MNE decides to make its original investment. This is particularly true in the case of tax legislation. It is difficult for an MNE to predict such government actions as they are often not flagged in advance to avoid discouraging new potential investors. MNEs may find that tax rates on their specialised activities are increased after they have incurred the initial investment. For example, in 2010 the Chilean Government increased taxes on copper mining from 5%, through a progressive tax, up to 14%.

Foreign Exchange Controls

Governments can also change the rules regarding currency and foreign exchange. For example, the government of a country hosting an MNE might promulgate laws preventing it converting its distributions to its owners into the currency of the MNE's home country, effectively locking in the profits made by the MNE into the host currency. In such extreme circumstances, governments prevent the movement of foreign currencies out of their jurisdiction. This blocking technique effectively locks the MNE's foreign currency holdings into the banking system of the host country.

Governments may also stipulate the exchange rates to be used for conversion of the host country currency into other currencies. A government that places these restrictions upon its currency clearly does not allow the market to set the exchange rate for their currency. Rather, they impose a rate that they believe will support some fiscal or political objective. Often in such cases an unofficial 'black market' rate develops, operating outside the conventional banking system. These imposed rates can differ substantially from the exchange rates used in unofficial markets.

Such situations arise because not all currencies trade freely on the world's foreign exchange markets. The greater the difference between the imposed rate and the rate that might occur if the market was allowed to operate freely, the greater the uncertainty for the MNE regarding the quantum of its future cash flows converted into the home currency.

Corruption

Transparency International, a voluntary body that champions open and transparent corporate and government behaviours, defines corruption as "the abuse of an entrusted power for private gain".

Corruption has been an issue for traders for centuries. Traders have either been the perpetrators of the corruption, such as in the case of smugglers and counterfeiters, or they have been the victims. In either case, the legitimate MNE will find itself facing corruption-related problems.

In countries where the government is corrupt, a MNE may find that its competitors are gaining an advantage by subscribing to the corruption culture. The MNE may also find that it is faced with the appalling prospect of being required to pay bribes in order to achieve its goals. The well-run MNE will always reject such situations, because well-run MNEs will adhere to a code of governance guiding management towards ethical and transparent behaviours. Paying bribes would certainly fall foul of such a code. (The issues relating to business ethics and MNEs are discussed in more detail in **Chapter 5**.)

It can be very challenging to factor into capital investment appraisal cash flow forecasts the effects of such corruption issues. Therefore, when appraising an investment, cognisance needs to be made for the 'unexpected' corruption factor. Somehow, management of the MNE must come up with a way of factoring these risks into the assessment process. The financial calculations of the investment can be made and an NPV calculated. The challenge remains as to how to factor in the effects of corruption on the investment cash flows.

In discussing political risks in **Chapter 7**, "Economic and Political Factors Impacting on International Business", we referred to the annual Corruptions Perceptions Index produced by Transparency International to facilitate an analysis and awareness of corruption.[4] MNEs can use such information to adjust their predicted cash flows to take account of the risk that might attach to the investment opportunity.

The existence of large bureaucracies within a country's administration system can often be a signal that the costs of doing business in that country will be high. While there may not be

---

[4] Transparency International is a non-governmental organisation that monitors and publicises corporate and political corruption in international development. See http://www.transparency.org/

corruption *per se*, there may be many points of contact between a MNE and the government bureaucracies, together with many regulations, which will tend to slow up business processes and add unforeseen costs to the operation of the MNE.

Transparency International has also ranked 28 countries based on the propensity of companies from those countries to pay bribes.[5] It is important for an MNE to be aware of such rankings. If an MNE is planning to be competing in its new potential market with a company from a country whose companies have a high propensity to pay bribes, then the MNE might attach greater uncertainty to its cash flow projections. The greater the uncertainty, the higher the return needed for investors to compensate for additional risks.

Companies from the Netherlands were found to be least likely to pay bribes while Russian companies were most likely to pay them. Companies from China were found to be the second-worst culprits in terms of their propensity to pay bribes. Given the size of Russia and China in terms of global trade these numbers make stark reading for an MNE that may be competing with companies from these countries.

Terrorism and Civil Unrest

Terrorism and civil unrest can add huge unforeseen costs to the operation of a MNE. In many parts of the world MNEs will need to factor in the cost of providing a high level of security in order to protect their assets or personnel. In Algeria, for example, oil companies need to provide security to such an extent that they are running the equivalent of private armies. The costs associated with such security provisions cannot be easily forecast. Sudden escalations in unrest can be unforeseen. Supplies of raw materials can be blocked, rendering production facilities useless. Goods can be prevented from leaving factories due to closed roads or ports and damaged infrastructure. An accountant sitting in her office in Athlone or Enniskillen may find it difficult to build the effects of such unrest into an investment's cash flow forecasts. Yet, that is what must be done to help ensure that the management of the MNE is making solid decisions, decisions that are likely to further the interests of its shareholders and other stakeholders.

Home Country Restrictions

The nature of political risk is not just associated with the policies of the governments of the host countries in which an MNE might be investing. The politics of the home country also present a risk. A home country government may change its view of relationships with another country, leading to unforeseen impacts on the MNE. For example, the EU imposed trade sanctions on Russia after the Ukrainian crisis in 2014. These sanctions could impact upon an Irish MNE operating in Russia or, indeed, an Irish manufacturer importing materials from Russia.

In **Example 12.3** below, the Irish Government in 1982 was eager to facilitate trade with Libya. However, as the years progressed the Libyan regime became more closely associated with global terrorist acts, which led to an increased amount of sanctions and embargos being placed on trade with Libya. These sanctions directly affected Irish MNEs doing business with Libya.

---

[5] www.transparency.org, Bribe Payers Index 2011.

EXAMPLE 12.3: IRELAND'S TRADE DEAL WITH LIBYA[6]

"Oil for meat, Libya

STATE RECORDS: An economic mission to trade Irish cattle and beef for crude Libyan oil was outlined in confidential records released by the Department of Foreign Affairs this week.

The trade mission in 1982, headed up by the then Minister for Agriculture Brian Lenihan, included high-profile businesspeople such as Larry Goodman of Anglo Irish Meats and Peter Evans of the Irish National Petroleum Corporation. The delegation also included the CEO of Coras Beostoic agus Feola, the Meat and Livestock Board.

Confidential records released under the National Archives' State Papers 30-year rule this week outline the trade deal negotiations.

Records stated the level of trade in live and dead meat between the two countries reached a record-breaking £120 million from 1980 to 1982. They show the Irish delegation wanted to increase its volume of dead meat supplied to Jamahirya. In return, the Libyans wanted Ireland to buy its crude oil among other requests.

Confidential records say Ireland supplied 150,000 cattle and 5,000 tonnes in 'dead beef' in 1981. The Libyans were looking to reduce live imports to 125,000 and increase 'dead beef' to 10,000. The Irish delegation was pushing for a decrease to 120,000 in live cattle and an increase to 15,000 tonnes beef.

State records reveal tense meetings got under way in Jamahiriya during the trade mission.

"Indications were that Libya was anxious to match these purchases with purchases by Ireland of Libyan crude oil," an official from the Department of Foreign Affairs outlined in documents.

State records show the Irish National Petroleum Corporation and the Irish Department of Industry and Energy felt that direct crude oil imports would be difficult to arrange because of "existing commitments with Saudi Arabia and the British National Oil Company and the fact that Libyan crude oil was generally unsuitable for refinery".

Department of Industry and Energy officials felt they at most could agree a once-off 100,000 tonnes of Libyan crude oil and then only at a discount.

During the visit, it was also agreed that surgical and medical training of Libyan graduates would be reviewed between the Medical Boards of Jervis Street Hospital and Richmond Hospital in Dublin.

Libyan officials were also keen to stress that substantial Irish contracts with its Department of Water were being finalised and the design of its first polytechnic college in Jamahiriya was being awarded to an Irish design consultant.

---

[6] Deeney, Lisa, "Oil for meat, Libya", Agriland, 4 January 2014. See https://www.agriland.ie/farming-news/oil-for-meat-libya/ (accessed May 2015).

Both sides also discussed training and education co-operation, particular in the areas of irrigation, ground water investigations and drilling of deep water wells.

The Irish delegation also agreed to consider purchasing Libyan caustic soda, hydrochloric acid, PVC powder, Urea and Methanol."

By 2011 the situation had changed dramatically. In response to the increasingly violent response by the Qadhafi regime to the protests and revolution occurring in Libya, the international community responded with a series of new trade sanctions against Libya aimed at Colonel Qadhafi, his family and associates, and his government. Companies were now advised to consider very carefully the impact of the new sanctions before proceeding with any business dealings with the country.

In rapid succession, the UN, US, EU and countries including the UK and Canada, adopted wide-ranging sanctions against Libya, including export restrictions, asset freezes and travel bans. Though focused mainly on financial transactions and trade in materials that could be used to promote violence, the sanctions were broadly drafted and had the potential to affect virtually any company that had business in Libya directly or indirectly. Companies doing business in Libya, therefore, had to be aware of – and adapt to – a rapidly changing legal environment.

Clearly, an MNE planning an investment in a foreign country needs not only to consider the political risk inherent in that country but also the political risk in the home country's relationships with that country. It is also pertinent to be aware of trading blocs of which the MNE's home country is a member, for example the EU. The relationship of the trading bloc with the host country may change, giving rise to trade sanctions or asset restrictions being imposed by the bloc on the host country, and with which the home country must comply as a consequence of its membership. In the Libyan example above, the Irish Government was obliged to ensure that Irish companies complied with the sanctions imposed at EU level. (Of course, this is not to imply that the Irish Government had anything other than full support for the sanctions being imposed at the time.)

Factoring Political Risk into Capital Expenditure Appraisal

There is much debate about how to factor political risk into the capital investment appraisal process. Some experts believe that political risk should be factored into an appraisal analysis by using a higher discount factor. Given that the discount rate to be chosen, r, for the return on equity can be expressed as:

$$r = r_f + \beta (r_m - r_f)$$

where
r = return on equity
r_f = risk-free return in home currency
β = the beta of the investment project, a measure of sensitivity of the non-diversifiable risk of the investment project to the market risk premium
r_m = rate of return of the home market, or sometimes the global market for a global MNE,

then the implication is that r will need to be higher to factor in the additional premium for the political risk. Using the components of the formula this additional premium could be included by adjusting upward the β of the investment project.

The capital asset pricing model (CAPM) used in this instance (see also **Chapter 11**) has the advantage of being simple – one just increases the discount factor on the basis that there is increased risk by adjusting the β. However, it is also somewhat arbitrary.

> For example, in considering an investment in Zambia, by how much should one adjust β to factor in political risk? One could increase the beta factor by 10%, 25%, or any number that seems to feel right. An accountant might apply their own judgement to the situation. Instinct might tell them that a project in Zambia is 25% more risky than a project in France and they would adjust the discount factor accordingly.

There is an alternative to adjusting the β in an arbitrary fashion, which is to use probability analysis to vary the cash-flow projections. In this way, the possible volatility in the expected cash flows is factored into the actual cash flows rather than into the discount rate being selected. (Remember: the discount rate will be a function of the β.) We have already seen how the capital structure of a project can affect its NPV. Selecting arbitrarily calculated discount factors using 'gut feel' or 'instinct' can give rise to projects being rejected that should have been accepted, and vice versa. In **Example 12.4** below Lulu Plc factors in political risk by using probabilities. It makes an assessment as to the likelihood of the different possible cash flow forecasts occurring. It then discounts these probability-adjusted cash flow forecasts to assess the investment project. Using this approach, Lulu avoids choosing an arbitrary adjustment to the β and, by implication, the return required from the investment, *r*.

Obviously, there is still some degree of estimation involved in this process since the selection of the probabilities of each cash flow option can never be absolutely certain. However, by adjusting the cash flow forecasts to take account of the political risk, the other variables of the CAPM can remain consistent with the MNE's investment project appraisal process, allowing for ready comparison between investment options.

EXAMPLE 12.4: FACTORING IN POLITICAL RISK

Lulu Plc is considering a gas project in Waziristan. Lulu's management expects the investment to be €75 million and it expects an income after costs of €50 million per annum for two years. Waziristan is very unstable politically. Lulu's discount factor for gas projects is 10%.

Calculate the NPV, ignoring the unstable nature of Waziristan.

$$\text{NPV} = -€75\text{m} + \frac{€50\text{m}}{1.1} + \frac{€50\text{m}}{1.1^2} = €11.78\text{m}$$

Since the NPV is positive, Lulu should undertake the project.

Lulu's management believes there is a 12% chance every year that Waziristan's Government will seize the asset and give no compensation. This changes the assessment of the project in the following ways:
- In Year 1 there is a 88% chance of €50 million of income and a 12% chance of no income.
- In Year 2 there is an 88% chance of some cash flow, this being the probability that the plant is not seized in Year 1.
- If there is cash flow in Year 2, there is an 88% chance that it will be €50 million. There is a 12% chance that it will be zero.
- Thus, for Year 2, there is a 0.88 × 0.88 = 0.774 chance of getting €50 million.

Applying the probabilities to the cash flows:
- we now adjust Year 1 cash flow to €50m × 0.88 = €44m; and
- Year 2 to €50m × 0.88 × 0.88= €38.72m.

Slotting these probability-reduced cash flows into the NPV calculation we get:

$$NPV = €75m + \frac{€44m}{1.1} + \frac{€38.72m}{1.1^2}$$
$$= -€75m + €40m + €32m$$
$$= -€3m$$

The NPV is negative and therefore Lulu should reject the project.

Clearly, there is an element of subjectivity in allocating a probability of an expropriation by the government of Waziristan at 12%.

Another approach could be to calculate what probability level of expropriation would produce an NPV of zero and then assess whether this represented a risk worth taking. In the case of Lulu, a 9.5% probability of expropriation produces a zero NPV. Therefore, if Lulu's management believes the chances of expropriation are lower than this, it should go ahead with the project. If it believes the probability of expropriation is higher than 9.5% it should reject the project.

As shown in **Example 12.4** a more thorough way to approach the problem of factoring in political risk is to calculate the various possible cash flows forecasts under different scenarios and use probability analysis to adjust these forecasts. Probability analysis in this instance involves the allocation of a probability to the various possible cash-flow forecasts from the investment project. For example, one could estimate that there is a 10% chance of Cash Flow A occurring, a 30% probability of Cash Flow B occurring, and so forth. Each cash flow forecast is reduced by the percentage likelihood of it occurring, that is, by the probability. Then, the probability adjusted cash flows are totalled, period by period. It is these totalled, adjusted cash flow forecasts that are then used to calculate the NPV.

One could argue that the probability analysis approach involves just as much subjectivity as adjusting the discount rate. To a certain extent this is true, but the more detailed approach of going through the cash flows does bring benefits. Each element of the cash flow can be considered. Not all elements of the project cash flows are subject to the same risk profile, and risks to cash flows further into the future are less impactful on the NPV calculation. Adjusting the discount factor or the beta doesn't readily account for this time effect of cash flows that are further out into the future. (The diminishing effect of time on discount factors means that later cash flows are discounted by smaller factors.)

If at all possible, it is always preferable that the management of the MNE endeavour to calculate the future cash flows of the investment project and adjust each separate element of those cash flows for the relevant political-risk probability. However, the simpler route of just adjusting the discount factor or the β upward is often taken.

These two methods, the simple upward adjustment of the discount factor and probability analysis of possible cash flows, can result in the same appraisal outcome in some circumstances.

If the discount factor adjustment quantum is calculated by reference to the effect of probability on future cash flows, the results can be the same under both methods, providing the effects are the same each year in which they occur.

In other words, if the probability of an expropriation is, for example, 15% each year, then it will be possible to calculate a discount factor adjustment that produces the same answer as applying the probability analysis approach to each individual year's cash-flow options. However, if the probabilities associated with each possible cash-flow outcome differ year to year, then it is preferable to use the probability analysis approach. The probability analysis approach will also give a more accurate assessment than the upward adjustment of the discount factor if the investment project has a terminal value.

Sources of Information on Political Risk

There are a number of sources that the MNE manager can consult in order to make an assessment as regards political risk. For example, the Economic Intelligence Unit (EIU), which forms part of The Economist Group, produces a risk index of countries which assesses four types of risk, including political risk. It further classifies political risk into two broad types: political stability and government effectiveness.

Table 12.1 below is the EIU's 2014 table of risk assessments for Zambia. You can see the two political risk components: political stability risk at 45 and the government effectiveness risk at 71, shown in bold on the table. Given our maxim, 'a risky euro is worth less than a safe euro', these risk factor scores can be particularly helpful in comparing risks between countries.

TABLE 12.1: OVERALL RISK ASSESSMENT: ZAMBIA[7]

RISK RATINGS	Current Rating	Quarter Score	Previous Rating	Quarter Score
Overall assessment	C	52	C	52
Security risk	B	32	B	32
Political stability risk	**C**	**45**	**C**	**45**
Government effectiveness risk	**D**	**71**	**D**	**71**
Legal & regulatory risk	C	58	C	58
Macroeconomic risk	C	60	C	60
Foreign trade & payments risk	C	50	C	50
Financial risk	C	54	C	54
Tax policy risk	B	31	B	31
Labour market risk	C	54	C	54
Infrastructure risk	D	62	D	62

Note: E = most risky; 100 = most risky.

Again from the EIU, **Table 12.2** below shows the scores and rating for Algeria:

---

[7] Viewswire.eiu.com/index.asp?layout=RKCountryVW3&country_id=890000289 (accessed May 2015).

TABLE 12.2: OVERALL RISK ASSESSMENT: ALGERIA[8]

RISK RATINGS	Current Rating	Current Score	Previous Rating	Previous Score
Overall assessment	D	63	D	63
Security risk	C	57	C	57
Political stability risk	**C**	**60**	**C**	**60**
Government effectiveness risk	**D**	**71**	**D**	**71**
Legal & regulatory risk	D	78	D	78
Macroeconomic risk	B	25	B	25
Foreign trade & payments risk	C	57	C	57
Financial risk	D	75	D	75
Tax policy risk	D	69	D	69
Labour market risk	D	75	D	71
Infrastructure risk	D	62	D	62

Note: E = most risky; 100 = most risky.

The political stability risk for Algeria is 60 versus Zambia at 45. These comparisons indicate that, all other things being equal, there are higher political stability risks in Algeria than in Zambia. Therefore, when adjusting the forecasted cash flows of otherwise similar investments one would expect to see bigger reductions in future adjusted cash flows for the Algerian project than the Zambian one.

(Note also: the security risk is higher in Algeria. Awareness of this should lead the MNE manager to forecast additional security costs for the project.)

The PRS Group also produces a monthly International Country Risk Guide (ICRG).[9] In June 2013, according to the ICRG, the political risk for Algeria was 56 (on a scale where 0 = most risky and 100 is no risk – the opposite of the EIU grading system).[10] Zambia had less political risk with a score of 62.5. The PRS Group's ratings also make assessments of future risk trends, including best case and worst case scenarios, out to five years in the future. So, what initially looks like a sea of guesswork, that is forecasting political risk, can be improved and enhanced by research and scientific methodology. Groups like EIU and PRS carry out detailed research into the countries they analyse. They use consistent methodologies across each country they assess, and each time they perform the exercise. This consistency means that the comparative information about a country over a given timeframe gives the MNE manager a measure of the trends concerning each type of risk. The consistency of analysis also allows for meaningful comparison between countries, as we did above for Zambia and Algeria. While it is still true that forecasting the future is an

---

8   Viewswire.eiu.com/index.asp?layout=RKCountryVW3&country_id=210000021 (accessed May 2015).

9   See https://www.prsgroup.com/

10   PRS Group, International Country Risk Guide, Volume XXXIV, Number 6, June 2013.

uncertain business, the MNE manager can inform herself as to what the probabilities of certain outcomes are before building the cash flow projections.

Strategies to Reduce Expropriation Risk

There are a number of strategies an MNE can adopt to reduce the risk of a host country's government seizing assets or expropriating a subsidiary, including:
- local debt funding;
- insurance;
- proprietary systems;
- local labour; and
- drawing cash quickly.

Each of these strategies is discussed in more detail below.

Local Debt Funding
This strategy involves the MNE funding its investment, at least partially, with locally sourced debt. In this way, creditors of the investment project are based locally and are likely to have an influence on the host country's government. If the government seizes the MNE's assets, the MNE can refuse to pay the sums due locally. The creditors will then seek to recover the monies they initially advanced to the MNE from the expropriating government. Thus, in considering any action, the host country's government will need to assess the hostility it may encounter locally.

The MNE will still be exposed on the equity element of the investment project's funding. Therefore, it may be in the interest of the MNE to have as much debt as possible in the investment project, preferably locally sourced. A derivation of this approach would be to borrow money for a project on a non-recourse basis. In this situation, the creditors of the investment project can only recover the money they have advanced from the investment project's proceeds or the sale of its assets. This means that if the assets are expropriated by the host country, the creditors will not be able to recoup their loans from the MNE. Remembering that a risky euro is worth less a safe euro, those providing the loans are likely to demand a higher return for lending into a project on a non-recourse basis. This higher cost of debt will increase the weighted average cost of capital (WACC) and consequently the discount rate for the project, meaning the cash flows will need to be larger than would otherwise be the case to generate a positive NPV.

Insurance
Many MNEs take out insurance to cover the risk of government expropriation. The Export Credit Guarantee Department (ECGD) provides such insurance in the UK, including Northern Ireland. The ECGD is a government department and operates under the name 'UK Export Finance'. The scheme primarily focuses on the provision of insurance to guarantee the recovery of debts but it can be extended to cover the risk of expropriation. In **Example 12.5** below, Bombardier, an aircraft manufacturer, is given support to enable it to sell its products, partially manufactured in Belfast, throughout the world. Through the help of the scheme, and its Canadian equivalent, risks of non-payment by foreign companies or states are minimised through elaborate insurance products. UK MNEs can also buy such insurance from commercial sources on the open market.

EXAMPLE 12.5: USE OF INSURANCE TO REDUCE EXPROPRIATION RISK[11]

UK Export Finance to support Northern Ireland aerospace exports

UK Export Finance will work in partnership with its Canadian equivalent to support sales of Bombardier's CSeries aircraft, which is part manufactured in Belfast.

UK Export Finance (UKEF), the UK's export credit agency, will participate in a programme of support for the new Bombardier CSeries aircraft. It will provide guarantees to its Canadian equivalent, Export Development Canada (EDC), to reflect the UK-manufactured content.

The wings of the aircraft are being manufactured at Bombardier's plant in Belfast, supporting up to 800 jobs directly and supporting a further 2000 jobs in the supply chain. UKEF will provide guarantees to EDC for around 20% of the value of loans extended by EDC to overseas buyers of the aircraft, reflecting the UK-manufactured proportion.

Bombardier and EDC announced the export credit support at the Farnborough Air Show on 14 July. Bombardier's investment in the UK, which has included a complex research and development programme, as well as the construction of a new factory, is one of the largest ever single inward investments in Northern Ireland. There are 495 orders and commitments for the aircraft, which successfully completed its first flight in 2013. First deliveries are expected in 2015.

UKEF has a long history of providing support to the UK aerospace sector. Its support for Bombardier aircraft will join its ongoing support for exports of Airbus aircraft and Rolls-Royce engines. Through its support for UK aerospace exports, UKEF is helping to increase the UK's exports and make the UK more competitive. Its support is provided in line with the terms of the OECD Aircraft Sector Understanding (ASU), which ensures a level playing field for such official support among signatory nations.

In Ireland the Department of Jobs, Enterprise and Innovation (DJEI) managed such schemes when they existed. However, the Export Credit Insurance Scheme, which was administered by the Department for many years, was suspended in 1998. Since then, though exporters have been able to avail of such insurance on the open market as commercial operators made such cover easily available, in early 2009 insurers began reducing or withdrawing cover and this led to some market failure in this sector.

In response to this problem, in mid-2009 the Irish Government arranged for a review of the export credit insurance market to be carried out by Forfás, the trade research and support agency (since August 2014, integrated with the DJEI). The resultant report concluded that there would be significant problems associated with a state scheme as sought. It was therefore decided to undertake a full-scale, forensic examination of the credit insurance market in Ireland, for which KPMG was commissioned. KPMG's report found that the introduction of a state-backed, short-term 'top-up' scheme would be expensive and of very limited impact

---

[11] Gov.UK, "UK Export Finance to support Northern Ireland aerospace exports", 14 July 2014. See https://www.gov.uk/government/news/uk-export-finance-to-support-northern-ireland-aerospace-exports (accessed May 2015).

and that a negligible number of jobs would be supported by such an initiative. The report was not published since it contained commercially sensitive information from the insurance companies, but it was referred to in the houses of the Oireachtas.[12] In addition, it noted that there were indications that the credit insurance market was showing signs of recovery and that the insurance companies would therefore begin to provide better levels of cover.

When carrying out an investment appraisal, a MNE should price the cost of insurance to cover expropriation. It can then deduct this cost from the cash flow projections which have been prepared on the basis of no expropriation risk. By subtracting the cost of the insurance from the cash flows, the MNE manager is effectively adjusting the cash flows for the expropriation risk. This adjusted cash flow can then be discounted at the appropriate rate. If the resultant NPV is positive the project can go ahead. Assuming the insurance quote is at an arm's-length commercial rate, the MNE does not need to actually take out the insurance when executing the project – the inclusion of the notional insurance cost is equivalent to doing a probability adjustment to the cash flows. (By 'arm's-length commercial rate' I mean a rate not subsidised by a government or trade support agency.)

Proprietary Systems

Another strategy to reduce the risk of an investment project being expropriated by a host country is to ensure that some element of proprietary input is needed for the project to work efficiently. For example, an automated factory might only work with computer systems that are owned and run from a server based in the MNE's home country. The factory in the host country cannot operate without these systems. Thus, if the host country's government seizes the assets it will be unable to operate them without the co-operation of the MNE as the systems driving the automation are located outside the host's jurisdiction.

Local Labour

The employment of local labour in the host country can be a useful strategy to minimise expropriation risk. However, while local employees can exert pressure on their government, as we saw in **Example 12.1** above, this strategy has limited effectiveness as the government may keep on the employees post-expropriation, thus reducing their efficacy as objectors.

Drawing Cash Quickly

It may seem obvious, but a risk of expropriation can be minimised by extracting as much cash as possible from the enterprise as quickly as possible. However, such harvesting of cash might be counter-productive because local management may become disenchanted with being starved of cash and performance can be adversely affected.

Many MNEs will allow some cash build-up in subsidiaries so that working capital and replacement capital expenditure can be financed locally, i.e. in the host country. As we have seen, using locally generated funds can reduce foreign exchange exposure risk. Therefore, minimising foreign exposure risk by allowing a build-up of cash in the foreign subsidiary can have a counter-weighing effect on the strategy for minimising expropriation risk through withdrawing cash quickly. Each MNE will need to weigh up the advantages and disadvantages of each approach depending on each unique set of circumstances.

---

12 *Seanad Éireann Debates*, Vol. 199, No. 5, Export Credit Insurance, 9 December 2009.

12.3 CULTURAL DIFFERENCES

In this chapter we have thus far focused on political risk. However, the MNE needs to assess the sensitivity of its predicted cash flows to other risk categories, such as the risks arising from cultural differences, and adjust the expected cash flows if necessary. We have discussed earlier in this chapter how political risk can be analysed by assessing and scoring the host country's attributes across a number of criteria. In particular, you will have noticed that some countries' propensity to corruption is higher than others. This propensity can be explained by cultural and structural differences that exist across different nations. Cultural differences extend beyond corruption and bribery. Indeed, the impact of the wider cultural differences upon an MNE's future activities will most likely be much more far-reaching than the corruption dimension alone. This means that an MNE must be cognisant of the cultural differences that exist between its operating locations. In addition, it must find some way of assessing the economic impact such cultural difference will have on future cash flows.

Different countries have different approaches to similar issues. Cultural differences can cause unforeseen deviations from forecasted cash flows unless the MNE's management makes itself aware of these cultural differences and factors them into the NPV analysis in some way. The cultural risk can be broken down into two areas:
- corporate culture internal to the MNE; and
- country culture.

We will cover corporate culture in more detail later in the next chapter (see **Chapter 13**, "Implementing Change in an International Environment"). Suffice to say at this juncture that an MNE cannot presuppose that organisational performance levels achieved in existing operations will be achieved in the new investment project being appraised, even with appropriate training. The MNE must be realistic when assessing the likelihood that the corporate culture of the existing organisation will be positively received and implemented in any new venture it invests in.

While stereotypes and generalisations are to be discouraged, it is fantasy to believe in the existence of an homogeneous global consumer market. While it is true that some global consumer brands have been able to achieve global market share, the success of Apple's iPhone springs to mind, even the ubiquitous iPhone has flexibility built into its design to cater for cultural differences. At its simplest, the user can choose the language that the iPhone's menus appear in. Apple realised that having a purely English-language device would not gain traction globally. It needed to provide an easy way for a user's own language to be incorporated into each device. In this way, Apple provided a route to gaining global traction through the customisation of its products for local cultural differences, in this case language, so that it broadened the appeal of its products. The truly global consumer market is still some time away.

It can be easier to forecast the effect of cultural differences upon the level of risk in capital investment appraisal when considering the end-user consumer market. It is much more difficult when considering the business operating environment and its impact. By this I mean that consumer behaviours can, to a certain degree, be predicted through the carrying out of appropriate market research and product testing. It is more challenging to figure out how the culture in a country will affect the efficacy of the MNE's operations, its management practices and the implementation of its action plans and processes. Business protocols differ widely across countries. Working hours, commercial etiquette and adherence to agreements are all treated differently in different parts of the world. Thus, the MNE manager must factor all of these nuances into their consideration of an investment's forecasted cash flows. While easier said than done, this is still possible.

Managers can research practices in the host country. They can involve themselves in trade associations and bilateral trade organisations. Through this type of networking an appreciation can be developed that allows managers to prepare their cash flows with greater understanding of the cultural nuances of the host country. The social psychologist Geert Hofstede provides useful comparative indicators for the cultural differences between countries.[13] These indicators can be used to assess the risks associated with certain cultural norms. (We go into more detail about how Geert Hofstede's research can be used in **Chapter 13**.

In the early 1990s when Musgrave Plc, an Irish-based multinational wholesale grocer, was considering an investment in Poland, it needed to assess the cultural risk attached to the potential investment. The nascent MNE sent executives to Poland to explore the business and consumer culture there at the time. The Zloty was not freely floating and many bureaucratic practices remained from the communist era.

The business proposition was extremely attractive, but the company felt that the cultural risk was too high and the investment proposal was rejected. Essentially, decades of communism had stifled the entrepreneurial flair of the Polish populace. The Musgrave model required an entrepreneur to operate the retail consumer-facing franchise, but the company felt that there would not be a ready supply of such entrepreneurs so soon after the fall of communism.

Cultural Differences and Risk

How does an MNE manager factor cultural risk into the investment appraisal process? One way of factoring in cultural risk is by adjusting the projected cash flows to take account of the probabilities of various outcomes. As mentioned before in this chapter, this can be done by applying probability ratios to expected cash flows. Another approach is to carry out sensitivity analysis, which necessitates the production of a number of NPV calculations for each analysed scenario. The MNE then considers each scenario and assesses it on the basis of the likelihood of its occurrence. For example, if the MNE has three possible ranges of cash flow, depending on different impacts of cultural issues, then it could either:
1. adjust the cash flows for the probability of each possible outcome; or
2. calculate three separate NPVs for each possibility and consider the results.

Where the second method is used, if all three NPVs were positive, then the project should go ahead. But what would happen if two were positive and the third was negative? The MNE would need to weigh up the likelihood of the third possibility occurring. In such a case the first method might produce a clearer answer. By adjusting the expected cash flows by the rates generated in the probability analysis, a clear positive or negative NPV will result. The MNE can then decide whether or not to proceed. The probability adjustments to the cash flows factor in all possibilities. If the outcome is a positive NPV, then the benefits of the two positive NPV scenarios calculated using the second method outweigh the negative of the third possible outcome, and the investment should proceed. In other words, if when using the second method some options produce positive NPVs and some produce negative NPVs, it is best to redo the NPV calculation using the first method, that is, the probability-adjusted cash flow NPV.

In **Example 12.6** below Bonnie Plc foresees three possible scenarios from its possible investment in Zedmania, each of which has a probability ascribed to it. Bonnie will produce cash flow

---

[13] See http://www.geerthofstede.nl/

projections for each of the three scenarios and then adjust the cash-flow projections to take account of their respective probabilities of occurrence.

EXAMPLE 12.6: CULTURAL ISSUES AND PROBABILITY ANALYSIS

Bonnie Plc, a Beeland company, is considering an investment in Zedmania. (Bonnie's discount rate for this type of investment project is 12%.) It assesses that the consumers in Zedmania might have resistance to its products. It foresees three possible outcomes:
1. Consumers reject Bonnie's price proposition and sales volumes per citizen will be 66% lower than in Buroland: 10% likelihood.
2. Some consumers will reject the proposition and sales will be 25% lower per citizen than in Buroland: 30% likelihood.
3. The products will be a success and sales per citizen will be comparable to Buroland: 60% likelihood.

Bonnie Plc prepares cash flow forecasts for each of the three scenarios. It then applies the probability ratio to each of the cash flow forecasts, i.e. multiply Cashflow Forecast 1 by 10%, Forecast 2 by 30%, and Forecast 3 by 60%. The adjusted cash flow forecasts are aggregated. The aggregated, probability-adjusted cash flows are discounted back by 12% and the NPV calculated. If the resultant NPV is positive, the investment project should proceed.

The other approach Bonnie could have used would be to perform three NPV calculations, one for each possible cash flow forecast. If all three were positive, then the project should proceed. If only two were positive, a judgement call would need to be made.

12.4 MISALIGNMENT OF GOALS BETWEEN PARENT AND SUBSIDIARY

As we saw in **Chapter 2**, agency theory explores the nature of the challenges that exist when the goals of an MNE and its stakeholders, especially shareholders, are out of alignment with the goals of its management. In the final analysis, all companies are run by people. All added value within an MNE originates with the spark of effort, motivation or energy of its people. When companies are run, managed and owned by the same person or group of people, agency theory does not present a major consideration. As companies grow, however, their ownership becomes divorced from their management, and managers can begin to further their own goals, sometimes justifying their actions to themselves and others as being in the best interest of the shareholders. Assurance of congruence between an MNE's goals and its management's goals is a key feature of good corporate governance.

The expansion internationally of firms presents a major risk of the relationship between the principals (the shareholders) and the agents (the MNE's management) becoming strained and conflicted. As MNEs grow, the distance, and therefore connection, both emotional and physical, between the shareholders and the management becomes stretched. Greater effort must be put in to the relationship by both parties to ensure alignment of goals. These tensions have become more pronounced in the last five decades as MNEs have grown in size and complexity (see **Appendix C.3**). This is especially so as movement of capital has become increasingly liberated. Improvements in communications systems, such as telephone and email, have helped alleviate the problem to some extent. These systems have helped subsidiaries, parent companies and shareholders to have greater communication than was the case in the past.

Take, for example, a retail MNE considering investing in a new opportunity in Italy, which it hopes will bring growth as well as a sense of excitement to the company. The organisation will be bigger, its reach will be further, the complexity greater and salaries will increase to compensate. However, the shareholders could possibly achieve the same results by investing in the new proposition directly themselves. They could buy the Italian chain directly themselves and not have the MNE, which they already own, complicate their structures by buying a business in a new international market. They do not need to use the original MNE as a vehicle for their investment. Therefore, it is critical that the MNE's management can explain not only that there are good returns to be generated from the new investment but also why the MNE should carry it out on behalf of the shareholders.

These reasons will need to be either that:
• the value of the existing MNE will be enhanced (e.g. by securing a source of supply at a preferential rate); or
• the MNE can extract more value from the investment than stand-alone investors.

Having made an investment for the right reasons an MNE can still find some of the possible ill effects of conflicts that arise in agency–principal relationships, which can impact upon its results. Just as the goals and motivations of an MNE's management can be misaligned with the shareholders' goals, so too can the goals of a subsidiary become misaligned with the goals of its parent. Most MNEs adopt a philosophy of delegating as much decision-making authority as possible to divisional management. Management practice over the decades has shown that this type of organisational system delivers a sense of ownership to local management and a responsiveness to local market issues that is difficult to achieve with a more centralised organisation structure.[14] For example, it would be difficult, if not impossible, for Kerry Group to manage its Brazilian operation entirely from Tralee, County Kerry. It must delegate some measure of authority to the local management.

But with delegation comes a cost. Local managers will want to do what is right for their division, their customers and their local market. Their individual goals can become the drivers of their behaviour and they can subordinate group goals to their own local goals, which can present a risk to the MNE. These risks are particularly prevalent in capital budgeting. In short, management's actions locally can work against the optimisation of shareholder returns.

When assessing an investment opportunity, the MNE must factor in considerations pertaining to the parent–subsidiary relationship. It should adjust its cash flows to best incorporate how these matters can impact upon those cash flows. For example, learning-curve assumptions could be adjusted, replacement capital expenditures increased or costs added to the project cash flows to cover management training and group-integration planning. Whatever approach is used to mitigate the effects of a misalignment of subsidiary goals with parent company goals, there is attendant risk and it must be considered in forecasting the cash flows and carrying out the investment appraisal.

---

[14] Bloom, N., Sadun, R. and Van Reenen, J. (2012), "The Organisation of Firms across Countries", *Quarterly Journal of Economics*, 127(4) 1663–1705.

12.5 CONCLUSION

In this chapter we have examined factors of a non-financial nature that need to be factored into investment appraisal by an MNE when considering a new investment opportunity. The main ones considered in the chapter were:
- political risk;
- cultural differences; and
- misalignment of goals between parent and subsidiary.

While these risks are difficult to quantify, we explored ways in which an MNE can attempt to measure risk of this nature and factor it into its appraisal processes. I encouraged MNEs to adjust the impacted elements of their cash flows using probability analysis to account for such risks. Alternatively, an MNE could adjust the discount factor. We also looked at how MNEs can adopt strategies that reduce political risk through financial structures or insurance.

In the next chapter we will examine how change is implemented in an MNE. Implementing change is difficult in all organisations but especially so in an MNE. This is because the international dimension of the organisation introduces complexities that create new challenges to change implementation. **Chapter 13** will explore techniques and approaches that the MNE can adopt to anticipate and overcome these challenges.

QUESTIONS

Self-test Questions

12.1   You are the financial controller of an Irish company considering a new investment opportunity in Belarus. How would you go about assessing the political risk attached to the project?

12.2   Sleeptight Hotels, a Belfast-based chain, has a hotel in Venezuela. It is concerned that it will be expropriated in two years' time but that compensation of £50 million will be paid. If the hotel is not expropriated it will be worth £200 million two years from now. An investor has offered to buy the hotel from Sleeptight for £80 million. Sleeptight uses 23% as its discount rate for hotels in South America when no expropriation risk is present. Evaluate whether Sleeptight should sell the hotel now.

12.3   How would you combine probability analysis into cash flow forecasts?

12.4   Name one source of objective data concerning political risk for a given country.

Thought-provoking Questions

Question 12.1

You are CFO of the European division of US-owned Good Banana Inc. Your company is considering buying a banana plantation in Honduras using retained earnings from the US dollar denominated company to finance the investment. The CEO of Good Banana wishes to run the new investment from the Irish division. Advise of the relevant risks that should be factored into the appraisal process and of strategies to mitigate those risks.

Question 12.2

You are the newly recruited management accountant for Big Dog Plc, the master franchise holder of a fast-food outlet. Big Dog assesses international expansion investment projects using a discount factor of 16%. Big Dog is considering expanding into Syria. It has produced the following cash flow projections:

(Numbers in €000s)
Year 0 Investment (€5,000)
Year 1 Inflow   800
Year 2 Inflow   900
Year 3 Inflow   980

It can sell the operation to a franchisee at the end of Year 3 for €4,500.

Big Dog believes that there is a 20% chance that at the end of Year 2 the business will be expropriated and that it will receive €3,000 compensation. Advise your new employer as to the best course of action; proceed with the investment or not.

Review Questions

(See Suggested Solutions to Review Questions in **Appendix B**.)

Question 12.1: BoneDri

Having read the BoneDri case study in **Appendix A**, what are the operational challenges that would need to be considered and planned for should BoneDri choose to establish a production facility in Bangladesh?

Question 12.2: Pillar Bank Plc

Having read the Pillar Bank Plc case study in **Appendix A**, discuss the challenges that Pillar Bank Plc might face in managing an overseas outsourcing contract and identify the steps it could take to address those challenges.

Question 12.3: Hughes Engineering Limited

Having read the Hughes Engineering Limited case study in **Appendix A**, discuss the practical issues Hughes Engineering Limited would need to consider in carrying out the project if it was successful in its bid to supply and install specialised machinery for ADP's new plant.

Question 12.4: Black Swan Inc

Having read the Black Swan Inc case study in **Appendix A**, detail the benefits and risks for Black Swan Inc of setting up a shared services centre.

Question 12.5: Trident Mobile Ltd

Having read the Trident Mobile Ltd case study in **Appendix A**, discuss the main operational and logistical issues for Trident Mobile Ltd in relation to setting up a new business in Kenya.

Question 12.6: Smart Bathroom Fittings Ltd

Having read the Smart Bathroom Fittings Ltd case study in **Appendix A**, discuss the practical cultural issues likely to arise when doing business in South Africa.

13

IMPLEMENTING CHANGE IN AN INTERNATIONAL CONTEXT

CONTENTS

LEARNING OBJECTIVES

Having read this chapter, you will understand:
- how to describe the main change theories of organisational change, including the McKinsey 7-S Model, the Nadler and Tushman and Burke and Litwin models, as well as Greiner's growth model;
- how to apply these theories to practical situations;
- the difference between planned change and emergent change;
- the roles of managers in MNEs in implementing change; and
- how to overcome challenges presented when implementing change in an MNE.

13.1 INTRODUCTION

In earlier chapters we examined the nature of MNEs and how international trade has grown, particularly in recent decades. We were introduced to some of the challenges that MNEs face, such as managing foreign exchange and assessing international capital investment opportunities. In the previous chapter I examined how non-financial issues, such as political instability, can be assessed and subsequently managed when appraising international invest-ments. In this chapter, we will now move on to consider how managers in an MNE can approach managing change in their organisations.

'Change is constant.' This seemingly contradictory phrase is heard in boardrooms and management conferences throughout the world. The increased pace of change has presented problems for businesses and has challenged pre-existing management theories in ways that were never envisaged.

Another phrase one might hear in a boardroom today is: 'If it's not broken, break it.' The essence of this expression is that if you think you do not need to change, you are wrong. 'Break' what you are doing in order to force yourself to change.

The harbingers of such change might just be consultancy firms selling services and programs to 'improve' your organisation. Three-letter acronyms such as TQM (total quality management), BPR (business process re-engineering) and ERP (enterprise resource planning) litter the inboxes of executives in today's MNE environment. There is a lot of 'noise' out there about noise, but is it really necessary?

Table 13.1 below shows the top 10 companies in the world according to *Fortune* magazine's Global 500 listing. Fortune rank the companies based on global revenue. Only two of the companies from the list in 1995 make it onto the list in 2014. The major Japanese corporations that peppered the 1995 list have disappeared from the list and Chinese companies, non-existent on the 1995 top 10, have now appeared on it. (Apple are just outside the Global top 10 at number 15.)

Based on this relatively crude listing, one can see that there is a lot of change, at least in the fortunes of the top 10 companies. Walmart's rise to the top is a direct result of its international expansion. In 1995 it was ranked 12th and in the intervening 19 years it has grown internationally to become a huge MNE and the world's largest company according to this table.

Of course, there are many ways to measure the size of a company. One could use market capitalisation, profits, number of employees or turnover. Whichever metric is used, the same answer will endure: the top 10 companies today are significantly different from the top 10 companies of two decades ago. The nature of change is such that this changed ranking applies throughout the world's corporations. It is indeed true that 'change is constant'.

TABLE 13.1: FORTUNE 500 GLOBAL TOP TEN 1995 V. 2014[1]

1995	2014
Mitsubishi	Walmart
Mitsui	Royal Dutch Shell
Itochu	Sinopec Group
Sumitomo	China Natural Petroleum
General Motors	Exxon Mobil
Marubeni Corporation	BP
Ford Motor Company	State Grid
Exxon Corporation	Volkswagen
Nisho Iwai	Toyota
Royal Dutch Shell	Glencore

---

[1] *Fortune* magazine's Global 500, www.fortune.com/global500/ (accessed June 2015).

But why is this? Why are companies that had the ability to grow and reach the top of the world rankings foundering only to be replaced by other companies that were not even 'on the radar' 20 years earlier? We will seek to answer this question in this chapter, to understand the nature of change, explore some theories about change management and look, finally, at how one implements change in an MNE.

13.2 FACTORS AFFECTING ORGANISATIONAL CHANGE

In this section we will discuss some of the factors driving organisational change, factors that have not yet been covered in this textbook. There are other external factors that also drive change and these have been discussed in their relevant chapters. This chapter is predominantly concerned with the 'human' aspect of managing change. We will explore here how managers deal with change and, particularly, the unique challenges that international organisations can present; how staff, customers, technology and legislation can drive the need for organisational change in an MNE. I will examine these drivers of change, paying particular attention to how they introduce complexity for the MNE manager, which flows from the fact that the same approaches to management challenges and change will not necessarily work throughout the globe.

Different countries require different responses and this can impact upon standardised approaches to business process and people management. The less the degree of standardisation in an MNE the more difficult it is to achieve some economies of scale, such as standardised operating procedures. The benefits of economies of scale, as we saw in **Chapter 2**, are often the reason for becoming an MNE in the first place. Therefore, it is crucial that an MNE can anticipate the variations to its policies and processes that will be required as it endeavours to introduce and manage change throughout the organisation.

Staff

An organisation is made up of people: its customers are people, its suppliers are people, and so forth. Business involves people and people change. For example, people change their jobs. Even if nothing else changed, the effect of staff joining and leaving companies produces changes that are difficult to assess and quantify. The staff turnover ratio for the *Fortune* 100 Best Companies to Work For in the US is 13%, meaning that 13% of employees leave each year. After eight years on average, there will be no one left in the organisation who was there eight years earlier and this dynamic is also happening in the companies with which each firm is interacting.

When someone joins a company, they bring with them something of their own history. They have learned how to apply their skills somewhere else. They have gained their competency in a different organisational environment. When someone leaves an organisation, some of the company's history goes with them. This is true irrespective of the level the person was at in the organisation. In whatever capacity, that person was serving the shareholders' need for wealth growth through adding value for the customer.

Some of the practices companies use to try to minimise the impact of staff turnover include:
- structured induction programmes;
- recruiting people that exhibit similar behaviours as the existing cadre of staff; many MNEs will have formally described the behaviour attributes that they expect employees to exhibit.

To minimise disruption when people leave they seek out new staff members that exhibit these traits and behaviour patterns;

- conducting exit interviews to see why people leave; and
- improving employment conditions to encourage people to stay.

The attempt to institutionalise the expected behaviours and knowledge base of an organisation is an understandable and well-intentioned goal. It is, however, a double-edged sword. By trying to preserve an organisation's *esprit de corps*, the company must stipulate how things are to be done, the behaviours expected and the procedures to be followed. This institutionalisation of behaviours can also lead to a resistance to change and, at its worst, an inability to change and a lack of innovation.

On the other hand, if an MNE adopts a *laissez faire* approach it can find that employees feel the company stands for nothing at all, that is has no core purpose or codified expectations of behaviour. The organisation will become known for a lack of consistency in its approach to customers, products and quality.

The following is a statement from the values section of an infamous company's corporate website: "a 'global corporate citizen' this company intends to conduct itself in accord with four capital-V Values: Respect, Integrity, Communication and Excellence".

Can you guess the company?[2]

The task of MNE management is to find the magic combination that ensures the desired balance between prescribing behaviours and competence while still retaining adaptability. Organisations attempt to do this by defining their values. Through defining values they outline clearly the underlying behavioural principles they wish to exhibit in the global marketplace. The problem is that these value statements can often be generic, vague or meaningless. We will see later on in this chapter how MNEs can come to grips with these challenges and avoid trying to foster a corporate culture and adaptability to change without being trite and ineffective.

National Culture and the Customer

Taken collectively, the aggregate of the needs and wants of a population and its societal mores can be described as its 'culture'. In the previous chapter we explored how varying cultures across different countries produced behavioural differences, which could impact upon an MNE's projected performance outcomes in the different regions in which it operates. We considered how these different possible outcomes could affect investment appraisal and how an MNE could factor in some of these uncertainties concerning cultural behaviours into its investment appraisal processes. Using research that compares countries cultural attributes across a number of criteria the MNE can help anticipate possible cultural impacts upon its projected outcomes. The same approach can be taken when considering how to manage change in an MNE and we will examine later in this chapter how an MNE can use research to plan for the unique challenges that executing change in an MNE brings.

---

2 Enron. See www.nytimes.com/2002/01/19/opinion/enron-s-vision-and-values-thing.html (accessed August 2015).

> *"When I was a child, I spoke as a child, I understood as a child, I thought as a child. When I became a man, I put away childish things."*
>
> Corinthians 13:11

We all change. Our needs change. As we get older, we mature, we desire and need different things. Since the global market is made up of people and people age, their needs are constantly changing. Even if there were no new technologies, markets would change by the force of changing demographics alone. Some countries, mainly in the developed world, have populations where the percentage of older people is increasing. In other countries, it is the percentage of younger people that is increasing. These increases are being brought about as infant mortality is tackled and health systems improve. Some developed countries are not replacing their deaths with births and their populations are falling. Other countries face the opposite challenge where their infrastructure and resources cannot cope with their growing populations. These changes in countries' demographics affect customer make up and bring about changes for global producers of goods and services, and the markets upon which they must focus their efforts.

As populations develop and grow, they also change. Subsistence farmers living in grinding poverty focus on getting through the day with enough food and water to survive. As such peoples develop and their standards of living improve, their expectations change. Their desires and needs change, becoming more complex and demanding and they increasingly become greater consumers of resources. MNEs provide returns to their shareholders by meeting these changing needs on a global basis. The MNE that can best provide for the needs of the changing consumer will succeed.

A MNE must adapt to more of these customer- and culture-driven changes than a purely domestic firm because it operates in more markets. One of the keys to understanding how to adapt to a country's culture is to have some construct or model that enables a MNE to understand different cultures and compare them to each other and to its home country's culture. Using such a model can help the MNE to quantify the nature of the challenges and opportunities presented by cultural differences and act accordingly.

There are many models of cultural difference. All of them seek to analyse a country's culture into identifiable dimensions that can be measured. For the purposes of our discussion, we will explore one such model. I have chosen the Geert Hofstede Six Dimensions Model as it has a large amount of supporting data for its findings and is readily accessible. Other models may be equally valid and all broadly attempt to achieve the same thing, i.e. inform decision-makers about likely differences between countries and cultures. Another model often used in business contexts is Trompenaars' Model of National Cultural Differences, developed by Fons Trompenaars and Charles Hampden-Turner.[3]

The Geert Hofstede Six Dimensions Model

Geert Hofstede, a Dutch academic and social psychologist, analysed how workplace values are influenced by national culture. He studied thousands of employee assessments carried out by IBM between 1967 and 1973, eventually covering 50 countries, and developed a model that could be used to measure culture in differing countries on a number of dimensions. He first identified four dimensions and, as further research was carried out, this expanded into six dimensions. Hofstede has always stressed that the country scores, of themselves, are meaningless; it is the comparison of one country to another that brings insights.

---

[3] Trompenaars, F. and Hampden-Turner, C. (1997) *Riding the Waves of Culture: Understanding Cultural Diversity in Global Business*. 2nd Edition, McGraw-Hill.

Hofstede's original analysis proposed that a county's culture could be statistically measured across four identifiably different dimensions. These four dimensions, called the Hofstede dimensions, are:
- power distance (PDI)
- individualism versus collectivism (IDV)
- masculinity versus femininity (MAS)
- uncertainty avoidance (UAI).

In the early 1990s, a fifth dimension was added, long-term orientation (LTO), following research by Michael Harris Bond, which involved surveys developed with the aid of Chinese academics. The surveys resulted in assessments on the LTO for an initial 23 countries.

By 2010 further research had been carried out by Michael Minkov. One of the outcomes of this more extensive work by Minkov was to replace the fifth dimension, LTO, with a broadly similar dimension, pragmatic v normative. Because of the extensive nature of Minkov's research, the fifth dimension could now be applied to 92 countries. Minkov's research also allowed the addition of a sixth dimension, indulgence v. restraint (IND). This sixth dimension could also be applied to the 93 countries that Minkov had statistical data for resulting from his research.

So, with the additional research carried over the years, especially by Minkov, Hofstede's original four dimensions have now become six.[4]

Hofstede's model is useful for understanding cultural difference between countries, not just for customers but also staff and suppliers. It can also be helpful in understanding the nature of political risk and country risk.

An MNE can use Hofstede's dimensions to compare different countries' values across the six dimensions. Such a comparison will allow the MNE to attempt to predict how its business model might be affected by the differences in cultural norms that exist between different countries. (**Chapter 18** provides some practical examples of how an MNE can use Hofstede's Six Dimensions Model in structuring performance measurement systems.)

In considering the nature of change for a MNE, one can see that cultural differences between the countries in which an MNE operates bring about the need for change. These changes may be needed in the products or services offered by the MNE or in its management practices or business models. The differences between countries means that the MNE is unlikely to be progressing its development at the same rate in each and every country in which it operates. The business model will be at different stages of evolution and development in each market because all business is a function of an interaction between the internal world of the business and the external world of its customers, suppliers and wider society. As consumption patterns change and alter across the MNE's business units, the overall make-up of the MNE's cash flows also changes. These changes alter the proportion of each country's share of the aggregate cash flow of the MNE, resulting in cash flow mixes that are constantly changing.

Technology

One of the key drivers of change for MNEs has been changes in available technology. For example, technological developments have allowed the greater integration of large

---

4 Hofstede, G., Hofstede, G.J. and Minkov, M (2010) *Cultures and Organizations: Software of the Mind.* Revised and Expanded 3rd Edition. New York: McGraw-Hill.

organisations, making them more manageable. Indeed, deregulation and liberalisation of the world's markets aside, it is difficult to see how MNEs of the size of today's largest corporations could be run without the Internet, broadband and other modern communication systems.

While the development of communications technology has been an enabler for the growth of MNEs, it has also created more competition. The speed to market has increased, thus increasing the need for responsiveness from MNEs. This itself brings about a need for change in the organisation.

New ways of meeting the age-old needs of consumers have also been brought about through new technologies. For example, cars satisfy a consumer's need for individual mobility in the way a horse may have done in the past. Mobile phones satisfy a consumer's need to communicate with people who are far away in the way smoke signals may have done in distant times. Technology has also created new consumer demand for products and services that did not exist before, e.g. the development of the camera brought about an entirely new consumer market for the taking of photographs and their subsequent display; the development of MP3 players created the market for downloadable music. The combination of mobile phone technologies, MP3 players and mobile broadband has created the market for music-streaming services, a market that did not exist in 2010. (Of course, all of these music systems are meeting the basic human need to either create or listen to music and rhythm.)

Thus, we can see that the need for organisations to change and adapt to new technology comes both from increased demand for goods and services and increased efficiency in operations derived from enabling technologies. Failure to anticipate and subsequently adapt to these changes is a route to decline.

Legislation

The final important source of change a MNE should consider are changes to the legislative codes in the countries in which it operates, which can require the organisation to implement new ways of doing things. They can also impact upon the returns available to shareholders, challenging some of the assumptions made when the original investments were made. For example, an increase in corporation taxes in a country will reduce the return available to the parent company.

EXAMPLE 13.1: SOUTH AFRICA AND RACIAL QUOTAS

The introduction of legally enforced racial quotas can mean a company will need to change its recruitment process and its workforce make-up. For example, in South Africa, the Employment Equity Act seeks to promote the advancement of people 'of colour, women and people with disabilities'. The Act requires organisations that employ more than 50 people to have action plans to improve the representation of the aforementioned groups in the workplace. They must also register these action plans with the SA Department of Labour. The action plans, and existing employment demographics, feed into a numerical scoring system, the Black Economic Empowerment scorecard. This scorecard is a factor in a company's ability to win government tenders. Therefore, an MNE that acquires an enterprise in South Africa will need to ensure that its action plans for the business incorporate the addressing of any issues that may flow from this legislation.

While many countries do not allow any discrimination between employees or job applicants on the grounds of gender, race or religion, many countries do. Those countries that do allow discrimination have programs that encourage such discrimination on the basis of 'affirmative action', i.e. discrimination in favour of a perceived minority or disadvantaged group. Countries with such programs included, Canada, Israel, India and Germany. In Northern Ireland there is a requirement to monitor and submit an annual census of the 'community background' and gender make-up of an employer's workforce. This census must also include an analysis of 'leavers' and those promoted. Where an employer's workforce demographics are out of alignment with the demographic of the community from which the workforce is drawn, the employer must take corrective actions to address the misalignment.[5] An MNE needs to be able to adapt to these changes and respond in a way that ensures the shareholders' interests are preserved whilst complying with the laws in each country in which it operates.

13.3 ORGANISATIONAL IMPLICATIONS OF CHANGE

We have seen how the environment in which an MNE operates is affected by changes to people, national cultures, technology and legislation. These change dimensions are similar to those one considers in carrying out a PESTEL (political, economic, social, technological and legal) analysis when contemplating expansion into a new market. (See **Chapter 7** for further details. See also Chapter 5 of Gallagher G., *Corporate Strategy for Irish Companies* (2nd Edition, Chartered Accountants Ireland, 2011).) This is because the attributes that make a market attractive for an MNE are, almost by definition, the same ones that, when they change, will bring about a need for change in the organisation.

If it is so straightforward to analyse the dimensions of change, then why do MNEs struggle to identify and adapt to these changes? In April 2011, Pascal Visee wrote in the *McKinsey Quarterly*: "Sometimes, multinationals mandate globally scaled solutions that cater to a theoretical average but have little relevance locally. Other times, multinationals tailor solutions too much to each local subsidiary's specific circumstances. Predictably, many of the scaling benefits and cost savings evaporate."[6]

Throughout this textbook I have emphasised balance and equilibrium. Shareholders balance their aversion to risk with their need for a return. The foreign exchange markets set exchange rates at the equilibrium point of supply and demand for a given currency. The same is true for a marketplace and the organisations that operate in it. The employees in an organisation at any moment in time are there because it meets their needs for employment, job satisfaction, work–life balance, challenge, etc. at that stage in their lives. Customers buy an MNE's goods and services because, at the specific price at that moment in time, it meets their needs.

However, such equilibrium points can shift and change. A customer may find that she can meet the same need at a lower price elsewhere – her equilibrium point changes, which does not mean that the equilibrium point for the business's employees will shift at the same time. For example, a checkout operator's pay does not drop just because an individual customer did not buy carrots this week because she found them too expensive. Indeed, the checkout operator's pay may not drop the

[5] www.equalityni.org/employers-service-providers/large-business/registration-and-monitoring/affirmative-action (accessed June 2015).
[6] Visee, P. (2015), "The globally effective enterprise", *McKinsey Quarterly*, April.

following week either when the customer this time rejects both the carrot and cucumber buying propositions. In this example, the changing behaviour of the customer does not impact upon the staff member, and if one multiplies this instance across the business's hundreds of employees and hundreds of thousands of transactions, it becomes apparent that the equilibrium of the business has established a degree of inertia, an inability to change quickly to changing demands.

The more complex an organisation's structure and business model the more difficult it will be to adapt to change (see **Appendix C.3**). At a granular level, an employee may not even care too much. Taking our example above to its extreme, the checkout operator will just apply for a new job in the fast-growing superstore that has just opened down the road. Accordingly, the organisation must find ways to adapt to change and to encourage its staff to embrace this change. For that to happen, its management must understand:

- the nature of change; and
- how to implement change in organisations.

We will examine these two topics in detail in the remainder of this chapter.

13.4 THE NATURE OF ORGANISATIONAL CHANGE

A theory is a structured explanation of how a system will change in response to a given impetus or stimulus. In this section, we consider a number of theories that have been developed concerning organisational change, theories which we would expect will help us to understand how an organisation will respond if certain stimuli act upon it. We would also expect that such theories will explain how and why one organisation is different from another.

As organisations are made up of people, theories of organisational change must explain **how** individuals change, **what** motivates them to change and **why** some people are more open to change than others. Organisational change theories also draw on knowledge of how individuals behave in groups, why people behave differently in groups and how group-change processes can be developed to produce better decision-making than can be achieved at the individual level.

While thinking and theories about change in organisations must incorporate both individual and group approaches to change, it must also be greater than the sum of these. This is because organisations (in this case MNEs) have many more stakeholders than just the individuals of which they are comprised. When taking a holistic view of an organisation one considers all the stakeholders, from the shareholders who own the MNE to the communities in which the MNE operates and the customers it serves.

To understand how all these elements interact with an organisation and how organisational change is thus brought about, it is useful to think of an organisation as an **open system**. Let us consider the two elements of this phrase.

Organisations as 'Systems'

First, a 'system' can be thought of as an arrangement of interconnected elements that, taken together, form a whole. The whole has its own identity and is not just an aggregate of the individual components, i.e. the system is greater than the sum of its parts. 'Greater' in this context does not necessarily mean 'superior'; it means that the system stands for something different to, and apart from, the individual elements taken at a granular level.

One often sees this concept in action in sporting contexts. For example, the Irish rugby team has an identity of its own that is different from, although comprising, the 15 people who are on the field at any one time. There are the other squad members, the backroom staff, the coaching specialists, the fans, the heritage, etc., all of which combine to make up what is the Irish rugby team. The team excels when the performance of the group is superior to the aggregate performance of the individuals. The team does not just go out on the pitch on its own. It needs to interact with other teams in order to perform. In this way, the team, the organisational system, is an **open** system, which is the second concept I want to introduce regarding organisational change theories.

Open and Closed Systems

Systems can be open or closed. In a closed system, the elements only interact with each other. In scientific experiments researchers often try to create closed systems so they can examine the interaction between one element of the system and another with no interference from external sources or other systems.

Organisations, on the other hand, are open systems. They are exposed to external stimuli from many sources external to the organisation system itself. For example, customers may demand greater quality, legislators can impose new regulations and competitors can sell similar products more cheaply. Therefore we describe an organisation as an open system, responding to stimuli from both (e.g. staff) internal and external sources (e.g. technology).

Systems Thinking

Open systems exist within a wider world system: a global set of open systems and sub-systems all interacting and reacting to each other in a constant state of flux. Thinking about organisations as open systems has allowed MNE managers to direct increasingly complex tasks and goals. This increased managerial competence has no doubt enabled MNEs to have an even greater reach than before.

When applying systems theory to change management we need to highlight that:
• A system comprises interdependent elements, whose interdependency requires the system to be thought of as a whole.
• The 'whole' system cannot be thought of as acting on its own – the organisational system itself is an element in a wider system.
• Each element within an organisational system will have a different view of what the system's goals are and of how it interacts with the other systems that exist in its operating environment.

There is a danger in organisational change management to forget that the theories and their attendant models are constructed approaches to thinking that allow us to understand organisations. MNE managers can be tempted into trying to make the organisation fit the theory rather than understanding that the theory is a construct to enable understanding.

The temptation to try to make an organisation fit the model increases as it becomes larger. Large MNEs will have many subsystems across the globe. They also have high degrees of functional specialisation. Often, while the human resource specialists know most about organisational change theory, they may not know much about the actual reality of the organisation's operations. In these situations, where the change theory experts are removed from the reality, their good intentions can founder as they try to impose theoretical change models.

Having considered this word of caution, we now move on to look at some change models.

Models of Organisational Change

When an architect is designing a building she will often make a small balsa wood model of it. In recent years, advances in technology have allowed designers to build three dimensional simulations of their projects on their computers. Magical virtual flying cameras whizz us through the rooms of the building, fly us high above for aerial views and help us picture what rooms would look like with a bigger door, smaller windows or purple walls. Such is our delight at seeing these virtual 3D architectural models that they feature heavily in TV design shows, such as Channel 4's *Grand Designs* and RTÉ's *Room to Improve*.

Organisational-change models will aid an MNE manager's understanding of the dynamics of its organisation and will help them identify the drivers of change and simulate change programmes in order to increase the chances of success. Remember: the best managers are those who can predict the consequences of their actions.

We will now look at some models of organisational change and how an MNE can use these models to improve decision-making within the organisation. These models are chosen as they have relatively widespread use in commercial environments, especially in MNEs. We will further examine how the models and frameworks can be used to manage and implement change.

McKinsey's 7-S Model

The management consultancy firm McKinsey developed an organisational-change model that can aid MNEs in understanding and managing change.[7] A key concept behind the 7-S Model is 'degree of fit'. In selecting running shoes for training for your next marathon there are a number of attributes you need the shoes to have. They need to be suitable for long-distance running on roads, support your individual gait and, of course, be the right size. You might also have a preference for shoes made in factories that comply with your ethical standards. The attributes that determine your shoe selection, therefore, depend upon your goal, your shoe size and your values. Extend this thinking to the organisation. The MNE manager must have a model that helps him envisage the organisation's 'fit' in terms of the goals it has set for itself and the values it wishes to adhere to in the pursuit of those goals. Back to our running shoe example: we may find a beautifully made shoe that fits exactly and is manufactured in a factory with the highest ethical standards, but it has a five-inch heel and a red-leather sole! It meets many of our requirements but won't help us achieve our goal.

The same thinking applies in the application of the 7-S Model, which we use to assess an organisation and to describe which of its elements need to change in order to achieve the organisation's desired state – its goal or an intermediate step along the way to achieving the goal. The '7 Ss' are:
- **S**trategy: the action plans a company has in place to respond to changes in its external environment.
- **S**tructure: the configuration of physical and intangible assets, together with people and how these are co-ordinated to achieve the organisation's objectives.
- **S**ystems: the procedures that support the organisational structure in its delivery of the strategy.
- **S**taff: employees, and associated processes to manage and develop them.
- **S**kills: the competencies the organisation has and how it develops them.
- **S**tyle: the culture of the organisation, combining both its management style and the belief system of the organisation itself.
- **S**hared values: the fundamental guiding principles and ideas around which the business is built.

---

[7] See www.mckinsey.com/insights/strategy/enduring_ideas_the_7-s_framework (accessed February 2015).

Figure 13.1 shows how these individual seven components of the framework interact with each other, with the shared values at the nucleus of the framework. However, it is worth noting that all elements of the framework exert some influence on each of the other elements.

The most revolutionary aspect of this model when it was first introduced in the 1970s was the idea that an organisation's effectiveness was not just about structure. The framework builds on the idea that an organisation's effectiveness is about its co-ordination, of which structure is just one element. Also, each of the seven elements is equally important, that is, they are not part of a hierarchy. The framework suggests that it will be difficult to progress on one element of the framework, for example, Systems, without progressing on the other six at the same time. This co-ordination of progression will give the reader some clues as to how an MNE can use the framework. The core idea is to understand how the organisation currently operates under each of the elements by doing an audit of the existing operation. Then, the MNE looks to see how each element will need to change in order to achieve a particular objective or set of objectives. The framework acts as a kind of checklist to ensure that all elements are captured in the action plans developed to support the change initiative and the achievement of the objectives.

FIGURE 13.1: McKINSEY 7-S FRAMEWORK[8]

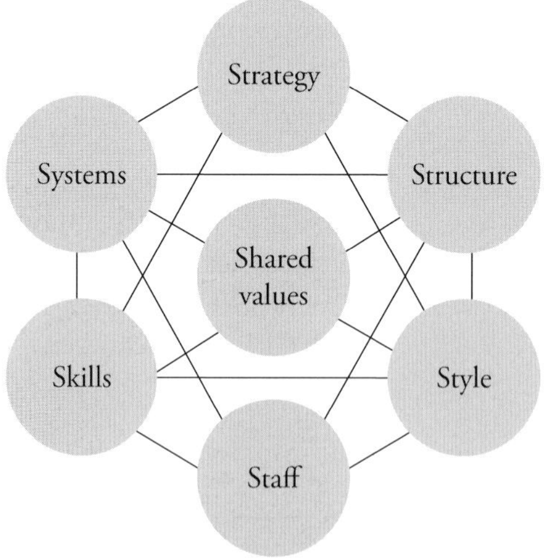

The Nadler and Tushman Change Model (The Congruence Model)

Developed in the 1980s, the Nadler and Tushman model (also called the 'congruence model') divides the organisation into inputs, processes and outputs.[9] It is referred to as the 'congruence model' because, like the McKinsey 7-S model, it addresses degrees of 'fit'; in other words, the model is concerned not only with the individual elements but also their

---

[8] Adapted from the McKinsey 7-S Model.

[9] Nadler, D.A. and Tushman, M.L., "A Diagnostic Model for Organisational Behaviour" in Hackman, J.R., Lawler, E.E. and Porter, L.W. (eds.) (1987), *Perspectives on Behaviour in Organisations.* New York: McGraw-Hill.

degree of fit with the needs of the organisation. The Nadler and Tushman model deals with some of the shortcomings in the McKinsey 7-S model in that it explicitly incorporates the external environment. Arguably, it is the external environment that has the most dramatic effect on an organisation over time. The model also diagrammatically represents how the outputs from the strategy execution feed back into the inputs, creating a continuous evolutionary process. This dynamic nature of the model is useful since organisations are constantly evolving, even if in some cases that evolution is toward extinction rather than growth.

The model is based on the idea that the organisation is an 'open system', capable of being influenced by, and influencing, other systems with which it interacts and the external environment.

Inputs to the organisational processes are the MNE's environment, its resources and its history. These inputs combine in different ways in different organisations to create the strategy. The strategy then inputs to the organisation shaping who (**people**) does what (**work**) and how (**informal structure and processes**). The inputs also shape how the people are organised (**formal structure**). These four organisational dimensions combine to produce the outputs, which are achieved at three levels: system, group and individual. The outputs then shape the inputs through a feedback loop. This is not as complex as it sounds. Essentially, the idea is that today's outputs will shape today's organisation which, in turn, shapes what it does tomorrow.

An MNE can use the model by first carrying out an audit of the existing elements of the model as they pertain to the organisation today. The outputs are then compared to the desired outputs and gaps in performance of actual output to desired output are identified. The MNE then analyses which inputs or elements of the model need to be changed in order to reduce the gaps between desired and actual outputs. In this way, the model guides the organisation toward congruence between actual and desired outputs. Let us examine the application of the Nadler and Tushman congruence model in more detail. Essentially, we are looking for where there is both congruence and incongruence between an organisation's objectives and what it is actually doing.

Step 1: Audit what is actually being done, i.e. analyse each of the four central elements, work, people, formal structure and informal structure separately. For example, for the work element the analysis would examine the nature of the work: is it mechanistic or does it require creativity; is it more important that it is done quickly or carefully, etc? Each element is analysed and documented.

Step 2: Interrelationships between the four elements: how each element interrelates with each of the other three is considered and described, thereby building up a structured picture of how the organisation processes activities. The MNE should focus particularly on identifying where there is congruence or incongruence between the elements and their interrelationships.

Step 3: Produce a plan to foster and maintain congruence: this final step involves producing the change plan, which will take what has been learned from the process thus far and turn it into specific actions and initiatives that will change the way things are done. The plan should seek to reinforce existing congruence and eliminate incongruence. As **Figure 13.2** suggests, the plan will be relevant at the system, or total organisation level, the business unit level and at the individual level.

FIGURE 13.2: NADLER AND TUSHMAN CONGRUENCE MODEL[10]

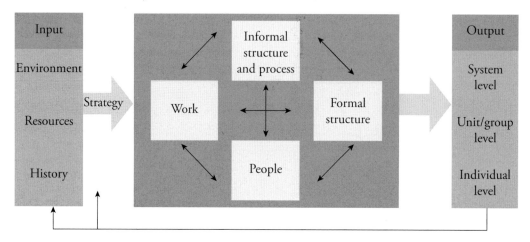

The Burke and Litwin Change Model

In the 1990s Warner Burke and George Litwin developed their model of organisational change, which was based on the concept of 'organisational climate'.[11] This 'climate' comprises the feelings and perceptions of the members of an organisation toward it. The model seeks to develop a causal framework that helps managers understand which organisational dimensions need to be changed and how these dimensions are to be linked in order to achieve the new goals. The model is complex and goes beyond the McKinsey 7-S and the Nadler and Tushman models in that it links change, how change is carried out and the ultimate connection between these two elements and performance. That is to say, the Burke and Litwin model tries to establish causal links between the need to change, how change is carried out, how people feel about how the change is carried out and, ultimately, the performance of the organisation and its effectiveness.

Burke and Litwin identify two types of change: transformational and transactional. As the names suggest transformational change is much more all-encompassing and is usually driven by external environmental factors, such as changes in customer-demand profiles or new technologies. These transformational changes in turn give rise to transactional changes, which are smaller, more minor in nature, and which affect individual actions, management and processes in the organisation. Transactional changes give rise to changes in how the individuals in the organisation feel about it, thus creating what Burke and Litwin term 'the climate'.

Figure 13.3 below shows the Burke and Litwin model. The key boxes are at the top and at the bottom. 'External Environment' represents the stimuli for change that come from the external environment, similar to what we discussed above in the Nadler and Tushman model. The box at bottom of the figure, labelled 'Individual and Organisational Performance', represents the outputs from the organisation. The model shows that the external environment is impacted upon by the outputs of the organisation, causing it to change. These changes, together with other changes, affect the external environment and feed into the organisation's need to change again. Thus, one can see that change, and the

---

10   Adapted from the article by Nadler and Tushman cited above.
11   Burke, W. and Litwin, G. (1992), "A Causal Model of Organisation Performance and Change", *Journal of Management*, Vol. 18, No. 3, 523–545.

FIGURE 13.3: THE BURKE AND LITWIN MODEL[12]

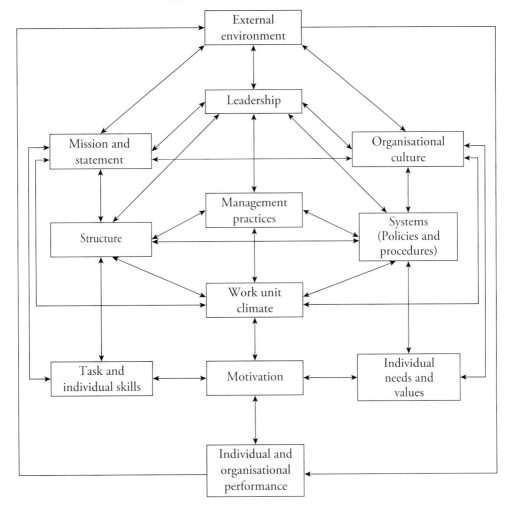

need to change, is constant, ongoing all the time, as the changing external environment creates the impetus for organisational change, which then causes the external environment to change, and so forth.

The other 12 boxes in the figure are the variables that Burke and Litwin believed were the best classifications or groupings of other major change dimensions. You can see that there is a degree of flow in the boxes from top to bottom. The environment impacts upon the organisation's leadership, culture, strategy and mission. This in turn leads to changes in systems, practices and structure. All of these combine to shape the climate of the work units. They also impact upon the individuals' skills and tasks and upon their needs and motivations, which are ultimately what drive performance. The collective performance then creates changes upon the external environment, and so forth.

---

12 Adapted from the Burke and Litwin article cited above.

One of the attractions of the Burke and Litwin model is that it links the external environment, the leadership of the organisation and the performance of individuals. In this way, the model connects individuals to the wider organisational strategies and goals.

Greneir's Growth Model

In 1972, Larry Greiner developed a model of how organisations evolve and develop over time. He finessed this model in 1998, creating a very useful framework for understanding an organisation's evolution and the need to change.[13]

Greiner proposed that organisations evolve and develop through different phases of growth from their inception to full maturity. These growth phases are relatively stable organisationally. However, as each growth phase nears its end, an organisational crisis tends to emerge, which requires a change in organisational focus and leadership approach. If this change does not occur, involving transition from one phase to the next by making necessary changes in underlying operating processes and management practices, then the organisation does not move forward to the next level of growth. It stagnates at its current level. As shown in **Figure 13.4** below, there are six growth phases; originally there were five, but Greiner added a sixth in the late 1990s having witnessed in the interim the inexorable growth of the MNE and realising that there was a sixth growth phase involving alliances. Each growth phase and its associated transition are discussed in the sections that follow.

Phase 1: Growth through Creativity The entrepreneurs who found an organisation are usually the ones running it at the start. This is the creative phase. The founders are involved in creating new products and markets. The organisation is still small; there are not many staff; communication is simple. Structures are informal and long hours of effort are rewarded by the value of the fledgling organisation rising, bringing increased wealth to the founders/owners.

As the organisation grows in size, more staff join and more external capital is sourced from fresh investors. Informal communication systems do not work as efficiently as they did when the organisation was smaller. Eventually, the organisation finds itself in what Greiner describes as a "leadership crisis". There is a need for a change in leadership style from entrepreneurial to managerial. Sometimes the founders will alter their own style but, more often, they will introduce professional managers to the organisation.

Phase 2: Growth through Direction Having successfully transitioned from the creative phase and dealt with the leadership crisis the organisation enters a growth phase characterised by 'direction'. Communication is more formal and budgets and targets begin to appear as performance measures. The organisation starts to separate into specialist functions like marketing or sales. Bonus and incentive schemes replace the stock ownership of the original founders.

As growth continues products and processes being managed become increasingly numerous and complex. It becomes impossible for the top management to issue directives about what needs to be done to manage all tasks. The staff who report to top management begin to know more about what needs to be done than the managers themselves. The organisation enters a new crisis phase, an autonomy crisis. New structures are needed where greater autonomy is granted to those further down the organisation hierarchy.

---

[13] Greiner, Larry E. (1998), "Evolution and Revolution as Organisations Grow", *Harvard Business Review*, May–June.

FIGURE 13.4: GRENEIR'S GROWTH MODEL[14]

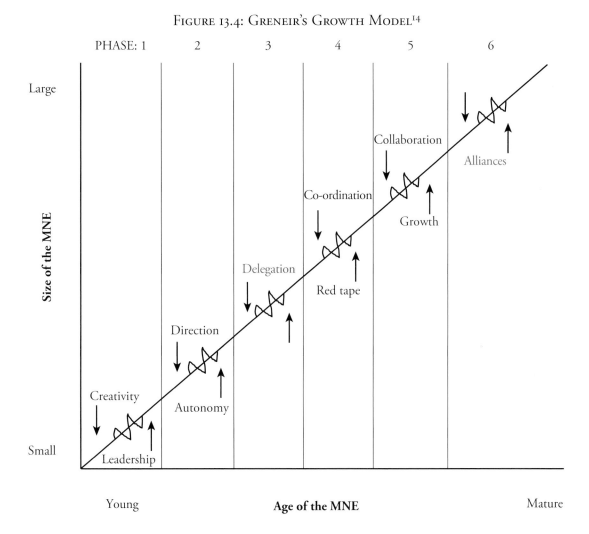

Phase 3: Growth through Delegation Middle managers are freed up by greater autonomy, with which they start to develop more products and markets. The organisation's top management spend more time reviewing higher level issues and monitoring performance. As the business grows the organisation increasingly relies upon middle managers' ability to lead their teams. At the same time, the directing top managers must 'let go' and avoid micro-managing. These strains often lead to organisational dysfunction and a new type of crisis, the **control** crisis, which can stifle growth. New ways of working need to be found that allow greater freedom to middle managers but at the same time ensure that the top managers remain in control of the strategy and direction of the business.[14]

Phase 4: Growth Through Co-ordination and Monitoring The organisation continues to grow as the business units that were previously acting autonomously now act in a co-ordinated way facilitated by top management. The central function allocates finance to projects and ensures investment projects carried out by the MNE's business units meet required return

---

[14] Adapted from the Larry Greiner article cited above.

targets and fit within its overall strategy. However, as the organisation continues to grow, these controls and co-ordination activities from the centre can begin to strangle initiative and creativity. Further growth becomes difficult to achieve and the organisation enters a **red-tape** crisis. New ways of working must be found that loosen up the centralised control functions in such a way as to encourage and foster collaborative working.

Phase 5: Growth through Collaboration In phases 2, 3 and 4 the organisation has grown through the application of various types of formal control structures, which are now replaced by teamwork and flexibility in a control framework unrecognisable when compared to the more formal control structures of earlier phases. Information systems need to be very sophisticated to allow teams to find and use the information they need to create new ways of working together. Reward systems are often structured around the achievement of team goals. Managers find themselves achieving results through being part of different project teams and initiatives, often more than one at the same time. Eventually, growth through collaboration is exhausted and any further growth must come from external partnerships and alliances. The **internal growth** crisis has been reached.

Phase 6: Growth through Extra-organisational Solutions Greiner revisited his growth model a number of times to test its relevance based on new and emerging trends in company growth patterns. The rise of the global firm and the organisational structures associated with some of the largest of these MNEs caused him to add a sixth stage. The resolution to the stagnating growth that occurs from the internal growth crisis is overcome by the formation of external alliances and collaborations with like-minded organisations. In the **growth through extra-organisational solutions** stage the MNE will be forming joint ventures. It may also begin to form mergers and to enter into outsourcing arrangements. Greiner's growth model finishes at this stage and does not propose a further 'crisis' that causes growth stagnation.

The growth rates achieved at the different stages will be different for each organisation. One of the main drivers will be the growth rate of the markets in which the MNE operates.

The value of Grenier's model is that it can help explain how the nature of the 'change challenge' can alter as the organisation develops. An MNE can apply the model by first determining where on the growth path it is, leading to conclusions on what type of organisational changes it faces if it is to continue to grow and prosper.

Finally, it is useful to consider how each of the three change models we have looked at could be combined with Grenier's growth model to produce a comprehensive understanding of the MNE's change environment.

Planned Change

The models of organisational change we have considered above propose change of a planned nature; they suggest that change takes place through the use of change models, planning tools and long-term organisational transformation. Indeed, Nadler and Tushman built on their change model by further proposing 10 principles that should guide an MNE manager in instituting large-scale change:
1. Diagnosis: analysis of the organisation, its strength and weaknesses, opportunities and threats and the implication of these for planning and strategy.
2. Vision: a description of the future desired state.
3. Energy: nothing will happen unless there is some effort put into change.

4. Centrality: the nature of the change must be clear and linked to the core strategy of the organisation.
5. The 'three-theme principle': only try to implement major change across a maximum of three themes at any one time. A 'theme' is a collection of tasks and activities that a change initiative might be organised around. In most MNEs a theme might be a large project or change initiative.
6. The 'magic leader': visible leadership is key to large-scale change.
7. Leadership is not enough: the leader must have broad base support to bring about change.
8. A planning/opportunism mix: successful major change involves a combination of planned change coupled with opportunistic actions.
9. 'Many bullets': while there might only be three major themes, many actions, small and large, need to be put in place, each re-enforcing the three change themes. There will be no silver bullet, rather many, many smaller bullets.
10. Investment and return: large-scale change involves the consumption of many resources and brings with it much risk. There should be a clear link between the investment and a measurable return commensurate with the risk.[15]

These 10 principles can be used to help guide the MNE manager through the treacherous task of managing and implementing change.

Emergent Change

> *"Everyone has a plan until they get punched in the face."*
>
> Mike Tyson

The models of organisational change we have discussed have a certain neatness and linearity to them. But, of course, change does not happen in a neat, linear fashion. In recent years there has been new thinking about the nature of change in organisations, which has evolved as managers realise that the success rate for major, planned change is not as high as they would like. Such failures pose the question: "Is there something wrong with our understanding of change?" Proponents of the idea of change as an emergent, non-linear process do not believe in the notion of planned major change. They see change as being a constantly evolving process within organisations. Some believe that, in trying to execute major change programmes, many MNEs are wasting their shareholders' money. Built-in adaptability is preferential to change capability.[16]

While, from an organisational perspective, thinking about emergent change is relatively new, it is not new in the history of ideas. For example, Field Marshal Helmuth von Moltke the Elder, a 19th-Century Prussian general and military strategist, once wrote that "no battle plan ever survives contact with the enemy".[17] By this he did not mean that planning, *per se*, is a waste of time.

---

[15] Nadler, D. and Tushman, M (1989), "Organisational Frame Bending: Principles for Managing Reorientation" *The Academy of Management Executive*, Vol. 3, No. 3, 194–204w.

[16] Dawson, P. (1994) *Organisational Change: A Processual Approach*. (London: Paul Chapman). Kanter, R.M. (1999) "Change is Everyone's Job: Managing the extended enterprise in a globally connected world" *Organisational Dynamics*, 28(1): 7–23.

[17] Moltke, Helmuth Graf von Militarische Werke, Vol. 2, Part 2, pp 33–40, found in Hughes, Daniel J. (ed.) (1993), *Moltke on the Art of War: Selected Writings*. Presidio Press: New York.

Rather, he believed that once a plan is put into action, the environment changes **as a result of the plan** and a new tactic must then be chosen. These thoughts echo Napoleon's who often commented that he went into battle with no plan of operations. Both were successful by dint of **planning how to be adaptable** on the battlefield and by being prepared to alter their tactics as the situation demanded.

While emergent change thinking is relatively new, a consensus seems to have evolved as to what proponents of the emergent change model propose:
• Change in an organisation is a continuous process of experimentation and adaptation.
• Organisational change is best achieved through small and medium-sized changes.
• Change is a disorganised process that happens at differing levels in the organisation over periods of months and years through different individual projects that are nonetheless inter-connected.
• Change is a socio-political process.
• Managers must foster experimentation and adaptation, not manage change.

These loose principles can be woven together to form a belief system about change which advocates that organisations be constructed or restructured to adapt more, as in the manner of living organisms rather than automated systems. By thinking of organisations as 'living', MNE managers can begin to connect sentient 'feeling' issues with harder tangibles, such as machinery and assets. To achieve this dynamic, an organisation's managers must somehow empower members of the organisation to act on the basis of their own motivations. Empowering organisations to behave in this way requires managers to operate differently from the traditional approach. They must somehow create the environment for this freedom of movement and expression while at the same time ensuring that the organisation's efforts are directed toward a shared goal that ultimately maximises wealth for the shareholders. The goal congruence that is needed to achieve this level of well-directed enthusiasm is not easily found. Indeed, such is the difficulty of achieving this level of flexibility, while remaining focused, that it can be argued that emergent change processes are just as fraught with execution risk as major planned change approaches, a dilemma leading us to our next section, in which we consider how to implement change in an MNE.

13.5 IMPLEMENTING ORGANISATIONAL CHANGE

Having identified the following:
• that change is needed,
• the desired future state, and
• what processes, structures and systems need to change,

and also having communicated the need for change, the organisation must now move to the implementation phase of the change. Most change programmes that fail do so at the implementation phase. While post-event analysis shows that the failures are partly due to poor performance in the earlier stages of the process, the majority of change programme failures arise from implementation failure.

As we have seen, an MNE is a more complex organisation than a purely domestic-based organisation, complexity that increases the execution risk on any change project. So, what steps can the management of an MNE take to ensure that the possibility of failure is reduced? How can the MNE ensure that the transition to the new desired state happens as smoothly as possible? These questions are addressed below.

Project Management

Over the last century, and particularly in the last 50 years, a new branch of business management practice has emerged. By examining successful change initiatives from the past and comparing them to failures, management theorists and practitioners have developed approaches that are more likely to produce successful outcomes. We refer to this body of work as the theory and practice of 'project management'.

Originating in the engineering field, the first project management techniques were mathematical in nature and involved scheduling tasks and projects in a sequential and logical manner. The two main ones were the 'critical path method' (CPM) and the 'project evaluation and review technique' (PERT). Many businesses seized on the opportunity to introduce elements of a scientific approach into the management of change in their organisations. By the 1960s, project management had established itself as a field of management study and practice in its own right.

There are many project management approaches. It is critical to select the one that is appropriate for a given MNE's culture and the nature of the change to be implemented. Some MNEs will adopt or tailor slightly, an existing approach for all projects in the business. This approach has the advantage of having a standardised approach to change management and the emergence of a consistent language in the organisation.

We will now look at the different possible project management approaches and give some guidelines as to how to select an appropriate process for a particular MNE.

The Traditional Approach

The traditional approach involves four stages combined with the activity of controlling and monitoring the project. As can be seen from **Figure 13.5** below, after the initiation phase the project moves into planning and design, which is followed by the execution phase. The execution phase is monitored and controlled. If anything goes off-track, then the design and planning is adjusted to take account of it and the execution activity is adjusted accordingly. At some point, the monitoring and controlling function will flag that the project goal has been achieved and the project will then move into the fourth and final phase. Many MNEs adopt this simple process-oriented approach or some derivation of it.

Lean Project Management

A suite of concepts has been brought together under a management approach called 'lean management' ('lean' being driven by the idea of achieving more with less waste). The project management approach with such a system is, not surprisingly, lean project management. This approach would

FIGURE 13.5: THE TRADITIONAL PROJECT MANAGEMENT PROCESS

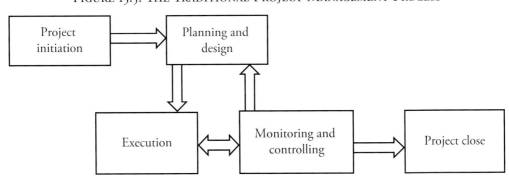

be pertinent in an organisation where the lean concept is applied to other business processes. In 'lean' organisations there is a high focus on 'lean' principles. Lean principles are driven by the concept of eliminating waste from business processes and practices, both physical and temporal waste. Lean project management approaches have this focus on waste elimination as their key driver. Two of the main lean project management processes are 'Six Sigma DMAIC' (define, measure, analyse, improve, control) and the Deming Cycle. Six Sigma project management processes focus on continuous improvement and data-driven added value management and measurement. It was developed at Motorola University by Bill Smith in 1986.[18] Originally focused on eliminating production variability, Six Sigma has now been combined with lean principles, which focus on eliminating waste, to produce Lean Six Sigma. This combination seeks to eliminate eight types of waste: **time, inventory, motion, waiting, over-production, over-processing, defects** and **skills** (also known as 'TIMWOODS'). At present there are many training programmes in Ireland that deliver skills and competence specifically in Lean Six Sigma. In a recognition of the importance of these skills for MNEs, Enterprise Ireland has published a directory (see Lean Education Directory (2015) available from www.enterprise-ireland.com.)

The Deming 14 Points method and its associated Deming Cycle[19] is the other main lean project management approach. Its focus is similar to Six Sigma in that it emphasised continuous improvement and statistical analysis of outputs and outcomes. Deming was an American statistician who worked in Japan in the late 1940s and early 1950s as it sought to rebuild its infrastructure after the Second World War. He espoused an approach to management that eliminated inefficiency through continuous improvement and taught it to hundreds of Japanese managers. Deming returned to the US in the late 1950s, where he led a quiet life until the 1970s. His ideas took hold in Japan and Japanese products stated to be superior in quality to their Western equivalents. This superiority became evident in the early 1970s, which led many MNEs in the West to examine why Japan had been able to excel. They realised that Deming's systematic approach was a critical dimension to the Japanese success. Western companies then began to implement total quality management (TQM) approaches advocated by Deming as a way of improving quality, efficiency and, ultimately, returns for shareholders.

Critical Chain Project Management

The critical chain project management (CCPM) approach was developed to factor uncertainty into project management throughout an organisation. Scarce resources for the whole organisation are identified and all change processes are assessed as to their criticality to the organisation and the achievement of its goals. The scarce resources are allocated to the projects that emerge as being most critical through a process called 'resource levelling'. This approach is particularly useful when there are a large number of projects being planned across the organisation.

PRINCE2

PRINCE2 ('projects in a controlled environment, version 2') is a generic project management approach that evolved in the 1990s. Its usefulness is in the use of a common language together with a very clearly defined project management framework. The PRINCE2 philosophy is focused on outputs and deliverables, which must be produced to an agreed quality and timeframe. Consequently, it is very much oriented toward clearly defined, unambiguous project mandates and goals and a well-defined project scope. A particular advantage of PRINCE2 is

---

[18] www.motorola.com/content/0,,3079,00.html (accessed May 2015).
[19] Deming, W. Edwards (1980), *Out of the Crisis*. MIT Press.

that it is used in so many MNEs that new recruits to an organisation can adapt quickly to their new organisation if they have prior experience of PRINCE2 project management approaches.

Agile Project Management

Agile project management is philosophically different from other project management approaches in that it is much more oriented toward a process view of human collaboration. In this approach, product project management is seen as a series of small tasks completed and brought to conclusion as the situation demands. It is an approach most often seen in creative industries. It does not favour large-scale planned change. One can see how proponents of emergent change theory would see advantages in agile project management as it seeks to avoid large-scale planned change.

Change Agents

Whichever project-management approach is adopted by an MNE, it will fall to the people in the organisation to execute the project. There are a number of roles that the organisation needs to consider when implementing a change project. Some of these roles are formal and some informal. In any case, these roles will exist, whether by appointment or not, in all successful projects. By this I mean that successful projects need people who will carry out particular tasks, both soft and hard, in the project management and execution process. 'Hard' tasks in this context means those tasks that are capable of precise definition, such as "weld item number 6087 to item number 4453 using process 45T". 'Soft' tasks are less capable of definition and are often classed as the 'messier' people-related issues. For example, "manage communication issues for the closure of Plant No: 34R". This task will involve many uncertainties since the people involved introduce emotional aspects to the task that can and will be difficult to predict.

With almost all organisational change, and more so with planned change, some people, or a group of people, will take responsibility for ensuring that the change is implemented. More formally we refer to these people as 'change agents'. A change agent is anyone who is involved in the implementation of change, supporting or sponsoring the initiative. A large or small number of people may be change agents, depending on the reach and scope of the project.

An organisation may also select people to be the change agents. This selection process may choose people from outside the organisation, or from different levels within the organisation. In any case, the change agents are formed into a project team. They need to have specific skills over and above their functional specialisation. Typically, they will have competence in specifying goals, communicating effectively, team-building and influencing skills.

Proponents of emergent change argue against this approach. They view change as iterative and expect all personnel to be able to execute the emergent changes needed as part of their day-to-day jobs. In organisations where change is managed with the emergent change philosophy, one would not expect to see project teams with special project management skills managing large-scale projects. Rather, change will be much more iterative, made up of constant, small adaptations to products, processes and structure. Change activity is led from within work groups as part of the everyday rhythm of the organisation.

Clearly, not all change can be managed this way. Large-scale infrastructure projects, such as building a bridge, require more traditional project and change management approaches. Thus, the selection of the change management technique will be a function of:
• the nature of the change required, and
• the culture and philosophy of the MNE.

Change Recipients

While change agents are the people tasked with executing the change, 'change recipients' are the people, or entities, whom the change will affect. Change agents can also be change recipients in that a person could be involved in a project that will also be impacted by the change. Indeed, in emergent change thinking the change agents are the internal change recipients.

The internal change recipients are those internal stakeholders that are affected by the change. Some individuals may welcome change and others may resist it, even though both sets of responses arise from the same input. The MNE manager must remember that every person is unique. Each individual will have their own perspective on an issue. Different personality types will also view change differently.

Past experience has shown that there is strong support for change when there are positive consequences not just for the MNE's organisation but also at an individual level. Change agents must ensure that change recipients' individual goals are capable of being connected to the MNE's organisational goals. This goal congruence is a strong predictor of the possible success of a change initiative.

Predictors of failure might be harder to discern but MNE change agents need to be mindful of possible measures to detect symptoms of underlying disquiet with the change process. At the extremes there may be evidence of misinformation or sabotage. Involving change recipients in the change process is crucial. The temptation is to remove a project team from day-to-day operations while they manage and execute the change. Their visibility in the organisation is reduced just at the time it should be increased. Indeed, sometimes projects are cloaked in secrecy. This may be necessary for commercial reasons, but change agents should anticipate the problems such secrecy might create down the road with change recipients.

13.6 CONCLUSION

Change is brought about by the recognition that there is a need to change in response to a stimulus from the external or internal environment. We looked at a number of theories about organisational change, including the McKinsey 7-S and the Nadler and Tushman approaches. Each presents different structured ways of thinking about organisational change for MNEs.

Two main schools of thought about change have evolved: the major planned change approach and the emergent change approach. The first focuses on transformational change while the latter focuses on small incremental changes and adaptability.

Implementing change in an MNE is ordinarily more complex than in an equivalently sized domestic enterprise. This is because the multi-location and multi-cultural dimensions to the MNE cause issues that are not present in the domestic firm. Tools exist to allow MNE managers to assess and analyse the potential challenges that the different countries within which an MNE is operating might present. Having identified the change that is needed and the possible challenges that exist in implementing it, the manager must go about the execution of the change. Many project change methodologies exist and the MNE must select the approach that is most suitable for its culture and the nature of the change being implemented.

QUESTIONS

Self-test Questions

13.1 What is the difference between major planned change and emergent change?

13.2 Describe one project management model.

13.3 Evaluate the McKinsey 7-S Model of change. Do you see any flaws with it?

13.4 Think about a recent change in your organisation. Who were the change agents and who were the change recipients? Was there much of an overlap?

Thought-provoking Questions

Question 13.1

You have just been appointed as management accountant in Gelotali Ltd, the Irish subsidiary of Gelo Plc, a Italian-based MNE with ice-cream manufacturing plants in 17 countries throughout the world. Your boss, Mark Eldon, has told you that the head office has told the local board of Gelotali Ltd that there will be a need to introduce a new manufacturing process into the Irish operation. This process will involve major change to the existing practices and processes in the Irish operation. He asks you to research how Gelotali might approach the changes envisaged.

Question 13.2

Your boss, the CEO/Founder of a small company, Iota Ltd, has told you that he has heard of Greiner's Growth model. He wonders whether it has any implications for Iota Ltd and asks you to produce a short paper with your thoughts. Iota is led by its founder and your boss, Billy Bounder. Billy is directly involved in almost all decisions and owns 99% of the company. His father owns the other 1% but is not involved with the business at all. The business grew at over 25% per annum for the first four years. Iota manufactures small components that are needed for the installation of electric gates. The customers are the fitters of such gates, both in industrial and domestic settings. Growth has begun to slow and many people in the business complain that Billy just hasn't the time to devote enough attention to all the issues that need to be managed. You sit down and begin to formulate your thoughts ...

Review Question

(See Suggested Solutions to Review Questions in **Appendix B**.)

Question 13.1

In discussing international trading, what is meant by the term 'culture'?

PART IV

TREASURY MANAGEMENT IN AN INTERNATIONAL ENVIRONMENT

In Part I of this book we looked at why organisations internationalise; in Part II we explored the economic factors influencing multinational enterprises (MNEs). In Part III we progressed to look at how international organisations make decisions. In this part, we will examine the treasury function in an international environment.

An MNE may organise itself on a centralised basis with a large degree of decision-making authority residing centrally at head office. Alternatively, it may organise itself on a more decentralised basis with greater power devolved to its operating divisions and business sub-units. Whichever structure it favours, the MNE will almost always have a centralised finance and treasury function. At its simplest, the MNE will need to produce group accounts, requiring it to consolidate accounting information at a central point. The MNE will almost always need a centralised treasury function to complement the finance function. This happens, not least because the MNE will need to consolidate its capital resources in order to make decisions about capital investments and dividend payments to shareholders. In the two chapters in this part we will explore how the treasury function operates in an MNE. In **Chapter 14** we explore the sources of finance available to the MNE and in **Chapter 15** we examine how the treasury function manages foreign exchange risk.

14

SOURCES OF FINANCE

LEARNING OBJECTIVES

Having read this chapter, you will understand:
- the two pillars of capital for the MNE: debt and equity;
- the sources of equity;
- the sources of finance;
- the different types of debt instruments, especially bonds;
- the bond markets and how they operate;
- other types of bank loans;
- how banks are the world's largest MNEs and how financial regulation can affect other MNE sources of debt; and
- how an MNE decides on the appropriate level of debt.

14.1 INTRODUCTION

On 9 June 2009, the Dublin-based Smurfit Kappa Group Plc ('SKG'), one of the world's largest integrated manufacturers of paper-based packaging products with operations in Europe and Latin America, announced that it was seeking the consent of its lenders to amendments to its senior credit facility agreement. The proposed amendments planned to significantly enhance SKG's financial flexibility, providing it with:
- the ability to raise longer-dated capital to refinance a portion of its existing senior facilities;
- extended maturity of its revolving credit facility; and
- increased leverage and interest cover covenant 'headroom'.

How do firms like SKG raise money, and from whom? What are the differences between an MNE's ability to raise money (and the sources of that money) and that of a purely domestic firm? How does the exchange rate play into the decision-making, if at all?

This chapter seeks to answer these questions and to explain how MNEs source the finance to carry out their activities and add value for shareholders. We will explore this topic in two main sections: first, we will look at how an MNE raises equity, and then we will consider how it raises debt financing. We have discussed in **Chapter 11** how these two pillars of finance combine to provide the long-term capital structure of an MNE. We also looked in that chapter at the balance to be achieved between debt and equity.

At the outset it is worth noting that different countries tend to have different appetites for the various forms of finance. Stock markets dominate the financial mix in the US, bonds dominate in Japan and bank loans tend to have a much higher share of the financing mix in Europe. In Japan, for example, the inability of their banks to provide loans after the financial crisis of the 1990s meant that MNEs had to tap into international bond markets for finance. This form of funding proved very successful for the top-end firms, such as Toyota. Will Europe follow suit after the financial crisis of 2008 and onward? It is conceivable that European banks, in a desire to shrink their balance sheets (also known as statements of financial position), will be less attracted to issuing loans. This in turn may lead to greater focus on bonds as a source of finance. If one thinks it through one can see that investors, many of whom lost money in the European banking crisis, were indirectly financing corporate European MNEs. The banks were using the investors' money to lend on to the European MNEs. When the MNEs were unable to pay their debts, the banks struggled. Perhaps in Europe over the coming years there will be a greater appetite for the issuance of bonds rather than relying on loans from the banks (though, of course, there is a certain scale needed to make a bond issuance worthwhile, most bond issuances tending to be for over €10 million).

While both are sources of debt finance, the distinction between bank loans and bonds is that bonds are issued directly to investors, who can then trade the bonds if they wish. Loans, bank loans in particular, are more restricted in terms of their tradeability and both parties will usually need to see out the full term of the loan.

Figure 14.1 opposite depicts the large array of sources of long-term finance available to an MNE. Essentially, however, they fall into two classes: equity and debt. In **Section 14.2** we explore sources of equity. In **Section 14.3** we then discuss sources of debt.

14.2 SOURCES OF EQUITY

A company raises money by selling its shares to investors. In return, the investors participate in the fortunes of the company in proportion to their 'share' of the company. Selling shares in a company to raise money is called 'equity finance'. Most large MNEs will list their shares on one or more stock markets, making them available to a wide pool of potential investors. Listing the shares on a stock market for the first time involves the '**primary market**', which is the market of investors who buy the shares the first time they are made available for purchase. This first-time offering is often called an 'IPO', or initial public offering. Once the shares are listed and have been bought for the first time they start being traded on the stock market. This subsequent buying and selling of the shares is the 'secondary market'. The price at which shares are being bought and sold for on the secondary market expresses investors' beliefs in the future fortunes of the company. This price is important for a MNE for three reasons:

1. it represents a view of the ultimate owners of the business as to its worth;
2. it sets a price from which the MNE can extrapolate the cost of new equity financing if needed; and
3. it can provide a way to align owners' interest with that of management and avoid the corrupting effects of agency (see the discussion of agency in **Chapters 5** and **12**).

FIGURE 14.1: SOURCES OF LONG-TERM CAPITAL

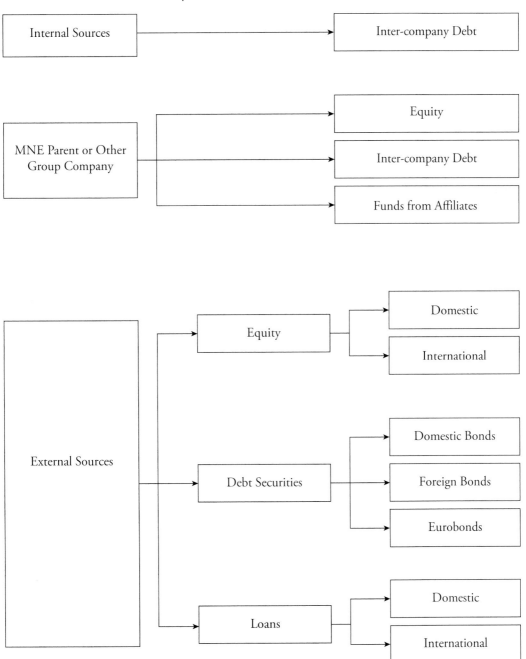

The second point above is of particular importance when an MNE is considering future fund-raising from equity. The higher the share price, the lower the percentage of the company that must be given away, or sold, in a new issue of shares to raise finance.

Most MNEs list their shares on international stock markets, normally those of the country in which they are headquartered. Often though, MNEs will list their shares on stock exchanges located in other countries. The 'stock market' comprises the companies that list their shares on exchanges. A 'stock exchange' is the infrastructure for trading those shares. For example, Marks & Spencer (M&S) is part of the stock market. The computer systems that allow the trading of M&S form part of the stock exchange. As mentioned, some MNEs list their shares on one or more exchanges, not necessarily the country of their head office. For example, Ryanair, the Dublin-based, low-cost airline, is listed on the Irish Stock Exchange, the London Stock Exchange and the NASDAQ. Ryanair would not go to the trouble of supporting these multiple listings if it was not of value to the company and its shareholders.

We will first explore the world's stock exchanges and then we will look at the advantages of listing on more than one exchange for an MNE.

International Stock Exchanges

Table 14.1 below shows the size of all the world's stock exchanges that are members of the World Federation of Exchanges (WFE) at the end of January 2015. The market capitalisation of the firms listed on the exchanges was over $67 trillion when converted to US dollars at the rates prevailing at the end of January 2015. Nearly 30% of the entire value of the aggregate of the world's stock exchanges is made up of the New York Stock Exchange (NYSE). (The London Stock Exchange left the WFE in late 2013 following a dispute about strategic direction of the organisation. Ironically, the WFE relocated to London from Paris in late 2013.)

TABLE 14.1: DOMESTIC MARKET CAPITALISATION (LOCAL CURRENCY)[1]
(in millions of local currencies)

Exchange	Cur.	2015 January
Americas		
Bermuda SE	BED	1 609.7
BM&FBOVESPA	BRL	2 129 953.2
Bolsa de Valores de Colombia	COP	326 794 812.8
Buenos Aires SE	ARA	515 925.3
Lima SE	PEI	227 650.5
Mexican Exchange	MXP	6 795 220.0
NASDAQ OMX	USD	6 830 968.0
NYSE	USD	19 222 875.6
Santiago SE	CLP	141 163 505.0
TMX Group	CAD	2 433 368.7
Asia-Pacific		
Australian SE	AUD	1 623 957.5
BSE India	INR	103 462 816.4
Bursa Malaysia	MYR	1 639 731.9

---

[1] World Federation of Exchanges members, www.world-exchanges.org/statistics/monthly-report (accessed July 2015).

Exchange	Cur.	2015 January
Colombo SE	LKR	3 042 260.7
HoChiMinh SE	VND	1056 445 951.7
Hong Kong Exchanges	HKD	25 772 620.3
Indonesia SE	IDR	5287 336 946.5
Japan Exchange Group – Osaka	JPY	NA
Japan Exchange Group – Tokyo	JPY	528 879 386.6
Korea Exchange	KRW	1367 714 694.0
National Stock Exchange India	INR	101 002 177.2
New Zealand Exchange	NZD	98 455.4
Philippine SE	PHP	12 303 271.4
Shanghai SE	CNY	24 499 623.7
Shenzhen SE	CNY	14 042 852.7
Singapore Exchange	SGD	1 021 698.5
Taipei Exchange	TWD	2 661 165.9
Taiwan SE Corp.	TWD	27 081 366.5
The Stock Exchange of Thailand	THB	15 034 665.9
Europe-Africa-Middle East		
Abu Dhabi SE	AED	409 313.0
Amman SE	JOD	17 827.7
Athens Exchange	EUR	36 554.3
Bahrain Bourse	BHD	8 329.0
BME Spanish Exchanges	EUR	833 796.2
Borsa Istanbul	TRY	533 270.3
Budapest SE	HUF	3 748 300.3
Casablanca SE	MAD	512 940.2
Cyprus SE	EUR	2 925.5
Deutsche Börse	EUR	1 559 292.0
Dubai Financial Market	AED	328 408.5
Egyptian Exchange	EGP	527 836.5
Euronext	EUR	2 939 410.0
Irish SE	EUR	121 018.0
Johannesburg SE	ZAR	11 004 015.2
Kazakhstan SE	KZT	3 893 667.5
Ljubljana SE	EUR	6 168.0

Exchange	Cur.	2015 January
Luxembourg SE	EUR	53 881.6
Malta SE	EUR	NA
Mauritius SE	MUR	271 670.4
Moscow Exchange	RUR	26 975 640.3
Muscat Securities Market	OMR	14 841.5
NASDAQ OMX Nordic Exchange	EUR	1 072 776.5
Nigerian Stock Exchange	NGN	9 855 202.0
Oslo Børs	NOK	1 716 500.5
Qatar Stock Exchange	QAR	648 789.4
Saudi Stock Exchange – Tadawul	SAR	1 918 730.7
SIX Swiss Exchange	CHF	1 385 708.5
Tel Aviv SE	ILS	774 137.0
Wiener Börse	EUR	81 192.3

At one point in the 1980s, Japan had the largest stock exchange in the world as measured by market capitalisation of its listed companies. As Japan's fortunes have waned so has the market capitalisation of its listed companies. Nonetheless, Japan remains the largest stock exchange by market capitalisation outside of the US. The London Stock Exchange, which is not a member of the World Federation of Exchanges (see above), has the third largest market (again by market capitalisation) at approximately $3,600 billion at January 2015.

Emerging Markets

One of the major changes in the last 20 years has been the emergence and growth of stock exchanges in the emerging economies of China, Brazil and India. **Table 14.2** below shows the scale of this growth in terms of market capitalisation values expressed as a percentage of GDP as at 31 December 2013. This measure is often used as an indicator of stock market development.

TABLE 14.2: MARKET CAPITALISATION AS A % OF GDP[2]

DEVELOPED MARKETS	%	EMERGING MARKETS	%
Ireland	87.3	Brazil	51.6
UK/Italy	74.1	China	78.8
US	155.1	India	157.1

From a brief examination of the above statistics we can deduce that the emerging markets are beginning to have, or in the case of India already have, well-developed stock exchanges in comparison to the size of their domestic economies. (The UK and Italy is combined as the

---

[2] Sources: table of GDP numbers are from www.imf.org/external/index.htm; stock market caps are from World Federation of Exchanges.

London Exchange Group is a combination of exchanges from both countries.) The UK on its own would have a ratio of well over 100%, but when it is combined with Italy's relatively low level the number falls to 74.1%. In Ireland the number is high at 87.3%, showing the effect of some large MNEs still remaining listed on the Irish Stock Exchange even though much of their activity is generated outside the country.

The Irish Stock Exchange ratio of market capitalisation to GDP raises an interesting question: why do companies, particularly MNEs, list on more than one exchange, i.e. cross-list? Ryanair, for example, is listed on the Irish Stock Exchange, the London Stock Exchange and the NASDAQ. We will discuss this below.

Cross-listing

The practice of listing shares on more than one stock exchange is called '**cross-listing**'. The main advantage to an MNE in cross-listing is that it reduces the cost of its capital, which in turn boosts the share price. There is a cost associated with listing on an exchange. Therefore, an MNE will only cross-list when the benefits outweigh the associated costs. Cross-listing also brings greater growth opportunities to a company by giving it access to a wider pool of investors. Detailed below are the main reasons for an MNE to cross-list.

Liquidity
Throughout this textbook we have repeated two maxims concerning value:
- a euro today is worth more than a euro tomorrow; and
- a safe euro is worth more than a risky euro.

To those maxims we can now add a third:
- **a liquid euro is worth more than an illiquid euro.**

Liquidity has a value in and of itself, which is reflected in the trading value of financial products on global markets and exchanges. The more liquid a stock is perceived to be, the lower the required return by investors in that share. This is because investors attribute a value to liquidity of a stock. All other things being equal, this will lead to a higher share price.

One of the reasons an MNE will cross-list its shares is to increase its liquidity by making the stock available to a wider market. Research has shown (see below) that total trading volumes increase once a share is listed on more than one market. Furthermore, the bid–offer spread narrows. Bid–offer spreads represent the difference between the price buyers are willing to pay for a share, the bid price, and the price at which sellers are willing to dispose of the share, the offer price. The gap between these two prices is called the 'spread'. A small gap is called a narrow spread and is often taken as a sign of high liquidity in a stock, meaning there are many willing buyers and sellers. Both these effects, a wider number of investors and more trading volume, support the belief that cross-listing can add value for an enterprise. Interestingly, if an MNE in a developed market cross-lists in an emerging market, research has also shown there is increased volume both on the home market and the new market. If an MNE is originally listed on an emerging market exchange, then the trading volume on the home exchange drops.[3] Therefore, an MNE with a listing on an emergent market exchange needs to factor in the reduced trading on the emergent market exchange in any decision it is making about cross-listing.

---

3   Halling, M. (2008), "Where is the market? Evidence from Cross-listings in the US" *Review of Financial Studies*, 21, 724–761.

Market Integration

By cross-listing on a foreign stock exchange an MNE makes its shares more available to foreign investors (effectively a form of capital liberalisation of the home market). The easier it is for investors to own shares in an MNE, the greater the trade in those shares and the more the price will reflect the real value of the company. When markets are integrated, the prices for shares of similar risk have the same returns. The price of a share sold on a market that is not well integrated with world markets will be lower than would otherwise be the case because the risk inherent in the share is borne by investors in the home market only. If the MNE can find ways for foreign investors to easily hold the share then the equity risk is shared among a wider set of shareholders and the cost of capital should fall.[4] This is especially true for MNEs from emerging market exchanges who seek to cross-list on developed market exchanges.

Expanded Shareholder Base

Cross-listing will expand the base of shareholders that may own an MNE's equity. One would think that an investor wanting to buy a particular publicly traded equity could buy that equity irrespective of what exchange it is listed upon. In practice, however, this is not the case. Investors may not even look at shares that are quoted on exchanges outside their home country. They may be prevented from doing so because of constraints on the portfolio they are managing together with restrictions on the existence of foreign shares in their portfolio. Constraints are often put on fund managers' portfolios, either self-imposed or by industry regulators, as to which countries' exchanges the fund manager may invest in. Also, there can be constraints on who can own and invest in certain shares. For example, in China there is a large number of classes of shares available to investors. However, some shares can only be bought by Chinese investors and other classes can only be bought by foreign investors. Sometimes, as in July 2015, the Chinese government restricts the sale of certain types of shares.

Corporate Governance

We have discussed agency theory in **Chapter 5**. A major concern of investors is that management or a small group of dominant shareholders may extract value from an MNE by diverting funds from the firm into projects or investments that are not made for the benefit of all the shareholders. Corporate governance regulations have evolved over time to protect investors from errant behaviour of this type. Not all countries have strong shareholder-protection legislation. Countries also differ in the degree of effort employed in enforcing what legislation they do have. By cross-listing in a country with a strong shareholder-protection code and enforcement track record, an MNE is sending a signal to the market about its willingness to adhere to the relevant codes.

Cross-listing in certain countries, such as the US, also exposes an MNE to the litigious environment prevalent in that country. There is a strong heritage in the US of disgruntled shareholders using the legal system to seek remedies for malpractice in the field of corporate governance. This heritage exists because history has shown that US courts provide a good outcome for such shareholders in genuine cases. Therefore, listing one's shares on exchanges where there is a strong record of corporate governance enforcement demonstrates the MNE's confidence in its own governance and the effectiveness of its strategies for delivering shareholder value in an open and transparent fashion. The removal of the agency costs associated with poor corporate governance should increase the free cash flow available for other more wealth-enhancing projects, and thus improve shareholder returns. ('Agency costs' is a term used

---

[4] Miller, D. (1999), "The market reaction to international cross listings: Evidence from depositary receipts", *Journal of Financial Economics* 51, 103–123.

to describe the hidden cost to an MNE of the misalignment between the goals and objectives of the MNE's management, and those of the MNE owners.)

Fundraising

The wider the shareholder base available to a firm, the more capital it should be able to raise. If a firm is restricted to its home market then its access to capital will be restricted to the available capital in that market. By cross-listing, an MNE will allow a wider pool of investors to buy shares in the firm. When accessing new capital for a new multinational investment project this can be particularly important. For example, for an Irish MNE listed on the Irish Stock Exchange that is considering a €2 billion project in Brazil, which it intends to fund through new equity, this investment would represent nearly 2% of the market capitalisation of the entire Irish stock market. If it cross-listed in Brazil, there would be two advantages:

- it would gain access to the larger Brazilian stock exchange and its investors would increase the size of the pool from which the capital could be raised; and
- Brazilian investors would be more likely to be able to appraise the project.

Cross-listings Arbitrage

Cross-listings arbitrage refers to the idea that arbitrageurs will buy and sell in the various exchanges on which a share is listed in such a way as to ensure that the exact same price is quoted for the share at the same time on all exchanges (see **Chapter 8** for a definition and more complete discussion of arbitrage.) Arbitrage activity increases the trading of a share since such trade is supplemental to the trading that would occur if the share had a listing on only one exchange. The arbitrage trading is also increased because of exchange rate movements. The movement in exchange rates on one exchange gives rise to momentary arbitrage opportunities on other exchanges denominated in a different currency. Arbitrageurs act quickly to exploit these small differences, leading to a speedy rebalancing of the quoted share price. In **Example 14.1** below I use real information from the various exchanges that CRH, the Irish Plc, has listings for.

EXAMPLE 14.1: CRH AND CROSS-LISTINGS ARBITRAGE

CRH is a company listed on three stock exchanges, the London Stock Exchange (LSE), the Irish Stock Exchange (ISE) and the New York Stock Exchange (NYSE, through an American depositary receipt (ADR) – see below). A glance at CRH's website on 18 November 2014 at 11.00 a.m. shows that there are three prices quoted for a share in CRH:

LSE: £13.62, ISE: €17.04 or NYSE: $21.45.

The exchange rates between these currencies at the same moment on 18 November 2014 is:

£0.79939 = €1 = $1.2526

Using these rates we should be able to restate the value of a CRH share on each of the exchanges to see if we can make a quick profit by exploiting the short-term price difference that might exist between the three exchanges. However, will this work?

If we start with a euro denominated share trading on the ISE worth €17.04. Converting this into Sterling at the rate of €1 = £0.79939 we get, €17.04 = £13.62, which is the same as the Stg£ price quoted for the share on the LSE, meaning there is no arbitrage opportunity.

Let's now try the NYSE. €17.04 converted into US dollars at €1 = $1.2526 implies a CRH share should be worth €17.04 × 1.2526 = $21.34. The price quoted for the CRH share in New York is $21.45, 11 cents more than we could achieve if we bought a share in euro and converted it into dollars. This might present an opportunity. Imagine we had €100,000 to invest. We could buy CRH shares on the ISE. We would get 100,000/17.04 = 5,868 shares for our money. We could then sell the shares on the NYSE for 5,868 × $21.45 = $125,868 and convert our dollar proceeds back into euro at the current exchange rate of €1 = $1.2526, getting €100,485. Hey presto … alchemy. We have turned our €100,000 into €100,485 and incurred no risk. Assuming the transaction costs are less than €485 we are onto a winner. But, when I go to complete this set of trades I find that the NYSE is not yet open and I cannot sell the shares in New York. So, we will wait until later in the day and see what the price is for the CRH shares in New York when that exchange opens.

By the time the NYSE opens the shares in CRH have moved to $21.39 and the shares on the ISE are €17.00 per share. The implied exchange rate of €17/$21.39 = 0.795 closely matched the official exchange rate quoted on the FOREX markets of 0.799. If arbitrage theory applies to trading in CRH shares, the difference between the derived rate and the actual exchange rate of 0.795 − 0.799 = 0.004 accounts for the transactions' costs and the service fee of the ADR depositary bank (see below). My easy money scheme is not going to work. The arbitrageurs working in the market have bought and sold CRH shares in such a fashion as to ensure that the exchange rate movements between the various exchanges where the share is listed are quickly taken account of in the share price quoted. The effect is that there is one universal price for the CRH share irrespective of which exchange it is traded on and in what currency.

If the market is efficient then there should be no opportunity to make a risk-free profit. In the above example, the profit-making plan should fail because the NYSE should adjust the instant it opens. This is because arbitrageurs operating in the market are constantly checking for the smallest of differences and adjusting share prices accordingly, often through the trading of huge volumes of shares at the thinnest of margins.

American Depositary Receipts (ADRs)

In **Example 14.1** above, I mentioned that the listing of CRH shares on the NYSE was by way of ADR. An ADR is a way that a non-US MNE can have its shares traded on a US exchange. An American depositary receipt (ADR) represents a specific number of shares in the home market of the MNE that are held by a US depositary bank. The US bank converts all dividends and other receipts generated by those shares into US dollars and charges a small fee for its services (Bank of New York Mellon dominates this market). The mechanism is needed since an MNE's results and dividends can only be recorded and paid in one currency. Therefore, a mechanism needs to be arrived at to allow the share to be listed in another currency. A number of actual shares in the MNE are allocated to the depositary bank and the ADRs are the instrument that is traded as a proxy for the actual shares, which are held by the bank.

There are three main levels of ADR:
- Level 1: these ADRs trade 'over-the-counter' meaning they are not listed on an exchange, they are traded between brokers and dealers. Only existing shares are traded. This is entirely a secondary market. There are few requirements and there is no requirement to comply with US GAAP.

- Level 2: these ADRs also represent existing shares, as with Level 1. In other words, no new capital is being raised. Unlike Level 1 ADRs, these ADRs trade on the major US exchanges. Consequently, they must comply with SEC (US Securities and Exchange Commission) listing regulations and file reconciliations of their accounts to US GAAP using Form 20-F.
- Level 3: ADRs are used to raise fresh equity. They are traded on the major US exchanges and must comply with SEC regulations and file complete reconciliations to US GAAP.

Global Depositary Receipts (GDRs)

In the 1980s, ADRs dominated the cross-listing market. However, as markets became increasingly global in nature and the movement of capital easier, global depositary receipts emerged. GDRs are similar to ADRs except that they trade on many different markets and settle in many different currencies. Nonetheless, the same basis principle applies. Such has been the growth in GDRs that they now dominate the cross-listing market. While other exchanges trade in GDRs, the New York exchange still accounts for over half of global trading in depositary receipts.

Globally Registered Shares (GRSs)

Globally registered shares are actual shares in a company traded across a number of global exchanges. Unlike GDRs they are not a receipt representing a share in the company deposited in trust in a bank's vaults. GRSs are not yet a major part of the cross-listing market as they tend to be more expensive to maintain than a GDR.

Private Placement

Up to now we have considered how an MNE can raise equity through a share placement or improve its cost of capital by cross-listing. The MNE may also raise fresh capital by way of a **private placing**, which is where the MNE raises money by selling shares privately rather than making them available for subscription publicly through an exchange. This approach tends to cost less than listing the shares on a stock exchange but has the downside of not providing equivalent liquidity for the investor. Because liquidity is limited, the pool of investors may be smaller than would be the case with a public offering. Also, remembering our third maxim that 'a liquid euro is worth more than an illiquid euro', the return required by the investors will most likely be higher than that required by a public offering. This additional higher return required by the providers of private equity pushes up the cost of capital, which can mean that projects are rejected that would otherwise have been undertaken by the MNE if it had had a lower return of equity requirement.

14.3 SOURCES OF DEBT

When companies are initially formed they will have funds provided by the initial investors or shareholders. They will also seek to raise funds from other providers, normally banks or grants from governments. The banks from which the funds will be sourced will typically be local, domestic banks.

As companies grow they will extend their reach and will begin to consider raising funds further afield, from banks in other countries or raising funds in other currencies.

In June 2014 Ladbrokes Group Finance Plc issued £100 million of bonds, to be redeemed in 2022 (eight years later). The company pays an interest rate of 5.125%. Ladbrokes are using the funds to finance their growth plans. Why did Ladbrokes issue a bond? How did they choose the rate of 5.125% and why did investors buy this bond?

In this section, we will examine the factors that influence an MNE's selection of its approaches to sourcing debt finance. We will begin by examining the sources of long-term capital that may be available to an MNE.

As we have seen in **Figure 14.1** above, the sources of long-term capital are wide and varied. An MNE may have some, most or all of these elements in its financing mix. Equity and bonds can be issued by a firm in either its home market or in a foreign market. These products can be sold on again in the secondary markets. This liquidity is attractive to investors and reduces the returns the MNE must make available for them. The MNE may also borrow money by way of loans from either external sources, such as banks, or from elsewhere within the group. The choices of 'sources of funds' that are available to the parent of the MNE are also often available through the MNE's subsidiary operating units. In other words, an MNE may source its long-term debt requirements by way of borrowing directly by the parent company or it may have its subsidiaries borrow the funds. The MNE may have a combination of both borrowing by the parent and by the subsidiaries. It may also borrow long-term funds in one country or subsidiary and deploy the funds through intercompany lending in another part of the enterprise.

With this array of choices, how does the manager in the MNE choose the optimum financing mix? To answer this question we must consider how an MNE borrows money for long-term capital needs. Normally, such borrowing is done by the issuance, by the MNE, of '**debt instruments**'. These are the financial instruments that underpin the obligations on a borrower. The obligations are given in return for the provision of the funds that have been borrowed by the MNE. Debt instruments include loan notes, bonds, mortgages, leases and other types of agreements between borrowers and lenders. The MNE manager must consider how to arrange these debt instruments in such a way as to optimise the financial position for the enterprise. To understand how the MNE manager may configure the array of possible debt instruments available to the MNE we must look at how debt instruments differ from one another; in other words, what choices are available to the MNE.

Attributes of Debt Instruments

The main attributes that differentiate different debt instruments are:
1. the currency in which they are denominated;
2. the interest they earn and when it must be paid;
3. their liquidity; and
4. their international characteristics.

The nature of each of these attributes is discussed below.

1. Currency

All debt instruments will be denominated in a specific currency, for example the euro, Sterling or the US dollar. An MNE manager will need to consider in what currency they should borrow the necessary funds. If a purely domestic company borrows in a foreign currency to gain a better interest rate, it is exposing itself to a foreign exchange risk, which is likely to erode any interest rate benefit. If, however, the company covered its risk by using financial instruments, such as currency swaps, the cost of such a risk-minimisation strategy would exactly equal the benefit from the lower interest rates (see **Chapter 15** for a description of how currency swaps operate).

So, it does not make sense for a domestic company to borrow in a foreign currency unless the company wishes to speculate on the foreign exchange markets (which is not a good business practice). However, for an MNE it makes perfect sense to borrow in a foreign currency. In **Example 11.11** in **Chapter 11** we contrasted the different NPV scenarios that arose when 'Scrod Plc' borrowed in Turkish Lira or in euro. If an MNE borrows in its home currency for cash flows that are in a foreign currency, it will expose itself to foreign exchange risk. If it borrows in the same currency as the cash flows for the project it will have an inbuilt foreign exchange hedge. This practice of balancing liabilities and assets/cash flows in the same currency is called **balance-sheet hedging**.

In some instances the treasury function in an MNE will borrow in a variety of currencies, thus introducing an internal portfolio diversification of the MNE's currency exposure. The treasurer may also use differing foreign exchange hedging instruments to reduce any risks that unnecessarily expose the MNE to foreign exchange risk.

BBVA has issued $1.5 billion of a new type of perpetual debt that can eventually be converted into equity, becoming the first European financial institution to strengthen its Tier I capital position through the new securities. The bond offering takes place only weeks after the approval of new capital regulation in Europe.

Given the growing importance of the total capital position of financial institutions, BBVA has decided to lead the market with an issuance of a new instrument that will compute as additional Tier I under CRD-IV (BIS III), as Capital Principal for the Bank of Spain and as Buffer Convertible Capital Securities for the European Banking Authority (EBA).

The instruments are perpetual, with a fully discretionary and non-cumulative coupon and are loss-absorbing through conversion into equity upon trigger events. The coupon was set at 9%, down 50 basis points from the initial guidance thanks to the strong demand. The issue was placed with qualified foreign investors, with an order book that exceeded $9 billion and with the participation of more than 400 investors. Between yesterday and today, BBVA marketed the product to potential investors in Singapore, Hong Kong, London and Zurich.

"We have substantially strengthened our capital base and we have led the market," said Manuel González Cid, chief financial officer of BBVA. "Once again, BBVA has had overwhelming support from international investors."[5]

---

2. Interest Rates and Maturation

The second key attribute of a debt instrument is the interest to be paid on the debt and when it must be repaid. When structuring their loans, MNEs should seek to avoid grouping repayments of the principal around the same date. This holds true in most cases unless there are large inflows of cash around a foreseeable date in the future. This might happen where a MNE has planned the sale of a major subsidiary, for example, in five years' time. It may then arrange its affairs such that a number of its loan principal repayments occur around the same time. Normally, though, an MNE needs to source long-term external funds to make a large investment of some type. Income from the investment over time ought to be enough to pay the interest on the loan and allow enough retained cash to be built up to repay the loan principal

---

5   See http://press.bbva.com/latest-contents/press-releases/bbva-first-european-issuer-of-new-generation-of-tier-i-instruments__9882-22-c-102652__.html (accessed November 2014).

when it falls due. Therefore, the MNE would ideally structure the loan interest and repayment dates so that they match the cash inflows from the investment project. In essence, MNEs tend to finance short-term debt requirements, such as working capital, out of short-term debt and to finance long-term capital needs out of long-term debt.

However, it is unlikely that an MNE will get things all its own way when borrowing funds or be able to issue debt instruments always on its own terms or demand repayment terms from a bank that are entirely in its favour. Normally, the term of the debt instrument will be dictated by the standards of the MNE's particular debt market and will be shaped by investor demand and expectation. For example, US corporate bonds are typically for periods of 20 to 30 years (see later in this chapter for a more complete description of bonds and Eurobonds.) Eurobonds, on the other hand, are issued with repayment timescales of typically five years. Clearly, the longer a bond is in issuance before its redemption date, the more often it is likely to be traded on the secondary bond markets. This means that the MNE may eventually find that the identity of its creditors change over time as holders of its debt instruments sell on the instruments to other banks or investors, which has implications for the relationship and stakeholder management practices of the MNE. Each time its debt instruments are sold to another party the MNE may need to invest effort in understanding the nature of the new relationship. Why has the investor bought the debt instrument? What are their needs? What do they understand about the business of the MNE?

Interest on debt may be **fixed** or **floating** and is paid to the holder at predetermined intervals. Floating rates are rates that vary over time according to a prevailing, independently set interbank rate, such as the London Interbank Overnight Rate (LIBOR). Variable rates will normally be short term while fixed rates tend to be for a longer timeframe. If short-term variable rates are lower than long-term fixed rates, an MNE might be tempted to borrow short term rather than long term. However, it is commonly accepted that long-term rates are just a weighted average of short-term rates combined with expectations in the movement of those rates. Market efficiencies would tend to support this theory since if it were not true, MNEs would always borrow short term when rates are below long-term rates (and vice versa) and therefore would never lose out. In real life, when it suits the purpose to which the funds will be put, MNEs will borrow at short-term variable rates even when there are lower long-term fixed rates available. The opposite is also true. It is difficult to be certain that long-term fixed rates are a simple extrapolation of short-term rates adjusted for expectations of movements in rates. This is because many things will change interest rates over the medium term and it is not possible to track which expectations came to pass and which did not and what effect they have on rates. In summary, therefore, it is better not to speculate on interest-rate movements but to source the lowest possible interest rate for the duration of the cash flows to which the capital raised is going to be allocated.

(We are discussing interest rates and maturation of debt instruments. We are especially focusing on bonds as they represent the most common type of debt instrument for raising long-term capital for an MNE.)

Some corporate bonds are issued with no expectation of their being redeemed. These bonds are called '**perpetuals**'. An advantage of issuing perpetual bonds, particularly in recent years, is to take advantage of low interest rates. While this may be the motivation for the bond issuer, from an investor's point of view the capital value of the bond will fall in value if interest rates deviate above expectations, a risk that will need to be factored into the interest rate the perpetual bond attracts. The potential fall in the capital value of the bond thereby negates the 'interest rate' benefit potential for the bond issuer, that is, the borrower.

3. Liquidity of Debt Instruments

Having considered the currency of debt instruments, repayment timeframes and interest rates, we will now look at their liquidity. The liquidity of a debt instrument represents a measure of the ability of the holder of the instrument, the lender, to be able to sell it to another party, i.e. the ability of the lender to be able to trade the debt instrument, effectively, to sell it.

Corporate bonds can be issued directly to the investing community and are then traded on the secondary bond markets. The interest rate attaching to a bond is normally fixed when the bond is issued. However, the de facto interest rate adjusts on the secondary market since the bond may change hands for a price different from the original issue price. This may happen because of a shift in interest rates or in the perceived risk profile of the bond issuer. For example, the Ladbrokes bond mentioned above was in units of £100. By November 2014, these bonds were trading at £101.20. We can calculate the interest rate implicit in this bond by solving the equation 5.125, the original interest rate, divided by 100 over 101.2, which gives:

$$x = 5.125\left(\frac{100}{101.2}\right) = 5.06$$

Thus the interest rate now being earned by an investor who bought the bond in November 2014 is 5.06%. The interest rate has fallen since the bond issued. This could be due to a number of factors, including falling interest rates generally or some issue relevant to the individual Ladbrokes' bond or the sector in which it operates.

In any case, the main thing to note in this example is that bonds can be traded on regulated bond markets after they have been issued, thus giving the investor some liquidity in the debt. In some instances, an MNE may buy back its own bonds if the price has fallen to such a degree as to make this a credible investment for the benefit of the shareholders.

As mentioned above, some debt, particularly in Europe, is sourced by MNEs from banks. Even debt secured from banks as against the issuance of bonds can be traded, depending on the nature of the loan agreements. Banks will lend long-term funds to the MNE. The banks, in turn, have 'borrowed' this money from their depositors, the money markets for shorter requirements or by issuing bonds themselves for longer term capital requirements. In these instances, the bank is an intermediary and this type of debt is called '**intermediated debt**'. It is normally not tradable, although the financial crisis has seen banks sell off their loan books in order to improve liquidity. In many instances the banks have been selling these distressed debts for below the original amount lent to the MNE, in other words, at a discount. In some instances shareholders in the relevant MNEs have actually been able to buy the debt of their own company at a discount to the 'face value' of the original loan note.

4. International Characteristics of Debt Instruments

Debt instruments are issued by a variety of organisations, including MNEs, governments and local authorities. They are also issued in a number of different countries and currencies. Thus, we can build up a matrix of the possible international characteristics a bond may exhibit from the perspective of the issuing entity:

	Issued by residents or domestic entities	Issued by non-residents or foreign entities
Domestic Currency	Domestic Bond	Foreign Bond
Foreign Currency	Eurobond	Eurobond

From the table above we can see that **Eurobonds** are the label given to bonds issued in foreign currencies whether by domestic entities or by foreign entities. For example, if an Irish Plc raised funds by issuing US dollar-denominated bonds, they would be Eurobonds. Likewise, if a Canadian company's Irish subsidiary raised funds by issuing US dollar bonds, they would also be Eurobonds.

A '**foreign bond**' is a bond issued by a foreign entity but in the domestic currency. For example, an Indian company issuing a Sterling-denominated bond would be a foreign bond from a Belfast perspective. Foreign bonds are normally subject to the regulations of the country in which they are issued, not the regulations in the country of the issuing company. Accordingly, an Indian company issuing Sterling bonds in the hope of attracting investors in London must comply with the regulations of the London Stock Exchange for the issuance of debt, not whatever regulations might apply in India.

The Bond Market

The main component of the bond markets on a global basis are **government bonds**, which are bonds issued by federal or sovereign governments together with certain local authorities. For example, Transport for London has issued £400 million of bonds to fund reductions in air pollution and help with climate change.[6]

At the end of 2014 there was just over US$100 trillion of bonds outstanding throughout the world.[7] Almost 50% of the total bond market is made up of bonds issued by governments. Taken together, US, Japanese and EU Member State government bonds account for almost all government bonds in issue. In emerging markets the government share of the bond market is much lower. Most bond issues still tend to be domestic bonds, that is, bonds issued by domestic entities in their home currency. Only 30% of the global bond market is made up of international bonds, though this is the fastest growing area of the bond market. Of the 50% of the bond market made up of issues by corporations, almost 80% is issued by financial institutions such as banks. Just over 10% (almost US$10 trillion) of the total global bond market is made up of issuances by non-financial corporations.

We will now explore the types of bonds and their relevant markets in some more detail. First, we will examine the currency of the bond issuance and how this might affect how and where it is bought and sold.

Domestic Corporate Bonds

Domestic bonds are issued by borrowers in the domestic market in the currency of that market. An MNE may issue a bond in its home market and currency to finance international expansion. An example would be the Ladbrokes bond issue described above. Domestic bonds are regulated by the governments in the countries in which they are issued. The main regulators are the Financial Services Authority (FSA) in the UK and the Securities and Exchange Commission (SEC) in the US. In Ireland bonds are traded on an exchange operated by the Irish Stock Exchange (ISE).

---

[6] See www.db.com/cr/en/concrete-deutsche-bank-supports-transport-for-londons-first-green-bond (accessed July 2015).

[7] Bank for International Settlements, *BIS Quarterly Review*, June 2015, Table 18.

To make sense for all parties, a bond issue would need to be at least €10 million in size. Amounts under this would not be economical since:

- the issuing entity would need a credit rating;
- investors would need to perform due diligence; and
- debt instruments (bonds) would need to be of a scale to interest bond traders.

Foreign Corporate Bonds

Foreign corporate bonds are issued by a foreign entity in a domestic market. Foreign bond issues are usually issued by MNEs. For example, UK-based Ineos Grangemouth Plc issued a €285 million bond on the Irish Stock Exchange. Ineos is raising the money to build a huge ethane holding tank in Scotland that will allow it to feed its refinery from US shale gas once North Sea gas supplies dry up. The MNE has raised euro since the construction contract for the new tank is with a euro-denominated German construction firm.[8] Interestingly, this bond was secured by a guarantee from the UK Government and could consequently be issued with a relatively low interest rate of 0.75%. It was issued on the Global Exchange Market (GEM) section of the ISE, where ISE deals with tradable debt instruments in many currencies. The ISE regulates the issuance of the debt and has listing regulations to which foreign MNEs must adhere when listing their debt on the market. The market provides both a primary and a secondary market, meaning that MNEs can raise money by listing their debt instruments. Also, investors can achieve liquidity by selling the instruments on the market. Most instruments listed on the GEM section of the ISE can also be bought on other stock exchanges.

Eurobonds

Though these types of bonds sound as if they are intrinsically connected with the euro currency, they are not. As we have seen, a Eurobond is a bond denominated in a currency other than the currency of the country in which it is issued. They should not be confused with European bonds, which are bonds backed collectively by all Eurozone countries. Indeed, over 70% of Eurobond issues are in US dollars.

Eurobonds have some special characteristics worth noting. Originally, they were bearer bonds meaning that whoever was in possession of the bond was the recipient of the interest payable and the ultimate bond redemption funds. When the Eurobond market was first developed, US withholding taxes could be avoided on bearer bonds. By the time these withholding tax breaks were removed the Eurobond market had been established. Eurobonds often have convertibility options allowing them to be converted into equity, or shares, in the issuing entity, which means that the lender who has purchased a Eurobond may, in certain circumstances, end up converting the bond into a given number of shares in the MNE that has issued the bond. The trigger event for a conversion right to apply is often a redemption date, i.e. if the bond is not repaid on a certain nominated day, the bondholder can convert the bond into a given percentage of the equity of the issuing entity.

Eurobonds normally have no covenants, meaning that there is little or no underpinning security. In the Ineos example above, the UK Government was prepared to give a guarantee to the bondholders that it would step in if Ineos did not repay the bond. This is not the normal situation with Eurobonds, however. The absence of underpinning security or collateral means Eurobonds often have a higher degree of risk for the investor than a bond backed with collateral.

---

[8] www.ineos.com/sites/grangemouth/news, press release 17 July 2014 (accessed December 2014).

The existence of these additional risks means that the issuer must have a good credit rating to succeed on the Eurobond market.

Most Eurobonds are underwritten by the investment banks involved in their issuance. The banks guarantee the issuer that they will buy any bonds that remain unsold in the market upon the initial issuance. This system of underwriting normally involves the main syndicate selling the bonds on to a wider group of banks in advance of the actual launch to the bond market. Though these banks are supposed to release the bonds onto the market so that they can be taken up by the final bond purchasers, this does not always happen and the larger underwriter banks tend to hold onto the bonds, thus causing a shortage on the market. This shortage can drive up the price of the bond, allowing the underwriter to make an additional profit when they do eventually sell the bonds they hold. In **Example 14.2** below the underwriters of Scrod Plc's bond issue hold back €20 million of bonds leading to an artificially lower supply of the bond on the market. The law of supply and demand will apply and the price will rise if the supply is constrained. The 'profit' made by the underwriter from such a practice is, in essence, a cost that the issuing entity could have avoided had all the bonds been released onto the market at the correct time.

EXAMPLE 14.2: EUROBOND ISSUANCE – AN UNDERWRITING CHALLENGE

A syndicate of four banks managing the issuance of €100 million of Eurobonds on behalf of Scrod Plc 'sell' on the bonds to the second and third stage underwriters in advance of the issue date. When the date arrives, the underwriters are supposed to release the bonds onto the various exchanges. Imagine that €20 million of bonds are withheld by some of the second- and third-stage underwriters. In that instance, the market does not receive the full €100 million of bonds but only €80 million. This problem is alleviated by only using underwriters that have delivered on their commitments in the past. By using underwriters that have a good track record, Scrod can ensure that the market for its bond issue is best served.

London is the main trading centre for Eurobonds. It provides both the initial fundraising primary market and the valuable secondary market. It is the secondary market that delivers the liquidity for the investor. It also allows a performance measure for the performance of the MNE. If an MNE's performance is strong, one would expect to see the MNE's risk profile improve, which should lead to an increase in value of bonds issued by the MNE on the secondary markets. Likewise, if the performance is poor, or investors lose confidence in the MNE, the value of the bonds will fall on the secondary market. Therefore, the trading of the bonds on the secondary markets can provide a good indication of the market sentiment toward the issuing entity or MNE. This market indication can be helpful, especially in cases where the MNE's shares are not publically traded. In other words, where there is no other market indicator with regard to performance.

The variation of a bond's selling price on the secondary market from its original par value or ultimate redemption value can be an indicator of the market's view of the risk attached to the MNE. Other macro issues such as interest rate movements can also affect the bond price. Therefore, it is important from an investor point of view to distinguish between macro-environmental impacts on bond prices and MNE- or sector-specific issues.

Global Bonds

A '**global bond**' is similar to a Eurobond in most respects. However, unlike a Eurobond, it can also be issued in the country whose currency is used to denominate the bond. For example, a global bond issued by a German MNE denominated in Sterling could be sold in the UK or any other market in which a Eurobond market operates. If the German MNE issued a Sterling Eurobond, then it would only be marketed in Eurobond markets outside the UK, i.e. outside of the country in whose currency the bond is denominated.

Bond Interest Rates and Rights

We have looked at the characteristics of corporate bonds relating to their currency denomination. We now turn to examine the ways in which bonds attract interest and other rights that investors have by purchasing them.

Straight Fixed-rate Bonds

Straight fixed-rate bonds have a maturity date set sometime in the future. On this date the holder of the bond will be repaid the face value of the bond. During the lifetime of the bond the bondholder receives interest payments at regular intervals. These interest rates are normally a fixed percentage of the face value of the bond. Approximately 70% of international bonds are straight-fixed rate bonds.

Zero-coupon Bonds

Zero-coupon bonds are a special class of straight fixed-rate bond. These bonds pay no interest rate during their lifetime. Despite this, zero-coupon bonds can attract investors because they are initially sold for less than their face value. The gap between the face value and the initial selling price represents the profit for the investor or purchaser of these types of bonds. Upon maturity, the bondholder can redeem them for face value from the issuer. The return on the zero-coupon bond is therefore the difference between the original price paid and the face value, a total gain from the investment known as the '**outset**'.

Zero-coupon bonds are attractive to potential investors because they do not need to be concerned about re-investing interim interest payments. The issuer has the benefit of not needing to provide for the cash outflows of the interest charges during the lifetime of the bond.

There is an implicit interest earned when an investor purchases a zero-coupon bond. In some countries this implicit interest is taxable even though no cash flow benefit accrues to the bondholder. The implicit interest rate for a zero-coupon bond is given by the formula:

$$zero\,coupon\,bond\,\,yield = \left(\frac{F}{PV} \right)^{\frac{1}{n}} - 1$$

where:
F = face value of the bond
PV = the issue price of the bond, i.e. its present value at date of issue
n = the number of periods remaining.

This formula can also be used when calculating yields for dates in between the original issue date and the final maturation. All other things being equal, a zero-coupon bond should increase in value as it moves toward its final maturity date. In **Example 14.3** below Scrod Plc's zero-coupon bond will increase in value as time goes by and the eventual redemption date approaches.

Example 14.3: The Workings of a Zero-coupon Eurobond

In 2014 Scrod Plc issues $50 million of zero-coupon Eurobonds on the New York Stock Exchange maturing in 10 years. The initial discount is 12%. Scrod will therefore raise $50m × (1 − .12) = $44m. It will need to have $50 million to repay its bondholders in 2024. In the meantime, the purchasers of the bond will have spent $44 million buying bonds that will pay them back $50 million in 10 years' time. In 2023 the value of the bonds will have increased, assuming no other changes in the fortunes of Scrod Plc or in interest rates. This is because investors in the bond know that in one year's time, 2024, they will be able to redeem the bond for its face value of $50 million.

Floating-rate Bonds

As the name suggests, floating-rate bonds are those whose interest rates are variable. The interest rate they attract is normally linked to a reference rate (such as LIBOR). Interest calculations are paid quarterly or semi-annually, normally consistent with the reference rate. For example, a bond paying interest quarterly might be referenced to the three-month LIBOR, which is set at the beginning of each quarter. Floating-rate bonds account for about 30% of the international bond market.

Equity-related Bonds

Equity-related bonds are bonds that have some connection to the equity of the issuing entity or MNE. Typically they fall into two categories:
• convertible bonds; and
• bonds with warrants.

Convertible bonds can be converted into equity in the issuing MNE by the bondholder. The number of shares into which the bond can convert is set at the time it is issued.

Bonds with warrants are similar except that the bond has attached to it a 'warrant', an entitlement, to purchase a certain amount of the issuing MNE's stock at a certain price.

Equity-related bonds can be worth more than their equivalent straight fixed-rate bond. This is because the conversion rights or the warrants have a value in and of themselves, which is in addition to the value inherent in the bond's redemption value. On the other hand, an MNE will not want to cede some of its equity if it does not need to since the effect of converting debt to equity is to dilute existing shareholder value. Therefore, the MNE will only issue bonds with warrants or conversion rights if it believes it is the most economical way for it to raise the long-term capital it needs. This is why equity-related bonds are normally issued when there is a higher degree of risk or uncertainty involved. For example, if a firm is issuing a bond in order to finance oil exploration, investors in the bond may feel that they are exposed if the project goes poorly but will not get a sufficient share in the upside if things go well. In this instance, they may find a bond with conversion rights more attractive. They get their interest and face value back if things do not go according to plan and they get a share of the equity upside if things go well.

From this oil industry example one can see that an investor in a convertible bond might be prepared to accept a lower coupon at the outset in return for a higher return if the project materialises successfully. In theory, the NPV of the two possible cash flows should be the same because the probability of success is the same in both cases: straight bond or convertible.

This means the future cash flows are the same and their discounted value will be the same, assuming the same investor with the same requirements. Therefore, the discounted cash flow values of the convertible bond could be used to calculate the implicit rate of return on a straight fixed-rate bond with no conversion rights.

The benefit to the issuer of a convertible bond is that the interest rate is lower at the outset. There is also the benefit of the existing shareholders not suffering any diminution in their control of the company until the conversion.

Interest Rate Swaps

While straight fixed-rate bonds are the type of bond that is issued most frequently, they are normally available only to highly rated governments and MNEs. Companies with poorer credit ratings (see discussion of credit rating at the end of this chapter) may not have access to fixed-rate bonds because investors are not keen to take a long-term view on the MNE due, in part, to their assessment of the risks attached to the projected cash flows. Another MNE may wish to take advantage of its ability to raise funds over the longer course but would wish to have short-term variable interest rates. While it could issue a floating-rate bond (see above), another option is to do an **interest rate swap** whereby the MNE would swap interest rate serving costs with an entity that has a variable or shorter term interest rate horizon. In order to have a swap, we need to have two parties with counter-balancing interest requirements – one who has fixed-rate bonds and the other having short-term variable-rate bonds.

Earlier in the chapter we mentioned that long-term interest rates are the aggregate of short-term rates plus expected movement in short-term rates. This means that an MNE engaging in an interest rate swap is really introducing timing differences to their cash flows that, due to the particular trading situations in which the MNE finds itself, suit its purposes.

For example, imagine an MNE with a fixed interest rate payment on its bonds and that the MNE's cash flows from its investment are well correlated to variable interest rates. Therefore, its cash flows before interest charges move up and down in a fashion correlated with the movement up and down of variable interest rates. From these varying cash flows it deducts its fixed interest rate costs, leading to even more pronounced relative variability on its post-interest charge cash flows. Rather than have a volatile profit statement that would flow from such pronounced variations in cash flows, it might 'swap' its fixed rates on its bonds with a borrower who has variable interest rate debt but has a need for fixed rates on his debt. An MNE may wish to have fixed-rate interest payments because it wants certainty as to its future cash flows. The counterparty may want variable rates because its own income has a strong relationship to interest rates. By matching its varying income with variable interest cost it is reducing the volatility of its earnings stream. Such arrangements are normally carried out by banks acting as intermediaries. Sometimes the bank acts as a 'matchmaker' and the two parties are aware of each other's existence and contract with each other. Other times, the bank will act as the market maker, taking the interest rates from each party and performing the middleman role, contracting with each party separately. The MNE may never know what party or parties are on the other side of the transaction.

International Banking

The growth of international trade has brought about a growth in international banking. Banking transactions are deemed to be 'international' if one of the parties is foreign or the

currency is not the domestic currency. For example, Bank of Ireland is involved in an international banking transaction if it:
• lends euro money to a Swiss-based MNE; or
• receives deposits from a US investor; or
• lends US dollars to a Dublin-based MNE.

Table 14.3 below shows the extent to which domestic banks in various countries are exposed to foreign-denominated claims. Of the global total of US$32,616 billion reported by the Bank for International Settlements (BIS), 29% is corporate related, the remainder government and banking-sector related. (For further details on BIS, see **Chapter 9**.) From the table one can also see that Ireland punches above its weight in terms of its banking sector's exposure to world markets, which is driven by the fact that the Republic of Ireland has been successful in both the foreign direct investment (FDI) and export markets and has a vibrant financial services sector based in the IFSC.

The types of loans captured in the above table include all international banking loans, including those made by domestic banks to domestic firms but in a foreign currency. This table is indicative of the major change that has happened in banking over the last three decades, i.e. the internationalisation of banks and a convergence of the banking model. Banks originally were involved in lending and deposit-taking. Insurance companies protected against risk and investment banks focused on capital-raising and redemption. However, as global banking regulations have been eased, banks have become more involved in all types of financial instruments. As they broadened their business offering, the banks also widened their geographic reach.

According to Forbes, and as shown in **Table 14.4** below, by 2015 the biggest companies in the world are banks.

TABLE 14.3: TOTAL FOREIGN CLAIMS ON BANKS BY COUNTRY 2014[9]

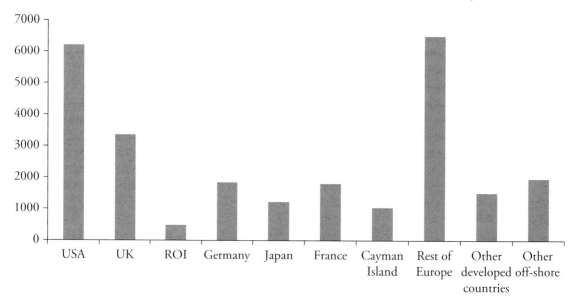

---

[9] www.BIS.org/statistics/constats.htm, Table 9A (accessed November 2014).

TABLE 14.4: BANKS AMONG THE TOP 10 GLOBAL COMPANIES [10]

Rank	Company	Country	Assets US$ bn	Market Value US$ bn
1	ICBC	China	3,322	278
2	China Construction Bank	China	2,698	213
3	Agricultural Bank of China	China	2,575	190
4	Bank of China	China	2,458	199
6	JP Morgan Chase	US	2,593	225
10	Wells Fargo	US	1,701	278

There are six banks in the top 10 companies in the world according to the 2015 Forbes Global 2000 list. More extraordinarily, four of these banks are Chinese. One can see that as international trade has grown, so have the banks that support that trade. Forbes used four metrics in calculating the table: sales, profits, assets and market value. While there is an element of subjectivity in deciding how to weight the metrics in relation to each other, for our purposes the message is clear: banks are pretty big these days.

The Basel Accord

As banks have grown in size they have become multinational giants. This has brought about the need for a banking supervisory framework that can stretch across borders and has a global reach.

A bank must source capital just like any other business and, like any other businesses this capital comes from its equity and its debt providers. The bank then invests the capital in income-producing assets, i.e. the loans it makes to its customers. The terminology can be confusing since loans are normally considered a liability. However, in the case of a bank its loans are actually the assets of the business, the investments it makes to produce future cash flows, to provide returns to its providers of capital.

In **Chapter 11** we considered how much debt an MNE should have in relation to the amount of its equity. The MNE manager must determine how much debt is appropriate. The level of debt and its sources are interrelated issues. We previously examined how increased levels of debt provide higher rates of returns to shareholders but with correspondingly increased levels of risk. In fact, there eventually comes a point where each additional percentage level of debt increases the overall cost of capital for the MNE because of the perceived risk of default on the total debt repayment. I hypothesised that this threshold debt level might be between 80% and 90% of total capital needs, depending on the industry. In banking, the debt to equity levels are higher, but how high should they be allowed to go?

In 1988, recognising the need for a global supervisory framework for banks, the G10 countries formed a committee consisting of the senior central bank officials from those countries[11] and formulated the '**Basel Accord**', which required that banks hold a capital value of at least 8%

---

[10] www.forbes.com/global2000 (accessed July 2015).

[11] G10 in 1988: Belgium, Canada, France, Germany, Italy, Japan, the Netherlands, Sweden, Switzerland (originally in association, hence 11 countries), the UK and the US.

of their assets. Straightforward, one would think. However, in recognition that not all of a bank's assets (these are loans, remember) have the same risk profile, they allowed the assets base to be calculated on a pro-forma basis depending on the type of asset the bank had. The 8% threshold was then applied to this 'pro-forma' calculated loan book. Government loans were excluded completely and interbank loans were only calculated at 20% of their par value. Thus, the two largest components of most banks' loan books were excluded or dramatically reduced for the purposes of the calculation. Only commercial loans and personal loans were given a full 100% weighting.

In addition, not all of a bank's activities fell into the original Basel Accord definition and as the years passed more account needed to be taken of off-balance sheet items and derivatives. Different weightings were given to each class of activity. By the mid-1990s, over 100 countries had adopted the Basel Accord capital requirement framework for their banks.

In the late 1990s and early 2000s, banks began to sell securitised assets. In simple terms, banks, especially in the US, would add together different types of loans into a 'bundle'. Some of these loans would be mortgages, some car loans and some other good quality loans. Taken together as an aggregate, the banks were able to give these loans a lower risk rating than the weighted average of the risk rating of each loan measured individually. The only logic for this could be that there was some element of risk eliminated through the diversity of the portfolio. For example, if you added mortgages on property in Washington, Florida and New York to car loans in California and popped in some asset-backed corporate loans made in Texas, it was possible to create a loan whose risk 'beta' was less than the weighted average of the risk 'betas' of all the component parts. This was arguably the case because some of the risk would be counter-weighted in that it was highly unlikely that Washington property would collapse at the same time as Texan industry. Mortgages in particular were believed to be low risk as they were ultimately secured on domestic properties, which were assumed to be only going up in value!

These aggregated loan portfolios were sold on between banks. Remember: the Basel Accord only attached a weighting of 20% to interbank debt. So, banks were able to create a money-making machine. The first step in starting up this money-making machine was for the banks to lend money in order to create assets from a bank's perspective. The banks lent money provided to them through their debt and equity capital. Then the loans were packaged and sold on to other banks or funds whose 'Basel weighting' was less than 100%. As a result, the sold-on loans carried a lower capital ratio requirement than the original loans, creating value in the banks. Put another way, loans that originally were classified as external and requiring a higher level of capital by the banks were replaced by inter-bank lending, which could be done with much less capital backing from the lending bank's perspective.

In 2004, US interest rates started to rise and the borrowers found themselves unable to repay their loans. This meant that the cash flows into the banks that had bought these loans began to falter. The loans needed to be written down, leading to huge capital losses. These losses were not backed with the requisite amount of capital and the balance sheets of the affected banks began to come under significant pressure, leading to the collapse of some banks. Other banks required state intervention to allow them to continue in existence.

By 2006, a new version of the Basel Accord, Basel II, had been agreed and implemented in Europe. It was complex in nature and endeavoured to calculate risk profiles of various asset types, including derivatives, and produce a capital reserve ratio for the banks from this array of risk types. The **capital reserve ratio** is an attempt to quantify how much capital a bank should have in relation to the amount of lending it has undertaken. Banks were allowed to use two types of assessment:

- the old weightings system but with externally set standards for the differing asset and derivative classes; and
- an internal ratings system, requiring external disclosure to a supervisory board.

One can see with hindsight the faults in Basel II, especially the second system, which relied so heavily on adequate disclosure, transparency and good supervisory practices.

Basel II was never implemented in the US, as the financial crisis of 2008 took hold before the accord could get off the ground. Banks began to write down the value of their loans, especially the collateralised debt securities as the mortgagees struggled to make repayments. Losses on the banks' balance sheets had a multiplier effect on their ability to lend. In order to preserve their capital ratios they had to reduce the amount of their assets, i.e. their lending. This meant demanding repayment of loans that they might otherwise have rolled over. Interbank loans, which, as we have seen, had only been weighted at 20% in the capital requirement system began to appear risky, especially after the collapse in 2007 of Northern Rock, a mortgage provider in the UK, and the later collapse of the US investment bank Lehman Brothers in September 2008. Banks were now faced with writing off completely, or substantially, any money owed to them by these institutions. This money had been lent with a draw on the lending bank's capital reserve of only 1.6%. (1.6% was the quantum of capital extant in banks at the time, meaning 98.4% of its assets were loans to customers.) But if it now had to be written off the effect would be a 100% hit to the bank's retained earnings and capital account. Put another way, a bank only had a reserve of €1.60 for every €100 it was owed by a fellow bank. The result: chaos.

The BIS and the central banks of the world combined to reflect lessons learned from the financial crisis in drawing up new banking standards, particularly as they pertain to adequacy of capital. The result was and is Basel III.

Basel III

An underlying cause of the global financial crisis was the build-up of excessive on- and off-balance sheet leverage in the banking system. In many cases, banks built up excessive leverage while apparently maintaining strong risk-based capital ratios. At the height of the crisis, financial markets forced the banking sector to reduce its leverage in a manner that amplified downward pressures on asset prices. This deleveraging exacerbated the 'feedback loop' between losses, falling bank capital and shrinking credit availability.

The deficiencies in financial regulation exposed by the financial crises of 2008–2009 led to a revisiting of Basel II. The idea was to increase the level of capital reserves that banks need to have. In 2011, the Basel III framework introduced a simple, transparent, non-risk-based 'leverage ratio' to act as a credible supplementary measure to the risk-based capital requirements. The **leverage ratio** is the ratio of a bank's capital reserves to the loans it has made. The 'non-risk' element meant that the leverage ratio was a simple ratio and would be 'blind' to the risk profile of the bank's loans. The leverage ratio is intended to:

- restrict the build-up of leverage in the banking sector to avoid destabilising deleveraging processes that can damage the broader financial system and the economy; and
- reinforce the risk-based requirements with a simple, non-risk-based 'backstop' measure.

The Basel Committee on Banking Supervision, made up of the central banks of the G10 countries, was of the view that:

- a simple leverage ratio framework is critical and complementary to the risk-based capital framework; and
- a credible leverage ratio is one that ensures broad and adequate capture of both the on- and off-balance sheet sources of banks' leverage.

Implementation of the leverage ratio requirements began with bank-level reporting to national supervisors of the leverage ratio and its components from 1 January 2013 and proceeded with public disclosure starting 1 January 2015. The Committee will continue monitoring the impact of these disclosure requirements. The final calibration, and any further adjustments to the definition, will be completed by 2017, with a view to migrating to a Pillar 1 (minimum capital requirement) treatment on 1 January 2018.

The Basel III leverage ratio is defined as:

$$\frac{Capital\ Measure}{Exposure\ measure} = Leverage\ Ratio$$

The Basel Committee will continue to test a minimum requirement of 3% for the leverage ratio during the parallel run period (i.e. from 1 January 2013 to 1 January 2017). The committee has set out additional transitional arrangements. The European Central Bank has been carrying out stress tests across all banks in the Eurozone countries. In part this is to satisfy itself that the banks are fit for purpose. It is also to ensure that banks have plans in place to address additional capital requirements they may have in anticipation of the full roll-out of Basel III requirements by 2017.

Why does any of this matter to an MNE? It matters because an MNE must have capital to expand and grow. That capital can only come from internal sources, such as retained earnings and equity, or external sources, such as loans and bond issues. The banks provide a vital conduit for external debt financing for MNEs. If the banks require higher returns or are constrained in their lending abilities, then the return on capital required by MNEs will rise. This rise in the return required reduces the value of an MNE and increases the hurdle which new projects have to achieve before they become appropriate investment projects.

Types of Bank Loan

We have covered how an MNE sources its finance from either equity or debt, and looked at the bond market as a source of debt. We will now consider the raising of loans from banks as another source of debt.

Term Loans

An MNE may borrow money from its bank with a repayment schedule over a fixed period, i.e. the 'term' of the loan. The loan may be secured on all assets of the company, specific assets or be completely unsecured. The interest rate may either be fixed or variable. The loan can sometimes be repaid early, with or without conditions.

Additionally, a loan may have certain performance criteria attached to it called '**covenants**'. Much of the time of the finance department of an MNE is spent either negotiating the terms of these covenants or ensuring the appropriate reporting is made to the lending bank to demonstrate

compliance with the terms set out in the covenants. The covenants usually cover thresholds of performance which must be achieved by the MNE. Examples of typical covenants include:
- achieving forecasted cash flows within agreed tolerance levels;
- capital expenditure ratios, e.g. only spending 50% of cash flow on capital expenditure in any one year;
- net and gross margin percentage targets;
- debt/equity ratios and other balance sheet ratios.

In an MNE with foreign currency cash flows[12] the management of these covenants can be particularly challenging. Exchange rate fluctuations outside the control of the MNE can affect the ratios, even when the underlying performance of the company is solid.

Eurocredits

Eurocredits are not termed thus because they are made in euro (as with Eurobonds the terminology is a confusing coincidence), rather they are loans that take place on the Eurocurrency market, which is the market where banks lend to and borrow from each other outside of their domestic jurisdictions. Such banks are known as 'Eurobanks'. They not only lend money to each other but also extend longer term loans to governments, other financial institutions and to MNEs. For example, when Bank of Ireland lends Stg£10 million to a client, this is an example of a Eurocredit.

Eurocredits have two distinguishing features that set them apart from debt instruments issued by domestic banks:
- they are usually syndicated; and
- they normally attract a floating interest charge linked to an independently set variable interest rate benchmark, such as LIBOR.

Syndicated Loans A syndicate is a group of banks that collaborate to make a loan. Syndicated loans normally arise because the lenders do not wish, for whatever reason, to take on the full risk of the loan, instead preferring to share out the risk between a wider number of banks. Typically, one bank will be the lead bank. This is the bank the MNE will involve itself with initially, which will then put together a wider group of banks who will agree to collaborate in the setting up of the loan. In some instances these banks may agree to participate in the loan only if the lead bank cannot secure sufficient willing participants. In this way, these banks provide an underwriting facility for the syndicate.

When the participants are finally agreed and the loan made, those that are actually providing the funds are called the 'participating banks'. One of the banks, often the lead bank, will be designated as the 'paying agent'. This is the bank that will act as the conduit for the cash flows. For example, the borrowing MNE will pay the interest on the loan to the paying agent, who will then distribute it on to the participating banks in the manner agreed at the outset between the members of syndicate.

Types of Eurocredit Loan There are two types of Eurocredit loan.
- **Term credits** Where the loan exists for a specific period of time, after the expiry of which the loan is due to be repaid.
- **Revolving credits** Here the borrower is afforded the choice of borrowing up to a fixed amount within a given timeframe. It differs from a term credit in that the MNE does not

---

[12] Some MNEs can operate in countries with the same currency, e.g. a French company with branches in Italy and Germany. All this MNE's cash flows will be in euro.

need to draw down the full amount of debt it has been sanctioned for. For example, an MNE might be allowed to borrow up to $10 million depending on its needs at any time over the next five years. The syndicate normally affords the borrower this choice in return for a commitment fee. From the borrower's perspective it means that the full loan does not need to be drawn down immediately.

Euronotes

Euronotes are a debt instrument issued on the euro currency markets and are short-term promissory notes normally underwritten by a syndicate of banks. While the notes typically mature within 12 months they are issued on a revolving basis, which means that when they mature they are replaced immediately by the next issue. This feature, called 'roll-over', often has a defined period for which the roll-overs will stay in place. For example, an MNE may issue six-month Euronotes rolling over every six months for up to five years.

Since Euronote loans mature within 12 months, their draw on the capital reserves of the banks are not as onerous as debts with longer terms. They have an advantage over bonds in that they are shorter term. For example, an MNE may not have full visibility of its debt requirements over the next year or so. Rather than issue a bond and possibly find itself with short-term surpluses that it needs to re-invest, it can borrow using Euronotes, thereby ensuring it has enough facilities to meet its debt requirement without actually taking on the longer term cost of a bond.

Euro Medium-term Notes

A number of MNEs have taken to bypassing intermediaries and issuing euro medium-term notes (euro-MTNs) directly to the market. These notes have maturity timeframes that sit between Euronotes and more conventional bonds, typically from as short as one year to seven years. There are a number of characteristics of euro-MTNs that set them apart from other debt instruments:
- issued periodically or continuously rather than all at once, meaning that the issuer can take advantage of improvements in yield curves;
- can be issued in relatively small denominations;
- costs of setting them up are lower;
- not underwritten;
- not public offerings, therefore funds can be raised discreetly.

The MNE would need to be raising at least €10 million to justify the costs associated with euro medium-term notes. Normally amounts raised would be larger, i.e. over €50 million.

Choosing the Appropriate Debt

We have seen that there is a vast array of financing options open to the MNE. In truth, most small and medium-sized MNEs will not have all these options available to them because the costs involved in putting together the debt instruments are too high for the amount of money being borrowed.

I have set out below a step-by-step method for selecting from possible debt options. This is just one approach; there are many others, though the principles will be the same or similar:
1. The MNE should decide how much it wishes to borrow. To do this it needs to assess the cash flow needs and to decide how much to finance by way of debt and how much from internal sources, such as retained earnings or fresh share capital, i.e. equity.

2. In choosing the type of external debt to take on, the MNE should consider the actual costs of putting the debt instrument together. (Treasurers will broadly know how much it costs to put together the various debt instruments discussed in this chapter.)

3. At this stage the MNE will know how much it wishes to borrow and which types of debt instrument it has the options of using. The next decision is to decide what currency it wishes the loan to be denominated in. While this decision can be shaped by the interest rates available, it is more likely to be a function of the NPV calculations and the level of balance sheet hedging provided by the various options (see **Chapter 11** for how currency choice can affect NPV calculations). The further out the terminal cash flows, the more an MNE will be exposed to foreign exchange rate risk if the cash flows are in a currency different to the currency in which the loan is denominated. The tax deductibility of the loan interest will also be a consideration. In some countries, interest on loans taken out in the host country is allowed as a deduction against profits but interest on inter-group loans is not.[13]

4. Having decided the currency in which it wishes to borrow, the MNE must next decide from what source it will borrow the money. Earlier in this chapter we saw how the international banking sector is now so developed that an MNE has a number of choices from which to source its debt. For example, an Irish Plc could borrow US dollars from an Irish bank, a US bank, a syndicate, a German bank, etc. The MNE will normally choose the source from which it can derive the best terms. The interest rates and the repayment schedules will only form one part of the mix of considerations of the terms. The MNE should also be concerned to ensure the minimum amount of collateral is given and the less constraining the covenants are the better.

This four-step approach will become much more complicated in practice because the steps will not be as neatly defined as I have set them out here. However, the same basic principles will still apply. Normally, an MNE will have laid down broad policies with regard to its levels of debt, the types of debt instruments it will pursue and its overall gearing levels. The more transparency there is on these matters, the easier it is for the finance team to arrange borrowing requirements. It will also be easier for the investor or lender to know what they are investing in or who they are lending to.

Comparing Costs

Step 4 of the process above involves the MNE comparing the costs of the various funding options. Care needs to be taken that all costs are considered. The temptation is to look at the headline interest rate and not fully understand other implications of the loan instrument. For example, it will generally be true that convertible bonds would attract a lower interest rate than a straight fixed-rate bond. However, the MNE management will need to bear in mind the dilution effect of the subsequent conversion and how the shareholders will respond to such a dilution. Another hidden cost can be the compliance costs of the covenant. Some covenants may prevent an MNE from raising further funds without renegotiating the terms of the loan, which could make the MNE locked out from other funding sources when it seeks to raise new funds in the future.

---

[13] At the time of writing this issue is a hot topic and I expect it still will be when you read it. Many MNEs have based themselves in Ireland, some to take advantage of Ireland's low corporation tax rate. By charging high interest rates and other charges to operating subsidiaries in high corporation tax countries, MNEs can effectively earn profits in Ireland from lending money across their groups. This topic is covered in more detail in the section on transfer pricing in **Chapter 16**.

All-in-Cost

To ensure that an MNE is comparing like with like when looking at debt selection options, the 'all-in-cost' (AIC) approach should be taken. The AIC approach involves calculating the IRR of all the future payments to the lender as against the net proceeds obtained from the lender at the outset.

Often a company will neglect to take account of certain elements of cash flows and focus instead on the headline interest rate. Care should also be given to the spread or loan margin. For example, if borrowing in Sterling, the rate of interest should be compared to the risk-free rate of interest in the market. The gap between the rate quoted and the risk-free rate indicates the premium the MNE is paying for borrowing the funds. Put another way, it is the return the lender requires to compensate for the risk factor in lending to the MNE. Different lenders may have different appetites for the risk associated with differing MNEs or the sectors in which they operate. This premium that the lender is proposing to charge is the most critical element of the interest rate differentials between the various lending options facing the MNE.

Credit Ratings

Various companies provide information on the creditworthiness of corporations and countries. Moody's Investor Services and Standard & Poor's (S&P) are the best known. They classify bonds in different classes depending on their assessment of the creditworthiness of the issuer. Three other major credit rating agencies are European Credit rating agency (Eurorating), the Japan Credit Rating Agency (JCR) and Fitch. Countries are issued sovereign creditworthiness ratings, which allow investors to compare different grades of quality of investment and adjust their required return accordingly.

Rating Action: Moody's downgrades Tesco's ratings to Baa3, short-term ratings to Prime-3 (P-3); Ratings remain on review for downgrade

London, 23 October 2014 – Moody's Investors Service downgraded to Baa3 from Baa2 the senior unsecured long-term ratings of Tesco Plc and its guaranteed subsidiaries. Concurrently, Moody's downgraded to Prime-3 (P-3) from Prime-2 (P-2) the short-term ratings of Tesco and its subsidiaries. All ratings remain on review for downgrade.

"We have downgraded Tesco's ratings because of the materially reduced trading profit for the first half of fiscal 2015 that is affected by the rapid structural changes in the UK retail grocery market as well as the ongoing uncertainties related to the investigation by the FCA into Tesco's accounting irregularities," says Sven Reinke, a Moody's Vice President–Senior Analyst and lead analyst for Tesco. "Even if the FCA concludes its investigation without material negative financial implications, Tesco faces huge operational challenges which continue to put its investment-grade rating at risk. The ongoing review will focus on the company's strategy to stabilize the trends in its operations, and improve its overall financial profile as it adapts to fundamental shifts within its home market. The outcome of the company's strategic review of its businesses, as well as the financial policies and business practices that its new management team will employ, will be critical elements of that assessment."[14]

(The effect of this downgrade was a further 4.5% fall in Tesco's share price on the back of a 15% fall in the preceding three weeks.)

---

[14] Moody's Investor Service, Global Credit Research, 23 October 2014. See https://www.moodys.com/research/Moodys-downgrades-Tescos-ratings-to-Baa3-short-term-ratings-to--PR_311079 (accessed May 2015).

The grades that a bond or a country can receive vary from AAA, which is the best quality, to C, which is the worst. There are 17 intermediate points on the scale between the highest and the lowest. Remember our maxim: 'a risky euro is worth less than a safe euro'. Applying this to the debt markets and using the credit rating agencies rating systems we can deduce that the better the quality of the creditworthiness, the lower the return required by investors. Therefore, it is in the interest of an MNE to ensure that it has as good a credit rating score as possible.

MNEs pay the rating agencies to grade their creditworthiness, which creates a possible conflict of interest. Some commentators have pointed out that this could have been one of the contributing factors to the financial crisis of 2007 onward, the argument being that credit rating agencies gave unduly favourable ratings to the products that were created through the alchemy of asset securitisation process, effectively creating an aggregate creditworthiness to the pooled debts that was better than the weighted average of the constituent parts. This allowed the appearance of value creation whereas in fact there was none. Whatever the rights and wrongs of those arguments, the ratings agencies still play a key role in the debt markets for MNEs.

Their role is two-fold: first, some lenders will only lend to MNEs that have a credit rating above a certain level, say A+. Consequently, the pool of available lenders is lower for MNEs who do not reach that threshold. As the laws of supply and demand prevail, the MNE will pay disproportionately more for their debt than competitors who are more highly rated. Therefore, it is a source of real competitive advantage if an MNE's rating is strong and it has, by implication, a lower cost of capital. It can borrow at a lower cost and, with this lower cost of capital, projects that its competitors might reject can be undertaken by the MNE. Accountants, and the finance function, play a critical role in driving competitive advantage through active management of the sources of finance for the MNE.

Secondly, since a risky euro is worth less than a safe euro, borrowers with lower grade ratings will need to pay more for their loans.

These two factors mean that access to funds will be increasingly more expensive as gradings disimprove. The rising cost of debt means that the return for shareholders worsens since they get their return from whatever is left over once the debt has been serviced. The effect of a downgrade on a share price can be quite dramatic on its price.

14.4 CONCLUSION

In this chapter we have seen that an MNE's capital is made up of two pillars: equity and debt. Equity can be sourced by the issuance of shares, normally on one or more of the world's stock exchanges. Some MNEs will seek to list on more than one stock exchange in pursuit of a lower cost of capital and a wider pool of potential investors. Foreign exchange differences should be minimal due to the arbitrage effect of efficient markets. MNEs may also raise money locally, as against in their home country, for the financing of projects and investments. In some instances, new external shareholders might be brought in to finance specific joint ventures or alliances with shareholder agreements in place to divide up the surpluses.

Debt can be obtained by the MNE by borrowing directly from a bank or by issuing bonds. Different markets have different appetites for the various forms of debt. An MNE should look to match its future cash flows with its debt repayment and servicing costs, both in terms of timing and currency. Bonds will trade on secondary markets after they issue, affording the investor some liquidity. This also gives the debt issuer an opportunity to get live market feedback as to the cost of capital, information that can be used for the calculation of NPVs for project appraisal.

There are a number of different debt instruments, each having its own particular characteristics, which means that an MNE has a number of choices to make in selecting the most appropriate debt instrument. The main differences between debt instruments are

- interest rates;
- maturity dates;
- tradability on the secondary markets;
- conversion rights;
- currency denomination;
- collateral and covenants.

Ratings agencies will score MNEs' creditworthiness; the riskier the MNE, the higher the cost of obtaining debt. Banks will also be constrained in their lending by their own credit ratings, the leverage ratio requirements of Basel III and their own government regulatory rules.

QUESTIONS

Self-test Questions

14.1 What are the three main sources of financing for an MNE?
14.2 Why is there a need for Basel III?
14.3 What is the difference between a straight fixed-rate bond and a floating-rate bond?
14.4 What does 'all in cost' mean?

Thought-provoking Questions

Question 14.1

You have just been appointed as the CFO of Allover Plc, an Irish building supplies business with subsidiaries in Poland, Brazil and Estonia. Your CEO has explained to you how the business is looking to raise $10 million to finance a new acquisition in the US. He has asked you for your thoughts about how Allover could source the finance for this investment. He said you should consider all possible options.

Question 14.2

You are an analyst for a small local newspaper based in Kerry. Your editor has asked you to prepare a short article on zero-coupon bonds. She wants you to explain what they are and how they differ from other types of bonds. "Remember," she said as you were about to leave her office, "our readers are not financial experts. Give me something in plain English."

Review Questions

(See Suggested Solutions to Review Questions in **Appendix B**.)

Question 14.1: BoneDri

Having read the BoneDri case study in **Appendix A**, identify the level of funding required to establish the operation in Bangladesh and recommend appropriate sources of finance for this.

Question 14.2: Hughes Engineering Limited

Having read the Hughes Engineering Limited case study in **Appendix A**, calculate the level of funding required and identify and develop some appropriate financing options for the project at hand.

Question 14.3: Stent Manufacturing Limited

Having read the Stent Manufacturing Limited case study in **Appendix A**, discuss the possible finance options available to Stent Manufacturing Limited in respect of this opportunity.

15

MANAGING FOREIGN EXCHANGE RISK

CONTENTS

SUMMARY OF LEARNING OBJECTIVES

Having read this chapter, you will understand:
- the three types of foreign exchange risk facing an MNE: transaction risk, economic risk and translation risk;
- how to identify ways to measure the exposure of an MNE to each of these types of risk;
- how to propose techniques to manage each type of risk;
- how to appraise the various techniques available to the MNE to manage foreign exchange risks and their associated costs;
- how to calculate the rate applicable to a forward contract; and
- at a high-level, how currency options are valued.

15.1 INTRODUCTION

Multinational enterprises (MNEs), by definition, do business in countries other than their own domestic economies. At their most basic they sell into or buy from companies and governments in foreign jurisdictions. As they develop and grow they will establish trading entities and manufacturing facilities in these foreign countries. All of this activity is in pursuit of returns for their shareholders.

In conducting international transactions, MNEs will find that they will have receipts or payments to make in currencies other than their domestic reporting currency. These cash flows need to be translated back into the home currency for the production of the consolidated accounts and so that they might eventually be disbursed to the MNE's shareholders. As we have seen in **Chapter 8**, the conversion rate that applies to such translation, called the '**exchange rate**', will depend on how much the foreign currency is worth in the MNE's domestic currency at a point in time.

Since an exchange rate is a variable beyond the control of an MNE it presents a risk to the MNE's future cash flows. A simple way of assessing managerial competence is to assess the ability of managers to predict the consequences of their actions. Shareholders invest in companies based upon performance predictions and disclosed risks to that performance. As exchange rate movements will be outside of the control of an MNE, its approach to the management of this risk must be disclosed.

The risks to which an MNE is exposed as a result of dealing in foreign currencies fall into three categories:
- transaction risk;
- economic risk;
- translation risk.

In this chapter we will explore the nature of each of these risk types, how to measure the risk and explain what techniques are available to the MNE to manage it.

15.2 TRANSACTION RISK

Transaction risk arises when a future cash transaction, either an inflow or an outflow, can be affected by an exchange rate fluctuation. In **Example 15.1** below you can see that Posh Stuff's risk exposure is connected to the transaction it undertakes, the purchase of 10,000 glasses in euro.

EXAMPLE 15.1: POSH STUFF (1) – TRANSACTION EXPOSURE

A Belfast-based department store, Posh Stuff, has bought crystal glassware from a Galway-based manufacturer, Glassy Eyes, at €100 for a set of six drinking goblets. It intends to sell the sets for £160 in its downtown Belfast store. It has ordered 10,000 sets for delivery in 30 days' time and has 60 days' credit from the date of delivery. Posh Stuff knows how many euro it will need to pay for each set of six glasses (€100) and for the entire order (€1,000,000), but it does not know how much Sterling it will need to make the payment. The amount of Sterling it will need will depend on the Sterling/euro exchange rate on the day it makes the payment, i.e. 90 days after it has placed the order (delivery is 30 days from the order and payment a further 60 days later). This uncertainty is called a '**foreign exchange transaction exposure**'. The clue is in the name. The exposure arises from the fact that a cash transaction is due to take place. These cash transactions are normally a result of a more fundamental trading transaction. In our example, the cash-flow transaction of paying for the glasses arises from the trading transaction of the Belfast department store ordering the 10,000 sets of glasses from the Galway manufacturer and agreeing the price of €100 for a set of six. The exposure arises directly from the timing difference between when the trading transaction (the sale) was agreed and when the cash transaction (the payment) takes place.

Whenever an MNE enters into a transaction that will involve a cash flow at some time in the future in a foreign currency, it has a foreign exchange transaction exposure risk. The risk arises because the **spot exchange rate**, the rate at which one currency is converted into another, that will prevail on the date in the future of the intended cash flow is not known at the time the transaction is being committed to. If an MNE has a transaction exposure it has three tasks it must carry out:
1. measure the transaction exposure risk;
2. decide whether to hedge, and if the answer is yes:
3. decide which hedging technique to use to manage the transaction risk.

1. Measuring Transaction Risk

The first task is to measure the level of transaction exposure, currency by currency. In **Example 15.1** above there was only one transaction. Posh Stuff has a future payment of €1,000,000 to make to Glassy Eyes that it needs to make in 90 days' time. In this example, it is easy to measure the total exposure: it is €1,000,000 in 90 days' time.

In most instances, however, there will be more than one transaction to take account of. The larger an MNE is, and the more markets in which it operates, the more complex will be its foreign exchange transactions. The MNE must have a systematic way of consolidating all its future known transactions in the various currencies in which it has exposures. It is the **net** exposures it is interested in, meaning that the MNE, taken as a whole, only has exposure to a particular exchange rate fluctuation on the net cash inflow/outflow of the given currency on a given day in the future. This is because it can match inflows with outflows in the same currency, meaning that the exposure only arises on the net difference between the two. In **Example 15.2** below Posh Stuff's euro exposure is only on €500,000 since it can offset the €1,500,000 cash inflow with the €1,000,000 outflow.

EXAMPLE 15.2: POSH STUFF (2) – NET TRANSACTION EXPOSURE

Posh Stuff had sold some of its own-brand, handmade furniture to Kanapee, a German home store chain, for €1,500,000. Kanapee is due to pay Posh Stuff on the same day that Posh Stuff is due to pay Glassy Eyes €1,000,000. When measuring their transaction exposure risk, Posh Stuff must look at the net exposure. It has €1,500,000 coming in and €1,000,000 going out. Therefore, its net exposure is that it has a net inflow of €500,000 in 90 days' time, i.e. a cash inflow of euro in 90 days' time. The exposure risk is due to the uncertainty as to how many pounds Sterling it will receive for the €500,000 since it cannot accurately predict the spot rate that will prevail on the day.

In a more complex environment it will be necessary to perform cash-flow projections into the future for all foreign currency cash flows and their associated timings. As the spot exchange rate is the exchange rate prevailing at any particular moment in time between one currency and another it is constantly changing, minute by minute, second by second. For most practical purposes it will suffice to perform the cash flow projections on a weekly basis, or daily if the sums are significant relative to the overall size of the business.

In an MNE there will need to be a central consolidating point, usually the treasury function, where the cash flows from all the subsidiary entities and investment projects are brought together and the net exposure calculated. This process cannot readily be done by each subsidiary since they will not have visibility of all the cash flows within the group.

Example 15.3 below shows why a centralised treasury function is critical for the effective management of foreign exchange risk in an MNE and the value of a centralised treasury function feeds into the wider issue of the organisational structures of MNEs (see **Chapter 3**).

Example 15.3: 'Moneybank' – Centralised Net Exposure Measurement

Moneybank has a subsidiary, Alpha, which has a $250,000 cash inflow in Week 10. Gamma, also a subsidiary of Moneybank, has a $200,000 outflow in Week 10. Therefore, Moneybank has a net inflow US dollar exposure in Week 10 of $50,000. This exposure is the net of the inflow in subsidiary Alpha of $250,000 and the outflow of $200,000 in subsidiary Gamma. Only at the Moneybank head office can the central treasury function see that the group exposure in Week 10 is a dollar inflow of $50,000. While Alpha and Gamma know about their own individual exposures they are unaware of each other's exposure. If the information was not collated and consolidated at group level, Alpha would believe it had an exposure of $250,000 and Gamma an exposure of $200,000. Together they would put in place strategies to cover $450,000 of exposures.

In the Moneybank example above, only two subsidiaries and two cash-flow events are considered. In real life things will normally be more complicated. There might be more subsidiaries involved, numerous currencies, and multiple foreign currency cash flows. MNEs must have systems and processes in place that allow for efficient capture of the salient information to afford ample time for the MNE to decide what action it wishes to take.

2. To Hedge or not to Hedge

Foreign currency translation: CRH's activities are conducted primarily in the local currency of the country of operation resulting in low levels of foreign currency transactional risk. The principal foreign exchange risks to which the consolidated financial statements are exposed pertain to adverse movements in reported results when translated into euro (which is the Group's reporting currency) together with declines in the euro value of the Group's net investments which are denominated in a wide basket of currencies other than the euro.[1]

Having identified its net exposures currency by currency, week by week (or day by day), the MNE must then decide whether to protect itself against some or all of the expected exposures. Most MNEs will have a policy agreed by the board of directors that will guide the finance function as to what steps to take. (It is important that shareholders are also aware of the policy as well as the MNE's approach to managing transaction exposure risk.)

As discussed in **Chapter 11**, Modigliani and Miller have proposed that only the non-diversifiable risk in a company should affect the value of the firm.[2] Since foreign exchange risk could be diversified at the personal level by the investor, the MNE need not undertake any risk mitigation strategies, or so the Modigliani–Miller Theorem might argue. In real life, however, the exact conditions underpinning the Modigliani–Miller Theorem do not often apply and investors will tend to reward predictable and steady cash flows with a lower cost of capital. Investors are unlikely to be able to assess the ongoing transaction risks in the MNE without access to all the transaction details. Rather, they will expect, rightly, that the MNE will manage these risks. The strategy of 'no surprises' really does pay.

---

[1] CRH, *Annual Report 2013*, p. 93.
[2] Modigliani, F. and Miller, M. (1958) "The Cost of Capital, Corporation Finance and the Theory of Investment" *American Economic Review* 48(3) 261–297.

Foreign exchange risk management [GSK]

Foreign currency transaction exposures arising on internal and external trade flows are not generally hedged. The Group's objective is to minimise the exposure of overseas operating subsidiaries to transaction risk by matching local currency income with local currency costs where possible. GSK's internal trading transactions are matched centrally and inter-company payment terms are managed to reduce foreign currency risk. Foreign currency cash flows can be hedged selectively under the management of Corporate Treasury and the Treasury Management Group (TMG). Where possible, GSK manages the cash surpluses or borrowing requirements of subsidiary companies centrally using forward contracts to hedge future repayments back into the originating currency. In order to reduce foreign currency translation exposure [see **Section 15.4** for an explanation of translation exposure], the Group seeks to denominate borrowings in the currencies of the principal assets and cash flows. These are primarily denominated in US dollars, euros and Sterling. Certain borrowings can be swapped into other currencies as required. Borrowings denominated in, or swapped into, foreign currencies that match investments in Group overseas assets may be treated as a hedge against the relevant assets. Forward contracts in major currencies are also used to reduce exposure to the Group's investment in overseas assets (see 'Net investment hedges' section of this note for further details). The TMG reviews the ratio of borrowings to assets for major currencies monthly.[3]

One can see from extracts above from the annual reports of the Irish-based CRH and London-quoted GSK that each company has a different approach to managing exchange rate transaction exposure. The key point is that the investors in these companies can assess their individual appetite to foreign exchange risk in an informed way. The finance and treasury functions also have clear guidelines as to what actions to take concerning this risk. In most cases an MNE will seek to minimise risk; in almost no situation would an MNE's board of directors or risk committee sanction speculation on the foreign exchange markets as a route to making or improving cash flow.

3. Managing Transaction Risk

Having decided that it will hedge some or all of its transaction exposure risk, the MNE must then decide which hedging technique to use. Not all techniques are suitable for all transaction exposure types. The decision about which technique to use will be made by reference to the company's policies, its appetite for risk and the cost of providing the cover.

Internal Techniques

Invoicing   The first, and possibly simplest, approach would be for the MNE to invoice in the foreign currency thereby avoiding the transaction risk. For example, Adidas, the sportswear manufacturer, services its Republic of Ireland retail customers from its UK division. Adidas UK invoices its Republic of Ireland (ROI) customers in Sterling. This means that Adidas UK avoids any exchange rate transaction risk on its receivables when collecting the cash from its customers in Ireland. On the other hand, Adidas's ROI retailer customers take on a transaction exposure as they will most likely sell the goods for euro in their stores. (Though Adidas is a German company whose accounts are in euro, one assumes that the company's practice of invoicing its ROI customers in Sterling hedges the exchange rate risk from the UK operating division's point of view.) In the following panel we can see the actual text of Adidas' hedging policy extracted from its 2013 annual accounts.

---

[3] GSK *Annual Report* 2013, p. 70.

Derivative financial transactions entered into with banks by Group Treasury (primarily forward currency and currency option transactions) are generally related to underlying transactions with Group companies. Hedge accounting is applied if there is a direct hedging relationship between these transactions. The net hedge presentation method is applied. The fair values of the hedges are matched and changes in value from the hedged risk which offset each other are not recognized. Unrealized losses are recognized in profit or loss only if they are not covered by unrealized gains in the hedge accounting. Derivative transactions that are not recognized using hedge accounting are measured individually at fair value. Any losses resulting from these transactions are recognized in profit or loss; gains are not recognized in excess of cost.[4]

Thus, an MNE may, after assessing its cash flow profile, adjust its invoicing processes to create internal hedging opportunities. In this way, by internally arranging its affairs in an appropriate way, it might be able to avoid the costs associated with using an externally provided technique. (We will examine the external techniques next.) It should be pointed out, however, that it is unlikely that the MNE could avoid all transaction risk by this method as the timings of the cash flows are unlikely to be smooth enough to match each other in timings and quantum every day. However, an MNE with predictable cash flows may find that such an approach can help minimise some transaction risk, if not all.

Leading and Lagging   As mentioned above, the first task of an MNE with possible foreign exchange transaction risk is to assess the level of its exposure. One measure the MNE may take to help reduce these net exposures is to change its invoicing. Changing the currency in which it bills its customers or trying to alter the currency with which it will pay its suppliers might also reduce its net exposures. Either approach involves gaining support from either its customers or suppliers.

Once the invoicing alternatives have been exhausted, the MNE can then look at trying to match cash flows by negotiating either delays or accelerations of either payments or receipts. For example, Posh Stuff might have a euro payment due in Month 6 of €100,000. It has a euro income in Month 7 of €120,000. It would be in its interest to try to have these transactions take place on the same day so that the euro income and outflow match each other and the net exposure on the day will only be €20,000.

One of the downsides of using leading and lagging as a technique to hedge transaction exposure is the detrimental effect it may have on supplier relationships. Suppliers expect, rightly, to be paid according to the agreed terms of trade. They will not appreciate delays in payments carried out for the hedging purposes of their customers with no benefit to themselves. Fractious relationships with suppliers can affect the supply of goods in extreme cases as suppliers may be reticent to supply if they think there will be delays in payment.

External Techniques

Futures   A 'future' is a contract to buy, or sell, a specified asset at a predetermined date and price. In the case of foreign exchange futures the specified asset will be an amount of currency. Futures are the first of the externally available techniques for managing transaction exposure risk that we will discuss. An MNE can enter into a **futures contract** to either buy or sell a given amount of a foreign currency at a specified time in the future at an agreed rate. The contract documentation is such that the obligations can be traded on a **futures market**, which allows

---

[4] Adidas Group, *Financial Statements for Adidas AG for the Year Ended 31 December 2013*, p. 7.

the MNE to close out the contract if it is no longer required. Since they are traded instruments, futures tend to have higher associated costs than other types of foreign exchange hedging instruments (see below). Currency futures are only available in the major currencies and are for specific standardised amounts. For example, the €/£Stg future trades in blocks of €125,000. Futures are traded on regulated exchanges. The largest one in the world is the CME Group, originally the Chicago Mercantile Exchange.

A major advantage of futures is that, since they are traded, they are marked to market each day. In other words, the market sets a value for futures every day, thereby allowing the MNE to know the value of their currency futures at any moment in time. The main advantage of the fact that futures are traded on an exchange is that the MNE holder of a future can close out their position whenever they choose. This is what normally happens; futures seldom run their full course and are closed out before the settlement date. An advantage to an MNE of futures is that it can use them to hedge uncertain cash flows and then close out the future if the expected cash-flow transaction does not arise.

In **Example 15.4** below, Bettabuild uses a futures contract to ensure it knows with certainty the euro cost of its bid to buy a property in Zurich, Switzerland. If the bid is unsuccessful then Bettabuild can close out the future by selling it on the exchange.

EXAMPLE 15.4: USING FUTURES TO HEDGE A POSSIBLE AUCTION BID

Bettabuild, a County Laois-based MNE is bidding to purchase a property in Zurich, Switzerland. The auction is taking place in 90 days' time and, if successful the contract will close 180 days after that, i.e. in 270 days. Bettabuild believes it can offer up to CHF50 million for the property. Bettabuild can enter into a **futures contract** today to give certainty as to its total cost in euro of the purchase if it wins the auction. The future would mature in 270 days. If Bettabuild loses at the auction in 90 days' time it can unwind the position after the auction.

The implicit value or loss of a future is realisable every day as its value adjusts to make the contracted exchange rate equal the actual exchange rate on the day. In **Example 15.5** we can see how the movement of the futures market cancels out any benefit to Blubear from unwinding its futures position as the spot exchange rate moves between Stg£ and the €.

EXAMPLE 15.5: VALUATION OF CURRENCY FUTURES

Blubear, based in Tralee, County Kerry, has a Stg£95,000 liability to a UK supplier that falls due in 180 days. It buys a future for €125,000 that can be exchanged for £95,000. This is an implicit rate of €1 = £0.76. Blubear now knows that its maximum liability is €125,000 since it can exchange €125,000 for £95,000 when the debt falls due. After 90 days has passed the spot exchange rate is €1 = £0.80; the annual Sterling interest rate is 6%, and the euro interest rate is 2%. Should Blubear keep the future or unwind its position?

Using simple mathematics we can work out the value of the future on Day 90: it is a function of the Day 90 spot exchange rate, the maturity exchange rate and the interest rate differential for the 90 days that have still to run on the future.

If Blubear sought to sell the future on Day 90, it would only get €117,595 for it, incurring a loss of €7,405. This is because the market adjusts the value of the future to take account of the daily movements in the spot exchange rate as time moves toward maturity. So, how are we able to work out that Blubear would only get €117,595 for the future?

The driving force behind the market adjustment to the value of the future works like this:

Blubear could borrow €117,018 on Day 90 at 2% interest, the euro annual interest rate. It could then exchange the euro it has borrowed of €117,018 @ 0.80 into £93,615. It then places the £93,615 on deposit at 6% per annum, the Sterling interest rate. In 90 days' time (Day 180 since it incurred the liability) the Sterling deposit will have earned interest of £1,385. This is calculated as $£93,615 \times \dfrac{0.06}{365} \times 90 = £1,385$.

Adding the interest to the amount on deposit, Blubear will have £93,615 + £1,385 = £95,000 in the account in 90 days' time. This is the amount of Sterling it needs to settle its foreseeable liability.

Back in Tralee, on the euro debt, it will owe the €117,018 it borrowed plus the interest accrued over the 90 days at 2% per annum, being $€117,018 \times \dfrac{0.02}{365} \times 90 = €577$. Adding the interest to the amount borrowed, Blubear will have to repay €117,018 + €577 = €117,595 to its bank.

Therefore, Blubear derives no advantage from exiting the future since the market value it will get for the future equals precisely the sum it will need to meet the Sterling liability in 90 days. The only reason Blubear would exit the future is if the liability no longer existed, or it wished to speculate on the foreign exchange rates. In its accounts Blubear has no need to recognise the loss since it has already booked the cost of meeting the liability as being €125,000 when it entered into the arrangement. The fall in value of the future at Day 90 is a function of the weakening of the €, from €1 = £0.80 to €1 = £0.76 and the difference in the interest rates between the two currencies, € = 2% and Stg = 6%.

Forward Contracts   Forward contracts are similar to futures in that they are contracts to exchange certain specified currencies at an agreed date in the future at an exchange rate agreed today. Since the exchange rate that exists at the specified time in the future is now immaterial, the MNE effectively avoids exchange rate risk. In essence, it secures a predictable exchange rate at the time it enters into the contract. We have seen in **Chapter 8** that the exchange rate agreed in the setting of the forward contract is not a 'guesstimate' of where the exchange spot rate might be at a specified time in the future. Rather, it is today's spot exchange rate adjusted for the interest rate differential between the two currencies over the timeframe involved. Imagine a spot rate of €1.00 = $1.10 today. € interest rates are 5% and the $ rate is 15%, per annum. We would then expect the forward rate for one year from now to be: $€1.00 = \$1.10 \left(\dfrac{1.15}{1.05} \right) = \$1.20$ (see **Chapter 8, Example 8.9**).

Forward contracts are bilateral agreements between an MNE and its bank. The contracts are not traded on the markets and normally complete their term. MNEs will tend to use forward contracts when they know the exact timing and quantum of their foreign exchange exposures.

In **Example 15.6** below Belfast retailer Posh Stuff is looking for a forward contract to deliver €500,000 in 70 days' time. The calculations show how the bank works out the forward contract rate. The example demonstrates that the forward contract is a function of today's spot rate and the interest rate differential between the two currencies, the € and Stg£ in this instance.

EXAMPLE 15.6: FORWARD CONTRACT RATES

Posh Stuff has calculated that it has a net euro income in Week 10 of €500,000. In order to hedge this exposure, it decides it will enter into a forward contract for exchange of €500,000 for Sterling in 10 weeks' time. The exchange rate at Week 0 is €1 = £0.85. Euro annual interest rates are 2% and Stg£ interest rates are 10%. Posh Stuff's bank quotes it an exchange rate for the contract of €1 = £0.863p. The bank calculated this rate as follows.

The bank will borrow on Day 0 the amount of euro it needs to complete the contract with Posh Stuff in 10 weeks' time, i.e. 70 days on from Day 0. Therefore, the bank needs to borrow an amount of euro on Day 0 that will equate to €500,000 in 70 days' time. This amount is €498,089, since €498,089 plus interest charged of €1,911 (498,089 × 2% per annum for 70 days) gives €500,000.

The bank takes the €498,089 it has borrowed and converts it into Sterling at the spot rate on Day 0, €1 = 0.85p and receives Stg£423,376, which it places on deposit at 10% per annum and after 70 days receives £8,119 interest. The bank adds this interest to the amount on deposit and has £431,495 after 70 days. The bank receives €500,000 from Posh Stuff on Day 70 and uses it to repay the loan plus the interest accrued. It then pays over to Posh Stuff the Sterling amount that was on deposit, plus the accrued interest earned, a total of £431,495. Therefore, the rate it quotes for the contract will be €500,000 = £431,495 or €1 = £0.863p.

Another way of showing this calculation is: $€1 = £0.85 \left(\dfrac{1 + \left(0.10 \times \dfrac{70}{365} \right)}{1 + \left(0.02 \times \dfrac{70}{365} \right)} \right) = £0.863$

In the above example, the bank receives no benefit from facilitating the transaction. In real life it would charge a fee, which fee could be worked into the rate charged or could be charged separately.

Using a forward contract for foreign exchange an MNE locks in an exchange rate when it enters into the contract. It therefore knows the exact value of the transaction in the reporting currency once it undertakes the contract.

As mentioned earlier, the forward contract exchange rate is not a forecast of what the rate might be on the maturity on the contract. Rather, it is a function of the rate today projected into the future using interest rate differentials. It is critical for the MNE manager to grasp this concept. There can be a temptation to look at entering into forward contracts as 'a bet' on what the exchange rate might be when the maturity date is reached. For example, an MNE may enter into a forward contract for £100,000 at an exchange rate with the euro of £1 = €1.25 in 90 days' time, a total euro expenditure of €125,000. When it comes to buying the Sterling in 90 days' time the actual rate might be £1 = €1.10. Had the MNE not entered into the forward contract, it would have been able to settle the Sterling liability for €110,000, €15,000 less than the cost associated with the forward contract.

It is important to realise that this €15,000 is not a real loss because the transaction and its associated foreign exchange rates were locked in at the time of the contract. Subsequent movements in the exchange rate have nothing to do with the forward contract and, it is worth adding, are not 'the fault' of the CFO or the finance function.

If an MNE is competing in a market where some of its competitors hedge their transactions and others do not, it can find itself at a competitive disadvantage to the market or an advantage if exchange rates go against the competitors' approach. We can explain this by returning to our earlier example involving Posh Stuff.

EXAMPLE 15.7: POSH STUFF (3) – GAINING A COMPETITIVE ADVANTAGE USING HEDGING

Posh Stuff buys glasses from Glassy Eye at €100 per set of six and will sell these in its Belfast store for £160. It enters into a forward contract when it orders the glasses at £1 = €0.80. Accordingly, each set will cost Posh Stuff £80, and it will sell the glasses for £160, making a gross margin of 50%. A competitor in Belfast, Risky Business, also buys sets of glasses from Glassy Eye at €100. However, Risky Business does not enter into a forward contract. By the time Risky Business pays for the glasses the exchange rate has moved: £1 is equal to €0.70 and, accordingly, Risky Business pays £70 for each set of glasses. Risky Business could now sell the glasses for the same price as Posh Stuff, £160, and make £90 gross margin, 56%, or it could drop its prices and undercut Posh Stuff. In this scenario Posh Stuff will find itself at a competitive disadvantage entirely due to its risk-management strategy. Of course, the exchange rate could have gone the other way and Risky Business could have found itself at a competitive disadvantage. An MNE will need to decide what strategy is appropriate for their business sector given the risk appetite of the MNE and the dynamics of its market place.

Probability Analysis and Forward Contracts All other things being equal, MNEs will endeavour to have predictable cash flows and to minimise risk of volatility in their earnings profile. They should adopt the hedging strategies that best achieve this.

Some MNEs will undertake risk-assessment analysis and attempt to predict the exchange rate that might prevail at the time of the realisation of the foreign currency cash flow and compare it to the rate available on the forward contracts market. They will use statistical techniques to do so. At its most basic level, an MNE will examine past exchange rates and calculate the statistical analytics associated with the past trends. These statistics will allow the MNE to produce a probability analysis of the likelihood of various exchange rates in the future, using the past as a guide. It can then compare the unhedged possible cash flows to the de-risked cash flow and make an assessment as to whether it is worth hedging. While some companies do engage in this type of probability analysis to assess the propensity of exchange rates to change, most commentators will advise that forecasting exchange rates is futile. As mentioned in **Chapter 8**, the FOREX market is close to one of perfect competition. Therefore, all known information is factored into the exchange rate. Nonetheless, I mention the practice because it can and does happen.

The use of probability analysis in this context can be illustrated with an extreme example. Imagine that the exchange rate between two currencies has never varied and has remained constant for five years. If an MNE was presented with an opportunity to have a forward contract with an associated cost, there would be a good argument to say it should not incur the forward contract bank charges and not enter into the contract since the probability of the rates changing is very low.

The mathematicians among you will spot that if the MNE truly believes that there is no chance of a variance in the exchange rate then, assuming the forward contract presents a varied rate, there is an opportunity to make money risk free, as illustrated in **Example 15.8** below:

EXAMPLE 15.8: HYPOTHETICAL RISK-FREE GAINS

Assume the rate is 1 Zolar = 4 Buro and that this rate has not changed for five years. Zimby Plc is offered a forward contract at 1 Zolar = 3 Buro. Zimby believes there is a 100% probability that the exchange rate will remain unchanged. Therefore, it has an opportunity to make money risk free. It sells Zolars and receives 4 Buro for each one. It executes the contract. It then sells the Buros back, receiving 0.33Z for each Buro. Since each Buro only cost it 0.25Z it will receive $\frac{0.33}{0.25}$ or 1.32 Zolars back for every Zolar it invested in the scheme. As the saying goes: 'money for jam'.

Forward Contracts and Interest Rate Spreads   Earlier in this section we saw that the forward contract rate is a function of the spot exchange rate and the interest rate differential between the two currencies. While this is broadly correct, there are subtleties involved. Banks do not pay the same interest rates on deposits as they charge on loans. In the worked examples above we have assumed, for simplicity, that the prevailing interest rates are pertinent to both lending and deposit rates. In reality, however, there is a difference between the two which represents the bank's profit margin. This 'spread', the difference between what a bank earns from its loans and what it pays out on deposits, can affect the dynamic in the bank's calculation of what rate it will offer in a forward contract. When interest rate differentials between the currencies involved are large, or one currency's interest rate is very low, these spreads can have a significant bearing on what rate may be quoted. This means that the forward rate quoted will not just be a function of the prevailing interest rates and the current spot exchange rate. It will also be a function of the individual bank's cost of capital, its margins and the liquidity of the overall market. Though these factors have a smaller bearing on the forward rate than current spot rate and risk-free interest rate differentials, when the amounts get very large, these small differences can have a big cash impact. This is why firms might undertake a probability analysis to see whether the costs associated with the forward contract are such that they may render the use of the contract too expensive.

Money Market Hedges   A **money market hedge** is another technique that an MNE can use to hedge its foreign exchange risks. The technique involves using the financial markets, that is, the money markets, in such a way as to reduce the risk of gains or losses on a known transaction risk. Essentially, a money market hedge involves an MNE using its own funds in a way that locks in the exchange rate exposure at the spot rate and minimises future risk. In **Example 15.9** below, a Galway-based MNE hedges its 90-day dollar exposure by acquiring the $1,000,000 it needs today and placing it on deposit until it is needed in 90 days' time to pay the creditor.

EXAMPLE 15.9: MONEY MARKET HEDGE

A Galway-based MNE has a payment to make to a creditor in a foreign currency (US dollars) in 90 days: $1,000,000. It can earn interest on dollar deposits of 2% per annum. To perform a money market hedge it would change euros into dollars at today's spot exchange rate and put the dollars on deposit for 90 days. Then, when the payment falls due in 90 days, the MNE takes the money out of the deposit account and pays its creditor. Obviously, it need only place on deposit the net amount of dollars. The aim is to have $1,000,000 in 90 days so the MNE will deposit whatever amount is needed that will, when the interest is added, equate to $1,000,000 in 90 days. The cost to the MNE for doing this is the actual or the opportunity cost of tying up the euro it needed to make the deposit in the first place.

For an MNE to be able to execute a money market hedge it needs to have access to the funds needed to execute the hedge transaction. In **Example 15.9** the MNE would need to have the euro equivalent of the $1,000,000 available for the 90 days. While the funds are tied up in the hedge, they are not available for other uses within the business. This is one of the main drawbacks of using a money market hedge.

Currency Options   The three external techniques for managing transaction exposure risk discussed thus far (futures, forward contracts and money market hedges) all involve an MNE entering into a commitment to complete the transaction or, if it exits early, it will have to pay any losses on the contract up to that point.

The ideal hedging product would protect the firm's cash-flow expectations from adverse movement in the exchange rate while allowing it to benefit from positive changes in the rate. Does such a technique exist, however? Well, this is what a **currency option** tries to do: a sophisticated financial product that allows for this 'have your cake and eat it' approach.

A **currency option**, as the name suggests, affords an MNE the choice to complete the transaction or not. Currency options can be bought from the foreign exchange trading department of most banks or from foreign exchange brokers. There are two types of currency option:
• currency call options; and
• currency put options.

The MNE will pay a premium in order to acquire an option. This premium is the cost of the option and will be paid whether the option is exercised or not.

Currency Call Options   A **currency call option** provides an MNE with the right to purchase a given amount of a foreign currency within a specified time into the future at an agreed rate. The agreed rate is called the '**exercise price**'. Unlike forward contracts, the MNE does not have to buy the currency before the option lapses. If during the period of the option the spot exchange rate moves in a direction that makes the actual spot rate better than the option spot rate, then the MNE would just let the option lapse and completes its transaction using the actual spot rate. In **Example 15.10** below Posh Stuff decides not to use its option since completing the transaction using the spot rate is more advantageous. It still has to pay the cost of the option, £10,000.

EXAMPLE 15.10: POSH STUFF (4) – CURRENCY CALL OPTION

Posh Stuff acquired an option to meet its liability of €1,000,000 to Glassy Eyes 90 days from now. The option rate was Stg£1 = €1.23. The cost of the option is 1p per €1 unit of the target currency. When the debt to Glassy Eyes falls due, the spot rate is £1 = €1.35.

Sterling has strengthened to such a degree as to make it more attractive for Posh Stuff to pay the liability at the spot rate. Therefore, Posh Stuff does not exercise the option and instead buys

402 ADVANCED PERFORMANCE MANAGEMENT: AN INTERNATIONAL PERSPECTIVE

the euros it needs at the spot rate. It will acquire €1,000,000 for £740,740, being $\dfrac{1,000,000}{1.35}$.

It will also pay the costs of the option. This is 1p for each euro option, giving 1,000,000 by 1p, which is a further £10,000. Adding the cost of the option to the cost of buying the euro at the spot rate gives a total cost of settling the €1,000,000 liability of £750,740.

Had Posh Stuff a forward contract at the same exchange rate instead of an option, then it would have had to fulfil the contract. In this instance, it would have paid £813,008 to acquire the euros it needed, being, 1,000,000 ÷ 1.35. The cost would have been £813,008 – 750,740 = £62,268, a greater cost to Posh Stuff than using the call option (assuming there are no fees for the forward contract).

Currency Put Options   A currency put option involves acquiring the right to sell a specified quantity of a given currency at a rate agreed up until a specified date. As with currency call options, the rate of exchange agreed is called the exercise price. In **Example 15.11** below Posh Stuff has an income in euro of €1,500,000 in 60 days' time. The option rate it acquires of €1 = £0.80 is better than the spot rate of €1 = £0.72 when the euros arrive. Therefore, Posh Stuff takes up its right to exercise the option. It sells the euros it receives from Kanapee to the bank at the agreed option price.

EXAMPLE 15.11: POSH STUFF (5) – CURRENCY PUT OPTION

Posh Stuff has a receivable from Kanapee Gmbh in Germany of €1,500,000, which it will get into its bank account in 60 days' time. Posh Stuff acquires a currency put option to sell €1,500,000 in return for Sterling in 60 days at a rate of €1 = £0.80. The option costs 1p per €1.

When the day arrives and the €1,500,000 comes in from Germany, the spot rate on the foreign exchange markets is €1 = £0.72. Posh Stuff will exercise its put option and exchange the euro it receives from Kanapee for £1,200,000. Its total proceeds will be £1,200,000 less the costs of £15,000 (1,500,000 × 1p), a net proceed of £1,185,000.

If it did not have the currency put option, Posh Stuff would have converted the euro to Sterling at the spot rate on the day and received £1,080,000. Therefore, Posh Stuff is better off by £105,000 (£1,185,000 − £1,080,000) by buying the currency put option.

Pricing of Currency Options   How does a bank or foreign exchange broker price an option? The bank must consider the likelihood of the currency option being called upon. For example, the spot exchange rate between the US dollar and the euro is €1 = $1.25. A bank is asked to price a put option for $1,000,000 at a rate of €1=$1.60 with a settlement date seven days from now. Since the bank would deem it highly improbable that the dollar would weaken by such a large amount in such a short time, the premium on the put option would be relatively low.

The same considerations are made by a bank in pricing a currency call option. Accordingly, we can say that a currency option's premium will be influenced by three factors:

$$P = f(S - X, T, \sigma)$$

where P = the option premium
S = the spot exchange rate
X = the exercise price (also called the 'strike price')
T = the time to maturity
σ = the volatility of the exchange rate between the two currencies

In other words, the premium of an option is a function of the spot rate, the exercise price, the time to maturity and, critically, the volatility of the exchange rate.

In considering the acquiring of currency option, an MNE can expect to pay a larger premium as any of the terms in the above formula increase. For example, the longer the time to maturity, the more expensive the premium to be paid for the option will be.

While, from a bank's perspective, the pricing of an option is a bit more scientific than just looking at the variables listed above and deciding what would be a sufficient premium for taking on the risks involved, since it is an attempt to predict the future it is not entirely scientific. Using analysis of past transactions, various predictive models have been developed for pricing options. By using these models, MNEs can develop some forecasts as to the likely costs associated with the options approach to hedging. This predictive activity can also allow them to build in these costs into their pricing models for the ultimate sale of whatever product they are making. (We must never lose sight of the fact that all this financial engineering and modelling is, or at least should be, driven by the carrying out of the core trade of the MNE.)

The model I will use to illustrate the factors included in such models is the currency option pricing model derived by Biger and Hull.[5] (There are other models, such as Garman Kohlhagen, but essentially they all work the same way.) The formula below, based on Biger and Hull's model, is for pricing for a euro-based MNE wishing to buy a call option in another currency:

$$C = e^{-\theta T} S.N(d_1) - e^{-rT} X.N(d_1 - \sigma\sqrt{T})$$

where C = the option premium

$$d_1 = \left\{ \ln\left(\frac{S}{X}\right) + \left(r - \theta + \left(\frac{\sigma^2}{2}\right) / \sqrt{T}\right)\right\} / \sigma$$

S = underlying spot exchange rate
X = exercise price
r = euro risk-free rate of interest
θ = foreign currency risk-free interest rate
σ = instantaneous standard deviation of the return on a holding of the foreign currency
T = options time maturity expressed as a fraction of a year
N = standard normal cumulative distribution.

---

[5] Biger, N. and Hull, J. (1983) "The Valuation of Currency Options", *Financial Management*, Vol. 12, No. 1, 24–28.

Most MNE finance managers will not need to know the mathematical derivation of the above formulae – they will just need to know that the formulae can be used to predict the cost of various currency put and call options. In this way, the MNE can work out the potential costs associated with various hedging techniques in order to best plan the business activity and associated pricing options.

The Biger Hull model is for the pricing of what are called **European** options. These are options that cannot be exercised until maturity date. American-style options can be exercised at any time up to maturity date. This additional feature means that American-style currency options are normally more expensive than European-style options.

Zero-cost (or Cylinder) Options   A **zero-cost** (or 'cylinder') option is a currency option where the bank or broker is prepared to offer the option at a zero cost to the MNE. The bank is prepared to do this in return for the MNE conceding any benefits that may accrue to the option outside predetermined ranges. Normally, an MNE will purchase a currency option in order to protect itself from adverse movements in the spot exchange rate. If the exchange rate moves to such a degree that the option will give rise to a profit, this is a bonus for the MNE. In a zero-cost option the MNE will give some of this upside to the bank.

For example, an MNE has paid a premium for an option to buy $500,000 for €400,000 in 90 days, an effective rate of $1 = €0.80. If the exchange rate moves to such an extent that the spot exchange rate in 90 days is $1 = €0.60, then the MNE will not exercise the option and acquire the $500,000 it needs for the €300,000. This means the rate moved in favour of the MNE and it will have had an unexpected gain. The costs of the premium paid for the option should be netted against the unexpected gain.

Though 'happy' with the gain, the MNE would not normally try to anticipate such windfalls into its cash-flow projections. Usually, the MNE will be prudent in the calculation of such cash-flow estimates. This gives rise to an opportunity. A bank may propose to the MNE that it puts a floor on the exchange rate in the currency option. In other words, the bank may say to the MNE that if the rate goes above $1 = €0.80 then it can exercise the option and protect its position. However, in return, if the rate goes below, say, $1 = €0.70, the MNE will exercise the option at that lower price and the bank will be the beneficiary. The MNE will pay €400,000 (the exercise price) to the bank in return for $500,000. The bank can then convert the €400,000 it receives into $571,428 using the current spot rate $1 = €0.70. The bank will have given the MNE $500,000 so it makes a gain on the transaction of $571,428 – $500,000 = $71,428. The attraction of this for the bank is that it can, using the formulas mentioned earlier, work out the value of options and price in a profit margin. The advantage for the MNE is that it will get the option at zero cost. Since the MNE is primarily interested in protecting itself against adverse movements it is not overly worried about trading away some of the upside of beneficial movements. It is a 'win/win' scenario.

At this point, the following summary table will help you recall and distinguish between the various types of external techniques available to the MNE to hedge against exposure to exchange rate risk.

SUMMARY OF HEDGING TECHNIQUES

Technique	To hedge cash expected inflows	To hedge expected outflows
Future	Sell a currency future on the futures market in the currency and amount of the expected receipt. Futures are in predetermined lot sizes so quantum may not exactly match requirements.	Buy a future in the currency you will be paying out, on the futures market for the amount and timing of your expected payment.
Forward	Negotiate a contract to sell a specific amount of a currency on a nominated date in the future at a specified price agreed at the outset of the contract.	Negotiate a contract to buy the amount of the foreign currency you need to make the payment.
Money Market Hedge	Borrow an amount in the currency you are going to receive and repay it when you receive the inflow.	Borrow your domestic currency such that the lump sum invested and interest earned equal the amount you need to pay in the future period. Convert it into the currency you need to make the payment in. Invest the foreign currency until you need it to make the payment at a specified price agreed at the outset of the contract.
Currency Option	Purchase a **put option** in the currency in which you are going to receive the inflow.	Buy a **call option** in the currency you will be paying out in for the amount you need.

There are couple of other techniques for managing exchange rate exposure risk worth mentioning.

Cross Hedging   Cross hedging is used when there are no hedging tools available for the currency involved. Imagine that the currency in Zambia, the Kwacha, has no hedging products connected with it. An Irish company has an exposure to Kwacha. It wishes to hedge this exposure. It notices that the movements in the Kwacha are strongly correlated with movements in the US dollar. In order to hedge its exposure, the Irish MNE can enter into appropriate hedging arrangements using the US dollar. Thus, when the Kwacha/euro exchange rate moves, the Irish MNE will be afforded some hedging benefit as the dollar/euro exchange rate should move in a similar fashion.

Non-deliverable Forward Contracts   Non-deliverable forward contracts (NDFs) are a relatively recent development. These are mainly used to hedge exposures in the currencies of developing economies. Similar in concept to a normal forward contract, a quantum of the currency is agreed for delivery or receipt at a specified date in the future at an agreed exchange rate. However, in the case of an NDF the total value of the contract is not executed at the settlement date. Rather, the difference between the contract exchange rate and the spot exchange rate on the settlement date is exchanged between the parties.

NDFs have the advantage of allowing one to avoid completing a transaction in a currency which may not have much liquidity or is in some other way unattractive. Only the net difference between the rates at the settlement date is exchanged between the parties. This difference could be priced in the more attractive currency. In this way, a counterparty in an NDF may never actual receive or disburse the 'unattractive' currency.

Long-term Transaction Risk

Most of the techniques for managing transaction exposure risk discussed so far in this chapter become more expensive as the time for which they are needed extends. This is because the range of possible outcomes increases over time. Therefore, the risk profile of any hedging instrument becomes more risky as the range of possible outcomes increases. Remember, a risky euro is worth less than a safe euro. Therefore, the more risky a proposition is, the more expensive it becomes. By implication, the longer a hedging instrument needs to stay in place, the more expensive it becomes. But MNEs may sometimes need to have techniques to manage foreign exchange risk in place for more than just the next 12 months or 18 months.

We will now explore a number of techniques available to the MNE to hedge against longer term foreign exchange exposure.

Long-term Forward Contracts

As stated, the cost of using some techniques becomes more expensive as the date to maturity extends. In recent years, however, the banks have developed long-term forward contracts. An MNE can now buy long-term forward contracts for periods of up to five years. These can be useful where a fixed price and term arrangement is involved and the company knows how much foreign exchange it needs to hedge over the duration of the contract. Rental incomes of a foreign property might be an example of such a predictable, long-term foreign currency cash inflow.

The mechanisms for executing long-term forward contracts are the same as those for short-term forward contracts and the principles are the same.

Currency Swaps

A popular way of hedging longer term foreign currency exposures is for the MNE to enter into a swap arrangement with a counterparty, either directly or indirectly, through a banking arrangement. The two parties agree to exchange their future cash flows. In today's marketplace the swaps are normally products sold by the banks with a spread price offered depending on whether the MNE is looking to sell or buy the future cash flows in the foreign currency. Let us examine an example.

EXAMPLE 15.12: A CURRENCY SWAP

Biagold is an Irish Plc. It borrows €10 million secured against its assets in Galway to make an investment in a cheese-processing plant in the US. The €10 million is repayable in five years' time. Biagold will have invested the money in a US plant where the assets and the income will be in US dollars. Biagold intends to repay the loan by selling the plant in five years, once it is up and running. The CFO of Biagold, Micky Chart, wants to ensure that the MNE is hedged against future exchange rate changes. He decides to explore a currency swap.

Blu Dragon is a US company that has just invested $12.5 million in an asset in Germany which it hopes to sell in five years. It is also concerned that when it translates the future euro sale proceeds back into US dollars that the exchange rate will expose it to unforeseen losses. Can Biagold and Blu Dragon come together and solve their respective problems? The answer is 'Yes'.

Biagold borrows the €10 million at 5%. Blu Dragon has borrowed its $12.5 million at 8%. The parties agree to a foreign currency swap. This works as follows.

Biagold will give the €10 million it has borrowed to Blu Dragon. Blu Dragon will give Biagold its $12.5 million. The amounts to be exchanged are decided by the spot rate on the day of the exchange: €1=$1.25. Biagold will pay Blu Dragons interest costs of $12.5 million @ 8% of $1 million per year. Blu Dragon will pay Biagold the interest of €500,000 per year that is accruing on the €10 million loan.

Future exchange rate change will affect the actual amounts to be paid between the parties.

At the interest payment date the interest liabilities between the two parties are converted at the spot rate. The net payment is made between the two depending on who owes who the net amount. Imagine that the interest falls due at the end of Year 1. The rate on the due date is €1 = $1.50. Applying the interest rate we can calculate that Biagold is owed €500,000 or $750,000 by Blu Dragon, and Blu Dragon in turn is owed $1 million or €660,000 by Biagold. At the end of Year 1 the net position is that Biagold owes Blu Dragon since its liability to Blu Dragon is greater than Blu Dragon's interest liability to it. Since the dollar interest charge is the greater, Biagold must pay dollars to Blu Dragon of $250,000, being $1 million – $750,000. Biagold will have paid its bank €500,000 in interest. It will have paid Blu Dragon $250,000. Therefore its total interest cost (in $) will be €500,000 paid to the bank (at €1 = $1.5) = $750,000 plus the $250,000 it pays Blu Dragon, bringing the total interest cost in $ to $1,000,000 for Year 1.

By the end of Year 2 the exchange rate has moved to €1 = $2.2. At this interest payment date Biagold owes Blu Dragon $1 million interest, which equates to €454,000 at the prevailing spot rate. Blu Dragon owes Biagold €500,000 interest. Since this is greater than the amount Biagold owes Blu Dragon, Blu Dragon must pay the net, in euro, to Biagold. Biagold pays its bank the €500,000 interest it owes on the original loan and gets the benefit of the €46,000 it receives from Blu Dragon, meaning a net servicing cost of €454,000. **Note** that this cost is the same as the $1,000,000 cost at the end of Year 2 spot rate.

The interest rate calculations continue to be made until the agreement ends. It is important that both parties protect themselves from the risk that each will be in existence at the end of the five years. This risk, known as **counterparty risk**, can normally be managed through the execution of various bank guarantees.

At the end of the five years Blu Dragon will give Biagold back its €10 million, which it will use to repay the loan it originally took out. Blu Dragon in turn will receive back its $12.5 million from Biagold. The technique has meant that the final re-exchange of liabilities has preserved the original spot exchange rate of €10 million = $12.5 million or €1 = $1.25.

When you work through the transactions involved in this foreign exchange swap you can see that each party is able to service its interest rate costs from the currency in which it has chosen to receive an income. Any shortfall is made up for by the counterparty. The excess interest charge that may fall to one party or the other is the price of putting the swap in place. On the other hand, since interest rates are linked to exchange rates through the interest rate parity principles (see **Chapter 8**) this cost is rationally incurred.

Parallel Loans

Parallel loans originated before currency swaps and they relate to the same desire, i.e. to manage foreign exchange exposures. They also arose before capital markets were as developed as they are now. MNEs may not always have been able to raise funds in the country in which they wanted to do business.

For example, an Irish Plc may have borrowed in euro to finance a project in Turkey. It would have preferred to borrow Turkish Lira at the time but it was unable to raise funds in the Turkish market. A Turkish MNE making an investment in Carlow at the same time needed euro. It could not borrow euro as it has no creditworthiness in Ireland. Instead, it borrowed Turkish Lira. In a parallel loan, the two MNEs swap their loans. The Irish MNE took on the Turkish Lira loan from the Turkish MNE, and vice versa. There was no right of offset in these arrangements and if the Turkish MNE stopped paying the Irish MNE the euro loan interest and principle, the Irish MNE would still have to pay back the Turkish Lira loan. This is why such loans are called 'parallel'; they operate on twin tracks and are not connected as regards their obligations. At first glance one might think that the Irish MNE could walk away from its Turkish obligations. However, this would be no more advisable than walking away from any loan arrangement. Therefore, parallel loans have a large degree of counterparty risk since the MNE could be hit with servicing both loans if the counterparty defaulted.

Borrowing Policy

Another way an MNE can manage its exposure to longer term foreign exchange transaction risk is to borrow in the currency to which it has transaction exposures. In this way the MNE can seek to reduce its transaction exposures by minimising the net exposure in any one currency.

However, it is not always easy for an MNE to borrow in the currency in which it foresees transaction risk. This can be for a number of reasons, including:
- lack of track record in the relevant country;
- lack of suitable collateral acceptable to a bank that can lend in the foreign currency;
- inability to forecast future cash flows by currency at the time the original loans are taken out.

These problems in trying to match foreign exchange debt with transaction cash flows are what lead MNEs to using other hedging instruments, such as those discussed above.

15.3 FOREIGN EXCHANGE ECONOMIC RISK

As we have seen, foreign exchange transaction risk exposure arises when an MNE can see that movements in exchange rates could affect the expected value of its future transaction-related cash flows. Put another way, the value in the domestic currency of specific future transactions are affected since, when they are translated into the domestic currency, a gain or loss may occur.

Transaction risk is a subset of wider financial risks which, for an MNE, relate to its overall exposure to movements in foreign exchange rates. The other two foreign exchange risk types are:
- economic risk; and
- translation risk.

Economic risk can be defined as the future cash-flow impact resulting from changes in the MNE's market arising from unexpected exchange rate movements. In other words, the MNE's market, for either its inputs or outputs, is altered by unexpected exchange rate movements. The alteration in the market affects the MNE's cash flow forecasts. In **Example 15.13** below an Irish company finds itself at an unexpected competitive disadvantage due to the weakening of the New Zealand dollar against the Turkish Lira.

EXAMPLE 15.13: ECONOMIC EXPOSURE

The demand for an MNE's goods can be affected by foreign exchange movements. For example, if an Irish company is competing in Turkey against a New Zealand company, changes in the exchange rate between the Turkish Lira (TRY) and the New Zealand dollar (NZ$) can affect the Irish company's expected returns. If the NZ$ weakened against the TRY then a New Zealand MNE may be able to drop its prices in the Turkish market leaving the euro denominated Irish MNE at a pricing disadvantage.

Measuring Economic Exposure

An MNE cannot manage economic exposure until such time as it can measure its exposure, which is quite challenging because of the number of variables concerned. As we have seen, when measuring transaction exposure the MNE can take predicted cash flows, currency by currency, and calculate the net exposure. It can then seek to hedge these exposures where appropriate. Economic exposure is at a more fundamental level and therefore requires a more fundamental assessment of the future cash flows. In particular, it involves trying to anticipate demand responses to various scenarios of exchange rate.

The first step for the MNE in assessing economic exposures is to calculate the forward cash-flow forecasts, currency by currency. These cash flow forecasts should look out into the future as far as is reasonable for the given MNE and its operational sector. For example, if the business has prepared three-year strategic plans, then it would make sense to use these as the basis for the currency-by-currency cash flow projections. The MNE should then carry out sensitivity analysis at various exchange rate scenarios. This sensitivity analysis should involve some element of historical assessment. By looking at historical exchange rate movements and overlaying them with past cash flow performance it may be possible to develop some predictive models. It is especially important to adjust supply and demand profiles to incorporate exchange rate movements at the various scenarios. Models can then be developed that can predict the impact on the MNE of differing exchange rate positions. Using these models the MNE can quantify the level of exposure and even make estimates as to what price it is worth paying to minimise these risks.

Clearly, this process is not entirely scientific. It is difficult to tell the future. But managers should be assessed by their ability to predict the consequences of their actions. Therefore, the manager in a better-run MNE will be able to predict the future cash flows of their business with greater accuracy than their peers in more poorly run competitors.

Managing Economic Risk

Having identified and quantified its economic exposure, the MNE can now set about deciding what risk-minimisation strategies to adopt.

Restructuring

An MNE might reorganise its operations in order to minimise economic risk. This process would involve shifting the source of some of its revenues to other currencies or countries, or changing the nature of its cost base.

EXAMPLE 15.15: MANAGING ECONOMIC RISK

To take our earlier example of the Irish MNE competing with a New Zealand MNE in the Turkish market a bit further. The Irish MNE could change its sourcing policy to buy more input goods from New Zealand. This way, any movement in the exchange rate would affect the Irish MNE in the same way as its competitor. The MNE might look at expanding into markets where the New Zealand dollar has historically moved in the same direction as the euro when both are expressed in the currency of the new market. Imagine that, historically, the New Zealand dollar and the euro have moved in tandem when exchanged with the Japanese Yen. An Irish MNE could reduce its economic exposure by selling into Japan.

It is not possible to give all the possible scenarios that might be adopted since the dynamic of each MNE will be different. The key point is that once an MNE has modelled its economic exposure this allows it to look at how it might reorganise operational structures to minimise exposure to economic risk.

Refinancing

One specific way of minimising economic exposure is to refinance the MNE in such a way that the net exposures are reduced. In choosing the refinanced structures it is important to be as certain as one can be that the economic risk has being properly assessed. Some risks, especially if derived from past data analysis, may not be due to economic exposure but other market factors. For example, an analysis of past data shows that a competing MNE from another currency jurisdiction has reduced prices at specific times in the past. A purely statistical analysis could correlate these reductions with foreign exchange rate movements. However, the competitor may have reduced prices because of a forward contract benefit rather than the movement in the exchange rate *per se*.

Pricing Strategies

The FOREX market does not always move against you. If an MNE predicts its economic exposure well it will see that sometimes the economic conditions that may give rise to adverse effects may also sometimes produce positive effects. One approach to managing economic risk can be to even-out the effects of exchange rate movements by adopting pricing strategies that allow for a buffer to be built up in the good times to soften the blows in the hard times.

EXAMPLE 15.16: PRICING STRATEGIES TO MANAGE ECONOMIC EXPOSURE

Returning to our example of the Irish MNE competing in the Turkish market with a New Zealand MNE, the drop in demand for the Irish MNE's production due to the depreciating NZ$ will not last forever. At some point the pendulum may shift. By being able to model the benefits of these shifts, the Irish MNE can adopt a competitive pricing strategy. It would price its products such that it makes some extra profit during the times the exchange rate is working in its favour to counter the times when the exchange rate is against it. The income statement of the Irish MNE will therefore display cyclical patterns, showing higher profit margins when the euro is weak versus the NZ$ and lower results when it is strong.

15.4 TRANSLATION RISK

Thus far in this chapter, we have looked at transaction risk and economic risk. Transaction risk is associated with the actual transactions that an MNE is engaged in or plans to engage in. As we have seen, a variety of hedging techniques can be used by the MNE to manage transaction risk.

Economic risk is more difficult to measure. It is associated with marketplace changes that occur as a result of unexpected foreign exchange rate movements. We have explored a number of strategies that an MNE can deploy to minimise the negative effects of economic risk.

We now move on to examine the third type of foreign exchange risk to which an MNE can be exposed: translation risk.

Translation risk arises from the unrealised gains or losses that can occur when an MNE prepares its consolidated accounts. The exposure is that the balance sheets (also known as statements of financial position) of subsidiary companies may give rise to unrealised gains and losses when translated into the reporting currency at the reporting date.

To understand translation risk more thoroughly we need to look at how the balance sheet (also known as statement of financial position) of an MNE is affected by movements in foreign exchange rates. The translation risk arises from the use of different rates to translate the profit and loss and the balance sheets of the MNE's subsidiary entities to produce the group accounts. The profit and loss transactions will be translated into the reporting currency at rates prevailing throughout the reporting period. The balance sheet, on the other hand, will be translated into the reporting currency at the rate prevailing at the reporting date. Therefore, the subsidiary's profit and loss account is translated into the reporting currency at a different rate than the balance sheet (unless, by pure coincidence, the rates prevailing through the year are equal to the rate at the reporting date).

In **Example 15.17** below the parent company needs to make an adjustment in its balance sheet of £100,000 to account for the unrealised gain that occurs when it translated the balance sheet of its Texan subsidiary. The gain arises as a result of translating the Year 1 profit and loss at $1 = £0.60 while translating the balance sheet at $1 = £0.65. Since the retained earnings from the profit and loss account represent the movement in the balance sheet net assets from one year to next, converting the items at different rates will always give rise to a translation difference upon consolidation.

EXAMPLE 15.17: TRANSLATION RISK

A Belfast-based MNE has a subsidiary in Austin, Texas. The transaction exposures of the dollar-denominated subsidiary are negligible. In Year 1, the Texan subsidiary generated $2 million profit. The average exchange rate during the year was 1$ = £0.60. Accordingly, when the Belfast entity was producing its consolidated group results it translated the results from the Texan subsidiary into £1.2 million. The following year, Year 2, the subsidiary made another $2 million. This time the average exchange rate was $1 = £0.50. This result would be translated into the consolidated accounts at £1 million. Therefore, the group accounts have shown a drop in profits of £200,000 between the two years even though the actual profitability in US dollars remained the same.

Consider further that the Texan subsidiary used its $2 million dollars in each year to acquire some fixed assets for its factory in Austin. The spot rates at the balance sheet date for Years 1 and 2 were $1 = £0.65 and £0.55 respectively. Now one has the situation where the profit in Year 1 is translated at the average rate, giving a profit and loss impact of £1.2 million. However, the corresponding balance sheet is translated at the balance sheet date and produces an asset value of £1.3 million. The translated profit does not equate to the balance sheet. In the consolidated accounts of the Belfast entity there is a balancing item needed of £100,000. This item is adjusted to the reserves of the company's consolidated accounts. The reserves have been adjusted as mentioned. The assets will also have been adjusted through the consolidation process. Therefore, the translation risk exposure is to the extent that profits are translated at a different exchange rate than the assets used to produce those profits due to timing differences.

Measuring Translation Risk

Measuring translation exposure is relatively straightforward in the near term if an MNE has good cash flow, profit and loss and balance sheet forecasting systems. The exposed numbers are easy to forecast. The exchange rate that might prevail is not quite as easy to calculate since it is not possible to predict with accuracy what the exchange rate will be at the balance sheet date.

Managing Translation Risk

Having identified the translation exposure, the MNE must decide whether to hedge this exposure. This is a matter of some debate. Since the exposures are not represented by real cash flows, one school of thought is that they should not be hedged since they do not represent a real loss. On the other hand, some argue that since the reserves available for ultimate distribution to the shareholders are either reduced or augmented by the translation loss, they are a real item and the risk to the movement should be managed.

An MNE may take out loans in the currencies to which it has translation risk exposure regarding its assets. In this way, it can minimise the translation effect since both the assets and liabilities will be in the same currency. The lower the net asset position in the respective currency, the lower the translation risk.

Some MNEs will enter into forward contracts that hedge the balance sheet exposure at the balance sheet date. One of constraints of this approach is that there are no underlying cash flows to underpin the forward contracts. The MNE might draw cash back to the centre in order to minimise translation risk and then lend the cash back out to the subsidiary when it needs it. This could be seen as just substituting translation risk with the transaction risk associated with the cash flows carried out for no other purpose. In other words, the MNE will have hedged the translation risk by using transaction risk-management techniques. These techniques are not without cost.

It can be argued that a loss due to a hedge contract will be a real loss in that real cash has been expended and will leave the group. A translation loss is not a real loss and only becomes one if and when an actual transaction occurs. Since a cash transaction can be hedged once the MNE knows it is going to carry out the transaction, that is the time to hedge using transaction hedging techniques. Most commentators believe that transparent reporting as to the currencies in which the MNE trades allows the investors to make their own minds up about translation risk. There are strong arguments to say that real cash should not be used to hedge against paper losses.

15.5 CONCLUSION

The risk exposures to MNEs from movements in foreign exchange fall into three categories:
- transaction risk;
- economic risk; and
- translation risk.

MNEs will adopt various strategies to minimise these risks. The strategy adopted will first depend on the MNE quantifying the exposure. This task normally falls to the finance function, involves the projection of cash flows and, importantly, working out the **net** exposure in each currency. This is most easily done when the finance function operates centrally and can carry out the task by examining the cash flow forecasts from all the entities that comprise the MNE.

Having identified the net exposures, the MNE then needs to decide whether to hedge the attendant risk and, if so, which hedging techniques to use. Various techniques can be used to manage foreign exchange transaction risk. The main ones are:
- futures;
- forward contracts;
- money market hedges;
- currency options.

For longer term exposures the MNE may use:
- currency swaps;
- parallel loans.

Economic risk exposure is difficult to measure and, consequently, foreign exchange economic risk is difficult to manage. However, it is possible to minimise economic exposures by restructuring operations and/or financing.

Translation risk occurs when the accounts for an MNE are consolidated to produce a group picture. Many would argue that translation gains and losses due to foreign exchange rates are not real losses and should not be hedged, that hedging costs real money, which should not be used to minimise paper losses.

In this part of the book, we have been discussing the treasury function in an MNE. **Chapter 14** examined how an MNE raises the long-term capital it needs, both equity from shareholders and debt capital from the financial markets. In **Chapter 15**, we examined how foreign-exchange risks are measured and managed in an MNE. Both these activities, sourcing finance and managing foreign exchange risk, have different aspects to them when compared to a purely domestic enterprise and we focused on these areas of difference, with **Chapter 14** in particular examining the unique challenges that being an MNE presents when raising capital.

In the next three chapters, which form **Part V**, "Management Systems in Multinational Enterprises", we will examine how other operating functions in an MNE are impacted upon by dint of operating in a multinational environment as compared to a purely domestically based enterprise. The first of these chapters, **Chapter 16**, will examine how an MNE sets the prices it charges for its goods and services. We will then examine what management information systems an MNE might use. The final chapter in this part will examine how managers manage performance in an MNE.

QUESTIONS

Self-test Questions

15.1 Posh Stuff, a Belfast-based department store, buys 30% of its supplies from euro denominated suppliers. It sells 20% of its stock to euro-denominated customers through its website. Advise Posh Stuff on what foreign exchange management strategies it might adopt.
15.2 How does a currency swap work?
15.3 Is the pricing of a currency option pure guesswork?
15.4 What are the differences between a future and a forward foreign exchange contract?

Thought-provoking Questions

Question 15.1

You are Peter Pound, the treasury accountant for AllOverUs Plc, (AOU). AOU is based in Mullingar, ROI, and has operating divisions in Spain, Poland, India and Brazil. Your CEO, Ivan Ginty, has proposed exploring decentralising all functions from the head to each of the operating divisions. He believes that this will reduce complexity and 'put power in the hands of local management' as he puts it. He has asked for your views on the proposal in respect of how it might affect the treasury function, especially the management of foreign exchange risks.

Question 15.2

You are Aisling Cooper and you have just been appointed to the Finance department of Crosby Plc. Crosby manufactures industrial cranes for use on building sites at its plant based in Ashford, Co. Wicklow. It has just sold a crane to a US firm for $23,000,000. The customer will pay for the crane in 120 days time. The CFO Martin Conbur is your boss. He has told you that Crosby needs to pay US import taxes of $5,000,000 in 120 days. He wants you to advise him on the following:
• Whether there is a foreign exchange risk.
• If there is a risk, how he can best manage it.
• Estimate the rate Crosby might be quoted for a forward contract

You have determined the following information:
   US$ interest rates 5% per annum
   € interest rates 9% per annum
   Current exchange rate €1 = $1.08

You take out a piece of paper and do some rough calculations.

Review Questions

(See Suggested Solutions to Review Questions in **Appendix B**.)

Question 15.1: Smart Bathroom Fittings Ltd

Having read the Smart Bathroom Fittings Ltd case study in **Appendix A**, discuss the forward contract rate offered to Smart Bathroom Fittings Ltd by its bank as well as possible financing considerations in relation to financing the investment.

Question 15.2: Hughes Engineering Limited

Having read the Hughes Engineering Limited case study in **Appendix A**, discuss how Hughes Engineering Limited could manage the foreign exchange exposure that would arise from undertaking the project.

PART V

MANAGEMENT SYSTEMS IN MULTINATIONAL ENTERPRISES

In Part IV we explored how the treasury function operates in a multinational enterprise (MNE), focusing particularly on the unique challenges that a multinational environment presents for managing sources of capital and foreign exchange risks.

In Part V we examine in more detail how other key management functions in the MNE are influenced by the multinational dimension. There are three chapters in this part of the book. In **Chapter 16** we explore the pricing strategies of MNEs. Setting the prices for goods and services is a critical activity, as it determines ultimate profitability. MNEs face unique challenges since they operate in different marketplaces with differing customer profiles. They are also often working in different currencies. Chapter 16 explains how the MNE can manage these challenges. We also examine some of the more technical issues that arise for MNEs with transfer pricing, i.e. setting prices for transfers of goods between divisions of a group.

In **Chapter 17** we look at systems MNE managers can use to run complex organisations that span a number of different countries, focusing on strategic enterprise management systems (SEMS). SEMS are information technology systems that span an entire MNE, allowing managers to share and utilise information to make and support strategic decisions and manage subsequent performance.

In the final chapter in this part, **Chapter 18**, we examine how MNEs manage their performance. Managing across borders presents its own unique difficulties, which must be overcome for an MNE to be successful. Management styles that work in one country may not work in another. Managers need to know how to adapt their management style to the different cultural climates they find themselves operating in. They also need tools and techniques that can standardise performance measurement while at the same time dealing with the operational diversity that prevails in MNEs.

By the end of Part V the reader should have a good grasp of the unique challenges that face managers in an MNE. In addition to grasping the challenges, you will understand some of the key tools and techniques available to overcome these challenges. The MNE is the pre-eminent commercial organisation of the modern era. Understanding how to manage an MNE and how it differs from single-country domestic organisations will be an increasingly important part of the knowledge base of managers and leaders of 21st-Century organisations.

16

INTERNATIONAL PRICING STRATEGIES

CONTENTS

LEARNING OBJECTIVES

Having read this chapter, you will understand:
- how products are selected for sale into international markets;
- a framework for assessing if products need adaptation for foreign markets;
- the variety of pricing strategies available to the MNE;
- the concept of transfer pricing; and
- the various transfer pricing methodologies.

16.1 INTRODUCTION

All businesses must ultimately serve customers and the ultimate customer pays for everything that leads up to and precedes the final point of consumption: raw materials, logistics and the supply chain, the manufacturing process, advertising costs – everything, right down (or up) to management bonuses! Therefore, deciding which products to make available to the customer, and what price to charge for those products, is one of the most critical activities any business enterprise needs to master. (In this textbook, the term 'product' is used to describe 'goods and services' *produced* by an MNE.)

In this chapter we will examine how MNEs decide which products to sell in international markets and how they decide whether to adapt those products or to leave them unchanged.

We will then proceed to examine how the setting of prices in an international environment differs from that of a purely domestic entity. Too often the setting of prices for an organisation is seen as a sub-set of the activities of its buying or sales functions. While these are critical to the execution of pricing decisions, the actual setting of pricing policy should be a matter for the most senior management within the organisation. In the early part of this chapter I will explain how pricing is critical to the overall cash-flow generating capability of MNEs. I will explain how pricing strategies play a fundamental part in the overall MNE's strategies. We will also examine the unique complexities in managing pricing strategies that the multinational environment presents. I will use the 'value chain' concept to help illustrate the critical role pricing strategies play in the success, or otherwise, of an MNE.

In the second half of the chapter we will examine transfer pricing, a facet of pricing unique to MNEs. Transfer pricing covers the not insignificant matter of the internal pricing of goods and services supplied by one part of an MNE to another part operating in another country. Since these internal prices affect the taxable profits generated in each country in which the MNE operates, the policies and practices adopted by MNEs are of particular interest to tax authorities and governments. Indeed, one of the largest reviews ever undertaken by the OECD has been on how to tackle corporate tax-planning strategies that exploit gaps in the current system and artificially transfer profits to more attractive taxation locations. The outcome of this review of 'base erosion and profit shifting' (BEPS) has led to the publication, in October 2015, of details of agreed actions. These actions have been agreed by the G20 nations and are likely to be the basis of transfer pricing for the foreseeable future.

16.2 THE VALUE CHAIN

As introduced in **Chapter 3**, the concept of the value chain provides a structured way of grasping the components that make up the total 'value proposition' of an enterprise, which is what the ultimate customer pays for.

The outputs of the value chain of one business can be an input into another firm's value chain, thereby contributing to a global interconnectivity of value chains. For example, Acerinox is a Spanish MNE that manufactures stainless steel. The output from its value chain, stainless steel, is an input to the value chain of Hochtief Aktiengesellschaft, a German construction company. Unless an MNE is completely vertically integrated,[1] it will be part of a wider value chain comprising the value chains of all other businesses involved in the process of creating the product.

---

[1] Vertical integration is an organisation structure where an MNE owns and manages all phases of the production process from the extraction of raw materials to the final sale of the product to the consumer. Very few businesses are fully vertically integrated. The oil industry provides examples of organisations that are almost completely vertically integrated. Some oil companies extract the oil from the earth, ship it, refine it, transport it to filling stations that they own and run themselves to be ultimately sold to the motorist.

FIGURE 16.1: THE VALUE CHAIN

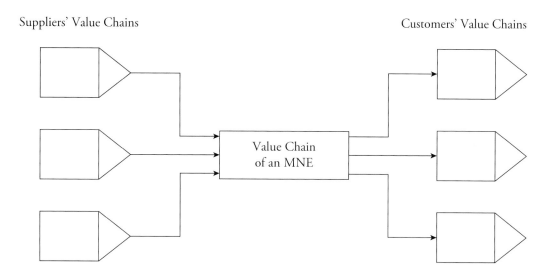

An MNE's position in the value chain for its product has a bearing on the pricing strategies, as we can see in **Example 16.1** below.

EXAMPLE 16.1: AN ENTERPRISE'S PLACE IN A VALUE CHAIN

Posh Stuff is a department store in Belfast. It has a jewellery department that sells gold and diamond rings. Posh Stuff buys its gold rings from Plan D'Or, a wholesaler in Paris. Plan D'Or buys from various manufacturers around the world. Its gold rings are mainly sourced from Eldorado Enterprises in Peru. Eldorado, in turn, sources its raw material from Rio Rioja Trading, a gold mine in Bolivia.

Nigel Bloom walks into Posh Stuff's jewellery department one Saturday morning to look at their array of gold rings. He considers their shape, gold content and price. When he is thinking about the price of the gold rings as an individual buyer, he is contemplating the value to him of the rings in front of him. In reality, he is assessing the cumulative effect of all the combined value chains and their associated pricing strategies that led to this point when Nigel Bloom buys his wife a ring.

When he finally settles on a ring and pays for it, he provides Posh Stuff with funds. These funds allow it to pay its wholesaler in Paris. The Parisian wholesaler can then pay the Peruvian manufacturer, which then must pay the Bolivian gold mine. Nigel Bloom is connected, through the purchases of the ring, with the value chain of all the interconnected entities that led to his ultimate purchase.

Of course, in real life the Bolivian gold mine does not have to wait until the gold ring is ultimately sold in Belfast to be paid. Modern financial systems and payment infrastructures mean that transactions are aggregated, payments are made upon agreed terms and invoices raised and settled at intermediate points along the interconnected value chains. Nonetheless, the fact remains, it is Nigel Bloom's ultimate purchase, and all the other Nigel Blooms in the world, that make up the cash flows that pay for the total value chain of gold rings. In this way we can see that consumer demand is the ultimate driver of almost all international trade (though there may be some exceptions to this, such as military spending).

Most MNEs realise the criticality of pricing strategies. Management consultants McKinsey have estimated that a 1% improvement in selling prices produces on average an almost 9% improvement in returns on capital. However, it is one thing to be aware of this, but another to act on it. Successful MNEs have solid pricing structures that allow them to make informed pricing decisions. They focus on their most critical processes, linking performance appraisal and price, and understand how they link in to the customer's perception of value. In the next section we will examine how successful MNEs formulate their pricing structures and how different pricing strategies can be deployed depending on market conditions.

16.3   PRODUCTS, PRICING AND THE MARKETING MIX

The 'marketing mix' is a concept used to describe the factors that combine to create value in a product or service. It involves five variables (all of which, conveniently, begin with the letter 'P'):
* Product
* Price
* Place
* Promotion
* People.

Since the five variable elements are interconnected, it is not possible to have an in-depth understanding of one without at least considering the other four. We will consider 'product', 'price' and 'promotion' from an MNE's perspective in this section; 'place' (see **Chapter 2**) and 'people' (see **Chapter 12**) are discussed elsewhere in the text.

The marketing mix will form the basis of an MNE's marketing plan. Small-scale changes to the five variable elements can be thought of as 'tactical' marketing while larger, more fundamental changes are considered as 'strategic'.

Normally, an MNE evolves from a domestic company (see **Chapter 2**) that sees an opportunity to market its products or services internationally. At the start of this journey is the decision regarding which of the nascent MNE's existing products or services will be chosen for the international market. Also to be considered is whether or not the product will need to be changed or adapted from the existing offering.

The decision whether to adapt the enterprise's existing products or services before launching internationally will be made after consideration of a number of factors. The MNE will need to understand the market it is proposing to enter, undertaking market research and assessment, often through conducting a trial or performing other types of test marketing.

Interestingly, Ireland is often chosen for such tests as the market is quite self-contained, being an island. There is also an advantage in that both the UK and the Eurozone markets can be tested on the island of Ireland without having to have a wide-scale launch. For example, a US MNE could launch a product in the Republic of Ireland and Northern Ireland without having to undertake a UK-wide or European-wide launch.

Figure 16.2 below shows the main competing pressures on an MNE in deciding whether or not to adapt its products (goods and/or services) for the international market. The 'product', at the centre of the diagram, can be a good produced or a service provided. On either side of the product box are lists of forces that act upon the marketplace for the product. The MNE should adapt its product to cater for the forces on the left-hand box, but should maintain a standardised product when the forces on the right-hand side are in existence. The MNE must decide which forces are the strongest and exercise the most influence on the product in the newly chosen/to be chosen marketplace.

If, for example, the left-hand side market forces are stronger then the MNE will adapt its product for the new market. However, it will need to have strategies in place to deal with the effect product adaptation will have regarding the forces on the right-hand side of the diagram. On the other hand, if it believes the right-hand forces are strongest, it will decide not to adapt the product. This means it will need plans to tackle the forces on the left-hand box.

In a further example, an MNE might adapt a product and find it loses economies of scale as a result of the adaptation. It will therefore need to get a higher price for the product or reduce the cost of manufacture some other way in order to preserve margins.

FIGURE 16.2: PRODUCT-ADAPTATION STRATEGIES FOR INTERNATIONAL EXPANSION

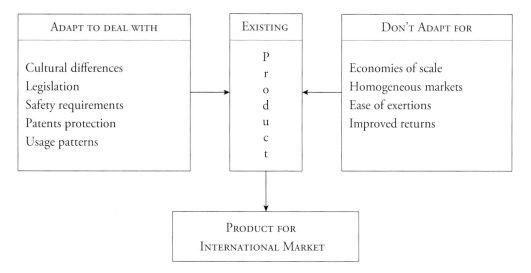

16.4 SELECTING PRODUCTS FOR INTERNATIONALISATION

There are a number of models an MNE can use in selecting products for internationalisation. The need for a structured model to help with the process is increased as the number of products the MNE has in its portfolio increases. These models therefore tend to be known as 'product portfolio analysis models'. In the following sections, we will explore two of the most commonly used models:
- the Boston Consulting Group (BCG) matrix; and
- the product life cycle.

The Boston Consulting Group (BCG) Matrix

The Boston Consulting Group (BCG) Matrix is a four-quadrant analytical technique that helps companies assess and plan their product portfolios. Each product or product group is analysed using the four-quadrant matrix shown in **Figure 16.3** below. A product's positioning on the matrix is dependent upon two variables: its relative market share, on the horizontal x-axis; and the rate of market growth for the product, on the vertical y-axis. Positioning according to these two variables causes each product to fall into one of the four quadrants on the matrix. Each quadrant has a label: 'dogs', 'cash cows', 'stars' and 'question marks'. The BCG Matrix proposes that the enterprise adopts a product strategy dependent upon which quadrant its product or products are positioned in. In simple terms, the BCG Matrix proposes that an enterprise should have a portfolio of products in each of the quadrants, the idea being to use the cash flow generated from the 'cash cows' to fund the growth of the 'stars'. The cash flow is also used to invest in the 'question marks' and eventually either turn them into 'stars', hopefully, or possibly 'dogs'. As the name suggests, 'dogs' are not appealing and enterprises should divest themselves of these products as soon as possible.

FIGURE 16.3: THE BCG MATRIX

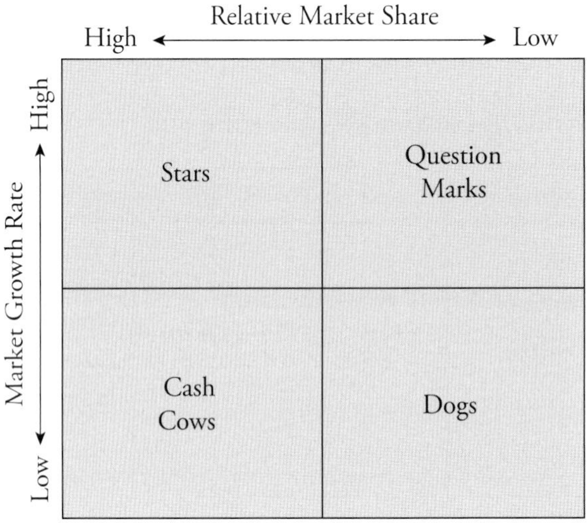

We can adapt and apply the BCG Matrix to an MNE's business by segmenting its product sales by geographic marketplace, as shown in **Figure 16.4**:

FIGURE 16.4: BCG MATRIX FOR A MNE IN FOUR MARKETS

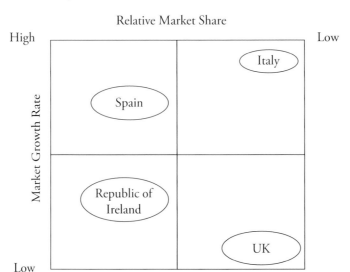

In doing so there are three variables to consider. First, the 'bubble' size for each country denotes the relative size of the MNE's sales in that country relative to the overall total relevant sales. Put another way, the bigger the bubble, the bigger the sales of the product or product category. If the UK bubble is twice the size of the Italy bubble, as in our example above, then the sales in the UK are twice the sales of Italy.

The second variable is the relative market share. In our example, the relative market share in the UK is high.

The third variable is the market growth rate. Again in our example, the growth rate of the UK market is low.

As we have seen, each quadrant of the BCG Matrix carries different characteristics and with them would go an associated recommended strategy. These can be summarised as follows:
- '**Dog**': low market growth rate/low market share. Strategy: '**divest**'.
- '**Cash Cow**': low market growth rate/high market share: Strategy: '**harvest**'.
- '**Question Mark**': high market growth/low market share: Strategy: '**decisions need to be made about the future**'. (i.e. further research and/or investment is needed before a final decision can be made).
- '**Star**': high market growth/high market share: Strategy: '**keep investing to maintain and grow market share**'.

By analysing its product portfolio using the BCG Matrix, an MNE can devise strategies for each of its geographic markets. Pricing strategies will form part of the marketing plan for each market. The BCG matrix is directly relevant to an MNE's pricing because once the MNE has assessed its positioning in each relevant market, it can set its prices accordingly. For example, it will pursue a growth strategy with its products categorised as 'stars'. Since it has a relatively low market share in these markets, it will use pricing policies and strategies that will further its growth ambitions. Many MNEs will have clear guidelines in their overall strategic plan as to what market position they wish to have. For example, Dublin-based DCC Plc has stated that:

> "DCC aims to be the number 1 or 2 operator in each of its markets. This is achieved through a consistent focus on increasing market shares organically and via value enhancing acquisitions."[2]

Clearly, the BCG Matrix model can help an MNE like DCC to structure its thinking about what strategies, including pricing strategies, to adopt in each market.

Product Life Cycle

Another useful tool that can be used for structured thinking about product strategies and associated pricing policies is the concept of product life cycle. Using the product life cycle model to set prices inextricably links pricing strategies with an MNE's wider business strategies. It is vital that pricing strategies fit within the overall business strategy for each product and, indeed, that pricing strategies are an integral component of the overall business strategy for the organisation. Pricing cannot be considered in isolation.

The product life cycle concept is built around the notion that products develop and progress through a cycle of change analogous to a natural life cycle. In its early days the product is created and, hopefully, starts to grow. It later matures and ultimately declines and dies. The model

---

[2] See http://www.dcc.ie/about-us/group-strategy.aspx (accessed June 2015).

proposes that at each of the four stages of the product's life cycle – creation, growth, maturity and decline – there are different types of purchaser for the product, who have differing views on price. The enterprise will price its products according to where it determines its products to be in their life cycle.

FIGURE 16.5: PRODUCT LIFE CYCLE AND CUSTOMER PROFILE

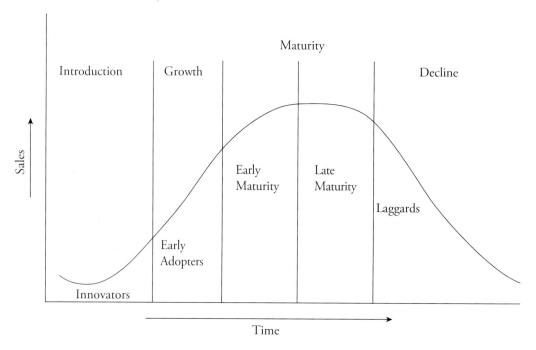

So, how does an MNE use this concept in setting its pricing strategies? The MNE can graph the life cycle of its product offerings in each market. The customer profile will be different for each stage of the product life cycle. Accordingly, the MNE must adapt the marketing plan for each product, including pricing policies, according to where each product is in its life cycle.

The pricing policy must be relevant to and reflect the target market. Innovators and early adopters are purchaser types attracted to products at the early stages of introduction and growth. They tend to be people who like to have the latest product and the most up-to-date version of a particular product type. They are not afraid to be seen to buy things that others do not have. For example, 'Innovators' will wear the Apple watch before other consumers. It will not matter to them that there is not yet, at the time of writing, a widespread acceptance of using this type of 'wearable' technology.

Early adopters tend to be less price-sensitive than consumers choosing a product in the 'late maturity' or 'laggards' phases. Late maturity purchasers tend to wait until products are tried and tested and have become commonplace. They will tend to be price-sensitive and will not purchase products they perceive to be expensive. 'Laggards' can sometimes find themselves paying higher prices for products as the supply begins to dwindle in response to reduced demand.

For example, vinyl records are now much more expensive than CDs or music downloads. The opposite was the case when CDs first arrived onto the music scene.

An MNE will find that its products may be at different stages of evolution in the different geographic markets in which it is operating (which is especially true for consumer products). Sometimes the company may try to accelerate the growth cycle of an existing product in a new market and launch it with a very attractive price in order to gain market share and move to early maturity as quickly as possible. However, it needs to ensure that pricing policy in one market does not jeopardise strategy in another geographically proximate market. For example, it is difficult for a product to be priced high in the Netherlands if it is sold cheaply in Belgium. This is one of the challenges for MNEs in deciding their expansion strategies.

EXAMPLES OF PRODUCT ADAPTATION AND STANDARDISATION

It is useful to illustrate the degree of product standardisation and adaptation that is undertaken by MNEs by considering some of the approaches taken by well-known MNE brands:

Coca-Cola   Standardised product, slight variations in packaging, variable pricing strategies

Toyota   Adaptation to comply with law (e.g. driving on the right)

Apple   Standardised product, almost standardised pricing

VISA   Standardised product

Samsung   Standardised products, variable prices

Hershey   Adaptation of product formula, adaptation of packaging, variable pricing

16.5 PRICING STRATEGIES FOR INTERNATIONAL MARKETS

Having decided which of its products it will sell internationally and the extent to which these need to be adapted, an MNE must then tackle the complexities of formulating a pricing strategy. In this section, we will consider some of the pricing strategies available to MNEs.

An MNE needs to decide whether to have a standard price in all its markets or whether to have adaptive pricing, but in internationalising its business it must first consider the risks of price escalation and how they might be avoided.

Export Price Escalation

We have seen how the internationalisation of a business introduces complexity. An MNE is more complex than a purely domestic firm, which in turn affects its pricing decisions. Even if the MNE intends to supply a foreign market with an existing, non-adapted product, as supplied in its home market, due to price escalation it is highly unlikely that the same pricing structure will deliver the same returns. In this context, **price escalation** is where the costs attaching to a product go up as it moves through the internationalisation process. Each step on its journey to a new, foreign market has the capacity to add cost. The factors that contribute to price escalation include:

- transport and shipping costs;
- storage;
- insurance;
- import duties and other taxes;
- agents' and distributors' fees;
- documentation costs associated with exporting (see **Chapter 10**).

These factors will add to the cost base of the products intended for export. The pricing will need to be adjusted accordingly if the MNE wishes to preserve margins. These price adjustments need to be factored into the wider pricing decision for the products involved. Factoring in these cost increasing considerations involves an assessment of what market position the MNE should take as regards its pricing strategy; should the prices be increased and, if so, how will this impact the attractiveness of the product to the customer? The price positioning of the product must correlate to the target market. An MNE cannot just put up its prices without understanding how this will affect the market. Another approach the MNE can take is to try to offset price escalation effects by adopting some of the strategies outlined below.

Strategies to Manage Export Price Escalation

An MNE will need to consider strategies to manage the possible effects of price escalation in order not to be at a competitive disadvantage compared to local suppliers:

- **Changing the Distribution Channel** The more nodes there are on the distribution channel, the more 'middlemen' there are taking a slice of the total margin available. A 'node' in this context represents a handling of the product, re-packaging, moving product from one place to another, and so forth. MNEs can explore ways to avoid middlemen. For example, direct selling to the end consumer is now a real possibility by using online sales.
- **Adapting the Product to Avoid Duties/Tariffs** Particular characteristics of a product may attract certain taxes, for example a tax-attracting ingredient such as alcohol. By altering the ingredients or the sizing of a product some host country taxes or tariffs may not apply. For example, in Ireland there is VAT on some biscuits but not on others depending on the level of chocolate in the product. An importer into the Republic of Ireland might lower the chocolate component in order to be able to sell the product without application of VAT. Obviously, it would be counterproductive to alter the product to such a degree as to render it unappealing. Such are the challenges facing MNEs.
- **Changing Pack Sizes** By decreasing pack sizes, a company can use a specific price point while absorbing the cost effects of price escalation factors. This strategy has been adopted increasingly in consumer products in recent years to ensure that price increases do not appear obvious. For example, a tube of toothpaste that was historically 100g and sold for £2.00 might still sell for £2.00 but would now weigh 85g. With clever packaging the product may even still look the same. This strategy may need to be adopted in entering a foreign market in order to absorb price escalation factors while remaining competitive.
- **Changing the Market Entry Strategy** When price escalation factors have a large impact on the costs and/or the product sector is especially price-sensitive, it may be necessary to revisit the market entry strategy. Price escalation features most highly as a product makes its way from being manufactured to the final market. By moving the manufacturing base closer to the final market, MNEs can reduce price escalation costs. Clearly, other costs have increased as the MNE has now opened another factory or commissioned a new manufacturing source.

The advantages will be balanced against the disadvantages. The evolution of this thinking is what leads to greater and greater internationalisation of MNEs.

- **Simplifying the Product Offer** Finally, the effect of price escalation can be managed by simplifying the product and removing unnecessary, value-added features offered in the home market. For example, a car may be sold with satellite navigation as standard in some markets, but the manufacturer may decide to dispense with this feature in developing markets so as to lower the total cost and to absorb the price escalation factors. By eliminating what might be termed 'frills', the MNE can absorb the price escalation factors and sell at a competitive price.

Standard Pricing

Standard pricing is where an MNE seeks to achieve the same price for its products in all international markets. Due to the variability of sales taxes and VAT, it is hard to execute standard pricing on consumer products. Nonetheless, some brands such as Apple seem to go quite close to having a standard price set by continent. Prices for Apple products in the Netherlands are very close to the prices prevailing in Dublin even though the sales taxes are different.

Other MNEs do not try to harmonise or standardise prices, and leave the price-setting to local management. This can sometimes lead to products being bought in bulk by traders in a lower-priced market for selling on in a higher-priced market in direct competition to the original manufacturing MNE. For example, if Wilkinson Sword supply Czech supermarkets at a low price, they may find that these products are bought in especially large quantities in the Czech Republic but are not sold in that market to consumers. Rather, they are exported from the Czech Republic to Ireland and are sold in Ireland in direct competition to the supplies from Wilkinson Sword themselves. This practice is called 'parallel importing' and the trade takes place on what is known as the 'grey' market. EU legislation is such that it enables, even encourages, such practices in order that there would be a convergence throughout the market of pricing and of free movement of goods.

Adaptive Pricing

Adaptive pricing is where the MNE will adapt its price to the local market conditions. **Figure 16.6** below shows how the selling price of an MNE's products may differ depending on the pricing strategy adopted in different markets. It is not simply a case of charging the highest price possible. According to the law of supply and demand, the higher the price charged, the lower the demand. In **Figure 16.6** six different pricing strategies are illustrated:

- bait pricing;
- market penetration pricing;
- competition-led pricing;
- demand-led pricing;
- premium pricing; and
- skimming.

The selling price increases from left to right. The first vertical line represents the variable cost of producing the product, the next vertical line the total cost of producing the product, i.e. variable cost plus fixed cost. The third vertical line represents the price a customer is willing to pay for the product. We can see from the chart that most pricing strategies are adapted to sell at prices above the total cost of production up to the price the customer is willing to pay. Some pricing strategies, however, will seek to sell at below total cost, and in some cases, even below variable cost.

FIGURE 16.6: RELATIVITIES OF MNE PRICING STRATEGIES

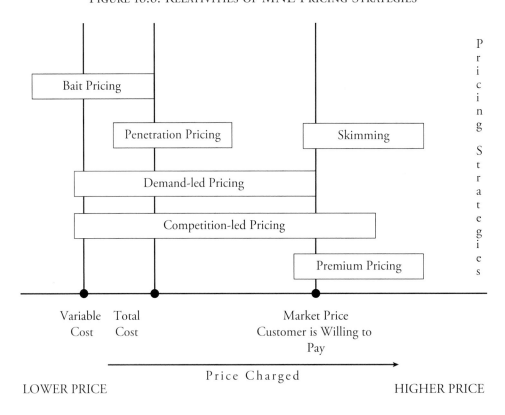

Figure 16.6 illustrates that an MNE must align its pricing strategy with its goals for the particular marketplace. At one end of the scale, an MNE will not be able to sell at prices below total cost for any length of time before its losses become unsustainable. At the other end of the scale, price skimming cannot be sustained over the longer term and prices will need to be discounted in order to maintain sales volumes. We will now look at these six pricing strategies in more detail, also explaining some other pricing strategies that an MNE may adopt.

Bait Pricing

Bait pricing is the approach where prices are set artificially low to attract customers. Once the customers have been 'hooked', the prices are increased or the price for peripherals and accessories are set high in order to recoup the losses on the initial sales. No MNE has ever made returns for its shareholders selling products at a loss so, in order to produce a return, other products must be sold at an unnecessarily higher price to compensate, or prices go up later. In other words, unless the sales of products at a loss are being subsidised by the sales of other products at very good margins, the MNE will eventually need to put up the prices of the loss-making products.

An example of bait pricing is a printer manufacturer pricing a desktop printer low but pricing its ink cartridges high. SKY TV, the satellite broadcaster, sells its set-top boxes at very low prices but seeks to recoup the costs from monthly subscriptions. In making it easy for customers to 'get into' the product or service, the idea is then to retain them and recover the original losses. However, if such customers keep changing suppliers, these strategies can become expensive to sustain.

Predatory Pricing

Predatory pricing is a form of bait pricing where the price chosen is so low it renders the competition unable to compete for any sustained period of time. In particular, it can be used where a larger MNE may subsidise its bait pricing from reserves it has generated outside the market to put a competitor without such reserves out of business. Over time, the company will then increase its prices in order to recover the initial costs of the bait pricing.

Some countries have outlawed this form of pricing on the basis that it is anti-competitive. The EU, Canada, the US and Australia all have laws restricting the use of predatory pricing to put one's competitors out of business. Other schools of thought argue that it provides low prices for customers and should not be prohibited in a free-market economy. In the Republic of Ireland, grocery products were prevented from being sold below cost for many years on the basis that this practice would ultimately lead to higher prices. The ban on below-cost selling of grocery products was removed in 2008. In the years that followed prices on some products fell while others increased and the overall effect was that price inflation in Irish grocery sector was the highest it had been for decades in the three years subsequent to the removal of the ban. While predatory pricing remains banned in all sectors, it is notoriously difficult to prove.

Market Penetration Pricing

Market penetration pricing is where an MNE will undercut its competitors' prices in order to gain market share. This strategy works best in markets where there is price elasticity, i.e. markets that are sensitive to pricing. A simple example is a special launch price for a product which will is available for a limited period, after which time it will rise to 'normal' levels. So endemic has market penetration pricing become in some sectors that launch price strategy has become the norm. Detergents, washing-up liquids and other household products are constantly launching new improved variations of their products at special prices.

There are fixed costs to be recovered in all markets in which an MNE operates. By gaining market share quickly, the MNE will more readily start to earn a contribution toward those fixed costs. For example, the company may establish a sales office on the ground in a new market, say Bulgaria. The Bulgarian-based sales office will sell products made in the MNE's home country. In order to start to recover the fixed cost of the sales office, the MNE may adopt market penetration pricing and once it has reached a reasonable market share, it can increase prices slightly and start to recover more of the fixed cost. Accordingly, the appropriateness of the strategy will be dependent on the price elasticity of the market, the ratio of fixed costs to variable costs and the size of the opportunity in relation to the MNE's overall scale.

Competition-led Pricing

Competition-led pricing involves an MNE selling its product or products on the basis of using a benchmark with the prices being charged by the competition. This is a common approach when entering a new market. It is not necessarily the case that the MNE will sell at the same price as its competitors, rather, it will set its own prices by reference to competitors' prices. For example, when the grocery discounters came to Ireland and the UK, they are believed to have set their pricing at a set percentage below the average prices of their competition. This means that the prices they sell at do not bear any relation to the prices they sell at in other geographical markets.

Similarly, an MNE may decide to sell a product in a new market at a price premium to competitors. For example, a new chocolate bar may be priced at 20% above the current market's most expensive chocolate bar. Such pricing may be part of a marketing strategy to convey quality or exclusivity, which might be real or imagined. The MNE will make an assessment, usually informed by research, as to what premium customers are willing to pay for their products versus an existing product in the marketplace.

The adoption of competition-led pricing can lead to problems where the MNE's products will be selling for different prices in similar markets, e.g. selling prices in the Netherlands may differ from those in Belgium, thus confusing or annoying customers. On the other hand, since the pricing is 'copied' from the competitor's pricing strategies, this factor should not lead to any major disadvantage unless the competitor only operates in one of the markets. For example, a Dutch yoghurt manufacturer sells its main product, a 200g tub, for €1.50 in the Netherlands. It decides to enter the Belgian market, where the market leader sells its equivalent product at €1.30. The Dutch manufacturer matches this price and sells into the Belgian market at €1.30. Customers back in the Netherlands will not be happy when they see that they are being charged 20c more. This type of risk is very real for MNEs adopting competition-led pricing strategies. When customers discover the price difference, they will need robust arguments to persuade them of the correctness of their pricing strategies. Sometimes an MNE will change some feature of a product in order to avoid direct comparison. In our example the MNE might reduce the pack size to 175g. While this may help make price comparison less transparent, it will also increase production costs since the product has been adapted for the Belgian market.

Demand-led Pricing

Demand-led strategy prices the product based on demand for it in the marketplace at a given time. An MNE following this approach must have some systematic way of assessing demand and allowing the price to fluctuate and vary in response to it. Demand-led pricing is a clear example of an adaptive price strategy whereby the MNE's prices in its target markets are set by the demand conditions prevailing in those markets. The best way to illustrate the concept is to consider an auction process. Prices are set by market demand. If the demand is strong, the price will rise, and vice versa. In today's commercial world MNEs will sell their products and services through tendering processes where they take part in auctions, often through virtual, online auctions. Prices will rise and fall depending on the level of demand. The pricing of hotel rooms is a good example of a demand-led pricing structure in operation. When demand for rooms increases due to a conference or concert being held nearby, prices increase.

Premium Pricing

Premium pricing involves setting prices at a high level, well above that needed to produce a 'normal' return. This approach is often adopted for the launch of new products or services into a new market. One of the thought processes behind such a strategy is that it is always easier to reduce prices later if market demand will not accept the higher prices. However, if the market *does* accept the higher prices, often because the MNE has a distinct or unique competitive advantage, the premium prices may last for some time. First-class travel on airlines is an example of a product that is priced at a premium level, often greater than the cost of the economy fare by a factor of many multiples. Passengers are willing to pay the premium price for the exclusivity, or comfort, of the service even though they know the cost of delivering the service bears no relationship to the price being charged.

> One can buy a white cotton T-shirt in Dunnes Stores for less than €4. One could also buy a white cotton T-shirt from Hugo Boss for €55, a 1,100% price difference. The Hugo Boss price strategy is not related to the production cost of the product but to a deep understanding of what the Hugo Boss target market will pay in return for the prestige of a designer brand.

It is often the case that if an MNE is trying to build a premium brand, it needs to support this with premium pricing. Customers expect there to be a relationship between quality and price, especially at the premium end of a market.

Skimming

All businesses will try to get the best price for their products or services. Skimming is an opportunistic pricing strategy that is at the upper reaches of this endeavour. It involves charging a price that customers know is above what the MNE would be prepared to take in normal circumstances. Often the customer has no choice. The product they need is essential for the customer and cannot be sourced elsewhere at a lower price.

Consider a situation where there are two suppliers of a component needed to operate a particular machine. A fire in one supplier's warehouse has rendered it unable to supply the market. The other supplier immediately increases its price to take account of the short-term opportunity. This is price skimming. It is different from demand-led pricing in that the demand for the product has not changed; rather, the price elasticity of the product has reduced, affording the remaining supplier a short-term opportunity to charge a higher price. Skimming is, by its nature, an opportunistic strategy and is not sustainable over time. Inventors of new products, especially medicines, are often accused of price skimming until patents run out. Then they are able to reduce the prices and still make a profit.

Early Cash Recovery

In some instances, MNEs will take a short-term view of their entry to a market, pricing products or services to maximise the early recovery of the cash invested. One might think that all pricing should be based on the extraction of maximum return over the shortest period of time. To some extent that is true, but an MNE will adopt a variety of techniques to set those prices. These techniques, some of which we have discussed above, provide the MNE with a structured framework upon which to base its prices.

The early cash recovery strategy is such a framework. The MNE will aim to recover investment in a given timeframe. In setting prices for products where there have been significant research and development costs, such as pharmaceutical products, the MNE may set its prices initially at such a level so as to recover its cash in investment in three years. In these cases, the actual selling price would bear some relation to the variable cost of producing the product but would also seek to recover the fixed cost as quickly as possible. This approach is suitable when the threat of an immediate new entrant is low but will rise over time. This approach can also be prevalent where the MNE detects a political or country risk associated with its investment in the foreign country and seeks to recoup its investments as soon as possible, viewing any subsequent sales after the cash has been recovered as a bonus.

Mark-up Pricing

Mark-up pricing is where an MNE sets a target mark-up on the cost per unit as a method for setting the price. For example, an MNE may wish to have a mark-up of 40%. It therefore adds 40% to its cost per unit in order to determine a selling price. If the product cost €120, the MNE would sell it for €120 + 40% = €168. Over time, the MNE develops knowledge of what mark-ups it needs on which categories of product to deliver the profits it requires. Obviously, the costs will differ by country, even if the product is the same, due to different distribution costs.

In this section we have covered standard pricing and adaptive pricing strategies that an MNE may adopt when trying to decide what prices to charge in its relevant markets. The MNE could have different pricing strategies for each marketplace, even for the same products. The key thing to note is that adaptive pricing strategies are much more prevalent for consumer goods than the use of standard prices. This is a result of the different nature of consumer markets across the globe. Industrial products that are sold to other businesses are more likely to have standard prices.

We now move on to the second half of this chapter, which is about transfer pricing. Transfer pricing covers the setting of prices for the transfers of products internally within the MNE. At first glance, one might think internal transfers should be no-one's business but the individual MNE's but, as you will see, the truth is very different.

16.6 TRANSFER PRICING

> A transfer price is an internal price set by an MNE which applies to the intra-company transfer of goods or services.

So far we have considered pricing strategies that an MNE may adopt in selling products to its external customers. In this section, we will examine how MNEs might set the prices for the internal selling of products between subsidiaries and between the parent and its subsidiaries.

In **Chapter 2** we were introduced to the motivations that drive the international expansion of domestic enterprises, which include seeking new markets in which to sell products and the use of cost advantages for the manufacture of goods or the provision of services. Some of these advantages are 'native' to a particular country, such as a ready availability of coal, and others are due to the availability of certain skill-sets and their low relative cost. Whatever the reason, MNEs will decide to make and develop products and services in and from geographic locations other than their home country. These will then be supplied to customers, either in the market in which they were made or in other countries. Such products may also be the inputs for the manufacturing process of another division of the same MNE. Two examples will help to illustrate this.

EXAMPLE 16.2: TRANSFER PRICES – ITALIAN ENGINES FOR ARGENTINIAN ASSEMBLY

A multinational car manufacturer assembles cars in Argentina for the South American market. It manufactures the car engines at its Italian division. The MNE must decide on what price to sell the engines from the Italian manufacturing division to the Argentinian assembly plant. This 'selling price' is called a transfer price.

An Irish luxury goods brand makes its finest crystal decanters at its factory in Poland. The decanters are transferred to finished goods depots and sold all over the world by its Ireland-based sales office. The MNE must decide on the transfer price, i.e. the price at which the Polish factory sells the final product to the sales office. The sales office will then set the prices to be charged to the external customers around the world using one or more of the pricing strategies mentioned earlier in this chapter.

At first glance, one might think it was straightforward to set a transfer price; that the entity making the product or supplying the service should charge their sister entity whatever it cost them to make it; that they should not seek to make a profit on their dealings within their own, wider organisation.

However, "hold on a minute", the supplying entity might protest, "we could sell these products in the external market for a higher price and make a profit." The argument would be made that the entity receiving the product or service should pay its sister company whatever price it would get in the open market. But it is not that simple. What is the open market price for a product that is essentially a 'work in progress'? The outputs from one part of an MNE transferred to another part of the MNE as inputs are most likely to be partially made or processed goods that form part of, or are combined with other inputs, to produce the final product that is sold on the external market. It is very difficult to say what the 'open market' price of such a partially complete product is. This open market valuation is made doubly difficult by the fact that the product or service will most likely be made in compliance with the MNE's own specifications or patents and that a directly comparable product on the open market is not readily available.

To counter these and other issues, a set of concepts has emerged that can be used in the setting of transfer prices. Before going on to examine the concepts we must first examine who is affected by the setting of transfer prices. In other words, who are the stakeholders? By understanding the different needs and wants of the stakeholders we can then see the merits or demerits of each of the different concepts in terms of their ability to meet the needs and wants of the differing stakeholder groups or, at a minimum, alleviate their concerns. The OECD has acted as the co-ordinating body to try to standardise these transfer pricing concepts. It has further sought to have member countries ratify the concepts through treaty arrangements. The legal basis giving effect to transfer pricing regulations has its genesis in the bilateral tax treaties that exist between most of the major developed countries. For example, the Republic of Ireland has 72 tax treaties and the UK has more than 100 tax treaties.

Stakeholders

Before considering the methods by which an MNE might calculate transfer prices it is worthwhile to consider the stakeholders involved in such transactions. We have seen that a transfer price is an internally set price which an MNE will use to 'price' intragroup transfers of goods or services. Since the selling price of one internal party is the purchase price of another internal party, taken together, they net out to zero. One could deduce from this that since internal pricing is a 'zero-sum game' it would be largely irrelevant in the wider scheme of things. However, this deduction would be wholly wrong. Transfer pricing has been and continues to be one of the most discussed topics arising from the growth of multinational corporations and the globalisation of manufacturing and the provision of services.

One of the hottest topics at the time of writing in international commerce and trade discussions is base erosion and profit shifting (BEPS). Countries are trying to agree between themselves through the auspices of the OECD how to tackle the exploitation of the non-standardisation of the global taxation system. The absence of a global taxation system means that some incomes are taxable if they arise in Country X but not if they arise in Country Y. The same anomalies apply to costs, some of which are allowable in some countries as deductions before calculating the tax payable but not allowable in others. Finally, of course, there are corporation tax rates. The Republic of Ireland, for example, has a low headline rate of 12.5%; the UK corporation tax rate is 20%. MNEs use transfer pricing to 'charge' for goods and services internally. They may locate their activities to optimise their tax position and exploit the lack of global harmonisation of tax codes. The OECD's BEPS project (base erosion and profit sharing) is an initiative to attempt to prevent the inappropriate use of the lack of global norms. We will return to BEPS later in this chapter.

Local Management

As discussed in **Chapter 18**, a manager's or management team's competence can be assessed on their ability to predict the consequences of their actions. Having assessed the MNE's environment(s) using a tool such as a PESTLE study (see **Chapter 7**), management will decide what strategy and action plan to adopt so that the MNE will achieve its goals. Where the entity or business unit is part of a larger organisation, the assessment will need to take into account the position the business unit fulfils in the wider MNE. In **Example 16.3** below both the Slovakian and the Austrian management will have an interest in how the transfer pricing system will work.

EXAMPLE 16.3: TRANSFER PRICING AND LOCAL MANAGEMENT:
A SLOVAKIAN/AUSTRIAN SCENARIO

A manufacturing plant in Slovakia makes components for a sister company in Austria. In this case, the management team will need to feed into the plans of the sister company to ensure overall alignment to the goals of the wider organisation. Transfer pricing affects both parties. The MNE's transfer pricing mechanism will dictate the selling price of the Slovakian component manufacturer. It will also dictate the cost price of the component for the Austrian assembly plant. In terms of performance measurement, a system that unfairly 'benefits' one party will, by implication, unfairly 'penalise' the other. The output of the Slovakian factory is sold, albeit internally, to the Austrian sister plant. If the transfer prices are set too high, the Slovakian plant may appear to be more efficient or effective than it actually is. Conversely, the Austrian plant will have higher inbound costs than might otherwise be the case, and the reverse also applies. Thus, both sets of local management will have an interest in how the transfer pricing mechanisms apply to their own performance measures.

It is possible to measure the performance of both plants on some other set of measures and not consider transfer prices at all. Using other measures might involve comparing number of units produced per hour of production uptime, or some other type of benchmarking approach other than prices. This approach, however, has its own set of challenges, as we will see below.

In many instances a manufacturing plant or business unit within an MNE makes a finished product that is then sold on through sales offices located in various countries. For example, in Ireland, BMW cars are sold through a combination of dealers and BMW sales offices. The cars are not made in Ireland. BMW must decide a pricing structure that 'sells' the cars to its Irish sales offices. The pricing process is further complicated by the fact that BMW must also supply the dealer network at prices that allow dealers to compete both with each other and with BMW's own sales effort. The transfer price into Ireland will also be compared to the transfer price into other countries by the local management, who would expect to see any differences to the prices charged to the Irish division compared to other European divisions being capable of explanation by the MNE's price-setting process and/or taxation and tariff differences.

Parent Company

The parent company or head office of an MNE will have a system for planning and co-ordinating the activity of its constituent parts. How developed the system is will be a function of the MNE's operating philosophy, which itself will be a function of the nature of the industry, the MNE's shareholders and customers, and the HR practices adopted by management. It will also be dependent to some degree on the culture of the countries in which the MNE operates.

One of the functions of the planning and co-ordinating process is to ensure that each operating unit is optimising its effectiveness within the overall MNE structure. Transfer pricing systems will impact on local management behaviours and, consequently, it is of utmost importance for the parent to ensure that its profit-optimisation goals are met through the effective setting of transfer prices. In other words, the transfer pricing system should support alignment of individual business units' goals to the overall goals of the MNE.

Trading Partners

Many MNEs will form joint ventures (JVs) with other entities in order to achieve a common goal, or are compelled to form JV alliances with governments in countries in which they wish to trade or manufacture. Whatever the reason behind the JV, the prices at which goods and services are bought or sold between it and other units of the MNE will be an important factor in the JV's overall success. These prices will be set by the MNE's transfer pricing system and its associated protocols.

Governments

The final stakeholders to mention are the governments of the countries in which the MNE is conducting its business. Governments rely on the revenue streams from taxation and are therefore interested in how transfer prices between units in an MNE are set. The profits of a business unit in Country A are dictated by the prices the unit can get for its products. When selling in the external market, these prices will be set by market forces. However, when set by some internal process, as transfer prices are, then a question can arise as to whether they prices are too high, or too low. A government will want to ensure that exporting divisions of MNEs do not set their selling prices to their sister divisions too low, thereby leading to less profits in the exporting country and, consequently, less tax revenue. Likewise, a government of a country in which an importing MNE is located will be motivated to ensure that the purchase price the MNE's division is paying for their inbound goods and services is not set too high, thereby reducing profits in the importing division with its consequent reduction in taxable profits.

Thus, governments want to have higher export transfer prices and lower import transfer prices for their countries. Because one government's export price is another government's import price the possibilities of tensions and conflicts are great. In order to bring some common understanding to transfer pricing, the OECD countries (including ROI and the UK), have signed treaties as to how transfer prices are to be agreed and set between divisions of MNEs operating in member countries. As mentioned above, the OECD is driving change in this area through the BEPS process, discussed further below.

Methods of Setting Transfer Pricing

As we have seen, transfer prices are the prices that an MNE will use to internally transfer goods and services between its differing operating units. On the face of it, this should be of interest to no-one but the management of the MNE since no external transactions have occurred. However, because the taxation of the activities of an MNE are collected at a country-by-country level, the tax payable in any one jurisdiction will be influenced by the transfer prices that have been set to govern these internal transactions. The tax authorities in the countries in which an MNE operates will be interested in the transfer prices it uses for the derivation and calculation of its tax liabilities. The MNE's internal method of charging for goods is its own business until such time as tax becomes involved. Once there is a taxation dimension, the transfer prices come under external scrutiny. It is true that an MNE could adopt one set of transfer prices for its internal management accounts and performance evaluation and a second, different, set of transfer prices for its tax calculations. In the main, though, MNEs will endeavour to produce their accounts in accordance with one set of transfer prices, if only to avoid complex reconciliations.

We have also seen how different stakeholders will respond differently to transfer prices. This is especially true for the performance management of business units which supply, or are supplied, by other business units within the MNE. The principle is that, within reason, the MNE should try to simulate true market conditions for the setting of the internal transfer prices. In this way, no manager can complain that their business unit's performance has been unfairly disadvantaged.

There are various methods by which an MNE can set its transfer prices. Each of the methods described below have been recognised by the OECD as being appropriate. Since the OECD's transfer pricing methods form part of the treaties between OECD member countries, the MNE can have some assurance that the application of one or more of these methods will not fall foul of the taxation authorities. While this is truer for OECD member countries than for other countries, taxation authorities may have differing degrees of evidential requirements for an MNE to demonstrate that its system complies with one or other of the methods. As you will see, most of the methods are linked to some type of external, market-set price. The MNE will need to be able to prove that the comparators and methodology it has chosen to set its transfer prices are sound and capable of being substantiated if scrutinised.

The Arm's Length Principle

When an MNE sells or buys goods or services from external entities, the prices for those goods and services are set by market forces, which respond to the economic pressures of the marketplace, especially the law of supply and demand. When an MNE is buying or selling goods or services internally between its business units, the same forces do not apply. Many MNEs will endeavour to simulate market forces in order to set internal prices. This is one way of mitigating the behavioural effects on local management discussed above. Transfer pricing should endeavour to simulate the prices that would be set if the entity was trading in the external market. This is **'the arm's length' principle** and it underpins, or is the benchmark for, all methods of setting transfer prices. (It is worth noting at this stage that such simulation is not without challenges, particularly where the internally traded good is a bespoke component being made for later integration into another product.)

Thus, the principle of arm's length pricing informs the organisational thinking of many MNEs in that they endeavour to create cultures of autonomy and empowerment within their divisions. In such decentralised organisations, the local business unit management team negotiate with their sister divisions to set transfer prices, thereby emulating the dynamics of a true market. In some cases they are empowered as if they were dealing with third-party customers or suppliers. This approach will not work in all industries or sectors, however. The greater the degree of specialisation or intellectual propriety involved, the less likely it is that either party within the MNE can transact with anyone other than their sister business unit.

> For example, Division X, part of an MNE, manufactures a component that has only one purpose, i.e. to fit into sister Division Y's production process. The manufacture of Division X's product is covered by patented technology and cannot be made by anyone else. Thus, it would be difficult to negotiate an arm's length price, as Division X is the only possible supplier for the component.

A key point is that while sometimes the organisational structure and negotiation dynamics of an MNE may actually create arm's length pricing, in many other cases it will be impossible to create the 'arm's length' price by internal negotiation and it will have to be derived using one of the methods explained below.

> There can be genuine pressures on an MNE to have non-market pricing for some internal transactions. Sometimes, these pressures can compete with each other. For example, an MNE may have produced a surplus of goods in one of its markets and wants to sell off the surplus at a loss, but not in its main market. It is prepared to sell the surplus at below its production cost. The surplus has arisen in Country A. At what price should the MNE transfer the surplus stock to its division in Country B, where it hopes to sell off the stock at below cost?
>
> All of these factors may affect transfer prices and the amount of profits accruing to associated enterprises within the MNE group. If it sells to the division in Country B at a knock-down price, it will incur the losses in Country A as well as off-setting these losses against the profits it made on the original sales in Country A. The taxation authorities in Country A may see that their income is being reduced by the losses, which have essentially allowed cheap prices in another country. Country B's government may be unhappy that products are being dumped in its market at below cost price, forcing local producers out of business.
>
> Even from this relatively simple example, one can see that the area of appropriate transfer prices and the application of the arm's length principle is a minefield of complexity.

The Arm's Length Principle, the OECD and Taxation The OECD is the international body to which countries have turned to devise and arbitrate on agreed approaches to transfer pricing. The OECD's main statement of the arm's length principle is in paragraph 1 of Article 9 (Associated Enterprises) of the OECD Model Tax Convention, which is the basis of bilateral tax treaties involving OECD member countries and an increasing number of non-member countries:

> "[Where] conditions are made or imposed between the two [associated] enterprises in their commercial or financial relations which differ from those which would be made between independent enterprises, then any profits which would, but for those conditions, have accrued to one of the enterprises, but, by reason of those conditions, have not so accrued, may be included in the profits of that enterprise and taxed accordingly."

> "1. Where
>
> a) an enterprise of a Contracting State participates directly or indirectly in the management, control or capital of an enterprise of the other Contracting State, or
>
> b) the same persons participate directly or indirectly in the management, control or capital of an enterprise of a Contracting State and an enterprise of the other Contracting State,
>
> and in either case conditions are made or imposed between the two enterprises in their commercial or financial relations which differ from those which would be made between independent enterprises, then any profits which would, but for those conditions, have accrued to one of the enterprises, but, by reason of those conditions, have not so accrued, may be included in the profits of that enterprise and taxed accordingly."[3]

One can see from this definition that if, for its own reasons, the MNE has a different approach to transfer pricing than the 'arm's length' principle, the authorities can adjust the taxable profits to bring them into line. This leaves plenty of scope for debate between tax authorities since adjusting profits upwards in one jurisdiction entails a mirror adjustment downward in the jurisdiction of the other division. Because the arm's length principle treats the members of an MNE group as if they were independent entities, attention is focused on the nature of the transactions between those members and on "whether the conditions there-of differ from the conditions that would be obtained in comparable uncontrolled transactions". An analysis is carried out which compares 'controlled' and 'uncontrolled' transactions. This 'comparability analysis' is at the heart of the application of the arm's length principle.

It is important to put the issue of comparability into perspective in order to emphasise the need for an approach that is balanced in terms of, on the one hand, its reliability and, on the other, the burden it creates for taxpayers and tax administrations. Paragraph 1 of Article 9 of the OECD Model Tax Convention is the foundation for comparability analyses because it introduces the need for:

> "• a comparison between conditions (including prices, but not only prices) made or imposed between associated enterprises and those which would be made between independent enterprises, in order to determine whether a re-writing of the accounts for the purposes of calculating tax liabilities of associated enterprises is authorised under Article 9 … ; and
>
> • a determination of the profits which would have accrued at arm's length, in order to determine the quantum of any re-writing of accounts."[4]

---

[3] Model Convention with Respect to Taxes on Income and on Capital (OECD, 2014).
[4] *Review of Comparability and of Profit Methods* (OECD, 2010).

The main purpose behind the OECD's application of the arm's length principle is not, as might be initially assumed, to ensure the taxation revenues are maximised. Rather it is because the OECD is founded upon the idea of free trade. Earlier in this text we saw how theories of free trade propose that all societies would benefit from increased international trade and collaboration and that such trade is best encouraged by ensuring a 'level playing field' for all competitors, free from artificial barriers or tariffs. The use of transfer pricing systems other than those that comply with the arm's length principle tend to alter the level playing field as they introduce competitive advantages that accrue solely from the taxation differences that exist in different jurisdictions. Accordingly, the arm's length principle seeks to have MNEs taxed in exactly the same fashion as if they were independent entities, thereby levelling the playing field.

Furthermore, and at the same time, the OECD asks tax authorities not to approach the issue of transfer pricing on the basis that MNEs intend to evade taxation. Although it is true that transfer pricing can be used for these purposes, the OECD points out that MNEs need *some* agreed system to price internal transfers and request it be presumed that they have adopted a legitimate approach.

If transfer prices do not reflect the arm's length principle, then the resultant taxation charges in a particular jurisdiction will be misstated, meaning that the taxation charge will differ from the charge that would have arisen had the MNE been transacting with an external entity. As we have seen, the OECD agreements between its member countries allow local taxation authorities to alter the transfer prices that an MNE has applied to its internal transactions to ones that will be used for the purposes of levying taxes. In summary, the system will seek to adjust transfer pricing agreements between an MNE's divisions to the extent that those transfer prices do not accord with the arm's length principle. This is an important concept to grasp. It is often the work of the finance team in the MNE to support its transfer pricing systems and provide such information as is needed by the taxation authorities to investigate the applicability of the system and its bona fides.

Effectiveness of the Arm's Length Principle The arm's length principle works in almost all cases and in some more effectively than in others, by which I mean that there are very clear external comparisons that can be devised and used for the comparability analysis. For example, if an MNE was mining copper in Zambia and selling it to its division in Germany, it should be readily possible to compare the price that these transactions would take place at if the two entities were independent of each other and not part of the same MNE group. The same is true if a company in Country B borrows money from its head office in Country A. It should be easy to determine what price the division would have had to pay on its borrowings if a company with a similar capital and financial profile were to borrow on the external money markets.

Nevertheless, there are some significant cases in which the arm's length principle is difficult and complicated to apply. The complications can arise when an MNE is involved in the integrated production of highly specialised goods, in unique intangibles, and/or in the provision of specialised services. Solutions exist to deal with such difficult cases, including the 'transactional profit-split' method (see below).

Some commentators see the arm's length principle as being flawed to its core because it seeks to 'level the playing field' by the elimination of taxation benefits arising from the multinational nature of the enterprise. It is argued that the arm's length principle imposes a 'false' transfer pricing structure on MNEs, which are as if they were sets of independent entities, which clearly they are not. For example, intra-group performance management may allow for superior cost performance in a division. Is it right, then, to impose an artificial price on transfers from this superior performing division as if it was an independent entity? There are difficulties in calculating fair ways to allocate the benefits of economies of scale in applying the arm's length principle. These complications also arise when faced with the benefits afforded an MNE through its superior integration.

Another problem with the effectiveness of the arm's length system is timing or, more accurately, time gaps between the calculations, the transactions and any subsequent investigation. The examination of the transactions between entities in an MNE by the taxation authorities happens often many years after the original transactions occurred, which puts additional administration burdens upon both the MNE and the taxation authorities. These costs can be high and can consume scarce resources, particularly within the finance department. For example, the OECD states the following:

> "The tax administration may also have to engage in this verification process perhaps some years after the transactions have taken place. The tax administration would review any supporting documentation prepared by the taxpayer to show that its transactions are consistent with the arm's length principle, and may also need to gather information about comparable uncontrolled transactions, the market conditions at the time the transactions took place, etc., for numerous and varied transactions. Such an undertaking usually becomes more difficult with the passage of time."[5]

Both tax administrations and MNEs frequently have difficulty in obtaining adequate information to apply the arm's length principle. Because the principle usually requires the comparison of the actual transfer prices applied by the MNE to uncontrolled transactions of a comparable nature carried out by other independent entities, there is a large data collection exercise involved. An MNE would be well advised to anticipate these investigations and prepare supporting comparison analysis at the time it is setting the transfer prices. This data will prove very useful in the event of any subsequent examination by the taxation authorities.

It is not easy to obtain the supporting information. For example, the most accurate comparative transactions may be being carried out by the MNE's closest competitors. These constraints mean that the MNE may not be able to prepare a full suite of complete information to support its transfer pricing decisions. In these instances, which will be common, both the MNE and the tax authorities will have to apply a degree of judgement.

However, even when one takes into account the above problems, the arm's length theory still provides the most solid principle to underpin the setting of transfer prices between associated entities in an MNE. The fact that an international consensus has evolved concerning the appropriateness of the arm's length principle means that we can be certain that it will have a role for the foreseeable future in the setting of transfer pricing.

Global Formulary Apportionment

Before we examine the more 'traditional' arm's length methods for calculating transfer prices, it is useful to consider the main competing concept to the arm's length principle: global

---

[5] *Review of Comparability and of Profit Methods: Revision of Chapters I-III of the Transfer Pricing Guidelines* (OECD, 2012).

formulary apportionment (GFA). (Though GFA is not in force as an **international** system for allocating profits between countries, it has been applied in some federal countries, such as Canada, as we shall see later.) GFA is believed by some commentators in this field to be a more equitable way to allocate MNE profits between taxation jurisdictions. We will now examine briefly the main concepts behind the GFA system.

As mentioned above, there are some who think that the arm's length principle is not the best way of calculating transfer prices between entities in an MNE. They believe that it is impossible to recreate a meaningful simulation of the transactions. In particular, they believe that some of the inherent benefits that underpin MNE strategies are lost by using the arm's length principle, namely economies of scale and tight vertical integration.

GFA works by looking at the global profits for an MNE and then, through the application of some formulaic apportionment, allocating profits to each of the countries in which the MNE operates. The taxation charge would then be made on the allocated profits in the respective jurisdictions. In **Example 16.4** below an Irish MNE has its profits allocated across the three jurisdictions in which it operates by reference to the relativity of its sales achieved in each of those jurisdictions.

EXAMPLE 16.4: GLOBAL FORMULARY APPORTIONMENT

An Irish MNE has made a €50 million profit for the year 2014. It operates in three countries, the Republic of Ireland, the UK and France. The sales in each of these markets are €100 million, €150 million and €250 million respectively.

The denominator used to allocate the profits are sales levels in each country.[6] Therefore, the applicable profits in each taxation jurisdiction are as follows:

$$\text{ROI} = \frac{100}{500} \times 50 = 10$$

$$\text{UK} = \frac{150}{500} \times 50 = 15$$

$$\text{France} = \frac{250}{500} \times 50 = 25$$

You can see from this approach that the idea is to come up with a way that taxes all the profits of the MNE somewhere. The key issue is what formula is appropriate to use to allocate the profits. In our simple example we used relative sale in each country to total sales as the basis of allocating the profits. However, imagine if the MNE in our example manufactured all the products it sold in a fourth country, e.g. China, but did not sell the product there, how would one then approach the allocation process?

---

[6] This is just a hypothetical example since GFA has not been internationally adopted. Sales are used as the denominator for the sake of simplicity. If GFA were ever introduced, I have no doubt the calculations would be much more complex. The same principle would apply, however, i.e. that the MNE's profits are allocated to each of the countries in which it transacts business by reference to an allocation formula.

Thus, there are three steps in applying GFA:
1. identify which units of the MNE make up the taxable entity;
2. determine the global profits;
3. establish the formula to be used in allocating the global profits. (The formula we used in **Example 16.4** was to allocate based on sales. The allocation can also be made on the basis of capital employed, costs, payroll charges or some combination of all four, or some other appropriate method.)

Though the GFA approach has not been generally adopted by the international community or the OECD as a method of allocating the taxable profits of MNEs, and is unlikely to have widespread international application any time soon, it has a distinct advantage over the arm's length approach to transfer pricing in that it requires significantly less administration. However, the selection of the formula to allocate the profits remains too contentious. An enterprise that has operations in a number of provinces in Canada will find its total profits will be split and allocated to each province by reference to the formula and taxed accordingly. It has, however, been used by local tax authorities within the Canadian federal taxation system. It is also used internally in some MNEs to allocate out to business units some centrally incurred overhead costs.

Arm's Length Transfer Pricing Methods

In this section we will examine three 'traditional' methods used to apply the arm's length principle to transfer pricing:
• the comparable uncontrolled price (CUP) method;
• the resale price method; and
• the cost plus method.

Comparable Uncontrolled Price (CUP) Method The CUP method is a particularly reliable method whereby an independent entity sells the same product as is sold between two associated units in an MNE. This method compares the price charged for the goods or services transferred between the associated business units of the MNE to the price charged in a comparable transaction in comparable circumstances in the real, external marketplace. If there is any difference between the two prices, the tax authorities may deem that the price is not in accordance with the arm's length principle and they can substitute the MNE's internally generated transfer price with the price identified in the comparable transaction.

The internally generated price is the 'controlled' price, the external market price is the 'uncontrolled' price, the distinction being that the MNE can control the prices it charges between its divisions while the external market is subject to real market forces, which the MNE cannot control. The controlled price flows from a controlled transaction. The uncontrolled price flows from an uncontrolled transaction. The transactions can be compared to each other for the purposes of the application of the arm's length principles if:
• any difference that exists between the two transactions being compared gives rise to a price difference;
• if the difference does give rise to a price difference, then it should be possible to adjust the prices accordingly with a reasonable degree of accuracy.

For example, the supply of copper between two divisions of a global MNE should be comparable to the supply of copper between a copper producer and a third-party customer. The difference between the transactions might be that one shipment originates in Zambia and the other in Angola. It should be possible to identify the difference in price that arises from the difference between the two transactions being compared.

Where an MNE can identify comparable transactions that are 'uncontrolled', the CUP method is preferable to all other methods. However, this may be easier said than done. Two transactions may look very similar at first examination, but small variations in the production process or the delivery timings can make the price differences quite high. Therefore, care must be taken by the MNE that it does not automatically select external, uncontrolled transactions without fully understanding how any differences will affect price.

The OECD's view of how an MNE should select comparable uncontrolled transactions is as follows:

> "In considering whether controlled and uncontrolled transactions are comparable, regard should be had to the effect on price of broader business functions other than just product comparability ... Where differences exist between the controlled and uncontrolled transactions or between the enterprises undertaking those transactions, it may be difficult to determine reasonably accurate adjustments to eliminate the effect on price. The difficulties that arise in attempting to make reasonably accurate adjustments should not routinely preclude the possible application of the CUP method. Practical considerations dictate a more flexible approach to enable the CUP method to be used and to be supplemented as necessary by other appropriate methods, all of which should be evaluated according to their relative accuracy. Every effort should be made to adjust the data so that it may be used appropriately in a CUP method."[7]

The key to the CUP method, and all other arm's length methods of transfer pricing, is to find transactions that are comparable and where differences that lead to price variations can be identified and adjusted for. In other words, find an identical uncontrolled transaction. If an identical uncontrolled transaction cannot be found, then the MNE must find one that is sufficiently similar as to allow readily identifiable reasons for why the prices between the two transactions might be different, and adjust for those.

For example, imagine an uncontrolled transaction whose only difference to the controlled transaction is the presence of some additional add-on feature, such as the addition of a paint finish. The price of the uncontrolled transaction can be adjusted for by the cost of the additional paint job in order to arrive at an arm's length uncontrolled transaction price.

The following examples illustrate the application of the CUP method. I have included an example where there is no adjustment needed to the price and also one in which, resulting from the comparison, an adjusted price can be deduced.

EXAMPLE 16.5: THE COMPARABLE UNCONTROLLED PRICE (CUP) METHOD

An independent enterprise sells unbranded Sri Lankan teabags of a similar type, quality and quantity as those sold between two associated business units of an MNE. Obviously, the sale by the independent enterprise is the uncontrolled transaction and the sale between the two units is the controlled transaction. We can then readily compare the two prices and see that they are in accord, assuming that the comparable sales take place at the same stage of the product's development and on comparable credit and delivery terms.

---

[7] *Review of Comparability and of Profit Methods: Revision of Chapters I-III of the Transfer Pricing Guidelines* (OECD, 2012).

If the only available uncontrolled transaction involves unbranded Kenyan teabags, it would be appropriate to inquire whether the difference in the tea or country of origin has a material effect on the price. For example, it could be asked whether the source of teabags commands a premium or requires a discount generally in the open market. Such information may be obtainable from commodity markets or may be deduced from dealer prices. If this difference has a material effect on price, some adjustments would be appropriate. If a reasonably accurate adjustment cannot be made, the reliability of the CUP method would be reduced and it might be necessary to select another, less direct method.

Another example is where the only difference between the sale of the Sri Lankan tea bags is the delivery and credit terms. In most instances the process can easily be adjusted to take account of additional premium or discount required to render the prices comparable. For example, if the controlled transaction price is for delivery 'ex-factory' while the uncontrolled transaction price is for 'FOB',[8] it should be possible to calculate the difference in price that would be applicable to these slightly different but well-defined variances.

As another example, assume an MNE business unit sells 1,000 tons of sugar for $80 per ton to a business unit within its MNE group. At the same time it sells 500 tons of the same grade of sugar for $100 per ton to an independent external customer. Here the controlled transaction between the MNE's units differs from the uncontrolled transaction only in the volume of the transaction, i.e. the number of tons sold. In this case, it should be possible by researching the sugar market in general to determine the appropriate discounts for increased volume of tonnage of sugar purchases. Once the MNE has determined the normal volume discounts that would apply for 1,000 versus 500 tons, it can see whether a price adjustment might be required to the $80.

(**Note:** the CUP method is preferable to the two other methods described below as it provides absolute evidence of the market price and uses this evidence to support the transfer price. However, an uncontrolled price may not always be available.)

Resale Price Method This method assumes that eventually a product or service transferred internally between associated business units in an MNE will be sold to a third party, either on its own or integrated into a finished product. In other words, eventually the products or services transferred through 'controlled' transactions within an MNE become 'uncontrolled' transactions as they will eventually be sold to an independent third party. This ultimate uncontrolled sale takes place at market prices and is, by definition, outside of the direct control of the MNE. This market price, the ultimate sale price to the independent customer, is called the 'resale price'.

The 'resale price' is then reduced by an appropriate gross margin, which is the deemed amount needed by the entity to cover the costs of its activities and receive an appropriate profit. The deducted gross margin is called the 'resale price margin'. It should be possible to work out appropriate rates of resale price margin by comparing the margins needed by independent entities transacting similar businesses and carrying out similar activities. This method works best when the MNE business unit selling on to the final external customer does not substantially alter the product being sold and is therefore more suited to sales and marketing type MNEs and distributors, where the products are manufactured on a grand scale in one location and shipped from there to a network of divisions around the globe for onward direct sales to the final customers.

---

[8] FOB ('free on board') is a shipping term meaning it is the seller's responsibility to cover the cost of getting the goods on board the nominated ship.

EXAMPLE 16.6: THE RESALE PRICE METHOD

A BMW sales office in Ireland sell cars to consumers. The gross margin on these transactions is externally comparable to the gross margin third-party dealers might earn on the same transaction. Essentially, the method involves working back from the resale price to determine an arm's length price. In our case, the BMW may be sold to an external customer for €40,000. An independent dealer might require a 15% margin to cover his costs and earn a profit. The MNE can then apply this resale price margin to the final resale price of its cars to derive the transfer price. In this case, therefore, a car selling for €40,000 would be 'bought' into the Irish division from the German parent at €34,000, being €40,000 less 15% resale price margin.

As with the CUP method, two transactions, a controlled one and an uncontrolled one, can only be used for the comparison to deduce the transfer price:
- if there are no differences between the two transactions, that would give rise to a price variation; or
- if there are such differences, they are capable of being identified and their impact on price can be adjusted with reasonable certainty.

One of the advantages of the resale price method over the CUP method is that differences in the products or services being sold may not require significant adjustment since the resale price margin required will be more or less the same. For example, if the controlled transaction was for a BMW 5 Series car selling for €40,000 and the uncontrolled transaction was for a 3 Series M Sport selling for €41,000, the resale price margin would be broadly similar, even though the actual products would be significantly different (for car aficionados at least). This situation arises because in these types of businesses the gross margin needed to carry out the value-added tasks is not so dependent on the attributes of the product being sold but of the activities being carried out. In other words, it takes the same amount of activity to sell a diesel car as it would for a petrol car. Indeed, one would expect that the resale price margin required of an Audi reseller would not differ substantially from those of a BMW or Mercedes distributor.

While the resale price method allows for a greater degree of product variability, the products being compared must still be comparable. It would be unreasonable to argue that distributors of television sets are comparable with distributors of motorbikes with regard to resale price margin. Even where the activities seems comparable, it is important to ensure that the underlying activities are comparable. For example, one distributor of televisions may guarantee 100% stock availability while another may sell on the basis of 'when it's gone, it's gone'. Clearly, there are increased costs associated with ensuring 100% stock availability. Therefore, a comparison between transactions of these two entities would need to take account of the higher margin needed by one versus the other to cover the additional costs of holding increased inventory.

EXAMPLE 16.7: THE RESALE PRICE METHOD (2)

There are two distributors selling televisions in the same market with the same brand name, 'Banjo'. Distributor A offers a warranty; Distributor B offers none. Distributor A does not sell the warranty as an added extra, rather he provides it 'free'. In order to compensate for the additional cost incurred, Distributor A charges a higher price and receives a higher gross margin. The resale price margin between the two transactions would need to be adjusted to take account of the different level of activity carried out by the two distributors.

As with CUP, for the resale price method to work we need to identify an uncontrolled transaction in the external world that can be compared to the controlled transaction. If we cannot find such an uncontrolled transaction, then the method cannot be applied.

Cost Plus Method Having already explored the two arm's length approaches to transfer pricing discussed above, CUP and resale price method, an MNE may find that neither is suitable as it cannot find a comparable uncontrolled transaction that works with either of the two methods. In this case it could turn to the cost plus method, which, as its name suggests, is where a transfer price is derived by calculating the appropriate costs for the goods or services being sold and then adding an appropriate mark-up. In other words, an MNE takes the cost and then 'plusses' a mark-up. It is clear that the two key variables are the costs apportioned to the product and the rate of the mark-up.

As with the other two arm's length principle methods, it is important that a comparable 'uncontrolled' transaction mark-up can be referenced in order to substantiate the mark-up rate chosen for the transfer price. This is not straightforward, however, since this method is often used for the transfer pricing of partially completed goods between one business unit and another within an MNE, because the resale price method and the CUP methods can present problems for the transfer of such products. The problems stem from the difficulty in finding comparable uncontrolled transactions for partially completed products, which is why the cost plus method may work. As with the CUP and resale price methods, an uncontrolled transaction is comparable to a controlled transaction for purposes of the cost plus method if one of two conditions is met:

"• None of the differences (if any) between the transactions being compared or between the enterprises undertaking those transactions materially affect the cost plus mark up in the open market; or

• Reasonably accurate adjustments can be made to eliminate the material effects of such differences."[9]

As with the resale price method, the cost plus method will probably require fewer adjustments than the CUP method because slight variations in the nature of the product in the controlled and uncontrolled transaction will be unlikely to give rise to a different mark-up percentage being applied, and accordingly the population of uncontrolled transactions suitable for comparison analysis will be higher.

EXAMPLE 16.8: THE COST PLUS METHOD (I)

Glassy Eye makes intricate glassware to a level just before final finishing and polishing, which is normally carried out by expert finishers. Glassy Eye sells a consignment to an independent glass finisher in Belfast. The mark-up on the €1 million cost of this consignment is 15%.

Near to Glassy Eye's factory is the manufacturing division of high-quality ceramics producer, Cracked Plate, whose manufacturing division supplies its sister business in Belfast with high-end, partially complete ceramic plates at a cost price of €1 million. The sister division in Belfast applies final glazes to the product and prepares it for sale to distributors and retailers.

---

[9] *Transfer Pricing Methods* (OECD, 2010).

Though at a product level there is quite a difference between glass ware and ceramics plates, the activities of the manufacturers could be deemed sufficiently similar to allow Cracked Plate to use the Glassy Eye transaction as a comparable uncontrolled transaction for the purposes of determining its transfer price using the cost plus method. In this case, it would first need to show that there are no comparable ceramic plate manufacturing transactions and that, therefore, it has not been able to use the CUP method. Since it is not supplying a finished product it will be unlikely to be able to find an uncontrolled transaction in which it could use the resale price method. Accordingly, having found no suitable comparable transaction for the other two arm's length principle transfer pricing methods, it finally identifies the Glassy Eye transaction and uses the 15% mark-up from that transaction to determine its own internal transfer price for the consignment of 'yet to be finished' ceramics that it is supplying to its associated division in Belfast. Glassy Eye and Cracked Plate will also need to have some system of information-sharing that both are comfortable does not expose them to any competitive disadvantage.

One of the complications of using the cost plus method, even if one does find a suitable uncontrolled transaction, is the determination of the costs to be included in the calculation. As all accountants will tell you, the allocation of costs to a particular product or activity can be more akin to an art than a science. For example, Cracked Plate may make many types of ceramics: some are highly specialised, taking a lot of labour to produce, but do not take up much warehouse or factory space to store; other products, though large and bulky, require little labour to produce. How should Cracked Plate allocate the overhead costs of the factory to each of these separate product categories in determining the base cost to be used in the cost plus system? Perhaps it should not allocate the overhead at all – it should just apply the direct manufacturing cost. If it does choose to use direct manufacturing cost only, then it will need to ensure that this is the same basis that is used by Glassy Eye in determining its mark-up for the sale of glassware to the Belfast finisher. In order to determine what base-line cost means in its comparison of uncontrolled transactions, Cracked Plate will need a certain degree of access to Glassy Eye's costing. However, this level of detailed information may not normally be available to MNEs as it is most likely to be commercially sensitive.

The comparison can be made even more complicated by the cost make-up underpinning the businesses involved in the cost plus transaction comparison. For example, one company may be renting its equipment while another may own its equipment outright. The basis of cost absorption will therefore be different. Nevertheless, this level of granular examination of the costs is needed to ensure that the comparison is valid and appropriate adjustments are made to correct any price differences that may arise. Again, referring to the OECD's guidelines:

"[I]t is particularly important to consider differences in the level and types of expenses – operating expenses and non-operating expenses including financing expenditures – associated with functions performed and risks assumed by the parties or transactions being compared. Consideration of these differences may indicate the following:

   a) If expenses reflect a functional difference (taking into account assets used and risks assumed) which has not been taken into account in applying the method, an adjustment to the cost plus mark up may be required.

b) If the expenses reflect additional functions that are distinct from the activities tested by the method, separate compensation for those functions may need to be determined. Such functions may for example amount to the provision of services for which an appropriate reward may be determined. Similarly, expenses that are the result of capital structures reflecting non-arm's length arrangements may require separate adjustment.

c) If differences in the expenses of the parties being compared merely reflect efficiencies or inefficiencies of the enterprises, as would normally be the case for supervisory, general, and administrative expenses, then no adjustment to the gross margin may be appropriate."[10]

Accounting Issues in Comparing Controlled and Uncontrolled Transactions Once an MNE is satisfied that it can accurately determine the base-line costs, it still needs to ensure that the accounting treatments of these costs are consistent between the controlled and uncontrolled transactions. The degree to which there are accounting inconsistencies will not prevent use of the cost plus method; the crucial factor is that the MNE must be able to make reasonably accurate adjustments to the mark-up rate it selects to negate the effect of those accounting treatment inconsistencies. The more adjustments that are needed, the more the cost plus method will become similar to an adjustment for net profits rather than gross profits, and the intention behind the cost plus method is that the gross operating mark-up required between the comparable transactions should be the same, or capable of reasonable adjustment. In choosing this method, the MNE is saying that the uncontrolled transaction is broadly in the same 'activity' sector as its own and therefore requires the same mark-up to cover indirect operating costs. However, the more an MNE needs to make adjustments between the two transactions to account for different treatments of costs, the more it becomes akin to saying that the two businesses need the same net margin to provide a return to shareholders on the capital employed rather than gross mark-up to cover indirect operating costs.

Costs can be broken down into three categories:
• direct manufacturing costs that can be applied to particular products, production runs or services produced;
• indirect manufacturing costs that can be reasonably allocated to product or services;
• operating costs that are not easily attributed to specific products or services.

Some MNEs will attempt to allocate all cost to products through the application of some formula or other. This becomes increasingly arbitrary when one gets to the allocation of indirect costs. For example, how does one allocate the taxation compliance costs incurred in Texas to a 'silicon chip' manufactured in Galway? In any case, the MNE will need to ensure that the transactions it is choosing for comparisons have the same, or at least adjustable, differences as its own cost structure.

It is not possible to be absolutely formulaic in determining rules to govern all cost allocation and absorption systems in the application of the cost plus system. Having said that, once MNEs do not lose sight of the arm's length principle, it should be possible to reasonably adjust for most circumstances, especially when the financial data that enables a comparison is available.

---

[10] *Review of Comparability and of Profit Methods: Revision of Chapters I-III of the Transfer Pricing Guidelines* (OECD, 2010).

EXAMPLE 16.9: THE COST PLUS METHOD (2)

Zimby Plc makes components for treadmills in Antrim, Northern Ireland. It supplies these components to its sister division in Poland where they are assembled into the finished product. It applies a 15% gross profit mark-up to determine its intra-MNE transfer price.

Crosbie Plc, also based in Northern Ireland, makes components for treadmills and supplies them to independent, third-party treadmill manufacturers. It achieves a selling price that gives it a 15% gross profit mark-up.

Zimby wishes to use the uncontrolled transactions of Crosbie to substantiate its transfer price methodology. Upon further examination, Zimby determines that Crosbie includes as direct certain costs that Zimby treats as administrative. These costs account for 10% of the total cost base used to calculate the gross profit mark-up in Crosbie, i.e. 10% of the costs that Crosbie has allocated to direct overhead and are included in the base cost used to calculate the 15% gross profit mark-up.

Zimby will need to adjust its cost base to be comparable to Crosbie or adjust Crosbie's calculated mark-up rate excluding those costs. The second of these options would look like this.

Crosbie cost base = €100

Crosbie gross profit mark-up 15% implies Crosbie selling price of €115

Adjust to equate Crosbie cost base to Zimby cost base

Crosbie adjusted cost base = €90

Crosbie gross profit mark-up is now $\dfrac{115-90}{90} = 27.78\%$

Therefore, this is the mark-up rate that Zimby should use to ensure comparability with Crosbie's uncontrolled transactions.

SUMMARY OF ARM'S LENGTH TRANSFER PRICING METHODS

There are three methods for calculating transfer prices using the arm's length principle:
- Comparable Uncontrolled Price (CUP);
- Resale Price;
- Cost Plus.

All three methods require that some degree of comparability can be undertaken. For the comparability to be valid, the controllable and uncontrollable transactions need to be compared across five variables:
- contractual terms;
- characteristics of the product or service;
- functional analysis;
- economic circumstances;
- business strategies.

The transactions being compared need to be assessed under these five headings. Where there is a disparity under any heading, an assessment needs to be made as to whether an appropriate adjustment to the price is possible. Either there is little or no price bearing difference between the transactions or, where there is a difference, the price effect should be capable of being determined and therefore adjusted. These adjustments are normally done in the preparation of the MNE's tax computation, which is normally prepared by the MNE's finance teams in conjunction with its tax advisors. In some instances, taxation authorities may impose deemed transfer prices on the MNE and assess a taxation liability accordingly. Usually there is a degree of consultation between the MNE's finance team, the tax advisors and the taxation authorities in the respective countries.

Other Transfer Pricing Methods

The three methods described above are ways of calculating transfer prices by reference to an uncontrollable transaction and performing an adjustment, if necessary, to arrive at the final transfer price. These methods are in accordance with the arm's length principle that should underpin all transfer pricing arrangements, at least for taxation purposes. While an MNE may adopt whatever transfer pricing system it wishes, it should be aware that the tax authorities in the relevant jurisdictions will adjust the systems applied if they believe they are not in accordance with the OECD guidelines and/or relevant tax codes and double taxation agreements.

However, not all transactions will satisfy the comparability tests outlined above. In such cases, an MNE must find another method of setting the transfer price. There are two methods that can help in these situations and these also have guidelines agreed between OECD member countries:
* the transactional net margin method; and
* the transactional profit split method.

Transactional Net Margin Method

The transactional net margin method is similar to the cost plus method in that it attempts to use an uncontrolled transaction profit level and apply it to the controlled transaction. An MNE would only use this method if it cannot find comparable transactions to apply the arm's length methods. Therefore, it is almost a given that there will be some degree of incompatibility between the parties being compared or that the financial information for the uncontrolled transaction is at a consolidated level.

EXAMPLE 16.10: TRANSACTIONAL NET MARGIN METHOD OF TRANSFER PRICING

A company, ZRB, makes mobile phones in the Czech Republic and transfers them to its distribution centre in Cork for onward sale across Europe. Another firm, HTP, also makes mobile phones in the Czech Republic but sells them on to resellers who apply their brand to the finished acquired product. HTP's net profit margin on its activities is 3%. ZRB could use this margin to calculate the attributable prices it charges its sister division in Cork for its products. ZRB will need to seek out and find an MNE like HTP that is willing to share information for the purposes of transfer pricing calculations.

The transactional net margin method will be unreliable if one of the parties applies some unique know-how to the product. For example, if one of the phone manufacturers above had included in its product a proprietary operating system that enhanced the handset in a way that could not be emulated, the comparisons between HTP and ZRB would become unreliable.

In this example we used a net-profit-to-sale calculation, though the method can use other net profit indicators, such as net profit to assets used or net profit to labour cost. It will be a feature of the industry sector as to which net profit indicator is most applicable.

Transactional Profit Split Method

The transactional profit split method seeks to:
- assess the total profit involved in a number of transfers between entities in an MNE;
- allocate the profits between the entities on some pre-determined basis.

Conceptually, one can see that there is a similarity between this method and the global formulary apportionment method (see above). It takes the ultimate profit attributable to the product or process and allocates the profit in such a way as to reasonably attribute profit to each transaction that makes up the final product.

One of the benefits of the transactional profit split method is that the analysis can be carried out without detailed cross reference to external third parties. Since the final sale of the product is an uncontrolled transaction, i.e. it is subject to market forces, this can then allow for a detailed examination of all the transfers that lead up to this point and allocate profit accordingly.

EXAMPLE 16.11: TRANSACTIONAL PROFIT SPLIT

A division of Scrod Plc manufactures a highly specialised product using an integrated manufacturing and supply chain involving three subsidiaries located in different countries. The division finally sells the finished goods from its sales division located in Ireland. Therefore, there are four entities involved: the three manufacturing subsidiaries and the sales division. The final profit can be determined by reference to the final selling price into the external market achieved by the sales division. This profit is then allocated across the four entities involved using an appropriate profit allocation method. Clearly there are two key variables involved here:
- the calculation of the attributable profit; and
- the allocation methodology.

Continuing with our example of Scrod Plc, let us assume the profit on the highly specialised machine was €2,000,000. Scrod has determined that the allocation of profits based on the net assets deployed in each of the four countries involved in the production and sale of the machine is a sound basis for the allocation of the €2,000,000. In the table below you can see how the €2,000,000 is allocated. The allocated profit would then form the basis of the taxation calculation and charge in each country, e.g. €222,000 would be subject to taxation in Ireland.

Division	Assets €million	Transactional Profit Split	Allocation of Profit €
Ireland	20	20 ÷ 180 = 11.1%	222,000
Poland	50	50 ÷ 180 = 27.8%	556,000
Czech Republic	80	80 ÷ 180 = 44.4%	888,000
Netherlands	30	30 ÷ 180 = 16.7%	334,000
Total	180	100%	2,000,000

In order to satisfy the tax authorities in **Example 16.11** above, Scrod Plc would need to demonstrate that it cannot reasonably apply any of the arm's length methods, that this method is reasonable and that there is a sound basis for the apportionment of the profits between the various business units. The main test that the tax authorities will apply is to see what would be the basis of the profit split between the entities had they been stand-alone. For example, if one of the activities used a large amount of fixed capital investment, one would expect to see a reasonable return on this investment.

Guidance for Application of the Transactional Profit Split Method

As we have seen, the transactional profit split method is used when it is not possible to use any of the three arm's length methods of CUP, resale price or cost plus. Though the OECD offers some guidelines on the transactional profit split method, it cannot provide for all possible outcomes in its application. Nonetheless, the overriding principle is to ensure that the split arrived at resembles, as closely as possible, the split that would have arisen had the associated business units involved in the transfers all been separate stand-alone entities.

In the extract below you can see how the OECD sets out its guideline for the use of the transactional profit split method:

"Under the transactional profit split method, the combined profits are to be split between the associated enterprises on an economically valid basis that approximates the division of profits that would have been anticipated and reflected in an agreement made at arm's length. In general, the determination of the combined profits to be split and of the splitting factors should:

- Be consistent with the functional analysis of the controlled transaction under review, and in particular reflect the allocation of risks among the parties,
- Be consistent with the determination of the combined profits to be split and of the splitting factors which would have been agreed between independent parties,
- Be consistent with the type of profit split approach (e.g. contribution analysis, residual analysis, and
- Be capable of being measured in a reliable manner."[11]

The approaches to profit splitting mentioned – contribution analysis and residual analysis – are not necessarily exhaustive or mutually exclusive. In other words, there may be other methods of profit-splitting analysis that are more appropriate.

Comparability Analysis

As mentioned throughout this discussion of transfer pricing, an MNE must be able to perform a comparability analysis if it is to use the arm's length transfer pricing methods of CUP, resale price or cost plus. In carrying out this analysis it is advisable to follow an agreed structure such as the one outlined by the OECD. Doing so would bring a degree of structure and formality

---

[11] *Review of Comparability and of Profit Methods: Revision of Chapters I-III of the Transfer Pricing Guidelines* (OECD, 2010).

to the derivation of internally generated transfer prices; it also lends itself to subsequent examination and robustness.

There will always be two main items under examination in the comparability analysis:
- the controlled transaction under review; and
- the uncontrolled transactions that are regarded as potentially comparable.

There are nine steps outlined by the OECD involved in carrying out the comparability analysis. But even before the analysis can be carried out the MNE must search for possible comparators, which may itself determine the transfer pricing methodology used. Clearly, this is an obvious 'chicken and egg' situation where the MNE may be led to select a transfer pricing method precisely because it is one where there are readily available comparators. The main driver in selecting the comparators is that the MNE is able to provide evidence that a conclusion about whether the controlled transactions being examined are consistent with the arm's length principle as described in paragraph 1 of Article 9 of the OECD Model Tax Convention can be arrived at.

> "As part of the process of selecting the most appropriate transfer pricing method and applying it, the comparability analysis always aims at finding the most reliable comparables. Thus, where it is possible to determine that some uncontrolled transactions have a lesser degree of comparability than others, they should be eliminated. This does not mean that there is a requirement for an exhaustive search of all possible sources of comparables as it is acknowledged that there are limitations in availability of information and that searches for comparables data can be burdensome."[12]

In all cases, it is considered appropriate that the MNE, or the tax authority if it is adjusting the MNE's selected transfer prices, provide the other parties with the supporting evidence and documentation that underpins their transfer price selection. This is particularly important for the MNE's finance team. If the MNE chooses a particular method, then it is important that all supporting documentation that fed into the decision be maintained and represented, if needed, in a fashion that allows ease of audit and examination. The MNE should bear in mind that the examination may be some years hence. Indeed, some of the assumptions made at the time of the selection of the transfer price may turn out subsequently to be mistaken. The main thing is that the MNE can demonstrate that at the time of selection, the transfer prices method selected was valid. In particular, one should bear in mind that there is some element of a sequential test process. By this I mean that if there are two possible sets of comparators available, the MNE should always use the one that is most amenable to external scrutiny, not the one that produces the optimal result for the MNE itself. Tax authorities will question why a complex route was chosen over an available easier route.

The Comparability Analysis Process

Outlined below is a typical process for performing a comparability analysis. While this approach is accepted good practice, it is not compulsory and any other search process leading to the identification of reliable comparables may be acceptable. Reliability of the outcome is more

---

12 *Review of Comparability and of Profit Methods: Revision of Chapters I-III of the Transfer Pricing Guidelines* (OECD, 2010), Chapter III, A, 3.2.

important than process (i.e. going through the process does not provide any guarantee that the outcome will be arm's length, and not going through the process does not imply that the outcome will not be arm's length).

NINE-STEP PROCESS FOR COMPARABILITY ANALYSIS

- **Step 1:** Determination of years to be covered.
- **Step 2:** Broad-based analysis of the taxpayer's circumstances.
- **Step 3:** Understanding the controlled transaction(s) under examination, based in particular on a functional analysis, in order to choose the tested party (where needed), the transfer pricing method most appropriate to the circumstances of the case, the financial indicator that will be tested (in the case of a transactional profit method) and identifying the significant comparability factors that should be taken into account.
- **Step 4:** Review of existing internal comparables, if any.
- **Step 5:** Determination of available sources of information on external comparables where such external comparables are needed, taking into account their relative reliability.
- **Step 6:** Selection of the most appropriate transfer pricing method and, depending on the method, determination of the relevant financial indicator (e.g. determination of the relevant net profit indicator in case of a transactional net margin method).
- **Step 7:** Identification of potential comparables: determining the key characteristics to be met by any uncontrolled transaction in order to be regarded as potentially comparable, based on the relevant factors identified in Step 3 and in accordance with the comparability factors.
- **Step 8:** Determination of and making comparability adjustments where appropriate.
- **Step 9:** Interpretation and use of data collected, determination of the arm's length remuneration.

In practice, this process is not linear. Steps 5 to 7 in particular might need to be carried out repeatedly until a satisfactory conclusion is reached, i.e. the most appropriate method is selected, especially because the examination of available sources of information may in some instances influence the selection of the transfer pricing method. For instance, in cases where it is not possible to find information on comparable transactions (Step 7) and/or to make reasonably accurate adjustments (Step 8), MNEs might have to select another transfer pricing method and repeat the process, starting from Step 4.

16.7 LEGAL ISSUES IN INTERNATIONAL PRICING AND PROMOTION

Though the transfer pricing environment and issues that we have covered in the previous section will have the most significant impact on an MNE when it is considering its internal pricing system to cover the transfer products between associates within the wider organisation, there are also legal considerations to be given to the external pricing model to be adopted.

Maximum Prices

In some countries the maximum price that can be charged for certain goods is set by regulation or law. The price may be below the market price for such products, which may give rise to some compensation schemes. In Paris after the French Revolution the city introduced a maximum price control for flour and a compensation scheme for millers. The scheme led to a fall in the price of flour but caused bakers from outside of Paris to flock to the city to buy the subsidised flour. This increased demand exacerbated the flour shortage and led to empty granaries and a healthy black market.

More recent examples include rent controls where landlords are prevented from raising rents to the market price and must preserve them at some predetermined rate. Another example is the EU-dictated maximum prices for 'mobile roaming' charges. Since 1 July 1 2014, the maximum price that can be charged for certain roaming services provided by mobile phone operators has been capped. Some would argue that this is a good thing as the operators were charging extortionate prices before the regulations came into force, while others argue that there is little competitive pressure on operators to reduce charges and the result is all operators charge the same, maximum price, even though they could charge less. (Interestingly, some consumers will actually buy a new mobile phone if they are visiting a foreign country and avail of normal local tariffs rather than pay the high roaming charges. The fact that this is a credible alternative suggests that there is an element of price skimming in the roaming market, even at the maximum prices set by the EU.)

Taxation

Taxes make up a large part of the price of some product categories. Tobacco and alcohol are taxed highly in some countries. If its products are affected, such high taxes mean that the MNE must adapt its pricing strategies and associated marketing techniques in these countries. The flexibility of using price as part of the marketing mix alters significantly as the tax element of the final price increases. The MNE will rarely have control over the tax portion of the price mix.

Regulated Industries

Some industries are regulated as far as price is concerned. In these industries, the price for the product is set by the regulator, or if not actually set by them, approved by them. In the UK, for example, OFWAT sets the prices that can be charged by the water industry.

In some industries there are tariffs applied to products if they are imported from or exported to certain markets. The political reasons for such tariffs can be complex and may have nothing to do with the sector itself but form part of some wider scheme of trade arrangements. Whatever the rationale, MNEs must cope with and understand the possible effects of such tariffs and quotas on their plans.

Consumer Protection

In order to protect consumers some price marketing in some countries is controlled. In Germany, for example, the advertising of certain types of discounts was prohibited by the regulators. This was done in order to prevent unfair competition between smaller and bigger shops. In the Republic of Ireland it was not allowed to price promote baby products. The belief was that by offering parents with young babies discounts on nappies, they could be seduced into supermarkets that would then get their discounts back by charging higher prices on other products. The prices for pharmaceutical products are often price controlled to prevent consumers who are ill from being overcharged for the medicines they need to recover.

BEPS

'BEPS' (base erosion and profit shifting) involves the use of tax-planning strategies to shift profits around an MNE to jurisdictions where there is little or no tax to be paid. It often involves using transfer pricing and intellectual property 'charges' to create profits in low tax countries while making little to no profit in high taxation countries. It is particularly detrimental to developing countries that have a low taxation base from personal income taxes or sales taxes due to the underdeveloped nature of their economies.

The BEPS process is the development of 15 specific action points that will equip governments with the tools and powers needed to address the issue. The CCAB-I in Ireland, representing accounting bodies operating in the Republic of Ireland and Northern Ireland, is making submissions at the time of writing to the OECD/G20 project team managing the process. The 15 action points were agreed in October 2015 by the OECD collaborative project teams. Subsequently they were adopted by the G20 nations and the US Department of the Treasury. The relevant countries will start implementation of the action plans as early as January 2016. The ROI 2015 Budget introduced legislation to give legal effect to some of the measures in the Republic of Ireland. Suffice to say that the 15 action points will increase the onus on MNEs based in Ireland or outside of Ireland to have full transparency on their transfer pricing actions and the basis upon which they calculate their tax charges in each jurisdiction in which they operate.

16.8 CONCLUSION

In this chapter we have seen the role pricing plays in the marketing mix. It is the most critical part of the mix since the price paid by the ultimate customer finances all the activities of the MNE and provides the ultimate return for the shareholder.

There are a number of pricing strategies that can be adopted depending on how the MNE wishes to position itself in the market and how it views its timescale in the relevant market place. MNEs will adapt their domestic price strategy to their foreign markets depending on its global marketing strategy, which will dictate the degree to which local price strategies will be different from the domestic market.

A particular issue for MNEs is the setting of prices for intra-company transfers of goods and services. We have seen that the arm's length principle must be applied to such transactions in order to comply with the OECD treaties. Three externally benchmarked pricing systems emerge: comparable uncontrolled price, cost plus and resale price. There are two systems also for setting prices where the external price is not readily comparable: the transaction profit split and the net profit split. We have also seen how the arm's length principle is superior to the global formulary split system.

MNEs are not always free to set whatever price they so choose. They often find that the products they sell, or the markets they operate in, are regulated insofar as pricing is concerned. The MNE must understand these regulations and how they impact on the marketing and pricing strategies to be adopted and the returns available in the relevant markets.

QUESTIONS

Self-test Questions

16.1 Describe the cost plus method of transfer pricing.

16.2 What pricing strategies might a car manufacturer adopt when entering a new country?

16.3 Why would a government impose a maximum price on a product?

16.4 What is premium pricing? Name some brands that apply premium pricing strategies.

Thought-provoking Questions

Question 16.1

You work as an accountant for Belle Enterprises (BE). BE manufactures accessories for pets at its plant in China. It has a good market share in the EU. It now intends to expand into the US. Your boss, the finance director, has asked you to prepare a paper that explains what pricing strategies BE should adopt when entering the US market.

Question 16.2

You have just joined Sheerbone Plc. Sheerbone manufactures components for bicycles, such as brakes, gear mechanisms and handlebars. It sells these components to bicycle manufacturers under its own brand, Sheer Speed. It makes the different parts of these components at a variety of factories located in Spain, Italy, China and India. The parts are then assembled into the final products at an assembly plant in Belfast. Sheerbone is head-quartered in Dublin, where the sales office is based. All sales are invoiced in euro from Dublin. Sales are 50% to Europe, 25% to the US and 25% to the rest of the world. The CEO has asked that you prepare a paper explaining 'this thing called transfer pricing'. He would like to understand how Sheerbone should charge for intra-group transfers of products.

Review Questions

(See Suggested Solutions to Review Questions in **Appendix B**.)

Question 16.1: R&D Investment

Having read the R&D Investment case study in **Appendix A**, outline an appropriate transfer pricing arrangement that might be used to charge for intercompany use of intellectual property and outline the particular issues that might arise in the context of the local firm and head office doing business across borders.

Question 16.2: Redbarn Brewery

Having read the Redbarn Brewery case study in **Appendix A**, outline the considerations for Redbarn Brewery in deciding its retail pricing strategy in international market-entry decisions and, in particular, the pricing decisions facing Redbarn Brewery in its expansion into the US market.

17

ENTERPRISE MANAGEMENT SYSTEMS

LEARNING OBJECTIVES

Having read this chapter, you will understand:
- the role of enterprise management systems (EMS) in the development and management of an MNE;
- how to appraise the challenges involved in the implementation of EMS;
- the various strategic enterprise management systems (SEMS) available to MNEs; and
- how the SEMS integrates functions in an MNE.

17.1 INTRODUCTION

In **Chapters 11** to **16** we have explored how decisions are made in a multinational enterprise (MNE), focusing particularly on where these decisions involve the expenditure and sourcing of capital, the management of risk and the pricing of products, both internal transfer pricing and pricing to the external customer. Clearly, there is a complexity of issues that the MNE manager needs to grasp in order to make the optimal decisions. In recent decades this decision-making has been greatly helped by improvements in information systems. In this chapter, we will consider contemporary developments in information systems that are used to support decision-making in the MNE.

There is complexity that comes with the growth of a business, which is all the greater in an MNE. By definition, an MNE has activities in more than one country. The multinational nature of its activities means that there is a greater challenge in managing the enterprise. In **Chapter 2** we saw how the rise of MNEs has been caused by a number of factors, one of which is the improvement in technology, which allowed for the management of larger enterprises with greater degrees of sophistication and integration. For example, the East India Company was a large global concern operating in Asia in the 1700s and 1800s. The degree of influence afforded its senior management at headquarters was somewhat less than that in an equivalent, modern organisation. Communication between branches and offices took weeks, if not months. Today, however, technology allows for immediate information flows concerning the operations of an MNE. It is possible for a UK-based, retailing MNE to know what sales are going through the tills in its Polish stores in real-time. The core issue these days is to know what data to collect, how to organise it and, most importantly, how to interpret it and act upon the findings.

17.2 DEVELOPMENTS IN INFORMATION SYSTEMS

Traditionally, MNEs used computers to simplify or automate previously time-consuming jobs within the business. For example, in manufacturing, systems were developed to aid process flows and speed up repetitive tasks or those requiring detailed calculations. Similarly, in the finance department, computer systems were used for accounting functions that previously required large numbers of manual calculations. Depending on how the organisation had internationalised, an MNE would have a plethora of systems, often operating in different languages, both human and machine, and all on different computer platforms. This complexity of information systems had a number of disadvantages:
- additional costs to the overall operation of the MNE;
- tardiness in the preparation of information and reporting; and
- inconsistencies in approaches to performing essentially the same task.

Most systems tended to be designed from the user's perspective. For example, the CFO might implement a receivables ledger system, while the logistics manager would install a vehicle-routing program and the head of manufacturing might introduce a materials-planning system. Though most of these computerised systems did improve the quality and/or reduce the cost of the activities they were designed to support, since each functional head was looking to improve their own process, systems were seldom integrated with each other. Indeed, they were often developed by specialist software firms that focused on the creation of applications for very specific sectors.

Systems in most MNEs became increasingly disparate, bespoke and unable to communicate with each other. Many MNEs grow by acquisition and newly acquired divisions would have previously developed their own systems. The new owners would want to standardise approaches and install their own systems, resulting in many acquisition benefits being delayed as systems integration projects stalled. Additionally, user-acceptance was difficult to achieve as each MNE business unit had an historical bias to its own in-house system. At a minimum, change was necessary, either at the parent MNE or the business unit level, and both would be difficult to achieve (see also **Chapter 13**).

While the computerisation of processes improved efficiency and effectiveness in MNEs over time, the lack of systems integration also presented problems for MNEs in achieving their goals. As supply chains grew, so did the need for systems to be able to communicate with one another.

For example, if a Belfast manufacturer is making components for assembly in France, there should be good communication between the two plants, language barriers aside. If the Belfast plant is making components for assembly in China, there will be greater challenges. These challenges are driven by: distance; language; time-zone differences; and culture.

By the 1980s, the global reach of MNEs was increasing and at the same time modern manufacturing principles were seeking to reduce waste and faulty output together with streamlining inventory-holding costs. Accountability to shareholders and the need for timely accounting grew, requiring MNEs to produce consolidated accounting numbers at a faster pace. IT departments grew in size and MNEs were constantly involved in writing interfaces that allowed the various systems to talk to each other. Many hours of analysis were spent in reconciling the information outputs from the various systems (which no doubt is still happening in 2015).

While these changes in manufacturing and accounting processes were happening, computer-processing power was also increasing at a dramatic rate, as was the capability of communications systems that connected computers through the Internet or through in-house networks or intranets. The coalescence of the needs of MNEs and the technological capability of computers and communications systems led to the development of systems that could, in theory, integrate all the functions of an MNE into one giant system. A 'Holy Grail' for information systems began to be envisaged: could one system be fully integrated into all aspects of the MNE's activities, dispensing once and for all with the disparate legacy systems?

17.3 STRATEGIC ENTERPRISE MANAGEMENT SYSTEMS (SEMS)

The strategic enterprise management system (SEMS) is the ultimate goal of information systems for the MNE. There are many other names and acronyms for such integrated systems. Among the most commonly used are:
- corporate performance management (CPM) systems;
- enterprise resource planning (ERP) systems; or
- business performance management (BPM) systems.

These acronyms can be used interchangeably. For example, in some texts 'SEMS' might be used to denote the consolidating dimension of an integrated system with other descriptors being used for the various components that comprise the overall system. However, for the purpose of this textbook, 'SEMS' will be used to describe an overall system integrated across the entire MNE.

The increase in global competition has increased the pressures on MNEs to reformulate their strategies quickly in response to the rapidly changing environment. They also need operational flexibility in order to implement these strategies effectively and in a timely fashion. These challenges have increased the need for the MNE to have robust and effective decision-making capability.

In order to achieve this, many MNEs have implemented integrated information systems into their businesses. The differing functional applications of these systems are connected to ensure efficient processing and timely, pertinent information, meaning that MNEs have been able to respond to their customers' needs more effectively than in the past. This delivers greater competitiveness.

One of the consequences of the development of more integrated information and decision-making systems has been the huge increase in the amount of information that MNEs have about their business, processes and customers. Capturing the data that flows from these systems and presenting it in a way that improves the speed and quality of decision-making is a goal of almost all MNEs. Using the systems to translate strategy into operational effectiveness is critical. MNEs that do this effectively will have a distinct advantage over those that do not.

Strategy Execution and Strategic Enterprise Management Systems

A major problem for today's MNE senior management is translating strategy into meaningful objectives to be executed by operational management. Execution must support an MNE's strategy, which must in turn be capable of being appropriately reformulated based on timely feedback from the front-line activities where the strategy is executed. Well-designed and executed SEMS processes allow an MNE to manage this critical feedback, which, together with good information from the environment, ought to be channelled back into the strategic management decision-making system. This information allows the strategy to be reformulated and the organisation can continuously improve and learn. Indeed, failure to complete the feedback loop can lead the organisation into repeating past errors or continuing to pursue ineffective strategies.

Strategies are designed to deliver on the value expectations of the stakeholder community with priority given, in most cases, to the shareholders. A structured way to assess the efficacy of the strategies and take corrective actions ensures that there is consistency in delivering to stakeholders. Using its SEMS, an MNE can link the individual activities of its workforce to its overall strategy. Corporate strategists can no longer operate in the back office: their activities must be integrated into the overall structure of an MNE and this is done most effectively through a SEMS.

The SEMS must support the management processes; particularly, the systems must allow the translation of overall MNE strategies into individual business unit strategies and, with further granularity, objectives for departments and individuals. This 'top-down' translation of strategy into objectives must be complemented by an equally important 'bottom-up' feedback loop. The SEMS must also be integrated in such a way so that managers are informed of performance at all stages through the business processes and how well they are integrated into their complementary processes in the MNE's value chain.

FIGURE 17.1: THE FUTURE IMPORTANCE OF THE STRATEGIC MANAGEMENT PROCESSES

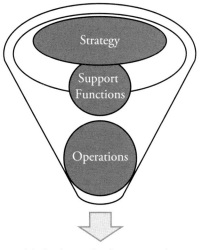

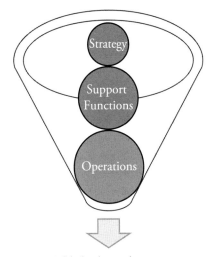

Added value – the future paradigm   Added value – the past

(Size of each shape represents the relative level of organisational effort.)

Figure 17.1 above shows that, in the past, the primary level of organisational effort needed to produce added value for stakeholders was focused on operational execution. The secondary level of organisational effort would then be focused on supporting operations and the least amount of effort would be on strategy. Into the future, effort levels will differ; there will be much less focus on the support functions and strategy will become a greater part of the organisation's efforts. Support functions will be increasingly outsourced, as indeed will much of the non-added value parts of operations. Thus, strategy formulation and its translation into operational excellence will become the hallmark of the successful.

17.4 VALUE-BASED MANAGEMENT

The concept of shareholder value has become more prevalent and important in recent decades, which has led to investors playing a much more active role in MNEs, particularly institutional investors trying to influence enterprise management in order to have strategy aligned with the objective of increasing short-term value rather than longevity (see the interview with Patrick Coveney, CEO Greencore Plc, in **Appendix C.3**). Since shareholdings in publicly quoted MNEs are liquid, investors can move their investments with relative ease; thus, investors' goals must be seen from the viewpoint of this liquidity. In contrast, an MNE's management may wish to work many years with the business and will value its longevity more than it will be valued by investors. In this example, one can see how shareholders' objectives and managers' objectives can become misaligned. Value-based management (VBM) seeks to address some of these misalignments.

Other stakeholder groups, such as employees, business partners and social interest groups, now have a greater say in an enterprise's policies. This means that when the enterprise is defining its strategy, their expectations must be taken into account in a similar way to those of the investors (see the discussion of stakeholder analysis in **Chapter 5**).

In order to satisfy these requirements, MNEs need to rethink the efficiency of their management processes and take the principles of value-based management (VBM) and the interests of stakeholders into greater account in their planning and performance-monitoring. VBM originated in the 1990s when private equity companies started to buy public limited companies and restructure them. Through this restructuring they managed to extract a value greater than the original acquisition price, leaving the original investors wondering how they had sold their companies for so little only to see the private equity buyers reap a fortune. They correctly intuited that the historical performance measurement approaches they had used for determining board performance were no longer appropriate, leading them to undervalue their shareholdings and, by implication, allowing executive management and boards to manage with such underperformance.

This dissatisfaction with historical performance management systems led to the VBM approach in which the assessment of management performance is not based purely on the profit streams generated year-to-year but on the return on the assets used by the business. VBM systems were developed to examine the drivers of shareholder value, some of which were not financial measures but other quantitative and qualitative measures of the MNE's performance. The key to successful use of VBM is to determine what drives value for the enterprise. The measures chosen should be based on these drivers of performance. As mentioned, they may be non-financial measures, such as customer satisfaction.

The development of SEMS has enabled value-based management in MNEs through new software applications that support this new type of management process, which leads us to consider one of the main features of this new approach to performance management and how it is inter-linked into the SEMS: the balanced scorecard.

The Balanced Scorecard: Link between Strategy and Performance

Many strategies fail to deliver their envisaged objectives, usually because of:
• poor strategy formulation;
• poor execution; or
• no execution capability.

This level of failure is also a reflection on the lack of suitability of historical management processes for today's business environment due to changes in the nature of strategic implementation, which over the last 50 years has been driven by two things:
• the growth in size and reach of organisations, as seen in the growth of MNEs; and
• the move from an industrial to a knowledge economy.

Taken together, these changes have fundamentally altered the skills needed to run and manage a modern MNE. In particular, the modern MNE must have systems in place that translate strategy into execution capability, which is what the SEMS does. The MNE must also have monitoring systems that allow management to track performance and to respond quickly to environmental changes or underperformance, which is where the **balanced scorecard** comes in.

The balanced scorecard (BSC) was first introduced in a 1992 *Harvard Business Review* article by Robert Kaplan and David Norton.[1] The BSC can be thought of as a technique used to translate strategy into terms that can be understood and communicated **throughout** the organisation. For example, while strategy is formulated in the boardroom, it is delivered on the 'shop floor'; therefore, a strategy that cannot be communicated to and acted upon will be destined to fail. The BSC is a technique used to carry out this critical task.

The BSC serves to clearly define what an organisation's strategy means in terms of performance. Defining these performance measures ensures that the strategy is sound, because if it cannot be defined clearly in terms suitable for inclusion in a balanced scorecard, then the strategy is flawed in its formulation. For example, a strategic goal, such as 'being the Number 1 in customer service', would be translated into clear metrics, such as 'all customer queries solved within four hours' or 'helpline phone calls answered within three rings', and so on. The BSC will, therefore, be a list of measureable performance outcomes that directly link an MNE's strategy with its operational execution. If the strategy is solid and the metrics on the scorecard are well chosen, monitoring of the metrics and the actions that follow will drive superior performance, leading to improved outcomes for all stakeholders.

Since VBM recognises that all stakeholders' needs must be considered in a well-functioning MNE, the balanced scorecard will contain metrics relevant to all significant stakeholder groups. For most organisations these stakeholders will be:
• customers;
• shareholders;
• staff;
• suppliers; and
• the wider community and environment.

---

[1] Kaplan, R.S. and Norton, D.P. (1992), "The Balanced Scorecard: Measures that Drive Performance", *Harvard Business Review,* January February, 71–79.

Consequently, one would expect a balanced scorecard to be the translation of the MNE's strategy into measures relevant to each of these stakeholder groups. The SEMS will provide the information that will then be consolidated into the BSC. Accordingly, one can see that the MNE's strategy is communicated to the organisation through the balanced scorecard and performance is measured using the scorecard, it having been populated with information that has been captured in the SEMS.

This integrated approach to strategic management is vital for the success of an MNE competing in today's global economy. Without it, an MNE will struggle to keep up with its competitors and will find its value creation potential dwindling and, ultimately, its shareholders will move elsewhere to get the returns they need.

Figure 17.2 shows a balanced scorecard for a wholesale grocer.

FIGURE 17.2: BALANCED SCORECARD FOR A WHOLESALER

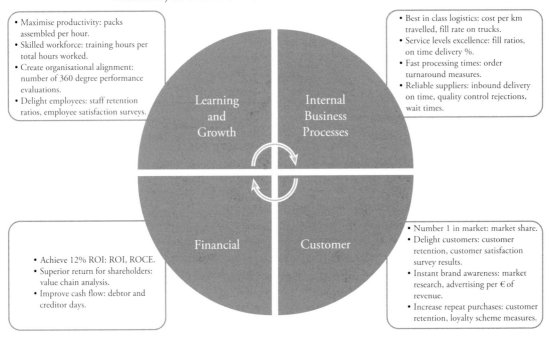

Once the organisation's strategy has been set out, various objectives are then set, broken down into one of the four quadrants: 'learning and growth', 'internal business processes', 'financial' and 'customer'. A number of measures are decided upon for each objective to monitor whether the objective is being achieved. For example, in **Figure 17.2** above one of the objectives in the 'customer' quadrant is to be number 1 in the market. The associated measure is market share.

The balanced scorecard becomes the reporting document used by the management team to steer the business to achieving its strategic goals. It is the first document examined at management meetings. By moving away from purely financial reporting the MNE can ensure it is monitoring all elements of its strategy.

The format of the balanced scorecard will often be a summary sheet, like the one in **Figure 17.2**, with backing sheets giving more detail. Often the objectives on the summary sheet might be colour-coded to give a quick feel for what is happening: green for objectives whose measures are on track, amber for those that need attention and red for the ones that are falling well behind. Such a simple colour-coding system can be extraordinarily effective in directing management effort to the areas that need attention.

17.5 DEVELOPMENTS IN MANAGEMENT ACCOUNTING

We have seen how MNEs manage the complexity of operating internationally through well-structured and integrated information systems, monitoring performance through management accounting applications that connect the strategy to operational execution using information that flows from the integrated information system. The balanced scorecard links strategy and performance, translating strategy into meaningful measures for stakeholders and propelling the MNE into actions that will deliver upon its strategic goals. We will now explore how and why management accounting has developed in order to help the modern MNE improve outcomes for all stakeholders.

In 1987, Robert Kaplan and Thomas Johnson made the case that management accountancy had become too reliant on financial reporting.[2] Identifying a number of important developments in business, they argued that management accounting practices lagged behind these changes. In particular, they pointed out that:

- Advances in computing performance had meant that many management accounting processes could now be computerised with ease.
- Modern manufacturing techniques had out-paced traditional standard-costing systems, leading to the development of more advanced management accounting approaches, which included non-financial measures such as downtime, production line changeover rates, rejections ratios, etc.
- Traditional management accounting systems allocated costs but did not facilitate an understanding of what was driving the costs. To address this gap in understanding, activity-based costing (ABC) was developed (though some would argue that ABC was merely a finessing of the concept that had always underpinned allocating costs to products and processes).
- Management accounting, with its roots in manufacturing, was concerned with day-to-day operations and did not provide a strategic outlook to help inform business managers. At the same time, hierarchical management philosophies were becoming outmoded with a greater move toward empowerment and delegation. Management accounting needed to provide frameworks that allowed for the management and measurement of performance in this new world. To that end, various new approaches were developed. These approaches fall within an overall classification of strategic management accounting and include:
  - **Competitor accounting:** assessment of the performance of rivals.
  - **Life-cycle values:** assessing the value of a product or a customer by calculating the net present value (NPV) of the future cash flows derived from that customer or product grouping.
  - **Benchmarking:** seeking out best practice performance measures for comparison of an MNE's performance.
  - **Intangible accounting:** endeavouring to value brands, intellectual capital and innovation.

---

[2] Johnson, H. and Kaplan, R. (1987). *Relevance Lost*. Boston, Mass.: Harvard Business School Press.

- ◦ **Environmental accounting:** measuring the environmental impact of an MNE's activities and seeking to assess the full environmental impact of decisions through the course of the lifetime of those decisions (for a good example of environmental accounting application in an MNE see www.toshiba.co.jp/env/en/management/account.htm).
- ◦ **Non-financial measures:** a move toward measuring non-financial performance, such as staff turnover, market research statistics, etc.

All of these developments have led to a revolution in management accounting, which has fed into the growth of MNEs and the management processes underpinning that growth. These processes are driven by a desire to manage with an empowered approach while ensuring overall alignment of an MNE's divisions with stakeholder goals. In this way, management accounting and its associated systems connect the organisation's performance to its strategy and enable improvements to both through a dynamic interaction. The BSC is the reporting construct that is used to make this connection. A further development, the **strategic scorecard**, is also used to connect strategy, action and performance. **Chapter 18** will demonstrate in more detail how these scorecards are used to measure and improve organisational performance.

17.6 DESIGNING A STRATEGIC ENTERPRISE MANAGEMENT SYSTEM

At its core, a SEMS collects data at its most basic level. It stores this data in a large-scale data warehousing system. The data is then extracted from the data warehouse by various analytical tools and aggregated, separated or collated into user-defined formats that support the business.

For example, the core data in a retail business is connected to the individual products that are sold through the tills. The system might capture all data about a product through its life cycle with the retailer, including its original purchase, the journey it made from its place of manufacture, etc., ending up with it eventually being sold to a customer.

Such analytical tools can be used to produce basic accounting data, presented in traditional formats. They can also be used for the preparation of much more complex information and analysis to help management of the MNE making business decisions. For example, in tracking a product's journey through a retail supply chain, a retailer can determine how often the product is handled, how long it has remained in inventory, reducing the number of times the data needs to be re-entered into the systems and so forth.

There are two major tasks facing the designer of a SEMS for a business:
- deciding on the core data elements and how they are to be captured; and
- choosing the analytical tools and their associated processes that will interrogate the data warehouse.

The designer of a SEMS does not have to start with a blank sheet of paper, however. Various developers of business systems have created SEMS that are available 'off-the-shelf', which has been one of the biggest changes in information systems design and implementation in the last 10 years. Traditionally, an MNE would write software from scratch or acquire it and modify it to its needs.

Since the data-warehousing approach captures 'raw' data at its source, the SEMS can be used across multiple industry types. Developers have also created modules that allow MNEs to speed up the implementation of SEMS through the use of the prior-developed modules, often called 'vanilla' modules. The advantages of less customisation are that development costs are lower, maintenance costs will be more efficient and the system is already tried and tested. For example, if inventory management is a priority area for an MNE, it could purchase a prior-developed inventory-management SEMS module from a recognised developer rather than develop a system from scratch itself. Interestingly, since many of these modules claim to represent best practice business process, MNEs are increasingly tailoring their business practices to fit the modules, whereas in the past information systems design was driven by the business process.

The debate on whether to adopt an off-the-shelf or customised SEMS is still not settled. One argument against off-the-shelf SEMS is that if all MNEs in a specific industry used the same SEMS then any competitive advantage derived from the SEMS would be eroded since all competitors are using the same systems. In other words, any competitive advantage that might have come from use of the systems is lost due to a homogenising effect.

To some extent, the homogenising effect does reduce competitive advantage: even the main developers of these systems will boast how their systems are already being used by a target customer's competitors,[3] highlighting that by buying the system you will not be falling behind your competitors. The critical thing is for management to be able to decide whether there is a sustainable competitive advantage to be gained from the system against how it is used. For example, all logistics firms use similar vehicles, yet its is no major competitive disadvantage to the homogeneity of the rolling fleet.

Furthermore, loss of competitive advantage due to a homogenising effect is a function of the specific industry in which the MNE operates and the degree of standardisation it wants to achieve in its own business. For example, when Walmart bought Asda in the UK, it did not change the Asda brand. It did, however, insist on installing its own systems into the UK business, despite the fact the Asda had recently installed new systems. Walmart wanted a standardised information system to apply to the enlarged group and believed its systems provided a competitive advantage.

Many large-scale implementations of SEMS have failed to deliver on what was initially expected of them and CFOs and CEOs have seen their careers run aground on the effort to introduce a fully-integrated SEMS only to find their organisations plagued with faulty applications, irreconcilable sets of information and frustrated employees and customers. Most of these problems arise from:
- poor systems requirement specification;
- delayed implementation; and
- overestimating the benefits that will accrue from the system.

Many of these problems can be avoided by following sound project management methodologies and not allowing the business to be seduced by the promise of great returns arising from costly systems implementation. MNE managers need to be very aware of the actual, achievable benefits that they can deliver for their shareholders and not be swayed by attraction of possible benefits that may be presented by sales function of the SEMS developers. Some SEMS implementations can cost over €100 million and rank as some of the largest capital investment programmes some MNEs will engage in. If the system has a clear business rationale, the path to success will be smoother. Accordingly, spending time specifying the business benefits at the outset, and quantifying those benefits, can save much heartache down the road.

---

[3] The main global developers and suppliers of SEMS are SAP, Oracle, and Business Objects. While there are many others, these three names would certainly be familiar to MNEs considering SEMS, even if they ultimately choose a different solution provider.

SEMS Architecture and Organisation Design

A strategic enterprise management system has an 'architecture', i.e. its overall system has a design structure that underpins and defines how it works, how it interacts with its environment and its users. This architecture should be aligned to the business structure and the overall strategic goals of the MNE. If there is a misalignment, then problems will occur. For example, trying to implement a fully integrated SEMS into a business that has a heavily decentralised business strategy will be fraught with problems and has a high chance of failure.

Figure 17.3 below shows a useful way of matching MNE strategy with a SEMS architecture.

FIGURE 17.3: MATCHING SEMS ARCHITECTURE WITH MNE STRATEGY

	Software	Architecture	Implementation
Decentralised	High levels of local customisation; devolved authority; local decision-making authority	Local, standalone systems and databases; local financial reporting systems	Phased roll-out; local IT supports and operators
Transnational	High level of customisation; centralised finance with local operations;	Integrated but hybrid approach; some standardised modules, some sourced locally	'Big bang' for some modules and phased or local for others
Global	Little customisation; central finance and operations	Centralised systems; hub structure	Big bang implementation; central IT function

It is worth noting how post-implementation analysis of problematic SEMS projects has revealed that one of the most common mistakes MNEs make is to treat SEMS implementation as an IT project. While there are, of course, major IT considerations to be grasped in the implementation of SEMS, the real drivers of the project should be the business leaders and business unit managers. Other stakeholders will also need to be involved in designing and implementing a SEMS, including customers. If SEMS design and implementation is left solely to the IT department, which will attempt to meet a wide diversity of users' needs, systems can become unduly complex and not fully integrated as far as business thinking is concerned.

17.7 IMPLEMENTING A STRATEGIC ENTERPRISE MANAGEMENT SYSTEM

We have seen how a SEMS will capture raw data elements and then allow all users of the system to configure the data in ways that meet their specific needs. Since all users access the same core, raw data, a SEMS implementation has the potential to impact everyone who interacts with or works in the organisation. Consequently, project planning for SEMS implementation needs to be far-ranging in its considerations. The main building-blocks will be:
- hardware installation;
- software installation;
- system configuration;

- customisation;
- data migration;
- integration;
- user training;
- user testing; and
- stakeholder analysis, especially customers.

SEMS implementation continues until the system becomes embedded in the organisation. Frequently, the new system will run in parallel for some time with legacy systems before going fully live. Though this approach has much to recommend it, there is one pitfall, which is that when running the systems in parallel, the user group of the new system tends to get most of the support. When the system goes live, the demands on the project implementation team escalate as new requirements and needs are discovered. Resources are directed to supporting the live users of the new system since their success or failure directly impacts upon the business results. The other user groups continue to run the older legacy systems while the project resources are spent supporting the live users. This situation can sometimes give rise to a resource constraint that negatively impacts upon business results.

This state of affairs can go unchecked for months, and often years. The result is that the MNE will have a partially installed SEMS and will carry the costs of maintaining two systems. For example, payroll systems can often be left until last by an implementation project or only be partially integrated. The direct labour element may be integrated into the SEMS for materials costing and labour allocations, but the payroll calculation system may sit outside the SEMS. Since the legacy system might be deemed to be working, it can often be left alone while focus is put on fixing or improving issues for the users who have gone live with the new system. This scenario means the MNE will have both its SEMS and its legacy payroll system operating at the same time. While this may not be a bad thing of itself, it means the project was not properly defined at the outset. And perhaps it is best for the needs of the business that there are disparate systems carrying out different functions. The payroll calculations in the various countries in which the MNE operates could be so different in nature that it does not make sense to try to have them all using the same payroll system. The key is to have robust project-planning processes so that this factor is identified early at the systems specification phase.

EXAMPLE 17.1: HOW A SEMS CAN GO WRONG[4]

Implementing large-scale information systems change is very challenging. Even the implementation of well understood systems, such as payroll, can produce unforeseen problems that can cost money and careers.

Before the creation of the HSE, the health service in Ireland was delivered through the operation of regional health boards. The Department of Health noticed that each of these boards had its own payroll system. They rightly believed that this involved a duplication of effort in each of the regional health boards. They foresaw a centralised system that would process the payroll for the entire health service. This system would allow for reduced costs since it would avoid the existing duplication. It would also improve the quality for

---

[4] For more see: Niall Hunter, "PPARS: a comedy of errors", 16 December 2005, www.irishhealth.com/article-html?id=8661 (accessed May 2015).

information being fed to the Department of Health. Since over 85% of the cost of running the health service is payroll and associated costs, centralising the payroll system would provide the department with a ready means to monitor costs and improve overall efficiency of the health service. To this end, a project was started in 1999 with the goal of centralising the payroll for the health service in Ireland. A budget of €9 million was agreed.

By the end of 2011 the system, now known as 'Personnel, Payroll and Related Systems' (PPARS) had cost a total of €201 million and was still not fully implemented. This delay in full implementation was all the more disappointing since during the lifetime of the project the regional health boards had been amalgamated into one overall health service, the HSE. Thus, even though there was now one overall organisation, the HSE was still not able to centralise and systemise one basic function.

By 2005 the project was paused and, eventually, a different path was chosen. The new path was to use an off-the-shelf system developed by SAP. By 2012, about half the HSE's 100,000 personnel were being paid through this system and 90% of staff records were held on the system.

The final cost was over 20 times the original budget. The example serves to illustrate that even a simple-sounding project can be mired in problems if there is no clarity about the project implementation and a clear understanding of the existing systems. Many people working in MNEs will find themselves involved in projects to implement new systems from time to time. They would do well to heed the lessons illustrated by the PPARS fiasco.

'Big Bang' or Phased Approach?

One of the major decisions an MNE will need to make concerning the implementation of a SEMS is whether to adopt the 'big bang' approach (instant changeover) or whether to phase the implementation. In some cases, an MNE will have no choice but to adopt a 'big bang' approach where the entire new system goes live throughout the business in a short, concentrated timespan. Factors that can lead an MNE to choose the 'big bang' approach include:

- **Integrated business** This may be the only option where an MNE is very tightly integrated and its customer offering is standardised across the business units that comprise the MNE.
- **Costly legacy systems** The existing legacy systems could have very costly maintenance contracts or be obsolete, leading to business risk. There may also be deadlines after which old systems may not be supported by the original vendors.
- **New offering** The MNE may be about to deploy a new customer offering or business process that adds value for the shareholders but can only be done with the new system.
- **Shock therapy** It can sometimes be more effective to instigate sustainable change by 'burning the bridges'. The culture of an organisation might be to resist change. The leadership of the MNE may deduce that to get the change that is needed to adopt the new systems, it is best to implement the new system across the board in one big bang.

Having pointed out the four reasons above that may lead an MNE to adopt a big bang approach, it should also be emphasised that implementing a SEMS using the 'big bang' approach in any enterprise is difficult. Doing so with complexities such as multiple sites, different languages, varied legislative and taxation codes, etc., is extremely challenging. It is advisable to adhere to the 'no surprises' maxim, meaning that there needs to be compelling business reasons for adopting an approach that would heighten the risk of unwelcome surprises.

Successful SEMS Implementation

The failure rate of SEMS implementations is higher than many business leaders would like to admit. In its 2015 ERP report, Panorama Consulting Solution, a US-based IT consultancy, reported that only 58% of respondents viewed their SEMS implementation as a success; 55% of SEMS implementations were over budget in terms of costs.[5] Examination of successful SEMS projects indicates some common factors that, if present in a planned implementation, will increase the chance of success and lower the risk of unwelcome surprises:

- **Strong project management capability** The organisation should have an agreed project management methodology, with well-trained project participants. The Institute of Project Management delivers such training in Ireland to a recognised international standard. The MNE should ensure its project team members are trained to the IPM standard or an equivalent.
- **Appointment of a project champion** A project champion is someone who acts as an organisational cheerleader for the project. This person can shepherd the project through its difficult moments and gain support for the initiative across the wider organisation.
- **Good business rationale and plan** It is crucial that any project has a well-grounded business rationale and it is wise to always ask the question: 'how will the customer enjoy the benefits of this project and how much more will they be willing to pay as a result?'
- **Collaborative teamwork culture** Project teams need to work well together and be trained to do so. Just as important is that the overall organisation understands the nature and benefit of good teamwork and values collaborative working environments.
- **Senior-level support** In the final analysis, any SEMS implementation will need support of some, if not all, of the senior management team. If there is no support, the project will be left either half-implemented or not implemented at all. It might seem obvious that senior figures in an organisation would support the implementation of a SEMS. However, not everyone believes in scientific measurement of performance; some managers who get to the top of the *ancien régime* are not so keen to see the old ways give way to the new.
- **Business process re-engineering** Traditionally, systems were designed to computerise the old manual processes. In a SEMS implementation it is important to rethink all the old systems and to redesign them to get the most of the new integrated approach. Even where a standalone process works well in isolation, it is unlikely to be optimal when considered in the wider context of an integrated system.
- **Excellent communication, both in the project and with the wider organisation** Not only does there need to be clarity about what is happening within the project but it is vital that the wider organisation is also kept up-to-speed. This wider communication is often neglected but it is vital to gaining organisation-wide acceptance once the system goes live.

These seven factors are easy to write down but are not easy to achieve. However, if an assessment of the SEMS implementation environment shows that any of these factors are absent, then the chances of success are lower.

17.8 CONCLUSION

The growth of the MNE has been meteoric in the last two decades. This growth has been partially enabled by advances in business technology, especially information systems. MNEs will seek to simplify their business systems and improve information quality and flows by implementing SEMS.

---

[5] See http://panorama-consulting.com/resource-centre/2015-erp-report/ (accessed October 2015).

These systems present significant improvements on the old legacy systems that developed over time since the original computerisation of business processes. The implementation of a SEMS is not without challenges, but these can be overcome by applying solid and well-understood approaches. The increased use of value-based management as a basis for assessing performance has increased the need for more comprehensive reporting of business performance for MNEs. The balanced scorecard integrates financial and non-financial measures in a reporting framework that allows for a more complete holistic performance measurement environment. The implementation of SEMS requires careful planning in order to ensure successful outcomes.

QUESTIONS

Self-test Questions

17.1 What are the reasons an MNE will opt for a 'big bang' implementation of a SEMS?
17.2 Scrod Plc has a decentralised organisational structure with heavily localised operations in the nine countries it operates in. What type of information systems architecture would be best suited to Scrod?
17.3 What benefits might be included in an MNE's assessment appraisal of implementing a SEMS?
17.4 What is a data warehouse?

Thought-provoking Questions

Question 17.1

You are the new accountant at ShivCat Plc (SC), a MNE manufacturer of vacuum cleaners based in Macroom, County Cork, Ireland. The business employs 1,600 people at three manufacturing sites in Poland, Slovakia and at Macroom. The head office is located at Macroom. Your boss, Aisling Springer, has asked you for some advice concerning a major new Strategic Enterprise Management System that SC had decided to implement before your arrival. Aisling is wondering what approach to adopt to the implementation project. She has asked you to prepare a short paper outlining the implementation options and some pros and cons of each option.

Question 17.2

Figgy Plc has just appointed you as a Project accountant. It is implementing a new enterprise-wide information system. Your boss is worried that the project implementation is beyond the competence of the existing organisation. She has asked you for some help. She suggests that you prepare a list of common features of successful implementation of large-scale SEMS. She would also like your thoughts about what skills you think are needed to make sure the SEMS implementation is a success.

Review Questions

(See Suggested Solutions to Review Questions in **Appendix B**.)

Question 17.1: TinyTots Baby Food Limited

Having read the TinyTots Baby Food Limited case study in **Appendix A**, identify the current problems in TinyTots Baby Food Limited's financial reporting system and suggest improvements, including how the reporting systems can support company strategy.

Question 17.2: EuroHub

Having read the EuroHub case study in **Appendix A**, evaluate the performance management system in EuroHub Ltd and make some preliminary recommendations on performance management within EuroHub (include performance measures, systems changes and incentives).

Question 17.3: Canam Inc

Having read the Canam Inc case study in **Appendix A**, prepare a brief memo to Martha with an initial list of the key requirements, which Canam Inc can incorporate into a Request for Proposal to be issued to a number of software vendors, in respect of a proposed new IT system.

Question 17.4: Canam Inc

Having read the Canam Inc case study in **Appendix A**, discuss the key challenges in implementing the system and what actions Canam Inc could take to mitigate these issues.

18

ORGANISATION DESIGN AND PERFORMANCE MEASUREMENT

Contents

Learning Objectives

Having read this chapter, you will understand:
- how MNEs structure themselves to optimise performance;
- the various performance measurement systems that MNEs use;
- how the strategic scorecard links strategic planning to individual performance;
- the use of KPIs in measuring performance;
- how cultural differences will shape the design of reward and bonus structures;
- how intellectual capital is the new frontline in performance management;
- how intellectual capital is measured; and
- the trends in management accounting that connect strategy to execution through measurement of both financial and non-financial metrics.

18.1 INTRODUCTION

In **Chapter 17** we looked at how MNEs capture and organise their information systems. In particular, we discussed the development of enterprise-wide management systems, which use the power and processing speeds of today's technology to inform MNE managers. Information is only part of the picture, however. MNE managers must use the information provided by their systems to stimulate and measure performance.

As with other management functions, the measurement of performance in MNEs is more complex than in purely domestic businesses due to the challenges presented by factors such as:
- multiple sites in different countries;
- language barriers;
- cultural differences;
- differing stages of development; and
- group structures.

In this chapter we will examine how:
- MNEs can overcome these challenges or at least mitigate them;
- the high-level design principles that underpin an effective performance measurement and appraisal system; and
- the criticality of aligning an MNE's organisation structure, as well as its performance measurement and appraisal systems, with its strategy.

We will also explore the critical link between individual performance measurement and organisational performance measurement. All organisations are made up of people, whose collective performance produces the organisational performance. It is clear, therefore, that there needs to be a link between the organisational performance measurement systems and the systems for reviewing individual performance.

In the final section of this chapter we will examine how non-financial performance measures have become increasingly important since the 1960s. The advent of value-based management (VBM) and other management approaches that look to measure performance across a number of metrics, not just financial, have led organisations to enhance performance measurement systems to incorporate non-financial measures in a structured way alongside the more traditional financial measures. (For more on VBM, see **Chapter 17**.) We will examine what systems the MNE can use to incorporate these non-financial considerations in a way that is structured and capable of analysis.

First, however, because it plays such a fundamental part in how performance is measured and how managers are held to account for their performance, we will consider the determinants of the organisation design.

18.2 ORGANISATION DESIGN

Rarely do the management of an MNE have the luxury of designing its organisation structure from scratch. Usually, the structure has evolved over time. What started as a small domestic organisation grows, new sites are opened, acquisitions are bolted on and new countries are expanded into. This organic process cannot be left unattended, however. If it were, the organisation structure would collapse through misalignment with company goals and lack of efficiency.

The capitalist model rewards profit-seeking enterprises. As discussed elsewhere in this text (see **Chapter 2**), MNEs have grown tremendously in the last 50 years and especially in the last 20 years. MNEs grow in size because they can meet customer needs more effectively than other organisational formats. The ability of MNEs to manage the complexity afforded by large organisation structures operating in various countries has become an enabling competence. MNEs that do not exhibit competence in this area will struggle to satisfy customers effectively and will eventually produce sub-optimal returns for their shareholders.

There is a significant body of research into how organisations ensure that their structures remain fit for purpose and aligned with their strategy and values; it is possible to discern structural patterns among successful MNEs. While we cannot do the research full justice in this text, we can summarise the key principles that have emerged. Understanding these principles is an important precursor to implementing performance management systems, which, in turn, will be part of the following 'feedback loop':

- goals are set by the MNE and are delivered by action plans executed through the organisation's structure;
- the outcomes of the actions are measured by the performance management system and fed back to the MNE's managers;
- goals and actions are then adjusted accordingly in order to fine-tune delivery.

The organisation's structure is an integral part of this dynamic process.

Performance and Organisation Design

Broadly, any group of people that collaborates to achieve a shared goal can be thought of as an organisation, the nature of which will be influenced by the task to be done and the characteristics of the people performing it. Thus, two different groups of people may organise themselves differently yet tackle and achieve the same task. Likewise, two groups of people organised along similar lines might achieve different tasks. We can infer from these observations that organisation design is influenced by factors that can be clustered around two main organising themes:

- the attributes of the task to be achieved; and
- the attributes of the people doing the task.

Maxim: **the task at hand should define the structure**.

Many texts describe organisation design as if the enterprise had a blank sheet of paper to work with. However, as mentioned, for practitioners in MNEs there will rarely be a blank sheet of paper; the legacy organisation structure will already exist. Therefore, if the organisation design needs to change, the management of an MNE will need to approach it mindful of the complexities of implementing such change **in an MNE** (see also **Chapter 13**).

If the two influencing factors shaping organisation design are the nature of the task to be done and the people to do it, and if an MNE already has an existing organisation structure comprised of the people carrying out the existing tasks of the MNE, the challenge therefore is to answer these two questions:

- How will the tasks to be achieved in the future differ from those being done today?
- What attributes are required of the people to achieve these tasks and how do they differ from the attributes of the current people?

The first of these questions regarding the tasks that need to be done is a strategic question – the formulation of strategy sets out what tasks need to be achieved by the organisation. The second question goes to the heart of organisation design. While the two factors interact, it is the strategic considerations that should always drive the organisation design. At the same time, while structure should follow strategy, one must also be realistic: there is little point in formulating a strategy that is beyond the capability of the organisation to implement.

While organisations are dynamic and evolutionary, the management of an MNE cannot force a change to which it is beyond the organisation's capability to adapt. Thus, the more adaptable an organisation's structure and people, the more strategic options it has available to it. This is the MNE's dilemma: flexible organisations may be less able to gain from economies of scale but can respond to strategic changes more readily than relatively inflexible structures with high degrees of specialisation that are excellent at achieving economies of scale but relatively poor at responding to strategic change.

Therefore, the first consideration of the organisation designer will be to assess the strategic plan **and** the propensity for the strategy to change. For example, an oil company that has found a well that will deliver oil for 10 years has a different strategic change profile than a smartphone manufacturer who may find its product is obsolete 12 months from now, replaced by the next enhanced iteration of telephone technology. Accordingly, each will have different approaches to organisation design.

Six Key Concepts in Organisation Design

At this stage it is worth presenting six concepts that are common to all organisation design challenges in MNEs and that are typically combined in the overall organisation design. These are clustered around the decision points that will need to be considered and, to a certain degree, are also descriptors of the labels and phrases one will hear and engage with when designing an organisation structure:

- **Organisation Chart** A diagrammatical representation of the organisation showing the formal relationships between the various roles, functions, entities, countries, etc.
- **Span of Control** The number of subordinates who report directly to one manager. The greater the span of control, the more direct reports a manager will have and the fewer the number of organisational layers between the most senior role in an MNE and the most junior.
- **Job Description** The specific tasks and standards required of a particular role.
- **Responsibility** The obligation on the occupier of a specific role to perform a certain task.
- **Authority** The right to direct someone in another role to carry out a task.
- **Accountability** The responsibility to carry out a task and report the outcome to someone else.

Definition of the Organisation's Tasks

Accurate definition of its tasks is the kernel of an MNE's organisation design: what tasks, who will do them and how they will account for their achievement or non-achievement to others in the organisation?

It is not possible for the organisation designer to be effective without a solid understanding of the nature of the tasks to be done. Yet, this is a common fault within MNEs. For example, specialists in organisation theory in the HR department can be tasked with designing an MNE's structure without having a sufficiently detailed understanding of the tasks required for it to achieve its goals. This is unfair on all parties involved. The specialists will design structures that work in theory but not in practice. It is a common refrain in MNEs that a specialist department like HR does not know what it is like at the 'coal-face'. Those at the 'coal-face' should help the specialists understand the activities and tasks that need to be done. Likewise, the specialists need to be open to such learnings and help the frontline operators understand that there are organisation design principles involved that, over time, have been shown to be more successful than just making it up on the spot. To be successful at this two-way information exchange requires good communication and openness. In an MNE it is vital that the specialists in one area understand, trust and value the specialists in the other areas in order to know how to perform the tasks to the required standards.

Relationships in an Organisation

Relationships between people in an MNE fall into two categories:
- **Formal** These are the relationships that are defined by the organisation's structure and are normally evident in an organisation chart together with the role descriptions.
- **Informal** The relationships that develop through the real-life interaction between people and departments. While these relationships cannot be captured in an organisational chart, they can be instrumental in achieving success or failure.

Formal relationships will typically fall into one of three types:
- **Line** This is where there is a formal relationship between roles where authority flows from one role down to the next, or accountability flows upward. An example would be a forklift driver who reports to the forklift supervisor, who in turn reports to the warehouse manager.
- **Functional** This is where a functional specialist has an authority over a role only to the extent that the role is concerned with that specific function. For example, a finance director can instruct the warehouse manager to record inventory movements in accordance with the specified internal control procedures. However, the finance director would not be able to instruct the warehouse manager on staff-rostering procedures.
- **Lateral** This type pf relationship exists between roles that are at the same level but in different departments. For example, the forklift supervisor might have a lateral relationship with the payroll supervisor.

When one considers these three relationship types, one can see the potential for tension between roles within a formal organisation structure. The purpose of organisation design is to achieve maximum effectiveness in carrying out tasks while at the same time minimising the potential tensions and conflicts that can and will arise. Some tension is natural, and even healthy in some circumstances, but only if it propels the organisation to achieving superior outcomes. If the tensions become destructive of value, then either the organisation design or the occupiers of the roles need to be changed.

Organisation Types

Organising a business to achieve its tasks, while ensuring effective relationships between roles, can be all the more complex in an MNE due to its multi-site nature as wells as the cultural and legacy considerations that will exist between its components. A balance must be struck between effective achievement of the task and efficacy of the overall organisation (see **Appendix C.3**). There are a number of structural designs available to the MNE.

Functional

This organisation will structure the line relationships by functional grouping. The finance director in Country A will report to the group finance director, not to the managing director in Country A.

This type of structure suits an MNE where there is one major product being produced for a global market with little or no tailoring to individual country needs. Remember our maxim: **the task at hand should define the structure**.

FIGURE 18.1: STRUCTURE BY FUNCTION

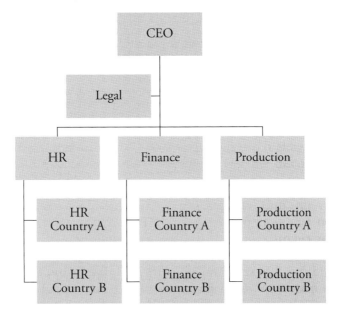

Geographic Area

In this organisation design the structure is set out by geographic area. This type of design is common in MNEs, especially where there is a degree of customisation to local markets required.

FIGURE 18.2: STRUCTURE BY GEOGRAPHICAL AREA

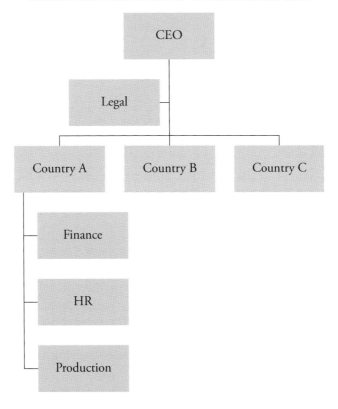

Product Type

In this structure the MNE is arranged by product type, which, though it allows for focus on delivering excellence in the particular product area, may result in duplication of certain overheads. The balance must be between the benefits achieved through the product focus and the additional costs of duplication.

FIGURE 18.3: STRUCTURE BY PRODUCT TYPE

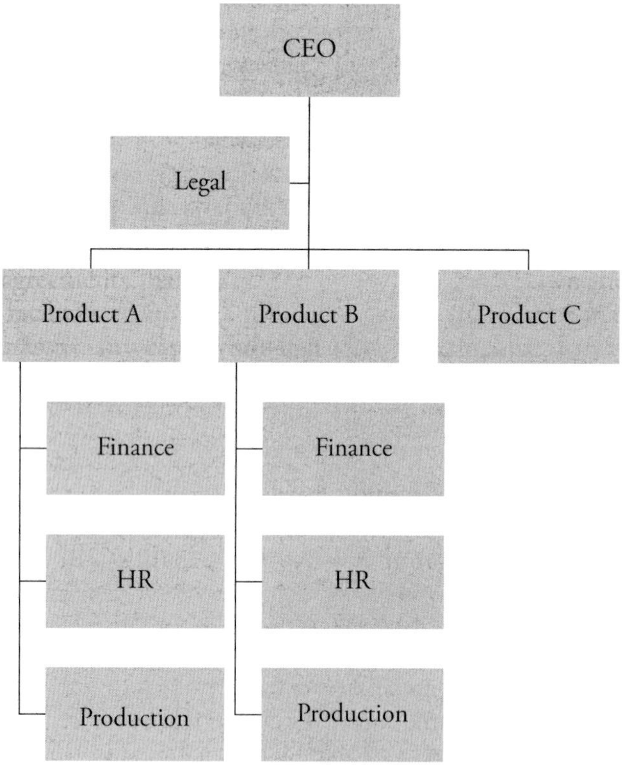

Customer Type

In this structure, the MNE organises itself around its customer types. This structure can work when different customer types require different services from the MNE, but it tends to add duplication in certain functions. There will also be co-ordination complications, leading to tensions in the formal organisation structure.

Hybrid Structure

We have seen that a possible drawback of some organisation structures is the duplication of functions and therefore costs. In order to overcome these drawbacks, some MNEs have organised themselves in what is termed a 'hybrid' structure, in which some functions are organised according to one principle, e.g. geography, and other functions organised to a specialty, e.g. finance. It is a hybrid of two or more organisation design principles in an effort to eliminate some of the drawbacks associated with choosing one design principle exclusively. Thus, production might be organised country by country, but finance might be a structure with a functional hierarchy. A hybrid structure requires careful consideration of the relationships and clarity of roles and responsibilities is critical.

FIGURE 18.4: STRUCTURE BY CUSTOMER TYPE

FIGURE 18.5: HYBRID STRUCTURE

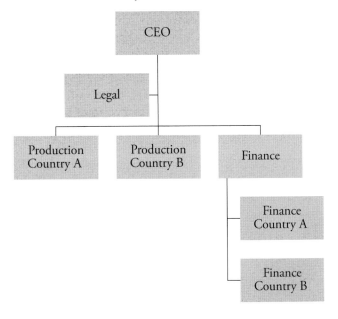

A hybrid structure can be very effective, especially where mature and open relationships exist between the functions of the organisation. However, it can become destructive of value when there are blurred lines of accountability. For example, in the organisation chart above, the finance manager in Country A reports to the head of finance for the group. However, in carrying out her day-to-day role she is based in Country A, interacting on a daily basis with her Country A colleagues. It requires a degree of sophistication for her to play her role in supporting the production function in Country A and at the same time reporting to her line manager, the head of finance for the entire MNE. The issues tend to come to a head around reporting of variances, internal control environment and capital expenditure planning and budgeting. (We will come back to these topics later in this chapter.)

Matrix Structure

Another organisation structure to consider is the matrix structure, which moves away from the old principle of unity of command and tries to avoid duplication of effort by having reporting lines that are both horizontal and vertical. For example, functional reporting might be on one axis and geographic or product reporting lines on the other axis.

	Finance	**Production**	**HR**
Country A			
Country B			
Country C			

In the matrix structure, a financial controller operating in Country A might find that she reports to the Country A managing director for some matters and to the group CFO on other matters. The possibility for confusion is obvious. Who, for example, would agree pay structures and bonuses? Which manager would set the performance targets for the Country A financial controller? How are priorities to be determined? The matrix structure has the advantage of reducing duplication and harnessing the best of all worlds in terms of organisational competency. However, it does have drawbacks, which stem from its complex nature and the dual-reporting lines. Organisations that implement matrix organisational structures need to have very well-defined descriptions of their target settings procedures and performance appraisal mechanisms.

Network Structure

The final organisation structure to consider is the network structure, which involves delegating tasks and responsibilities to a number of specialised units in order to produce a good or service for customers. The units may be subsidiaries of the MNE or outsourced to external companies or service providers. The main attributes of a network structure are:
- specialised units – each independent unit is highly specialised and can complete its own specified tasks independently of the other units;
- autonomy – each unit will be highly autonomous, deciding how it will achieve the completion of the tasks assigned; and
- central hub – the centre through which all tasks in the network are described and allocated out to the units.

Figure 18.6 depicts how a simple network organisation structure might work.

FIGURE 18.6: SIMPLE NETWORK STRUCTURE

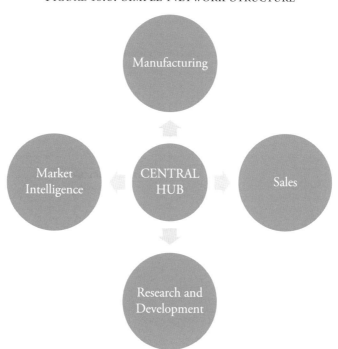

As can be seen in **Figure 18.6**, the central hub allocates the tasks out to each unit. The units may be internal to the MNE or may be external service providers or joint venture operations. The advantages of the network structure is that they can be cost-effective, geographically distributed and allow access to specialists that the MNE would not be able to develop 'in house'. The disadvantages are the difficulty in co-ordinating autonomous units, lack of central control and risk to intellectual property, since some units can glean critical intelligence about the MNE's products, processes, customers, etc.

Organisation Designs of Multinational Enterprises

As organisation structures have developed in MNEs,[1] four organisation patterns have emerged and most MNEs will be structured broadly according to one of following:

- **Global** The headquarters is in control of the whole organisation, with little local customisation or differentiation. This structure normally suits a highly integrated production process of a standardised product. An example of a global organisation structure is **Apple**, a hugely successful company selling its products globally. Apple products are highly standardised and decision-making concerning product design and pricing is tightly controlled from its headquarters.
- **International** The parent company transfers knowledge out to the divisions but allows some local customisation in order to better meet customer needs. An example of an international organisation design is the logistics provider **DHL**. Major decisions on branding and systems are 'dictated' from the centre, but there is also local adaptation to cater for individual market differences.

---

[1] In this text, to facilitate the reading experience we have used 'multinational enterprise' (MNE) to refer to any enterprise that has an international trading dimension, although we are normally discussing entities with a business unit in more than one country.

- **Transnational** A structure where the business units in each country specialise in a dimension of the overall MNE's processes in order to achieve efficiency and expertise. The units are interdependent but have a high degree of local autonomy as to how to fulfil their part of the value-chain proposition. **Nestlé**, the consumer foods giant, has organised itself on a transnational basis. It has 'embraced' complexity and turned it into a driver of business prosperity.[2] Accordingly, it has organised the MNE by allowing specialisation on a country-by-country basis where it makes sense to the achievement of the overall goals of the enterprise.
- **Multinational** Each country is almost completely standalone in its operations, drawing little direction from the centre. Such MNEs will have small headquarters that pull together finance and treasury functions and interact with the shareholders. Warren Buffet heads up **Berkshire Hathaway**, a huge MNE that allows its divisions almost complete autonomy in business decision-making. Some of its business units are MNEs in their own right and organise themselves in the fashion that best suits their individual business needs.

These four terms or labels for organisation structures are often incorrectly used as synonyms of each other. It is worth remembering the differences, however, in their cultures and ways of operating. MNEs will organise themselves differently depending on many things, including the nature of the markets they serve, the complexity of their processes and their organisational heritage. The MNE manager must try to identify both the existing structure and the structure that will best suit the MNE's marketplace and culture. The tasks that are needed to be done, and the people to do them, will be a function of the marketplace and the culture in which the MNE is operating. They must also try to ensure that the organisation moves toward bridging any gap that exists between these two structures, i.e. the existing one and the one best suited to the MNE's purpose. Bridging this gap is a route to superior performance for the MNE.

18.3 ORGANISATION DESIGN AND INDIVIDUAL PERFORMANCE REVIEW

The structure of an MNE involves how its people, its individuals, are organised into groups or collectives that are responsible for carrying out designated tasks in the furtherance of the achievement of the overall objectives of the enterprise. Thus, individual tasks combine to become collective tasks, which then further combine to produce the organisation's tasks.

By implication, therefore, the most efficient and effective MNEs have strong alignment between individual, collective and overall organisational tasks and objectives. Likewise, the performance targets of the individual should be connected to the performance targets of the group and organisation to which he or she belongs. The aggregate of all the collective performance targets in the MNE should add up to the MNE's performance targets.

If an individual's performance is linked, through the organisation's structure and strategy, to the MNE's overall performance, individual performance measurement is also connected to organisational performance measurement.

In the rest of this chapter, we will explore how individual performance is reviewed or measured and how it is connected to organisational performance measurement. We will then go on to

---

[2] Peter Brabeck-Letmathe, Chairman Nestle S.A., "Complexity Versus Corporate Efficiency", www.linkedin.com/pulse/20130923112052-230883806-complexity-versus-corporate-efficiency (accessed July 2015).

examine how organisational performance is measured, focusing on the use of strategic scorecards, which combine financial and non-financial measures in the furtherance of the achievement of the overall MNE's strategic goals. We will then consider the measurement of intellectual capital, which is increasingly the source of real wealth creation within MNEs, as the 'knowledge economy' gains in importance at the expense of more traditional types of manufacturing and production.

I will now examine individual performance review in MNEs in more detail.

Individual Performance Review

Performance review of the individuals who make up an organisation involves a number of key stages or activities:

- **Set Plans** Performance review will usually involve a dialogue between a reviewer, typically a manager, and a reviewee, typically someone reporting to the manager. The initial discussion will involve setting and agreeing plans, which will be for a specific timeframe and will dovetail with the organisation's overall objectives.
- **Measure Performance** Having agreed the plans, the reviewer and reviewee will agree a measuring system in order to monitor performance. There will be intermediate measure points to allow review of progress on an ongoing basis.
- **Give Feedback** The reviewer and reviewee will agree intermediate feedback sessions where the performance measurements will be reviewed. These sessions will be two-way: the reviewer will give feedback on how well the objectives are being met; and the reviewee will explain the nature of the support needed to achieve the objectives and whether this is being received or not.
- **Agree Improvements** Following on from the feedback session, the parties will agree on which improvements need to be made to the action plans of both sides in order to improve outcomes and more effectively achieve the objectives.

These four stages are interlinked in an improvement cycle where each concept feeds into the next concept, as illustrated in **Figure 18.7**.

FIGURE 18.7: PERFORMANCE REVIEW CYCLE

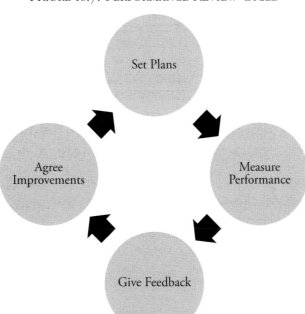

The MNE will need to have processes in place to carry out each of the stages in the cycle shown in **Figure 18.7**. At an individual level, these plans will be agreed with the line manager to which the person is accountable.

Importantly, the aggregation of all the individual plans in a department should equate to the department's plan. (I use the term 'department' to denote collectives of individuals organised around specific tasks, activities or functions.) In turn, the total of all the departmental plans should be the business unit's plan. The total of all the business unit plans should be the plan for the MNE as a whole. Therefore, the performance management system needs to integrate the overall plan of the MNE to the individual performance of all the members of the organisation and do so in a way that is not cumbersome and unwieldy. Advances in information technology have accelerated and improved these measurement and appraisal processes. In turn, this has improved the ability of complex MNEs to manage their affairs and compete effectively with more nimble local organisations.

Having considered, at a very high level, how individual performance should be reviewed, we will now examine how an organisation's performance can be measured. It is important that an MNE can connect individual performance review with overall organisational performance measurement. These connections can be made through the planning and budgeting process.

Planning and Budgeting

Investors make their decisions about investing in MNEs based on their expectation of a given return and their appetite for the associated risk. Some investors can tolerate a volatile return curve as it may suit their investment portfolio or their particular risk profile. In general, however, investors value a smooth return curve. Remember: a safe euro is worth more than a risky euro. In essence, this means that the greater the certainty of the returns, the more valuable the cash flows are to investors and the higher the price they will pay for those cash flows. It is therefore of primary interest to investors, and consequently an MNE's management, that MNEs can predict the consequences of their actions. Through such predictions they can give guidance to investors about likely future returns.

Indeed, in publicly quoted companies directors are legally required to warn the investor market if they feel the previously issued expectations are not going to be met. These profit warnings, if they have to be issued, are often career-ending events for CFOs and CEOs because the investor community expect the managers of an MNE to be capable of predicting its future results. The temptation of playing it safe and forecasting lower numbers is also problematic and will tend to lower the share price. Reporting earnings with a bumper set of results that were unpredicted will not win any 'brownie points'; investors who sold their shares based on the lower returns forecast will feel much aggrieved, and rightly so. Underestimating the forecasts is just as unfair to the investment community as exaggerating the forecasts or getting them plain wrong.

The short-term nature of some reward systems is such that individuals in an MNE may seek to 'under-promise' and 'over-deliver'. The managers then get rewarded with bonuses or good performance reviews for over-achieving targets. This behaviour is easily understandable as human nature generally tends toward the cautious rather than the reckless. Nonetheless, deliberately setting low targets causes under-performance within organisations, which the investor ultimately has to finance.

Thus, forecasting an MNE's results is a critical management function. But how does the management of an organisation as complex as an MNE go about creating such forecasts? Once created, how does the MNE ensure that the business is on track to achieve the results or, if off track, take timely corrective action to avoid calamity?

Planning

In order to forecast the returns available to its investors, an MNE must have a planning process. This could be a process which receives inputs, considers those inputs in some way, and turns them into outputs. The outputs are the plans for the business.

MNEs go about their strategic planning process in a number of ways. Almost always they will start with an analysis of their external environment and their internal capabilities. They will use frameworks such as PESTEL and SWOT analysis (see Chapters 5 and 6, of Gallagher, G., *Corporate Strategy for Irish Companies* (Chartered Accountants, 2011)). PESTEL, which stands for political, economic, social, technological, ecological and legal, is a useful acronym for considering what elements of the external world might impact upon the MNE. Likewise, SWOT (strengths, weaknesses, opportunities and threats) is a useful approach for gauging internal capability, i.e. strengths and weaknesses, with external impacts, i.e. opportunities and threats. From this analysis the MNE will derive a number of possible future scenarios from which it will choose the most desirable, having reference to its current situation and the overall aims and mission of the business. Understanding the future desired state and comparing it to the existing situation gives rise to a gap between the two positions. The MNE's strategic plans are designed to bridge this gap.

No matter what approach is used, all strategic planning will in some way resemble this process. The main difference between businesses will be the degree to which their analysis is forward-looking. Though most MNEs will set plans for three to five years, others may take an incremental approach and have shorter time horizons. (For a good example of how an MNE goes about strategic planning, see the essay by Jim Woulfe, CEO of Dairygold, in **Appendix C.1**.)

It is important to distinguish strategic planning from operational planning, and they differ in two significant aspects:
- strategic planning will be more holistic, involving the entire organisation and its stakeholders; and
- strategic plans will normally cover a longer time period.

An MNE will need to incorporate all its operating business in the planning process. This can be particularly challenging in an MNE where the outputs from one division are driven by the demand curve in another. In these situations there needs to be a reconciliation of the plans and an integration of the planning process to ensure meaningful outputs.

The plans, unit by unit, are consolidated, interrogated, questioned and reconciled until eventually they can be used as an overall strategic plan by the organisation to run its affairs. The strategic plan, therefore, should be dynamic in nature, capable of being changed according to environmental circumstances. In order for it to be dynamic it needs to come about through a process that is nimble and easy to put together. If it is cumbersome and complicated, then it will not be capable of the necessary adaptation.

The degree of adaptation that might be required is a function of the commercial environment in which the MNE operates, which in turn relates to the organisation's structure being a function of its operating environment (as we saw earlier in this chapter). Therefore, the planning process should also reflect the organisation's structure. A decentralised organisation will need to have a planning process that reflects it, operationally and culturally. A highly integrated and centralised MNE organisation structure will need a planning process driven from the centre.

FIGURE 18.8: ENVIRONMENT LINKING TO PLANNING THROUGH STRUCTURE

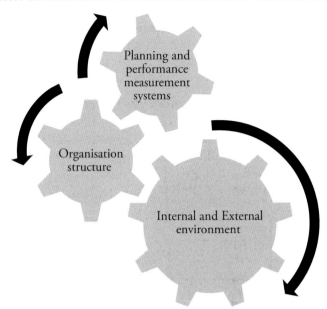

The planning process will produce an output, i.e. a plan, which will be used to allocate resources in the business and to assess financing needs. It will also be used to guide future returns for shareholders and investors. Normally, the first year of the plan will be prepared in more detail, usually by integrating it into the **budgeting process**. We will now turn to a high-level outline of how the budgeting process works in an MNE.

Budgeting

Having prepared a strategic plan, the MNE must now translate this plan into actions that will be executed by the organisation. Many strategic plans fail to deliver the promised results. Most commentators believe this is not due to the inadequacies of the plans *per se*, but rather the execution capability of the organisation. An average strategy brilliantly executed will produce better returns than a brilliant strategy executed with average capability. So, MNEs should not just have a good strategic plan but should also have the means to implement it.

The first step in translating the plan into actions is to incorporate the strategic planning process into the budgeting cycle. In the past, the budgeting cycle was predominantly a process driven by the finance department. It still is, but now the process needs to include both financial and non-financial measures, and ideally tie individual performance targets in with the strategic plan. While this degree of integration sounds straightforward, it rarely is.

"We typically lose out when a market commoditises and we no longer differentiate, further aggravated by being too slow or expensive."

"The matrix [structure] is too slow. We are in a turbulent market with many low cost competitors. We need short communication lines, quick decisions, alertness – we've got to be able to adapt fast."

These two quotations are from senior executives in the same company, Philips, the global electronics MNE. The first quote is from 2013, made by the Chairman Frans van Houten in a paper for the MIT Center for Information Systems Research. The second is from a product manager at Philips and appeared in article in *Management Today* in 1978. Thirty-five years apart, these statements reveal that the need for adaptive capabilities in an MNE's structure and planning process is perennial.[3]

In any group of people there is room for misunderstanding, all the more so when the group is trying to achieve a common objective. There may even be disagreements about what the objective actually is. When one considers the complexity of an MNE, one can quickly see how the possibility for misunderstanding and disagreement can grow dramatically. To ease such pressures, an MNE needs an excellent infrastructure for communication and the budgeting process needs to be integrated with this communication system.

A budget is an attempt to produce a simulation of possible future outcomes against which performance can be measured. Usually, just one possible future scenario is agreed on as the budget. Some MNEs will adopt a two- or three-scenario approach, having a target budget supplemented by a 'best case' and/or 'worst case' scenario. They do this so that they can have a range of possible outcomes. Having this range (worst case, target, best case) supports risk management as it allows the MNE management to assess what the downside risks can be of under-performance. For example, the finance director might see that in the worst case scenario the MNE may need to borrow additional funds, leading her to arrange additional contingency funding. However, adding these extra dimensions to budget-setting can overly complicate an already complex process.

In order to effectively connect the strategic plan to the budgeting cycle, the budget will need to forecast more than just financial numbers. It will also need to include non-financial measures, which in many respects are just as critical. Legacy budgeting systems have led to financial measures dominating the budgeting process. While this is understandable since, in the final analysis, investors want financial returns for their investment in an MNE, it is important to remember that financial returns are an output from the non-financial elements of a business. An apple orchard may produce a measureable financial return, but only if the apples grow and are harvested.

The well-known aphorism springs to mind: 'Not everything that matters can be measured, and not everything that is measured matters.' It would be wise for financial planners in MNEs to apply this in their financial planning and budgeting, to encapsulate what is important to the business and its stakeholders.

Though many minds in business are psychologically blocked in attaching importance to non-financial measures, this can, and must, be done in order to translate plans into actions. Financial planners need to consider what are the main drivers of performance in the business and, having identified them, ascertain how they are best measured. Sometimes the best measures will be financial, e.g. revenue or cash flow generated. Other times the measures will be non-financial, e.g. faults per 1,000 units. In **Example 18.1** below Topaz measures litres of fuel sold per fore-court as its main performance metric. The business has determined that this measure is one of the key indicators of its performance.

---

[3] Wouter, A. (2014), "The Past and Future of Global Organisations", *McKinsey Quarterly*, September.

EXAMPLE 18.1: NON-FINANCIAL MEASURES: TOPAZ

Topaz, the Irish fuel retailer, measures forecourt performance in terms of throughput of litres of fuel, not its euro or Sterling sales value. This choice was made because the individual forecourt manager cannot set the price of fuel, which is mainly made up of taxes and the global commodity price of oil. The forecourt manager is responsible for the volume of fuel dispensed through the forecourt. The forecourt results are aggregated up to produce a total litre volume result which is compared to the budget. The budget is set in litre volume, not euro or Sterling value.

Balanced scorecards (see also **Chapter 17**) and strategic scorecards are now widely used as reporting tools. These scorecards can capture both financial and non-financial metrics and using their SEMS, organisations can report actuals against these measures. We will examine the strategic scorecard in some more detail below.

The Strategic Scorecard

The International Federation of Accountants (IFAC) and the Chartered Institute of Management Accountants (CIMA) have jointly developed a Strategic Scorecard^{TM} framework to connect strategic goals to MNE performance. Like many tools in management performance it consists of a four-quadrant framework.

FIGURE 18.9: STRATEGIC SCORECARD[4]

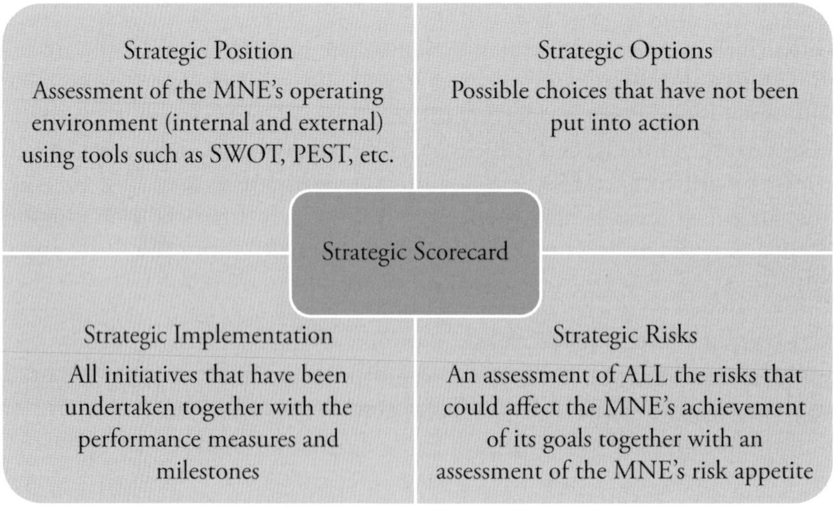

The strategic scorecard provides a link between strategy and implementation. It also connects risks into the assessment process and, in a major addition, includes strategic options not being followed by the business. This allows the MNE to be reminded that there are strategic options other than the ones it has chosen that might be chosen in the future.

While in **Figure 18.9** the strategic scorecard is a neat four-quadrant diagram, the reality will, of course, be more complex. The purpose of the diagram is to show the dimensions and

---

[4] Author's adaptation from IFAC.org, Enterprise Governance – Getting The Balance Right (2004).

considerations that are involved. Each component will need to be supported by further analysis, information and documentation behind each of the four quadrants. The scorecard should ideally be capable of linking up individual performance targets and measures, through consolidation processes, to the overall performance of the MNE. In this way, individual performance can be linked to the overall goals of the MNE.

Target Setting

The bottom left quadrant of the Strategic Scorecard in **Figure 18.9** represents the measurement of strategic implementation. The idea is that the MNE will have devised targets against which it can measure its performance. The targets will be derived from the outcomes associated with successful implementation of the strategy. But how does an MNE set these targets and, in particular, how can it link individuals' targets with those of the overall enterprise?

The 'SMART' approach is one of the best ways that MNEs can set targets, both at an individual and an organisational level. As shown in **Figure 18.10** below, the acronym 'SMART' stands for: specific, measureable, action-oriented, realistic and time-bound. Though this may appear to be rather simplistic in the context of some of the other concepts and models discussed in this textbook, if more MNE managers set clear targets by reference to these five attributes they would quickly see an increase in the performance and capability of their organisations.

The SMART framework can be used at all levels of an MNE. Using it to set integrated targets, the overall goals of the MNE can be cascaded down through organisation to meaningful individual goals. The strategic scorecard, in turn, can be used to aggregate the performance of individuals upward to the MNE's board, providing the crucial governance link between the shareholders and investors and the management of the MNE. The use of SMART targets and strategic scorecards together with SEMS (see **Chapter 17**) will increase the chances of successful strategic implementation in almost all cases.

Figure 18.10: Setting 'SMART' Targets

S	• Specific • Well-defined and unambiguous
M	• Measureable • Have specific measures that will demonstrate that the target has been achieved
A	• Action-oriented • Agree specific actions that are going to be carried out. Use action verbs such as finish, build, complete
R	• Realistic • The resources are available to carry out the tasks needed to achieve the target
T	• Time-bound • The target must be complete by a certain time. Milestones should be completed by specified dates

18.4 KEY PERFORMANCE INDICATORS (KPIs)

Earlier in this chapter we examined how MNEs are designed around clusters of activities or tasks required to deliver the outcomes that their customers will pay for. These activities are carried out by individuals working together with their colleagues, in teams, departments or functional groupings. How well these activities are carried out, i.e. their performance, must be measured. This is best done by setting SMART goals for individuals, the departments and functions they comprise and for the overall MNE. Actual performance against these goals or targets is measured using the MNE's information systems.

However, not all activities are as equally critical to the ultimate performance of the total MNE. If managers were given all the activity performance measures for the entire MNE, they would become overwhelmed with information. **Key performance indicators** (KPIs) prioritise certain activities and their measurement, cut through any surfeit of information and allow MNE managers to quickly determine performance achieved.

KPIs are performance measures 'indicating' progress towards a target. Their use has increased over the last three decades, especially as the use of balanced and strategic scorecards have become more widespread. The ability of managers to 'drill down' into KPIs has been greatly enhanced in recent years by the introduction of SEMS (see **Chapter 17**).

> KPIs can be set at all levels in an MNE. For example, a nightshift supervisor in Plant 3 in Romania might have KPIs that are linked to the productivity and quality of output on his specific shifts. The production director for the entire MNE, on the other hand, will be looking at KPIs relevant to overall production, perhaps by country. If there is a performance variance against the target in Romania, he may then seek, by exception, more detailed KPIs in order to explore the reason for the variance.

Selection of KPIs

As we have seen, the strategic objectives of an MNE can be broken down into 'SMART' targets with which, in turn, the performance goals of individual employees can be agreed. Importantly, an individual's goals are connected to the overall MNE's targets through the organisation structure. The more effectively individual goals are aligned with the overall MNEs targets, the more effective the performance of the MNE will be.

The selection of KPIs is vital to the efficacy of the overall performance measurement system. A KPI is linked to the 'M' of the smart target, i.e. measurement. KPIs are an indicator of performance toward achievement of a target.

> For example, imagine the target is to reach sales of €4.8 million in Zedmania. The KPI could be the sale achieved each month in Zedmania. Therefore, one of the MNE's monthly KPIs could be to have sales in Zedmania of €400,000 (12 months × €400,000 = €4.8 million).

Thus, there is a link between the selection of SMART targets and the selection of KPIs. SMART targets must be selected such that performance against them can be measured. Likewise, KPIs must be selected that can act as indicators of progress toward the achievement of a target. Essentially, you cannot select one without selecting the other.

Hierarchy of KPIs

KPIs are linked to SMART targets and SMART targets are set at all levels in the MNE, i.e. they are set for individuals, departments, functions, country business units and, at the top of this hierarchy, the entire MNE. Therefore, KPIs are also relevant at all levels in the organisation. Individual employees will have KPIs that are relevant to their personal performance and associated SMART targets. The department in which the employee works will have its KPIs. These KPIs will be a function of the aggregate of individual employees' KPIs and of the performance necessary to meet the demands of other departments in the organisation. KPIs will be summarised, aggregated and totalled as the number of individuals involved grows until finally one reaches the highest levels of the organisation structure, the top management team or the board. It should be possible to connect the KPIs for the total organisation, through a series of 'drill downs' to the KPIs of the individual.

The resultant architecture of KPIs in an MNE is that the KPIs should mirror the SMART targets and that both should mirror the organisation structure. **Example 18.2** below shows how each element of the organisation structure has an associated SMART target and associated KPI.

EXAMPLE 18.2: SETTING 'SMART' TARGETS

In this illustration, at the lowest level of the organisation hierarchy for the production line controllers there is just one target and its associated KPI (units per hour), though in reality, of course, a production line controller will have more than one target to meet. The production line controller for Line T has a target of 24,000 units of production for each eight-hour shift. Her KPI is the number of units produced per hour, thus focusing on progress toward the target. The controller of Line R has a target of 16,000 units per eight-hour shift. His target is lower as the machines on Line R are older and slower than on Line T. His KPI is also the number of units produced per hour.

Both controllers are part of a team that make up Shift 2, the supervisor of which has a target of producing 40,000 units per shift, 16,000 units from Line R and 24,000 units from Line T. The KPI for shift supervisors is total units produced per hour. If the hourly production drops below what is needed to reach 40,000 per shift, the supervisor can drill down into the data and see which production line is slipping behind.

The Shift 2 supervisor works at Factory B and reports to the Factory B Production Manager. The Shift 1 supervisor, whose shift target is 60,000 units per shift, also reports to the Factory B Production Manager. The Factory B Production Manager has a weekly production target of 700,000 units. This is made up of the Shift 1 target of 60,000 units per shift for seven shifts a week, equals 420,000, plus the Shift 2 target of 40,000 units per shift times seven shifts a week, 280,000, giving 700,000 units per week. The Factory B Production Manager's KPI is units produced per day. She monitors this KPI to ensure that the progress toward the weekly target in on track.

The MNE has another factory, Factory A, where the weekly target is 800,000 units. Both production managers at Factory A and B report to the Production Director, who has a monthly production target of 6 million units, being 700,000 units a week for four weeks from Factory B, equalling 2.8 million units, plus 800,000 units per week from Factory A for four weeks giving 3.2 million units and making a total four-weekly target of 6 million units. His KPI is the number of units produced per week.

The Production Director reports in turn to the CEO, whose target for production is 78 million units per annum, being 6 million units per four-week period for 13 reporting periods in a year. The CEO's KPI is the number of units produced per month, which indicates how progress is being made toward the overall annual target. For example, after four reporting periods she would expect to see that production is at 24 million units, being 6 million units per four-week period for four reporting periods. If production was only at 22 million units, she would be able to 'drill down' through the KPIs of her reports until she found the source of the variance. Corrective action could then be taken to get production numbers back on track.

Example 18.2 presents a simple scenario in order to illustrate the concept of KPIs. In reality, there will be more than one product, more than one SMART target and more than one KPI. Nonetheless, the principle remains the same: SMART targets are set for components of the organisation structure and progress toward the targets is measured using KPIs. Deviations from target results are picked up quickly and corrective actions taken.

Reconciliation of KPIs

Sometimes, however, interdepartmental KPIs are not reconciled, leading to misalignment within the MNE, as illustrated in **Example 18.3** below.

EXAMPLE 18.3: RECONCILIATION OF KPIs

In 2012, the production department of an Irish manufacturer had a KPI of producing 1,000 tonnes of processed material for sale by its sales offices in Portugal and Spain. When one added up the individual sales targets of each of the Portuguese salesforce, one arrived at a total sales target for Portugal of €4 million for 2012. The aggregate of Spanish sales was €7 million. The overall MNE target price per tonne, set by the marketing department, was €12,000 for 2012. Therefore, taking the production target of 1,000 tonnes and multiplying it by the target sales price of €12,000 per tonne, gives total sales for 2012 of €12 million. However, if you add the Portuguese sales target (€4m) to the Spanish sales target (€7m), you get a total sales target of €11 million. The sales teams are chasing sales targets of €11 million while the derived target of the production and marketing departments is €12 million. The two targets and their associated KPIs must be reconciled and a consistent set of targets decided upon.

The reconciliation issue in the above example arises in a fairly straightforward scenario of one product, one manufacturing plant and two sales forces. The complexity in most MNEs will be much greater, with more products, different currencies and more countries. It is important that the MNE has a system for ensuring that all its KPIs are aligned toward achieving the same goals. It is normally the finance department that ensures that the consolidation of the targets and associated KPIs for the entire group reconcile to each other resulting in a consistent overall target for the MNE.

18.5 MOTIVATION, INCENTIVES AND BONUSES

We have discussed how individual performance review works (setting plans, measuring performance, giving feedback and agreeing improvements, which leads to setting new plans, and so forth.) We also examined the setting of SMART targets and looked at how the strategic scorecard can be used to connect strategy to individual plans, as well as a means of monitoring performance.

All of this assumes that managers will adopt these approaches and performance measurements. However, why would managers in an MNE engage with any of this? In fact, what motivates managers and employees generally? Can systems be designed that will help maximise motivation within the context of performance review?

The investors in an MNE are rewarded by the returns they receive, which derive not just from the capital they have invested but from the ways in which the individuals in the MNE have used that capital. As we have seen in earlier chapters, agency theory demonstrates that the personal goals of an MNE's management might not be clearly aligned with those of its investors and shareholders. Corporate governance and reporting frameworks have been designed to make executives more accountable for their actions. Using the strategic scorecard, boards can assess the degree of alignment between the investors' needs and risk appetites and management's goal setting and performance. Into this dynamic comes the thorny issue of whether and how to use reward systems to align management and individual performance with the shareholders' goals, 'thorny' because if there is one topic bound to excite comment and sometimes outcry it is executive bonuses.

An MNE must try to reward results that are aligned with its investors' expectations. Many businesses do this by providing shares or, more often, share options to executives so that if the share price increases, they also benefit. One of the downsides of this approach has been that the executives rarely suffer when the share price declines. This is because the way many of these schemes operate is that the executives rarely have to risk their own capital. Rather, they have an option to acquire shares at a preferential price, if they so choose. If the share price falls, the executive does not exercise the option and therefore has lost none of their own money. There is also a risk of short-term actions being taken by management to boost the share price.

Various approaches have been taken to develop structures to align the interests of employees and executives with those of investors and shareholders, the most important being the independence of a board committee tasked to govern issues regarding remuneration. It is the role of an organisation's **remuneration committee** to approve all major pay and incentive schemes. In order to work effectively it should be a board committee and independent of the executive management of the enterprise. (*The UK Corporate Governance Code* (see **Chapter 5**) provides a useful structure for the composition of a remuneration sub-committee of the board.) It is also crucial that at least some of the members of the committee are sufficiently knowledgeable about the industry to know which goals and targets will most accurately measure success. (We have seen, for example, how in the banking crisis senior executives were receiving bonuses while their decisions were bringing about wholesale destruction of shareholder value.)

In MNEs, the issue becomes more challenging as not all cultures have the same approach to bonuses, and different nationalities may have different expectations of the leadership function in their employer. Different cultures expect different things from their business leaders. These different expectations can pose challenges for an MNE, especially if it wishes to standardise its management philosophy across different countries and cultures. We will now look at some pointers as to how managers can anticipate which type of reward systems will work in which culture types.

The Power Distance Relationship

As we saw in **Chapter 12**, power distance (PD) was one of the five dimensions of national culture developed by Geert Hofstede. While all five dimensions have some impact on the managerial approach to be used in the host country, PD is the one that most impacts motivation and reward systems.

Societies that are high on the PD scale will tend toward obedience of their superiors, and employees will quickly delineate between those who have power in the hierarchy and those who do not. Subordinates expect proactivity from their superiors and do not expect consultation. They expect and respond best to instruction. Consequently, countries with high PD scores will have bureaucratic organisation structures with low spans of control.

On the other hand, employees in countries with low PD scores will expect high levels of engagement and empowerment. They will expect their views to be sought out and will be surprised and demotivated by management practices that do not embrace this ethos. Consequently, while the organisation structures may be flatter, decision-making will certainly be slower than in countries with high PD scores. However, decisions may be of a better quality and be more likely to gain widespread acceptance.

The design of reward systems will need to take into account the likely response from employees given the cultural predisposition in the host country. It is unlikely that any employee anywhere would reject the chance to have more money in their pay packet at the end of the month or the year. The skill of the MNE manager is to calculate how to structure the reward system so that it motivates the behaviours which will lead to the desired outcomes.

Usually, the approach is to get the employee to 'think like an owner' and to reward them based on the subsequent outcomes. However, this is unlikely to be successful in a culture with a high PD score, and indeed may be a waste of money. In high PD cultures employees will expect to be told what to do and then carry out their instructions accordingly. Furthermore, they will not think that they should report back when things go awry as the expectation is that the leadership function will spot any deviations to plan. In these circumstances it will be necessary to have a senior management team in the host country that is aligned with the shareholders' needs and ready for the arduous task of managing in a directive way. In this type of system one would expect there to be a large disparity between the rewards for the people at the top of the hierarchy and those lower down.

The opposite would be the case in countries with a low PD score, where there will be a greater degree of team decision-making and consensus-building. Therefore, directive, micromanaging styles will not work as effectively and rewards will need to be shared out more equally.

Individualism vs Collectivism

Into this mix we should include another of Hofstede's measures, individualism, which indicates the degree of societal cohesiveness. In countries with a high individualism score, individuals are loosely connected to each other and the expectation for individuals to be responsible for their own successes or failures is high. If a country has a low PD score but a high individualism score, one would expect to find individual performance rewarded. The low PD score in these countries does not necessarily lead to greater teamwork since the individual feels quite disconnected from their fellow employees. The US, for example, has a high score on individualism and a low score on PD. This means that the culture will lend itself to empowered management styles with individual goal-reward systems.

On the other hand, the Philippines has a low individualism score and a high PD score. Here one would expect to see autocratic styles where people will essentially do what they are told. Reward structures will be basic. If there are bonus schemes, they will most likely be best suited to the achievement of team goals.

Japan has a relatively high PD score and a relatively low individualism score. In Japan, therefore, we would expect to see consensus-building management styles coupled with team goals and team-based reward structures.

Ireland scores relatively low on PD at 28 and scores 70 on individualism, compared to the latest UK scores of 35 on PD and 89 on individualism.[5] These scores suggest that in Ireland there is a comparably lower readiness to accept directive management styles than in the UK. On the other hand, the propensity toward collectivism is also stronger in Ireland than in the UK, although both are relatively individualistic compared to China, which scores only 20 on that scale.

Figure 18.11 below highlights the disparity of results that can arise from an assessment of just six countries on three of the scales from Geert Hofstede: power distance (PD), individualism (Ind) and uncertainty avoidance (UA). This disparity means that different approaches would need to be taken by MNE managers with regard to motivation and reward systems in these different countries.

---

[5] Source: www.geert-hofstede.com/countries (accessed May 2015).

FIGURE 18.11: NATIONAL CULTURE DIMENSION SCORES[6]

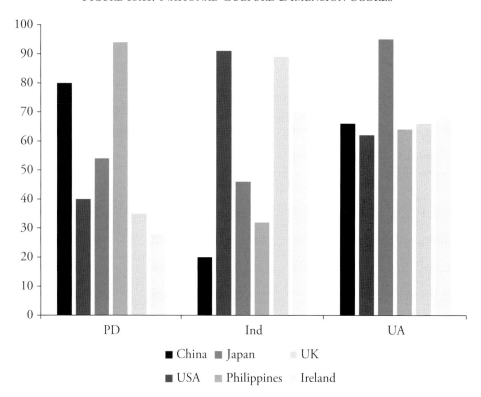

Uncertainty Avoidance

Another dimension that can impact upon reward system selection is uncertainty avoidance (UA), which measures a national culture's predisposition to avoid uncertainty. Since all business returns are a reward for the taking on of risk, all investors have some risk appetite. In order to align investor–employees interests it is useful to consider whether the investor appetite for risk in a particular investment is in alignment with the employees in the MNE. From **Figure 18.11** we can see that the UA score for Japan is high, which leads one to suppose that the culture that will dominate in an MNE's subsidiary in Japan will be one of caution. The Japanese subsidiary will try to avoid any uncertainty, plan carefully and methodically to have all eventualities considered before progressing with any actions. Decision-making is likely to be slow but thorough. If the MNE is in a sector that requires fast decision-making, an intuitive management style or an individualist approach, then the scores in Japan would suggest that there may be problems with a subsidiary there fitting in with the management culture required.

It is important to remember that these scores are only part of a methodology that MNEs can use in setting reward structures. It is also vital to remember that a country's predisposed culture need not necessarily be the one extant in an MNE; culture can be set and fostered by the MNE itself. The important thing is to recognise that some organisational cultures will be in harmony with the country's predisposition and sometimes an MNE may find itself in counter-cultural mode.

Why is any of this relevant to the MNE manager in connection with performance measurement? The MNE must decide how to organise its resources, especially people, to perform the tasks

---

[6] Source: www.geert-hofstede.com/countries (accessed May 2015).

required to deliver on its targets. It then needs to set SMART goals for each individual in the organisation, which should aggregate to achieve the targets of the MNE. The strategic scorecard can be used to measure performance against these targets, using the strategic implementation quadrant (see **Figure 18.9, p.492**). The other three quadrants will assess whether the targets remain relevant by assessing the MNE's strategic position, other options and strategic risks. (See **Chapter 17** for an example of a balanced scorecard, which is similar to a strategic scorecard. The 'learning and growth' top-left quadrant in the example in **Figure 17.2** includes measures to ensure alignment between the organisation's goals and those of the individuals who make up the organisation.)

The organisation's individuals need to be rewarded for their endeavours on behalf of the MNE. These rewards will be a combination of basic salary, bonuses and other incentives. The challenge for the MNE is that the different cultures in which it operates will be motivated by different types of reward structure. Individuals in different countries will attach different levels of importance to teamwork and individual performance. MNEs can use cultural measurement tools such as those from Geert Hofstede, to try to anticipate how employees in different countries will react to various types of management styles and reward structures. The complexity of performance measurement in different countries can be managed through the use of these tools.

18.6 VALUE-BASED MANAGEMENT AND PERFORMANCE MEASUREMENT

Chapter 17 examined how the success of private equity companies in extracting value from MNEs has led to changes in how MNE performance is measured and managed. Shareholders agreed to sell their investments only to find the new owners extracting hitherto unseen value from the enterprises. The previous shareholders would probably have accepted the private equity offers because they represented better value than that represented in the MNE's existing accounts or as expressed by management. The new private equity owners were able to recover their initial investments and make substantial profits by adopting a different approach from the MNE post-acquisition. This led investors to question how they were valuing companies and, in particular, how could unlocked value be better demonstrated in the financial statements of an MNE.

This thinking led to the development of value-based management (VBM) in which a more holistic view of the MNE is taken. The VBM approach tries to assess asset values and associated cash flows over longer periods into the future and to avoid the under-valuations that had occurred in the past. The obvious danger is not to be seduced into over-valuations.

In considering the potential value of assets hidden from view, the developers of these concepts began to consider **intangible assets**, which are assets that have no physical presence but, nonetheless, add value to an MNE by being a source of, or augmenting, future cash flows.

Intangible Assets

The valuation of an intangible asset is not entirely scientific and calls for a degree of subjective judgement. Despite this, approaches have developed that afford at least some degree of standardisation in the valuations of intangibles. Accounting standards have been drawn up concerning the valuation of the **goodwill** that arises upon acquisitions and its treatment in subsequent financial statements of the enterprise. Placing a value on brands or intellectual capital is more difficult since the value may have evolved over time and be associated with a certain *je ne sais quoi* or 'X-Factor' of success rather than something readily identifiable. However, when investors are appraising an MNE's future potential cash flows, they are in no doubt that its brands and intellectual capital will contribute to the stability of those cash flows and, often, directly to the quantum as well. For example, the social media giant Facebook has almost no asset value but is worth billions of dollars. The gap between the asset value and the market value must represent an intangible asset that will, in the future, generate cash flow returns for the investor. (Click 'Like' if you agree with this statement.)

Intellectual Capital

There is no worldwide standard definition of intellectual capital. For the purpose of this text, we will adopt a definition that is consistent with the MERITUM guidelines.[7]

Intangible assets are those intangibles that can be placed on an MNE's balance sheet (also known as a statement of financial position) in accordance with understood and agreed accounting principles. They normally arise from the expenditure of cash on some externally acquired right or entitlement. The accounting rules are well defined and applied with a degree of standardisation across MNEs, although there is still some work to be done in arriving at consistent treatment.

Intellectual capital (IC) is a collective noun denoting other intangible assets of a business that will not appear on its balance sheet but nonetheless represent value for the business and its stakeholders. Examples of IC are intellectual property (e.g. patents), the skills and knowhow of a design team or the customer relationships developed by a sales force. While, it is important that an MNE manages its IC, doing so it is not without its problems. First, how do you value IC? Secondly, how do you 'manage' it?

Valuation of Intellectual Capital

Why is it so difficult to value intellectual capital? Traditional accounting systems were designed to measure actual physical resources and their movements. This sufficed in an age where ownership of physical capital and assets was the route to wealth and success. In more recent decades, knowledge and creativity have become more important. Technological advances have meant that these more ephemeral assets can now add as much, if not more, value to a business than its physical assets, but accounting systems have not yet caught up. How do you put a value on creativity and measure intellectual capital?

Valuation of IC is linked to performance measurement. The change in value of the IC represents a change in the value of the enterprise. For example, if the IC of an MNE increases by 200%, then this additional value is of interest to investors in the MNE, which is why it is important to be able to measure IC in a consistent way at regular intervals. I associate the use of non-financial measures with the measurement of intellectual capital because, if the financial measures are capable of being captured through traditional accounting systems, then non-financial measures can be thought of as measures of performance derived from some organisational attribute different from purely financial performance.

Intellectual capital has a strange attribute in that what is valuable to one business may be valueless to another. For example, a supermarket chain in Ireland called Quinnsworth/Crazy Prices/Stewarts was taken over by Tesco in 1997. The brand names of the previous business had an undoubted value to its trading operation. However, when Tesco bought the business, it ascribed no value to the brand names and dropped them within a year.

---

[7] The MERITUM Project is the output from a collective of European universities which attempted to standardise approaches to intangibles and to intellectual capital, in particular. The 'MERITUM Guidelines' are contained in the Final Report of the MERITUM Project, published 20 April 2001. See cordis.europa.eu/documents/documentlibrary/70781341EN6.pdf (accessed May 2015).

As shown in **Figure 18.12** below, the MERITUM Project has classified intellectual capital into three categories:
- human capital – the knowledge that employees take with them when they leave;
- relational capital – resources linked to an organisation's relationships with the external world, such as those with suppliers, customers, shareholders;
- organisational capital, which is made up of the pool of knowledge that stays with the enterprise at the end of each day. It comprises:
  - intellectual property, such as patents, copyrights, licences;
  - infrastructure assets such as, routines and processes, culture, databases, and so forth.

FIGURE 18.12: CLASSIFICATION OF INTELLECTUAL CAPITAL[8]

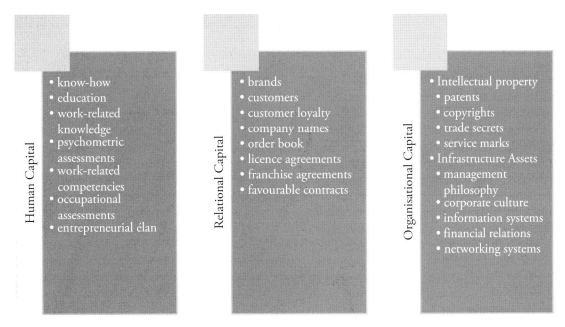

Figure 18.12 highlights the importance of intellectual capital. A large percentage of the overall value of an MNE could be categorised as 'intellectual capital' depending on its business sector, which is why is so important that it is managed. As introduced in **Chapter 17**, the balanced scorecard and the strategic scorecard provide structured approaches to managing IC together with the more usual financial measures of an enterprise.

Measurement of Intellectual Capital – Generic Models

In this section we will now look at three generic models that can be used for the measurement of intellectual capital. I use the term 'generic' to differentiate these models from ones which have evolved from models specifically designed and applied internally by individual companies.

The Balanced Scorecard and the Strategic Scorecard

As introduced in **Chapter 17**, Robert Kaplan and David Norton developed the idea of the balanced scorecard (BSC) in 1992,[9] their first exposition of which was in an article for the

---

[8] Adapted from the Final Report of the MERITUM Project (see n.7).

[9] Kaplan, R.S. and Norton, D.P., "The Balanced Scorecard: Measures that Drive Performance" (1992) *Harvard Business Review* (January February) 71–79.

Harvard Business Review. Kaplan and Norton had researched how successful companies were managing and measuring the return on their assets employed, in particular on their intangible assets. The result of this research led them to believe that successful managers needed to measure their performance with the same degree of effort and precision as scientists. This revelation was hardly new, but what Kaplan and Norton did was to apply measurement thinking to intangible assets, assets which had previously been largely ignored as far as management and financial reporting was concerned. The BSC was a method for connecting the organisation's strategy to its operational performance through the setting of financial and non-financial targets and the measurement of performance against those targets.

Kaplan and Norton divided measurement into four categories: financial, customer, internal business process, and learning and growth. In order to arrive at pertinent and relevant measures Kaplan and Norton proposed that the MNE should ask itself the following questions while formulating the measures:

- **Financial** To succeed financially, how should we appear to our shareholders?
- **Customer** To achieve our vision, how should we appear to our customers?
- **Internal Business Process** To satisfy our shareholders and our customers, what business processes must we excel at?
- **Learning and Growth** To achieve our vision, how will we sustain our ability to change and improve?

The task for the MNE is to decide on what measures would be appropriate in each of these four measurement quadrants. These measures should directly relate to the activities and tasks the MNE has set itself for the achievement of its strategic goals. For example, one of the measures in the customer quadrant could be the measure of the longevity of customer relationships. Thus, if the industry average is that a customer sticks with a supplier for three years, then the MNE might aim to have the best customer relationships in its industry. It might define this as having customers stay with it for twice as long as the industry average. Thus, the target would be to have customers stay for six years. The BSC process will help determine the measure and then provide the reporting mechanism to communicate the performance against the target. In the example given, the MNE is trying to measure and attribute value to the intangible asset of customer relationships and loyalty. It is in this way that the BSC is seen as a generic measurement tool for intellectual capital and intangible assets.

As discussed in detail earlier in this chapter, IFAC and CIMA have produced an iteration of the balanced scorecard called the Strategic Scorecard. While it also has four categories of measurement, they are more strategic in emphasis than the balanced scorecard.

The Performance Prism

The performance prism was first developed at the Cranfield School of Management, in collaboration with the management consultancy firm Accenture, by Andy Neely, Chris Adams, and Mike Kennerly.[10] The developers of the performance prism called the framework a "second-generation model for performance management". While first-generation models attempted to capture the idea that performance measurement was not just about measuring financial performance but should also examine non-financials measures, they were still looking at all measures from the perspective of the investor. Put another way, they were

---

[10] Neely, A., Adams, C. and Kennerley, M. (2002). *The Performance Prism*. London: Financial Times/ Prentice Hall.

measuring financial and non-financial factors with a view to encouraging behaviours that would maximise, in the end, shareholder value.

The performance prism goes further: it postulates that other stakeholder needs must be met, not just those of the investors and shareholders, in order to optimise returns within the MNE.

For example, one often hears senior managers say that 'our employees are our greatest asset'. Sometimes the employees smile inwardly when they hear this, knowing that the firm in question does not back up such grandiose statements by its systems, behaviours or processes. But, imagine if it did. Imagine a firm where this statement, 'our employees are our greatest assets', was supported by aligned systems, processes and behaviours. This is what the performance prism seeks to encourage, and not just for employees but also for other stakeholders. Thus, the performance prism attempts to encapsulate measures appropriate for the following stakeholders:
- investors/shareholders;
- customers;
- employees;
- suppliers; and
- community and regulators.

The reason the developers of the performance prism felt there was a need for this new 'second-generation' framework was threefold:
1. first-generation frameworks only focus on one or two stakeholders;
2. MNEs should expect some reciprocal contribution from stakeholders; and
3. MNE managers need to recognise that measuring and acting on one set of drivers does not necessarily lead to improvements across the organisation.

How does the performance prism work? The organisation is assessed and analysed based around five themes or facets, which are the five sides of the performance prism.

FIGURE 18.13: THE FIVE FACETS OF THE PERFORMANCE PRISM

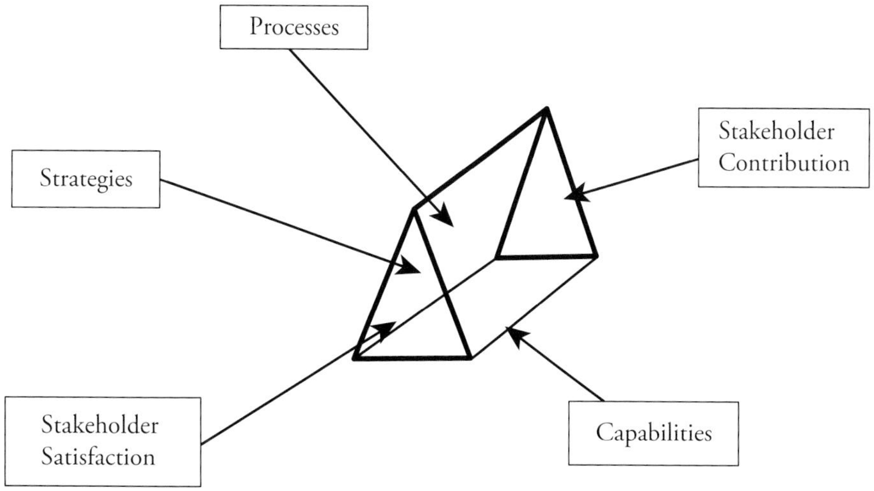

The five facets are organised as 'faces' of a transparent prism through which the organisation can be viewed. The framework endeavours to capture the complexity and, more importantly, the inter-relationship between the facets, the drivers of performance and the stakeholder population. In this way, the performance prism links many of the aspects of the strategic planning processes most MNEs will undertake:

- **Stakeholder Satisfaction** This zones in on who the MNE's stakeholders are and what they want from the organisation. We saw in **Chapter 3** how to carry out a stakeholder analysis. There are a number of tools that can help the MNE identify, and to some degree prioritise, their stakeholder groupings.
- **Stakeholder Contribution** One of the differentiating features of the performance prism, this analysis will identify what the MNE wants from its stakeholders. This facet explicitly recognises that there is, or ought to be, a reciprocal relationship between the organisation and its stakeholders. For example, the organisation may need fresh capital from investors, or new skills from employees.
- **Strategies** This facet encompasses which routes have been chosen to achieve the goals that have emerged from the first two stakeholder-focused facets. These emerge because satisfying stakeholder needs must be the goal of all organisations. The strategies are a powerful distinguishing feature of the performance prism as they are the paths chosen to achieve the goals. Often MNEs can use models that confuse goals with strategies, which leads to the selection of inappropriate performance measures. The measures should be chosen once the strategies have been identified and will assess how well the strategies are being implemented and communicated. The measurement system should also assess the degree to which strategies throughout the organisation are aligned and remain relevant to shifting stakeholder needs.
- **Processes** These are the business activities that combine to support and deliver the strategies. Having identified the processes, the MNE will select appropriate measures and targets that ensure that the processes are being carried out effectively and that they support the strategies. In particular, it is important to prioritise which processes are most critical and focus effort on these. It is neither possible nor desirable to include measures of all processes. Many business process re-engineering initiatives will come from the assessments of the processes in terms of their fit *vis-à-vis* an MNE's strategies.
- **Capabilities** This facet is concerned with the people, practices, technologies and infrastructure required to make the MNE's processes work. The necessary organisational capabilities must exist to support the processes identified. Such capabilities would include technical competence of staff, information systems, trucks and warehouses, etc.

One can readily see the linkage between the facets. The strategies are the path to achieving the goals which satisfy stakeholder needs. The processes support those strategies and the capabilities are reflective of the organisation's ability to make good on those processes. There is an element of 'chicken and egg', however, in that an organisation may not have the capabilities to support the processes that deliver the strategies to achieve the goals. In such cases, the performance prism should help highlight these shortcomings. If the obtaining of the correct capabilities is not possible, then processes will need to be redesigned, or strategies revisited. In extreme cases, goals will need to be reassessed or stakeholders' needs reprioritised.

In summary, the performance prism provides a framework of performance measurement and control that links the critical facets of MNEs. It is particularly valuable in measuring non-financial aspects, including intellectual capital and intangibles.

The Knowledge Assets Map

The knowledge assets map approach views the organisation (the MNE for our purposes) as a repository of pockets of knowledge, which are assets from which value is derived, value which translates either directly or indirectly into ways of meeting stakeholder needs.

Thus, the knowledge assets map approach seeks to identify the pockets of knowledge in an MNE and assess value on the basis of their contribution to meeting stakeholder needs. The two main sources of these pockets of knowledge are:
- relationships, which are related to the MNE's stakeholders and personnel; and
- structural resources, which are related to the tangible and intangible environment of the MNE.

Figure 18.14 below is adapted from the knowledge assets mapping system proposed by Bernard Marr and Giovanni Schiuma (two of the earliest writers in this field) and demonstrates this approach.

FIGURE 18.14: A GENERIC KNOWLEDGE ASSETS MAP[11]

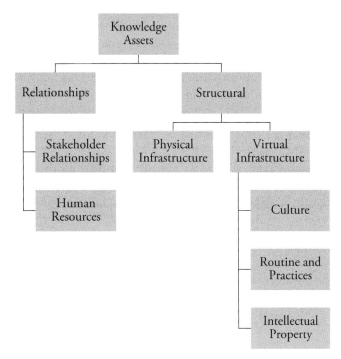

The left-hand side of the knowledge map shown in **Figure 18.14** represents the knowledge pockets of the organisation primarily identified with relationships between stakeholders, both individual personal relationships and relationships between the MNE and stakeholder groups and institutions. The relationships are grouped into two main categories: stakeholder relationships and human resources. The distinction between the two is that the stakeholder relationships cover all the external relationships between the organisation and its environment, such as franchise agreements, banking relationships or customer loyalty schemes, while the human resources dimension covers the internal relationships between the people and departments

---

[11] Marr, B. and Schiuma, G. (2001). "Measurement and Managing Intellectual Capital and Knowledge Assets in New Economy Organisations" in *Handbook of Performance Management*. London: Gee.

working in the organisation. These internal relationships could involve technical competency, organisational capability, motivation, interdepartmental harmony, etc. An organisation that has seamless integration and communication between its people has a significant competitive advantage. On the other hand, some MNEs set up healthy competition for resources and results between its internal stakeholders as a way to foster improved performance. In either case, value can be derived from the pockets of knowledge that arise from these relationships.

The right-hand side of the knowledge assets map covers structural resources, split between obvious physical infrastructure, such as buildings, IT systems, etc., and virtual infrastructure, which is broken down into three further sub-classifications: culture, routine and practices, and intellectual property.

Culture is hard to define and attach value to, but, as consumers, we can almost always tell when we are interacting with an organisation that has a strong culture, either positive or negative. For example, when visiting the EuroDisney theme park just outside Paris, one cannot but be impressed by the strong sense of fun and fantasy conveyed by all the staff one interacts with. The formal culture is set by the organisation's mission and its value statements. The informal culture is set by how it actually adheres to the aspirations set out in the formal statements. If management actions do not align with the corporate philosophy and value system, the result will be cynicism and value-destruction.

'Routines and practices' are the tasks and processes the organisation has built up over time and involve the ways in which things actually 'get things done'. Senior managers can often neglect to understand that it is through the aggregation of all these routines and practices that value is eventually added within the MNE.

The final knowledge pocket among an MNE's (virtual) structural resources is intellectual property. This could include the know-how, trademarks (brands), patents, copyright material and other intellectual property assets that the organisation will use to gain competitive advantage and add value.

Using the knowledge map to measure intellectual capital involves:
• identifying the organisation's knowledge assets and classifying them according to the structure in **Figure 18.14**;
• apportioning value to each of the assets and selecting measures with which to monitor the knowledge asset;
• prioritising those assets that are truly critical to the organisation's success; and
• setting performance targets and measuring actual performance against those targets, taking corrective action when needed.

It is vital that the performance measures are selected with true understanding of the MNE's structure and goals. Measure the wrong things and one will definitely get the wrong results as people focus on what they are being measured on. The temptation is to view the exercise as intellectual or hypothetical, which would be to miss the very real opportunities that can arise from looking at the MNE afresh using the knowledge assets map.

The Value-added Approach to Measuring Intellectual Capital

In 1996, George Robinson and Brian Kleiner devised a two-part framework for the measurement and valuation of intellectual capital.[12] It powerfully connected to the well-regarded value chain concept developed by Michael Porter (see **Chapter 3, Figure 3.2**) with the economic

---

[12] Robinson, G. and Kleiner, B. (1996). "How to measure an organization's intellectual capital", *Managerial Auditing Journal*, 11(8), 36–39.

added value (EVA) concept developed by New York consultancy group, Stern Stewart. Porter's value chain looks at an organisation as a system, where inputs are processed into outputs that customers buy. The inputs, processes and outputs are supported by expert functions within the organisational structure, such as human resources or procurement, all of which combine to produce something (a product or service) that customers are willing to pay for. The basic premise is that the customer will pay more for the output than the aggregated cost of all the functions and this excess is called the 'added value'.

The EVA system proposes that organisations should adopt projects that produce returns greater than the cost of capital. The EVA framework can be used to analyse where activities and projects are adding superior returns based on cost of capital and where the organisation is consuming capital resources without compensatory returns.

Robinson and Kleiner's idea was to combine these two concepts so that each component of the value chain is assessed according to the EVA framework. This simple idea poses many practical problems in terms of its calculation, the main problems falling into two areas:
- assessing the capital attributable to activities where the main driver of value is intellectual capital, such as the research and development department; and
- attributing or apportioning a share of the company's proceeds from customers to a particular activity. For example, how much of what a customer pays for a product can be attributed to the streamlined activity-based costing system that supports the manufacturing process.

Nonetheless, the process of examining its value chain in order to assess the EVA of each component can help an organisation determine where it is inefficient or uneconomical with resources. It can likewise identify where superlative performance is being achieved. The objectivity of the process is crucial to achieving the benefits that can flow. Sometimes the people in an MNE who know most about a particular process are the people who actually carry out the process. Simplistically, they may seem to be the best people to do the EVA for that part of the value chain. However, there is a risk that they may be biased in their assessment. Often, in order to avoid such natural bias and subjectivity, the EVA for each part of the value chain is carried out independently, or even better, by people from another part of the organisation. This does make the process longer but substantially improves the resulting analysis.

A real advantage of this approach is that it links well-known concepts (the value chain and EVA) in a way that can be readily understood by all stakeholders. Therefore, communication, a critical ingredient in any improvement programme in an MNE, can be aided greatly. It is difficult to overstate the importance of communication in delivering meaningful change and improvement, especially in driving the value enhancement of intellectual capital.

The Value Creation Index

This is an analytical process that seeks to explain the market value of an organisation in terms of non-financial measures. The US business publication *Forbes* surveyed its readers to ask them what the drivers of corporate value were. The results were then correlated with share-price movements and market valuations to produce a statistically robust list of what intellectual capital assets affect share prices. The top eight drivers were:
1. customer satisfaction;
2. ability to attract talented employees;
3. innovation;
4. brand investment;

5. technology;
6. alliances;
7. quality of major processes, products or services; and
8. environmental performance, e.g. when BP's share price fell dramatically after the Gulf of Mexico disaster.

MNE managers can use this value-creation index to assess their own performance, identifying where they excel and where they need to improve. One thing that emerged from the research was that the drivers of share price are different for different industry types. Some would further argue that each company has, or ought to have, its own unique set of drivers.[13] Nonetheless, assuming that there are industry-specific drivers and associated ranking, this approach allows the organisation to identify where it needs to improve in order to add more value for investors.

Market or Value-based Approach to Measuring Intellectual Capital

This is an appealing framework for measuring intellectual capital as its core premise is that the value of an organisation's IC is the difference between its market value and the value of its net assets.

A simple way of calculating the value of an organisation's intellectual capital is to take the difference between its market value (the number of shares in issue multiplied by the market value of the share) and the net book value of its assets. This can be done with a minimum of information, and the gap between the two figures indicates the inherent upside the market sees in the share price, an upside that can only be delivered by intangible asset values (unless the book value of the assets significantly undervalues those assets, for whatever reason).

However, the simplicity of the calculation is also its drawback – it ascribes only one value and classification to intellectual capital, though it might be possible to reconcile this single figure to a more detailed breakdown of IC using some of the other measurement systems described above.

Another drawback is that accounting standards have developed over the years and some balance sheets now include amounts for certain intangible assets. Goodwill on acquisitions, in particular, can be a large asset in many acquisitive Plc's balance sheets. This would have to be taken into account when doing the value-based calculation.

A further disadvantage of this approach to measuring IC applies particularly to MNEs where each subsidiary has its accounts prepared in accordance with its own local accounting standards and laws. These are consolidated to produce the group accounts. Therefore, at a group level, there is a certain netting of IC calculations where positive figures for some entities are negated by negative results in other subsidiaries. The sprawling nature of large MNEs such as Unilever, for example, renders the calculation at the total enterprise level almost meaningless.

Tobin's q

'Tobin's q' is a system devised by James Tobin in 1969.[14] The idea behind it is not too dissimilar from measuring the gap between net assets and market value used in the value-based approach.

---

13 Khavandkar, J. (2009). *Intellectual Capital: Management, Development and Measurement Models*. Tehran: Iran Ministry for Science: Research and Technology Press.
14 Tobin, J. (1969). "A General Equilibrium Approach To Monetary Theory", *Journal of Money, Credit and Banking*, 1(1), 15.

The difference is that the ratio of one to the other is calculated and the trend of the derived ratio is also tracked.

There are a number of different ways to work out the calculation, but the simplest is:

$$\text{Tobin's } q = \frac{\text{Equity Market Value} + \text{Liabilities Market Value}}{\text{Equity Book Value} + \text{Liabilities Book Value}}$$

When $q>1$, the firm has a market value greater than its assets at book value, which suggests the existence of intellectual capital. How the q ratio moves over time can then be tracked, helping MNE managers to assess whether the value of their intellectual capital is rising or falling. The q ratio for the individual firm can be compared to the q ratio for the market as a whole, or the industry sector, allowing the organisation to determine its performance *vis-à-vis* competitors. Tobin's q can also be used for other analysis, particularly the efficiency of capital and whether more funds can be raised from the markets, and so forth; however, this is beyond the scope of this book.

Calculated Intangible Value (CIV)

This is a fairly straight forward method of working out the value of IC from stock market available information. It involves calculating the return on capital for the immediate preceding three years and using this return level to derive an appropriate excess performance level that can be attributed to IC. This calculated excess performance is then adjusted for corporation tax and the net present value of the after-tax premium is worked out using the organisation's cost of capital. (An MNE's cost of capital and/or its WACC is often freely available from stock market analysts' reports on public companies. See **Chapter 11** for a more complete description of WACC and cost of capital.)

The seven steps are:

Step 1: Work out the average pre-tax profit of the last three years.

Step 2: Get the average year-end tangible assets for the last three years.

Step 3: Calculate a return on assets figure based on the two averages that have just been calculated.

Step 4: Find the industry sector average return on assets for the same period.

Step 5: Subtract the industry average rate of return from the company's average return rate and apply this derived rate to the average year-end tangible assets. This is the excess return.

Step 6: Reduce this excess by the average corporation tax of the same preceding three-year period.

Step 7: Calculate the NPV of this derived after-tax excess return using the company's cost of capital as the discount rate.

The calculated number can be used in two ways. First, it can be used as an absolute calculation to say that, of the total market value of an enterprise, this figure is the amount that can be attributable to intellectual capital. Secondly, the CIV can be tracked from year to year, allowing managers to see whether it is increasing or decreasing. Companies with a stated desire to grow through innovation or superior human resource performance would expect to see the CIV increasing. If it is not, alarm bells should be going off.

Another value of CIV is that it allows comparison between organisations. Such comparisons can inspire superior performance and develop greater understanding of one's competitors and marketplace.

Matching Assets to Earnings – The Baruch Lev Method

This system is similar to the CIV method as it attempts to calculate normalised returns on tangible assets and subtract this from the actual returns and impute the difference to intellectual capital. Baruch Lev[15] usefully defined assets as a source of future benefits. He postulated that the returns to organisations (including MNEs) derived from three types of asset: physical assets, such as buildings; financial assets, such as stocks or bonds; and finally, intangible assets. By isolating the normalised return from the financial and physical assets, it ought to be possible to calculate the return on the intangible assets. By applying an appropriate discount rate to the return on intangible assets, an intellectual capital valuation can be arrived at.

There are five steps to the Baruch Lev calculation:

Step 1: Calculate the average of the last three years' annual earnings together with the next three years' consensus forecast.

Step 2: Assess the average after-tax return rate on the firm's financial assets for the same six-year period. Arrive at average after-tax earnings on financial assets.

Step 3: Calculate the average physical assets held for the same six-year period and apply the industry average expected after-tax return rate on physical assets. Arrive at average after-tax earnings on physical assets.

Step 4: Add the average after-tax earnings for financial and physical assets together and subtract this total from the overall average after-tax earnings calculated at Step 1. We now have a derived figure for the after-tax return on intangible assets.

Step 5: Using an appropriate discount rate, impute a value to the after-tax average earnings calculated at Step 4. This is the balance sheet value of the intellectual capital.

Clearly, the selection of the discount rate at Step 5 is a major determinant of the value of the intellectual capital. This figure need not be entirely arbitrary. Since the return on the other two components of the assets structure is known (i.e. the financial assets and the physical assets, as is the overall cost of capital for the business) a derived rate can be worked out using statistical correlation methods. Lev suggested 10.5% as a discount rate for intellectual capital calculations.

Interestingly, if you use all the methods suggested by Lev to value physical, financial and intangible assets you can derive a value for a business which may differ from the actual market value on the stock market. You could use this system to guide your buying and selling of shares. If you really had confidence in the Baruch Lev model, you could become a millionaire very quickly and give up the 'day job' just by exploiting under- and over-valued shares based on the analysis.

Human Resource Accounting (HRA)

This is a system designed to quantify the economic value of the people in an organisation. Various models have been described over the years but, as one might expect, it is very difficult to value knowledge and experience. Indeed, once such a value has been ascribed, what is then done with it? Inter-firm comparisons and benchmarking would only be of value if all MNEs used the same measurement system and methodology and, most importantly, were equally objective.

Value-added Intellectual Capital Coefficient

This is an approach that measures the difference between sales and all input costs, except labour costs, and divides this difference by intellectual capital costs, which are approximated to be all labour costs. Put another way, it calculates a new profit figure, i.e. profit before labour costs,

---

15 Lev, B. (2001). *Intangibles*. Washington, D.C.: Brookings Institution Press.

and divides this number by the total labour cost. The more effective every € of labour cost, then the higher the ratio should be.

For example, if total labour cost was €1 million and total profit was €3 million then the ratio would be 4, i.e. €3 million profit, add back €1 million labour costs, giving €4 million divided by €1 million labour, producing a ratio of 4. This number essentially means that every € of labour produces €4 of profit out of which the labour cost must be paid. The remainder is for the investors.

The coefficient's simplicity is its attraction: the higher the number, the more effective the use of intellectual capital. However, its simplicity is also a drawback. A capital-intensive automated manufacturing plant may produce high profits when compared to a relatively low labour cost; the profits may not look quite so high, however, when the cost of the huge investment in automation is taken into account.

Measurement of Intellectual Capital – Non-generic, Individual Company Models

The preceding section dealt with the generic models that have evolved to measure intellectual capital and through its measurement improve performance and results for stakeholders. Some companies have adopted an individual approach and developed their own 'in-house' frameworks for measuring IC. Indeed, some have found their own models so successful that they have discovered a market for selling consultancy services, which has meant that frameworks that were originally organisation-specific have gained wider acceptance and application.

There is a two-fold value in considering these individual, non-generic company models. First, they appear to have added value in their respective organisations and, secondly, they are capable of being used in organisations other than the ones for which they were originally designed.

The most commonly used non-generic models are:
- Skandia's Navigator
- Ericsson's Cockpit Communicator
- Celemi's Intangible Assets Monitor
- Bates Gruppen's CompanyIQ Measurement System.

Each of these models was developed 'in house' by the eponymous MNE. Their aim is similar to the generic models in that they seek to establish a structured method of measuring, and thus managing, performance of intangible assets. They each have been successfully used in many MNEs, not just those in which they were first developed.

18.7 CONCLUSION

We have seen in this chapter that performance measurement is a complex but vital part of the management of an MNE. We looked at how an MNE might organise its operating units to optimise performance; how its performance measurement is shaped to some degree by the way it organises itself, which is driven partly by industry type, customer needs and management philosophy.

Developments in management accounting concepts, in particular the balanced scorecard, have led to increasingly sophisticated ways of connecting strategic planning to business performance measurement. The balanced scorecard has also allowed the measurement of performance across financial and non-financial metrics. The importance of intellectual capital (IC) to MNEs has increased in the last 50 years. It can be said that this form of capital is now the single biggest determinant of the future profitability of an MNE. Therefore, understanding how to value IC and compare different MNEs has become vital for investors and other stakeholders. Standard accounting practices and balance sheet valuation systems have lagged this development according to many commentators, and new (but still flawed) systems for valuing IC have been developed. The valuation systems are flawed in that they still call for some degree of subjective assessment and/or lack a standardised approach. Dealing with these flaws and the development of better IC valuation systems will continue to be at the forefront of accounting theory and discussion for the decades ahead. However, it is not just an academic debate: MNE managers must grasp that superior returns for investors and other stakeholders will come from excelling in the management of intangible assets and knowledge management. The successful MNEs of the future will be those that do this best.

QUESTIONS

Self-test Questions

18.1 From publicly available information, make some estimates as to the value of the intellectual capital of Google.
18.2 Why would reward systems differ from country to country?
18.3 What factors should an MNE consider when designing and shaping its organisation structure?
18.4 Taking an MNE you know, try to draw their organisation chart from publicly available information. Can you discern what organisation design principle it has used?

Review Questions

(See Suggested Solutions to Review Questions in **Appendix B**.)

Question 18.1: Kebabs Ltd

Having read the Kebabs Ltd case study in **Appendix A**, draft and outline a strategic scorecard for Kebabs Ltd, integrating a range of information and measures relevant to the company. Comment on the measures and relate the content of the scorecard back to the strategy of Kebabs Ltd.

Question 18.2: Boyne Aviation Limited

Having read the Boyne Aviation Limited case study in **Appendix A**, evaluate the current results of Boyne Aviation Limited in terms of finance and operations and compare them with the low-cost operator KPIs.

Question 18.3: Natural Food Company

Having read the Natural Food Company case study in **Appendix A**, evaluate the suitability of the Artisan Food Company against Natural Food's scorecard and assess whether it is a suitable takeover target.

Question 18.4: EuroHub

Having read the EuroHub case study in **Appendix A**, analyse the financial performance of the three lines of business (LOBs) within EuroHub and comment on any issues you see emerging from this analysis.

Question 18.5: Canam Inc

Having read the Canam Inc case study in **Appendix A**, prepare a memo for Jeff Welsh on the performance of Canam Europe for 2013 and include your thoughts on what, if any, additional KPIs Canam Inc should include in its performance scorecard in the future.

APPENDICES

CONTENTS

Appendix A

CASE STUDIES

Contents

BLACK SWAN INC

(Based on Chartered Accountants Ireland, FAE Autumn 2012, Simulation 3)

Black Swan Inc is a fast-growing US internet services company with turnover doubling over the past three years. It was established eight years ago and now has operations in 35 countries globally. Its EMEA (Europe, Middle East and Africa) HQ is in Ireland and it has country offices in nine countries across Europe, which principally focus on sales to local markets.

You are Dave Brennan, a newly hired financial analyst in the EMEA HQ, reporting to Andrew Doyle, the EMEA head of finance. Since joining Black Swan, you have been working on a project to standardise and improve the reporting pack that each European country sends to EMEA HQ on a monthly basis. This project was initiated in response to an accounting issue in Italy three months ago. As you complete your work, you realise that Black Swan would benefit from implementing a global accounting package sooner rather than later. Your current project is almost finished. It will soon be time to start into something new, so you are not surprised when Andrew calls you into his office on his return from a global finance meeting in San Francisco with the CFO, Rick Stanley.

"Rick has asked me to look into setting up a shared services centre (SSC) for finance for the EMEA region. He is happy with the progress in EMEA to date and feels that there is good long-term growth potential. However, he thinks that an EMEA-wide SSC will provide a better platform to support entry into new countries. Rick wishes to minimise the growth of finance and administration costs, which have been increasing steadily in recent years. So I need you to prepare an outline business case for the proposed SSC (see **Appendix 1**). This should include a high level financial cost–benefit analysis (estimated approximate annual cost savings and indicative implementation costs). It should also include an assessment of the wider business benefits of establishing an SSC and the potential risk factors involved. I want you to prepare the analysis using US$, as this will make it easier for Rick to evaluate.

"In terms of where the SSC should be located, you should consider a couple of options. You should include Ireland as a potential option. There are many SSCs already based in Ireland – these will be important in terms of finding suitably qualified staff. I also think we might be able to secure some grant funding from the IDA/InvestNI to cover staff-training costs. Rick wants us to look at Eastern Europe, too. He has heard that many US companies are setting up there. In fact, he has sent me a recent article from the *Wall Street Times,* which you should read (see **Appendix 2**). I would like you to include Poland as an alternative option in the business case. The choice of location will be a very sensitive issue, particularly with the local heads of finance, so I would like you to cover this in the business case document by outlining the key factors we need to consider in location selection other than cost."

As a starting point, Andrew hands you a file of preliminary data on the current finance operations. Relevant extracts are replicated in **Appendix 1**, together with some notes you took at the meeting. **Appendix 2** contains a copy of the article in the *Wall Street Times.*

"So let's get working on this as I would like to have a draft ready by the middle of next week. If you need anything let me know and remember that this is highly confidential. In general, finance people don't think 'shared services – what a brilliant idea'. They think, 'there goes my job', and start looking for another one."

The next day you start to put together the draft business case report. You note that any tax implications are being handled separately by your tax advisors and can therefore be ignored at this stage.

Appendix 1: Notes from Meeting with Andrew Doyle

Details of current finance data (headcount, costs, salary levels, activities) received from Andrew

	Ireland	England	France	Italy	Poland	Spain	Netherlands	Germany	Sweden	Total
Financial accounting	3	6	5	3	2	3	3	4	3	32
Billing and collections	4	14	15	14	7	9	7	12	8	90
Accounts payable	3	6	6	5	3	5	4	5	3	40
Payroll	2	4	5	4	2	3	3	4	3	30
Statutory accounts	2	2	2	2	2	2	2	2	2	18
Tax and treasury	3	–	–	–	–	–	–	–	–	3
Consolidation	5	–	–	–	–	–	–	–	–	5
Total FTEs*	22	32	33	28	16	22	19	27	19	218
Cost per FTE* US$000	60	68	70	58	45	58	64	64	68	62.67
Total finance cost US$000	1,320	2,176	2,310	1,624	720	1,276	1,216	1,728	1,292	13,662

*FTE – full-time equivalent employee

- In Ireland, EMEA consolidation, tax and treasury activities are performed in addition to the activities listed above. This results in the average cost per finance employee in Ireland being 10% higher than it would otherwise be.
- The accounts are maintained using US GAAP and adjustments are posted to prepare local GAAP accounts for statutory accounting purposes.
- The aim of establishing the SSC is to slim down the country finance functions and migrate as many activities as practical into a single EMEA SSC. It is envisaged that all finance activities will migrate to the SSC, with the exception of statutory accounting, consolidation and tax and treasury, which will remain in Ireland. Based on Andrew's knowledge and experience, headcount savings of about 15% can be achieved in an SSC through economies of scale within financial accounting, billing and collections, accounts payable, and payroll.
- The country finance teams currently use a variety of accounting packages to process accounting transactions. The plan is to implement a single accounting system as part of the SSC implementation in order to facilitate standardisation. It is estimated that this would cost US$0.9 million. External consultancy implementation support would cost an additional US$0.6 million.
- The estimated timeframe for implementation (including systems) is nine months. Each country would be migrated into the SSC on a sequential basis at a rate of one country per month. For each country migration there would be overlap payroll costs of one month's payroll to cover the training of new staff in the new SSC.
- Although existing finance staff would be offered positions in the SSC, it is unlikely that any would decide to relocate. Therefore, new staff would need to be hired for the SCC. The cost of hiring new staff is estimated to be 10% of the SSC's first year payroll.

- Half of the existing finance staff working in finance functions that are to be transferred to the SSC could be redeployed into other areas of the business, but the jobs of the other half would need to be made redundant. Based on average length of service and local redundancy regulations, it is estimated that the redundancy payments would equate to three months' pay using the current average annual salary of US$62,670.
- All other costs associated with the SSC are expected to stay broadly neutral.

Appendix 2: Newspaper Extract from the *Wall Street Times*

Poland – at the heart of Europe (Max Hunter, Warsaw correspondent)

Poland and Ukraine recently completed a successful hosting of the European Soccer Championships. Although neither team had much success on the field of play – both teams were eliminated before the knock-out stages – Poland is enjoying some success on the economic front.

Since the collapse of communism in 1989, Poland has adopted a free-market economy. Although some remnants of Eastern Bloc bureaucracy remain, the country is intent on modernisation. Poland became a member of the European Union in 2004 and has ambitions to join the Eurozone in 2016, if the euro still exists! (The Polish currency is the Zloty, which is worth about 30 US cents.)

The Polish economy has performed better than most of its European neighbours over the past five years, with GDP growth averaging in excess of 4%. With its population of over 38 million and a location in the heart of Europe, Poland is enjoying increasing success in attracting foreign businesses. Many household names have established manufacturing operations in Poland, particularly in the automotive and electronics sectors. With over two million students in higher education, Poland has also attracted some services and outsourcing operations, including IBM, Citigroup and Bank of New York Mellon.

So, for US corporations looking to increase their presence in Europe, Poland is worth considering.

BONEDRI

(Based on Chartered Accountants Ireland, FAE Autumn 2014, Simulation 2)

You are Jack Doyle. You qualified as a chartered accountant two years ago and have recently transferred to the management consulting department of a large accountancy practice. You previously worked in the audit department; however, you were keen to get some broader experience as a platform to getting a job in industry in the future. It is now February 2014.

You have been asked to attend a meeting with Conor Murray, managing director of BoneDri Limited (BoneDri), a successful Irish company that is engaged in the design and manufacture of high-quality outdoor clothing. You have been informed by your partner that Conor has some ideas about expanding the business overseas and he would like a 'fresh pair of eyes' to look at the proposal.

You review the client file and note the following: BoneDri has been a client of the firm since it was set up six years ago and it has been a real success story. It is 100% owned by Conor Murray, who won a prestigious national competition as Entrepreneur of the Year in 2012. (An extract of the article that appeared in the national press in December 2012 is replicated in **Appendix 1**.)

The following day Conor meets you at BoneDri's production facility. After a tour of the factory you get down to business over a coffee in the canteen. Conor highlights where he is looking for input into his proposal.

"The business is performing well but I need to think about the next stage of our development. Within a couple of years we are likely to reach production capacity, so we are considering opening a new production facility in South East Asia. This would also give us a foothold in the Asian market, which I see as having excellent growth potential for our branded products. I went to South East Asia last year as part of a trade mission and visited a number of countries. I am thinking of Bangladesh as a location for the factory. There are a number of textile manufacturers based there and I believe costs are rising significantly in China, so I have ruled out that location option. Therefore, I would like you to give me your considered views on the following.

- The financial implications of such a move and any other key factors that should be considered, i.e. does this make sense or would it be better to increase capacity in Ireland?
- The operational and strategic issues that would need to be considered in operating a large part of our business overseas.
- Having read about the collapse of a factory in Dhaka, Bangladesh, which resulted in over 1,000 workers being killed, needless to say I am concerned about corporate and social responsibility there. Given your firm's extensive network, could you outline in the report the key issues of corporate and social responsibility that I should be concerned about and what we can do about them.

"So to summarise, initially I would like you to prepare a briefing report for me on these matters and get back to me as soon as possible. You will need to meet with David Carson, our operations director, and Imelda Quinn, our finance director. I know from talking to Imelda that she would be interested in your views on how the factory in Bangladesh might be financed. They will provide you with more detailed information and relevant data."

The same day, you meet with David Carson and Imelda Quinn. The meeting notes and comments are included in **Appendices 2** and **3**, respectively.

Appendix 1: Extract from National Newspaper Article – December 2012

Conor Murray of BoneDri wins Entrepreneur of the Year 2012

Conor Murray, managing director of BoneDri, picked up the 11th Entrepreneur of the Year award at a ceremony in The Four Seasons Hotel last night.

BoneDri is that rare thing in Ireland these days, a local innovation-led success story with export potential! It was founded in 2006 by Conor Murray, who owns 100% of the company. BoneDri designs and manufactures stylish, high-quality outdoor wear such as rainwear, base layers, and tee-shirts using the latest synthetic fabrics. BoneDri designs and manufactures product under its own brand for sale in Ireland and the UK and it also manufactures under contract for leading brands, such as Oregon Sports, Ultimate Performance and K2.

BoneDri was set up in Ireland by local man Conor Murray six years ago. "From day one we were focused on designing high-quality, lightweight, comfortable and stylish products for the outdoor enthusiast, which we saw as a rapidly growing segment. We had the best laboratory weather conditions on our doorstep given the changeable weather conditions in Ireland," he joked.

"It was also very important to me to be 'green' in every way possible. Our customers value and recognise that we are an environmentally sound business committed to making our products in a sustainable manner."

BoneDri has grown rapidly in recent years. Revenues exceeded €/£50 million in 2012 on sales of nearly 10 million garments. It now employs over 400 staff at its factory in Ireland and is the major employer in the local town.

Appendix 2: Notes of Meeting with David Carson, Operations Director

Conor and Imelda are keen to further investigate the opening of a factory in Bangladesh. David can understand their perspective and agrees that costs would certainly be lower. The estimates of revenues, production volumes and unit costs are outlined below.

However, cost is not the only consideration: the quality would also have to be right. David would require a team to go out to get the factory running to BoneDri's quality standards. BoneDri's customers are very demanding and are sticklers for on-time delivery.

Consideration would also need to be given to the impact on production staff in Ireland. Increasing production overseas would mean reducing it locally in the short term. Clearly, this would mean layoffs and/or reduced working hours for staff. David has estimated that 50 staff may have to be made redundant, resulting in redundancy costs of about €/£0.5 million. However, there are quite a few things to be considered before taking this approach.

	Notes	2012 actual	2013 actual	2014 forecast	2015	2016	2017	2018
Sales (units – millions)	N1	9.4	10.5	12	13.5	15	16.5	18
Average selling price €/£	N2	5.7	5.5	5.4	5.2	5.0	5.0	5.0
Revenue €/£		53.6	57.8	64.8	70.2	75.0	82.5	90.0
Planned Production								
Ireland (units – millions)	N3	9.4	10.5	8	8.5	9	9.5	10
Bangladesh (units – millions)	N3	–	–	4	5	6	7	8
Unit Cost								
Ireland (with extra shift) €/£	N4	4.4	4.4	4.4	4.5	4.6	4.7	4.9
Bangladesh €/£	N4	n/a	n/a	3.3	3.5	3.7	3.9	4.1

N1 Sales Sales of 9.4 million garments in 2012; expect sales to double to 18 million by 2018.

N2 Sales Price Continually under pressure from major customers to reduce price because of increased competition in this market; average sales price in 2012 was €/£5.70; expect this trend to continue over the coming years but it is hoped to stem the reduction through increased sales of the branded BoneDri product range; expect average sales price to decline to €/£5.0 by 2016 and level off after that.

N3 Production Capacity Production capacity of 12 million units in the Irish factory; anticipated to reach full capacity by the end of 2014; it is for this reason that a facility in Bangladesh is being considered. The new factory should provide additional capacity of 12 million units per annum and could be operational during 2014; it is expected to start production levels at four million units and gradually increase this over the following years. The other option is to put on an extra shift in Ireland, which would give an additional production capacity of six million units per annum. It is estimated that it would cost an extra €/£1 million in 2014 in capital expenditure to modify the Irish factory to put on an extra shift.

N4 Unit Costs Production costs are significantly cheaper in Bangladesh; however, given that BoneDri's major customers are based in Ireland and the UK, although shipping costs would be higher, there would be substantial savings on unit costs. It is worth noting that the differential would likely be eroded over time because of higher wage-rate inflation in developing countries. Unit costs in Ireland are likely to remain reasonably stable over the medium term; however, costs for the extra shift in Ireland would be a little higher than current costs because of shift premiums.

Appendix 3: Comments Made by Imelda Quinn, Finance Director, During Recent Meeting

"I have been saying to Conor for a couple of years that this is the direction we need to take. Costs are significantly cheaper in Asia and every major manufacturer worth its salt has operations there. I am sure David gave you our costings. The savings we can make are significant.

"Generally, when making long-range investment decisions, we look at discounted cash flows. Conor doesn't like to look beyond five years, as he believes that the world is too uncertain to make any reasonable forecasts for more than five years. Typically we use a discount factor of 10%, which is higher than our average borrowing rate. We also tend to ignore tax implications at the initial phase of analysis until we are satisfied that the investment proposal stacks up on its own merits.

"I engaged a local engineering firm to prepare an estimate of the costs of building a facility in Bangladesh. It took a while to get it completed, but it was a comprehensive report. They estimated that the site and construction costs would be US$17 million with a further US$0.5 million in 'planning fees and permits', which they assured me they could get given their connections with local government. David told me that we should factor in an additional US$2 million for the costs of commissioning the factory and getting it operational (note: US$ to €/£ exchange rate is 1.30:1).

"I would be interested in your views on how we should finance this. We currently have €/£5.5 million in bank debt (summarised below) and our other primary source of capital is equity/retained earnings of €/£4.8 million. We are currently generating about €/£3 million per annum in EBITDA. Perhaps you could prepare a brief note for me on our likely options for funding the capital investment and your views on the options."

Schedule of Bank Facilities

Loan	Terms	Facility €/£ million	Balance End 2012 €/£ million
Term loan – Ireland factory	Eight years to end 2016 repayable in equal annual instalments – APR 6%	6.0	3.0
Working capital facility	Revolving facility to be reviewed annually – APR 7%	2.0	2.0
Overdraft facility	To be reviewed annually – APR 9%	0.5	0.5

BOYNE AVIATION LIMITED

(Based on Chartered Accountants Ireland, FAE Autumn 2012, Simulation 1)

You are Ann O'Leary and you work as an assistant management consultant for Blue Consulting (Blue), having recently qualified as a chartered accountant at a large national firm. Blue has recently been engaged by an airline, Boyne Aviation Limited (Boyne), to look at various aspects of its business.

Boyne is an Irish-owned airline that has been operating since 1990. Joe Burke was an operations manager for a large, international airline company in the 1980s. He left this role in 1989 and, together with his brother Mark, started the company. Boyne initially organised charter flights to Mediterranean holiday destinations as well as to overseas sporting events. Mark had gained many years of marketing experience in the family-owned travel agency business, which had been started by his grandfather.

In its first decade of trading Boyne expanded from a flight charter business to a standard airline, offering scheduled services between small airports in Ireland, Great Britain and France. This development reflected the relative higher margins available on scheduled services. Profits on regional routes have benefited from grants available from the Irish Government. These grants are provided on a rolling five-year period; the amounts available are determined by the Government's regional development agenda and the availability of funds. These grants have not been available in the last two years.

After many years of profitable growth and expansion, recent falls in passenger numbers, along with increases in aviation fuel prices, have put a lot of pressure on Boyne's profitability, with losses arising in 2011 and 2012. Boyne has been discounting its fares to try and maintain acceptable load factors. In particular, the Irish low-cost carrier Lion Air, together with the economic downturn, has adversely impacted on customer-buying patterns. Increasing numbers of customers are displaying price sensitivity and opting for lower-cost services.

Boyne is proud of the full service experience it has offered its passengers since 1990. This has enabled it to achieve a high level of customer loyalty and repeat business. It has maintained good relations with travel agents through whom most of its flights are booked. The airline has an excellent safety record. Historically, it has made effective use of its fleet with sub-leases of planes being offered in off-peak times to increase utilisation. However, Boyne has not been able to sub-lease planes in the past two years.

Your boss, Derek Trimble, has recently met with Joe Burke and James Murphy (Boyne's finance director). They discussed the various challenges facing the business and, in particular, how Blue could help Boyne to improve its performance both operationally and financially.

Derek has requested that you work with him on this assignment, knowing that you were involved in the audit of other airlines at the chartered accountancy practice where you qualified. Derek hands you a file (see extracts in **Appendix 1**) and asks you to review the data and draft a report on the performance of Boyne for the past two years and compare it to industry key performance indicators (KPIs). **Appendix 1** contains the management accounts for Boyne, along with a report summarising recent European airline performance, including a section on industry best practice KPIs.

In addition, Derek asks you to consider what Boyne would have to do to change its business model if it were to move from being a full-service airline to a low-cost operator. He suggests you outline your thoughts on this in the form of a briefing paper suitable for consideration by Boyne's board. In preparing this briefing paper, Derek indicates that you should consider what a low-cost operation's results and KPIs might look like if the identified low-cost operator KPIs were applied to Boyne's 2012 accounts. He suggests proceeding on the assumption that reducing average revenue per passenger to €/£100 would increase the load factor to 75%. Furthermore, Derek notes that these low-cost operators are generating operating margins of about 10%.

On completion of the meeting with Derek, you get some coffee on the way back to your desk and begin reading the file.

Appendix 1

Key Performance Indicators for Top Three Low-cost Airlines in Europe

Staff costs as % of revenue	21%
Average cost per employee (€/£)	40,000
Fuel costs as % of revenue	23%
Other operational costs as % of revenue*	24%
Airport costs as % of revenue	22%
Average revenue per passenger (€/£)	100
Average load factor	75%
Passengers per employee	2,000
Employees per aircraft	40

*Other operational costs include aircraft depreciation and maintenance.

Boyne Aviation Limited
Income Statement (Summary)
for the 12 months to June

	2011 €/£000	2012 €/£000
Revenue	66,120	65,653
Staff Costs	15,960	17,000
Fuel Costs	19,000	19,000
Other Operational Costs	18,000	17,900
Airport Costs	15,500	15,000
	68,460	68,900
Operating Profit/(Loss)	−2,340	−3,247

Boyne Aviation Limited
Key Performance Indicators

	2011	2012
Passenger numbers	580,000	581,000
Employees	380	400
Number of aircraft	9	9
Revenue per passenger (€/£)	114	113
Load factor	65%	65%
Average costs per employee (€/£)	42,000	42,500
Passengers per employee	1,526	1,453
Employees per aircraft	42	44
Revenue per aircraft (€/£000)	7,347	7,295

CANAM INC

(Based on Chartered Accountants Ireland, FAE Autumn 2014, Simulation 3)

You are Alan Hughes, a management accountant working for Martha Kramer, vice president of finance and head of the finance team in Europe for Canam Inc (Canam). Canam is a US NASDAQ-quoted corporation headquartered in San Diego. It is engaged in the development, manufacture and sale of cancer diagnostic devices and equipment and had revenues of US$400 million in 2012. It sells its products mainly to hospitals and medical centres through its locally-based sales offices and subsidiaries.

Canam has its European headquarters in Ireland. It was set up three years ago to manage the company's expansion into European markets. During a hectic three years, Canam has set up local subsidiaries in major European countries to penetrate local healthcare markets, which for the most part are dominated by State-owned/State-funded healthcare providers. All products are sourced from the parent company and shipped into a central warehouse in Ireland prior to being shipped to customers across Europe.

It is January 2014 and Martha calls you into her office. "Hi Alan, I have two pieces of work I want you to help me with. First, I want to share with you the details of a finance project I am seriously considering. I have decided that we should bite the bullet and implement a single enterprise IT system for Europe. As you know, following the opening of offices in Italy and the Netherlands this year – both of which have performed very well – we currently have eight subsidiaries across Europe. With sales going so well, our US headquarters is looking at opening offices in a further six countries in Europe over the next two years. The longer we leave it, the more difficult and costly it will be to implement a new IT system. I have spoken to our Global CFO, Jeff Welsh, and he is behind the idea in principle and has given me the go ahead to do some preliminary work.

"I would like you to prepare a brief memo for me with an initial list of our key requirements, which we can incorporate into a 'Request for Proposal' to be issued to a number of software vendors. The financial controllers from our European subsidiaries were in town this week for a meeting. I took the opportunity to discuss this matter with them and hear their views on issues with the current system and what their key requirements from any new system would be. Could you also include in the memo your assessment of the key challenges in implementing the system and what actions we could take to mitigate these issues – a summary table will suffice."

Martha continues, "Secondly, I need to prepare a memo for Jeff Welsh on the performance of Canam Europe for 2013. Overall, I thought we performed well. Growth was fantastic but gross margin was below expectations. It's difficult to get visibility on gross margin until year-end because of customer rebates and discounts. Could you look at the numbers and prepare a draft memo? Keep it brief. You might also pick up some useful information from the notes from my meeting with the financial controllers. One final point: in the memo could you also include your thoughts on what, if any, additional KPIs we should include in our performance scorecard in the future? We can then build this into the requirements for the new IT system. Thanks, Alan."

You spend the rest of the day reviewing the financial data and notes you received from Martha (**Appendices 1** and **2** respectively), and you begin to prepare the two memos for her. You agree with Martha that the time is right to implement a single enterprise IT system for Europe. Each of the subsidiaries currently uses a different accounting package. Italy does all accounting and analysis on spreadsheets, while France's accounting is outsourced to a small local firm. In the beginning this meant that subsidiaries got up and running quickly, but the disparate systems are proving to be a hindrance now. It is already a nightmare doing the consolidation, and in particular getting intercompany accounts to net out. Getting reliable revenue forecasts is also problematic, not to mention doing any serious analysis on customer/product profitability. Expenses are classified differently across subsidiaries, making meaningful comparison impossible. In spite of the effort involved in implementation, you look forward to getting a system that is fit for purpose and can grow with Canam.

Appendix 1: Canam Europe Performance Scorecard 2013

	Actual 2013	Budget 2013	Prior Year 2012
Revenue (US$000)	61,400	60,000	45,600
Gross profit (US$000)	29,500	31,000	25,100
Gross margin %	*48%*	*52%*	*55%*
Operating expenses (US$000)	18,400	18,000	15,800
Operating expenses (% of revenue)	*30%*	*30%*	*35%*
Net profit	**11,100**	**13,000**	**9,300**
Net profit (% of rev)	***18%***	***22%***	***20%***
Headcount at year-end	180	165	125
Average payroll cost per employee (US$000)	64.2	61.0	62.0
Customer numbers	140	120	68
Average US$/€ exchange rate	1.30	1.40	1.40

Appendix 2: Meeting Notes – Comments by Financial Controllers From European Subsidiaries

- Currently there is no facility to keep track of monthly revenue forecasts made by account managers and to compare them with actual revenues made. (**Note:** account managers are responsible for sales to, and relationship management of, customers. They report to country managers.)
- Currently there is no facility for customers to make orders or to make payments online. Tracking shipments from the US and the central warehouse in Ireland is difficult.
- The sales team keeps its own records of customer information, including contact details, which are often different from those that we maintain in the system. This was an issue for us as a number of our key sales staff left us during the year. Customers were not happy about having to 're-educate' our people on their operations and requirements.
- Currently we can't get detailed analysis of revenues or expenses, which we need to answer queries from the country manager or from Martha Kramer at month-end.
- Customers often dispute invoices, saying that they were promised special discounts by the account managers. There are so many different discounts/allowances and promotions, which change frequently. It's not clear to me what the approval process is. Sometimes we have difficulty in controlling discounts given to customers by account managers because frequently no written record is kept. This has resulted in a number of complaints by customers, not to mention the need for late adjustments at year-end to book additional discounts and allowances.
- Although we haven't had many bad debts to date, I am concerned that this might not be the case in the future as we don't have up-to-date credit limits. This year we doubled our customer base and, with further expansion into new markets, having current credit limits will be vital.
- For 2013, a number of intercompany invoices came in after the year-end that we hadn't accrued for because we had no record of the purchase order. This arose on purchases of the new mobile diagnostic model that was introduced in September. The product was a major success, contributing about US$5 million in sales in the final quarter – although the introductory discount of 30% undoubtedly helped!
- Sales team expense claims are manual and the supporting receipts often go missing. There are also frequent delays in approval and processing, which causes grief from the sales team.

- Currency is an issue. All intercompany invoices are denominated in US Dollars (US$), whereas our sales prices are set in euros (€). We need to report to corporate in US$, whereas we need to prepare statutory accounts in €.
- Preparation of local statutory accounts is cumbersome, with many adjustments required to management accounts.
- We need to ensure implementation doesn't deflect staff from sales activity.
- Will additional resources be made available to support the implementation? Will head office bear all costs of implementation?

EUROHUB

(Based on Chartered Accountants Ireland, FAE Autumn 2013, Simulation 2)

You are Jack Collins, a newly promoted manager working in the advisory services department of a large accounting firm, PDQ. Your firm has been engaged by EuroHub, a small growing Irish private company, to perform an 'operational review' of the business.

The engagement partner, Nathalie Fox, calls you into her office to brief you on the engagement and your role: "Hi Jack, congratulations on your promotion to manager! It is well deserved.

"As you know, we are extremely busy at the moment. We have recently won a project with a new client, EuroHub. Although EuroHub is a relatively small company, it is growing rapidly and performing well. It has three separate lines of business (LOBs), namely: LOB 1 Customer Support; LOB 2 E-commerce Order Fulfilment; and LOB 3 Electronic Contract Manufacturing Services. It was established in 1996 to take advantage of the opening up of the Single European Market and has grown steadily over the years. The growth in internet sales over the past five years has been particularly advantageous to EuroHub."

Nathalie continues, "EuroHub is privately owned. John Stapleton owns 65% of the shares, the three LOB managers own 5% each and 20% was recently acquired by a venture capital company for €/£2 million to fund the expansion of their business within the Chinese market.

As EuroHub is at a crossroads in its growth cycle, John felt that it would be a good idea to get an independent view of the business and has asked PDQ to perform an operational review of EuroHub. John mentioned that he has focused his time on developing and expanding the business over the last few years and has not spent much time on internal IT systems. However, he does feel that EuroHub may have outgrown its management information systems. Although EuroHub now has three LOBs, the financial performance data is combined, which can make it difficult to analyse each LOB. John also mentioned that he tends to focus on revenues and revenue growth, as he knows each of the LOBs earns a good margin. You should meet with EuroHub's financial controller, Kate Carson, to get more detailed information (see **Appendix 1** for notes of the meeting with Kate).

"Also, as I mentioned earlier, a venture capital company has recently invested €/£2 million in EuroHub to fund growth opportunities with Chinese companies. As a result, EuroHub has recently had a number of enquiries from Chinese manufacturers seeking to establish an online presence in the European market. These companies are particularly interested in having a base in Europe to manage sales orders, logistics and customer service. John is interested in our ideas on how EuroHub might target the Chinese market.

"So to summarise on what I would like you to do:
- briefly analyse the performance of the three LOBs from a financial perspective and highlight any relevant insights you may have;
- develop some preliminary recommendations on performance management within EuroHub (performance measures, systems changes, incentives); and
- outline any of the potential options open to EuroHub to develop a presence within the Chinese market (market entry strategy) and develop a preliminary recommendation on the best way forward."

Nathalie concludes, "I would like you to draft the relevant sections of the report dealing with the above areas by next week and let me know if you have any problems or need help. Thanks, Jack."

Appendix 1: Extract from Notes of Meeting with Kate Carson, Financial Controller of EuroHub

- Summary management accounts for 2012 (and comparative 2011 figures) are outlined below. EuroHub uses an 'off the shelf' accounting package for small and medium-sized companies. It has basic functionality (including general ledger, invoicing, payments, payroll, e-banking) and it has been broadly sufficient for EuroHub's needs. The biggest limitation is that it does not allow transactions to be separately analysed in terms of the different LOBs, but Kate believes this is available as an upgrade.

	2012 €/£000	2011 €/£000
Revenue	10,400	8,700
Cost of sales		
Direct labour	(3,800)	(3,000)
Direct materials	(800)	(720)
Transport	(2,400)	(2,080)
Total cost of sales	(7,000)	(5,800)
Gross margin	3,400	2,900
Operating expenses		
Administration salaries	(540)	(500)
LOB manager salaries	(240)	(240)
LOB manager bonuses	(105)	–
Telecoms	(240)	(200)
Rent and rates	(720)	(720)
Depreciation machinery and equipment	(290)	(290)
Bad debts	(60)	(20)
Interest expense	(100)	(100)
Other expenses	(140)	(130)
Total operating expenses	(2,435)	(2,200)
Profit before tax	965	700
Tax	(110)	(85)
Profit after tax	855	615

- Financial information is accumulated on a company-wide basis. However, revenues and headcount details are tracked separately for each of EuroHub's three LOBs. Details are as follows:

	Revenue 2012 €/£000	*Revenue* *2011* *€/£000*	Growth %	Headcount 2012	Avg. salary 2012 €/£
LOB 1 Customer support	2,100	*1,000*	110%	60	27,500
LOB 2 E-commerce order fulfilment	5,100	*4,100*	24%	30	35,000
LOB 3 Electronic contract manufacturing service	3,200	*3,600*	–11%	25	44,000
Total	10,400	*8,700*	20%	115	

- Last year EuroHub appointed a separate manager for each LOB to ensure there was a sharper focus on each of the LOBs. John thinks this has made a big difference and revenue for 2012 was up 20% overall on 2011. The growth in LOB 1 has been particularly strong, and has more than doubled during the year. The LOB 2 manager is a very strong salesman and he has won a large contract from a US company, although I think we priced it very competitively. LOB 3 had lower revenues in 2012 as this business tends to be uneven.

- EuroHub has a base of just over 100 customers in total. LOB 2 is the most mature business and has 75 customers headquartered in Europe and the US. LOB 1 has grown quickly and now has 25 customers. EuroHub also provides e-commerce order fulfilment services to one or two of these LOB 1 customers. In 2012 LOB 3 had five customers. John thinks there is an opportunity to sell more of our services to our customers in each LOB and this is something we have been encouraging the LOB managers to do.
- All transport costs relate to LOB 2 and direct materials relate to LOB 3.
- Each of the LOB managers is paid €/£80,000. There is also a bonus incentive scheme in operation whereby they are paid 5% of new revenues won during the year within their own LOB. Not all the LOB managers are happy with this system. Each manager also has been given a 5% equity stake as a long-term incentive.
- EuroHub operates from a single site, which contains factory, warehouse and office space. The allocation of space is approximately 20%/30%/40% for LOB 1/LOB 2/LOB 3 respectively. The remaining space (10%) is used by administration staff.
- EuroHub has plant and equipment with a net book value (NBV) of €/£2.9 million, which is being depreciated at a rate of 10% per annum on a straight-line basis. The majority (€/£2 million) relates to plant and equipment for LOB 3. The remaining assets are spread evenly between LOB 1, LOB 2 and administration.
- Approximately 5% of the telecom costs relate to administrative office usage. The remaining 95% is split 50% for LOB 1 and 45% for LOB 2.

Accounts receivable at the end of 2012 amounted to €/£1,665,000, of which €/£230,000 related to LOB 1, €/£1,120,000 related to LOB 2 and €/£315,000 related to LOB 3. One of the LOB 1 customers went into liquidation in 2012, resulting in a bad debt of €/£60,000 that has been fully provided for at year-end.

HUGHES ENGINEERING LIMITED

(Based on Chartered Accountants Ireland, FAE Autumn 2013, Simulation 3)

You are Ciara Lennon, a financial accountant working with Hughes Engineering Limited (Hughes), an Irish engineering company engaged in the design, manufacture and installation of specialist components for agri-business processing plants in Ireland and continental Europe. Hughes was set up by Ger Hughes 10 years ago.

You joined Hughes last year after you qualified as a chartered accountant, as you were keen to get more commercial experience. You have not been disappointed. Since you joined Hughes the company has won a number of international contracts and you have been involved in contract pricing as well as the routine monthly close cycle.

Ger has recently returned from a government-led trade mission to the Middle East and calls you into his office for a briefing meeting with the operations director, Mark Naughton, who accompanied Ger on the mission. "What a trip," Ger begins. "There's no recession in the Middle East. Usually when I go on these trips I hope to build some contacts for the future. On this trip Mark and I got talking to the CEO of Arabian Dairy Processing Company (ADP), the largest dairy processing company in the Middle East. He told us that ADP is looking to increase capacity and is planning to build a large new plant in the Middle East to cater for this increase in capacity. To cut a long story short, the CEO invited us to submit a bid to supply and install specialised machinery for ADP's new plant. This is a fantastic opportunity for us to break into the Middle East market.

"The bid is due in six weeks so we haven't got a lot of time. Ciara, I need you to start working on this. Mark will provide you with all the details you need. We understand that it will be a very competitive tender process, with some big players from Germany and France interested. Given that the contract provides us with the opportunity to break into a new market with growth potential, I will need you to calculate the most competitive price range for the bid. This should range from (a) the lowest price we could bid to break-even to (b) the price we could bid to maintain our normal profit margins on manufacturing and installation. Please include these in a briefing document for me, together with your perspective on the practical issues we would need to consider in carrying out the project if we were successful with the bid."

That afternoon you meet with Mark to get his perspective on the estimated costs to carry out the project. You like working with Mark. For an engineer he is not too technical and understands the needs of finance people! Your notes from the conversation are contained in **Appendix 1**.

Later you meet Ger who tells you, "I bumped into our bank manager last night at a Chamber of Commerce function. I updated him on our trading performance and prospects. In fact, I mentioned that we had a great opportunity in the Middle East. He asked me if we have sufficient finance. To be honest, I wasn't 100% sure and said I would look into it. So could you include in the briefing document an approximate estimate of how much funding we would need for the Middle East project if we were successful with the bid and an outline of the potential financing options. Oh and one last thing! ADP would like the bid to be priced in US\$. The current exchange rate is €/£1 = US\$1.25. I want to make sure we don't get exposed to any FX risk on this. Could you also include a piece in the briefing document on how we might manage any exposure?"

You set to work on the document immediately.

Appendix 1: Notes from Meeting with Mark Naughton on the ADP Bid

- The contract includes the manufacture and installation of specialist machinery to be used in a new dairy processing plant in the Middle East. The manufacture, installation and completion of the project is estimated to take 24 months.
- Specialist components will be manufactured at our plant in Ireland. The manufacture and delivery of the machinery will take six months. The cost of direct materials required for the manufacturing is estimated to be €/£900,000. Direct labour and direct overhead will be incurred at the same levels for this contract as incurred in 2012.

- Installation will be complex. It will mean four engineers on-site full-time for the first 12 months and six engineers for the final six months. A contract project manager will need to be hired for the duration of the installation as we have no spare capacity at the moment. Contract project managers are usually available for €/£90,000 per annum. Out-of-pocket costs for overseas staff (travel, accommodation and related expenses) usually amount to about €/£200 per day.
- The contract is at a fixed price. Final payment will be made when the contract has been certified by ADP engineers on completion. However, a payment on account of 30% will be made when the order is placed and a further 30% after 12 months.
- A summary income statement for 2012 is set out below. Hughes operates two revenue and cost centres:
  - engineering and manufacturing; and
  - installation and servicing.

Hughes Engineering Limited
INCOME STATEMENT (SUMMARY)
for the year ended 31 December 2012

	Engineering and manufacturing €/£000	Installation and servicing €/£000	Total €/£000
Revenue	26,250	6,125	32,375
Direct materials	(6,300)	–	(6,300)
Direct labour	(7,875)	(3,750)	(11,625)
Direct overhead	(4,725)	–	(4,725)
Plant depreciation	(2,100)	–	(2,100)
Cost of sales	(21,000)	(3,750)	(24,750)
Gross margin	5,250	2,375	7,625
SGA expenses			(3,990)
Interest			(360)
Profit before tax			3,275
Tax			(380)
Profit after tax			2,895

Notes
1. Hughes has 215 employees (125 in the engineering and manufacturing division, 50 in installation and servicing and 40 in administration). For busy periods, Hughes has access to a pool of contract labour that is paid the same average wage rate as existing engineering and manufacturing employees.
2. Approximately two-thirds of direct materials are sourced from European-based suppliers (denominated in €/£). The remaining one-third of direct materials is sourced from US suppliers (credit terms – payment in US$ on receipt).
3. Direct overhead principally includes: factory rent, consumables, power, light and heat, insurance, rates and freight costs.
4. Installation and servicing employees are normally charged to clients on a daily basis at a rate of €/£700 per day. Employee working days are 250 days per annum.
5. Selling, general and administration (SGA) expenses principally include salaries for administration employees (marketing, finance, HR and IT), telecom costs, office rent and rates.
6. Hughes has a revolving working capital facility of €/£6 million, which incurs interest at a rate of 6% per annum.

KEBABS LTD

(Based on Chartered Accountants Ireland, FAE Autumn 2010, Simulation 1)

You are a chartered accountant working as a strategy consultant for BS Consultants (BSC), a business consultancy. You are summoned to the office of your boss, Maria Rooney. She advises that you are to be assigned to assist a client: Kebabs Ltd (Kebabs). Kebabs is facing some performance measurement challenges and is considering an overseas investment.

She states: "As you know, Kebabs is an Irish fast-food restaurant chain. I understand from our client that the recent performance of the group has been somewhat disappointing. We are due to meet with Michael Courtney, the managing director, next week to discuss ways in which the current performance management system might be developed (to include a scorecard or similar) to assist in monitoring performance." Maria says that perhaps Kebabs has lost its way and is sending a confused message to its customers.

She adds: "In particular, I want you to identify relevant performance measures on key areas of its operations. You might also consider if the measures in use are adequately aligned to the business's strategy and also whether the non-financial measures available are adequate. Any suggestions for improvement as well as an indication of limitations will be appreciated by our client, though at this stage we will wish to have an outline of proposed measures to be used in the future."

She finishes by saying: "Look, you know my style. Let's get the structure and layout right with any detail as an appendix. We can sit down early next week and review what you have prepared." She then hands over a bundle of documents relevant to Kebabs and extracts from its management accounts and business plans (replicated in **Appendix 1** and **Appendix 2**).

You return to your desk and start reading the documentation. You note the importance attached by Kebabs to environmental issues and realise this warrants particular consideration in your proposal. Just as you are getting into the detail of the documents, Maria gives you a call. "Michael has phoned to ask if he can call in and talk through an investment opportunity. He's been keen to expand for some time and this opportunity has arisen in Germany. As you're going to be involved with Kebabs anyway, I think you should join the meeting and complete the initial evaluation of the project opportunity."

Later, at the meeting with Michael Courtney, he provides some background on the possible expansion into Germany. He notes that, "Kebabs is considering entering the German market, possibly through the acquisition of a local fast-food chain. The ideas are at an early stage with the expectation that any acquisition would be kitted out with the Irish company's livery (adapted as appropriate to German and local needs)."

You comment that the German fast-food market has grown substantially over the last few years and within that kebabs are the most popular fast-food item. However, the kebab market is primarily serviced by owner-managed small outlets. You express an opinion that a branded chain of kebab shops with a standardised offering in a more modern style environment might well appeal to a larger section of the German population. Little did you think that your late night visits to kebab shops at the Munich Beer Fest all those years ago would someday be relevant in your working life!

At the end of the meeting with Michael you agreed to prepare a short memorandum that outlines the possible market entry routes that might be considered in entering the German market and a brief assessment of key issues that may arise and how these might be addressed.

Appendix 1: Background on Kebabs Ltd prepared by Maria Rooney

Michael Courtney formed Kebabs Ltd in 1992. This followed his completion of an MBA at a local university. During his studies he had travelled to Turkey and saw the popularity of kebabs and related fast-food as a niche to be explored. His first restaurant opened in late 1992. Additional restaurants followed and there is now a chain of 25 restaurants all over the island of Ireland.

The restaurant format is a simple one. Customers have a choice of kebab offerings with a variety of seasonings. A range of additional offerings, including chips, breads and soft drinks, supplement this. From the start the company has prided itself on offering an innovative menu at reasonable prices. All offerings are branded and trademarks are used wherever possible.

The company has an in-house innovation team that combines seasoning and sauces from around the world. The recent launch of a kebab with a guacamole sauce was a great hit. The innovation has resulted in the company being recognised by Food Ireland, a government agency responsible for promoting the food industry generally. A number of awards have been received by the company since it was launched.

Cleanliness and hygiene are key and the restaurants are maintained to a high standard. Michael Courtney has been known to comment that the water consumption at his restaurants is very high, which ensures that they are very hygienic.

As with many fast-food restaurants the product comes in a series of polystyrene and other wrapping, all branded with the Kebabs name. This has given rise to some adverse comments from local environmental groups as not being sustainable. Litter in the environs of some restaurants has given rise to some restaurants being labelled litter 'black spots'. Michael is adamant that the format he has established is consistent with the provision of hygienic food.

Each restaurant has a manager who is responsible for all aspects of the operation. Initially each restaurant was operated on standardised lines, but over time each has been given greater autonomy in an effort to have greater responsiveness to customers and local conditions. This autonomy has been supported by the gathering of standard monthly performance data for each restaurant and comparing them on a number of key measures. (Additional information is available in **Appendix 2**.)

Extracts from the company's strategic plan (prepared in late 2009) include the following key goals for the group in 2010:
- increase margins in each restaurant by 2%;
- reduce returns by customers by 10% over rates in 2009; and
- maintain the high quality of the food.

The possible overseas expansion was not mentioned in the plan and I suspect that this idea has only emerged over recent months.

Appendix 2: Financial Performance Summary and Extract Prepared by Maria Rooney from Kebabs Ltd

MANAGEMENT ACCOUNTS AND SUMMARY FINANCIAL INFORMATION

Kebabs' financial performance in its first few years has been strong. Its rapid expansion did cause some initial cash flow problems, though these were resolved in 1998 with an investment by a local venture capitalist.

Summarised extracts from the most recent years are (all figures are €/£ millions):

Year	2006	2007	2008	2009
Turnover	19.1	21.6	23.2	22.8
Gross profit	6.3	7.5	7.8	7.2
Net profit	3.7	4.1	4.0	3.5

In recent years the performance has been impacted by increased local competition from pizza chains and burger outlets. Competitors have responded to the economic difficulties by reducing their prices and these have proven to be popular with their customers.

Kebabs monitors the performance of each restaurant and an example of the typical monthly evaluation data is provided in the following table (data for month of June 2010, the latest month for which such information is available):

	Restaurant X	Restaurant Y
Location	City centre	Regional town
Financial information:		
	€/£000	**€/£000**
Monthly turnover	85	62
Food purchases	32	22
Packaging used	2	3
Labour costs	18	16
Other direct overheads	3	2
Gross margin	**30**	**19**
Rent	10	5
Other expenses	5	4
Net profit	**15**	**10**
Cash generated	16	11
Capital employed	220	195
Other information:		
Number of meals served	10,520	8,350
Restaurant area	210 sq metres	160 sq metres
Purchases rejected	0.5%	2%
Wastage	5%	2%
Water consumed	150,000 litres	120,000 litres
% of time opened (Note 1)	85%	95%
Customer satisfaction rating	60%	65%
New offerings (year to date)	2	1
Average lead time to introduce new offering	3 months	1 month

Note 1: the restaurants remain open for about 16 hours per day on average.

NATURAL FOOD COMPANY

(Based on Chartered Accountants Ireland, FAE Autumn 2013, Simulation 1)

You are Barry Forde, a chartered accountant who qualified with an accounting firm in Ireland and later transferred to its Boston office. Last year you left the accounting firm to join one of the firm's fastest growing clients, Natural Food Company (Natural Food) as a business development manager. You report directly to Bob Tierney, senior vice president for strategy and corporate affairs, and your main job is to identify and evaluate potential acquisition targets.

Natural Food is quoted on the NASDAQ exchange and, based on its latest financial results (2012), had revenues of US$1.2 billion and profits of US$70 million. Natural Food is a leading natural and organic food company, with operations in the US and Canada. Natural Food has multiple brands and a consumer focus on health, wellness and nutrition. According to its website, Natural Food is "committed to implementing environmentally sound business practices and manufacturing processes". Natural Food is looking to buy a business in the UK or Ireland in order to expand its international footprint and is particularly keen on extending its organic product range.

You have just completed a whirlwind two-day trip to Ireland to have a look at a potential acquisition target, Artisan Food Company Limited (AFC). During the trip you met with AFC's founders and joint-managing directors, Kate Doyle and Jen Crowley. You were very impressed with Kate and Jen as they created AFC from scratch. Although quite different in personality, both Kate and Jen were engaging, enthusiastic and very knowledgeable about their niche segment. You also met with AFC's chairman, Dan Buggy, a retired bank manager and a friend of Jen's father. You would like to have visited one or two of AFC's suppliers, but unfortunately that was not possible on this trip.

As you sit in your comfortable business-class seat on the flight back to Boston you prepare to write your report. You gather together your meeting notes from your trip (**Appendix 1**) and summary financial information (**Appendix 2**).

As always, there are two things you need to cover in your reports to Bob: (a) a financial assessment of the target company, noting whether it meets the criteria set by Natural Food, and (b) an assessment of the acquisition target against Natural Food's strategic scorecard (**Appendix 3**). You also note to yourself before you start that Bob is a stickler for concise reports with clear recommendations.

Appendix 1: Meeting Notes on Artisan Food Company

Background Information on AFC

- AFC is a successful Irish company engaged in making and selling a range of chilled, ready-made food products such as soups and health snacks. Based in Ireland, it was set up eight years ago by two college friends, Kate Doyle and Jen Crowley. Kate is the driver behind food quality and product development, whereas Jen has a flair for marketing, having previously worked for a multinational food company as a brand manager.
- It is jointly owned 75% by Jen and Kate, 5% by the chairman Dan Buggy, and the remaining 20% by Enterprise Ireland/Invest NI, which invested in AFC three years ago to help it expand its product range.
- AFC mainly sells under its own brand and its products are distributed through most major food retailers and convenience stores in Ireland.
- AFC employs 20 people in sales, marketing, order-fulfilment and research. Manufacturing is outsourced to a small number of local suppliers.

Meeting with Jen/Kate to Discuss Sales Trends and Product Developments

1. **Soups**
   - Soups are where AFC started. Kate managed to source some fantastic local organic suppliers and started making soups from a rented kitchen. After five years the production was outsourced to a local food-processing company to allow for the focus on sales and promotion.
   - "The brand has gone from strength to strength and we are now the No. 1 independent producer of organic soups in Ireland."
   - In early 2013 AFC was contracted by a German discount supermarket to produce an own-brand soup for its 'luxury' label in Ireland. The consumer response has been favourable and, based on sales for the first quarter of 2013, AFC expects annual revenues to be €/£2 million from this contract.
   - According to Jen, "We are very excited about this development because it may give us a platform to extend this arrangement to mainland Europe. However, they know how to drive a bargain; our gross margin on this contract will only be 50% of our 2012 gross margin on our branded product. Inevitably there will be some cannibalisation of sales, but so far it looks like this will only be about 10% of revenues of our branded product."

2. **Health Snacks**
   - This range is performing strongly and generates a good margin. We expect sales to increase by approximately 25% in 2013 but, at the same time, would expect costs to stay in line with 2012 figures.

3. **New Products**
   - There is nothing else in the sales pipeline for 2013, but AFC continues to develop products for the future. AFC continues to invest in research and development (R&D) and there have been some early thoughts on introducing a 'Simply Italian Range' in 2014. Kate commented that, "It is early days, but we hope to carry out some consumer and market research later this year. Our research programme is important to us. It has served us well to date. We generally budget to spend 1% of revenues on R&D."

Meeting with Chairman, Dan Buggy

- "AFC is a great little business. There has been quite a bit of interest in AFC from a few large food companies. However, at this stage in our growth cycle, we think that there may be merit in joining forces with the right large player with global reach and the resources to promote our brands. We would possibly be interested in offers in the €/£5 million price region."
- "Jen and Kate are very dynamic ladies and have really put everything into AFC's development. They are very 'hands on' and are involved in all aspects of the business. At times they were getting stretched, so about a year ago AFC hired a general manager from one of the major Irish food companies, but sadly that didn't work out and the general manager has taken a claim against AFC on the grounds of constructive dismissal. AFC's legal advisors don't think there is much chance of it succeeding, but a provision of €/£60,000 has been included in the 2012 accounts."
- "We think that the recent industry issue of food traceability will be positive for us given our focus on high-quality organic ingredients. Consumers are becoming much more aware of food quality and provenance. One of our suppliers is being investigated by the Food Safety Authority, but we think it's just a routine check. They have informed us that the results of the investigation will be out next month. We have conducted our own testing and the results have been excellent with no issues arising. So we are not concerned."

Appendix 2

Artisan Food Company Limited
SELECTED FINANCIAL INFORMATION
year ended 31 December 2012

	€/£000
Revenue	4,800
Cost of sales	(3,300)
Gross profit	**1,500**
Sales and marketing costs	(520)
Administration expenses	(360)
Research and development costs	(50)
Operating profit	**570**
Finance costs	(75)
Profit before tax	**495**
Tax	(62)
Profit after tax	**433**

ANALYSIS OF REVENUE AND GROSS PROFIT
for 2012

	Soup	**Health Snacks**	**Total**
Revenue (€/£000)	3,600	1,200	4,800
Gross profit (€/£000)	1,080	420	1,500
Gross margin (%)	30%	35%	31.25%

Appendix 3

Natural Food Company
STRATEGIC SCORECARD (EXTRACT)
(Senior VP, Strategy and Corporate Affairs) – June 2013

Item/issue	Strategic Importance (H/M/L)	Current Status
Strategic position		
1. Industry consolidation – independent producers are being acquired by large food companies for scale efficiencies.	H	Monitoring merger and acquisition activity within the sector.
2. Natural Food is looking to expand its operations in developed markets and, in particular, North America and Europe.	H	Natural Food has an active programme in place to identify potential targets.
Strategic options		
1. Launch existing products into new markets.	M	Under review.
2. Enter new markets through acquisition or through joint venture (selection criteria: (a) maximum price to be paid – P/E multiple 10 times 'normalised earnings'; (b) strong growth potential; (c) strong local market positioning).	H	US$50 million acquisition made in France in January 2013. Currently being integrated into Natural Food.
Strategic risks		
1. Reputational damage to brands from food-contamination scares.	H	Continuous programme of quality assurance and testing procedures.
2. Increased focus on high-quality, 'own brand' fresh/chilled products by supermarket chains.	M	Continuing to invest in the promotion and marketing of Natural Food brands.
3. Management stretch/overreach.	H	Under review. May need to recruit a VP for Europe.

PILLAR BANK PLC

(Based on Chartered Accountants Ireland, FAE Autumn 2014, Simulation 1)

You are Lucy Kenny, a project financial accountant working for Declan Mullen, the finance director for Pillar Bank Plc based in Ireland.

Pillar Bank Plc (the Bank) is a large Irish bank engaged in retail banking. Its recent history has been troubled to say the least. It has racked up operating losses in each of the past three years because of credit losses on its loan book, which resulted in it being taken over by the State. Twelve months ago, the Bank hired a new chief executive from a Canadian bank, who is on a mission to shake things up and bring the bank back to profitability. One of the key initiatives being undertaken is an enterprise-wide restructuring programme. As part of this programme, many aspects of the Bank's activities are being looked at (see **Appendix 1** for a recent press statement from the new CEO).

Earlier today, Declan called you into his office. "The new CEO has gone mad on this cost reduction agenda. It's not as if we hadn't taken costs out before he came on board. We haven't hired anyone in three years because of the recruitment embargo and with all the retirements and departures we are now short-staffed in a number of departments! Anyway, one of the options he wants the Bank to look at is outsourcing back-office functions to a third-party provider. He told me that most banks in North America use outsourcing extensively.

"Ken Byrne, the Head of Operations, and I have had early discussions on the suitability of certain activities for outsourcing. Ken is not keen on outsourcing. Apparently about 10 years ago, before I joined, the Bank entered into an outsourcing contract for IT development and it was a mess. Staff complained about IT response times and it ended up costing more than originally budgeted. Quite frankly, it nearly cost Ken his job. Ken has given me an internal memo that one of his team prepared on this issue about three months ago." Declan hands you a copy of the memo (see **Appendix 2**).

Declan continues, "Also, last week I met with the CEO of Beta Solutions (Beta), a large Indian outsourcing provider. We had a preliminary discussion about outsourcing generally in the financial services sector and the Bank's current strategy. I asked him to send me a brief outline of Beta and what they could potentially do for us. I also asked him to indicate pricing and terms. "Declan hands you a copy of the response from Beta (see executive summary in **Appendix 3**).

Declan goes on to say, "I understand that you recently attended a conference on outsourcing in financial services, so you can put your knowledge to use and work on this with me. I would like you to review the memo from Ken and critically evaluate its findings, considering what Beta has come back with. You should prepare a report on your evaluation. You should also include an outline of the practical issues involved in using the services of an overseas provider. Outsourcing contracts often look good on paper but can be difficult to operate in practice. You should ignore any possible tax implications at this point."

Appendix 1: Extract from Recent Press Statement Made by the New CEO

"2012 was another difficult year for the Bank. Trading conditions remain tough but they have stabilised. However, since I took up my new role 12 months ago, we have started our journey towards rebuilding a sustainable, competitive retail banking business in Ireland by going 'back to basics'.

"Over the next 18–24 months, our key focus areas will be as follows.
- Reduce our cost base – we will ensure that our cost base is of a scale to meet our business needs going forward. Our operating costs in 2012 were €/£200 million and we plan to reduce our cost base by a further 10%. This will mean further voluntary redundancies.
- Optimise our cost of funds – currently our average cost of funds stands at 8%. We will look to reduce this over the next 12 months through a more balanced source of funding.

- Improve customer service and access – there will be no reduction in our commitment to serve and support our customers. We plan to invest in internet and mobile channels to improve our customers' ability to access us at a time and place that suits them.
- Manage our arrears portfolio.

"Finally, I want to acknowledge and thank our staff for their efforts over the past year. Since I was appointed I have seen extraordinary effort from our staff in overcoming difficult challenges.

"We look forward with cautious optimism to the year ahead."

Appendix 2: Internal Memo on Outsourcing

To: Ken Byrne, Operations Director
From: A.N. Other
Subject: Outsourcing Back-office Functions – Strictly Private and Confidential

Background

The purpose of this memo is to consider the feasibility of outsourcing the following back-office functions.

Function	Current payroll cost €/£ million	Current head count	Average length of service of employees (years)
IT help desk	2.25	50	8
e-banking customer support	3.60	120	4
HR operations	1.65	30	9
Accounts payable	3.15	70	7
	10.65	**270**	

Financial Evaluation

The functions within the scope of this review have a payroll cost of €/£10.65 million for 270 employees. The approach taken was to estimate savings and costs over the next five years (the usual length of outsourcing contracts) and calculate the NPV of cash flows using a discount factor of 12% (the norm for capital projects).

Based on discussions with Apex Consulting (Apex), the global consultancy, average ongoing savings from outsourcing contracts within the financial services sector is 30%. It is also normal for outsourcing companies to charge an upfront transition fee of €/£10,000 per role to cover the cost of training and 'onboarding' new people. Therefore, I have used this information in my calculations.

The key cost will be redundancy costs. For the last restructuring programme within the Bank, we paid six weeks' redundancy for each year of service, so I have used this multiple in the calculations. I assumed an average length of service of 7 years based on the range for the functions we are considering.

Apex recommended that we include €/£2 million for consulting costs as outsourcing projects are notoriously difficult to implement (as we know from prior experience!). Although the annual savings of €/£3.2 million are substantial, the costs associated with the transition would outweigh the benefits. The NPV of the cash inflows and outflows is a negative €/£1.6 million.

	€/£ million	Narrative
Annual saving	3.2	[30% of €/£10.65m] *per* Apex Consulting
5 years' saving	11.7	NPV @ 12%

	€/£ million	€/£ million	Narrative
Upfront costs:			
– Redundancy	8.6		[Average salary €/£39,444 × 7 years of service × 6 weeks divided by 52 weeks × 270 employees]
– Consulting	2.0		*Per* Apex Consulting
– Transition charge	2.7		[270 employees × €/£10,000]
Sub total		**13.3**	

NPV @12% = −1.6

Other Factors

In addition to the financial evaluation, there are a number of key qualitative considerations that would need to be taken into account, namely:
- there would likely be significant adverse publicity and it would have a negative effect on morale;
- I believe that inflation rates in India would erode benefits;
- the Bank's track record in managing outsourcing contracts is not favourable;
- the length of the contract would reduce the Bank's operational flexibility; and
- would we get Regulatory approval?

Conclusion

Given the financial and non-financial analysis, I do not recommend pursuing outsourcing at this stage.

Appendix 3: Executive Summary of Response from Beta Solutions to Pillar Bank Plc

About Beta Solutions

Beta Solutions (Beta) was founded in 1988 and now has over 50,000 employees worldwide. Most of the world's largest companies and many smaller companies have engaged in outsourcing for a variety of reasons, including to reduce costs, expand capabilities and increase flexibility. Outsourcing is very common in the financial services sector: over 90% of the world's top 100 banks have engaged outsourcing providers.

Beta has over 500 clients based in North America and Europe, including 100 financial institutions (40 banks). We provide outsourcing solutions for a wide variety of activities, but primarily information technology (IT), back office and customer services/support. Most services are provided from low-cost locations in and around Bangalore and Pune in India. Virtually all of our employees are English-speaking university graduates.

Indicative Terms/Arrangements for Pillar Bank Plc – Subject to Detailed Negotiation

- We understand that Pillar Bank Plc is currently considering outsourcing approximately 200–300 roles in a variety of functions.
- Outsourcing contracts typically operate on a role-for-role basis. However, over a period of three years we aim to reduce headcount by 10% through business process redesign. This is in addition to the savings arising from lower salaries in India.
- Average cost per associate (i.e. Beta employee) is currently US$32,500 (€/£25,000 at current US$/€/£ exchange rate of 1.30). Costs increase in line with inflation in India.
- Beta normally charges a management fee of 5% on top of this.
- There is usually a once-off set-up/transition cost. This varies for each contract, but is typically in the region of US$13,000 per role, but for contracts of over 100 roles it is fixed at US$1.3 million.
- Associates will be based in Beta's financial services centre in Bangalore, India, and will work a standard eight-hour day according to Irish time zones.
- The minimum term is typically three to five years. Most clients opt for five years.

R&D INVESTMENT

(Based on Chartered Accountants Ireland, FAE Autumn 2010, Simulation 3)

You, Charlie Powell, are an Irish chartered accountant working within a subsidiary of a US multinational enterprise (MNE) involved in manufacturing specialised engineering components. The materials and components used in the manufacturing process are sourced from a range of worldwide suppliers and group companies, and following assembly in Ireland these are sold to customers based in the European, African and Middle East (EMEA) markets.

You have been employed in the role of a management accountant for the last two years. The economic downturn has been a difficult time for the company. The Irish subsidiary is suffering from a loss of competitiveness and in response to this there is an active proposal to move the company's Irish activities 'up the value chain'.

A preliminary proposal is being prepared that aims to develop a research and development centre (R&D) in Ireland for the group. You recently received a memo from the chief executive of the Irish company indicating that you are to be part of a team established to progress this matter. (A copy of the memo is given as **Appendix 1**.)

The finance director, Mary Murray, summons you to her office. She indicates that she has been extremely busy dealing with a number of other key areas, such as securing sufficient credit from the company's bankers, and thus has not had a chance to focus on the planned development. "Look, I will be tied up on other matters for the next few days. I would like you to prepare a memorandum for the CEO and me, outlining how we can present the competitive advantages of locating an R&D facility in Ireland. You might consider if there is a suitable model that presents this and, more importantly, how this might be used to make a case to head office in the United States as a basis for developing our proposal. At this stage you might give me your preliminary thoughts on the issues that might be included. Let's sit down shortly and discuss what you come up with." With that you notice Mary looking at her watch and clearly it is time to return to your desk.

You sit down and begin to plan your ideas. You want to make a good impression as you have not had an opportunity like this before. You notice a message inviting you to a meeting later that day in Mary's office pop into your e-mail inbox. It's time to get moving.

Appendix 1

MEMO
To: Charlie Powell
From: John Purcell, CEO

Charlie

Many thanks for agreeing to assist the team looking at developing ideas for the research and development centre that we are proposing to establish in Ireland. The intention would be to use the planned facility to undertake key projects for the wider group and to license the resulting intellectual property (IP) to other members of the group. I know you are presently working with Mary on Ireland and its competitive advantages, but someone mentioned about transfer pricing implications. I know, roughly, what transfer pricing is but you might outline for me appropriate transfer pricing arrangements that we should use and the implications if we were to get it wrong. *(Please don't consider any tax issues – I've got my tax people looking at those.)*

You might drop me an email with your views.

Regards
John

REDBARN BREWERY

(Based on Chartered Accountants Ireland, FAE Autumn 2012, Simulation 2)

Redbarn Brewery (Redbarn) is an Irish microbrewery established 10 years ago by Stephen Ryan. Prior to that Stephen owned a number of pubs. He has an interest in beer and for many years experimented with home brewing. He created a few excellent beers and, being the type of person constantly on the lookout for new projects, decided he would set up a microbrewery. In order to make the investment, he sold his pubs to finance the construction of the microbrewery.

You are the financial controller of Redbarn. You have gained a reasonable level of knowledge of the brewing industry in the two years you have worked with the finance director, John Anderson. The business has shown good profits over the years. You prepare the monthly management accounts, cash flow statements, take care of tax compliance and perform various other assignments as they arise. One such assignment has just come up.

One of Redbarn's low alcohol but full-tasting fruit beers, Redbarn Gold, won a number of gold medal awards at a recent international craft beer competition held in New York, where much enthusiasm was shown for the new beer. The production process of Redbarn is innovative since it has been possible to produce the beer directly from the initial brewing process, while similar products require an additional process to reduce the level of alcohol. Redbarn is currently in discussion with its lawyers about patenting this new production process. For the moment, Stephen is not disclosing the type of malted barley and amount of hops/fruit he uses in his new brewing process.

At a recently held board meeting, it was decided that the company would look at various ways of entering the market in the US. John has given you the task of preparing a draft report covering the options for presentation to the board. It was agreed that Joe Wiley, operations and sales director, would do research and gather data on the US market, which he will give to you to assist you in preparing your report. (An extract of his research is included in **Appendix 1**.)

John has explained to you that he wants the report to help the board decide if it makes financial sense (taking into account potential risks under the various options assessed) to enter the US market and, if so, given the present circumstances of Redbarn, what the best market-entry strategy would be for the company. The option initially discussed was licensing a US company to produce the beer (see **Appendix 1**). John informs you about an approach made by one of the companies Stephen met in New York: a large brewery, Ryton Ales, based in Concord, New Hampshire.

A few days after your meeting with John, Joe advises you that Ryton Ales has suggested a joint venture (JV) between both companies, as this might be more appropriate than the licensing option. It was agreed that John would travel to Concord to meet with the CFO of Ryton Ales to discuss both the JV and licensing options. John has asked you to include both options in your report.

He also asks that you prepare a separate memo to him outlining the main issues you think should be discussed and addressed at the meeting in Concord, covering both the JV and licensing options, and to consider the implications for your finance function if the JV option is chosen. In the meantime, Ryton Ales have sent an outline of their JV proposal (see **Appendix 1**).

A few days later, Joe drops by your desk and comments on the JV proposal. He says that he thinks (in reference to the JV proposal from Ryton) it would be a mistake to price Redbarn Gold lower than that of other premium beers. He thinks the strategy should be to match the competitors' prices at retail but to allow the extra margin to stay with off-licences/bar-restaurants. This would leave the off-licences/bar-restaurants with an effective margin of higher than the standard 100% and 200% respectively and would encourage them to push sales over other premium beers. He asks for your thoughts on this as a pricing strategy for Redbarn Gold in the US market and you agree to prepare a memo for him.

Appendix 1

Note re US Craft-beer Market

While the consumption of beer in the US has fallen over the last number of years, the market for local, non-mass-produced bottled beers grew by 50% between 2008 and 2011. Recent US revenue from sales of beer is approaching US$100 billion, of which craft beer sales were US$8 billion. Sales from microbreweries and artisan producers are increasing, as many consumers are becoming more selective in their choice of alcoholic beverages and less inclined to drink the mass-produced beers from the larger breweries. "Consumers have developed a taste for very high quality, independent brews," writes the editor of *Beer Monthly*. "People are moving out of mass-produced, domestic brands and trading up to premium-priced craft beers."

Licence

A memorandum of understanding between Redbarn and Ryton Ales has been prepared by Joe on the licensing option. This would allow the New Hampshire brewery to produce the beer for sale in the US for an exclusive period of six years, starting in 2013. This would be in return for an initial, upfront payment of US$200,000 plus a royalty of $2 per case sold. Based on its experience of selling premium beers, Ryton Ales is confident that there will be a high demand for this beer and is happy to guarantee royalty payments based on a minimum of 80,000 cases in 2013, rising by 8% per year until 2018 when the initial licence agreement is proposed to end. Ryton would be responsible for any excise duty arising.

Extract of Joint Venture Proposal from Ryton Ales

Ryton Ales has proposed a 50:50 joint venture to produce this beer in its brewery near Concord. It has produced some projections based on its knowledge of the market for low-alcohol beers in New Hampshire and the surrounding states. Ryton Ales presently has spare capacity in its brewery and has been trying to develop a low-alcohol beer to complement its existing range. However, its bottling plant would require an investment of US$1 million to allow for the extra production, half of which would be payable by Redbarn. It estimates it could sell 110,000 cases in 2013, increasing by 5% per year until 2018 and direct costs, including distribution, would be 50% of wholesale value. US state and federal taxes of 40% would be payable on profits. In addition, in return for the use of its brewery, it is looking for the JV to pay it US$100,000 per year.

Pricing Strategy

Ryton Ales agrees with Joe's estimate of a sales price of $24 per case, which would mean a unit wholesale price of $2. It advises that off-licences would expect a mark-up of 100% and bar-restaurants a mark-up of 200%. This would mean a retail price of $4 and $6, respectively. This would result in a retail-sales price of about 20% less than other premium beers in the market.

Working Assumptions

Rate to use: €/£1.00 = US$1.40. You can assume that the exchange rate remains the same for each year.

John advises using a discount rate of 10% in any present value calculations and not to consider any economic value beyond the period under evaluation.

For the purposes of any calculations, assume that any corporation tax (ROI rate 12.5%/NI rate 24%) is paid in the same year as income is earned.

SMART BATHROOM FITTINGS LTD

(Based on Chartered Accountants Ireland, FAE Autumn 2010, Simulation 2)

You, Mary Conway, are a newly qualified Irish chartered accountant who has recently joined a successful Irish manufacturer of household plumbing devices in the role of financial analyst. The Company, which trades as Smart Bathroom Fittings Ltd (SBF) has developed a range of 'smart' plumbing devices that are designed to ensure they have a positive environmental impact. For example, SBF's most successful product is a toilet plumbing device that minimises water consumption. The device is a relatively high cost item that is seen as a value-added accessory in luxury homes.

You have been with SBF for the last six months and are gradually finding your feet. You are sitting at your desk, sipping your morning latté, when the finance director (Billy Murray, FCA) calls you to his office. He quickly outlines the issue he seeks your assistance with. He states: "SBF has performed well over recent years with the significant construction boom. With the dramatic economic slowdown and reduced activity in the construction sector, the outlook in Ireland is extremely limited."

Billy proceeds to outline the future options and then says: "I believe that international expansion is the way ahead for this business. I have extracted a number of economic statistics for a range of countries." He hands over the schedule to you (see **Appendix 1**).

He continues: "I know you are not an economist – nor do I want one to explain the jargon to me. However, I need your views on the key insights that the schedule provides and how this might impact on any potential investment decision. I am particularly interested in what they tell us about the economic attractiveness of each country." He finishes by saying: "Can you prepare a note for me on the schedule, highlighting any limitations you consider arising over the data provided? I will need it by the end of the week." With that he indicates that he has an urgent meeting with the managing director and you head for the door armed with the schedule.

As you settle back at your desk, you reflect that you want to make a good impression and you begin to analyse the data as a basis for preparing your report.

Six weeks later Billy advises you that the board, having taken your report into consideration along with other information available to them, is now considering South Africa as the preferred country for investment. The overall strategy is to acquire an existing plumbing distributor and to use this as a basis for driving sales within South Africa and the southern African region generally. You will be required to advise on any potential investment. A possible target has been identified, Rand Plumbing Supplies, and Billy calls you to a meeting to brief you on the relevant information for your analysis.

At the meeting Billy indicates that a preliminary estimate of cash flows has been helpfully provided by the target company's management (included as **Appendix 2**). He explains that the company is privately owned and has been trading successfully for 25 years, but notes: "Given that the owner–manager is planning to retire soon, I believe we need to move fast as I understand he is considering a number of alternatives other than an offer from us. On the basis of initial talks, I expect the investment to be in the region of South African Rand (ZAR) 4.5 million." He goes on to add that the managing director and the board would like confirmation that the investment has a payback period of five years or less and makes financial sense. The required (euro/Sterling) cost of capital is 10%.

As you gather your thoughts, you murmur something about tax and he responds: "Tax issues between Ireland and South Africa have yet to be examined in any detail. Just make an appropriate assumption until we get a chance to discuss in more detail with our tax advisors." He finishes the meeting by suggesting that you should also consider any sensitivity or other factors that are relevant to the evaluation: "Let's sit down next week and review what you have come up with."

You look at the figures provided and upload them into a spreadsheet. You are conscious that there are many aspects of overseas investment that you will need to brush up on. You have taken note of Billy's comment about tax, but realise that your South African tax knowledge is virtually non-existent. A quick call to the company accountants yields enough basic tax information to complete the initial valuations as follows.

- The normal corporation tax rate in South Africa is 40% per annum.
- As a means of attracting inward investment, the South African government offers a special rate of tax of 10% for the first four years of any investment.
- For appraisal purposes, you've confirmed that it's OK to assume that tax is payable in South Africa and in Ireland at the same time and this arises in the year after the profits arise.
- You assume that the capital allowances available are the same as the depreciation charged in the accounts.
- You agree that any tax computation will be subject to separate tax review.
- They've also indicated that you should be aware that although the €/£ to ZAR exchange rate is presently €/£1 to ZAR10.15, the ZAR is anticipated to weaken each year against the euro/Sterling over the duration of the investment, moving in line with the long-term interest rate differential between the euro/Sterling area and South Africa. The current interest rates are 3% for the euro/Sterling area and 12.4% for South Africa. The level of political uncertainty in South Africa makes it difficult to be certain if these rates will prevail, however inflation is expected to remain higher than in Ireland.
- As you settle in to working through the numbers, a message pops up on your screen. It is an e-mail from Billy. The relevant extract is replicated in **Appendix 3**.

Appendix 1: Data for 2009

Country	South Africa	Brazil	Zimbabwe	India	Ireland
Population	49m	199m	11.4m	1.16bn	4.2m
Interest rates	11.5%	20.48%	N/A	6%	3%
Inflation	7.2%	4.2%	Hyper	7.8%	−1.7%
GDP (using PPP USD)	$488.6bn	$2.04 trillion est.	$2bn	$3.56 trillion	$177bn
GDP growth	−1.9%	0.1% est.	3.7% est.	6.5% est.	−7.5% est.
GDP per capita (PPP)	$10,000	$10,200	$200	$3,100	$42,200
Unemployment	24%	7.4%	68%	10.7%	12%
Current account balance	−$15.6bn	−$11.28bn	−$597m	−$8.4bn	−$5.3bn
Public debt as % of GDP	35.7%	46.8%	304%	59.6%	64%

Note: for comparative purposes, all financial data is in US Dollars converted using a purchasing power parity (PPP) methodology. N/A: not available. All figures are taken from *World Fact Book*.

Appendix 2

Rand Plumbing Supplies (Pty) Ltd
INDICATIVE ESTIMATE OF PRELIMINARY CASH FLOWS FOR INVESTMENT PURPOSES
(All figures are ZAR million)

Year	2011	2012	2013	2014	2015
Revenue	7.5	7.8	8.1	8.4	14.6
Outflows	(4.2)	(4.1)	(5.3)	(5.5)	(9.5)
Depreciation	(0.8)	(0.9)	(0.8)	(0.8)	(1.0)
Accounting profit	2.50	2.8	2.0	2.1	4.10
Taxation	(0.25)	(0.28)	(0.20)	(0.21)	(1.64)
Profit after tax	2.25	2.52	1.8	1.89	2.46

Appendix 3: E-mail from Billy Murray

To: Mary Conway
From: Billy Murray
Subject: Some Considerations Regarding the South African Investment

Mary,

Many thanks for your assistance with the appraisal of the South African investment. I am looking forward to visiting there soon to discuss the proposal in more detail.

I have been in touch with the owner of Rand Plumbing Supplies (Ron du Plessis) and he has sent me an extract of some issues from a local trade journal that has highlighted some factors that may impact on our investment. (These are included as an attachment.) I would like you to include a note on the cultural factors that may affect us in how we do business in South Africa.

If we go ahead with this – it will cost us about €/£450,000 or 4.5 million ZAR, which I think we will – we will have to arrange to borrow. According to the existing heads of terms agreed with Rand Plumbing Supplies the money in ZAR would be payable three months from signing the contract to purchase Rand Plumbing Supplies. I mentioned this potential investment to our bank manager last week and he gave me a few options in relation to financing the deal. One was for our bank to lend the money and for us to enter into a forward exchange contract to close out any exchange risk on the three-month gap to payment. Further to that conversation he has sent me an e-mail giving me an example of a forward contract rate if we were to sign the deal for the purchase of Rand Plumbing Supplies. I don't know much about forward contracts – what do you think? (See e-mail in **Appendix 4**.)

Billy

Attachment: Assessment of the South African Market

South Africa is a country with many different ethnic groups and cultures and the legacy of the apartheid era remains strong, with a large gap between the wealthy and the poor of the country.

The transfer of power in 1994 from the minority apartheid government to the democratically elected African National Congress government generated a large amount of optimism that has not, over time, translated into a better standard of living for the majority of South Africans. However those previously excluded from political power have benefited economically and a large black middle class has emerged. South Africa experienced high economic growth in the post-apartheid period.

House-building in the Johannesburg area has been greatly impacted by the recent economic downturn. Despite this there remains significant pressure on the government to expand the provision of housing to lower income groups. Many of these were affected by the restrictions imposed during the apartheid era. Despite initial high hopes of the ANC government to address the major housing deficit, progress has been slow.

The factors that have contributed to the slow progress include lack of available suitable land, bureaucratic inefficiency and corruption. A number of senior local authority managers have recently been imprisoned following a corruption scandal in the local housing procurement programme. Following intervention of a Government minister, the sentences were suspended.

High-income groups remain a small niche market in the region. The demand for housing and expansion has been constrained by emigration and security concerns, with many homeowners investing heavily in security arrangements given the high crime rates.

Lower income groups continue to be impacted by poverty and HIV, in particular. The high rate of unemployment and underemployment has impacted on crime rates and access to water in some townships remains a challenge.

Appendix 4: E-mail Extract

Billy,

It was great to meet you last week and I hope the negotiations on the South African deal go well.

You mentioned that the deal will cost you ZAR4.5 million. Subject to approval by our credit committee, I think we would look favourably on advancing finance for this if you decide to proceed. Given the three-month gap between signing the contract and paying for the company – I mentioned to you the possibility of you taking out a foreign exchange contract with us. This would mean you would close out any exchange risk on paying in ZAR between the time you agree to buy the company and the time you have to pay for it. You would know the euro/Sterling value of your loan liability at the time of buying the company.

As an example, if you were to buy the company today and were to enter into a forward exchange today, we could offer you the following forward rate: the current exchange rate €/£1 to ZAR is 10.15 and we would be able to offer you a 90-day forward exchange rate of ZAR10.19.

Regards
Manager

You look up the money market interest rates and see that euro/Sterling 90-day rate is 0.75% and ZAR is 3.1% both based on 90-/360-day convention.

STENT MANUFACTURING LIMITED

(Based on Chartered Accountants Ireland, FAE Autumn 2011, Simulation 3)

Dr Darren Gibson spent many years in the US where, after qualifying as a doctor, he was involved in the research and development of medical stents that provide less intrusive medical solutions than full heart surgery for patients with heart problems. Stents are small manufactured tubes about 1 cm long made from precious metal alloys and are inserted in patients to keep blocked arteries open.

In 1990 Darren returned to Ireland where he set up a successful company, Stent Manufacturing Limited (Stent), manufacturing drug eluting stents (DES). DES are used in hospitals mainly in Ireland, Great Britain (GB) and Germany. As well as keeping blocked arteries open, these stents secrete small amounts of medicine over time to prevent blood clotting around the stents.

You are the recently appointed financial controller of Stent. The company grew substantially in the early years and benefited from venture capital investment, which provided the funds for the construction of the Irish manufacturing plant and the significant amounts invested in research and development and medical trials.

Darren has stepped back from the day-to-day running of the company and is now the chairman of the board. At a recent meeting Dick Jones, the company managing director, outlined the new corporate strategy that the board was developing. In summary it was that Stent would expand its manufacturing and research and development facilities outside of Ireland in order to increase sales and retain its position as the most innovative supplier of its particular type of stent. He explained that it was important to be close to the users of their product, to enable a constant exchange of information on the product's effectiveness. He argued that good communication with the medical profession was key to sales and continued innovation. He hoped that the choice of location would support the new strategy. It would also give governmental regulatory agencies easier access to the company processes and manufacturing facilities.

Dick stated the two most obvious locations for a new plant would either be the south-east of England or southern Germany. Great Britain is the most important market for Stent Manufacturing Limited and has provided the majority of the company's sales since inception.

After the meeting with Dick your boss, Brian Murphy, who has been the finance director for the last year, comes by your desk. He discusses the proposal with you and you volunteer to do some research and prepare a memo on the new plans. He is happy with this and says initially he would like to understand the broad cost implications of choosing either England or Germany. He explains that the sales price that can be charged by the company is probably not that relevant in deciding where to locate the facility and, as you are aware, the stent profit margin is extremely high. He adds that the stent buying decisions are normally made by the cardiologists and that quality and successful surgical outcomes, rather than price, drive the purchase decision. Brian reminds you of the company's mission statement, which is "to be the manufacturer of the highest quality drug eluting stents in the European market".

You ask Brian why the company does not supply to the US market and he responds that, although the product has US Federal Drugs Agency approval, the board has taken the view that, as the US stent manufacturers dominate that market, the company should concentrate on the European market at this time. Brian adds that it will be difficult to raise the substantial amount of funds necessary for this project in Ireland at the present time, even though Stent is a highly profitable company. He also states that the venture capital companies that would have previously backed this project now see the company as too mature for their type of investment and suggests that lack of finance might stop this project going ahead. You decide to give this some attention in your report.

You clear your desk and begin your work. The preliminary results of your research are in **Appendix 1**.

A week later Dick Jones asks how you are getting on with the project – you tell him broadly what you are doing and he responds that the cost of manufacture will only give half the story when deciding on the location for the new plant. When he leaves you realise what he meant and instantly you decide you had better broaden your thinking and expand your report.

Appendix 1

You meet with the head of manufacturing, John Childs, who oversaw the construction of the current facility in Ireland and discuss with him the broad requirements of a new facility. He says he already has some ideas for the 'next generation' stent manufacturing plant and would hope to improve significantly on the current facility. He says it's a pity it will not be built here in Ireland, but qualifies it by acknowledging the need for the company to expand overseas.

The new factory will be 3,000 square metres and take 12 months to build – the same length of time in each country.

You have gathered the following information:

Stent Manufacturing Limited

	GB	Germany
Total cost to develop new facility €/£000	50,000	70,000
Initial annual production in thousands of units	400	400
Fixed annual costs, including R&D €/£000	30,000	33,000
Other variable annual costs €/£000	5,000	6,500
Variable labour – thousands of hours payable per year	192	198
Average wage cost rate per hour €/£	19	21
Factory life	10 years	10 years

You extract the following information from the company's management accounts:

Year to	Jun 2010 €/£000	Jun 2011 €/£000	% increase	Potential Market €/£000	% of Market 2011
Sales					
Ireland	19,000	20,000	5%	50,000	40%
Great Britain	83,000	85,000	2%	220,000	39%
Germany	13,000	16,000	23%	280,000	6%
Other European	5,000	8,000	60%	600,000	1%
	120,000	129,000	8%		

TINYTOTS BABY FOOD LIMITED

(Based on Chartered Accountants Ireland, FAE Autumn 2011, Simulation 2)

TinyTots Baby Food Limited (TinyTots) is an Irish-based company that has been in business for 20 years. It was established in 1990 by Grace Smiley when her friends asked her for the recipes of the puréed vegetable dishes she prepared for her twin girls. Grace had a background in food science and had worked in the dairy industry. Supported by her local Enterprise Board, Grace started manufacturing and selling to local supermarkets.

The company has grown from that time to be one of the largest manufacturers and suppliers of organic baby food in the European market with a turnover of €/£180 million and employing 400 people.

Grace attributes much of the success to the energy and drive of one of her first employees, Mark Chandler. Mark was initially employed as production manager of the small manufacturing facility and is now the managing director. One of Mark's biggest decisions was to purchase a French company four years ago which also manufactures organic baby food. This was to facilitate an expansion into the Continental market.

You work for Brown Consulting as an associate director. Two weeks ago, you were called into a meeting with your boss, James Brown. The firm had recently been engaged by TinyTots to advise on a number of issues. James explained to you that, while turnover at TinyTots is still growing, profitability has fallen and Mark Chandler feels, even though they are all working harder than ever, they are having difficulty in managing parts of the business. Mark is of the view that the board at times appears to lack quality information, which prevents it from making decisions and that the company is not reaching its potential. In addition, the French subsidiary is losing money. Last week you spent three days at the head office of TinyTots and two days at the offices of the French subsidiary. The notes you made during your visits are in **Appendix 1**.

Yesterday you met with James to discuss your initial findings. You tell him you think some kind of reorganisation is necessary. He agrees and asks you to come up with a new structure that would help the company overcome its present problems along with a rationale for it. In addition, he also suggests you come up with an exit strategy in respect of the French manufacturing facility in the event that TinyTots may decide to close that plant, bearing in mind the wholesale side appears to be profitable.

You also discuss with James the poor quality of management information and he suggests that perhaps you should look at it from a strategic enterprise management system perspective and the problems TinyTots may face in implementing such a system. You agree to do this at a summary level and return to your desk to start your report.

Appendix 1

At the Irish head office of TinyTots you meet with Grace, Mark Chandler and Brian Jones, the finance director, and take the following notes.

Mark explains that the strategy of TinyTots is to be number one or two in terms of sales in the European organic baby food market within the next five years. At present, from information it has on sales of its competitors, it is number 20. TinyTots supplies a number of the large supermarket chains in the British Isles from its Irish base. The turnover has doubled in the last five years. The French subsidiary supplies the company's customers on the Continent. You get a sense that Grace is disappointed with the recent results of the Group and, in particular, the decision to buy the French subsidiary.

The company sells 10 types of baby food, some of which they manufacture themselves, the rest bought in from other manufacturers and subsequently sold under the TinyTots brand. The manufacturing divisions sell their products to the wholesaling divisions in their respective countries, who in turn sell and distribute to the retailers.

All of the company's own products are produced in the two factories in Ireland and France. The group head of manufacturing, who is based in Ireland, has spent time at the French plant, but little progress has been made in making it profitable.

You ask Brian for the group's product profitability information, which you presume would be part of the management accounts. Brian tells you that each of the divisions produces its own management accounts and his team consolidate in summary form into group accounts for the board and the company's banks, but the divisions don't report sales and cost of sales by product to Head Office.

In order to keep control over the raw material buying decisions and to achieve bulk discounts, all procurement authorisation is done through the Irish Head Office.

You take a copy of the organisational chart and the consolidated management profit or loss account (which are below). After the meeting Brian takes you aside and says he has been concerned about the management information system for some time – that it appeared to provide the necessary information when TinyTots had only the Irish operation to worry about but the French company has its own way of doing things and information is sometimes hard to come by. As a result of the language barrier, the French subsidiary maintains its own computer hardware and accounting system, which were inherited from the previous owners.

TinyTots Baby Food Limited
ORGANISATIONAL STRUCTURE

Managing Director

Group Head of Manufacturing	General Manager (Ireland)	General Manager (France)	Marketing Director	Finance Director
Ireland	Marketing	Marketing		
France	Sales and Distribution	Sales and Distribution		
	Finance and Admin	Finance and Admin		Finance and HR
Quality				Admin (Head Office)
				Group Procurement

On your visit to the French subsidiary you meet with the general manager, Jean Depaul. Amongst other things, you discuss with him the French trading results, with which he is quite pleased. He reckons they maintained their wholesale profit at approx. €/£1.2 million in the face of difficult trading conditions. When you ask about the performance of the manufacturing side, he says that low demand for those products means the factory is operating below capacity and so is making a loss. However, the marketing director in Ireland is working on increasing sales on the Continent. He adds that after preparing their own month-end accounts, his finance team produce the figures for the French manufacturing plant and send them over to the head of manufacturing in Ireland for review.

TinyTots Baby Food Limited
DIVISIONS

2010	Manufacturing Ireland €/£000	Wholesale Ireland €/£000	Manufacturing France €/£000	Wholesale France €/£000	Head Office* €/£000	2010 Total €/£000
Sales	55,000	110,000	25,000	72,000	−80,000	182,000
Cost of sales						
Internal	0	55,000	0	25,000	−80,000	0
External	48,000	43,000	25,100	41,000		157,100
						0
Gross profit	7,000	12,000	−100	6,000		24,900
GP %	12.7%	10.9%	−0.4%	8.3%		13.7%
						0
Admin costs	5,100	10,000	2,600	4,840	0	22,540
PBT	1,900	2,000	−2,700	1,160	0	2,360
Admin as % sales	9.3%	9.1%	10.4%	6.7%		12.4%
PBT as % sales	3.5%	1.8%	−10.8%	1.6%		1.3%

* Head office adjustment on sales/cost of sales is to contra out intercompany sales.

While total turnover for 2009 was a little less than the above, divisional performance was similar and mirrored that of 2010.

TRIDENT MOBILE LTD

(Based on Chartered Accountants Ireland, FAE Autumn 2011, Simulation 1)

Trident Mobile Ltd (Trident) is an Irish mobile phone company that has been operating in the Irish market for the last 10 years. It has a 40% market share and is number two in the Irish market.

Trident is looking to leverage its experience in successfully running a mobile phone company by acquiring a mobile phone licence in another country and starting a new company there. Trident has a reputation as being a socially responsible company and considers this to be a key part of its success to date and is committed to this as part of its ongoing strategy.

You are the management accountant in the commercial department. Over the last two years you have spent your time looking at the profitability of the various bundles offered by Trident and analysing profitability by customer profile and corporate groupings. Much of your work involves modelling the financial effect of proposed changes to the various bundles of call minutes, texts and internet access offered by Trident. The commercial department also monitors competitor offerings and assesses the effect of these on competitor profitability and the likely attractiveness that their offerings may have for Trident customers.

Your boss, John Greene, commercial director, has, at a recent meeting, informed you of a bigger project the company is about to undertake. He stated that Trident's board has decided to bid for a mobile phone licence in Kenya. In addition, it is of the opinion that in order to achieve critical mass and create a successful business in the African market, it will need to operate in at least one other African country. John gives you a file on the project (extracts **Appendix 2**) and asks you to meet with Jenny Wilson, who is the project manager for the expansion into Africa. You have enjoyed working with Jenny in the past and look forward to getting stuck into this project. John asks you to review the figures and prepare a report on the amount that Trident should bid for the Kenyan licence. You agree to include a note of any key risks as part of this report on the valuation. In addition, he asks you to review the economic data in the file (**Appendix 2**) to see if it would be of help to Trident in deciding where else to invest in Africa.

After your meeting with Jenny (see **Appendix 1**) you return to your desk and start work.

The next morning John drops by to see how you are getting on. He also raises the possible practical and cultural problems Trident might face in doing business in a country like Kenya. You agree to do a brief note for him outlining your thoughts.

Given the importance Trident places on social responsibility, you also decide to cover this area in your report.

Appendix 1: Notes on Kenyan Project

Jenny tells you she has been working on this project for the last few months and has spent a week in Kenya meeting their telecoms regulator, looking at the competition and planning the entry strategy. She tells you that, based on preliminary work, Kenya was chosen as the target country but that now Trident wants to rework the figures to firm up the bid price for this second round of licence sales in the Kenyan telecoms market.

It has been agreed that a well-connected businessman in Kenya will hold 5% of the shares in Trident Kenya; however, at this point, it is not anticipated that he will fund any of the capital expenditure or provide any investment in the new company. He has, however, experience in raising funds in the Kenyan bond market and Trident expects to use this source for funding.

You record the following brief notes at the meeting:
- Kenya population – 40 million;
- capital expenditure forecast of KES5,000 million per annum in 2012 and 2013;
- the licence will give Trident the right to operate in Kenya for a minimum period of 12 years;
- expected average revenue per customer: KES4,800 per year, starting in January 2013;

- expected market penetration is 2.5% of the Kenyan population by the end of year 2013, rising by 50% each year until 2016 after which customer growth is expected to be minimal. It is assumed that new subscribers will be spread evenly over the year. In their first year with Trident subscribers will, on average, pay 50% of the annual expected revenue and thereafter KES4,800 per year;
- cost of sales will be 60% of the revenue. Cost of sales includes overheads and the costs of routing calls through other providers. The corporation tax rate in Kenya is 30% and is paid one year in arrears. Capital allowances of 33.3% per year are allowed against revenue on all capital expenditure;
- Trident uses a real discount rate of 8% on all projects. Projected long-term Kenyan interest rates are 11% while those in euro/Sterling are expected to be 4%;
- Kenyan shilling (KES) exchange rate to euro/Sterling is currently 100.

Appendix 2: Background Information on African Mobile Phone Market

Extract from Recent News Article on the African Mobile Phone Market

Africa is a continent of more than 1 billion people and has seen the largest increase in the world in mobile phone use over the last decade. Market penetration has grown from 200 million users in 2005 to 400 million in 2010 and is forecast to grow to 55% (550 million subscribers) over the next three years.

Many of the world's largest mobile phone companies have entered the African market over the last decade, particularly those from countries that previously had a colonial presence on the continent.

Historically, many mobile phone companies were of the opinion that African countries were not sufficiently economically developed to support the level of discretionary spending by customers necessary to create a commercially viable industry. However, in recent years mobile phone technology has significantly boosted economic activity on a continent where long distances and a previously poor communication network was a barrier to trade. Mobile phones are used by migrant workers to transfer funds back to remote villages and by urban food market traders to communicate with suppliers to reduce over-supply and maintain prices. It is not uncommon for users in developing countries to spend 15% of disposable income on mobile phone usage.

ECONOMIC DATA

African Economic Outlook 2010 – OECD							
	Population Thousands	Land Area Sq km Thousands	GDP US$ million	Annual Real GDP Growth %	Inflation %	Mobile Penetration* %	Number of Competitors in Market
Tanzania	43,739	945	53,167	7	12	40	5
Zambia	12,935	753	19,606	5	13	35	3
Malawi	15,263	118	8,395	5	9	22	4
Uganda	32,710	241	46,632	8	10	45	4
Mozambique	22,894	802	21,746	8	3	25	2
Kenya	40,000	593	62,423	4	7	55	4

* Mobile phone penetration figures are not from OECD.

Appendix B

SUGGESTED SOLUTIONS TO REVIEW QUESTIONS

Index of Solutions Relating to Case Studies

Index of Solutions

BLACK SWAN INC

Note to Andrew Doyle

PRIVATE AND CONFIDENTIAL

Re: Draft Outline Business Case for EMEA SSC

Further to our meeting last week I have attached a draft outline business case for the set-up of a finance shared service centre (SSC) for EMEA. The business case is based on the information you provided.

The draft outline business case covers the following:
- a high level financial business case (costs/benefits) of setting up an SSC in either Ireland or Poland;
- the wider benefits of establishing an SSC;
- key risk factors which should be considered; and
- the key criteria we should consider for the selection of a suitable location.

Let me know when suits to discuss,

Dave Brennan

Draft Outline Business Case for Set-up of a Finance Shared Services Centre for EMEA

STRICTLY PRIVATE AND CONFIDENTIAL

1. Introduction and Purpose of Document

Black Swan has been growing rapidly in EMEA. Revenues have more than doubled over the past three years. This growth trend is expected to continue as more sales offices are opened across EMEA.

Black Swan currently employs 218 people in finance across nine countries at an annual cost of US$13.7 million. Senior management is currently considering the finance organisation structure in the light of Black Swan's growth plans. The objectives include:
- ensure scalability/operational flexibility;
- ensure efficient and (relatively) low-cost operations; and
- ensure a strong control environment.

To achieve these objectives senior management are considering the establishment of a shared services centre (SSC) for finance. This will mean consolidating as many finance activities as practicable in a single location to support the local offices. At this early stage two possible locations for the SSC have been identified: Ireland – as it is the EMEA HQ and a popular choice for many international companies; and Poland – which has lower salaries than most parts of Europe.

The purpose of this document is to outline the high-level business case for changing the finance organisation. Specifically it covers:
- the financial business case (costs/benefits) of setting up an SSC in either Ireland or Poland;
- the wider benefits of establishing an SSC;
- risk factors that need to be considered; and
- the key criteria we should consider in the selection of a suitable location.

The document has been prepared on the basis of preliminary data on current finance costs provided by Andrew Doyle.

Clearly, we will need to validate the baseline data and undertake more detailed analysis before we make any final decisions.

Solution 11.2: Black Swan Inc

> **Evaluate and assess the opportunity facing Black Swan in establishing a finance shared services centre in EMEA from a financial and non-financial perspective. In addition, estimate the annual cost savings and the investment required for set-up.**

2. Financial Considerations

The following table summarises the estimated financial implications of setting up an SSC based on the preliminary data set out in Appendix 1:

	FTE	SSC – Ireland	SSC – Poland
		US$000	**US$000**
Current finance	218	13,662	13,662
Future finance (Note 1)	190	10,260	8,550
Annual saving (Note 2)		**3,177**	**4,654**
Implementation cost			
New systems		900	900
Consultancy		600	600
Redundancy (Note 3)		1,504	1,504
Staff overlap (Note 4)		738	615
Recruitment (Note 5)		886	738
Implementation cost		**4,628**	**4,357**
Contingency		**500**	**500**
Total		**5,128**	**4,857**

The key points to be noted are as follows.
- Our current cost of finance is US$13.7 million for 218 finance staff (average cost per FTE – US$62,670).
- By setting up an SSC we can reduce staffing levels by 28 to 190. Of this total, about 164 staff will be based in the SSC and 26 will remain in the individual countries. These savings will be derived from bigger spans of control, and improved productivity levels.
- In addition, we can reduce our payroll cost by locating the SSC in a country where salary levels are comparatively lower. In Ireland, the average cost per FTE is US$54,000 and in Poland it is US$45,000. As these rates are lower than our average cost across EMEA, considerable savings can be achieved.
- The net effect of lower headcount levels and lower average salaries for SSC staff is a potential annual saving of approximately US$3.177 million for an Irish-based SSC and approximately US$4.654 million for a Polish-based SSC.
- Clearly, we will need to validate the data/assumptions on which this is based and perform a detailed assessment of possible location options in advance as there are other criteria apart from salary levels that we will need to take into consideration. I have outlined the other factors I think we will need to consider for location selection in Section 3 of this document.
- There are likely to be significant costs associated with the set-up. My initial estimate is that implementation will cost in the region of US$4.6 million (Poland – slightly less at US$4.3 million). The main costs are as follows.
  - Redundancy – I have assumed that only half of the existing finance team will be redeployed and redundancy payments will amount to about three months' salary, which results in a redundancy cost of approximately US$1.5 million. Clearly, the number of redundancies and the payments we make will have a material impact on the business case so we will need to refine this estimate in due course.
  - New systems and consultancy support – as part of the SSC implementation we will roll out the new global financial software. I have estimated a cost of US$1.5 million for this.

- o Recruitment agency costs for hiring new staff were estimated at 10% of salaries.
  - o Overlap payroll cost for the period when we are training in new staff. I have estimated one month's payroll for this.
  - o I have also included contingency of US$500,000.
- Given annual savings of between US$3.2 million and US$4.7 million, the SSC will deliver a payback of the implementation cost between 12 months and 19 months. Given this return the SSC looks like a worthwhile investment.
- In addition, the SSC will deliver wider benefits to Black Swan. These are outlined in Section 3.
- Notwithstanding this there are some risk factors that we will need to consider, which I have also outlined in Section 4.

Solution 12.4: Black Swan Inc

> **Detail the benefits and risks for Black Swan Inc of setting up a shared services centre.**

3. Wider benefits of SSC

In addition to the financial benefits of setting up an SSC, there are a number of other benefits to be gained including the following.
- It provides a platform for growth. Black Swan is planning to open many new sales offices in EMEA over the next few years. It will be quicker and easier for an existing SSC to set up financial processes (such as billing, collections, payments) for the new offices rather than having to set up a separate finance function for each new sales office.
- It will benefit Black Swan to have standardised finance processes that, apart from being more efficient, will improve the control environment. This is important given the problems we had in Italy earlier in the year.
- It will facilitate the roll-out of the new enterprise computing software that Black Swan is planning to implement globally.
- It will free up the residual finance team in the country offices to provide more value-added advice to management rather than spending their time on routine transaction processing.

4. Risk Factors

Notwithstanding the benefits, there are a number of risk factors we will need to take into consideration.
- Loss of 'corporate memory'. The existing members of staff have built up considerable knowledge of customers, suppliers, transaction history and processes. We would lose this experience in the creation of an SSC. We could mitigate this by clearly documenting our processes in advance and ensuring enough time for a proper handover. In this regard we may need to look at extending the training-in time, which would push up the implementation cost.
- Some finance staff will undoubtedly leave when they learn about our plans, which will cause disruption. We might want to consider retention bonuses for selected key employees. Again, this would push up implementation costs.
- There may be resistance from the existing finance management and team. Clear and consistent communications will be key. We will need to get existing finance management buy-in from the outset.

Solution 4.2: Black Swan Inc

> **Advise on the key factors to be considered in selecting an appropriate location for a shared services centre investment and how to attract FDI for businesses operating in Ireland.**

5. Location Assessment

The location of the SSC will have a critical impact on the cost and quality of services being provided so it is important that we consider a number of alternatives. The key factors we will need to consider as part of the assessment are as follows.

- Salary levels for finance staff and salary inflation levels. The benefits of using a low-cost location can be quickly eroded if labour inflation rates are high.
- Other costs, such as office rents, telecommunications and utilities, need to be considered.
- The availability of skilled labour and foreign language skills. This is key – if there is a shortage of finance skills, it will impact on service levels and ultimately push up costs.
- Availability of grants and subsidies for job creation and/or to offset training costs.
- Availability of suitable office space.
- Time-zone compatibility.
- Work permit issues if we need to bring in foreign workers.

At this stage we have only looked at two possible options, Ireland and Poland; prior to finalising we will need to do a more detailed assessment. Notwithstanding this they are good place to start.

1. **Ireland** Ireland is the location of choice for setting up a European base for many multinationals, particularly US corporations. The availability of skilled labour is high due to the number of universities and the existing footprint of SSCs already based here. Unit labour costs are lower than other parts of Europe and payroll inflation is low. Many foreign workers are already based here, so language skills do not tend to be an issue. In addition the Government, through the IDA/InvestNI, is very supportive of foreign direct investment and grants/subsidies are often available for setting up in certain regions. Finally, our EMEA HQ is based here and we have available finance resources that could lead the project.

2. **Poland** Poland is also a popular base for FDI principally because of its low labour costs. Many German and US firms have established operations there although they have been primarily manufacturing rather than services. Availability of labour is generally good, with more than two million currently in higher education. The Government is supportive of FDI and makes grants available. It has been in the EU since 2004 but it is not in the Eurozone. Infrastructure, although improving, is still relatively underdeveloped and it has a reputation for being bureaucratic.

6. *Conclusions*

- Based on preliminary data there is a strong financial case for establishing an SSC for EMEA.
- In addition to the financial benefits, an SSC would also facilitate the achievement of our objective of improved control environment and a platform for scaling-up the business.
- It is not without risks. The principal risks relate to the loss of organisational knowledge and experience, and potential resistance from finance management, but there are actions we can take to mitigate these risks.
- The location of the SSC will be an important and sensitive issue. We will need to perform an objective assessment as part of feasibility analysis. However, both Ireland and Poland look like attractive options. Our existing EMEA HQ in Ireland will provide a solid base for managing the implementation and is perceived as a low-risk location given availability of skills and the footprint of existing SSCs based there. Nevertheless, from a financial perspective Poland does have lower implementation costs and salary costs.
- In conclusion, the SSC option looks attractive based on preliminary analysis so we should proceed to the next stage and prepare a detailed feasibility assessment and business case.

Notes and Workings

Note 1: Headcount Analysis

	Current	Future Total	Future country	Future SSC
Financial accounting	32	27	–	27
Billing and collections	90	77	–	77
Accounts payable	40	34	–	34
Payroll	30	26	–	26
Statutory accounts and compliance	18	18	18	–
Tax and treasury	3	3	3	–
Consolidation/Financial analysis	5	5	5	–
Total	218	190	26	164

Note: 15% reduction for financial accounting, billing and collections, accounts payable and payroll results in headcount saving of 28 (i.e. 218 – 190).

Note 2: Annual Payroll Saving

	Ireland – SSC	Poland – SSC
Current average salary for finance	US$62,670	US$62,670
Future SSC salary	US$54,000	US$45,000
Saving per head	US$8,670	US$17,670
SSC headcount	164	164
Total rate saving	US$1.422m	US$2.899m
Headcount saving (28 × US$62,670)	US$1.755m	US$1.755m
Total payroll saving	**US$3.177m**	**US$4.654m**

Note 3: Redundancy Calculation

192 displaced roles × 50% [made redundant] × US$62,670 [average salary] × 3/12 [3 months' pay] = US$1.504m.

Note 4: Staff Overlap Cost

Ireland SSC: 164 SSC roles × US$54,000 × 1/12 [1 month's training] = US$0.738m.
Poland SSC: 164 SSC roles × US$45,000 × 1/12 [1 month's training] = US$0.615m.

Note 5: Hiring Cost

Ireland SSC: 164 × US$54,000 × 10% = US$0.886m.
Poland SSC: 164 × US$45,000 × 10% = US$0.738m.

BONEDRI

Report for Conor Murray on Potential Investment in SE Asia

STRICTLY PRIVATE AND CONFIDENTIAL

1. *Introduction and Purpose of Document*

BoneDri is currently evaluating options to increase its production capacity to meet expected increased sales demand over the next five years. Specifically it is considering opening a new production facility in Bangladesh.

The purpose of this report is to outline our views on this proposal. Specifically it covers the following.
- The financial implications of the proposal compared with increasing capacity in Ireland. (We have used DCF analysis for the five-year period 2014–2018.)
- Other factors that should be considered as part of the decision.
- The operational and strategic factors that would need to be considered in operating a significant part of the business overseas.
- Finally, it also deals with the corporate and social responsibility issues to be addressed and how BoneDri could address these issues.

The document has been prepared on the basis of data/forecasts provided by David Carson and Imelda Quinn.

We would be delighted to meet you in due course to take you through our analysis and findings and answer any queries you may have.

2. *Executive Summary*

- The proposed strategy to diversify production and markets appears to be sound.
- The proposed investment in Bangladesh yields a positive NPV in excess of €/£11 million based on the assumptions you provided.
- However, we believe there are many other factors to be considered prior to finalising your decision, including:
  - the investment required (€/£15 million) is considerable, so availability and cost of funding will be critical factors;
  - sensitivity analysis, particularly in relation to sales forecasts, should be undertaken; and
  - other options, such as sub-contracting or a local partnership, should be considered in more detail.

There are considerable operational challenges for a company of BoneDri's size in relation to managing a significant part of the business in Asia, which should not be underestimated.

Solution 11.6: BoneDri

> **Consider the financial implications of establishing a factory in Bangladesh and discuss any other key factors that should be considered (i.e. does this make sense or would it be better to increase capacity in Ireland?).**

3. *Evaluation*

Financial Analysis We have calculated the net present value of incremental savings associated with increasing production capacity by opening a factory in Bangladesh. The analysis is set out in **Appendix I** to this report (see attached spreadsheet). Based on the financial analysis, opening a factory in Bangladesh would yield cost savings with a positive NPV of €/£11.4 million (before tax) compared with increasing capacity in Ireland. This is a very significant saving over five years and arises because of the substantial cost differential between Ireland and Bangladesh. As the relative proportion of production is moved overseas, the annual savings get larger.

The key assumptions on which this analysis is based are:
- forecast sales (and hence production) doubling from 9.4 million in 2012 to 18 million in 2018;
- the split of production between Ireland and Bangladesh, and the forecast future costs of production in both Ireland and Bangladesh are based on data supplied by David Carson;
- estimates of factory set-up costs amounting to a total of US$19.5 million (€/£15 million) as supplied by Imelda Quinn;
- cash flows beyond 2018 have been ignored;
- a US$–€/£ exchange rate of 1.30 has been used; and
- tax has not been considered at this stage.

Other Factors to be Considered There is no doubt that, based on this preliminary financial analysis, the savings are considerable. Furthermore, it would provide a foothold in Asia which could be a long-term growth market for the BoneDri brand.

Notwithstanding this there are a number of other factors that BoneDri should consider prior to making a final decision.
- *Reliability of Forecasts* Clearly the financial analysis is dependent on the accuracy of the forecasts. The critical assumption relates to forecast sales, which are expected to double over the next six years. Given the scale of the investment (€/£15 million) we would suggest performing some sensitivity analysis prior to making a final decision.
- *Reputational Impact Locally* The decision to relocate part of the business overseas is likely to negatively impact BoneDri's reputation in Ireland, particularly if layoffs take place, which is likely. The impact could be mitigated by a clear communication strategy.
- *Impact on Brand* Consideration should be given to the impact on the BoneDri brand as an ethical company given the perception of exploitation of workers in certain SE Asian countries. Again, it would be possible to mitigate this through voluntary external factory inspections and clear communications.
- *Management and Control of Business Overseas* The shift of a considerable part of the business overseas to Bangladesh would have considerable operational consequences for BoneDri in terms of management control (see section 4 below).
- *Availability and Cost of Funding* We have prepared a high-level note for Imelda Quinn on long-term funding, which we have included at the end of this report.

Conclusion We can understand why Bangladesh is under serious consideration given that it is the world's second-largest manufacturer of ready-made garments after China. Based on the financial analysis, the potential investment in Bangladesh looks favourable with a positive NPV in excess of €/£11 million.

However, we would recommend more detailed analysis prior to finalising this decision. There may be other options worth considering, such as using a sub-contractor in SE Asia to manufacture garments. This would avoid or postpone the significant investment in capital and management time and would provide a degree of protection if sales demand is lower than expected.

Solution 12.1: BoneDri

> **What are the operational challenges that would need to be considered and planned for should BoneDri choose to establish a production facility in Bangladesh?**

4. Operational and Strategic Issues of Operating a Business Overseas

From a strategic perspective, establishing a large business in a low-cost developing country in Asia has certain advantages for BoneDri.

As you noted, it provides a foothold in the enormous and rapidly growing Asian market – luxury branded products have performed very well there over the past decade. In addition, the lower cost base will give BoneDri some protection against declining margins in core markets. However, the establishment of a production facility in a foreign location over 5,000 miles away from Ireland would present new operational challenges that would need to be considered and planned for. The principal issues would be as follows.

- **Management control** BoneDri is a still a relatively young company with a small management team. Managing a business on two continents is likely to stretch management. There may be a need to bring in one or two experienced managers for the new operation and relocate some key employees until BoneDri has bedded-in the new operation.
- **Longer Lead Times to European Markets** Bangladesh is over 5,000 miles from the UK and Ireland, which is currently where BoneDri's major customers are based. Delivery lead times will be longer, so supply chain and inventory management will be more critical.
- **Ensuring Quality** BoneDri has a reputation for producing high-quality clothing. It will be vital to ensure that it maintains quality standards in the new facility to maintain this reputation.
- **Hiring and Training Suitably Skilled Staff** This is related to the point above. In setting up any operation overseas it is important to understand the local labour market and know where and how to source staff with the right skills.
- **Complying with Local Laws and Regulations** Local laws and regulations can be very different (and onerous) in overseas markets. It is important for BoneDri to obtain a thorough understanding of these laws/regulations and any permits required. We would suggest that BoneDri secure the services of a local law firm and/or accountants to advise on what is required.
- **Security of Intellectual Property** As a producer of high-quality branded produce, BoneDri would need to consider how to secure its intellectual property rights (designs, logos, etc.) to avoid cheaper produce appearing on the grey market and damaging the brand.
- **Dealing with the Potential Issue of Corrupt Payments** In the information provided by Imelda Quinn, she alluded to a payment to cover 'planning fees and permits'. In order to protect both the reputation of the company and its officers, BoneDri will need to establish clear guidelines around this type of payment. Corrupt payments and bribes are not victimless and are contrary to the ethical business principles of BoneDri. Any payments of this type will need to be investigated further and their purpose will have to be determined. BoneDri should engage the services of a local reputable professional services firm to obtain clear advice on the status of these payments. Our firm, which has a global network, may be able to help in this regard. If these payments are corrupt/bribes, then BoneDri should consider an alternative location for its expansion.
- **Inflation/Cost Control** Clearly a key advantage of setting up in a developing economy is the lower wage structure. However, this advantage can get eroded over time as wage inflation is often higher than in developed economies.

Solution 5.3: BoneDri

> **Outline the key issues of corporate and social responsibility that BoneDri will need to consider should it choose to establish a production facility in Bangladesh and what it can do to address these.**

5. *Corporate and Social Responsibility Issues and Actions*

The final issue you asked me to consider are the corporate and social responsibility issues that might arise with an investment in a developing economy and some of the actions that could be taken to deal with these issues.

Clearly this is an important matter for BoneDri given its reputation as an environmentally sound business. If BoneDri goes ahead with the establishment of its own operation, it will have more control than if it was to simply sub-contract to local suppliers.

CSR Issues to Consider:
- ensuring workplace health and safety;
- ensuring humane and fair standards of pay, working hours, conditions, rest periods, etc;
- relations with local communities;
- sustainability issues, such as water conservation, emissions and waste, and energy conservation;
- building standards and workplace facilities and conditions; and
- the apparent local societal acceptance of corrupt payments to make business operations run more smoothly.

Potential CSR Actions   There is a range of actions BoneDri could consider in relation to addressing CSR concerns in a developing economy.

- Having clear and transparent CSR policies and standards (including potentially appointing an executive with responsibility for implementing the policy), which are likely to exceed local requirements (policies should cover things like employee welfare, working conditions, recruitment policy, sustainability, bribes, etc.).
- Providing training and education to employees to help them develop their skills.
- Getting involved with local communities, for example, getting involved in schooling programmes and medical programmes, potentially in partnership with local government.
- Sourcing from reputable suppliers and insisting on a process to audit/inspect suppliers.
- Agreeing to voluntary inspections from independent organisations.

Solution 14.1: BoneDri

> **Identify the level of funding required to establish the operation in Bangladesh and recommend appropriate sources of finance for this.**

Briefing Note for Imelda Quinn on Funding

Introduction   BoneDri is considering a significant investment in a new plant in a developing country. In connection with this you have asked me to prepare a high level briefing note on funding options. I understand that the scale of the required funding is approximately US$19.5 million (€/£15 million).

Funding Options   Broadly speaking you have two major options:
1. to fund all, or part, of the investment with debt (probably a term loan similar to the existing loan on the Irish factory); or
2. to raise some additional equity to fund some, or all, of the investment.

Debt/Long-term Loan   BoneDri has a current debt–equity ratio of approximately 50/50, which is declining with the ongoing repayment of the existing term loan. Funding the entire investment (€/£15 million) with debt would push the debt level in 2014 to approximately €/£19 million and the debt–equity ratio 80/20 or 70/30. This is very high and servicing this level of debt would put pressure on the business. If the terms of the loan were similar to those of the existing loan, interest and capital payments would amount to nearly €/£4 million in 2015–16 and drop to circa €/£3 million from 2017 onwards. Given current EBITDA levels of €/£3 million, this looks extremely tight.

However, there is likely to be some capacity to fund part of the investment with debt. I would recommend initiating discussions with your bank to get a sounding on lending availability and preparing forecasts of future cash flows (EBITDA) to facilitate these discussions.

BoneDri should also consider whether it makes sense to borrow in €/£ or US$. This will depend on its overall hedging strategy. Prior to finalising its decision, BoneDri should prepare a forecast of cash flows in each currency.

Equity   It is likely that BoneDri would need to obtain external equity funding to finance all, or part, of the investment.

As a private company the likely options are through a venture capital company or possibly through a consortium of high net-worth investors. Clearly this will mean diluting ownership of the company. The investors will also want a view on a medium-term exit strategy for their investment.

However, it could also provide an opportunity to get expertise of Asian markets through the new investors.

Conclusion   The long-term funding of the business should be viewed as part of a broader strategy on where BoneDri's management sees the business going over the next five years rather than as part of a single (albeit large) capital investment. In our view the next step for BoneDri's management is to prepare a business plan for the next five years covering opportunities, strategy, investments required, cash flows and risk management.

As well as helping management to confirm its views and get buy-in from the team, it is something that will be required by bankers or new investors.

We would welcome the opportunity to discuss this with you and Conor in more detail.

Appendix 1: Financial Analysis for BoneDri

	2011	2012	2013f	2014f	2015f	2016f	2017f	2018f
Forecast Revenues								
Units (millions)	8.4	9.4	10.5	12	13.5	15	16.5	18
Option A – produced in Ireland only (millions of units)	8.4	9.4	10.5	12	13.5	15	16.5	18
Option B – produced in Ireland (millions of units)	8.4	9.4	10.5	8	8.5	9	9.5	10
Option B – produced in Bangladesh (millions of units)				4	5	6	7	8
Average sales price per unit (€/£)	6.00	5.70	5.50	5.40	5.20	5.00	5.00	5.00
Revenue (€/£m)	50.4	53.58	57.75	64.8	70.2	75	82.5	90
Unit costs under each option								
Option A – Ireland only (€/£)	4.4	4.4	4.4	4.4	4.5	4.6	4.7	4.9
Option B – Ireland (€/£)				4.4	4.4	4.4	4.4	4.4
Option B – Bangladesh (€/£)				3.3	3.5	3.7	3.9	4.1
Total cost Option A (€/£ million)				52.8	60.75	69	77.55	88.2
Total cost Option B (€/£ million)				48.4	54.9	61.8	69.1	76.8
Relevant Cash Flows								
Savings (A – B) (€/£ million)				4.4	5.85	7.2	8.45	11.4
New factory cost/modification costs not required (€/£ million)			−15	1				
Redundancy cost (€/£ million)				−0.5				
Net cash flows (€/£ million)			−15	4.9	5.85	7.2	8.45	11.4
DCF (€/£ million) @ 10%			11.41					

BOYNE AVIATION LIMITED

Report on Performance of Boyne Aviation Limited

Executive Summary

Boyne Aviation Limited (Boyne) is an Irish-owned airline operating between Ireland and a number of destinations in Great Britain and France. It has been in business since 1990, but results for 2011 and 2012 have been poor with operating losses of €5.6 million. I have compared the results of Boyne with those of other low-cost operators by focusing on some standard key performance indicators (KPIs). My analysis shows there are a number of significant differentiators between Boyne and the low-cost operators. It would appear that Boyne is incurring the costs of a full service airline but not enjoying the premium airfares.

Airline profits tend to be cyclical, with poor years following a number of profitable years. However, the last few years have seen many European airlines fail due to competition from low-cost operators. Airlines now tend to operate full service on long-haul flights where passengers are happy to pay premiums for a better service. As Boyne operates on short-haul routes its business model is facing stiff competition.

Solution 18.2: Boyne Aviation Limited

> **Evaluate the current results of Boyne Aviation in terms of finance and operations and compare them with the low-cost operator KPIs.**

Commentary on Boyne

Revenue Revenue per passenger has fallen marginally from €/£114 in 2011 to €/£113 in 2012 and this compares with an average KPI revenue in the industry of €/£100 (see **Appendix I** below). The figure for Boyne is probably consistent with it being somewhere between a full-service provider and a low-cost operator, however the recent load factor of 65% shows that the airline is flying with a lot of empty seats. This may be because the fares are too expensive when compared to other airlines' or compared to other available forms of transport. Passenger numbers in 2012 were static when compared to 2011. There is a relationship between passenger fares and load factor and cheaper fares would normally result in more passengers flying and an increase in load factor. Increasing airline revenue depends on optimising this relationship as decreasing fares should result in increasing the load factor but may reduce overall airline revenue. When compared to full-service airlines, low-cost operators seek to raise additional revenue for providing additional services like priority boarding, extra baggage, choosing seats, etc. This provides the low-cost operators with valuable extra revenue that full-service airlines provide free of charge. By charging these extra fees as optional extras, low-cost operators can keep their advertised initial fares low and so allow favourable comparison with the competition.

Costs The operational costs of Boyne are much higher than those of the low-cost operators. Some of these may be a result of Boyne operating as a full-service airline, however that would not explain why, for example, fuel costs are a higher percentage of turnover.

Staff costs are 26% of revenue in 2012 as opposed to 21% for the low-cost operators. These costs are a function of average staff cost multiplied by the number of people employed. Average salary costs are higher than the average salary costs of the low-cost operators and the number of passengers per employee is lower. Full-service airlines tend to be more unionised with better salaries, pension plans and benefits.

Fuel costs, at 29% of revenue, are greater than the industry average of 23%. This is unrelated to the level of service offered; however, fuel costs vary between airlines and depend greatly on each airline's fuel-buying strategy. Most airlines hedge their fuel costs, to some degree, by buying fuel options at fixed prices. The success of an airline's hedging strategy will determine its fuel spend relative to other airlines. If Boyne had managed to purchase its fuel in line with the industry KPI, it would have saved approximately €4 million.

Airport costs, at 22.8% of revenue, compare favourably with the industry KPI. These charges would include fees charged by airport companies on a per head basis plus costs of baggage handling, etc. Low-cost operators tend to operate from secondary airports with the extra cost of travelling to city centres being paid separately by the passengers. These secondary airports charge lower landing fees than the main airports and this is reflected in air-ticket prices. Most airlines outsource their baggage handling and costs may not be directly comparable if baggage is handled in-house by Boyne.

Other Operational Costs Other operational costs include the cost of aircraft depreciation and maintenance. In comparison to the industry KPI figure, Boyne's other operational costs are high and would require further investigation to find out the drivers of these costs. Age of aircraft and aircraft mix and how aircraft maintenance is contracted for will have a bearing on how these costs compare with competitors. Low-cost operators tend to use one type of aircraft as much as possible, which reduces maintenance costs, the amount of spare parts and costs of training of both on-board and maintenance staff.

Boyne is currently following a strategy of offering its customers a full service and is incurring the associated costs; however, in trying to compete with the low-cost operators, it is discounting fares. The result is Boyne incurring operating losses. Boyne's management has to agree on the marketing strategy it will follow given the business environment it is working in and put in place an operational plan to achieve profitability.

Solution 2.2: Boyne Aviation Limited

> **Detail the actions Boyne Aviation Limited should take in terms of managing costs and revenues in order to change the business model to that of a low-cost operator and prepare a forecast statement of income and expenditure for Boyne using industry KPIs.**

BRIEFING PAPER

To: Board of Boyne Aviation
Re: Boyne operating as a low-cost operator

Boyne is making significant losses under its current strategy. One of the options available to it is to move from being a full-service airline to a low-cost operator. Low-cost operators worldwide tend to have similar characteristics. These are, from the customer point of view:
- low fares;
- flights servicing secondary airports that are further from main cities than the main airports;
- point-to-point services that do not guarantee connections to on-going flights;
- extra charges for on-board meals/drinks;
- extra charges for any non-carry-on luggage;
- online booking; and
- lower levels of customer service.

Other non-customer characteristics are:
- a higher utilisation of aircraft;
- a lower number of staff per passenger;
- staff working longer hours and lower basic salaries; and
- using one type of aircraft to reduce maintenance and training costs and to enable easier transfer between aircraft of pilots and on-board staff.

Addressing both Revenue and Costs in Order to Reposition Boyne

I have taken Boyne's 2012 accounts and have adjusted them to reflect the low-cost operator KPIs (see **Appendix I** below). I have considered what actions would have to be taken in order for Boyne to move towards being a low-cost operator.

Revenue Boyne's average revenue per passenger was €/£113 in 2012 and its load factor was 65%. While it would be difficult to accurately predict the increase in passenger numbers were Boyne to reduce fares, the airline is presently more expensive than its competitors. I acknowledge that the other airlines are not necessarily operating on the same routes as Boyne and passengers may not necessarily have alternatives, however a reduction in passenger fares should result in an increase in numbers booking with Boyne. By applying the low-cost KPIs and reducing average air fare, Boyne should see an increase in its passenger-load factor and an increase in revenue.

Revenue management is a complex part of running an airline. In my adjusted statement of income and expenditure (see **Appendix I** below), I have assumed that a reduction in airfare to €/£100 will result in an increase in the load factor to 75%. Market research may provide better information on the likely consumer reaction to a reduction in fares.

Boyne continues to use travel agents for booking and so the cost to the passenger is higher than the revenue shown in the accounts. Boyne should offer its passengers online booking facilities and possibly telephone booking. In doing this it should be able to provide its passengers with lower fares.

Costs
Staff Costs Staff costs are, more so than fuel or other costs, under the control of Boyne management.

Staff numbers per passenger and per aircraft are higher than those of the low-cost operators. Boyne should look at the drivers of these staff costs. Staff pay is normally made up of a number of items – contracted basic pay, overtime, various allowances and benefits. It may be that costs could be reduced by way of negotiating reductions in the extra pay and allowances without affecting basic pay. As staff numbers are currently higher than the low-cost operators, Boyne should look at where the additional staff are currently deployed and look at ways of reducing employee numbers. Low-cost operators generally achieve greater productivity from their employees, for example, by having cabin staff managing the boarding process and aircraft cleaning.

Reduction of employee numbers may be achieved by way of a voluntary redundancy scheme. If this were not to deliver the necessary numbers, then a compulsory scheme might be considered. Such a plan would involve negotiations with the unions and Boyne may consider a HR consultancy firm to help with this.

Outsourcing some activities may also reduce payroll costs.

Maintaining employee morale would be crucial if a redundancy scheme was to be implemented and Boyne's management would have to manage this process in the context of company survival in the face of competition.

Fuel Costs Boyne should look at its fuel-buying strategy and establish why its fuel costs are a higher percentage of costs than their competitors'. It may be that it has entered into expensive fuel-hedging contracts in the past and these have driven up their costs. It may also be due to the use of inefficient aircrafts.

Fuel surcharges have not been popular with passengers.

Other Operational Costs Other operational costs, at 27%, are also higher than those of competitors and are likely to include costs like aircraft depreciation/leasing, maintenance, on-board catering, back-office costs, advertising, etc.

Boyne should look at the drivers of these costs and determine how they could be reduced.

The use of a single type of aircraft can reduce buying and maintenance costs significantly. Quicker turnaround times at airports would mean higher aircraft utilisation and hence lower costs.

Lower aircraft specifications, at the expense of passenger comfort, can also reduce costs (for example, non-reclining seats, no aircraft blinds and higher density seating).

There is no guarantee that by changing to a low-cost model Boyne could operate profitably. Scale of operations and competition are big influencing factors in airline profitability and Boyne is very small in airline terms.

APPENDIX 1: BOYNE AVIATION – STATEMENT OF PROFIT OR LOSS BASED ON INDUSTRY KPIS

12 months to June	2011 €/£000		2012 €/£000		Adjusted 2012 €/£000		Industry KPI
Revenue	66,120		65,653		67,038		
Staff costs	15,960	24.1%	17,000	25.9%	14,078	21.0%	21%
Fuel costs	19,000	28.7%	19,000	28.9%	15,419	23.0%	23%
Other operational costs	18,000	27.2%	17,900	27.3%	16,089	24.0%	24%
Airport costs	15,500	23.4%	15,000	22.8%	14,748	22.0%	22%
	68,460		68,900		60,335		
Operating profit/(loss)	–2,340	–3.5%	–3,247	–4.9%	6,704	10.0%	10%
Passenger numbers	580,000		581,000		670,384		
Employees	380		400		352		
Number of aircraft	9		9		9		
Revenue per passenger (€/£)	114		113		100		100
Load factor	65%		65%		75%		75%
Average Staff Costs	42,000		42,500		40,000		40,000
Passengers per employee	1,526		1,453		1,905		2,000
Employees per aircraft	42		44		39		40
Revenue per aircraft (€/£000)	7,347		7,295		7,449		8,000

CANAM INC

Memo on Proposed Enterprise System Implementation

To: Martha Kramer
From: Alan Hughes
Date: January 2014

STRICTLY PRIVATE AND CONFIDENTIAL

1. Introduction

Canam Europe is at the early stages of considering the implementation of a Single Enterprise System for all subsidiaries.

The purpose of this memo is: (a) to set out some initial views on key requirements for the system; and (b) set out some potential implementation challenges and what steps we should take to mitigate these issues. The memo has been prepared on the basis of a workshop with the country financial controllers and a preliminary discussion with Martha Kramer.

This should be considered as a starting point. At a later stage I think we will need to run more detailed workshops to flesh out requirements in more detail.

Solution 17.3: Canam Inc

> **Prepare a brief memo to Martha with an initial list of the key requirements, which Canam Inc can incorporate into a Request for Proposal to be issued to a number of software vendors, in respect of a proposed new IT system.**

2. Key Requirements for Proposed Single Enterprise System

Transaction Accounting
- General ledger with automated monthly close processing.
- Consolidation management, including intercompany netting. Need to facilitate integrated and standardised chart of accounts to ensure consistency of classification.
- Sales and accounts receivable management, including billing, discounts, credit limits and credit decisions. We will also need to standardise our approval process for discounts and allowances. Workflow could be beneficial with appropriate limits of approval authorities built in.
- Customer self-service for sales and payments.
- Purchase order/invoice processing using workflow. Electronic payments.
- Multi-currency capability.
- Travel and expense management (online self-service data entry, rules-based processing, online approval, workflow driven).

Budgeting, Forecasting and Business Intelligence
- Robust planning and budgeting integrated with monthly management accounts.
- Cost/expenses 'drill down' capability.
- Business intelligence tools, including customer and product profitability; sales forecasts.
- Corporate performance scorecard to track KPIs.

Other
- Consider customer-relationship management to enable account management by the local sales teams incorporating details of all major customers and prospects (key contact details; sales history; contact history).
- Governance and risk control framework will be important given some of the current weaknesses we have in our control environment.
- Ability to maintain both local statutory records and management accounts within the general ledger.
- System needs to be scalable to accommodate new subsidiaries.

Solution 17.4: Canam Inc

> **Discuss the key challenges in implementing the system and what actions Canam Inc could take to mitigate these issues.**

3. Key Implementation Challenges and Mitigating Actions

Implementation Challenge	Mitigating actions
Lack of senior management commitment	• Articulate a clear and compelling vision of what we plan to achieve and why we are doing this. This should include a written business case. • Visible leadership from the top (you and Jeff, and the country controllers).
Lack of buy-in and ownership by subsidiaries	• Involve those impacted in the planning and design. The initial workshop was a good start, but we will need to widen to the subsidiary finance teams. • Ensure regular two-way communications. • Align performance management and rewards with the project (in other words, bonuses should be partially dependent on successful implementation).

Implementation Challenge	Mitigating actions
Implementation does not achieve the desired results	• Ensure that scope is clear at the outset with tight controls over changes to agreed scope. • Establish performance measures for desired changes (cycle times, error rates, etc.).
Significant implementation delays and cost overruns	• Develop a comprehensive explicit implementation plan. • Ensure adequate skilled resources (we may need to get external support here). • Ensure we have adequate project management to track progress, and facilitate timely decision-making. This may be an area where I can play a role.
Implementation deflects local management from 'the day job'	• Local controllers are concerned that the implementation will affect revenue-generating activity; therefore, we need to ensure adequate resources are made available for the implementation. (We may need external support.) • We should also incorporate successful implementation into management-performance goals/objectives.

Solution 18.5: Canam Inc

> **Prepare a memo for Jeff Welsh on the performance of Canam Europe for 2013 and include your thoughts on what, if any, additional KPIs Canam Inc should include in its performance scorecard in the future.**

MEMO ON CANAM PERFORMANCE SCORECARD AND KPIs

To: Martha Kramer
From: Alan Hughes
Date: January 2014

STRICTLY PRIVATE AND CONFIDENTIAL

1. Introduction

The purpose of this memo is: (a) to review the performance of Canam Europe for 2013 based on the performance scorecard; and (b) set out my thoughts on additional KPIs that should be considered in the future for a more balanced view of performance.

2. Performance Review – Key Points

Revenues and Growth
- Canam Europe recorded strong growth for 2013. Revenues at US$61.4 million were up 35% on 2012 and were marginally ahead of budget.
- The key drivers of growth were: (a) the opening of new offices in Italy and the Netherlands; (b) the increased penetration of existing markets (Canam Europe more than doubled customer numbers from 68 to 140); and (c) the success of the new mobile diagnostic model, which contributed US$5 million to revenues in Q4.
- Revenue numbers were adversely impacted by the decline in the value of the US$ against the €/£ during the year. On a like-for-like basis, revenues were up 45% on 2012 and 10% on budget. I have dealt with the impact of currency movements below.

Gross Profit/Margin
- Gross margin for 2013 was 48% compared to 55% in 2012 and a budget of 52%.
- This is partially explained by the decline in the value of the US$ (see below) but other factors came into play.

- The new mobile diagnostic product sold at an introductory discount of 30%, which resulted in a lower GM in Q4. I have estimated that the lower margin on this product arising from the introductory discount was c. US$2 million (US$5 million/70% × 30%). Adjusting GM for this special discount would increase GM by 3% to 51%, which is close to budget.

Operating Expenses
- Operating expenses, at US$ 18.4 million, were up 16% on 2012 and were broadly in line with budget.
- The reason for the increase was higher payroll costs arising from increased headcount, which at year-end stood at 180, up from 125 a year earlier. This was due to the opening of two new offices and also our sales team was enhanced to support the strong revenue growth.

Currency impact and Overall Profitability
- Overall, Canam Europe had a strong performance in 2013. We recorded a net profit of US$11.1 million, which was nearly 20% ahead of 2012.
- However, it was nearly US$2 million behind budget, which was mainly due to exchange-rate movements. As previously noted, the weakening of the US$ had a significant impact on our performance for the year given that we sell in euro and intercompany pricing on our product is in US$. I have prepared a brief summary of performance on a like-for-like basis (i.e. restating results using the 2012 exchange rate).
- Consideration should be given to asking corporation headquarters to set intercompany prices in euro.

	2013 Actual	2013 Restated	Budget	2012
Revenue (US$000)	61,400	66,123	60,000	45,600
Gross Profit (US$000)	29,500	34,223	31,000	25,100
Gross Margin %	*48%*	*52%*	*55%*	*52%*
Operating Costs (US$000)	18,400	19,815	18,000	15,800
Net Profit (US$000)	11,100	14,408	13,000	9,300
Average US$/€ exchange rate	1.30	1.40	1.40	1.40

3. Additional KPIs

The KPIs used in our current scorecard are principally financially focussed. We should consider including some additional KPIs that focus on other important dimensions of the business, such as:
- customers,
- employees/talent, and
- internal business processes.

During 2013 our financial performance was strong; particularly our revenue growth. However, with the rapid growth some worrying signs appeared that, if not addressed, could cause the business some problems in the future, notably the following.
- Anecdotally there appeared to have been quite a few customer disputes in relation to pricing, delivery and service. We don't have a good understanding of customer satisfaction. We should consider developing a measure of customer satisfaction using surveys and other data (product returns, unplanned discounts, etc.). Additionally, we should track discounts given to customers. We need to tighten controls in this area, which I have addressed in the memo on system requirements.
- Given the nature of our product and customers it is important to have knowledgeable staff who establish long-term relationships with our customers. There were some customer issues this year related to sales staff turnover. Therefore, we need to keep track of employee turnover (particularly customer-focussed staff) and employee satisfaction. Perhaps we could look to conduct an employee survey each year.
- Process efficiency: given the growth in the scale and geographic spread of our business, we should keep track of cycle times from customer order to delivery to the customer.

Therefore, I would suggest that we consider adding some of the following KPIs to our performance score-card. When we decide which ones we plan to implement, we must ensure that we can capture the data relatively easily.

- Customer satisfaction index.
- % revenue from new customers.
- Employee turnover.
- Customer/sales staff turnover.
- Employee satisfaction index.
- Account managers' average professional competence (years).
- Admin staff as a percentage of total staff.
- Sales order to delivery cycle time.
- Discounts/allowances as % of revenue.

EUROHUB

Draft Extract for Operational Review Report to EuroHub

STRICTLY PRIVATE AND CONFIDENTIAL

Introduction

In connection with our project for EuroHub to perform an operational review of the business, I have prepared a draft report extract dealing with the specific areas you asked me to cover, namely:

- an analysis of the relative performance of the three LOBs within EuroHub;
- diagnosis and recommendations in relation to EuroHub's system of performance management; and
- an analysis of the options open to EuroHub in relation to its Chinese market-entry strategy.

If you have any queries in relation to this document, please let me know.

Solution 18.4: EuroHub

> **Analyse the financial performance of the three lines of business (LOBs) within EuroHub and comment on any issues you see emerging from this analysis.**

1. LOB performance Review Analysis

Introduction We have prepared a review of EuroHub as a whole and the relative performance of the three LOBs for 2012 based on management accounts for the y/e 31/12/12 and data provided by the financial controller. We have not validated the information provided as it did not form part of the scope of the review.

Overall the business is performing strongly with revenue growth of 20%. Gross margin has remained healthy at 33%. Overheads have increased by 10%, however much of the increase relates to LOB-manager bonuses (€/£105,000) and a bad debt (€/£60,000) in LOB 1 Customer Support. Taking these factors into consideration the business has maintained strong control over overheads. This has translated into strong growth in profits. PBT of €/£965,000 is up 38% on last year. However, the overall picture masks some significant variations in the three LOBs, as is evident from the table below.

	LOB 1 Customer Service	LOB 2 E-commerce Order Fulfilment	LOB 3 Electronic Contract Manufacturing
Revenue (€/£000)	2,100	5,100	3,200
Revenue growth YoY	*110%*	*24%*	*−11%*
Gross margin (€/£000)	450	1,650	1,300
Gross Margin: %	*21%*	*32%*	*41%*
Contribution (€/£000)	−39	1166	*732*
Contribution (%)	*−2%*	*23%*	*23%*
Estimate of capital invested (€/£000)	530	1,420	2,315
Return on capital (%)	*−7.3%*	*82.1%*	*31.6%*
Days sales outstanding	40	80	36

(For detailed workings, see **Appendix I** below.)

2. Observations on LOB Performance

(a) LOB 1 Customer Support
- This LOB experienced the strongest revenue growth in the current year, more than doubling from €1 million to €2.1 million.
- However, this is a lower-margin business (21%) and overheads are relatively high. After a bad debt of €60,000 it made a negative contribution to central overhead of €39,000.
- The increase in the number of customers and revenues in the current year was clearly at the expense of gross margin. This LOB should focus on pushing up gross margin and maybe should consider weeding out some very low margin customers if price increases are not possible.

(b) LOB 2 E-commerce Order Fulfilment
- This LOB is performing extremely well.
- Revenue is up 24% and it now constitutes nearly 50% of revenues.
- Gross margin is a healthy 32% and it makes a contribution of €1,166,000 (23% of revenue), which equates to a return of about 80% on the capital tied up in this LOB.
- The only area of concern for this LOB is the speed of collection of accounts receivable. Days sales outstanding (DSO) are 80 days, over double the level for the other LOBs. This LOB should increase its focus on collection for this business in the future.

(c) LOB 3 Electronic Contract Manufacturing Service
- This LOB is also performing well. Gross margin is very strong at 41% and it earned a contribution of €732,000 in 2012 (23% of revenues).
- However, revenues declined by 11% in the current year. It has a relatively small customer base (five customers), which makes it prone to larger fluctuations in revenues.
- It has a higher fixed cost base than the other LOBs, so any increases in revenue will flow to the bottom-line. This LOB should put increased effort into winning new customers in the future.
- Working capital management appears to be strong. DSO are the lowest in the business at 36 days.

Solution 17.2: EuroHub

> **Evaluate the performance management system in EuroHub Ltd and make some preliminary recommendations on performance management within EuroHub (include performance measures, systems changes and incentives).**

3. Assessment of LOB Performance Management System

Overview of Current System Your performance management system has three main components: (a) the financial and other recording systems that capture relevant performance information; (b) the measures or KPIs used to monitor performance; and (c) the incentives/rewards for management to achieve the organisation's goals. Our understanding of your current system is as follows:

- a basic financial accounting package where costs are not separately allocated to LOB;
- a focus on revenues and revenue growth to measure the performance of each LOB; and
- a bonus system for the three LOB managers, which is based exclusively on sales growth.

Diagnosis There are a number of issues with the current system, which we have outlined below.

1. LOB performance is not transparent as the financial system does not capture and allocate costs against each LOB. Hence it is difficult to monitor profitability performance of each LOB on an ongoing basis. Also, currency issues may pose problems.
2. The KPIs used to measure the performance of each LOB are too narrow. They focus solely on revenue and revenue growth. They do not include any measure of LOB profitability. Furthermore, no account is taken of other important organisational goals, such as customer satisfaction, operational efficiency, employee satisfaction or working capital management.
3. The LOB manager bonus system is skewed. Managers are paid a bonus of 5% of revenue growth. Clearly this incentivises managers to win new business but it takes no account of profitability or sustainability of revenue. In 2012 the manager LOB 1 Customer Support earned the highest bonus, even though this LOB was not profitable. In addition, the manager of LOB 3 Electronic Contract Manufacturing Services earned no bonus, even though this LOB was quite profitable.
4. Very few of your customers buy services from more than one LOB and yet there is very little incentive for the managers to cross-sell with the current reward system.

Recommendations The good news is that many of these issues can be fixed relatively easily and without significant investment. We recommend the following.

1. We understand that the financial application has an upgrade that can facilitate multiple divisions with revenues/costs separately allocated. We recommend that you consider purchasing and implementing this upgrade. This would require changes to the chart of accounts and the setting-up of new management reporting templates. We recommend that you put in place a project to implement the necessary changes (under the leadership of the FC).
2. We recommend that you broaden the suite of measures used to monitor LOB performance. Many organisations use the 'balanced scorecard' approach to performance measurement whereby they identify and track financial and non-financial measures that are key to long-term success. We recommend that EuroHub adopts this approach. While you may wish to consider what are the key performance indicators for the business as a whole and for each of the LOBs, we have set out below some suggestions:
   - revenue vs. budget/revenue growth;
   - gross margin %;
   - contribution;
   - customer satisfaction rating (this can be determined from annual feedback surveys and/or using data from operational systems, e.g. on time delivery, service resolution statistics, etc.);
   - employee satisfaction (this can be determined by an annual online survey or by churn rates); and
   - days sales outstanding (DSO) is a useful measure for tracking working capital invested in accounts receivable.
3. We recommend that you revisit the incentive plan for LOB managers. Although it is simple, transparent and incentivises sales, it is too narrowly focused. We suggest that you introduce two components to the bonus scheme. (a) One component based on overall company performance (e.g. profitability). This might be a percentage of company profit over a particular level. (b) A second component based on LOB performance using a balanced set of objectives (aligned to KPIs). These should be agreed upfront with each LOB manager and assessed at the end of the year by you in a formal performance review meeting with the manager. This component might be at your discretion but within certain defined parameters, e.g. bonus of 30% of salary for on-target performance; 30%–50% for above-target performance and 0%–30% for below-target performance.

Solution 3.4: EuroHub

> **Discuss the various market entry strategies available to EuroHub in entering the Chinese market and recommend the most appropriate strategy.**

4. Chinese Market Entry Strategy

Introduction The Chinese market has been identified as an attractive source of new clients. EuroHub has received a number of enquiries from Chinese manufacturers seeking to get a foothold in the European market. Consequently there is evidence that an opportunity exists for EuroHub to act as their customer support/logistics agent.

You have asked us to outline our views on the market entry options and the most appropriate strategy for EuroHub.

Options We believe there are three potential options for market entry:
1. *Appoint Irish-based China Sales Manager* This would involve appointing a home-based sales manager dedicated to the Chinese market. This manager would be engaged in developing a list of target companies, screening the target companies by sending an introductory e-mail directing them to the website, which will need to be updated to include a Chinese translated version. Once leads are generated, follow-up calls by a Chinese-speaking business development agent could be made. Finally, it will be important for EuroHub to send the sales manager to China to meet directly with the prospects to secure new business. It is unlikely that Chinese businesses will commit to a business relationship without face-to-face contact. This is the least expensive option.
2. *Establish a Sales Office in China* This would involve setting up a small office in China with a skeleton staff. It might initially be simply a sales manager and an office support person. From this base the sales manager would conduct broadly the same activities as for the direct sales from home office option. However, in addition the sales manager could make many more sales calls, attend trade fairs and generally establish more of a presence.
3. *Joint Venture* This would involve identifying a Chinese company to act as EuroHub's representative on the ground in China. The partner would bring its local knowledge of the Chinese market and its contacts. EuroHub would provide service delivery to clients. The joint venture (JV) could involve some sharing of the initial investment and profits arising from Chinese clients would flow to the JV and be shared in the manner agreed at the outset as part of the initial agreement. This option is more complex than the other options as it involves shared control and ownership. Finding the right partner is critical and due diligence would be necessary.

Recommendation As each of these options has differing levels of cost and investment (€/£ and management time), the optimal strategy depends on market potential (potential revenues and profitability). It is probably too early to call at this stage.

We recommend that EuroHub pursues an incremental approach. First, as a 'no regrets' first step, EuroHub should hire a Chinese business development manager (on a contract basis initially), whose role would be: (a) to implement the direct sales model immediately, including making some targeted sales visits to China; (b) to assess whether there are competitors to EuroHub already providing this service; (c) to investigate whether there are any suitable JV partners; and (d) to evaluate the best long-term market-entry strategy for EuroHub.

APPENDIX 1: DETAILED ANALYSIS OF LOB PROFITABILITY AND WORKINGS

(All amounts in €/£000)	LOB 1 Customer Support	LOB 2 E-commerce Order Fulfilment	LOB 3 Electronic Contract Manufacturing Services	Admin
Revenue	**2,100**	**5,100**	**3,200**	**n/a**
Direct labour	1,650	1,050	1,100	n/a
Direct materials	–	–	800	n/a
Transport	–	2,400	–	n/a
Cost of sales	1,650	3,450	1,900	n/a
Gross Margin	**450**	**1,650**	**1,300**	**n/a**
Admin salaries	–	–	–	540
LOB managers' salaries	80	80	80	–
LOB managers' bonuses	55	50	–	–
Telecoms	120	108	–	12
Rent and rates	144	216	288	72
Depreciation on machinery and equipment	30	30	200	30
Bad debts	60	–	–	–
Interest expense				100
Other admin expenses		–		140
Total overheads	**489**	**484**	**568**	**894**
Contribution	**–39**	**1166**	**732**	**–894**

ESTIMATE OF CAPITAL INVESTED

I do not have full figures for capital invested, but have used the total of fixed assets and receivables as an estimate for illustrative purposes.

(All amounts in €/£000)	LOB 1 Customer Support	LOB 2 E-commerce Order Fulfilment	LOB 3 Electronic Contract Manufacturing Services
Plant and Equipment (€/£2.9 million total) *€/£2 million in LOB 3 Electronic Contract Manufacturing Services* *Balance split evenly between other two LOBs and administration*	300	300	2,000
Trade Receivables	230	1,120	315
Estimate of Capital Invested	**530**	**1,420**	**2,315**

HUGHES ENGINEERING LIMITED

Discussion Document in Relation to Arabian Dairy Processing (ADP) Bid

STRICTLY PRIVATE AND CONFIDENTIAL

1. Introduction and Purpose of Document

Hughes Engineering has the opportunity to submit a bid to Arabian Dairy Processing Company (ADP) in connection with the manufacture, supply and installation of specialist machinery for a new plant.

The purpose of this document is to provide management with some analysis relevant to the bid. Specifically it covers:
- an estimate of the possible bid pricing range (from breakeven to 'normal' profitability);
- practical issues that would need to be considered if Hughes Engineering is awarded the contract;
- an estimate of the additional funding required for the contract and an analysis of possible financing options; and
- a consideration of potential FX exposures and how they might be managed.

The document has been prepared on the basis of data provided by Mark Naughton, indicative cost estimates and the 2012 income statement.

2. Executive Summary

- I have estimated that the bid pricing range should be in the region of €/£3.84 million (breakeven) to €/£5.53 million (to achieve normal profit margins).
- Given that the contract provides us with an opportunity to break into a new market with growth potential, I recommend we price keenly as it is likely to be a very competitive tender process. However, as it is a fixed-price contract with an inherent risk of overrun, I recommend that we do not price it too close to breakeven or we could end up losing money. Perhaps somewhere between €/£4.5 million and €/£5.0 million would be worth considering.
- The estimated funding requirement for the contract is between €/£1.35 million and €/£1.9 million depending on how we price the bid. The higher amount is required if we price at breakeven cost. Ideally we should try to finance this through a short-term working capital loan or overdraft from our bankers.
- If we decide on a longer term growth strategy into new markets, we may wish to consider bringing in some additional equity, potentially through a VC.
- FX exposures would arise on this contract as revenues will be in US$ and costs will be predominantly in €/£. However, I believe that most of the risk will be naturally hedged internally given that we source the bulk of our direct materials in US$ from US suppliers.
- Given the location of the installation in the Middle East and the relative scale of the contract, there would be a number of important issues to address if we were to be successful in winning the bid, including employee resourcing, management and control, and contract jurisdiction.

Solution 11.4: Hughes Engineering Limited

> **Calculate the most competitive price range for the bid to supply and install specialised machinery for ADP's new plant. This should range from: (a) the lowest price Hughes could bid to breakeven to (b) the price Hughes could bid to maintain its normal profit margins on manufacturing and installation.**

3. Tender Price Range

As instructed I have prepared potential bid pricing for two scenarios: (a) the price at which we would breakeven; and (b) the price at which we would earn our normal level of profit.

Based on my analysis I have estimated that the bid pricing range should be in the region of €/£3.84 million to €/£5.53 million (or US$4.8 million to US$6.9 million). The detailed calculations are set out below in **Appendix I**.

	Breakeven	Normal Profit
Manufacturing (€/£000)	2,700	3,750
Installation (€/£000)	1,010	1,710
Funding (€/£000)	133	72
Total (€/£000)	**3,843**	**5,532**
Total (US$000)	**4,804**	**6,915**

The key assumptions used in this calculation are:
- manufacturing direct labour and direct overhead will be incurred at the same levels for this contract as incurred on all contracts for 2012;
- factory depreciation is not included in the breakeven scenario as this would not be an incremental cost for this contract;
- a mark-up of 25% (GM 20%) has been applied to manufacturing cost in the 'normal profit' scenario; this is the average mark-up we achieved in 2012;
- installation engineers have been included at average salary cost for the breakeven scenario and at normal charge out rates for the 'normal profit' scenario (i.e. at €/£700 per day);
- the cost of a contract project manager has been included at a rate of €/£90,000 p.a. for 18 months;
- out-of-pocket travel and accommodation expenses have been included at a rate of €/£200 per day for each engineer on-site;
- funding cost has been estimated based on estimated cash flows for the project and using an interest rate of 6% (see section 5 of this discussion document for estimated cash flows);
- the US$ range has been calculated using an exchange rate of €/£1 = US$1.25; and
- no contingency has been built into either cost estimate.

Solution 12.3: Hughes Engineering Limited

> **Discuss the practical issues Hughes Engineering Limited would need to consider in carrying out the project if it were successful in its bid to supply and install specialised machinery for ADP's new plant.**

4. Practical Issues with Doing Business in a Multicultural Environment

There is no doubt that this contract would represent a huge opportunity for Hughes Engineering Limited. It would provide a platform for further growth in the Middle East and would enhance our reputation globally. The European market is going through a recession so it is important for us to diversify geographically into new markets.

Notwithstanding this, there would be a number of issues we would need to consider and manage if we were to win the ADP contract, including the following.
- **Fixed Price Contract** I understand that ADP wants a fixed-price contract. Given the risk of overruns we would need to build some contingency into our pricing and also ensure that the contract is worded tightly so that we are not exposed to factors outside of our control. In this regard we should ensure we have appropriate legal advice.

- **Scale** This is a relatively large contract. It is about 15–20% of the size of our current operations. We would need to scale-up our resources for this and ensure that it did not adversely impact our current projects and customers.

- **Control** The Middle East is a relatively distant location for us, so it would be more difficult to manage a contract there. We would need to ensure we have a very experienced project manager on the ground there.

- **Employee Issues** Eighteen months overseas in the Middle East is a long time. It may be difficult to get engineers to relocate overseas for this contract. We will have to consider incentives (allowances, additional flights, etc.) or rotating staff on this contract for periods of (say) six months. Another option would be for us to hire some engineers on a contract basis specifically for this project.

- **FX Exposure** Given that the contract would be in US dollars and our costs would be predominantly in €/£, we would need to manage our foreign exchange exposure. I have dealt with this in more detail below in section 6 of this discussion document.

- **Local Issues and Legal Jurisdiction** We will need to determine whether there are any local permits required or additional local taxes. Further, we will need to consider the contract jurisdiction in the event of a dispute. Ideally the contract would be drawn up under Irish/UK law, but this may not be possible. Another option might be to specify an international court (such as the International Court of Justice) for jurisdiction. Our legal advisors will be able to help us here.

- **Social, Cultural and Political Issues** We will need to be aware of the social, cultural and political sensitivities of operating in a different country. Some further research and perhaps a more formal due diligence may be required. The Middle East is a vast area, with numerous internal differences. As a guideline, think of some of the cultural differences which exist within Europe alone.

Solution 14.2: Hughes Engineering Limited

> **Calculate the level of funding required and identify and develop some appropriate financing options for the project at hand.**

5. Estimate of Funding Required and Financing Options

Our funding requirement varies over the life of the contract (24 months: six months for manufacturing and a further 18 months for installation) given the timing of payments from ADP. In addition, the level of funding required depends on the price at which we bid the contract. I have estimated the range of funding based on the two pricing scenarios, i.e. breakeven and 'normal profitability', which I have rounded to €/£3.8 million and €/£5.5 million respectively. The outflows will be the same regardless of pricing.

The results are set out in the table below (detailed workings are below in **Appendix I**).

(All amounts in €/£000)	0–6 months	6–12 months	12–18 months	18–24 months	Total
Outflows	(2,700)	(295)	(295)	(420)	(3,710)
Inflows – breakeven	1,140	–	1,140	1,520	3,800
Inflows – normal profit	1,650	–	1,650	2,200	5,500
Net cum. inflows (outflows) – breakeven	**(1,560)**	**(1,855)**	**(1,010)**	**90**	
Net cum. inflows (outflows) – normal profit	**(1,050)**	**(1,345)**	**10**	**1,790**	

On the basis of the analysis, the peak funding requirement will be in the range €/£1.35 million to €/£1.9 million.

The simplest way to finance this requirement would be through a term working-capital loan from our bankers (duration: 18–24 months). This is the most straightforward approach. We would need to discuss whether additional security would be required. We might also want to consider borrowing in US$ to provide a hedge against foreign currency risk (see section 6 of this discussion document).

Another option would be to obtain additional equity, either through existing shareholders or potentially bringing in a VC to provide growth funding. This might be worth considering if we decided to pursue a growth strategy in new markets. The advantage is that we would not incur interest costs, however it would lead to a dilution of ownership.

On balance I would recommend the loan option given that our funding requirement is only for 18–24 months.

Solution 15.2: Hughes Engineering Limited

> **Discuss how Hughes Engineering Limited could manage the foreign exchange exposure that would arise from undertaking the project.**

6. FX Considerations

The final issue you asked me to consider is the potential foreign exchange exposure (FX) on this contract. The FX exposure arises because the revenues from the contract are in US$ and the majority of costs will be in €/£. If we did not hedge this risk, we would expose the company to the impact of the movement of the €/£ exchange rate against the US$. If the US$ weakened against the €/£ over the two years of the contract, we would receive less €/£ revenue than expected and this would impact negatively on the profitability of the contract. The key methods of managing FX exposure are:

- **internal netting of currency flows** – this involves looking at inflows and outflows in all foreign currencies and determining whether exposures can be netted against each other;
- **FX contract** – a second method is to enter into a FX contract to sell a specified amount of US$ at a specified future date(s) at an agreed rate;
- **money market hedge** – this method involves borrowing foreign currency (US$) upfront, converting it to €/£ immediately and placing the €/£ funds on deposit. The FX loan will then be repaid when the US$ are received from ADP under the payment terms; and
- **FX option** – finally, we could buy an option to sell US$ in the future at an agreed rate. Under this method we could decide to exercise the option if the US$ weakened against the €/£. On the other hand, if the US$ strengthened, we could let the option lapse and realise the FX gain.

Given that we source a third of our materials from the US in US$ there is likely to be a natural internal hedge for part of our US$ exposure. This is the cheapest and best form of hedging and I would recommend we look at this first. Last year we purchased about €/£2.1 million of direct materials from the US so over two years this will probably cover much of our exposure on this contract (it will depend on how we price it); however, we will need to forecast inflows and outflows by month to see if there is any net exposure.

For any net exposure we will need to decide how or whether we wish to hedge. If it is significant (say over €/£200,000), I suggest we hedge. Possibly we could obtain part of the bank loan in US$ as a money market hedge.

The FX option may be best as we are looking at a tender process and our bid may not be successful and if it is not successful, the maximum loss would be the premium paid.

APPENDIX 1: DETAILED WORKINGS OF BID PRICE

	Notes	Breakeven €/£000	Normal €/£000
Manufacturing cost			
Direct materials		900	900
Direct labour	1	1,125	1,125
Direct overhead	2	675	675
Plant depreciation	3	–	300
Direct cost		2,700	3,000
Normal Gross Margin	4	–	750
Sub-total		2,700	3,750

Installation cost			
Engineers – first 12 months	5, 6	300	700
Engineers – final 6 months	5, 6	225	525
Project manager cost – first 12 months	7	90	90
Project manager cost – final 6 months	7	45	45
Out-of-pocket expenses – first 12 months	8	200	200
Out-of-pocket expenses – final 6 months	8	150	150
Sub-total		1,010	1,710
Funding cost	10	133	72
Bid range (€/£000)		3,843	5,532
Bid range (US$000) at €/£1 = US$1.25		4,804	6,915

NOTES
1. **Direct Labour** – direct materials €/£900 × 1.25 (as in 2012).
2. **Direct Overhead** – direct materials €/£900 × 0.75 (as in 2012).
3. **Plant Depreciation** – not applicable for breakeven; direct materials €/£900 × 0.33 (as in 2012).
4. **Gross Margin** – per 2012 results mark-up was 25% (i.e. 20% gross margin).
5. **Installation Breakeven** – four engineers × 12 months × average salary €/£75,000 (€/£3,750,000/50 employees) for Year 1 and six engineers × six months' average salary €/£75,000 for final six months.
6. **Installation Normal Profit** – four engineers × €/£700 per day × 250 days for Year 1; and six engineers × €/£700 per day for 125 days (six months) for final six months.
7. **Project Manager** – €/£90,000 for Year 1 and €/£45,000 for final six months.
8. **Out-of-pocket Costs** – Year 1: four engineers × €/£1,000 per week for 50 weeks = €/£200,000; Year 2: six engineers × €/£1,000 per week for 25 weeks = €/£150,000.
9. **Cash Flows** – outflows will be the same under both scenarios. 0–6 months: all costs €/£2,700,000; 6–12 months: engineers €/£150,000 + project manager €/£45,000 + out-of-pocket expenses €/£100,000 = €/£295,000; 12–18 months: as for previous six months; 18–24 months: engineers €/£225,000 + project manager €/£45,000 + out-of-pocket expenses €/£150,000.
10. **Funding Cost** – calculated based on net cash flows at 6%. Outflows as above. Inflows depend on bid price. Two scenarios calculated – bid price of €/£3.8 million (breakeven) and bid price of €/£5.5 million (normal profit). Inflows are spread 30% at beginning (first six months); 30% midway through contract (12–18 months) and 40% on completion (18–24 months).

KEBABS LTD

Solution 18.1: Kebabs Ltd

> **Draft and outline a strategic scorecard for Kebabs Ltd, integrating a range of information and measures relevant to the company. Comment on the measures and relate the content of the scorecard back to the strategy of Kebabs Ltd.**

I have drafted the strategic scorecard that I believe could prove useful for Kebabs Ltd.

STRATEGIC SCORECARD: KEBABS LTD

	City Centre	Regional
Financial measures		
Gross margin %	35.3%	30.6%
Net margin %	17.6%	16.1%
ROCE	6.8%	5.1%
Sales per sq metre	€/£405	€/£388
Customer measures		
Customer satisfaction	60%	65%
Food returns	0.5%	2%
Average waiting time		
Innovation measures		
New offerings (year to date)	2	1
Average lead time to introduce new offering	3 months	1 month
Operational measures		
Average spend per meal	€/£8.08	€/£7.43
Labour cost per meal	€/£1.71	€/£1.92
Wastage %	5%	2%
% of time opened	85%	95%
Water usage per meal	14.26 litres	14.37 litres

The above are some suggested metrics that may be used as a basis for assessing the performance of each fast-food restaurant however:
- data like this is really only useful over time where it can be compared against the same metrics for previous periods;
- there are no existing standards against which these may be compared: while the city-centre restaurant is more profitable than the regional one, we have no idea of competitive factors at play or different cost bases;
- key performance indicators can be built up over time and additional ones developed against which performance can be evaluated;
- it would be useful to compare the performance of Kebabs against other fast-food retailers, particularly the best performers, therefore I would suggest calculating similar metrics for competitors from accounts and other information available against which we could compare performance;
- in addition, we could look at other non-financial metrics that would be aligned with strategic and other priorities suggested, like use of packaging materials and cleanliness of the areas outside of our fast-food restaurants.

Ideally, the selected measures (or key performance indicators (KPIs)) should be chosen based on the agreed strategic priorities. In the material presented the following three strategies have been identified:
- to increase margins in each restaurant by 2%;
- to reduce returns by customers by 10% over rates in 2009;
- to maintain the high quality of the food.

We do not have the rates in the previous year to enable us to identify the longer-term profitability or the level of returns. It can be commented that the stated strategies are more operational goals rather than strategic. Indeed, the note suggests that there is no mention of the German expansion. This suggests that the operation of the business focuses on the area of operations and the area of strategy needs to be developed in the future.

Kebabs should revisit its strategy and decide what is being offered to the public. Is it competing on price or on quality – or is it selling an environmentally friendly experience? For example, if it were to offer the latter, then it should showcase its environmental credentials when fitting out its restaurants in terms of sustainable building and lighting, look closely at its choice of packaging (e.g. cut out the use of polystyrene), monitor water usage, ensure the areas outside of its restaurants are kept clean, use solar for heating hot water, etc. It would standardise this across all of its restaurants and make sure the public is aware of what it does and how it differentiates from the competition. It cannot satisfy all of the market with a mixed message. I suggest it carry out a SWOT analysis and decide what part of the market it is targeting. With this information it would be easier to plan and align suitable metrics and performance measurements against the agreed strategy.

The question includes reference to waste and waste disposal and environmental issues generally. This is discussed below.

Solution 5.1: Kebabs Ltd

> **Discuss the environmental concerns arising from the information presented and devise key performance indicators (KPIs) as to how these can be monitored and managed.**

Environmental Reporting

Environmental management accounting covers the physical information (on the use, flows and fates of energy, waters and materials (including wastes)) and money metrics covers environmentally related costs, earnings and savings (source: UN Expert Group on EMA (2001)).

In terms of the details given, there are a number of environmental issues that have been highlighted. These are now considered with their implications and possible metrics to quantify each issue:

Issue	Implication	Possible Metrics
Water consumption is high, additional legislation and increased focus from local councils is planned for this area.	Level of usage is likely to be metered, with possible penalties for wastage. Usage of water is presented as a key factor in maintaining hygiene in restaurants. (Alternative materials might be used.)	• Total water consumed in restaurant for the period. • Consumption per meal served could be estimated. • Targets for usage could be set with monitoring of usage against these.
Usage of packaging.	Fast food uses non-biodegradable packaging and this is often disposed of in an unsustainable manner. Restaurants have been identified as litter black spots giving rise to possible fines and bad publicity.	• Level of packaging consumed could be monitored. • Litter fines incurred could be monitored. • Adverse publicity might be assessed.
Materials used and wasted.	Food products need to be monitored to ensure health and safety standards are maintained. Ideally, wastage should be minimised by cooking on a demand basis.	• Total materials used (volume and cost measures) also by customer or meal served. • Level of materials returned (may be indicative of quality issues). • Level of wastage generated.
Other areas could include electricity or energy usage or atmospheric pollutants, etc.	Likely that the State may wish to monitor these and ensure best practice.	• This could include electricity usage in each restaurant compared to a standard, etc.

Other Possible Commentary

It is not clear, however, whether the company is committed to being environmentally responsible (included in what is termed 'corporate social responsibility'). Ideally we should clarify the company's objectives (for example, to be seen as 'green' and environmentally friendly or merely to comply with the law) and then work with management to agree priorities and how these will be developed going forward. It would be important that there is a consistent message for staff in this area and ideally a 'compliance' or tick box attitude should be avoided. Without knowing the company's overall position and where it wishes to go, it is difficult to be more specific.

Kebabs could calculate its existing carbon footprint from its present activities and take positive steps to reduce this and become carbon-neutral in its business activities. Ways of reducing its carbon footprint include using environmentally friendly sources of energy, recycling and reducing waste. In addition, it is possible to buy carbon credits to offset its carbon footprint further. If its strategy was to offer its customers an environmentally friendly experience, a neutral carbon footprint would reinforce that strategy.

Solution 3.1: Kebabs Ltd

> **Identify the potential market-entry routes for Kebabs into the German market and discuss the key issues relating to each option. Recommend the most suitable market-entry option.**

MEMO

Re Kebabs Ltd – Possible Market Entry Routes into German Market

Before examining the possible market-entry methods, it should be noted that it would be normal to carry out a screening of possible markets. This is designed to ensure that the markets are viable and worthy of development and investment.

Germany has the largest population of any country in Europe and its fast-food industry is less developed than that of Ireland.

I have noted below a number of ways in which Kebabs may enter the German market. As Kebabs is a fast-food company the traditional market-entry methods such as exporting and direct sales do not apply.

Possible Market Entry Methods and Issues to be Addressed

Possible Market-entry Method	Issues to be Addressed
Foreign direct investment: acquiring an existing business or establishing our own business directly and branding as Kebabs.	This would require significant financial resources to undertake. Significant cultural and other factors are likely to arise. As we have only operated in Ireland, establishing such an operation could be considered to be quite risky.
	The success of this investment may be constrained by our management and financial resources and time available. The advantage of directly investing, however, is 100% control and all of the returns.
Joint venture (JV) operation: here we would partner with an existing company or other partners.	This would reduce the required potential investment and if our partners are well selected, there could be sharing of expertise and resources.
	Managing and co-ordinating such an operation is likely to be more complex and problematic. This is a possibility if Kebabs were to identify a suitable partner where each would bring complementary skills to the JV, i.e. Kebabs' branding and operational systems, German partner's local knowledge and staff.
Licensing arrangement with a third-party organisation in our target market.	It should be possible to license our expertise and other know-how to a third party. This is a relatively low risk method and generates cash up-front. This is not common in the fast-food business.
Franchising arrangement to one or more franchisees in the target market.	This is an extension of the licensing arrangement and is popular with fast-food businesses. Typically the investor overseas enters into a contract, which gives them access to our know-how, our trademarks and other livery and logos. Kebabs would have a defined agreement identifying what it is offering and the terms required by the franchisee. (Franchisee selection and monitoring is likely to be a key factor.)
	Standard operating and procedural manuals would need to be provided by Kebabs to franchisees along with back-up support in all areas of the business.
	At this stage Kebabs does not have a presence in Germany and is unknown to the German public, therefore it would have difficulty in attracting suitable franchisees.

Concluding Comments International expansion is a high-risk activity. Kebabs needs to consider if it has the necessary resources (finance, expertise, time) to develop and nurture the potential target. The information presented makes a more detailed analysis difficult at this stage, however significant operational and cultural challenges appear likely.

Perhaps Kebabs might look at a more considered approach to this investment opportunity before taking any final decisions. Kebabs is now entering a more mature stage of its business life cycle where strategic focus is perhaps more important than before. There may not be the internal skills, knowledge or experience in Kebabs to drive this forward. A partnership or JV-type arrangement is likely to be more appropriate. More information is needed to develop our ideas further.

NATURAL FOOD COMPANY

Draft Report on Artisan Food Company

STRICTLY PRIVATE AND CONFIDENTIAL

Introduction

In connection with Natural Food's initiative to identify suitable acquisition targets in Europe, I met with the founder owners of Artisan Food Company (AFC), a small Irish food company, on a two-day visit to their operations. AFC is engaged in making and distributing a range of high-quality, chilled food products, including soups and health snacks. The purpose of this draft report is to:

- outline my financial assessment of AFC; and
- consider whether it is aligned with the strategic scorecard of Natural Food.

If you have any queries in relation to this document, please let me know.

Executive Summary

- Going forward AFC has projected annualised revenues of €/£6.7 million; annualised profits of €/£0.73 million; and has good growth prospects in Ireland and possibly in other markets in Europe.
- The indicative price range of €/£5 million would give a prospective P/E of 6.8 and this fits within the financial parameters set by Natural Food.
- The acquisition would be aligned with Natural Food's strategic scorecard.
  - It would give us a foothold in the Irish market and provide a platform for growth.
  - AFC product range is organic, which is in our 'sweet spot'.
  - The founders are dynamic, have a track record of success in developing and marketing new products and would be an addition to our management team in Europe.
- In conclusion I would consider AFC to be an excellent fit for Natural Food and recommend that we take it to the next stage of analysis and discussion.
- However, there are some important points for detailed follow-up, as follows:
  - AFC outsources food production to third parties. We need to meet with suppliers to get a better understanding of the quality of food production and supply chain processes,
  - we need to review the latest revenue and gross margin to ensure it is in line with the forecasts provided, which are significantly improved on 2012 performance.

Solution 11.3: Natural Food Company

> **Evaluate and assess the international investment opportunity for Natural Food Company in relation to the Artisan Food Company and recommend whether or not the company should proceed with the acquisition.**

1. Financial Assessment of Artisan Food Company

Introduction   The latest financial information available was for 2012. I understand from discussions with the owners that performance has improved significantly in 2013. I have based my analysis on forecast sales and margins (obtained through discussion), which I have annualised to facilitate comparison with 2012 (see below). Clearly, we will need to validate this information at a later stage if we decide to proceed.

Key Points/Highlights

- Significant sales growth of 40% forecast for 2013 due principally to the impact of a new contract with a German discount retailer (€/£2 million) and the annualised impact of new products introduced in 2012.
- Gross profit margin is expected to decline from 31% to 27% again due to the new contract, which has a gross margin of 15%, which is 50% of the margin on our branded product.
- I have analysed sales and gross margin below in **Note 1**.

- Broadly speaking, expenses are expected to remain flat. The reduction in admin expenses relates to a one-off item in the 2012 accounts. Presumably as the business grows there will be upward pressure on expenses, but we may be able to achieve synergies in this area on a pan-European/global level.
- AFC continues to invest in developing new products and budgets, c. 1% in revenues each year.
- The tax rate in Ireland is a favourable 12.5% (ROI)/24% (NI).
- Forecast normalised PAT for 2013 is c. €/£730,000 – approximately 70% higher than 2012 levels.

(All data in €/£000)	Notes	2013 Annualised Forecast	2012 Actual
Revenue	1	6,740	4,800
Cost of sales		4,943	3,300
Gross profit	1	1,797	1,500
Sales and marketing costs		520	520
Administration expenses		300	360
Research and development		67	50
Finance costs		75	75
Profit before tax		835	495
Tax		104	62
Profit after tax		730	433

Note 1: Revenue and Gross Margin

	Soup – Existing Brands	Soup – New Brand	Snacks	Total
Revenue 2012 (€/£000)	3,600	–	1,200	4,800
Forecast growth	*–10%*	*new*	*25%*	
Revenue 2013 (forecast) (€/£000)	3,240	2,000	1,500	6,740
Gross profit 2012 (€/£000)	1,080	n/a	420	1,500
Gross margin 2012	*30%*	*–*	*35%*	*30%*
Gross margin 2013 (forecast)	*30%*	*15%*	*35%*	*26%*
Gross profit 2013 (forecast) (€/£000)	972	300	525	1,797

Conclusion

- Going forward AFC has projected annualised revenues of €/£6.74 million; annualised profits of c. €/£0.73 million; and has good growth prospects in Ireland and possibly in other markets in Europe.
- The indicative price range of €/£5 million would give a prospective P/E of 6.8 and this fits within the financial parameters set by Natural Food.
- However, there are some important points for detailed follow-up, as follows:
  - AFC outsources food production to third parties. We need to meet with suppliers to get a better understanding of the quality of food production and supply chain processes;
  - we need to review latest revenue and gross margin to ensure it is in line with the forecasts provided which are significantly improved on 2012 performance.

Solution 18.3: Natural Food Company

> **Evaluate the suitability of the Artisan Food Company against Natural Food's scorecard and assess whether it is a suitable takeover target.**

2. Assessment against Strategic Scorecard

Item/issue	Strategic Importance (H/M/L)	Assessment
Strategic Position		
1. Industry consolidation.	H	Our competitors are buying up small independent producers. This acquisition would increase our footprint in Europe and give us greater global reach.
2. Natural Food is looking to expand its operations in developed markets, in particular North America and Europe.	H	AFC would give Natural Food a foothold in the Irish market and provide a platform for growth into Europe, particularly given the listing with the major European retail multiples.
Strategic Options		
1. Launch existing products into new markets.	M	n/a
2. Enter new markets through acquisitions or through joint ventures.	H	Consistent with strategy.
Strategic Risks		
1. Reputational damage to brands from food-contamination scares.	H	Need to assess the potential risk of reputational damage arising from the investigation of one of AFC's outsourced manufacturers.
2. Increased focus on high-quality, 'own brand' fresh/chilled products by supermarket chains.	M	AFC has entered into a distribution arrangement with a German discount chain. We will need to determine if, on a long-term basis, this is in line with our strategy. The contract currently contributes a net €/£120,000 to PAT so it would not be a deal-breaker if we decided not to pursue this strategy.
3. Management stretch/overreach	H	The potential acquisition could further stretch management given that we are currently grappling with the integration of our new French acquisition, however it is relatively small-scale and the experience of the key personnel in AFC could prove to be a valuable addition.

PILLAR BANK PLC

Internal Report for Finance Director on Outsourcing

STRICTLY PRIVATE AND CONFIDENTIAL

1. Introduction

Pillar Bank Plc (the Bank) is currently considering whether outsourcing certain back-office functions makes commercial sense. This is being looked at as part of an enterprise-wide restructuring programme.

In this regard you have asked me to review and critically evaluate a previous internal report prepared by Operations taking into consideration additional data we have obtained from Beta Solutions, a global outsource provider (I have included both documents in appendices to this report).

You have also asked me to include in this report the key issues and challenges that the Bank would face in managing a substantial overseas outsource contract.

Solution 11.5: Pillar Bank Plc

> **Review the memo from Ken in relation to outsourcing and critically evaluate its findings, considering the information with which Beta has provided Pillar Bank Plc.**

2. *Critical Evaluation of Internal Report*

Financial Assessment   The operations department's internal memo (the memo) concludes that outsourcing the functions under consideration would generate a negative NPV of €/£1.6 million. In my view the analysis is based on a number of critical assumptions that could be challenged or which, in the light of additional information, are out of date. Specifically:

- Beta has indicated that the transition charge would be capped at €/£1 million (US$1.3 million). The memo includes a fee of €/£2.7 million.
- The memo assumes all staff would be made redundant. There may be an opportunity to redeploy staff into areas where we are currently recruiting. We could look to redeploy some staff given shortages, and increased focus on mobile/internet platforms may mean a reduced redundancy cost.
- The memo assumes a consultancy cost of €/£2 million. I agree that resources will be required for implementation, but we could look to reduce this estimated cost by tendering consultancy services and/or by using internal project resources.
- The memo takes average savings at 30% (€/£3.2 million p.a.). Using the specific data supplied by Beta, the savings would be closer to €/£3.6 million p.a.
- The memo ignores potential savings after Year 5.
- Beta indicates that it seeks to reduce headcount by 10% over three years through business process redesign (BPR). This upside on BPR is not factored into the memo.
- The memo does not consider functions individually. It is relatively more attractive to outsource certain functions. For example, the annual savings on eBanking support are much lower than for other functions. We should run the analysis looking at different options. eBanking support might be an area that we would not be keen to outsource as we are increasing our focus on mobile/internet platforms.
- The memo uses a discount factor of 12%. One could argue that this should be closer to 8%, which is our current cost of funds.
- I have prepared an alternative NPV calculation with updated assumptions and it shows a positive NPV of circa €/£4 million (see **Appendix I** to this report).

Non-financial Assessment
- We should **not** consider outsourcing customer support as it is a key plank of future strategy and savings are lower.
- The Financial Regulator's approval may not be an issue given the services outsourced as they are not core banking activities, such as credit assessment and risk management.
- Beta has a strong track record and expertise in the areas we are looking to outsource.
- The CEO has already signalled redundancies so this should not be a major issue.
- The Bank's track record in outsourcing is an issue but it can learn from past mistakes.
- Inflation may be an issue but perhaps we can negotiate with Beta.
- Ditto on term. Beta's CEO has indicated that a contract could be for three years.
- A proportion of the Bank's fixed costs will become variable.
- We will need to consider the impact of US$ to €/£ exchange rate as the contract is priced in US$. Potentially we could look to negotiate the contract in €/£.

Conclusion
- Outsourcing could potentially deliver substantial savings – the Bank is looking to reduce costs by €/£20 million and this could provide up to €/£4 million in savings.
- The non-financial issues highlighted could be managed.
- Therefore we should explore our outsourcing options in more detail.

Solution 12.2: Pillar Bank Plc

> **Discuss the challenges that Pillar Bank Plc might face in managing an overseas outsourcing contract and identify the steps it could take to address those challenges.**

3. *Managing Overseas Outsourcing Contract – Issues*

I have set out in the table below the key challenges we might face in managing an overseas outsourcing contract. We should also discuss the issues with Operations as I am sure there are lessons that we can learn from our previous outsourcing contract.

Challenges	Steps we could take to address these challenges
Managing the transition.	The transition to an outsourcer needs to be managed carefully. We need to factor in enough time to do a proper handover, with 'parallel running' for a short period of time. We would also need to ensure that we have good communications with those impacted (externally/internally).
Loss of organisational knowledge.	Given that the average length of service in the relevant functions is seven years, there is a lot of embedded knowledge in our workforce. We would need to ensure adequate training/handover time to allow for knowledge transfer. We could also ensure that processes, policies and relevant historical information is well documented.
Cultural and language issues.	Although all the outsourcing staff will be English-speaking, there may be issues with dialects/pronunciation. We should consider minimising the outsourcing of functions dealing directly with customers. In saying that, a number of UK and Irish companies have outsourced customer roles so it may not be as big an issue now as it was five years ago.
Managing service levels and quality.	I understand that there was an issue with response times in the previous outsourcing contract so we would need to be careful here. We would need to ensure that we put in place quantitative and qualitative metrics to measure performance and track this regularly at service meetings. We should also ensure that the contract is tightly written to avoid ambiguity.
Managing cost escalations.	I understand that in our previous outsourcing contract costs were higher than anticipated. Again we will need to ensure that the contract is clear. We should put in place clear rules around approving variations. We should also ensure that we have adequate resources on our side to manage the arrangement. Good governance can help here with regular service review meetings.
Time-zone differences.	India is five hours ahead of Ireland so we would need to factor this into the contract and ensure that service is provided for the hours we want.

PILLAR BANK PLC – REVISED WORKINGS FOR REDUNDANCY COSTS – BY DEPARTMENT

Service Area	Current cost €/£000	Average salary by dept €	Head-count	Average length of service	Business criticality	Future salary cost €	Future payroll cost €/£000	Management fee 5% €/£000	Future total cost €/£000	Savings p.a. €/£000	Imp. cost €/£000	Redundancy cost €/£000	Set-up cost €/£000	Payback Years
IT helpdesk	2,250	45,000	50	8	medium	25,000	1,250	62.5	1,312.5	937.5	2,577	2,077	500	2.75
eBanking customer support	3,600	30,000	120	4	medium	25,000	3,000	150	3,150.0	450.0	2,862	1,662	1,200	6.36
HR Operations	1,650	55,000	30	9	low	25,000	750	37.5	787.5	862.5	2,013	1,713	300	2.33
Accounts payable	3,150	45,000	70	7	low	25,000	1,750	87.5	1,837.5	1,312.5	3,244	2,544	700	2.47
Sub-total	10,650		270				6,750	337.5	7,087.5	3,562.5**	10,696	7,996*	2,700	3.00

Average salary cost per memo to Ken Byrne (KB) = €/£39,444, with seven years' average length of service.

DCF of Outsourcing Back-office Functions (Original and Revised)

	Original per memo €/£000	Notes/assumptions	Revised €/£000	Notes/assumptions
Redundancy	8,600	€/£39,444 × 7 years × 6/52 weeks × 270 employees	**7,996**	See * above
Set-up	2,700	270 × €/£10,000	1,000	Capped at €/£1 million
Consultancy	2,000		1,000	Negotiate and use some internal resources
Sub-total – implementation cost	*13,300*		*9,996*	
Annual savings	3,195		**3,562.5**	See ** above current cost of funds
Disc. factor	12%		8%	
NPV	−1,591.73		3,914.70	

R&D INVESTMENT

To: John Purcell / Mary Murray
From: Charlie Powell
Re: Gaining competitive advantage in the Irish market
Date: day/month/year

Further to our meeting, this memo focuses on two key points relating to competitiveness in the Irish market:
• overall strategic competitiveness;
• issues to be aware of relating to the use of transfer pricing practices to enable the intercompany charging of IP.

Solution 4.1: R&D Investment

> **Use Porter's Diamond Model to aid R&D Investment to present the competitive advantages of locating an R&D facility in Ireland.**

During the decade starting in the mid-1990s Ireland developed as one of the most successful countries in the global economy. Large inflows of capital into Ireland's open economy along with a flexible and well-educated workforce created much economic growth.

In the early part of this decade a shortage of labour started driving labour costs to uncompetitive levels and started to erode our competitive advantage.

Most countries go through three main stages in their economic development in terms of how they interface internationally. These main stages are: resource driven, investment driven and innovation driven. Ireland is probably between the investment-driven and innovation-driven stages. It is aware that it has lost its competitive edge in terms of labour cost, but is actively positioning itself to be more innovation driven.

The model I've used to assess competitiveness is Porter's Diamond. It is used to focus on competitive advantages of countries. It provides a useful starting point, as the focus of our discussion is on the establishment of the R&D centre in Ireland. In terms of competitive advantage, this is divided into four elements that interact. I've given a brief overview of each element and discussed its relevance to our own situation.

1. Factor Conditions

Porter differentiates between basic input factors (natural resources, unskilled labour, etc.), which are largely inherited and do not guarantee a competitive advantage, and advanced factors (such as an educated workforce, R&D capacity and infrastructure), which are typically key.

Assessment Ireland does not have an abundance of natural resources, unlike a country, for example, like Russia; however, it does have some significant input factors. Ireland's infrastructure is comparatively strong following significant state investment in infrastructure (roads) and Ireland is well serviced with ports. Airport links are well developed, both regionally and internationally. The State has made significant investment in education and there is a strong supply of experienced workers and graduates to meet the needs of international high-tech companies. Significant investment is being made by the State to support research and development and favourable tax treatment of expenditure on R&D is available to increase Ireland's attractiveness.

2. Demand Conditions: The Home Market

A large home market that is reactive to customer needs is likely to stimulate innovation and generate significant scale to support international expansion.

Assessment The Irish market is relatively small and heavily dependent on the international market. However, as a member of the EU, Ireland provides access to a significant European market. The Irish market is relatively sophisticated. Demanding and aware of global trends; it is used to service the high-quality needs of the world's top multinational enterprises.

3. Related and Supporting Industries (Cluster Effect)

The existence of related and supporting suppliers can be a key basis for building and maintaining a centre of excellence. The presence of clusters of similar and related industries can be a major competitive factor insofar as companies 'feed' on each other's innovation and create a pool of experienced employees that can easily transfer between similar industries, bringing specialist skills.

Assessment Ireland has positioned itself well in such sectors as pharmaceuticals and IT. Many pharmaceutical companies have located in Ireland, attracted initially by grants and favourable tax rates, but staying here due to the presence of supporting industries (amongst other reasons). Some of the larger US MNEs, like Boston Scientific, carry out significant research on new products in Ireland. Links to universities are likely to be important in this regard and highly relevant to MNEs when deciding where to locate an R&D centre. Access to appropriate international tax and legal advice is also important.

4. Firm Strategy Structure and Rivalry

Certain countries display an affinity to particular industries (e.g. Germany and engineering). There can be factors that make a country attractive due to national priorities (e.g. Israel and agriculture and defence) or a high level of local competition in terms of building national champions. Some countries have an affinity to, and take pride in, their association with particular industries, e.g. Italy and fashion design. In addition, local rivalry between similar firms can help companies develop their competitive skills further and so help in expanding abroad.

Assessment Parts of Ireland have a strong tradition in engineering, particularly Northern Ireland in heavy engineering, e.g. shipbuilding and aircraft manufacturing. Light and precision engineering is carried out by many companies in the Shannon region. US high-tech multinational manufacturing companies have based their European manufacturing and sales in Ireland.

Solution 16.1: R&D Investment

> **Outline an appropriate transfer pricing arrangement that might be used to charge for intercompany use of intellectual property and outline the particular issues that might arise in the context of the local firm and head office doing business across borders.**

BY E-MAIL TO JOHN PURCELL

Further to your memo of ddmmyy

We are looking at the possibility of developing an R&D centre in Ireland for the Group and charging other Group companies for use of the resulting intellectual property. We will have to decide on a method and a basis for arriving at the amounts to be charged that reflect commercial reality and avoid difficulty with any revenue authorities.

Transfer pricing arises where one part of a group of companies charges another part of the group for goods or services supplied. In many cases the transfer price is not an open market price as there may or may not be an 'open market' for, in our case, the services supplied. Transfer pricing can be used in order that the profit on the transaction is earned in a low tax regime like the Republic of Ireland; however, we must comply with the OECD rules in relation to calculating transfer prices on an arm's length basis so as not to attract accusations of artificially inflating profits in order to reduce taxation payable in other jurisdictions. From a state perspective, national tax authorities are interested in transfer prices as they will be concerned about the potential loss of tax revenue in the country in question. This is not a matter that would typically be of concern to the revenue authorities in the Republic of Ireland as low corporation tax rates typically 'attract' profits. In Northern Ireland the corporation tax rates are higher and so the tax authorities may be concerned that revenue from IP has been understated and transferred at less than market price so as to reduce the UK corporation tax payable.

There are a number of approaches to transfer pricing:

Market Price In this case the tax authorities are unlikely to challenge the transfer price as this is set by the external market.

Transfer at Below Market Price This might be used in situations such as:
- where the importing country has a lower rate of tax on profits than the exporting country and profits are artificially moved to the importing country with a distorting impact on appraisal and management motivation;
- where the importing country applies high tariff barriers, a lower price might be set to enable a lower or more realistic market price to be used.

Transfer at Above the Market Price Reasons for this might include:
- where the importing country taxes profit at a higher rate than the exporting country;
- where dividend repatriation is restricted;
- if there is a fear of expropriation of assets by a foreign government, the company may wish to retain funds in the exporting (safer) country.

In our case there will probably be no external market to determine the correct price to charge, therefore it may be necessary to set a transfer price on a cost plus basis or equivalent. In order to ensure that goal congruence occurs, it will be necessary to ensure that the objectives of the purchasing and selling divisions are aligned by examining the cost structures in both operations. A straight cost plus model can discourage efficiency as any inefficiency in the producing division is passed on to the receiving division. A negotiated price may be used in some cases where the actual price set is based on the negotiating 'power' of both parties.

Alternatively, an initial fee could be agreed on a fellow group company using the intellectual property with an ongoing charge based on a percentage of the selling price.

Overall, the operation of the new division would involve the Irish operation undertaking research and development, resulting in the creation of intellectual property. This would then be licensed to other group members. Additionally, it may be possible to transfer existing group intellectual property to the Irish subsidiary, which is then licensed to other group members.

REDBARN BREWERY

REPORT TO BOARD OF REDBARN BREWERY

Re: Proposed Expansion in the US Market

Executive Summary Due to the recent success of Redbarn's newly developed low alcohol product, the company is considering expansion opportunities. Redbarn is looking at the possibility of entering the US market and the two options being considered are entering into either a joint venture agreement or a licensing agreement with a US company based in New Hampshire.

I have calculated the NPV of each of the options being considered by the board and discussed some of the factors and limitations that may affect the resulting NPV. I have also considered the market-entry strategy that Redbarn should pursue in its expansion into the US market.

The US is a large and mature market and one in which many Irish companies have successfully done business. Trading links between our two countries are well established with good transport links and a mature financial infrastructure.

Solution 11.1: Redbarn Brewery

> **Assess the financial outcome of the various investment options open to Redbarn Brewery and consider the various risks relating to the analysis.**

JOINT VENTURE

	2012	2013	2014	2014	2016	2017	2018
Cases		110,000	115,500	121,275	127,339	133,706	140,391
	US$	US$	US$	US$	US$	US$	US$
Sales		2,640,000	2,772,000	2,910,600	3,056,130	3,208,937	3,369,383
Direct costs		(1,320,000)	(1,386,000)	(1,455,300)	(1,528,065)	(1,604,468)	(1,684,692)
Gross profit		1,320,000	1,386,000	1,455,300	1,528,065	1,604,468	1,684,692
Factory usage		(100,000)	(100,000)	(100,000)	(100,000)	(100,000)	(100,000)
PBT		1,220,000	1,286,000	1,355,300	1,428,065	1,504,468	1,584,692
Investment	(1,000,000)						
Tax		(488,000)	(514,400)	(542,120)	(571,226)	(601,787)	(633,877)
PAT	(1,000,000)	732,000	771,600	813,180	856,839	902,681	950,815
50%	(500,000)	366,000	385,800	406,590	428,420	451,340	475,407
	€/£	€/£	€/£	€/£	€/£	€/£	€/£
€/£ @ 1.4	(357,143)	261,429	275,571	290,421	306,014	322,386	339,577
Discount factor (10%)	1.000	0.909	0.826	0.751	0.683	0.621	0.564
	(357,143)	237,639	227,622	218,106	209,008	200,202	191,521
JV NPV	**926,955**						

LICENCE

	2012	2013	2014	2015	2016	2017	2018
Fee (**US$**)	200,000						
Royalty: **Cases**		80,000	86,400	93,312	100,777	108,839	117,546
@ US$2 (**US$**)	–	160,000	172,800	186,624	201,554	217,678	235,092
Income (**US$**)	200,000	160,000	172,800	186,624	201,554	217,678	235,092
	€/£	€/£	€/£	€/£	€/£	€/£	€/£
Income €/£	142,857	114,286	123,429	133,303	143,967	155,484	167,923
Discount factor 10%	1.000	0.909	0.826	0.751	0.683	0.621	0.564
PBT (ROI)	142,857	103,886	101,952	100,110	98,330	96,556	94,709
Tax @ 12.5%	17,857	12,986	12,744	12,514	12,291	12,069	11,839
ROI	125,000	90,900	89,208	87,597	86,038	84,486	82,870
PBT (NI)	142,857	103,886	101,952	100,110	98,330	96,556	94,709
Tax @ 24%	34,286	24,933	24,468	24,027	23,599	23,173	22,730
NI	108,571	78,953	77,484	76,084	74,730	73,382	71,979

Licence NPV ROI	**646,099**
Licence NPV NI	**561,184**

Risks Attaching to the Calculated NPVs

- Currency risk of US$ to €/£. A weakening in US$ will reduce the value of the NPV in €/£.
- Sales risk regarding the number of cases sold.
- Debt-collection risk with US distributor.
- Operational risk regarding the production in the US.
- Reaction of competitors to the new product.
- How appropriate is the discount rate used and the effect of relative inflation on the discount rate?

Sensitivity Analysis

Sensitivity analysis of the two options, particularly of the JV option, would provide the board with further valuable information and help it in making a decision. There are a number key assumptions used in arriving at the net present values. For example, an exchange rate of US$1.4 to €/£ has been used. If the US$ weakened over time and the rate was US$1.5 to €/£, the positive NPV would fall. Calculating the NPVs using different assumptions would show how sensitive the positive NPVs would be, given changes in the key assumptions. Redbarn could take steps to mitigate some of these key risks by considering hedging the cash flows. Similar analysis could be carried out on remodelling the NPVs based on different sales projections of cases of beer sold.

Redbarn has developed a new production process and is currently in discussions with its lawyers about patenting this process. In entering into a JV or licensing option it will be imparting this knowledge to its partner and it will have to include legal protection of this knowledge in any agreement.

If Redbarn were looking to limit its exposure and overall investment in the US, the licensing option is probably the best one for Redbarn as the NPV is relatively guaranteed. However, it is also the option over which Redbarn has the least amount of influence on the subsequent outcome.

The JV option shows the highest NPV of €/£926,000. This figure is dependent upon the sales being achieved. However, we would have to consider how the $500,000 initial investment would be funded. If the finance was raised in the US and not subject to a parent company guarantee from Ireland, the exposure for Redbarn would be less than if raised in Ireland by Redbarn. Any ROI/NI tax on remittances should be covered by double taxation treaties with the US. One advantage of the JV option is that Redbarn will be in a position to influence decisions that may grow revenue and profit in the future.

Solution 3.3: Redbarn Brewery

> **Detail the considerations surrounding the various market-entry strategies open to Redbarn Brewery in entering the US market.**

The method of entry into a market can determine the success or failure of the expansion and I will consider each of the two options below.

Joint Venture

A joint venture is normally entered into by two organisations when they believe that their respective complementary skill-sets can work together to the economic benefit of both. In this case, Redbarn has produced a product that both companies believe will sell well in the US market; however, it does not have a manufacturing or marketing presence in the US. Ryton Ales is an established brewery and successfully sells beer in the US market.

Joint ventures normally carry a lower risk of market entry for new products than direct exporting. However, with the sharing of risk comes the sharing of profits.

The correct choice of joint venture partners is critical for success. Redbarn will have to consider such matters as:
- how the respective corporate cultures will work together. Redbarn is a relatively small company and Ryton Ales may welcome the innovation and energy that small successful companies bring to the market;
- the commitment of top management to the project is important so that the necessary resources are made available and the necessary decisions are taken to advance the project;
- the relative importance of the joint venture to each company – while the JV would obviously be important to Redbarn, its importance to Ryton Ales would be critical in determining how successful the JV could be.

The benefits of a joint venture in this case are clear insofar as Redbarn does not have the capacity to produce in the US and does not currently have the marketing and distribution knowledge to operate in that market. Redbarn would also benefit from the experience that Ryton Ales has gained in the US in beer production and marketing.

Licence

Licensing carries a lower risk of market entry than either directly exporting or a joint venture. The benefit of licensing to Redbarn is that it does not involve an upfront investment apart from management resource. In this case, Ryton Ales has proposed paying Redbarn an upfront fee plus an amount per case sold. It has also guaranteed a minimum number of cases per year. There would probably not be any exit costs associated with the licence option when the licence term comes to an end.

While the licence option would afford Redbarn a source of revenue that is less risky than the JV option, the JV option offers more potential in the longer term to benefit the company.

Solution 6.1: Redbarn Brewery

> **Detail the practical issues that Redbarn Brewery would need to address in negotiating any joint venture/licensing agreement and, in addition, detail the practical implications for the finance function in Ireland if the joint venture were to be established.**

MEMO

To:	John Anderson
From:	Financial Controller
Re:	Meeting with Ryton Ales regarding possible joint venture/licensing agreement

You asked me to consider the issues that should be discussed and addressed at your forthcoming meeting with Ryton Ales and in addition to consider the implications a JV option would have for our Irish business.

(a) Issues to be Discussed with Ryton Ales

The meeting will afford the opportunity to agree a 'Heads of Terms' document covering both the JV and licence options. I would suggest that a discussion document be sent in advance of the meeting so that both sides have the opportunity to consider their positions. Issues to be addressed and considered at the meeting are as follows.

Joint Venture
- The legal status of the JV, i.e. incorporated or not.
- Intellectual rights over the new process: who will own it; can Redbarn charge a fee into the JV for its use?
- Why a JV with Ryton Ales; what complementary skills will both sides bring to the JV?
- Has Ryton Ales the distribution network and marketing skills to promote the beer?
- How will decisions be made – a separate JV board? How will split decisions be taken?
- Is the US$100,000 rent figure justified?
- How would Redbarn get on with Ryton Ales – are their corporate cultures similar?
- HR issues – will Redbarn supply any of the employees – brewers, etc.? Will the JV be an opportunity for our employees to gain experience of US production and marketing?
- How financially strong is Ryton Ales, how long trading, what is its reputation in the premium brewing market?
- What would be the structure of any board with representation from each side?
- Form and timing of monthly reporting.
- Redbarn's rights to information from JV.
- How important would the JV be to Ryton Ales? If it is a very small part of its business, it may not get the attention from Ryton's board it would need to become a success in the US. Redbarn will have to ensure that Ryton is not just using the JV to get access to the new production process developed by Redbarn.
- What will happen when the JV ends?

Licence

- The commercial terms, including upfront payment and basis for licence fee.
- The timing and currency of any payments, US$ or home currency. Fees receivable in €/£ would need to be protected from currency risk.
- How the intellectual property rights of Redbarn will be protected under the agreement.
- The term of the agreement, terms of any extension of the licence agreement and how it would end.
- The rights Redbarn will have to determine if the correct licence fee is paid – certified by auditor, etc.
- The rights of Redbarn to set prices and agree marketing strategy under the agreement.
- The rights that Redbarn will have to ensure that the quality of the product is maintained.
- Which legal jurisdiction will apply, US or Irish, in the event of disagreement?

(b) Implications for Irish Finance Function of the Joint Venture Option

If Redbarn were to enter into a joint venture with Ryton Ales in the US, it will have particular reporting implications for the company in Ireland.

It has yet to be decided if the joint venture would be incorporated or unincorporated; this could affect how the results of the US JV would be incorporated within the Irish results.

Redbarn will have to consider how best to report the monthly results of the JV, either by incorporating them into its own management accounts or presenting a separate set of figures to the board.

Being a 50/50 partner, Redbarn will be able to influence how the JV will report and measure performance. Redbarn will be in a position to determine the format in which it will receive the monthly accounts. Receiving the figures in US$ will give it a better appreciation of the underlying commercial environment in the US; however, this will mean having to translate them into local currency for consolidation with the Irish accounts. This should include actual figures, budgets and forecasts, etc. The JV will have to produce the figures to fit in with Redbarn's reporting schedule and this would mean agreeing a reporting calendar with the finance team of Ryton Ales.

Redbarn may be able to request the monthly results in an electronic format that can be imported directly into its own accounting system, taking account of foreign exchange differences and US GAAP.

Redbarn will also have to incorporate the figures into its annual statutory accounts, which will mean producing group accounts. Consolidation will be by way of proportional consolidation or equity accounting.

The JV will produce accounts in US$ and the figures will have to be translated each month into €/£. Intercompany accounts with the JV will have to be set up and reconciled each month to capture any transactions.

Redbarn will have to consider if it has sufficient capacity within its existing finance department to deal with the extra workload that may arise.

Redbarn will need to ensure that it will comply with any US filing regulations and double taxation treaties. Redbarn will also need to ensure that its company constitution allows it to enter into joint venture agreements.

Solution 16.2: Redbarn Brewery

> **Outline the considerations for Redbarn Brewery in deciding its retail pricing strategy in international market-entry decisions and, in particular, the pricing decisions facing Redbarn Brewery in its expansion into the US market.**

MEMO

To: Joe Wiley
From: Financial Controller
Re: Pricing Strategy

There are a number of important considerations to take into account when determining a pricing strategy. In this case Redbarn is considering the price point for its premium low alcohol beer in the US.

Pricing decisions are determined by a number of factors, including:

- **Organisational Objectives** – what does the company want to achieve: building market share; creating brand awareness; profit?
- **Company Costs** – Companies should set prices so as make a profit on their operations. For this reason, they must fully understand their cost structure. Sometimes companies will, as part of a marketing strategy to grow market share, sell below cost. This is where a company would have other profitable products to cover the losses and be part of a definite and measureable strategy to gain market share. It is normally used when a product already has a presence in the market. It would not be advisable in the case of Redbarn Gold as it is a new beer and price discounting would suggest low quality.
- **Customer Demand** – High customer demand gives the seller more control over pricing. Redbarn is introducing a new product into the market, but the market for premium beers is already well established and price points are in existence for the various segments of that market.
- **Competition** – Competition for premium beers in the US market is high and Redbarn will have to price according to the existing market. If its prices are out of line with the premium beers already on sale, it is unlikely they will be successful. Redbarn will have to decide how it is going to compete and with what competitive advantage. As it has a premium product, it should probably compete on quality while matching prices of similar products.
- **Distribution Issues** – A successful distribution strategy will be important in determining the outcome of Redbarn's expansion into the US. Distributors like Ryton Ales will be part of the chain, along with retailers between Redbarn and the consumer. Therefore, Redbarn will have to agree with Ryton Ales and retailers the marketing and pricing strategy. It would be difficult for it to do this from Ireland, given its small size, and so the choice of partner in the US is key to the success of the launch to ensure the distribution and that product placement reflects the premium quality.

Companies will always set prices according to their strategic objectives and consider the effect on their bottom-line. If Redbarn decides to proceed with this JV or the licensing option it will depend on Ryton Ales to a large extent for its marketing, distribution and pricing knowledge of the US market.

Given that the JV will be selling a premium low alcohol beer, this will influence its pricing decision. High quality is associated with high price and so the price should be set equal to or higher than the competition. Price gives a signal to a customer and a low price suggests low quality.

I would disagree with Ryton's suggestion that the price be set lower than that of other premium beers. I think that the beer should be retailed on the basis of quality and matching the price of other premium beers. On this basis, retailers would achieve a margin on Redbarn Gold higher than that of other beers, which would encourage them to push the product over other beers. Once the beer achieves some traction in the market, Redbarn could revisit the pricing strategy.

SMART BATHROOM FITTINGS LTD

Solution 8.1: Smart Bathroom Fittings Ltd

> **Analyse the economic data presented in Appendix 1 and comment on the relative attractiveness of each of the countries for Smart Bathroom Fittings Ltd in expanding internationally. Comment on the limitations of the data provided.**

Memo to Billy Murray

Re: Overview of 2009 Economic Data

I understand that we are looking at the potential of an overseas investment. I have reviewed the schedule you gave me. The economic strength, political and economic stability and future growth of a country's economy will be an important part of the decision where to invest. The use of economic indicators is an important tool in analysing the relative attractiveness of economies. It is important to note the relationship between economic indicators like the ones given. For example, the GDP per capita of a country may look high but when looked at in conjunction with the size of a population, it may indicate that a market is too small to enter.

Key Insights Provided by the Data

Population A large population is indicative of a large potential market. In the context of the data provided, India is by far the largest market, though with a relatively low GDP per capita, the number of people who are likely to afford our luxury product is likely to be limited. In terms of population and GDP per capita, both Brazil and South Africa would appear to be more attractive.

Interest Rates The interest rate set by its central bank can also tell us a lot about a country's economy. Central banks will normally increase the interest rate when they think inflation is running too high. Brazil had a big problem with inflation in the 1990s and the rate shown of 20% reflects its attempts to keep it low. However, the downside of high interest rates can be an increase in exchange rates (as long as inflation is controlled) – making exports more expensive. High interest rates also depress local consumption, especially for discretionary goods and home improvements.

Inflation The level of inflation is indicative of how fast prices are rising. There are a number of drivers of inflation, including low interest rates and increasing the money supply. High inflation can reflect weak monetary policy (excessive government spending funded by borrowing), bottlenecks in the economy or excessive demand chasing too few goods. Inflation in both South Africa and India appears to be relatively high. Countries with high inflation relative to their trading partners generally see a depreciation in the value of their currency. The hyperinflation in Zimbabwe means that it would be a very difficult economy in which to operate. Ireland is suffering from deflation, a sign that economic activity is falling.

Economic Growth South Africa and Ireland are both suffering the effects of the current downturn. Brazil is just 'breaking even', while India is doing well. Zimbabwe is also doing well after a disastrous number of years, though this shows the danger of looking at just one indicator. The other indicators for Zimbabwe show a country with very high inflation, very low GDP per capita and high debt problems. The higher the growth, generally the more attractive is the potential investment country. However, too high a level of growth over a period of time can result in a subsequent correction, which can depress an economy for many years. Economic growth in an economy stimulates demand in construction and refurbishment, an important area for Smart.

Unemployment A pool of appropriately trained workers is something that any investor will wish to see. Zimbabwe and South Africa have high levels of unemployment and this may be indicative of significant structural long-term problems. However, a very low rate of unemployment may suggest a lack of available employees and upward pressure on pay rates.

GDP per Capita As noted earlier, the level of income will be an indicator of the level of potential spending power. Obviously, people on low income will not be buying expensive plumbing devices for their bathrooms. Other considerations might be the level of income spread within a population. It would be useful to have a breakdown of GDP per capita between (say) the top 25% of each population versus the rest. That would help us in positioning products and identifying potential market segments.

Current Account Balance How a country is performing in terms of current account (imports less exports) is an indicator of the strength of its economy and any deficit will have to be funded by borrowings. A high deficit that is driven by spending on consumer goods is not a welcome development, whereas one based on capital goods to facilitate building of capacity is generally favourable. In addition, current account deficits should be looked at in conjunction with other indicators, like inflation. For example, South Africa's current account deficit and its inflation rate of 7.2% would suggest a future weakening of its currency exchange rate against countries with better balance of payment positions and lower inflation.

Public Debt as % of GDP   The level of public debt is indicative of the dominance of the state in the economy. A high level of debt will create significant challenges as this will have to be funded by taxes and may depress economic growth in the future.

The data given only allows for a brief overview.   The limitations of the analysis are as follows:
- We have only got data for one year: we would normally like to assess the trend over the longer term and in particular, historical data for previous years and forecasted data for future years.
- Additional commentary is needed: there is no commentary on the data to put it in any context. Without such detail it is hard to be prescriptive.
- Weightings: we have no indicators as to which factors are considered to be more important in our analysis.
- Comparability: we have assumed that all data is drawn up on a comparable basis. Figures for Zimbabwe are likely to be less reliable than for some other countries.
- Cultural and other factors: each of the countries is subject to different cultural and other factors that are not reflected in the numbers.
- The accuracy of the data should be checked and supported by other sources.
- This data would be used as a screening tool to identify potential markets only at a macro-economic level – it would not be the basis on which to make an investment decision.

Solution 11.9: Smart Bathroom Fittings Ltd

> **Evaluate the possible investment by Smart Bathroom Fittings Ltd in South Africa from both a qualitative and quantitative perspective.**

The euro discount rate given is 10%. There are two ways to find the NPV:
1. convert cash flows to euro and discount at 10%; or
2. discount the ZAR cash flows at the equivalent discount rate in ZAR and then convert the NPV to euro at the spot rate.

Under the first method the exchange rate will change each year, and under the second method the ZAR NPV is translated to the home currency at the spot rate. Both methods should give the same result.

The data is incomplete in that working capital has been ignored as well as terminal value. Of specific concern is that the numbers have been prepared by the target company and this needs to be challenged. Sensitivity analysis is needed, too. The numbers as presented show a 'hockey stick' pattern!

> Tutorial Note: two methods are shown here, but either is appropriate.

NPV	2010 ZAR million	2011 ZAR million	2012 ZAR million	2013 ZAR million	2014 ZAR million	2015 ZAR million	2016 ZAR million
Revenue		7.500	7.800	8.100	8.400	14.600	
Outflows		−4.200	−4.100	−5.300	−5.500	−9.500	
Investment	−4.500	0.000					
Tax			−0.250	−0.280	−0.200	−0.210	−1.640
ZAR (million)	−4.500	3.300	3.450	2.520	2.700	4.890	−1.640
Method 1							
Exchange rate	10.150	11.076	12.087	13.190	14.394	15.708	17.141
	€/£ million	€/£ million	€/£ million	€/£ million	€/£ million	€/£ million	€/£ million
	−0.443	0.298	0.285	0.191	0.188	0.311	−0.096
Discount factor (10%)	1.000	0.909	0.826	0.751	0.683	0.621	0.565
€/£ (million)	−0.443	0.271	0.236	0.143	0.128	0.193	−0.054
NPV €/£ (million)	**0.474**						
Method 2							
ZAR (million)	−4.500	3.300	3.450	2.520	2.700	4.890	−1.640
Discount factor (20%)	1	0.833	0.694	0.579	0.482	0.402	0.335
	−4.500	2.749	2.394	1.459	1.301	1.966	−0.549
NPV ZAR (million)	**4.820**	@10.15					
NPV €/£ (million)	**0.4749**						

$$\text{ZAR discount rate} = \text{current discount rate} \times \frac{(1+i)}{(1+i)} = 1.10 \times \frac{1.124}{1.03} = 1.200 \text{ (i.e. 20\% discount rate)}$$

$$\text{Exchange rate in future} = \text{current exchange rate} \times \frac{(1+r)}{(1+r)}$$

$$\text{Exchange rate for 2011} = 10.15 \times \frac{1.124}{1.03} = 11.076$$

The rates for each of the years 2012–2016 are calculated similarly, i.e. by taking the previous year's rate, multiplying it by 1.124 and dividing it by 1.03.

Taxation (Ireland)

Additionally, there may be incremental tax payable in Ireland (2.5% payable for the first four years for companies based in ROI; 20% for those based in NI). This would presumably only arise if the company was deemed resident in Ireland, i.e. managed from Ireland.

The project meets the payback criteria of less than five years and has a positive net present value. However, the NPV is fairly marginal and before making a final decision one should consider some of the sensitivity factors below.

Limitations of Data and Sensitivity Analysis Requirement

The primary limitation is that the numbers have been prepared by the vendor. Without the carrying out of an appropriate due diligence, these estimates should be treated with caution. The data as presented does not include any of the following matters:

- working capital requirements and how these might change over the duration of the project;
- possible terminal values;
- funding issues – these do not appear to have been considered and it is possible that a different cost of capital may be needed to reflect the different financing arrangements or different business and operational risks.

Sensitivity Analysis

The numbers appear to be relatively static with a large, unexplained increase in revenue in the final year. Given the figures have been prepared by the target company itself, these forecasts would have to be reviewed.

The NPV of €/£474,000 is very marginal in terms of an investment in an overseas company and a fall in revenue of 20% would deliver a negative NPV.

Before proceeding the following matters should be considered.

- Due diligence: a full due diligence review of Rand Plumbing Supplies is needed. What is being acquired in terms of assets (and liabilities)? How have the projections been prepared? What is the legal status of the company, organisational structure of the business, key employees and age profile, key customers and potential? We also need to consider what warranties/indemnities we require (if any) from the existing owners in relation to unrecorded liabilities.
- Risk analysis: consideration should be given to the risks prevailing in the business and how these might be managed.
- Other information: additional information should be sought, including additional financial and management accounts for the last number of years to see if they support the projections made, trade references and bank references.
- Additionally, we should assess if there are any factors that could be influential, such as ability to remit funds, security factors, etc., which may affect the investment decision.
- We would have to understand the involvement of Mr du Plessis in the business as he is due to retire. How important is he to the current business?
- If Mr du Plessis is important to the success of Rand, is there some way he can continue to be involved, perhaps as a minority shareholder or as a non-executive director for a number of years?
- We need to consider how we could add value to Rand from a strategic and operational perspective. If we cannot, should we be investing?
- The projected figures do not take account of any potential sales of our Irish products in the South African market – is this a possibility?
- Does the potential return justify our involvement, given the potential difficulty of owning a business in South Africa and the Irish management resources that it would consume?
- Is an investment in South Africa aligned with the strategy of Smart Bathroom Fittings Ltd; will it add to the value of our company?
- We should consider what legal and financial advisors to use in South Africa.

Notwithstanding the marginal NPV, any investment in this case should be treated with caution and at this stage it is difficult to see how one could recommend proceeding until some of these concerns have been addressed.

Solution 12.6: Smart Bathroom Fittings Ltd

> **Discuss the practical cultural issues likely to arise when doing business in South Africa.**

Cultural awareness is critical when doing business in a foreign country. Business success is based on creating trust and mutually beneficial relationships. Cultural awareness and sensitivity to local customs and practices, and familiarity with recent history, can be critical in developing relationships and trust. At a business level, it is important to be familiar with particular business customs when doing business overseas.

- Cultural practices of customers and consumers, e.g. as regards giving and receiving credit and whether such terms are honoured.
- Distribution systems: in some countries the distribution systems can be quite different from those in Ireland, with multiple layers and local agreements that can make access difficult to newcomers. However, South Africa is the main access route to all of southern Africa as their ports are well developed.
- Different business practices: in some countries the giving of gifts is seen as a normal part of doing business, but such practices could lead to potential corruption.
- National differences: South Africa is a multi-ethnic environment with a legacy of apartheid, which could impact on any investment.
- Perceptions of Ireland: Ireland is generally favourably viewed in South Africa and we may be able to leverage this.
- Many languages are spoken in South Africa, though the common business language is English.
- Political instability may be a factor: nationalisation of foreign-owned businesses is a risk, possibly mitigated by having a suitable South African on the board to ease our way in local negotiations.
- The people of South Africa are a mix of African, English and Afrikaans and awareness of their respective cultures and history is important when doing business.
- Affirmative action in favour of the black majority in South Africa and in favour of black-owned companies is government policy and is seen as a way to redress some of the inequality of previous South African governments.

Specific issues have been raised in Appendix 3 and there are a number of ways in which these may be managed.

Issue raised	Concern	How this might be handled
Significant downturn in house-building due to economic downturn.	Future prospects have been affected. Has the full impact been reflected in the projections? How will this impact on our sector?	Some additional information may be sought on planned house-building levels, as well as population statistics. Sector we are aiming at is probably a minority wealthy sector.
Pressure from Government to address deficit for indigenous population.	Likely political pressure, which may impact on the sector.	Seek assurances over how this might be handled/obtain insurance.
Identified political corruption.	Will we be affected by corruption (e.g. giving bribes) to ensure we are successful?	Seek independent advice – perhaps consult local embassy officials.
High economic disparity among groups. Many of these are affected by emigration and security concerns.	Is the sector we are aiming at sufficiently large and sustainable?	Some consultations with trade representatives and others may provide some assurance on these.
Impact of HIV and other factors on parts of the population.	Not likely to be a key issue in terms of the target market (but could indirectly impact on staff).	

Solution 15.1: Smart Bathroom Fittings Ltd

> **Discuss the forward contract rate offered to Smart Bathroom Fittings Ltd by its bank as well as possible financing considerations in relation to financing the investment.**

MEMO TO BILLY MURRAY

Re: Forward exchange contract

I refer to the e-mail you received from the bank manager in relation to a forward exchange contract.

A forward exchange contract is an agreement to buy a pre-determined amount of a foreign currency at an agreed rate and on a specified future date.

My understanding of his proposal is as follows.

If we agree to buy Rand Plumbing Supplies, we will be committed to paying ZAR4.5 million three months after signing.

We will enter into a forward exchange contract fixing the rate at which we will buy ZAR.

When the time comes to pay for Rand Plumbing supplies, the bank will advance us the money by way of loan in €/£ and we will use that to purchase ZAR at the pre-agreed exchange rate.

In theory this is an option for us; however, I have two difficulties with it:

1. The rate quoted by the bank based on the figures given is too expensive. I have recalculated the figures and estimate the contract rate should be about 10.39. The difference involved is not large, given the relatively small size of the potential investment, but I think we should ask for the basis of the calculation. I am aware that this was a sample quote from the bank.

Forward Exchange rate calculation

$$10.15 \times \frac{(1+(0.031\%))}{(1+(0.0075\%))} = \frac{1.031}{1.0075} = 10.39$$

2. While we may be able to get a loan for this investment from our local bank manager to finance this investment, it would make more sense to arrange finance in South Africa for the following reasons:
   - revenues earned in ZAR can be used to pay the interest and capital, thus eliminating the need to transfer money from our own bank and avoiding any losses due to exchange rate fluctuations;
   - on consolidation of the results of Rand Plumbing Supplies with our own, we can match any potential translation losses on assets with translation gains;
   - perhaps you can arrange to meet with a bank in South Africa on your forthcoming visit?

STENT MANUFACTURING LIMITED

MEMO

To: Brian Murphy, Finance Director
From: Financial Controller
Re: Proposal re location of new manufacturing facility

I refer to our recent discussions and the briefing from Dick Jones regarding the location of the new stent-manufacturing facility. It is clear that making the correct decision in relation to the location of the new facility is critical to the future success of our company.

I met with John Childs, who provided me with a lot of the cost data I have used in this report. To help in my analysis I have used Ohmae's 5Cs model, which is used as a tool to help assess new business environments from a strategic marketing point of view. (A number of models could be used to structure this answer, among them the McKinsey 7-S model, Porter's Diamond (see Gallagher, *Corporate Strategies for Irish Companies*, p.160) or Ohmae's 5Cs, which is elaborated upon in this suggested solution.)

Solution 11.7: Stent Manufacturing Limited

> **Compare the option of setting up an operation in Germany to that of South-East England from both a financial and non-financial perspective and advise Stent Manufacturing Limited as to how it should proceed.**

I believe that the location of this facility is less about cost and more about being consistent with the expansion strategy that Stent is now employing. It is important that the company aligns its strategic objectives with its market requirements. The location of the new facility is to be either England or Germany. I have considered both countries using the 5 Cs of Ohmae's model, which are: the customer, the company, competition, currency volatility and country. In addition to the 5 Cs, I also analysed the costing information supplied by John.

Customers   The buying decision for our products is made by the cardiologists who insert the stents into their patients. The buyers are not especially price-sensitive as the cost is relatively insignificant relative to the overall cost of the surgery and the additional life expectancy that patients achieve after a successful operation. It would appear that cardiologists in Great Britian (GB) are already happy to purchase our stents as we are seen as a 'home' producer. However, our sales into the German market at present suggest a low level of market penetration. If we were to have a facility in Germany, I would expect a large increase in sales as German cardiologists would be effectively using a German-manufactured product. Being based in Germany would allow better communication and a more effective transfer of knowledge between German cardiologists and our German-based facility. Presently, we have 6% of the German market and sales have grown 23% in the last year; however, there is potential to grow our share of the market by locating a plant in Germany. In addition, a German-based plant would allow easier access to other European markets, particularly the northern and eastern European markets.

Currency   From a currency perspective GB would be a better location if Stent Manufacturing Limited is presently based in NI and Germany would be better if Stent Manufacturing Limited is based in ROI. There are no restrictions in repatriating profits from either country. There are no real long-term issues in terms of currency volatility. One consideration may be matching the currency of the source of finance with the project's revenue stream. Obviously, a company based in GB selling to customers on the Continent will face currency exposure.

Competition   There is significant competition in both countries, as can be seen from the percentage of the total market that we hold. However, we are operating in a market that would be expected to grow over the coming years. As the market matures we can probably expect prices to fall, though quality will always be an important differentiator. We have 39% of the GB market as opposed to only 6% of the German market. Both the GB and the German markets are similar in size, but there is far more potential in the German market. A greater understanding of the German and European markets would be necessary to ensure there are no significant barriers to Stent increasing its sales in the German market. Having a presence in Germany will allow us to compete better in that market.

Country   In terms of country, GB would be a better fit as it is English-speaking, has a similar legal system, similar culture and a business environment that an Irish company would be familiar and comfortable with. As regards the language barrier in Germany, it is likely that the senior managers that Stent would employ to get a German facility up and running would be English-speaking, meaning that would not necessarily be a barrier to a successful start-up. Both counties are members of the EU and so some convergence of standards and regulation can be expected, and local laws should not be a barrier to operating successfully.

I would imagine both countries would welcome investment from this type of industry and make available state aid, advice, etc. A full PEST analysis may be relevant here to compare both countries. Both countries would have the necessary skilled labour and graduates available, but location within each country would have to be taken into account to confirm this.

Company   Stent Manufacturing Limited has demonstrated its ability to produce and sell its products into both the GB and German markets. The next step of actually starting a manufacturing facility in one of these countries will be difficult. By reason of distance and language, a move to GB would be relatively easier, though Germany has a long history of high-quality manufacturing and so the infrastructure to support Stent will be available.

Stent wishes to become a larger supplier in the market and the board has stated that it is part of the company's strategy to create a facility elsewhere in Europe in order to expand its customer base. From an investor point of view, a growth in sales will deliver more profit to the bottom-line.

Costings   I have done a quick analysis of the costings in terms of the relative cost per item produced. The calculations show that manufacturing in GB will be approximately 16% cheaper and while this is significant to the bottom line (€/£7 million in profit), the strategic advantage of having a German facility and the potential increase in sales will outweigh this extra cost. On balance, I think it would be better for Stent to locate the facility in Germany.

COST PER UNIT PER YEAR

	GB (000)s	Germany (000)s
Factory	5,000	7,000
Fixed, including R&D	30,000	33,000
Variable	5,000	6,500
Labour	3,648	4,158
	43,648	50,658
Units	400,000	400,000
Average cost	109.12	126.65

Solution 14.3: Stent Manufacturing Limited

Discuss the possible finance options available to Stent Manufacturing Limited in respect of this opportunity.

Sources of Finance for this Project

With the current difficult situation in Irish banks, it would be difficult to raise finance here. (Northern Ireland may be a little easier with access to GB banks.) Even though the project is viable, the shortage of capital available in the Irish banks means that good projects will still find it very difficult to raise finance.

Stent is a profitable company creating a product for which demand is increasing and in need of at least €/£70 million of funding (plus working capital). I do not know what amount of funds are available internally, but assuming that we do need to raise a large amount of capital there are other options available to us apart from Irish banks.

The issues that we should consider are:
- costs of finance and the effect on the company's overall cost of capital – the lower the cost of capital for this project, the greater the value that will be added to shareholders;
- relative taxation treatments;
- dividend remittance issues;
- matching the currency of repayments and revenue;
- matching the timing of finance repayments with the revenue from the new project;
- the amount of money that has to be raised;
- the period over which the finance will be repaid.

Brian Murphy suggests that venture capital companies would consider Stent to be too mature for financing; however, given that Stent is considering a flotation sometime in the near future, venture capital companies or private equity companies would certainly consider this as a good investment as they could take an equity stake and divest in a relatively short period of time when the company floats.

Other possible sources of finance would include:
- Eurobonds, which are long-term loans that can be traded by holders on a secondary market. Issue costs are high but interest rates are normally lower than bank finance for companies with a good credit rating. (Pension funds are generally active buyers of Eurobonds.)
- Banks in the country in which the facility will be constructed. German and GB banks would be far more willing to lend funds to a company manufacturing a profitable product in their own country than a company based in Ireland. It may be easier to arrange finance if a separate subsidiary were to be set up in Germany or GB (with guarantees, where necessary, from the Irish parent).
- Stent should also consider the availability of government grants for both capital construction and employment. A lot of manufacturing firms are locating to countries with cheaper labour and so new projects like that being proposed by Stent are keenly sought after.

TINYTOTS BABY FOOD LIMITED

BRIEFING PAPER

To: James Brown – Brown Consulting
Re: TinyTots Baby Food Limited
Date: xx yy September

James,

Further to our recent discussion, please find below a summary of my findings relating to TinyTots Baby Food Limited. If you have any queries, please let me know.

Kind regards

UR Employee
Associate Director

TinyTots Baby Food Limited is a manufacturer and wholesaler of organic baby food. It commenced producing 20 years ago at a time when this market was in its infancy. It has grown profitably over the years and four years ago expanded into the continental European market. However, it is experiencing difficulties in managing this expansion. At the present time its organisational structure does not sufficiently support its business strategy. In addition, the reporting systems do not provide the type of information necessary to manage this size of business and will not support the company in its stated objective of successfully growing the turnover profitably.

Solution 2.1: TinyTots Baby Food Limited

> **Propose and explain a new structure that would help the company overcome the present problems being experienced with the international expansion.**

It is important for MNEs to properly align their organisational structure with their strategy taking into account the needs of their customers. As companies grow, particularly where this involves international expansion, organisational structure becomes more important. A company structure that works in the early stages of growth is often characterised by a lot of hands-on management by the original founders. This can often lead to all decisions being referred up the chain and to a paralysis in decision-making. It appears that the current organisational structure of TinyTots does not support the business needs of the group.

The French subsidiary has not been sufficiently integrated into the business and it is unclear from the existing structure who has managerial responsibility for the manufacturing facility in France. While Jean Depaul is happy to discuss the profitable wholesale business in France, it appears that the French manufacturing side is under the responsibility of the Irish-based head of manufacturing. This does not work, as the results demonstrate, and will probably lead to decisions being made by Mr Depaul that are good for the TinyTots wholesale business in France but not for the group as a whole.

It is important for TinyTots to decide how it wishes to structure its business. There are a number of possibilities in how it may accomplish this.

The model I have suggested here is that the business reorganises itself by country, with both manufacturing and wholesaling under the control of country managers. In addition, I would suggest that all of the main finance and administration functions are done in a shared services centre based at the Irish head office. This structure would eliminate any sub-optimal decision-making as regards the transfer pricing between the manufacturing and wholesaling operations. In addition, the company will save costs in centralising the finance and administration departments and it will be easier to standardise information-gathering and reporting because full control of this will remain at head office.

ORGANISATIONAL STRUCTURE FOR TINYTOTS BABY FOOD

Additional points that could be made:

- Board to put in place appropriate strategy aligned with objectives and targets for each country. In this case the board should put in place a suitable structure, treating each of the companies as separate profit centres with their own budgets and targets set each year.
- As procurement is critical to profitability, place it within the responsibility of country managers.
- French manufacturing (assuming it remains) should be placed within the responsibility of the French general manager.
- Responsibility for quality control should be separate to the manufacturing function.
- Finance and administration should be at a central location, in order to reduce costs and to standardise collection of information and reporting.
- Remove differentiation between manufacturing and wholesaling with one division manufacturing, selling and distributing to the retailers.
- Understanding the product sales mix and each product's contribution to profit would help in making the correct decision for the most suitable structure. It may be that a small number of the products deliver most of the profit.

The French general manager holds the view that losses in that facility are due to insufficient sales and appears to believe that responsibility for increasing sales lies with the director of marketing in Ireland.

Depending on the view of the board regarding the possibility of increasing sales from the French manufacturing plant, one option is to close this factory to stem the losses and produce for the French market from the Irish plant.

Solution 3.2: TinyTots Baby Food Limited

> **Develop an exit strategy for the manufacturing plant that will maintain TinyTots' operational capability and enhance company value.**

The international expansion of TinyTots suggests that the company has outgrown its current management structure whereby day-to-day operational control by the top management was possible. Reorganisation by the board should include the board setting strategy and ensuring that the individual companies have sufficient resources and the right people to manage the daily operations, from there on managing the business by monitoring the individual profit centres against agreed budgets.

Making the general manager for France responsible for the French manufacturing division may deliver better results because, at present, it is the only division making losses. However, TinyTots should consider the possibility of closing the French manufacturing plant as it has incurred losses of over €/£5 million over the last two years. I would suggest the board prepares a detailed strategic plan for the French operation to consider its viability. If this is not deemed appropriate, the board should prepare an exit strategy that would include such matters as:

- considering ways in which the French wholesale division can be supplied from the Irish plant;
- consider if it is viable to continue buying from the existing French raw material suppliers to supply the Irish manufacturing plant on a commercial basis;

- consider if employees from manufacturing can be redeployed on the wholesale side;
- ensure the French wholesale customers will continue to purchase from TinyTots even if the product is not manufactured in France;
- consider a phased closure of the French plant together with a phased introduction of increased production in the Irish plant. This will help maintain supplies to the French wholesale business and sales to the French customers;
- plan for the logistics of supplying the French wholesale division from Ireland, taking into account the possible need to lengthen order times;
- review any commitments, such as property lease terms, that the French subsidiary may have entered into;
- calculate the costs of closing the manufacturing plant taking into consideration, for example, employment contracts, repayable grants and phased factory shutdown.

Solution 17.1: TinyTots Baby Food Limited

> **Identify the current problems in TinyTots Baby Food Limited's financial reporting system and suggest improvements, including how the reporting systems can support company strategy.**

There is room for significant improvement in the reporting systems of TinyTots and a reorganisation of the group offers an opportunity to develop this in alignment with its organisational structure. A strategic enterprise management system approach would allow the company to structure its reporting system to monitor its performance against the goals and objectives set by the board.

The current reporting structure of TinyTots displays the problems often encountered by companies that have outgrown their current reporting systems. This includes such issues as:

- The management accounting function not developed beyond a basic scorekeeping role. TinyTots needs to identify the information it requires from its accounting system to provide the data needed to manage its business, including full profitably data by product for each of the markets into which it sells.
- Poor underlying information systems. The FD has discussed the lack of good information in the organisation, which at present seems to produce only that necessary to prepare statutory accounts. Financial information for annual audited accounts is historical in nature and does not in itself aid decision-making to drive expansion and model where the business will be in future periods.
- The ambiguous business strategy in TinyTots does not help the individual directors for Ireland and France to understand what is expected of them or to determine their respective responsibilities in relation to their business.
- Lack of appropriate project and change management skills at a group level seems to be an issue in TinyTots. The level of change necessary has to be driven at the highest level to ensure adequate resources are made available and the whole organisation understands the importance of the changes in systems.
- The performance measures set by boards must be adequately aligned with the strategy of the company. In the case of TinyTots, growth in turnover appears to be an important part of the strategy; therefore the performance measurement system needs to monitor sales by product and country against budgets and forecasts to ensure there is constant focus on what is necessary to meet the company's strategic targets.

TRIDENT MOBILE LTD

NOTE TO JOHN GREENE

PRIVATE AND CONFIDENTIAL

Re: Bid Price for Kenyan Mobile Phone Licence

Further to our meeting last week, I have reviewed the file and together with information from Jenny Wilson have calculated a possible bid price for the Kenyan mobile phone licence. I also discuss below other issues that I think Trident should take into account before making a decision.

Based on my calculations, the potential bid amount that I arrive at is €/£100 million. However, I would not anticipate we would bid this price for the licence and would expect this to be discounted after taking in many other risk factors. In addition, we need to consider the amount that other mobile phone companies will bid for these licences and the amounts bid for the previous licences.

You also asked me to consider what other African markets we should consider entering (using the basic economic data in the file). Based on my analysis, I recommend we look closely at Uganda and Tanzania in particular, though further information is required before any decision could realistically be taken.

As discussed, I have also considered the likely practical issues to be considered when setting up a business in Kenya and I've explained some of the issues to be further explored when considering the application of a CSR policy.

Solution 11.8: Trident Mobile Ltd

> **Evaluate the possible investment by Trident Mobile Ltd in Kenya from both qualitative and quantitative perspectives and suggest a bid price for the contract.**

This figure is arrived at using a discounted cash-flow methodology which places a higher current value on cash that will be generated in the near future than cash that will be received in later years.

For a company the size of Trident, this represents a very large potential investment and requires detailed consideration of issues on a number of levels.

The resulting NPV calculation is based on a number of critical assumptions made and I would suggest further work is carried out on some of these assumptions. Additional market analysis of the Kenyan market would give us better information on the likely spend per customer and the level of market penetration we could expect to achieve. Of the bid amount calculated, 85% relates to cash flows arising in Years 6 to 12. Many companies will ignore cash flows beyond (say) six years due to their inherent uncertainty and there would certainly be an argument here to discount them further. Twelve years is a very long timespan to consider for an investment in this area of technology and advances in technology might well make the current business model obsolete – this should also be considered in arriving at a bid price. (Investment in a fixed-line infrastructure looked like a good long-term strategy for Eircom; however, technology advances have provided customers with many alternatives.)

We have assumed capital expenditure of KES5 billion for the first two years but have not allowed for any capital expenditure after that time. We need to understand if this is realistic in terms of the 12-year time span.

Assuming that the main finance for this project is available from the capital markets in Kenya, Trident will have to consider how it will remit profits back to Ireland. We will have to ensure there are no barriers to extracting profits in hard currency and also take into account local taxation implications. I would expect this to be covered in the bid submission documents.

Trident should also consider alternative ways of arriving at a bid price – such as applying a value to the likely number of customers it may be expected to gain over a suitable period and also looking at previous bids by existing providers in Kenya.

There are a number of other risks that we need to take into account in considering this investment.

Political Risk Investment in African countries can be subject to significant political risk. There may be no guarantee that future rulers will consider themselves bound by decisions or contracts entered into by previous administrations. In order to mitigate this, it would be important that any deal is conducted fully in accordance with Kenyan law and that international protocols are followed. It would also be important that good relations are maintained, as far as possible, with the different political parties in the country. One way of mitigating this political risk is to source funding for the investment from the local Kenyan finance market.

Operational Risk   Starting a business in an overseas country carries with it a large amount of operational risk. Doing so in many African countries carries a greater risk insofar as the business support structure is far less developed than in more developed countries. Organisations setting up in an African country would need to be prepared to be far more self-sufficient and bring in to the country many of the resources that they might expect to find in more developed countries. Trident should expect and budget for: delays in getting the infrastructure set up, issues with maintenance of equipment, possible power shortages, problems finding suitably qualified staff, a banking system that will not be as developed as Ireland's, etc.

Commercial Risk   In order for the business to be commercially viable, Trident will have to attract a large customer base and will need a suitable marketing plan and develop a network to sell the airtime. Most sales would be by way of prepaid cards and a distribution network will have to be developed to achieve this. The margins payable to the distributors will be critical in this and will have to be comparable or higher than the competition.

Legal System   The legal system in Kenya originally evolved from that in place when it was a British colony and so should be comparable to that of Ireland/UK. However, local practices can be expected to be different. Given the high-profile nature of the investment, the likely difficult negotiations with Government and the many contractual relations that will be developed, it would be important for Trident to retain as an advisor one of the better and larger legal firms in Kenya. We should do some research on this to ensure we do not encounter avoidable problems in getting this new project operational.

Other relevant issues that should be considered before making a final decision:
- What value to place on the long-term element of the earnings – is it safe to assume 12 years?
- What are our competitors likely to bid for the rights?
- Contractual issues – if a contract is breached, can Trident pursue for assets outside of Kenya?
- How can Trident reduce the risk further, given the potentially large amount of the investment?
- How will a deal be financed – is local finance available?
- What is the likely level of involvement of the local partner?

CUSTOMER NUMBERS

| | 2013 | 2014 | 2015 | 2016 | 2017 |
	000	000	000	000	000
Opening	–	1,000	1,500	2,250	3,375
New	1,000	500	750	1,125	–
Closing	1,000	1,500	2,250	3,375	3,375

(Based on 2.5% of population in 2013, rising by 50% each year until 2016, and then minimal growth.)

NPV CALCULATIONS

	2012	2013	2014	2015	2016	2017	Remainder
Average revenue per head	–	KES4.8	KES4.8	KES4.8	KES4.8	KES4.8	
	KES million	KES million	KES million	KES million	KES million	KES million	KES million
Income (Note 1)	–	2,400	6,000	9,000	13,502	16,200	16,200
Cost of sales (60%)		–1,440	–3,600	–5,400	–8,101	–9,720	–9,720
	–	960	2,400	3,600	5,401	6,480	6,480
Capital	–5,000	–5,000	–				
Total net cash	–5,000	–4,040	2,400	3,600	5,401	6,480	6,480
Taxation (see below)	–	–	–	–	–	–709	–1,944
	–5,000	–4,040	2,400	3,600	5,401	5,771	4,536
Value of remaining annual income (Note 2)							18,872
Discount rates 15% (Note 3)	1.000	0.870	0.756	0.658	0.572	0.497	0.497
NPV	**–5,000**	**–3,515**	**1,814**	**2,369**	**3,089**	**2,868**	**9,379**

NPV short term	**1,626**
NPV longer term	**9,379**
Final tax payment	**–317** (–1944 × 0.163)
KES(million)	**10,688** = €/£106,884,414 @ 95% = €/£ 101,540,193

Taxation Workings

	KES million	KES million	KES million	KES million	KES million	KES million
Income	–	960	2,400	3,600	5,401	6,480
Capital allowance	–	–3,333	–3,333	–3,333	–	–
Loss b/f			–2,373	–3,306	–3,039	–
	–	–2,373	–3,306	–3,039	2,362	6,480
Tax @ 30%			0	0	–709	1,944

Notes:
1. Assumed that new subscribers will pay 50% of the annual expected income (on average) in their year of joining.
2. Annual income after 2017 is obtained by applying a seven-year annuity factor to the annual amount of KES4,536 million (KES4,536 million × 4.1603 = KES18,872 million). This gives a projected income for 12 years in total.
3. The appropriate discount rate is estimated as:
   (1 + real discount rate) × (1 + long-term Kenyan rate) ÷ (1 + projected long-term domestic rate) = (1.08 × 1.11) ÷ 1.04 = 1.15 (i.e. discount rate of 15%).

Solution 8.2: Trident Mobile Ltd

> **Analyse the economic data presented in Appendix 1 and comment on the relative attractiveness of each of the countries for Trident Mobile Ltd in expanding internationally. Comment on the limitations of the data provided.**

We know that the African mobile phone market is forecast to grow substantially over the next few years and will probably deliver the highest growth rates in the world. However, African economies are less developed than elsewhere in the world and discretionary spending in general per head of population is far less than more developed countries. Notwithstanding this, many African countries have sufficient economic activity to support a mobile phone industry.

GDP/Population   While GDP per head of population is important in terms of affordability, the size of the population will also determine the potential size of the market.

	Population 000s	GDP per head US$	Population per Sq Km
Tanzania	43,739	1,216	46
Zambia	12,935	1,516	17
Malawi	15,263	550	129
Uganda	32,710	1,426	136
Mozambique	22,894	950	29
Kenya	40,000	1,561	67

After Kenya, the next highest GDP per head is Zambia at $1,516 per head and Uganda at $1,426 per head. Tanzania's GDP per head also appears high enough to support a growing mobile phone industry. The size of the population in Uganda and Tanzania makes those countries more attractive in terms of market size compared with, say, Zambia and Malawi. The GDP figures, however, do not show the distribution of income within the populations and it is likely that large disparities will exist between the richest and the poorest citizens of those countries. This is critical, as it is unlikely that people below a certain income level would use a mobile phone.

Annual Growth in GDP   All of the countries included in the file show high levels of real GDP growth, which suggests growing economies. This is a positive sign as a growing GDP generally means more income in the hands of consumers. However, if this level of growth were to continue over a number of years, inflation would become a problem, which in turn would reduce the value of the currency and the earnings when remitted to Ireland (assuming lower levels of inflation in Ireland). High levels of inflation are reported in Zambia, Tanzania and Uganda, which, if they were to continue, could depress future economic growth.

Population per Sq Km   A higher density of population per square km would suggest a lower network construction cost as less infrastructure has to be built to reach a higher number of customers. This, however, assumes a fairly even distribution of population and does not take account of urban population density. In general it would mean that the cost per customer of constructing a network in Uganda would be cheaper than the cost in Tanzania or Zambia.

Mobile Penetration/Competition   The lowest mobile phone market penetration is in Malawi; however, this is the country with the lowest GDP per head of population. Zambia and Uganda have similar GDPs per head to Kenya but their market penetration rates are lower; therefore, there is immediate potential for growth in these markets. There is existing competition in all of the countries but we do not have, at this stage, their respective market percentages.

Based on the data given I would suggest we would look at Uganda and Tanzania based on GDP per head of population and market size. Though the GDP for Zambia is higher, the total population is smaller, which will limit the size of the market.

The above is a very brief overview and I would suggest we conduct further economic analysis and market research. Further information that would be useful in making a decision would be: geographic distribution of population within countries; distribution of GDP per head to see how representative the average is; a PEST analysis, as mentioned elsewhere in my workings; information on the existing mobile phone companies, the size of the markets and their market shares. Also, the data given was for one year only – additional years would give better information because economic trends could then be discerned.

Solution 12.5: Trident Mobile Ltd

> **Discuss the main operational and logistical issues for Trident Mobile Ltd in relation to setting up a new business in Kenya.**

There are likely to be many practical issues for Trident in doing business in Kenya or other African countries. These include:

- Arranging for employees from Ireland to work in Kenya. Issues arising here would include the form of expatriot employment contracts, local housing, local employment taxation, local healthcare provision, country allowances and incentives to relocate in Kenya, etc. Many UK businesses have a long history of placing expatriate employees in African countries for years of service; however, with better communications and easier transport I imagine Trident would place staff in Africa on short to medium contracts according to the needs of the Kenyan company. For example, the initial construction phase would require a different type of manager than the revenue growth stage.
- Finding adequately educated and trained staff to get the company operational is likely to take some time and may include a number of our HR staff relocating to Kenya for a time. A mobile phone company is likely to be an attractive employer for many people and I suggest that placing ads in newspapers and organising roadshows in local universities would be a good way of attracting new staff.
- Trident will have to carefully choose its local professional legal and financial advisors. It may be that we could use the local offices of our own audit firm – this may ease our entry into Kenya.
- Trident will need local banking facilities for its own transactional needs and also banking in relation to receiving monies from subscribers. Banking facilities will not be as developed as in Ireland.
- Prepaid phone cards are likely to be the main method of receiving money from subscribers and a network of sellers will have to be set up.
- Advertising is likely to be key in attracting new subscribers and a marketing strategy suitable for Kenya will have to be created. This is where local knowledge would be invaluable. There is no guarantee that a marketing plan drawn up in Dublin would work in Kenya, where there would be many different cultural references.
- Before Trident is in a position to sell to subscribers it has to construct a network. Although we have done this in Ireland, constructing in Kenya will be significantly different and should be the subject of its own project plan with a separate, dedicated team.
- A detailed business plan, including organisation structure and geographical locations, should be prepared, taking into account Kenyan needs. Employing people with experience of Kenyan business and, if possible, Kenyan mobile phone company experience, would reduce the difficulties we may face.
- Language will not be a problem as the main business language in Kenya is English.

Solution 5.2: Trident Mobile Ltd

> **What are the key points that Trident Mobile Ltd will need to consider in terms of developing a corporate social responsibility policy in respect of its proposed operation in Kenya?**

In common with other mobile phone companies, Trident looks beyond acting in the sole interests of its shareholders and takes into account its corporate, environmental and social responsibility to all stakeholders. These stakeholders include the Government, local communities, consumers, employees, environmental agencies and other interest groups.

In expanding into Kenya, Trident is likely to become a high-profile company and this affords it the opportunity to advance its CSR policy. CSR is unlikely to be as advanced in African companies as it is in the West and so may give Trident a competitive advantage relative to other mobile phone companies.

The kind of CSR opportunities that may arise in Kenya would be:
- encouraging smaller local businesses as suppliers to Trident, helping them with the procurement process and standard setting, etc.;
- forming good relations with the Kenyan Government – perhaps partnering with Government to help with educational/health programs;
- operate according to the highest environmental standards available; ensuring suppliers also act in an environmentally responsible manner in their dealings with Trident through suitable contract terms;
- operate an excellent HR policy in relation to rewards, health and further education – perhaps forming partnerships with local Kenyan schools/health clinics;
- providing training and education to their sub-contractors/suppliers;
- maintaining excellent relations with local communities;
- ensuring Trident acts ethically in all its dealings with official bodies, gaining a reputation for doing so.

While following a CSR policy may be common in Western countries, it is likely to be difficult to do fully in Kenya as many of the concepts will not be developed in the minds of the public. For example, environmental concerns might not be uppermost in the minds of the Kenyan people. Barriers to bribery and corruption are likely to be lower than in Ireland or the UK and employment law will not be as advanced as in Western countries. For this reason, resulting operating costs may well be higher than for other mobile phone companies. However, in the longer term, we would make some strategic gains as business standards improve across the board in Kenya.

It has been suggested that a local businessman will have a 5% interest in the business for no investment. Some countries insist that a minimum shareholding percentage is held locally and I do not know if that is the case in Kenya. However, it should be noted that there are both advantages and disadvantages to this set-up.

In favour of this is that, on the basis that he is an experienced Kenyan businessman, he is likely to have contacts in both financial and government circles and so could facilitate the introduction of Trident into Kenya. His team may also be able to advise on the local culture, the typical problems we will face and advise on recruitment.

On the other hand, this businessman will take 5% of the value of the company. There is also the risk that his influence is limited to one political group and may not survive a change in Government. It is important that we carry out a due diligence on this individual to ensure that he is ethical in his dealings and is likely to continue to have influence were a change in power to take place.

OTHER SOLUTIONS

(**Note:** the solutions to these questions are not related to a particular case.)

Solution 7.1

From a legal perspective the word 'property' means a resource over which a business or individual has a right of ownership. Therefore property can include land and buildings, natural resources, such as minerals, etc., as well as intellectual property rights. Property rights refer to the legal rights over the use to which a resource is put and the use of any income that may be derived from that resource. While almost all countries have laws that protect property rights, in many countries these laws may not be fully enforced and property rights are violated.

In countries with weak legal systems, crimes such as theft, blackmail and piracy can be common. For example, in the years following the collapse of communism in Russia in the mid-1990s, the Russian Mafia employed tactics like blackmail to extract money from businessmen and if protection money was not forthcoming, violent retribution was common. In 1995 and 1996 alone over 500 contract killings of businessmen occurred annually.

In some countries, the violation of property rights occurs when public officials (e.g. politicians and government officials) extort income, resources or the property itself from the property owners. This can be done through legal mechanisms, such as taxation, taking assets into state ownership without compensation being attached, or perhaps, illegal means, such as demanding bribes. Some examples include the Marcos government in the Philippines in the 1970s and 1980s as well as President Suharto in Indonesia until the 1990s, who demanded bribes for letting foreign companies set up in their countries. While no country can be considered free of corruption, large differences do exist in their attitude to it. Where the rule of law is tight, violators are punished by the full force of the law whereas in other countries politicians and bureaucrats openly flout the law.

How does this impact on MNEs? There is evidence that high levels of corruption significantly reduce the levels of foreign direct investment, level of international trade and economic growth rate in a country. If profits and resources are siphoned off by politicians, bureaucrats and/or organised crime, then both foreign and domestic investors will be much slower to invest in a country as the rate of return they will receive is much diminished from that which they would expect in a country without corruption.

In some cases laws have been passed making it illegal for a company to bribe government officials in another country. In 1997, trade and finance ministers from the member states of the OECD adopted the Convention on Combating Bribery of Foreign Public Officials in International Business Transactions. This obliges member states to make the bribery of foreign public officials a criminal offence.

Solution 9.1

The International Monetary Fund (IMF) was established at the Bretton Woods Conference in 1944. Most countries of the world are members of the IMF. The three broad aims of the IMF are to:
1. promote international monetary co-operation, and to establish a code of conduct for making international payments;
2. provide financial support to countries with temporary balance of payments deficits;
3. promote high employment, sustainable economic growth and reduce poverty.

When the IMF and World Bank were set up in the 1940s, one of the key things they hoped to achieve was currency stability and to ensure this they introduced a US Dollar-based gold-standard system. This meant that each country established a par value for their currency against the US Dollar, which was in turn pegged against gold (at $35 per ounce). Each country then had to maintain its exchange rate within $+/-1\%$ of the par value by buying or selling currencies. However, this system of effectively fixed exchange rates collapsed in the 1970s due to inflation in the US and a series of balance of trade deficits, and as a result the major currencies have fluctuated against each other since then.

Solution 9.2

The World Bank (more properly called the International Bank for Reconstruction and Development (IBRD)) began operations in 1946, with the reconstruction of war-damaged economies as one of its objectives. Today, its chief aim is to supplement private finance and lend money on a commercial basis for capital projects. Loans are usually direct to governments or government agencies, for a long-term period of over 10 years (typically 20 years). Lending is usually tied to specific projects, although the Bank's lending policy has been more flexible in recent years.

The World Bank's funds are obtained from capital subscriptions by member countries of the IMF, its profits, and borrowing. The major source of funds is borrowing, and the World Bank makes bond issues on the world's capital markets (e.g. New York).

World Bank lending is for projects concerned with the development of agriculture, electricity, transport, etc. The cost of World Bank loans was (and still is) high to developing countries, and in 1960 the International Development Association (IDA), a subsidiary of the World Bank, was set up to provide 'soft' loans, i.e. loans at a low cost with easy repayment terms, to less developed countries, for similar types of projects financed by the World Bank.

Because the IDA acts as a concessionary arm of the World Bank, lending money on easy terms, it is a potentially valuable source of finance for developing countries.

The IDA makes loans for 50 years without interest and charges only a service fee.

Many of the IDA's most needy members in Africa have seen their economies contract over the past 20 years. The appeal of IDA loans to these countries, and the need for such loans to help development, should therefore be readily apparent to you.

Solution 9.3

The Bank for International Settlements (BIS) is the banker for the central banks of other countries. It is situated in Basel, where it was founded in 1930. Most of its deposits are from the central banks of various countries and some are shareholders and represented on its board. It is a profit-making institution and lends money at commercial rates. The Bank of England, for example, has a 10% stake in the BIS.

The main functions of the BIS are to:
1. promote co-operation between central banks;
2. provide facilities for international co-operation.

Solution 10.1

A bill of exchange (sometimes called a 'draft') is an instrument commonly used in international commerce to effect a transaction. It is an order written by a seller (exporter) instructing an importer or its agent to pay a specified amount of money at a specified time. If properly drawn, these bills of exchange can become negotiable instruments providing a convenient mechanism for financing the movement of international goods.

The advantages of payment by means of a bill of exchange in international trade are as follows.
1. A convenient method of collecting payments from foreign buyers.
2. The exporter can seek immediate finance using term bills of exchange instead of having to wait until the period of credit expires (i.e. until the maturity of the bill). At the same time, the foreign buyer is allowed the full period of credit before payment is made.
3. On payment, the foreign buyer keeps the bill as evidence of payment, so that a bill of exchange also serves as a receipt.
4. If a bill of exchange is dishonoured, it may be used by the drawer to pursue payment by means of legal action in the drawee's country.
5. The buyer's bank might add its name to a term bill, to indicate that it **guarantees** payment at maturity. On the continent of Europe, this procedure is known as 'avalising' bills of exchange.

Solution 10.2

Export factoring is essentially the same as factoring domestic trade debts. Factoring is an arrangement to have debts collected by a factor company, which advances a proportion of the money it is due to collect. The main aspects of factoring are:
- administration of the client's invoicing, sales accounting and debt-collection services;
- credit protection for the client's debts, whereby the factor takes over the risk of loss from bad debts and so 'insures' the client against such losses. This service is also referred to as 'debt underwriting' or the 'purchase of a client's debts'. The factor usually purchases these debts 'without recourse' to the client, which means that if the client's debtors do not pay what they owe, the factor will not ask for his money back from the client;
- making payments to the client in advance of collecting the debts. This is sometimes referred to as 'factor finance' because the factor is providing cash to the client against outstanding debts.

The benefits of factoring for a business customer include the following:
- the business can pay its suppliers promptly, and so be able to take advantage of any early payment discounts that are available;
- optimum stock levels can be maintained, because the business will have enough cash to pay for the stocks it needs;

- growth can be financed through sales rather than by injecting fresh capital;
- the business gets finance linked to its volume of sales. In contrast, overdraft limits tend to be determined by historical balance sheets;
- the managers of the business do not have to spend their time on the problems of slow-paying debtors;
- the business does not incur the costs of running its own sales ledger department.

Factoring, as compared with 'forfaiting' (see **Review Question 10.3**), is widely regarded as an appropriate mechanism for trade finance and collection of receivables for small to medium-sized exporters, especially where there is a flow of small-scale contracts. A factoring service typically offers prepayment of up to 80% against approved invoices. Service charges vary between around 0.75% and 3% of total invoice value, plus finance charges at levels comparable to bank overdraft rates for those taking advantage of prepayment arrangements.

Solution 10.3

Forfaiting is a method of providing medium-term (say, three to five years) export finance that originated in Switzerland and Germany, where it is still very common. It has normally been used for export sales involving capital goods (machinery, etc.) where payments will be made over a number of years. Forfaiting is also used as a short-term financing tool. Forfaiting became very popular in the 1990s when companies were dealing with the break-up of the Soviet Union as all the political and commercial risk of non-payment by the importer was carried by the guaranteeing bank.

Forfaiting is a method of export finance whereby a bank purchases from a company a number of sales invoices or promissory notes, usually obtaining a guarantee of payment of the invoices or notes. It works as follows.
1. An exporter of capital goods finds an overseas buyer who wants medium-term credit to finance the purchase. The buyer must be willing:
    (a) to pay some of the cost (perhaps 15%) at once;
    (b) to pay the balance in **regular instalments** (perhaps every six months), normally for the next five years.
2. The buyer will either:
    (a) issue a series of promissory notes; or
    (b) accept a series of drafts with a final maturity date, say, five years ahead but providing for regular payments over this time: in other words, a series of promissory notes maturing every six months, usually each for the same amount.
3. If the buyer has a very good credit standing, the exporter might not ask for the promissory notes (or drafts) to be guaranteed. In most cases, however, the buyer will be required to find a bank that is willing to guarantee (avalise) the notes or drafts.
4. At the same time, the exporter must find a bank that is willing to be a 'forfaiter'. Some banks specialise in this type of finance.
5. Forfaiting is the business of discounting (negotiating) medium-term promissory drafts or bills. Discounting is normally at a fixed rate, notified by the bank (forfaiter) to the exporter when the financing arrangement is made. If the exporter arranges forfaiting with a bank before the export contract is signed with the buyer, the exporter will be able to incorporate the cost of discounting into the contract price.
6. The exporter will deliver the goods and receive the avalised promissory notes or accepted bills. He will then sell them to the forfaiter, who will purchase them without recourse to the exporter. The forfaiter must now bear the risk, i.e.:
    (a) risks of non-payment;
    (b) political risks in the buyer's country;
    (c) the transfer risk that the buyer's country might be unable to meet its foreign exchange obligations;
    (d) the foreign exchange risk. The forfaiter holds the promissory notes and has paid cash to the exporter, and therefore it is the forfaiter who accepts the exchange risk;
    (e) the collection of payment from the avalising bank.

The diagram below should help to clarify the procedures.

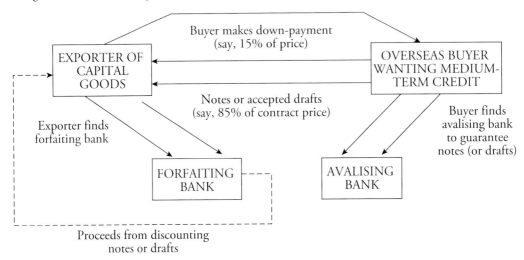

Forfaiting can be an expensive choice, and arranging it takes time. However, it can be a useful way of enabling trade to occur in cases where other methods of ensuring payment and smooth cash flow are not certain, and in cases where trade may not be possible by other means.

Solution 10.4

Letters of credit provide a method of payment in international trade which gives the exporter a risk-free method of obtaining payment.

At the same time, documentary credits are a method of obtaining short-term finance from a bank, for working capital. This is because a bank might agree to discount or negotiate a bill of exchange, and so:
- the exporter receives immediate payment of the amount due to him, less the discount, instead of having to wait for payment until the end of the credit period allowed to the buyer;
- the buyer is able to get a period of credit before having to pay for the imports.

Banks may advance pre-shipment finance to help with manufacture.

The buyer (a foreign buyer, or a UK/Ireland importer) and the seller (a UK/Ireland exporter or a foreign supplier) first of all agree a contract for the sale of the goods, which provides for payment through a documentary credit.

The buyer then requests a bank in his country to issue a letter of credit in favour of the exporter. Typically, the bank will look at the creditworthiness of the buyer (it may even request a cash deposit or other form of collateral against the letter). This bank that issues the letter of credit is known as the 'issuing bank'. The buyer is known as the 'applicant' for the credit and the exporter is known as the 'beneficiary' (because he receives the benefits).

The issuing bank, by issuing its letter of credit, guarantees payment to the beneficiary. Banks are involved in the credits, not in the underlying contracts.

The issuing bank asks a bank in the exporter's country to advise the credit to the exporter. This bank is known as the 'advising bank'. The advising bank agrees to handle the credit (on terms arranged with the issuing bank), but does not normally make any commitment itself to guarantee payment to the exporter.

The advising bank (in the exporter's country) might be required by the issuing bank to add its own 'confirmation' to the credit. The advising bank would then be adding its own guarantee of payment to the guarantee already provided by the issuing bank. If it does confirm the credit, it is then known as the confirming bank. Thus, a confirmed letter of credit carries the guarantees of two banks, usually one in the exporter's country (the confirming bank) and one in the buyer's country (the issuing bank).

The cost of issuing a letter of credit is usually borne by the buyer.

A documentary credit arrangement must be made between the exporter, the buyer and participating banks before the export sale takes place. Documentary credits are slow to arrange and administratively cumbersome; however, they might be considered essential where the risk of non-payment is high, or when dealing for the first time with an unknown buyer.

Solution 10.5

Export credit insurance is insurance against the risk of non-payment by foreign customers for export debts. Not all exporters take out export credit insurance because premiums are very high and the benefits are sometimes not fully appreciated; but, if they do, they will obtain an insurance policy from a private insurance company that deals in export credit insurance.

Though exporters can pursue non-paying customers through the courts in order to obtain payment, export credit insurance may still be necessary because:
- if a credit customer defaults on payment, the task of pursuing the case through the courts will be lengthy, and it might be a long time before payment is eventually obtained;
- there are various reasons why non-payment might happen. Export credit insurance provides insurance against non-payment for a variety of risks in addition to the buyer's failure to pay on time. The types of risk covered are described later.

Export credit insurance is not essential, especially when exporters are reasonably confident that all their customers are trustworthy.

Solution 13.1

Culture is a direct determinant of demand and ways to do business. It can have a huge role in how a company operates abroad. It may lead an organisation to focus its international activities on locations belonging to the same ethnic, religious or cultural groups that are served in the domestic market. Export activities may be concentrated into locations where management feels 'comfortable'. It can affect how you do business in a country right down to who you should have running your subsidiary operations in a location.

International business is different from domestic business because countries are different. Sometimes it is necessary when operating in another country to customise the product and service offerings to appeal to the tastes and preferences of the local culture. Business success across different countries requires what is called 'cross-cultural literacy' (an understanding of how cultural differences across and within nations can affect the way business is practised). In general, success in a foreign country requires an MNE to understand and then adapt to the culture of its host country.

There is also a direct link between culture and the cost of doing business within that culture. For example, different cultures may be more or less supportive of the capitalist mode of operation and this may in turn increase or decrease the cost of doing business. Therefore, Japan's huge growth in the 1960s, 1970s and 1980s was helped in no small measure by cultural factors conducive to capitalism, while it is argued that stagnation in the UK economy in the 1960s and 1970s was partially linked to conflict between well-drawn class barriers.

When doing business abroad the MNE manager needs to be aware of the dangers of self-referencing, or judging events with reference to our own experiences and self-perceptions, which can lead to misconceptions. Therefore, when you wear a suit and another person dresses casually, when others may not look you in the eye, when they smile and you are earnest, you need to note that such information or behaviour may not mean what you think it does. Thus, cultural adaptation is a skill a MNE manager needs to develop when operating in a different country and this can involve down-playing the importance of first impressions and limiting the urge to self-reference.

'Culture' can be defined as a system of values and norms shared among a group of people that, when taken together, constitute a design for living. Culture is reflected in an individual's perception of observed events, their personal interactions and in the selection of appropriate responses to social situations. 'Values' can be defined as abstract ideas about what a group believes to be good, right and desirable. By 'norms', we mean the social rules and guidelines that prescribe appropriate behaviour in particular situations.

Values form the bedrock of a society and provide the context within which that society's norms are established. They will include things such as attitude towards individual freedom, democracy, truth, justice, honesty, loyalty, social obligations, collective responsibility, the role of women, love, sex, marriage, etc. In practical terms, democratic, free-market capitalism is a reflection of a philosophical value system that emphasises individual freedom.

An example of how cultures can differ is in relation to the concept of time. Some cultures, such as the US and Northern Europe, place a great emphasis on the value of time ('time is money'), whereas Latin, Arabic and Mediterranean cultures have a more elastic relationship with time. Doing business in either culture requires the other to respect and adapt as necessary. As an example of norms at work, in Japan the presentation of a business card is critical as it represents one's status, which is important in a hierarchical culture. To receive a card and not read it carefully is considered rude by the Japanese.

APPENDIX C

THE VIEW FROM THE TOP OF IRISH MULTINATIONAL ENTERPRISES

CONTENTS

Appendix C.1
BUILDING A SUCCESSFUL INTERNATIONAL BUSINESS

Jim Woulfe, Chief Executive, Dairygold Co-Operative Society

Background

Dairygold is Ireland's leading farmer-owned co-operative. From our Munster base, our food ingredients business processes almost one billion litres of milk (nearly 20% of the total Irish milk pool) from 3,000 farmer suppliers each year, into high-quality dairy products. Our agribusiness manufactures and sells feed and fertiliser; it is Ireland's largest grain buyer and processes this grain together with other ingredients into quality animal feeds, which in turn are sold to our milk suppliers and a wide range of other customers. In addition, we operate a substantial network of Munster-based retail stores supplying an extensive range of farm inputs and hardware.

Our business model has developed over 100 years through the heritage, provenance and tradition of the farmers who supply us with our raw materials, together with leading-edge dairy-processing technology and expertise. Over that time Dairygold has been involved in many businesses, including branded consumer foods.

Dairygold in 2014 is a lean, fit-for-purpose food and food ingredients manufacturer. Our philosophy of maximising our member suppliers' income from farming by maximising the value we add to current and future milk and grain supply and by minimising the costs of farm inputs, while growing the net asset value of the business in a sustainable way, is at the heart of our business. These principles have seen Dairygold's turnover grow to €850 million, with an EBITDA of €50 million, while paying members leading prices for their inputs. The business is supported by a highly skilled and motivated staff of 1,150, working throughout our businesses in Ireland, the UK, France, Germany and Spain.

The Irish dairy industry produces in excess of six times the domestic requirement for dairy produce, which results in our products being destined primarily for export markets, making it critical for Dairygold to be an internationally driven organisation. Our dairy product mix includes cheddar and continental-style cheeses, butter and dairy powders, including casein and speciality ingredients such as demin whey powders. Our cheddar and demineralised whey powder factories are the largest in Europe, providing us with significant scale and a competitive advantage. Dairygold has significant technical ability, demonstrated by the production of Ireland's only PDO (Protected Designation of Origin) cheese, Imokilly Regato, and by our linkages with the world's most well-known and successful baby-food brands using our demineralised whey and other ingredients in the production of their high-end products.

Our route to market is built on a twin-track approach involving key strategic customers and partnerships in the B2B (business to business) sector supplying quality dairy ingredients to both the food manufacturing and food service sectors and the B2C (business to consumer) sector through a long-standing strategic relationship with the Irish Dairy Board (IDB).

Dairygold's Strategic Plan to 2020

Dairygold's detailed strategic plan, like many successful businesses, has profitable growth as a central objective. We have a target to grow our international sales by 60% from 2014 to 2020, following the abolition of EU milk quotas from April 2015, through increasing sales volumes and maximising added-value opportunities. In summary, Dairygold will realise its robust, sustainable strategic plan by incorporating quality milk supply, efficient and modular processing capability and optimising routes to market in an overall balanced financing model that maximises return and minimises risk. Strategic planning has often been compared with "peeling an onion", a process of peeling back layers of information, critically analysing, forecasting and financial modelling to determine a core set of strategic objectives and clear deliverables.

Dairygold commenced with an analysis of the macro trends for core dairy business. Attempting to predict the future is not an exact science; however, there is consensus amongst researchers around the following core elements: world population and urbanisation will increase, incomes in the developing world will rise and diets in these economies, which are predominantly milk deficit regions, will become more westernised. In summary, dairy demand is set to rise by *c.* 100 billion litres worldwide by 2020, *c.* 2.5% per annum with supply projected to increase by *c.* 2% per annum, with volatility prevailing in individual years.

Using tools such as the Boston Matrix, Porter's Five Forces, Decision Tree Methodologies and also customised strategic analysis criteria, Dairygold developed its investment plan to 2020, with *c.* €200 million being invested in infrastructure and technical capability, routes to market and working capital requirements.

Where every single kilogram of additional product will be required to be sold directly or indirectly into export markets, the plan leverages off Dairygold's current success in export markets, but demands the development of new international markets in developing countries, where significant demand growth is being projected.

Selling into International Markets

There are a number of ways in which a business drives sales growth in international markets – such as partnerships with key customers, acquisition of businesses offering routes to market, partnering with agents and distributors, or by developing direct export sales. Dairygold's growth and success over the past number of years has been driven by focusing on all of these channels. Successful partnerships are built on compatible philosophies, combined with each of their respective strengths, delivering incremental benefits to both organisations. To develop new international markets Dairygold applies and draws on the successful experiences of the past.

In the B2C channel, Dairygold has developed and grown a very successful partnership in consumer branded products with the IDB. Products such as Kerrygold Butter for the German market, Kerrygold Whole Milk Powder for international markets in the Middle East and North Africa (MENA) and sub-Saharan Africa, Kerrygold Regato Cheese for the Greek market and Pilgrims Choice Cheese for the UK market, have been incredibly successful. This partnership approach spans the entire supply chain – from production, product innovation, development and sales and marketing.

In the B2B channel, we have developed very successful long-term strategic partnerships with a large number of global blue-chip companies. Two such examples include Danone plc and Tine Co-Op. For Danone, Dairygold prepares and supplies significant volumes of key ingredients with functional attributes for the production of leading, globally branded infant milk formula products. This relationship has incrementally developed based on the quality of product Dairygold is providing together with the technical relationship that continues to enhance the functionality of the finished product.

Tine Co-Op is Norway's largest milk processor (95% of Norwegian supply); Dairygold produces Jarlsberg Cheese for TINE a leading international branded product, number 1 imported table cheese into the USA. This relationship has been evolved due to Dairygold's technical competencies and has enabled Dairygold increase its sales of speciality cheese to export markets, expanding its product portfolio and capability.

The following elements are vital for successful strategic partnerships: a synergistic opportunity, capability to deliver and, above all, partners whom you respect and trust that you will be able to do business with over the long term. To mitigate risk, all business partnerships and commercial agreements must be underpinned by robust legal agreements.

Dairygold has been successful in developing export markets through vertical integration acquisitions of businesses that already purchase products that we produce. We have implemented this strategy in the UK where, more than two decades ago, we acquired Haslington Cheese, a major supplier of formatted cheese to the UK food ingredients and food service sectors. This business was a large cheese buyer and through its acquisition, Dairygold displaced cheese produced by its competitors and secured an outlet for its own products from Ireland in an 'added value' way. Subsequently, in the mid-2000s, through the growth and development of this business, we acquired Dan Dairies, another UK business, which offered a complementary product offering to our core customer base.

In addition to the route to market strategies outlined above, Dairygold has also been extremely active in developing direct export sales from Ireland. While our core market is the UK and mainland Europe, we are increasingly focused on the growth markets of China, MENA, Russia and sub-Saharan Africa. Our approach involves extensive market research, with the objective of identifying the opportunities that are most aligned to our unique selling point (USP), in order to allow us to develop a secure competitive position. In this regard, the assistance of IDB, Bord Bia and Enterprise Ireland is essential through organising trade shows and trade missions, and providing market intelligence and networking opportunities. This enables us to develop contacts and build relationships to provide a platform for growth which involves working with distributors or agents who either operate on our behalf or in conjunction with us. There are a number of practical reasons for doing this, such as the distance to market or the complexity of importation requirements versus our scale in a given market.

We also develop direct contacts with primary end-users and operate the full supply chain. The advantages to doing this include capturing the maximum margin possible in the transaction and also ensuring a deeper relationship with the customer, which will ensure we are their preferred supplier and on top of their contact list when they are procuring product. This enables us to directly track changing market requirements and to quickly adapt our approach to product development and innovation.

Following the success of this approach, we operate from sales offices in Mainz, Germany, and in Barcelona, Spain, both of which are critical to ensuring that we have the right level of direct interaction with key customers and the most up-to-date market intelligence available.

Risks and Challenges

The development of international export markets provides significant opportunities, but also brings with it challenges and risks. There are particular risks that relate to export markets that a purely domestic business may not experience.

Currency risk is a key challenge. For Dairygold, US Dollar and GBP Sterling are the key foreign currencies in which we sell. We enjoy a partial natural hedge in GBP Sterling as we purchase significant quantities of Sterling-denominated natural gas, while we operate a strict hedging policy in US Dollar through the use of forward contracts.

Geo-political risk is a significant challenge and it can have serious implications for international businesses. For example, we have been investing significant resources since 2012 in developing the Russian market for casein and cheese products. The 2014 Russian sanctions are having a serious impact on the success already achieved in this market. To mitigate this type of risk we endeavour to operate in a wide range of markets, so that if one market is closed, we will have adequate alternative markets for our product.

Credit risk is another significant risk. We operate strict credit control policies: if we cannot secure credit insurance on a customer, we will use instruments such as letters of credit and bills of exchange, or seek cash in advance or cash against documents. In a relatively low-margin business such as Dairygold's, it is imperative that we are only exposed to the least credit risk possible.

Cultural risks must also be recognised as an exporter serving global markets. Every country, in every part of the globe, has its own unique culture, customs and character and it is the understanding of these that can determine the success or failure of a business relationship. Of course, this diversity brings with it the ability to enrich our own perspectives of the world and shape our own business strategies. Equally, the naturally friendly and hospitable nature of the Irish culture assists in mitigating these cultural challenges.

The Key to Success

An organisation's culture and strategy are the key principles on which to develop and grow a successful business and a successful international strategy must be a core element of the overall business strategy. The business needs to have clear goals and objectives before it commences the development of export markets, which involves significant time, energy and organisational focus and brings an entirely new set of risks and challenges to the business. However, for a business such as Dairygold, these are the markets in which it must operate. This requires revisiting and capitalising on its key strengths and building its strategy based on the principles that have led to its success: knowing the market, minimising risk and, above all, being close to its customers and ensuring that they are front and centre at all times. In this way, Dairygold will continue to maximise its market returns and deliver on its primary goal, which is to ensure that its members get the best possible returns.

Appendix C.2

NTR IN THE USA 2004–2009: RENEWABLE ENERGY – SOLAR THERMAL

MICHAEL WALSH, FORMER GROUP FINANCE DIRECTOR, NTR

In the years 2004 to 2008, NTR had considerable success in the US. Through its subsidiary, Airtricity, NTR had entered the US market in 2004 and over the following four years developed several hundred megawatts ('MWs') of wind-generating capacity in the wind market in West Texas (the ERCOT region).

As a result the Group had gained a very significant understanding of and insight into the electrical energy sector in the US and in particular into the renewable subset of that sector.

Following the sale and monetisation, the West Link Toll Bridge in 2007, and the subsequent sale of Airtricity, NTR had very significant cash resources.

A significant return of capital to shareholders (€250 million) followed.

The Group's success in the US, and the market understanding that that success had instilled in the Group, led to further analysis of American business development opportunities for the Group.

After considerable research, the Group developed an investment thesis based on the emerging renewables sector in the US. The strategic proposition for the investment thesis was underpinned by the broad themes of climate change, security of energy supply and general resource depletion.

Accordingly, investments were made in three sectors: solar, wind and recycling.

In all cases the approach taken was to invest in existing businesses, with strong local partners that could benefit from NTR's capital and strong business development credentials. [See **Chapter 3** for more on how MNEs expand internationally.]

From the outset, good progress was made across all three businesses:
- Wind: NTR had a good partner with a track record in development that needed capital to both develop and to own and operate wind farms in the US Midwest.
- Solar: identified a technology commercialisation opportunity (not a technology development opportunity – the relevant technology had been around for many years within the the Department of Defence – but had not been produced and installed at a commercial scale).
- Recycling: a basic opportunity for consolidation in a large but still extremely fragmented market.

So far, so good; all were well-worn paths to business-building.

This essay is not an attempt to write a history of NTR's experience in the US, but rather to concentrate on one particular element of the NTR story and to seek to understand some of the lessons arising from it.

In the solar business ('SES') the objective was to develop and construct two significant solar parks in the Mojave Desert and the Imperial Valley in Southern California.

To do this would require the manufacturing and installation of the generating units ('Suncatchers') at scale (tens of thousands of units) in order to deliver both the capital cost reductions and operating efficiencies that together would reduce the cost of power generation (LCOE) to competitive levels, combined with the need to reach the significant scale required for the Californian market.

To finance projects of this scale would also require significant non-equity funding, mainly through bank project finance and Government-backed funding.

Huge progress was achieved on both these fronts, but in particular in relation to manufacturing. Partnerships were formed with well-respected auto-industry component manufacturers, in both the US and Canada, to supply and install metal components and engines in to what would essentially be an assembly operation, not dissimilar to the manufacturing and assembly model deployed in the auto industry over many decades.

So what happened?

Well, the history of the financial crisis post-Lehman Brothers has been well documented. The emergence of the crisis made securing the necessary project financing virtually impossible in the 'off-risk' environment that pertained for a number of years following the onset of the crisis.

Less well known, but arguably of much more significance, were the cost reductions achieved in photo voltaic solar panels ('solar PV'), which had the effect of opening up a huge cost advantage for solar PV over the Suncatcher technology being backed by SES, with the result that despite the cost reductions achieved with Suncatcher, the relative competitiveness of Suncatcher to solar PV was undermined.

This dramatic reduction in solar PV cost was a result of the greater than $50 billion of investment in Chinese panel manufacturers, supported by the Chinese Government, in an effort, ultimately successful, to secure a dominant position in the market for solar energy technology. In the period 2007–2010, the delivered cost of utility scale solar PV fell from mid-20 cents per kwh to 12–13 cents on a like-for-like basis – a rate of cost reduction that simply could not be matched by any solar thermal technology.

SES therefore found itself with a technology which, along with all solar thermal technologies, had become uncompetitive relative to solar PV, and which therefore could not be project financed.

With a technology that was now fundamentally uneconomic, what was left to do was to orchestrate an orderly retreat from and wind up of the business in a way that was fair and equitable for all involved and which simultaneously would not threaten the remainder of the Group. Internally, this became known as the "Cut off your arm to save your life" decision.

Arguably, the most difficult decision facing the Group was not necessarily the decision to wind up the business but the decision which preceded it, i.e. to actually acknowledge that the business was not going to succeed and to gain institutional acceptance of this fact. This is entirely unsurprising as so much capital, both financial and human, had been invested in the project and the hopes and aspirations of so many committed and talented people were riding on a successful outcome.

Once that decision was made, however, the process of orchestrating an orderly exit from the solar business (and in the process stemming the cash haemorrhage that it was costing the Group) proceeded apace.

So, what are the key lessons/takeaways?

First, whilst attention to detail will always be crucial, the need to maintain a thorough understanding of changing market dynamics is absolute; a market-changing factor like the emerging solar PV cost advantage will derail even the most perfectly executed business development plan.

Secondly, an ability to respond rapidly and flexibly once changed circumstances have been (correctly) identified is a must.

Both of these are of particular importance when a significant portion of an organisation's resources, and its reputation, have been invested in the project at hand.

Finally, to end on a positive note, whilst much has been written about NTR's challenges in recent years, the fact remains that having stabilised the Group's finances, the Group has since returned a further €100 million to shareholders (by way of a share buy-back in December 2013) and at today's share price [early 2015] has a market capitalisation of €230 million.

Appendix C.3

FROM IRISH SUGAR TO GLOBAL CONVENIENCE FOOD

Author's Interview with Patrick Coveney, Chief Executive, Greencore Plc[1]

EM: What motivated Greencore to expand internationally from its very core Irish roots and, in particular, what cultural challenges, as against the financial ones, does running an international business present? Also, does being Irish bring any solutions to those challenges – is there something uniquely beneficial about being Irish in the internationalisation context?

PC: I guess there were really two stages of the internationalisation of Greencore and, in both instances, the core factor behind that internationalisation was growth. [See **Chapter 2**, Why Businesses become Multinational.]

If you go back to the creation of Greencore in 1991, what was privatised was an Irish business which was highly profitable, centred on a sugar monopoly business, which had been running – and running very effectively – for nearly 70 years at that point. That generated tonnes of cash, which had been under state ownership, largely used to fund employment-generating enterprises on the island of Ireland, a small number of which made some money, but the overall performance of the group was largely dependent on one business, which was the Irish sugar business.

So, as a public company, with a board that viewed growth as a way of generating shareholder value, the Greencore portfolio wasn't structurally set up to do that. They generated a lot of cash, with very high returns but actually it was structurally capped by the European sugar regime in terms of how much sugar it could produce.

In response, the business went through two stages of extending its footprint into the UK. The first was to take some of the ingredient businesses that they knew a fair bit about, principally malt, and scale up that business in the UK. Secondly, Greencore put its toe in the water in the late 1990s into a variety of relatively small food manufacturing businesses, which built some knowledge of what it would take to supply assembled food, typically to grocery retailers.

On the back of that experience, and under pressure to deploy its strong balance sheet to try and source growth, Greencore bought a company called Hazlewood Foods in 2001. [See **Chapter 3**, **Section 3.8**, Foreign Direct Investment.] That strategy changed the shape of our business; Greencore moved from effectively an 'island of Ireland' ingredients business, to a two-country, two-division business, where we had an ingredients business which was the old Greencore and then a new convenience foods business centred on the Hazlewood acquisition. Hazlewood was an entrepreneurial business that had over-invested, lost an element of control and capital discipline and Greencore bought it. So, from 2001, for

---
[1] November 2014.

about the next six years, Greencore ran those two divisions side by side, and at the end of that period, or coming to the end of that period, the sugar business ended overnight. It was a regulated business and when the regulation changed it became uneconomic to both grow sugar and process sugar, and so the business that had provided all the cash and had shaped the culture and the operating norms of the business was stopped. We then made a strategic decision in the interests of both growth and returns to do three things:

The first was to continue the exit from ingredients by getting rid of all the rest – to focus the group entirely on what we call convenience foods.

Secondly, we sought to scale up our convenience foods business in the UK through a combination of strong organic growth, which was consumer-driven, and acquisitions that strengthened the category positions that we were already in.

And third, we took a decision, having spent the best part of 18 months working it through, to extend our convenience food footprint in the United States.

Those decisions: exiting ingredients; scaling up our UK business through a combination of organic growth and complementary M&A; and building a business from scratch in the United States, were what created the portfolio, organisation and growth that we have today.

EM: You mention there being a strong balance sheet in the late 1990s. So, why was it in the interests of shareholders, whoever they were at that time, that you would make such major decisions, effectively sowing the seeds of a major change in the whole nature of the business, rather than just giving them their money back and letting them invest in similar companies if they so wished? Greencore had no core heritage in what you were moving into.

[See **Chapter 11**, Investment Appraisal Techniques.]

PC: Yeah, a very good question. Actually, quite a number of shareholders thought it was a bad idea and shared that perspective very publicly with the board. And you know, the truth is, the heritage of Greencore, its knowledge base, its capability and its ways of working, did not fully equip it to operate the Hazlewood Foods portfolio. I would distinguish the acquisition of the portfolio, and the portfolio reshaping, from the operational and commercial management. Greencore actually had both an excellent set of leaders and a corporate capability in asset configuration – what's in, what's out, what do we need to do to reduce debt. So the business was quite effective at pruning the Hazlewood portfolio, but struggled for several years to actually manage the residual businesses for growth and performance. In a way, that lends some credence to the characterisation that the Hazlewood acquisition was a highly risky transaction that brought the business into a geographic market, a set of product markets and business area types that the group had little previous history of operating in.

EM: And if you apply that to Greencore's most recent expansion into the US that you mentioned when you were explaining about the motivations, why, from a business perspective, the United States as against any other market?

PC: I will make two points on that. I think the business decision to extend our convenience food footprint into another geography was very consistent with a view that we wanted to use the capabilities and knowledge in ways of working that we had refined. [See **Chapter 12**.] Hazlewood had pockets of excellent performance, we had just to go out and find them. Then, there was the question of scaling them up, codifying that capability and figuring out what would be appropriate in other markets and what would not. But the Hazlewood acquisition is very open to the challenge that this was an entirely different type of business – because it really was. Whereas the extension of Greencore Convenience Foods, a largely UK business, to our Greencore USA business is at least consistent with trying to replicate a common set of capabilities and ways of working.

Now to the question as to specifically why we chose the United States. This was driven by two things: first, an assessment of the market, which was initially a desk-based market understanding, informed through a combination of analysis and history. We actually had a series of historic trading relationships in continental Europe; we had businesses in The Netherlands, Belgium and France, and that experience, plus our knowledge from the UK, led us to seek out a series of things and avoid a series of other things. For example, it is very important to have flexible, relatively low-cost labour, consumers who already have a track record of buying chilled prepared food and retailers who are tangibly investing in building a chilled prepared food range. Secondly, we had a view that if we were going to build a business in a new geography, it needed to be in a geography that, if we could get it working, would be scalable and material, relative to our UK business, which was already creating half a billion euro in revenue at the time. So, in other words, while building a material business in smaller markets might have been material in the context of those markets, it would not have materially changed the breadth and the balance of our portfolio over time. So, the US stacked up very well in that regard.

Also, I think our board were informed by several other things: first, some of our individual board members had personal histories and others food industry histories, involving Irish companies successfully extending to the US, be that Kerry Foods, Glanbia, IAWS in food, or the personal histories in financial services and in hotels. [See **Chapter 4**.]

I should balance that by saying there were some of our other non-executive directors who came at this issue more from their UK corporate experience. They actually had deep scepticism about whether or not a UK food company, be it a manufacturer or retailer, could build a successful business in the United States.

But perhaps a more important factor than all of this analysis was that we got specific inbound enquiries and requests for help from several US retailers – from Kroger, from Stop & Shop, from the Del-Haize Group and from WeightWatchers (a brand owner that had traded with us in the UK, who was looking for a licensed partner in chilled food). [See **Chapter 2**.] So those inbound requests to both understand how our food business was working and how chilled food worked at scale gave us momentum and confidence.

It was at an interesting time, 2007–2008, in that this coincided with the much-hyped arrival of Tesco into the United States. The Tesco entry created a genuine fear amongst the incumbent US retailers that a scaled-up Tesco proposition leveraging their fresh food history and economic model from the UK, with the margin structure attached to that at the time, could become a real-scale player in the United States. And so there was a desire on the part of the incumbent retailers to get ahead of Tesco and figure out how they would build the chilled prepared foods skills and ranges that would give them more defensibility against Tesco.

And then there was the Walmart factor. Walmart was crushing the competition, in terms of its economic model, with its general merchandise and ambient and frozen propositions that it had. However, its system was less well set-up then to be able to do fresh prepared food. And so, the more regional, more 'food-focused' retailers felt that doing fresh food well would give them a point of difference versus Walmart. So, those competitive or potential competitor dynamics generated a lot of inbound interest into the UK, and into manufacturers like us.

So, put all that together: the collective expertise of our board; an 'outside-in' market assessment fuelled by having put two feet on the ground for 18 months meeting everyone, visiting manufacturers, retailers, reporting back, under no urgency to act, just to learn what was there; and then a series of pretty detailed, full-on customer requests, pulling us to the market, led to our decision to enter into the US. The irony, though, is that despite all of that, we made a complete mess of it at first!

EM: Explain what happened.

PC: The business and strategy that we started with didn't work at all. We've since changed it entirely.

EM: Did you buy it?

PC: Yes, we bought a business but we then invested a lot into it. Our CAPEX into the initial business we bought probably equated to the consideration. So we spent 35 or 40 million Dollars buying it; we spent nearly the same again in upgrading the facility and extending it.

Our strategy was to focus on what the Americans call 'whole meal replacement'; a broad set of products, sold into the deli team, much of it merchandised on the deli counter, catering to a wide variety of product needs that would provide fresh, accurately portioned, safe food to consumers. This proposition would also enable the store teams to decommission a lot of the labour that they had in the deli and/or decommission some of the external commissary kitchens that they had. That was our business. In a UK context, it leveraged most from the ready meal part of our portfolio, in terms of the kind of manufacturing processes that were attached to that, but we also did salads, side dishes, some portioned desserts, some quiche and and some soup. We had a very wide variety of products types; at one point, for our largest customer at the time (Hannaford), we had almost 200 stock lines, and not far off that, going into Stop & Shop; and it was a disaster!

EM: Why do you say that?

PC: It was a disaster because of three things actually. First, we were a 'jack of all trades but a master of none'. So, we were reasonably effective in making all the stuff, but there were always some other players that were better than us. There were large regional salad players who were lower cost than us and there were specialist prepared meal providers who were better quality than us. So we lacked, beyond an ability to aggregate, a point of distinctiveness. The second problem was that the commitment that the retailers had around supporting the supply chain, investing capital in-store and driving marketing, didn't come through. They shied away from delivering the level of in-store labour reduction that was core to the economic model. A third problem, which I think was terminal, was that the propositions didn't work with consumers.

That being said, I will make two points about that learning process. First, one thing that we did very well was that we were actually open to learning. While we started with a view that "this is what we think will work", we were very good at not being a prisoner of it or being tied down by it – we avoided saying, "this works in the UK, therefore we must make it work here". We did some research work where we thought this was what was going to work; when it then transpired that it wasn't working, we began to question it and from there we adapted and tried new things, with lots of initial support from retailers.

Secondly, I remember shortly after we entered into the US, I met a very senior executive in Kerry Foods who asked me about the acquisition. He asked: "how much did you spend on it?" When I told him the amount we had spent on the acquisition, he said, "can you afford to lose all that?" and I replied: "Yeah, we probably could. It would be reputationally embarrassing, but economically we could. I mean, it might cost me my job but the business can survive." His response was intriguing: "Yeah, that's important because it won't be worth anything in the end." This showed me that that's the price of learning about the market – and it turned out to be very true.

EM: You have articulated in the Annual Report a strategic long-term mission, goal and vision. My question is, in the corporate governance dynamic, does the executive management need the board to vote on a move such as expanding into the US? Or, since it's in accordance with the long-term mission, can the executive management just press on, as long as it achieves the required returns? Can the executive management say to the board: "We're going to do this", and unless it involved raising fresh funds or breaching debt/equity ratios, they'd be allowed to go on with it? [See **Chapter 5, Section 5.8**, Corporate Governance.]

PC: The narrow answer to your question is that our policy would not have allowed the executive to deliver that strategy without specifically engaging with the board on it – and, actually, to be precise about it, at that point in time any capital decision that involved the expenditure of more than a million pounds, on anything at all, was referred to the board for decision. But more broadly, I don't know what a board would be for if it wasn't engaged in decisions of this type. The way that I have run this business for the last seven years is with a very, very candid level of engagement with my board.

EM: Is there an informal dynamic between executive management and non-executive directors that helps your strategy evolve?

PC: Well, where theory meets practice, as you begin to move from direction-setting to strategic execution, you do, of course, want to tap into the judgement and experience of your board. That's what they are there for. One of the things we have done, for example, is that as our strategy has changed, we have worked to internationalise our board more. So, we have people with direct, first-hand experience of running businesses in America on our board now.

We have former senior executives of United Biscuits and Glanbia on our board, and John Herlihy who has current experience and a lot of involvement and commitment with Google in the States right now. We have quite a lot of US experience on our board but that's not what drives our strategy. I think it's absolutely the job of the CEO and executive management to propose a strategy to the board. Once that strategy is set, it's then the job of the board to keep that strategy on course from a governance perspective.

EM: They say culture is set from the top; you have the board, you have the executive management headed by yourself and you have 'The Greencore Way', the company's way of doing things, what it stands for. So, how do you infuse The Greencore Way into people who may not be highly paid – this low-cost, flexible labour force that you talk about, many of whom would know little about Ireland?

PC: Well, actually, you won't see any reference to Ireland in 'The Greencore Way', for a start. We have some Irish leaders in the business, but we don't think about ourselves as imposing the Irishness of the business or those leaders on the rest of the business. Nor do we impose the Britishness of our operating sites on the rest of the business.

Let's talk about The Greencore Way for a second, and give you the context for this: a big, big part of what we were trying to do as a business between 2007 (when I became CEO) and early 2013 was about massive portfolio change. To give you one reference point, if I go back three years and one month, which is just before we closed the Uniq acquisition, there are more sites in our business today that weren't in our portfolio three years ago than legacy sites – we have 25 sites across the group, 13 of them are new to Greencore in the last three years. Twelve of them were there before.

So, we ran the business consistent with, first of all, a need to establish basic financial and operating controls across these new sites. [See **Chapter 13**, Implementing Change in an International Context.] We then had to complete the exit from the ingredients business as we divested 15 different types of businesses in that period. We scaled up our UK business through strong organic growth, buying six sites between Uniq and International Cuisine. We sold our business in continental Europe. We sold our water business. We were scaling up our US business, and so we ran the whole group with my focus, as CEO, being on getting the strategy and the portfolio right, and I had a Chief Operating Officer providing the day-to-day operating control of the business.

All of that established a portfolio that was bang in line with what we wanted it to be, given the strategy that we had. Once we created it, it became apparent very quickly that it was working. This became apparent to executive management a little earlier than it did to the board and much earlier than it became apparent to our shareholders and some external onlookers. What was clear to me then was that we were largely done with the portfolio change and we needed to focus on capability, culture and people to really get value from the strategy that we had created. A number of things were necessary to do that: one was for me to be much more 'hands on' in those areas, so I removed the role of COO to have a much simpler strategy and reporting lines. This move brought the senior leaders of the business closer to me and closer to the board. I set up an entity described in our Annual Report as our 'Group Executive Board' (GEB).

We also suddenly realised we were quite a big business, which was performing well, and that a lot of the ways by which we had run the business were now inconsistent with what we wanted. We had run the business as an accumulation of sites. We didn't have a common systems platform. We didn't have a common way of thinking about HR and, actually, we'd never had a HR Director who'd been successful across the whole group. By way of example, we had many pockets of good practice, but they were just that, pockets. So, what we then tried to do was show that the culture of a business is led from the top, though that it should not be imposed from the top. If I put it a little bit differently, you can't wish your culture to be something; it has to evolve from what the business is, albeit directed, tweaked and pulled together by the business leaders.

EM:　That leads on to my next question, Patrick, which is connected to culture. Take your Salt Lake City locations, in Utah, an alcohol-free state, culturally different to the UK or Ireland. How does the organisation connect to its employees in Salt Lake City? If you are to be relevant to your customers and to your shareholders, ultimately you have to be doing something in Utah as a group that a stand-alone Utah organisation couldn't do.

PC:　The magic here is in the principles of The Greencore Way – it's in the fact that we actually want local autonomy and local entrepreneurship, but we want the benefits of the group to add to that. [See **Chapter 18**, Organisation Design and Performance Measurement.] So, Salt Lake City connects into our group well and does so in a number of different ways. First, it's connected in a customer sense because 7-Eleven are important customers, our most important customer in Salt Lake City. We also have a big 7-Eleven agenda in Fredericksburg, in Chicago, in Minneapolis and in Brockton.

Then we have some formal processes that run through our group which are the same wherever you go: how we do food safety, financial reporting and standard expectations around budgeting and forecasting. As it relates to me, Salt Lake City gets aggregated into our US division and reports to me and our Group CFO, Alan Williams, monthly through the same process with which all of our sites report. We have a programme called 'Lean Greencore', which is how we share best practice in manufacturing and build a pipe-line of continuous improvement initiatives, sharing both processes to generate initiatives and specific ideas that have worked in analogous plants – Salt Lake City is as much a part of this as any other site. And, thirdly, there is our method of employee engagement, which is common across all of our sites. Of course, some of the processes or incentive models have to be different, purely because of geographic reasons, but the fundamental policies and processes are the same right across our group.

EM:　In what sense does the company believe in scientific management? In other words, that 'management' is a practice that can be taught, that it is capable of being written down and described to others and so therefore can be inculcated? You believe in using analysis to make decisions, to aid decision-making, but not in the absence of intuition. But is it analysis first, guided by intuition rather than intuition first and then we make the analysis fit?

PC:　Yes, I think that's right, although you can end up forming habits; if decisions look and feel similar to previous ones, you can often end up relying on intuition, sometimes too much, actually. You have to discipline yourself to make sure that you understand the decision you're making there and then. It's an interesting point on scientific management that I would somewhat agree with, but not fully. I think if you were to ask my team about my leadership style and what I value in other people, I think they would say something like: "Patrick looks for leaders not managers", which is somewhat connected to my belief that management can be taught, but leadership less so. So, of course, we have to have leaders and managers; if you are in a management role in Northampton or Manton Wood and you have got up to 3,000 people working in your facility every day in the height of the summer, with demanding orders, when you're trying to produce four million units a week, you need to have a decent labour-scheduling system, proper line automation, running those lines at high speed, and you need to have consistent application of product. And so, it will look and feel like a Frederick Taylor scientific management process for the 21st Century. But actually you also need to have people who can inspire others, with an intuition around people and customers, and who can build relationships, and who are curious. I end up valuing those skills more.

EM:　If you've 10,000 people, obviously 9,800 of them have got to be excellent executors of whatever it is they have to do in the service of the customer and the shareholder. As well as that, however, you hope they are also encouraged to exhibit other values that ground them as people.

PC:　Absolutely. I recall taking one of the senior leadership team of Starbucks around our facility at Park Royal in London. I would know him well, and we were six months into the roll-out of our multi-regional programme with them and he was pushing to move a big slug of additional business to us on the basis of what he was learning about how we did things. There was some resistance internally, but the more senior levels in Starbucks have autonomy. We had a brilliant, brilliant tour around our plant in Park Royal, which probably embodied the Greencore values better than anywhere else at the time. This guy, who in his previous job had run all of the internal Starbucks factories, commented on two things that struck him: "This is the best factory I've ever been in," he said, adding that it wasn't the factory's assets or otherwise, but that, "I've never seen a level of engagement like this".

EM: Moving onto some financial questions, would you have different hurdle rates on your NPV calculation for different types of businesses? For example, would risky ones have higher hurdle rates?

PC: No. We run with our group WACC on everything, which is around 8.0%. [See **Chapter 11**, Investment Appraisal Techniques.]

EM: Other companies take their WACC plus 4 to take account of risk, while if it was an absolutely steady state, sometimes they might even do something at lower than their WACC because it has a lower risk than their current risk profile.

PC: Again, I think we probably exercise some kind of qualitative judgement on that. So, where a team, either a division or within a division, has a track record of always delivering to plan, then their projects will be looked on more benignly. The majority of our projects that we approve in this kind of enhancement CAPEX process, which is slightly different from the new factory build stuff, will have a payback of a year or two years, so with IRRs which are way up, you know, 50% plus, and of course we like that.

But we don't just like it because it's good; we like it because it's reflective of the dynamics of our business. Half our SKUs are new every year. So, if we are getting a project that has a payback of six years, who knows where our portfolio is going to be. Then, it is not going to feel right, not because it can't be modelled but because it's just inconsistent with what our business is.

If I contrast it with Glanbia, where I am a non-executive director on the board, they have a fabulous set of businesses, but one of the big signature businesses is global cheese production. They are the largest cheese producer in America and they have to put big, big CAPEX towards those cheese plants that are going to run for the next 30 years. Now, you know, some of the IRRs that they are running with on those projects are 10–11%. But actually that process, producing American cheese, is a predictable one in terms of what it is going to look like, and the capital intensity of things attached to it.

EM: You've been unbelievably open and generous with your time. It's been a fascinating story and very relevant to readers interested in international expansion from an Irish perspective. Thank you.

Index